CASSANDRA
✳ EASON'S ✳
COMPLETE
BOOK OF
SPELLS

CASSANDRA * EASON'S * COMPLETE BOOK OF SPELLS

Ancient & Modern Spells for the Solitary Witch

quantum

LONDON • NEW YORK • TORONTO • SYDNEY

quantum

An imprint of W. Foulsham and Co. Ltd
The Publishing House, Bennetts Close, Cippenham, Slough,
Berkshire, SL1 5AP, England

ISBN 0-572-03001-0

Cover illustration by Jurgen Ziewe

A CIP record for this book is available from the British Library

The moral right of the author has been asserted

Printed in Great Britain by Creative Print and Design (Wales), Ebbw Vale

CONTENTS

INTRODUCTION

Magic and spell-casting are part of a living tradition. This tradition includes the secret formulae and ceremonies of formal witches and magicians throughout the ages and the homelier wisdom of our ancestors. Our forebears regularly carried out simple family rituals for abundance and protection of their homes, animals, crops and tools, and devised recipes for love or healing that were handed down orally through the generations.

This book draws on a number of formal and informal systems from around the world and through the ages to create a working modern spell book that you can refer to both for resolving everyday concerns and for increasing your own psychic and magical powers. It also provides a basis for creating your own spells, so that you can add to the magical traditions of the past and pass on some of your insights to your descendants. Pages 665–70 are designed to give you all the information you need to do this. They include charts and information on basic magical knowledge and symbols. It is a good idea to copy the spells you find most useful in this book, together with any adaptations you have made, into a book of your own. To this you can add your own spells, seasonal celebrations and personal ceremonies for healing or protection.

Like any good recipe book, this book contains spells you can carry out in a hurry using the basic contents of your store cupboard when the need is most pressing. There are also more detailed rituals for those quieter times when you can work at the most appropriate moon or sun phase, using crystals, incenses and herbs you have collected over the months and keep specially for magic in a cupboard or box in your home. I have also given instructions for casting the most important spell of all: the one for bringing to fruition your greatest – and perhaps secret – wish or desire.

What is magic?

Magic is the psychic energy that is generated when you use your own mind power, amplified by natural energies (from the moon, the sun, the Earth, herbs, crystals, clay, wax and so on), to bring into actuality what you wish to manifest.

When we talk about spells, we are usually referring to more informal, but no less powerful, formulae. Spells tend to use simple materials, words and actions. They are performed on a particular occasion, with the intention of transforming a wish into reality – hopefully in the near future. The word 'ritual' is fairly interchangeable with 'spell', but it is often applied, as in this book, to more complex and organised magical workings, or ones with a less immediately tangible, and sometimes longer-term, results.

In relation to spells and rituals, the adjectives 'magic', 'psychic' and 'spiritual' are likewise more or less interchangeable. I have tended to use the word 'spiritual' in connection with healing spells, prayers and invoked deity forms from different traditions. Do not worry about adopting – or, indeed, mixing – deity names from different cultures and religions. You are not summoning up these gods nor being blasphemous. The deities (male or female) are all aspects of a higher positive energy and help you to focus on the particular powers you need in your spell.

Magic can involve formal rituals and require precise materials, detailed preparations and complex pre-ordained steps. Such ceremonies are usually set down by one of the many organised magical traditions and entail the use of specially purchased or crafted tools, such as wands and swords, that are kept especially for rites. At the other end of the scale is the everyday practitioner who works at the kitchen table when the children are in bed, or at weekends in the countryside, borrowing from the garden and the larder, and making use of the sunshine and the rain – together with, perhaps, a twig wand – to weave her magic. Neither form of magic is better. This book steers a middle course, adapting concepts from the magic of different lands and ages, formal and informal, so you can try out ideas in your home and garden, on weekends and holidays, and find a style that suits you. Generally, I have given substitute locations or materials – if, for example, you cannot go to the sea and do not want get up at five in the morning in the middle of winter. But occasionally I have noted that the conditions and materials are integral to the spell, and you should wait until the conditions are right and the materials are available, or else use a different spell.

The origins of magic

Formal magic became an organised system 5,000 years ago in ancient Egypt and has evolved over the centuries in many different directions. But the first rituals were carried out long before the appearance of civilisation as we would recognise it. We know of ritual dances and ceremonies (probably related to the hunt) from cave drawings dating back tens of thousands of years. One of the surviving records of magical practices is the Dancing Sorcerer, a cave painting at Les Trois Frères in the French Pyrenees, which dates from about 14000 BCE. The sorcerer is painted in black and stands high above the animals also depicted on the walls.

Folk magic celebrating the seasonal changes and using them as a source of power is a heritage that we all share. It has been a part of every culture in every place around the world. These celebrations have entered the modern Christian calendar as Christmas, Easter and Harvest Festival. In almost every country in the world there are celebrations, too, around new year.

Not all magic was (or is) positive. The ancient Egyptians performed vicious curse rites against enemies. Medieval European and Scandinavian magicians – and, indeed, a minority of early twentieth-century occultists – manipulated angelic and demonic energies and sometimes got themselves into all kinds of psychological trouble in what was basically a quest for personal power.

You can read more about the origins of magic and witchcraft in my book *A Guide to Practical Witchcraft and Magick Spells* (Foulsham/Quantum, 2001).

White magic

This book contains only positive spells, or white magic. My own magical tradition is an ancient Water Witch path, and I have great respect for covens and formal magical practitioners, almost all of whom work positively for the general good and healing. I practise as a solitary witch and am also a trained Druidess, or nature priestess. But magic is as valid in the kitchen as on the wildest moorland, and even if you are new to magic you can carry out very effective spells if your intentions are good and your heart pure. The almost lost traditions of family and domestic magic are reviving, and working alone or with friends and family will and must always be a vital and rich strand of magical practice.

The rules of magic

White magic is highly ethical and, like most forms of spirituality, adheres to a moral code. In magic you are accountable for the energies you send out, so you can't just say sorry and wipe out a curse or nasty sending with an absolution from on high. The following four rules are a basic code of conduct to which all practitioners of white magic adhere.

Rule 1: If it harm none, do what you will.
A magical practitioner does not have carte blanche to carry out magical workings regardless of their consequences for others (or for nature). That means you can't curse your enemies, or even people you think are doing wrong to the vulnerable. Nor can you draw or bind someone to you against their will, albeit in the name of love. Psychology is a close relation of magic and psychic work, and if you manipulate others, neither you nor they will be truly happy. Love should be based on freedom, and success on effort and talent, not on manoeuvring someone else out of a job or causing them to make mistakes.

Rule 2: What you send out returns threefold.
This rule means that whatever energies you send out in your magic will return to you with three times the intensity. Send out love and generosity and good things will come bouncing back. Carry out healing spells for others and you will find yourself healed in the ways you most need. Send out with malice or anger and they will likewise return in unexpected ways. This rule is also one of the most powerful forms of mental and psychic defence, for it means that you can simply bounce back any nasty feelings sent your way.

Rule 3: Enough for your needs and a little more.

Spell-casting is more than writing a psychic shopping list and involves some form of payback. It is, of course, valid to ask in spells for what you and your family need. If you are worried sick about money, you can't focus on the needs of the planet or the health of the dog down the road effectively. However, asking for a big win on the Lottery is not considered ethical and is likely to rebound on you. Generally, if you ask for help through a spell, you will get a little more than you asked for, as long as your requests are reasonable.

Rule 4: Keep the balance.

This rule is about a kind of cosmic payback. If you ask for something in a spell, you should always give a little in return to a person, animal or place in need. This doesn't have to be money but could be in the form of time or help. By doing this you will increase the positive energies at large in the cosmos, so ensuring that they are there for you if you have a problem in the future.

If you are going through a really good patch in your life, don't abandon spell-casting but direct your spells to healing others (perhaps people you don't know so well), addressing global concerns, and sending out blessings. Under the threefold law (Rule 2), good things will come into your life as a result of your altruism. Our distant ancestors knew this, and surviving indigenous cultures remain aware that we are all co-responsible for the turning of the world and the cycle of the seasons and that by performing positive rituals and actions we can assist Mother Nature in her work. Modern ecological movements also recognise that when people absolve themselves of spiritual responsibility for the planet and its creatures, neglect and destruction more readily occur.

Different kinds of magic

The spells in the book fall in to three main categories, although in practice a single spell may have elements that belong in more than one category. A spell might, for example, work to remove sorrow (banishing magic) and increase confidence (attracting magic).

Attracting magic

This is also sometimes called sympathetic magic, as it involves using a symbol or symbolic action to imitate what you wish to attract into your life. You might, for example, add a coin to a pot daily to encourage the steady accumulation of material resources, or you might keep a tiny doll in a cradle next to your bed in order to help you to conceive. Deosil (clockwise) movements signify attracting energies.

Banishing magic

Banishing can be a very positive form of magic for getting rid of debt. As well as creating magical energies to reduce the problem, it can galvanise your personal money-making strategies and release you from the panic that sometimes freezes us into inaction in a crisis. Where people are concerned, it is possible to banish any hold they have over you. If, for example, a destructive ex-partner still has an influence over your life, you can reduce it by burning a cord in a candle flame so that it breaks. If the emotional blackmail is strong, you may have to repeat the spell several times, but eventually you will be able to walk away mentally free (if not physically). It is best to leave the rest to karmic laws, rather than attempting to banish the offending person to outer darkness till hell freezes over – under the threefold law (see page 9), this will only rebound upon you. Banishing magic generally involves widdershins (anti-clockwise) movements.

Binding magic

This kind of magic needs care but is very effective. You can, for example, bind a partner in fidelity – perhaps by tying a ribbon to hold two dolls, representing the marriage, face to face. If the spell is to be ethical, however, it is necessary to add the words 'if it is right to be', so that you allow free will in yourself and in your partner. For the sake of ethics, it may also be a good idea to put a time limit on the spell, perhaps fixing it for a few days when one of you will be away on a business trip that may offer a lot of temptation. Be aware, however, that if you or partner want to stray, the marriage will not be happy even if you use magic to bind yourselves together for eternity.

The five stages of a spell

Every spell or ritual includes five stages. These stages usually include both words (often repetitive ones that create a rhythm and build up energies) and actions (again, often repetitive, or following a sequence). Both words and actions become more intense as the spell progresses. However, some spells rely purely on words or purely on actions. The ancient Egyptians believed that words were intrinsically powerful and that by speaking your intention you were creating the necessary energy for it to manifest in reality. They also used symbols, which they animated or empowered with words during the ritual.

In informal spellcasting, the stages run into one another, whereas in formal magic they are more distinct – and there may be a preliminary circle-casting ceremony (see pages 13 and 655) to create an enclosed concentrated area of power that is also protected from outside influences.

Stage 1: Defining the focus

This is the most important part of the spell in many ways. It involves clarifying the purpose of the spell and identifying the symbol that will represent it. You can use absolutely anything for a symbol – herbs, a crystal, a tarot card, a representative miniature item (such as a silver heart locket for love or a toy plane for travel) and so on. Alternatively, you can write your wish or need on a piece of paper, or use a photograph of the person you wish to help or heal. The spell begins as you name aloud the intention of the spell and any specific details, for example:

I seek healing for my mother, who is undergoing a stomach operation tomorrow.

Stage 2: Action
Next, you transform your spoken wish into reality by endowing the symbol with life and power. You might do this by chanting or singing words that express the wish, or walking slowly around the symbol, perhaps banging a drum or a cymbal. Another common method, which I have used in a number of the spells in this book, is to pass the symbol through or over the four magical substances that symbolise the elements. Salt, placed in the North, is used for Earth; incense, placed in the East, is used for Air; a candle, placed in the South, is used for Fire; and a cup or dish of water, placed in the West, is used for Water. The elemental substances are arranged in a circle or square around the symbol and are picked up each in turn, usually starting with salt in the North and proceeding deosil (clockwise). The combination of the four elements generates power in the symbol. (See pages 684–86 for more on the elements.)

Stage 3: Raising the power
This is the most active and powerful part of the spell, and involves building up the speed and intensity of the action started in Stage 2. You might repeat the chant louder, dance faster or drum with greater intensity until you feel that you have reached a peak of power. This moves the parcel of energy invested in your desire at ever-increasing speed from the thought plane to reality. Another method involves enchanting the symbol by passing your hands, palms down and flat, a few centimetres above the symbol, your power hand (the one you write with) deosil (clockwise), and your receptive hand simultaneously widdershins (anti-clockwise). Once you have established the rhythm, you can build up a faster and faster pace. (If you prefer to go anti-clockwise with your power hand and clockwise with your receptive hand that is fine, as long as you are consistent.) A third method is to hold a lighted incense stick in each hand, moving your power hand deosil and your receptive hand simultaneously widdershins a few centimetres above the symbol so that the smoke spirals, again, creating a rhythm. If you have a written wish you might also burn it in the flame.

Stage 4: Releasing the power
You will know when it is the moment to release the power. You may feel as if you are driving with the hand brake on or as if you are a balloon about to burst. When you are ready, release the power into the cosmos with a final shout of an end line of a chant or words such as: 'The power is free' or 'The power is mine'. You might, alternatively, end the spell by suddenly extinguishing a candle and sending the light to the subject of the spell or to yourself. If you were enchanting the symbol using your hands, you could throw them wide above your head and bring them down vertically like slashing knives or plunge your incense sticks into a dish of water. At this point the flash of released energy should bring the wish into actuality, although you may have to do some earthly work to get it to the right place, i.e. into your life or your bank account.

Stage 5: Grounding the power

At the conclusion of any spell, you need to bring yourself back to everyday reality – otherwise your mind will buzz all night and you will find yourself becoming irritable. To do this you could sit on the ground and press your hands and feet on to the earth, so allowing excess unfocused energy drain out. Alternatively, you could stand with your feet apart and your hands by your side, fingers pointing downwards, and feel yourself gradually slowing down and your body and mind relaxing. Afterwards, clear and wash any tools and sit quietly, perhaps eating a light meal and playing gentle music. You might also like to tend plants or make plans for your first practical steps towards fulfilment of the spell.

Psychic protection

If you practise magic with honest intent and calm mind, you are protected. But as an extra safeguard you may wish, before you begin, to ask in your own words for the protection of your personal deity, guardian or spirit guide, or visualise angels standing in the four corners of the room. You could also set four white pillar candles at the centre of each wall, asking that light from them stand sentinel while you work. Light the candles deosil (clockwise), beginning with the one on the northern wall. Extinguish them in reverse order after the ritual. If you like, you can name the candles for the Archangels – Uriel in the North, Raphael in the East, Michael in the South and Gabriel in the West (see pages 680–82 for more information about Archangels).

Another method of defence is to cast a simple deosil (clockwise) circle with the index finger or your power hand (the one you write with), about waist high. Alternatively, use a pointed crystal, held it in your power hand, to draw a waist-high circle of imaginary light around where you will be working. You could say as you cast your circle:

May the circle that is cast forever be unbroken. May the love of the God/Goddess/Light be forever in my heart.

After the spell and initial grounding (before the clearing up), walk the circle in the opposite direction to the one in which you cast it, picturing the light coiling back into your finger or crystal. Say:

The circle be open but never shall be broken. May the love of the God/Goddess/Light remain forever in my heart. I thank you wise guardian(s) for your protection.

PART I

Spells for Love

Most people want someone special to love and to love them in return. Still today, with a high divorce rate in our society, we wish for happy-ever-after – and, even with the odds against us, there is no reason why we should not have it. Of course, we all make mistakes: we may enter a permanent relationship for the wrong reasons; we may marry someone who has problems from the past that make them unable to give and receive love. And we are no longer prepared to live in an unhappy relationship as our grandparents and great-grandparents often did.

For each of us there is, I believe, a number of people who could make us happy in a love relationship. It is just a question of coming together with one of them in the right place at the right time. That is true whether we are seeking our first love or looking for a permanent relationship second, third or even fourth time around.

Love spells have traditionally been used to identify a lover and then to call him or her. In Chapter 2, I have drawn together a number of these old spells, not just for interest value but because they work and because they often identify someone in our present world whom we had thought of simply as a friend or had dismissed because we were still dreaming of handsome princes or lovely princesses.

Love spells, ancient and modern, work by opening us to the possibility of love so that we give out the right signals – not desperation but an open heart and mind. You know that when the sun is shining, the bathroom scales are having a light day and you are wearing your favourite outfit, you feel good and the world smiles back. Love spells have the same effect. What is more, they open the telepathic channels so that not only are we more receptive to love but people who would make us happy are also drawn into our circle.

There are two provisos with love spells. Firstly, if you are calling a specific person as a lover, you should add (either silently or aloud): 'if it is right to be'. Secondly, you should never call a person who is already in a relationship that has a chance of survival. Neither unwilling love nor stolen love is a good basis for a lasting relationship or a faithful lover.

1 SPELLS FOR ATTRACTING NEW LOVE

The spells in this chapter are all adaptations of love spells I have created or collected from various people over 15 years of research and that I know have worked. Some of them are modern versions of older rituals. Try these and the older forms in Chapter 2 and see which you prefer.

A word of warning: if you are already in a good relationship, do not carry out these spells. Work instead with the spells for commitment and fidelity in Chapters 3 and 4 respectively. If you have doubts about your current relationship, talk them over with your partner and try working the spells for reconciliation in Chapter 6. You will only muddy the waters if you look for new love while you are still involved.

A rose spell to attract the right person into your life

I make no apologies for the fact that the first spell in this book has appeared in other formats in previous books of mine. It is by far the most successful love spell I have used.

When I attend healing festivals I get through at least two vases of roses carrying out this spell, and many satisfied people return with partners the following year. On one occasion, in Malmö, Sweden, an 80-year-old woman I had worked it for went rushing off back to her sheltered accommodation, clutching her burnt petals, to invite the man in the next apartment to come with her on her weekly trip to Copenhagen. The spell works for both calling a current lover who is being over-reticent and attracting an as yet unknown lover.

You will need
6 roses, preferably pink and perfumed, which are fresh but not damp; a map of your local area, state or country, or a world map if you want a lover from far away; a vase; a pure white or beeswax candle in a holder; a metal tray.

Timing
As soon after the crescent moon as possible, although any night up to the one before the full moon is okay. It is good but not essential to be able to see the moon in the sky.

The spell
* Set the map on a table.
* Scatter five of the roses across the map, as you do so saying:
Near or far, by land and sea,
A lover true I call to me.
* Light the white candle and set it, in its holder, on the tray.
* Take up the sixth rose (six being the number of Venus, Roman goddess of love). From it remove five petals and set them next to the base of the candle-holder, as you do so saying:
Come my love, come to me,
If it is right to be.
Come my love and with me stay;
Stay forever and a day.
* Taking care not to burn yourself, hold each of the five petals in the candle flame in turn, allowing each to catch fire in one corner. As you do so, say:
Burn a pathway to my door;
Five rose petals now are four.
Four to three in candle fire,
Bringing closer my desire.
From three to two I burn the rose;
Love no hesitation shows.
From two to one till there is none;
The spell is done; come lover, come.
* Leave the petals to burn out on the tray. They need only be partly burnt.
* Blow out the candle and send the light with a private unspoken message of love, to wherever your lover – known or unknown – may be.
* Place all six roses, including the one with the missing petals, in a vase of water and leave it near a window facing the front of your home.
* Carefully collect the burnt petals or their ash and bury them under a fruit tree, rose bush or fast-growing plant. If you do not have a garden, use an indoor tub. As you do so, recite the following verse five times:
Near or far, by land and sea,
A lover true I call to me.
* When the roses die, bury the one with the missing petals close to where you buried the burned petals, repeating the 'Near or far' verse five times.
* If necessary, repeat the spell the following month.

A simple rose-scattering spell to draw a lover into your life

I have encountered a number of simple spells that involve scattering roses along an actual physical pathway to draw a lover into your life. The traditional spells call for five roses, which should be scattered from the end of the road to your front door.

However, unless your street happens to be deserted, it is probably easier to create a symbolic pathway of love with your rose petals.

Begin scattering them at the end of your garden path and finish at your door. This way you will avoid the hazard of helpful people en route telling you that you have dropped a rose, or chasing after you and handing the dropped roses back, which rather detracts from the magic!

You will need
5 pink or red roses, or 5 pink or red flowers with plentiful petals; a container for the petals; a small open box or dish.

Timing
Any night from the crescent moon to the night before the full moon.

The spell
* Plan your route before you start to work. Any pathway will do as long as you begin outside your house and end at the front door. You can adapt this ritual to suit the layout of your home. If you have paths around the side of the house, you could use them to create a longer symbolic route along which your future — or maybe reluctant — lover will be drawn.
* Take your five roses and, one by one, slowly pluck off the petals, placing them in the container. As you do so, say over and over again:
So I make the path of love.
Love follow it and find me.
* Go to the furthest point on your pathway of love and begin to walk the path, scattering the petals in a trail behind you as you walk and repeating the chant softly and continuously, aloud or to yourself.
* Scatter the final petals on your doorstep or in your entrance porch.
* Open your front door and say:
Love enter and be welcome.
* Step inside and pick up five petals from the doorstep. Stand in the open doorway, facing outwards, and repeat the second chant three times.
* Go in and close the door. Set the five petals in the box or dish, on a window ledge facing the street or main entrance. If possible, leave a light shining in or near a street-facing window until you go to bed.
* Bury the dead petals from the box or dish either beneath a green plant outside the front door or in a plant pot near the entrance to your house. The wind will carry the rest away.
* Repeat monthly until love comes.

An incense pathway spell to call lasting love into your life

This pathway spell uses incense smoke to represent the pathway. Fragrance was believed by ancient Egyptians to contain the essence of the deities and so to transfer magical energies to the user (see page 41 for an ancient Egyptian incense spell).

The following is a modern love ritual that uses six different floral love incense sticks, six being the number of Venus and of love. However, you can use six incense sticks of the same fragrance if it is easier. If you are working indoors, use small sticks so that you are not overwhelmed by the fragrance, and make sure the room is well ventilated.

You will need
6 incense sticks chosen from the following fragrances: carnation, jasmine, lavender, lilac, lily of the valley, lotus, mimosa, rose and ylang-ylang (apple and strawberry are Venus fruits and are good alternatives to floral fragrances); an incense-holder for each stick – the long wooden ones that collect the ash are ideal, but you can also improvise with metal, glass or ceramic jars or bottles; a tub of mixed pink and green glass nuggets, or small rose quartz and jade crystals; a stiff piece of white paper or card; a small drawstring bag.

Timing
Lovely at sunset, when the smoke rises against the last light. If you are working outdoors, or near a window, the light of the setting sun may be reflected over the ritual.

The spell
* Set the six incense sticks in the holders in a row on a flat surface, beginning with the one nearest towards you. The row need not be long.
* On either side make a pathway of alternate rose quartz and jade crystals (Venus's stones) or pink and green glass nuggets (Venus's colours).
* Light the stick nearest to you, saying: *I call my love in fragrance, wherever he/she may be.*
* Light the second stick, saying: *I call my love in fragrance to find his/her way to me.*
* Light the third stick, saying: *I call my love in fragrance that love will deeper grow.*
* Light the fourth stick, saying: *I call my love in fragrance, happiness to know.*
* Light the fifth stick, saying: *I call my love in fragrance that she/he will never stray.*
* Light the sixth stick, saying: *I call my love in fragrance, forever and a day.*
* Leave the incense to burn and allow images to form in the curling smoke that may suggest how and where you will meet your new love.
* When the incense is burnt through, scoop a small amount of the ashes from each stick onto the paper or card. Shake the ashes gently, as you do so reciting all six chants in order.
* Look at the ash formation through half-closed eyes. It will appear as a scene of you and your love or perhaps one or two initials of a person who could make you happy. If you can see nothing, stare hard at the ash picture, close your eyes, open them, blink and say the first words that come into your head. This is a good way of breaking through the barriers of your conscious, analytical mind, which is excellent at problem-solving but struggles with magical insights.
* Put the glass nuggets or crystals in the drawstring bag and set it by your bed. As you drift into sleep, imagine yourself walking along the crystal pathway to where your love is waiting.

A crescent moon spell for love and trust if you have been hurt by a previous lover

If we have been hurt by love, we sometimes close down the channels through which we convey the desire for love and friendship to the world. Even if we have decided, on a conscious level, that we are ready to start again, our unconscious mind may still be holding back. When we then get no response, we may feel quite wrongly that we are unattractive or unworthy of love. This is a very gentle spell to rekindle from within us new confidence and a willingness to try again (see also the hospitality spell on page 151 if you are not quite ready to love again).

Do not feel that after doing this spell you have to take drastic measures to meet new people, for instance by joining a dating agency – unless you want to. Usually the new love begins as a friendship or a shared interest with someone who will be found in places you already regularly visit. He or she may turn up unexpectedly at work, perhaps at a business gathering or a get-together with one of your colleagues after hours. The meeting may be the result of a chance introduction or may come about through a friend of a friend or a relative. Relax and let love come to you in its own time. Once you have opened the psychic doorway to the possibility of love, it will not be too long arriving.

This spell follows the old practice of wishing on the crescent moon by turning silver over three times (see also the moon spells on pages 183–5).

You will need

A silver heart (such as a locket or charm), or a small pink rose quartz crystal (sometimes available in a heart shape), or – if you can get neither a silver heart nor a rose quartz crystal – a pink or clear glass nugget; a white flower or blossom, or 3 ivy or other evergreen leaves; a pink scarf or piece of material.

Timing

The night you can first see the crescent moon in the sky. If it is cloudy, wait for the first clear night.

The spell

* Go out into the open air – your garden, your balcony or any open space. Hold the silver heart, rose quartz crystal (symbol of gentle love) or glass nugget in your power hand (the one you write with) and turn it over three times, repeating each time you do so:

  One for love, you moon above, send love to me.

  Two for love, you moon above, fidelity.

  Three for love, you moon above, eternally.

* Leave the heart, crystal or glass with the flower or ivy leaves on the pink scarf for three further nights, each evening before you go to bed repeating the love chant three times.

* On the fifth night of the spell, repeat the chant just once. Return the flower or leaves to any patch of earth but do not bury it.

* On the sixth night of the spell, do something to make yourself happy: perhaps going to the cinema, having a luxury bubble bath or visiting friends or family, but do not seek love actively.

A white flower and moon spell to make someone you like notice you

White flowers are associated with the moon and moon goddesses in a number of cultures. Some of these flowers, such as white jasmine and mimosa blossom, are most fragrant at night. The link between the moon and love goes back thousands of years to the time when human fertility was first linked with lunar phases.

In our affluent modern culture, we can obtain white flowers or blossoms throughout the year, making it possible for us to carry out flower love spells all year round. This spell involves making moon water (see page 93 for another spell using moon water).

You will need

A clear glass or silver-coloured bowl; 9 small white flowers or blossoms; some still mineral water; a smooth stick from a tree (preferably a moon tree such as the willow or another tree that grows near water) or a pointed crystal quartz; a small bright pink ribbon long enough to tie in a bow.

Timing

A waxing moon bright enough to cast a silver or golden glow in the sky, and preferably into a bowl of water.

The spell

* Go out into the open air, taking with you the bowl, white flowers, mineral water and stick or crystal quartz.
* Half fill the bowl with water and, moving deosil (clockwise) encircle it with the white flowers.
* Stir the water nine times deosil with the stick or crystal, as you do so saying:

Moon of increase, let love grow
That (name) may love show.
Moon shine down your beauteous light;
Make me beloved to his/her sight.

Leave the water overnight.

* In the morning, when you wake, sprinkle nine drops of your newly created moon water over the ribbon, as you do so repeating the chant three times.
* Tie the ribbon in a bow and wear or carry it hidden for nine days, and thereafter on any occasion when you know the person you like will be present.
* Bottle the remainder of the water so that you can splash it on your wrists when the object of your affection is near.

A white rose and candle spell for a secret love

In the language of flowers, which became popular during Victorian times, a white rose signified secrecy. This belief came from a much older tradition, in which a white rose with the Latin words *sub rosa* written beneath would be painted over the doorway to a house or banqueting hall. This signified that whatever was heard from a guest within would remain secret.

There may be many reasons why we cannot of speak our love. Perhaps we or the person we love are not free to express that love without hurting innocent people. There may be family or even community or religious disapproval in some sections of society, or a policy at work that forbids office relationships.

This spell strengthens the links of secret love even if they are no more than secret smiles, whispered words, e-mails, brief meetings or stolen kisses. It will also help if you love someone for whom it may in the future be possible to express your love openly but for whom you must now conceal your feelings.

You will need

A white rosebud; 2 white or beeswax candles; a sharp metal nail or a very fine silver-coloured screwdriver or a small paper knife or (if you can find one) a long thorn from a rose bush; a slender vase for the rosebud.

Timing

A cloudy night before the full moon.

The spell

* Working indoors, light the first candle and close the curtains of the room so that the candle sheds the only light.
* Using the engraving tool, about halfway down the second candle carefully inscribe your initials and those of your secret love, enclosed by a heart. Work in silence and take care not to break the candle.
* Light the second candle from the first and then extinguish the first candle. Say:

Under the rose we love, sub rosa, sub rosa, sub rosa. Yet one day we shall walk in the light together that all may see and rejoice in our love.

* Pick up the rosebud and whisper a private message to your love.
* Extinguish the candle and sit in the darkness, holding the rose and picturing the day you and your love will be together.
* When you are ready, turn on the light and place your rosebud in water, in the vase, between the candles.
* Every evening you are home, re-light both candles and leave them to burn for five minutes. Hold the rose so that the light shines in it and repeat the secret words of love in your heart while focusing on future happiness. Continue this practice until the symbol on the candle has burnt through and disappeared.
* When the rose has died, cast the browned petals into any flowing water. The spell is now done. You can repeat it with new candles and a fresh rosebud whenever you feel dispirited.

A tarot card spell for romance

Tarot cards are popular ingredients in all kinds of spells because the card images are so rich and provide a powerful focus for attracting good things and caring people into your life.

You do not need to know how to read tarot cards to carry out tarot spells, although as you work with certain cards your intuition will give you all kinds of insights that subsequently prove accurate. Indeed, many people become expert tarot readers as a result of working with tarot cards in magic.

Still today, many of us want a romance in which we can cherish someone and be cherished in return. In our fast, modern culture, which places the emphasis on sexual performance, this vital aspect of partnership may be forgotten. Not every relationship becomes a long-term commitment, but those heady golden days – especially of an early love or a brief but wonderful encounter later in life – can be so special that we treasure the memories forever.

This spell will also work if you want to rekindle romance within an existing relationship in which the demands of third parties or just everyday life have temporarily obscured the reason you came together in the first place.

You will need

A tarot pack; 2 pale-green and 1 dark-green candle, or 3 white candles; 3 suitable candle-holders; a stick of rose or lavender incense; a square pink scarf or piece of material at least 35 × 35 cm/ 13 × 13 in; some white writing paper; a red pen, or alternatively a quill pen or a sharpened feather and a bottle of red ink (if you choose a quill or feather, you might like to practise writing with it before you cast the spell); an envelope; your favourite fragrance.

Timing

Late at night, the day before you plan a romantic surprise or are going to a party or social event where you hope to meet someone new (see also the Valentine's day flower love charm on pages 47–9).

The spell

* Look through the tarot pack and from the court cards (Kings, Queens, Knights and Pages) choose a card to represent yourself and a card to represent the partner you seek. The Kings and Queens are ideal if you are in your thirties or older and are seeking romance. The Knights and Pages are suitable to represent younger men and women respectively, and for first love at any age. The Pentacles characters are reliable, home-loving, patient and loyal. The Cups (or Chalices) characters are romantic, idealistic, caring and imaginative. The Wands (or Staves) characters are exciting, passionate, eager for new places and experiences, and very creative. Finally, the Swords characters are logical, cautious in love but totally devoted when committed, assertive, honest, and associated with thinking and the mind. You can choose two cards of the same suit or mix and match. If you are a same-sex couple, you can choose two cards of the same gender.
* Look through the tarot pack again and find the Lovers card from the major arcana (the picture cards, which do not belong to any suit). Keep this card to one side for use later.

- Set all three candles in a row. If you are using green candles, set the dark-green one in the centre. Each candle should be about 15 cm/6 in from the central one.
- Spread the scarf in front of the candles – where wax will not drip on it when the candles are lit.
- On the scarf, set the card you have chosen to represent you, placing it below the pale-green candle on the left. Place the Lovers card below the dark-green candle. Place the card representing your potential romantic partner beneath the pale-green candle on the right.
- Light the central candle. Pick up the Lovers card, holding it so that it is still in front of the dark green candle and say:
  So shall it be; romantically entwined are we.
  Replace the card.
- From the central candle, light the candle representing you, as you do so saying:
  So shall I be radiant in your sight.
- Place this card beneath the Lovers card, as you do so saying:
  Love so gentle, love so true, so I welcome you into my heart.
- Light the third candle, representing your lover, as you do so saying:

Love without question, love without doubt.
I ask only your care and loving company.
- Set this card beneath your own card and the Lovers, but say nothing.
- By the light of the candles, write a romantic letter to your love, known or unknown, using the red pen or quill. You are not going to send this letter, so you can be as poetic as you wish. You can quote from a favourite love poem if you like, or make up one of your own.
- When you have finished writing, fold the paper and slip it inside the envelope. Write 'To my love' or the lover's name on the envelope and seal it with the green candle wax. Then dab a drop of the fragrance in the corners of the envelope.
- Blow out first your own candle and then the lover's, as you do so seeing each light join with that of the central candle.
- Set the envelope on the scarf, in front of the dark green candle. When the candle is burnt through, wrap the envelope in the pink scarf and keep it safely in a dark place such as a drawer. Keep the love letter – if all works well you can give it to your love on your wedding day. Repeat the spell if necessary.

A candle, copper and mirror love spell

Many of the older love spells involve projecting the image of a loved one or future lover from one's unconscious mind into a mirror by candlelight, since the mirror was believed to reflect the soul or essence of a person. I have recorded two of these older spells on pages 58 and 61. A lot of modern spells also use a mirror to manifest an image of a future love, or maybe a present friend who could become more.

There are countless mirror spells. The following two are among my favourites. The first uses a technique called 'seeing clear' and relies on looking through a circle, in this case of copper. Copper is the metal of the love goddess Venus and attracts love, while giving a glimpse into the future through its circular gateway to other dimensions.

You will need

A round or oval mirror propped against a wall, on a table or on a fitted unit (a 3-sided mirror is very effective); 2 pink or green candles; a copper bracelet (available very cheaply in pharmacies and health food stores) or a circle of copper wire shaped into a bracelet (copper wire will shape easily without tools); a stick of rose incense.

Timing

After sunset, on a Friday.

The spell

* Light the rose incense (the fragrance of Venus) in front of the mirror so that the smoke is reflected in the centre of the mirror.
* On either side and slightly in front of the incense, set the candles, so that they too are reflected in the mirror. Do not light them yet.
* In front of the incense, so that it lies directly between the candles, place the copper bracelet.
* Sit or stand facing the mirror, so that your face is reflected through the smoke between the candles.
* Light the left-hand candle, as you do so saying:
This is my love that burns bright. I call my love, known or unknown, through candle flame this night.
* Light the right-hand candle, as you do so saying:
This candle is for my love, known or unknown. Burn bright that I may see your face tonight.
* Pass the copper bracelet carefully over or through the left-hand candle flame, as you do so saying:
Through candle fire, I call you. Show yourself in the glass that we may be joined in spirit.

* Now pass the bracelet through the incense smoke, as you do so saying:
Through the skies I call sight of you through this circle of love.
* Finally, pass the bracelet carefully over or through the right-hand candle flame, as you do so saying:
Through candle flame I call you. Show yourself in the glass that we may be joined in our hearts.
* Hold the bracelet so that through it you can see the incense smoke and beyond that into the mirror, and say:
Known or unknown, let me see your face.
* Still holding the bracelet, close your eyes and allow a picture to build up in your mind's eye of a distant face or figure coming nearer through the mist. When the form is close enough for you to identify it, open your eyes, look into the copper circle reflected in the mirror and say:
Let me know you, who will become as dear as my own self.
You will see the image, small but clear, framed within the copper circle like a cameo.
* Put down the bracelet and imagine the face looking over your shoulder and smiling into the mirror. Say:
Welcome into my life.
* Blow out the candles, first your own and then your lover's, sending the light of both to wherever he or she may be.
* If the face was of a friend or colleague, take time to get to know this person better; love may grow spontaneously. If you saw no one, try the spell again in a week's time. This does not mean that you will not find love but merely that now is not the time to see the face.

A three-night candle and mirror ritual to attract or strengthen new love

This spell is good for attracting a specific person whom you like a lot, or for strengthening feelings after first or early dates if you feel that the new person in your life could make you happy. The spell will also help to hasten connection if one or both of you are shy or afraid of being hurt. Because mirrors are reflective surfaces, they have the capacity, especially by candlelight, to break through conscious barriers and open channels to higher states of awareness where magical connections can happen – hence the large number of magic mirrors in fairy tales.

You will need

I short pink candle; I short green candle; a large metal tray; a round or oval mirror propped against a wall, on a table or fitted unit (a 3-sided mirror is very effective); an old pen or pencil, a knitting needle or pointed object suitable for inscribing in warm wax.

Timing

On the three nights before the night of the full moon, after dark.

The spell

* On the first night, set the two candles on the tray, the pink one (representing you) at the left-hand end of the tray, and the green one (representing your lover) at the right-hand end, placing them so that their glow will be reflected in the mirror.
* Light the pink candle and then light the green candle from the pink, as you do so saying:
Flame and flare, connect us in lovingness.
* Look between the candles into the mirror and softly call the name of your love. Now move the candles slightly closer, as you do so saying:
So do we move nearer to each other's heart.

* Blow out the green candle and then the pink, looking into the afterglow in the mirror. If you see an image of your love in the glass, smile back, but do not force the image to come. Many people just see mistiness in the centre of the mirror.
* On the second night, light the green candle first, and then light the pink candle from the green, as you do so repeating the first chant.
* Again look between the candles and call your lover's name softly. Now move the candles even closer, as you do so repeating the second chant.
* Blow out the pink candle and then the green one. The image of your love may be clearer in the afterglow reflected in the mirror. If it isn't, visualise the image in the glass.
* On the third night, light the pink candle, and then light the green candle from the pink, repeating the first chant.
* Look between candles into the mirror and call your lover's name softly. Now move the candles so close that they touch. Say:
Our hearts touch. So are we joined in tenderness.
* Look into the mirror over the candles. See your face and that of the other person close in the two flames and becoming one. If you still cannot see this, use your imagination – our most powerful psychic tool – to create the joint image in the glass.
* Let the candles burn down and, using your inscribing tool, in the mingled wax draw a heart with your initials entwined. Keep it as a love token.

A seven-day lodestone or magnet ritual to increase the romantic interest of a potential lover

Lodestone magic is known in cultures as old as that of ancient Greece. A lodestone is a piece of naturally magnetic iron ore. In modern lodestone rituals, block magnets (rather than the horseshoe kind), with positive and negative polarities at either end, are often substituted. You can buy lodestones in mineral and New Age stores; find a pair by seeing which attract. The more jagged ones tend to have a male/positive polarity. You can also buy a pair by mail order. Lodestones work equally well for same-sex relationship love spells.

This spell is ideal if you have found someone you like a lot but who, though friendly, does not seem to regard you in a romantic way. It will also work well if you have been out with someone a few times but the relationship is not progressing, perhaps because he or she is shy or fears rejection. With this spell you should add silently, either at the end of each day's working or once on the seventh day, 'if it is right to be' – the lack of interest may be because the chemistry is just not right.

You will need

2 lodestones that attract or 2 block magnets with positive/negative poles at the ends; a flat surface such as a stone slab, fireproof chopping board or tray (not metal); a tall red candle in a holder (or the type of candle that has 7 wicks); 2 sheets of white paper; a red pen; a small red drawstring bag; magnetic sand or iron filings (obtainable from hardware stores), or alternatively some patchouli essential oil.

Timing

The hour after sunset, on seven consecutive days, beginning on a Friday.

The spell

* Identify which is your lodestone or magnet and which belongs to your intended lover, then set them at either end of the surface, with the attracting ends facing each other.
* Using the red ink, write your name, as given on your birth certificate, in the form of a triangle on a sheet of the paper. Set the piece of paper beside the appropriate lodestone or magnet.
* Do the same for your intended lover, using as full a name as you know. If necessary, you may be able to make an excuse to see his ID card or driving licence.
* Place the red candle behind the two lodestones or magnets and in the centre, so that it forms the point of a triangle (with the two lodestones as the base). Light the candle. Red is the colour traditionally used in lodestone magic, and the triangle is a symbol of lovers coming together.
* Let the candle burn one-seventh of the way down (or, if you are using a seven-wick candle, burn down one wick), as it burns saying:
Friday is the day of love; may my lover closer move.
* Before you extinguish the candle, move the lodestones slightly closer together; then, as you put out the candle, send the light into the cosmos to amplify and fall as radiance around you.
* Repeat these steps each evening for the next six days, until on Thursday the lodestones or magnets are together in front of the candle. Substitute the appropriate day name in the chant.

- On Friday, put the lodestones or magnets and the folded names together in the drawstring bag and add the magnetic sand or iron filings. Alternatively, anoint the lodestones with a single drop of the patchouli essential oil before placing them in the bag. As you fill the bag, repeat the chant.
- Take the magnets or lodestones out of the bag every Friday and add more iron sand or iron filings, or re-anoint them, as you do so, reciting the day rhyme.

A magnet spell to attract an unknown lover

Some spells actually work better with a magnet than a lodestone. Like lodestones, magnets are also used in sympathetic magic to symbolically draw pins or iron nails that represent love energies or people into your life. The attracting energies are magically transferred to the actual situation.

You will need

A horseshoe magnet; a box of pins or tiny iron tacks; 6 small tea-lights or tiny white candles in holders.

Timing

Between the crescent and the full moon, preferably after dark.

The spell

- On any flat surface, indoors or in a sheltered place, arrange the tea-lights however you like over a small area. Light the tea-lights, as you do so saying:

From North or South, East or West,
Let him/her come who loves me best.
The lights will act as your guiding beacons.
- Scatter the pins or tacks around the lights, as you do so, repeating the chant.
- Holding the magnet in your power hand (the one you write with), turn round nine times deosil (clockwise), as you do so saying faster and faster:
As magnet draws iron and flowers the bee,
I call true love to come to me.
- Use the magnet to draw the pins, as you work repeating both chants.
- Put the magnet and pins on a window ledge to face the nearest ocean (even if it is hundreds of miles away). Leave them there until the full moon or, if you do the spell near the full moon, until the next crescent moon

A magnet and mirror spell to attract an unknown lover

This spell has the same purpose as the previous one but adds romance and atmosphere.

You will need

A round mirror; a pink fabric heart; pins or tacks; a horseshoe magnet; a green tablecloth; 6 small silver candles.

Timing

Any six days during the waxing moon, just before you go to bed.

The spell

- Cover a table with the cloth and place the mirror flat in the centre. Place the silver candles in a circle around the mirror, so that their glow is reflected.
- Scatter the pins in a deosil (clockwise) circle around the candles, repeating six times as you do so:
As pins are drawn, like bee to flower,
I call my love to me this hour.

- In a deosil sweep, make a circle with the magnet, picking up all the pins and repeating until they are all attracted:

  As pins are drawn, like moths to light,
  Come love to me, come to my sight.

- When you have all the pins on the magnet, place it on top of the heart, and place the heart in the centre of the mirror.

- Gaze down into the mirror in the candle light, trying not to cast your own reflection in it, and say:

  In silver light, love so bright;
  Like moth to flame, my love I claim.

- Blow out the candles in reverse order of lighting. Do not attempt to look for an image of your future love in the mirror.

- Repeat these steps for five more days. On the last night, as you blow out the sixth candle, look full in the mirror and you may see an image of your love. Even if you do not see anything, love will come into your life within six moons.

A rose quartz or amethyst spell to dream of the one you love

Pink rose quartz and purple amethyst are traditionally associated with dreams, and many of the old love spells involve placing an amethyst with a symbol of your love. This symbol may be a lock of your love's hair entwined in yours to establish the telepathic link between you. In this way you can dream of your lover, and hopefully he or she of you at the same time, a wonderful way of being together if you are separated by distance or circumstances. It is also a good way of mending quarrels. If you do not have a lock of your love's hair, you can still carry out the spell by engraving the wax heart with your entwined initials.

You will need

A small pink candle; a metal tray; a rose petal for each week or month you have been together (if long-term partners, use years as a measure for the petals); entwined hair (optional); a sharp silver paper knife or thin screwdriver; a piece of unpolished amethyst or rose quartz, or if you can find one, a rose quartz or amethyst heart-shaped crystal.

Timing

Before bed.

The spell

- Light the pink candle on the metal tray. Set the crystal on the tray so that the light shines on it but wax cannot fall on it. Leave the candle to melt in a pool of wax while you write a love letter or poem.

- Just before the candle has melted, hold the crystal above it and repeat seven times:

  I call my love in dreams tonight.

- While the wax is still soft, press the petals and hair into it, repeating the chant seven times. If you are not using hair, write your entwined initials in the wax with the knife or screwdriver and enclose in a drawn heart shape.

- Cut a heart shape in the wax and gently ease it out as soon as the wax is hard.

- Put the heart by your bed and the amethyst on top of the heart. Recite the chant as you fall asleep.

An oil bath ritual for a first date or a social event where you hope to meet someone new

Ninth-tenths of attractiveness is self-confidence. We all know physically unremarkable people who are like a honey pot, with people of both sexes swarming round them. The secret is an intangible magic and a radiant glow that the finest make-up artist or most expensive fashion designer cannot create.

The following is a simple bath ritual that can also be adapted to a shower. It is a spell I have recommended to people of all ages, and it has been a great success. It works equally well with young people and those returning to the social scene after a divorce or separation, or after grieving for a partner who has died. Men sometimes prefer to substitute pine and sandalwood oils and adapt the words.

You will need

A small bar of lavender-, rose- or sandalwood-scented soap; a paper knife or nail file; lavender and rose essential oils or two concentrated oil-based bath foams in these fragrances; scented rose or lavender tea-lights in holders; some CDs of gentle music and a CD player suitable for the bathroom (optional).

Timing

Before you go out, or before the person you like arrives for a meal or a drink at your home.

The spell

* Run a bath. Light the tea-lights, arrange them around the bathroom and extinguish the main bathroom light.

* Sitting in the bathroom, use the paper knife or nail file to carve into the soap the word 'beauty', 'radiance' or any other word that describes the magnetism you desire. Recite the chosen word over and over again as you engrave the soap.

* When the bath is ready, get in and add two or three drops of the lavender oil a drop at a time. For each drop of lavender, say:
Flow with love, flow with radiance. Radiant I am and radiant will I be, for all to see.

* Now add two or three drops of the rose oil a drop at a time. For each drop of rose say:
Flow with beauty, flow with harmony. Beautiful I am and beautiful shall I be. So all shall see.

* Drop the soap into the water, as you do so saying:
Melt fears. Lovely I am and lovely will I be to he/she who waits for me.

* Enjoy a leisurely bath by candlelight, perhaps with gentle music.

* When you have finished your bath, get out but leave the soap in the water until it has melted. Then run cold water into the bath, swirling it around and letting the dissolved soap flow down the plug hole as you chant:
Fear and doubts flow from me,
In the water to the sea;
Remain no more to trouble me.
Radiance I see and radiant will I be.

* Go out or wait for your guest, and have a lovely time.

A fragrance spell to make you irresistible

It can be quite nerve-wracking to go out socially if you have been rejected or betrayed in love or if you have lost your confidence for any reason. Meeting someone at the place or event you go to who obviously admires you can be a terrific ego booster, even if it's no more than an evening's flirtation. As I said earlier, if you feel good about yourself, then others will perceive you positively. Men as well as women can use this spell, empowering a favourite after-shave or cologne.

You will need

A gold-coloured or vibrant-orange candle; a paper knife or thin gold-coloured screwdriver or sharp metal nail; a bottle of your favourite fragrance.

Timing

Within 24 hours before the planned event or social occasion.

The spell

- Using the paper knife, screwdriver or nail, engrave the initial of your first name about halfway down the candle. Around the initial engrave a circle of radiating rays to represent the sun. As you work, picture yourself at the social event you plan to attend surrounded by friendly people. If it is to be a quieter gathering, such as a dinner party, visualise yourself in the midst of good company. As your imagination creates the scene, your unconscious mind may reveal an image of a person who obviously finds you attractive. It may be someone you already know but with whom you had not previously clicked emotionally. If the figure is shadowy, do not force the image. Once you get to the social event, you may find that there is more than one competitor for your attention, or the person you encounter there may invite you to meet a new circle of friends where you will find your new romance.

- Light the candle and set your fragrance bottle so that the light shines on it but wax does not drip on the bottle, as you do so saying:
Fragrance of mine, be filled with light,
That I may likewise shine this night.
Fragrance of mine, be filled with treasure;
Make every moment purest pleasure.
I am as the sun.

- Leave the candle to burn down and before you go out anoint your pulse points with the fragrance, as you do so saying:
I am the sun; I am pure fragrance.

- Take a tiny phial of the fragrance with you to the event so that you can put a drop of it on each of your wrists if you begin to lose your confidence.

A crossroads spell to bring a desired person into your life

There are a number of traditional spells in which a would-be lover leaves a circle of dried beans at a crossroads where the intended will step over them. Alternatively, he or she uses the soil from the desired person's shoe print to grow the love. Shoe prints are a way of transferring the personal essence of the object of love without using stolen nail clippings and so on – a practice that seems to me to be too intrusive and manipulative.

I know of one American 30-something who used a modern form of this spell when she wanted to date her boss. She pretended to drop her corn chips – in a circle – outside the executive elevator. Unfortunately, before her boss stepped out, the cleaner had vacuumed them up!

You will need

A receptacle suitable for collecting a little earth (see also step I for alternatives); a small cardboard or wooden box with a lid; a personal item of your own, such as an earring, a button or some soil from your own footprint; a spoonful of sugar.

Timing

Traditionally a summer spell, but you can carry it out any time.

The spell

* First of all you need to obtain a small amount of earth over which your beloved has stepped. You may need to be ingenious, for example, spilling a plant pot in the office just as the person you like is walking by, or dropping something in a flower bed and asking him or her to help you retrieve it. Alternatively, if you can temporarily get hold of a shoe belonging to your intended, rub a crystal or stone over the sole to absorb the essence. Another possibility is to leave a dried pea or bean on the floor – in lieu of a circle of beans, which might be too obvious unless you can make your circle in grass. As I said, ingenuity is the key to success.

* Take the soil, bean or crystal imprinted with the would-be lover's essence and set it in the box together with the personal item of your own, sprinkling the sugar over both items.

* Close the box, as you do so saying: *Our pathways cross, our lives touch; hearts connect and love grows in sweetness.*

* If there is a crossroads or other intersection handy, bury the box there. You could, for instance use a large plant pot in a reception area you both cross or a bush in a park where you both walk your dogs. Failing that, create a symbolic intersection in your garden by marking a cross in the earth in front of a bush and bury the box there. As you work, repeat the chant three times.

* Try to encounter the would-be lover regularly at an intersection over the following days.

A love spell bag for growing feelings with someone who has entered your world

Spell bags appear in almost every culture and time (see also page 197) as a way of releasing magical energies slowly and continuously. Love spell bags are traditionally very tiny so that they can be carried or worn. However, the modern ones I create do not have the intimate additions of the earlier ones, such as stolen pubic or head hairs, or drops of blood. I believe that love spells should help to bring out mutual and willing attraction. This is much healthier, and in the long term more likely to lead to lasting love than are more manipulative techniques.

You will need

A very small pink fabric drawstring bag or a small pink circle of cloth and a red cord long enough to tie around the top of the cloth and knot three times; a tiny silver-coloured or red velvet heart; a small pale-blue lace agate or rose quartz charm; a few dried rose petals or lavender heads, or 3 pinches of dried rosemary (mix all three if you wish, reducing the amount of each); a pinch of dried mint; a slender silver-coloured chain, fastened to symbolise love without end; a tea-light or very small white candle; a hand bell of any kind, preferably silver-coloured; a white cloth.

Timing

Love spell bags should be made at 10 pm on a Friday if possible. If you can, begin at precisely 10 o'clock – if you can hear a chiming clock that is especially magical.

The spell

* Spread the white cloth and assemble the ingredients of the bag – the heart, agate or rose quartz charm, flowers and herbs, and chain – in a circle. You can leave the herbs in their original containers if you like. Put the bag or cloth circle and cord in the centre of the circle and place the candle behind it, still within the circle.

* Draw the curtains and light the candle, so that the room is dimly lit. If you are able to hear a clock chime 10 o'clock as you start to prepare the bag, ring the bell ten times in time with it. Otherwise, ring the bell ten times when it is 10 o'clock by your watch or clock.

* Put the heart; then the crystal; then the rose, lavender or rosemary; then the mint; and finally the chain, one by one, into the bag or on the pink fabric circle, working in silence.

* Pull the drawstring or gather up the circle of fabric and tie the gathered ends with the cord. Tie three knots in the drawstring or cord, one above the other. Say nothing.

* Ring the bell ten times and extinguish the light.

* Sit in the darkness and, holding the bag between your hands, whisper ten times:
Night and darkness speak his/her name;
Silently I do the same.
With passing days may this spell grow;
When fragrance passes, his/her love show.

* Keep the spell bag with you always until the fragrance fades. The spell is then done, and if it is right to be, your intended will notice you.

A spell bag to bring fun and excitement into your life

Even the most level-headed of us crave fun and excitement at times — perhaps because we are about to settle down or because we have just escaped from a controlling relationship. Having a person (or persons) around who flirts with us, offers us trips to Paris or sends us flowers can help to put the sparkle back into our life. Just occasionally those fun romances can turn into the real thing, but even if yours doesn't, it is good to be the centre of attention sometimes. The following spell bag will kick-start your charisma in a big way. The power will last only for a few evenings, until the herbs in the bag wilt, but you can always make another bag

You will need

A small circle of red cloth and a scarlet ribbon, or a drawstring purse big enough to hold a tiny crystal; I sprig of fresh mint and I sprig of fresh thyme (available from supermarkets); a sprinkling of ginger or cinnamon; a tiny clear quartz crystal or a clear glass nugget; sandalwood or orange essential oil.

Timing

A day when you are going out on the town or to a celebration.

The spell

* Spread out your ingredients and open the circle of cloth or the purse.
* Place the mint on the cloth or into the bag. As you do so, say:
  Mint for excitement.
* Place the thyme on the cloth or into the bag. As you do so, say:
  Thyme for admiration.
* Place the ginger or cinnamon on the cloth or into the bag. As you do so, say:
  Ginger / cinnamon to make my heart glad and my eyes sparkle.
* Place the crystal or glass on the cloth or into the bag. As you do so, say:
  Crystal / glass clear for life and laughter and lovely times ahead.
* Sprinkle one or two drops of the orange or sandalwood on the cloth or into the bag. As you do so, say:
  Orange / sandalwood for warmth and radiance.
* Tie the cloth with the ribbon or fasten the purse, securing it with three knots and saying as you do so:
  So bind together, wind you knots. Hold firm, that life may be kind and grant me this evening of joy.
* When you go out, attach the spell bag to the inside of your handbag or to a piece of clothing where it will not be seen. Have a good time.

A mist spell to bring the perfect lover

Sometimes we discover, to our cost, that a seemingly perfect lover is not all he or she seemed. This spell is not intended to bring you the most physically attractive or wealthiest companion (unless that is what you ask for – after all, it is your spell); rather it is meant to attract the kind of love that is perfect for you spiritually and emotionally.

Mist has always been considered magical because, as it clears in small patches, it is believed to give glimpses of other dimensions. It has long been held that mist can carry our words to people from afar if we call them through it. The magical Isle of Avalon, identified as present-day Glastonbury in Somerset, England, was, according to myth, always shrouded in mist so that none could find it unless they were meant to do so. Even today, as you drive over the flat plains towards Glastonbury there is often a mist followed by a sudden break in the cloud that reveals the Tor looming upwards very close before the sky completely clears. A mist spell performed on the Tor will be extremely powerful; however, you don't have to go to Glastonbury to perform a mist spell effectively. A mist in your garden, by the sea or on a balcony will do just fine. If the need is urgent, use a steamy bathroom.

You will need

A small torch.

Timing

When there is natural mist, if possible.

The spell

* Stand in the mist and turn round nine times slowly, as you do so saying:
  Where are you, my love? I seek you through the mists of time. Love, I light the way. You have only to follow.
* Switch on the torch and cast the beam directly ahead, as you do so continuing to repeat the words, and turn slowly so that the beam casts a series of 'pathways'.
* Gradually stop turning and let the words fade softly into the mist.
* Go indoors and light a lamp at the window of a high-up room, leaving the lamp there until the mist clears.

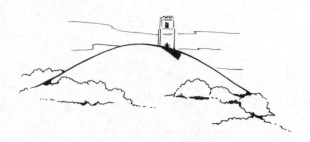

A ritual to find your twin soul

The Greek philosopher Plato described twin souls 2,500 years ago: 'When one of them meets the other half, the actual half of himself, the pair are lost in an amazement of love and friendship and intimacy and one will not be out of the other's sight even for a moment.' Like Plato, some people today believe that there is one special person for us in this lifetime and that only with them will we experience total unity and bliss. It is said that when we meet them we will recognise them, and even that we have known and been with them in previous incarnations.

This spell is a shorter adaptation of one I created some time ago and allows the powers of nature rather than the spell-caster to direct the outcome. It is intended to call your other half, and some who have used it are convinced that it has called the spiritual twin with whom their destiny is entwined; however, it can also be used to call those with whom we can enjoy close love connections although they are not our soul mate. Because in this spell you are seeking your twin soul as opposed to someone who would simply make you happy, you may have to be patient or make a special trip to fulfil the ideal criteria for the ritual.

You will need

9 gold coins with holes – for example old Spanish 25-peseta coins or well polished Chinese divinatory coins – or small looped gold-coloured earrings; 9 white flowers; 9 grapes or any other small fruits; a basket made of rushes, raffia or any other natural undyed substance; a sandy beach (by a tidal river will do).

Timing

At the full moon, when the tide is about to turn, preferably during the evening. Use a tide table to find the best time. Take care in tidal waters – even rivers – and do not wade out; the currents can be strong and quick-changing.

The spell

* Go to the beach at the appropriate time, carrying your coins, flowers and grapes in the basket.
* Look around the beach for a stick and then, in an area that will be washed by the tide, use it to draw a circle in the sand. Inside the circle, make a tiny sandcastle and, in a spiral around the base of the castle, write your name and the date, together with the following words:
I call my twin soul, by the power of the turning sea, to find me, wherever she/he may be.
As you write the words, it is best to add, either in your head or out loud:
If it is right to be and will cause no hurt to others.
* As the tide turns, paddle into the water and set the basket afloat, as you do so saying:
Twin soul, if it's meant to be,
Find your way back home to me.
Far away or nearer lands,
Come my love and take my hands.
* Hold your hands high above your head and then outstretched towards the sea. You will feel the breeze rippling them, and perhaps the touch of your twin from across the waves.

A seven-day spell to help you give out the right vibes to attract a lover

Pink flowers are associated with the awakening of love. When we open ourselves to the possibility of love, we give out vibes that make others respond positively to us. This spell is like opening a window to love, which may be difficult if you have been hurt in the past or lost confidence in yourself.

You will need
A bunch of pink flowers.

Timing
Early afternoon on the first day and thereafter in the morning.

The spell
* On the first afternoon, go to a park or garden (your own or a public one) where there is a circular flower bed with blooming flowers, preferably pink (for new love).

* Walk around the flower bed nine times deosil (clockwise) with open arms, saying continuously, either softly or silently:
I welcome love into my life.
* On the way home, buy a bunch of pink flowers.
* When you get home, hold them, still in the cellophane, and turn around nine times, repeating the chant.
* Put the flowers in a vase and place it where you can walk all around it.
* When you get up on each of the following six days, walk around the vase nine times deosil, repeating the chant continuously.
* When the flowers die, pluck the petals and collect them in a bowl. Scatter the petals to the wind outdoors, repeating the chant.

2 Traditional Spells For Identifying a Lover and Attracting Love

While there are traditional spells for many purposes (you will find them throughout this book), love spells are far and away the most common type. For this reason, I have devoted a whole chapter to them. The traditional love spells in this book constitute only a fraction of the folk love rituals in existence. I have recorded them because I would hate to see them get lost among the vast numbers of modern love spells that are being created. These old spells tell us of the lives and dreams of our ancestors, while at the same time having a freshness and innocence that can give hope to modern lovers.

I have discovered these spells in research and travel extending over 15 years. They come mainly from eastern and western Europe, the Mediterranean and Scandinavia, and have been passed down through an oral tradition. Many travelled with the colonists to America, Australia, New Zealand and South Africa. I also found a folk heritage that I had not expected in Egypt, when I made a research trip to the country in 2003. More recent religious traditions had not eradicated ancient love spells dating from the time of the Pharaohs, which have passed into popular knowledge almost entirely by word of mouth. I was lucky enough to be invited into homes where this hidden tradition thrives.

Traditional love spells usually have a dual purpose: to identify a lover or confirm that a chosen lover is the right one and then to call that lover. They were generally carried out at one of the seasonal or yearly change points – such as midsummer, halloween (the beginning of the Celtic year) or new year – because at such times energies were especially fluid and so magic was considered more likely to work. In Christian times, a number of saints were thought to be kindly disposed to lovers, and so love spells were worked on their saint's day (either before or after worship at church). Such seasonal love rituals are a good alternative to the modern commercialised celebration of St Valentine's day and can help us to become more aware of subtle changes in the passing year.

You might ask why we should practise spells involving archaic words and actions (such as sticking pins in a pincushion) that seem either homely or downright strange in the modern world. The answer is that words that have been spoken and actions that have been taken in love and hope over hundreds of years or more become endowed with the positive emotions of previous spell-casters. By repeating them we are able to tap into that source of power and thus to strengthen our own spell.

What's more, the old spells to identify a lover contain some remarkably sound psychology. They work on the same principle as all divination: the questioner selects by a seemingly random process letters or words that give the name of the person who will be right for them. Some would argue that the name of the person comes from the deep unconscious of the questioner – an area of wisdom where the barriers of past, present and future are not clearly drawn. Others would say that it comes from a guardian angel. In fact these are not contradictory views but simply different ways of explaining the same phenomenon. The spell acts to make the divinatory powers more accurate and also to create a psychic connection with the known or unknown lover.

The divinations in these spells do not usually refer to a man or woman from the other side of the world (unless you intend to travel there in the near future) or to a love ten years hence, but to someone who is around you at present in some capacity – perhaps a friend of a friend or a colleague. Imagine, for example, that the name Alan Jones appears in a divination. You may know an Alan Jones who works in Accounts, but you have never spoken to him, because you are lusting after Mike Collins, who lives with his girlfriend in the nextdoor flat. In this case, perhaps your subconscious is giving you a nudge in the right direction. Sometimes it is simply a question of recognising the right person in your everyday life rather than waiting in vain for the dream lover.

The same cautions apply to these traditional love spells as to those in Chapter 1: namely, that you should not work them if you are already in a strong relationship (the spells for commitment and fidelity in Chapters 3 and 4 respectively are more appropriate). If you have doubts about your current relationship, discuss them with your partner and try working the spells for reconciliation in Chapter 6.

An ancient Egyptian myrrh and oil ritual for a good lover

I found this spell at an exhibition at the British Museum in London some years ago, but it was not until I went to Egypt that I was able to buy the sacred lotus essence it requires. I have since discovered that you can buy lotus essential oil in other countries through aromatherapy suppliers. I have adapted the spell slightly, since the original involves embalming a fish with myrrh, which may not be to the modern taste! (The fish is a fertility symbol.)

Much Egyptian magic relies on words, sometimes spoken by the spell-caster in the voice of a god or goddess — a way of borrowing the power of the deity for magical purposes (see pages 143 and 146). Speak the words slowly. Though this is traditionally a woman's spell, men can take on the role of Hathor, the love goddess, or change the words of the spell and speak as the sun god Ra, Hathor's father.

You will need

Lotus oil (a few drops of lotus essential oil diluted in a carrier oil) or lotus cologne; 8 myrrh incense sticks and a single holder; a deep bowl; some rose petals (if you can pick them fresh just before the ritual, that will make it even more special, or you can pluck petals from roses bought from a florist's); a rose bush in the garden or small rose in a pot; some cod liver oil or a kelp-based oil (optional); a small wooden spoon.

Timing

Dawn and late evening on the seventh day before the full moon, then the following six nights and the night of full moon.

The spell

❋ At dawn or in the early morning of the seventh day before the full moon, pour about three teaspoonfuls of lotus oil or cologne into the bowl, as you do so saying:
I, Hathor, ask you Father Ra to fill this sacred bowl with your magical light that love may light on me and those who call my name.

❋ Add a teaspoonful of the fish oil if you are using it, and a few rose petals. Cover the bowl and leave the mix where light can fall on it until dark.

❋ After dark on the same day, light a myrrh incense stick near the bowl. Stir the mixture seven times deosil (clockwise) and say:
I, Hathor, send thee a husband / wife true to be, eternally. So I decree and it shall be.
Leave the incense stick to burn through.

❋ Repeat the incense lighting, stirring and chanting on the next six nights (before the full moon).

❋ On the eighth night of the spell, the night of the full moon itself, light the myrrh incense stick and rub just a little of the oil mix in the centre of your forehead, repeating the nightly chant three times.

❋ Pour any excess mixture into the soil around the rose bush, burying the petals contained in the mix.

An ancient Egyptian Hathor love-knot ritual to attract lasting love

Knots, used for binding someone in love, have been associated with love magic since ancient Babylonian times. Most famous as a focus for love-knot magic are the seven daughters of Hathor, the sisters of Fate or Destiny (who also protect children and young women from harm).

Hathor is the ancient Egyptian goddess who, assisted by her daughters, presides over women, marriage, beauty, fertility, music and dance. Ancient Egyptian women prayed to Lady Hathor or her daughters for a husband; today in Cairo young women appeal to the same deities through the use of this and similar spells.

The seven daughters of Hathor are represented in love spells by seven separate red ribbons or cords, which are tied together in the spell. The daughters have special ritual names that can easily be memorised: Lady of the House of Jubilation, Lady of the Stormy Sky, Lady from the Land of Silence, Lady from under the Black Earth, Lady with Hair of Fire, Lady of the Sacred Land, and Lady whose name Flourishes through Power.

If you have been betrayed in love or have never found the right person, this ritual is a good way to attract into your life someone who will stay – as the ancient Egyptians used to say, 'so long as the sun shines and the waters flow' (see page 78 for a love charm using this concept). I am told that, unlike other spells, this one often attracts a lover from further afield – in the case of the girls I spoke to, from other parts of Egypt. Western women I know of who have tried this spell have become involved in holiday romances that were something a little more than just pleasant flirtations.

This spell is traditionally practised on a flat roof, but any outdoor place or upstairs facing a window will do just as well. Men as well as women of all ages can use it with success.

You will need
7 red ribbons or cords (curtain cord is good) of equal lengths, each no more than 15 cm/6 in long; a red candle

Timing
The hour before sunset, Hathor's special time.

The spell
* Practise the seven names of Hathor's daughters so that you can recite them. If you prefer, you can just call each 'Lady Hathor'.
* Light the red candle (red is the colour sacred to Hathor) and set the seven cords in front of it, one in front of the other.
* Take up two cords and tie them together, as you do so saying:
  Lady of the House of Jubilation, I ask that she/he may come to me. Hathor guide the way.

- Take up the third cord and tie it to the second, as you do so saying:
  Lady of the Stormy Sky, I ask that she/he may accept me as I am. Hathor guide the way.
- Take up the fourth cord and tie it to the third, as you do so saying:
  Lady from the Land of Silence, I ask that she/he may be kind and gentle in word and action. Hathor guide the way.
- Take up the fifth cord and tie it to the fourth, as you do so saying:
  Lady from under the Black Earth, may she/he grow to love me more each day. Hathor guide the way.
- Take up the sixth cord and tie it to the fifth, as you do so saying:
  Lady with Hair of Fire, may she/he be faithful and never give me cause to doubt. Hathor guide the way.
- Take up the seventh cord and tie it to the sixth, as you do so saying:
  Lady of the Sacred Land, may our love grow deeper with the years. Hathor guide the way.
- Tie the seventh cord to the first cord to make a circle, as you do so saying:
  Lady whose name Flourishes through Power, may there be always unity through bad times as well as good, so long as the sun shines and the water flows. Hathor guide the way.
- Let the candle burn through and leave the circle of knots indoors, near your bedroom window, so that it catches the first light of dawn.
- On the next dawn or when you wake, untie both ends of the final knot that makes the circle, as you do so reciting its chant. Leave the untied cord in front of the others.
- Working in reverse order of tying, untie a single cord each morning until all the cords are untied. As you work, recite the appropriate chant and leave the untied cords one in front of the other.
- When all the knots are untied, bury the cords beneath a fruit-bearing tree (traditionally a fig tree; however, these are not that common in modern Cairo).
- Wait a week, and if your love has not come, repeat the spell. Wait a further month, and if your love still has not come, repeat the spell again – Egyptian magic tends to be slow but powerful: the energies are building. In the meantime make sure you go out as usual, perhaps finding new interests but not actively seeking love (for example in a singles bar) unless this is something you actively want to do.

A new year's eve love ritual for naming your true love

The turning of the year is a natural time for love divination, especially if love has been slow to come during the previous year. Because Christianity was grafted on to old pagan customs by order of Pope Gregory (who sent St Augustine to England in 597 CE), the Bible and the saints became part of folk magic, and remained so well into the twentieth century. Indeed, I can remember this spell being played as a party game at new year in my childhood in the 1950s (see also page 71).

You will need

A small Bible (the St James's version is best); a door key; 26 slips of paper; a black pen; a long red ribbon.

Timing

At midnight on new year's eve

The spell

* In the Bible find the Songs of Solomon (Chapter 8, verses 6 and 7) and recite the words:
  Set me as a seal upon thine heart, as a seal upon thine arm, for love is as strong as death ... Many waters cannot quench love, neither can floods drown it. If a man would give all the substance of his house for love, he would be contented.
  Place the key in this page of the Bible and set the Bible down in the centre of the floor.

* Kneeling in front of the Bible, write the letters of the alphabet one on each of the pieces of paper. Shuffle the letters and place them at random face down in a circle around the Bible, leaving a space between the first and last letters.

* Remove the key from the bible and tie it on to the ribbon.

* Holding the ribbon with your wedding ring finger, walk around the outside of the circle of letters deosil (clockwise), allowing the key to swing over each of the letters and moving from one to the other slowly. Continue walking (making more than one circle if necessary) until the key remains still over one of the letters. This letter is the first initial of your true love, who may be known or unknown to you.

* Collect up the letters, shuffle them once more and replace them at random face down in a circle around the Bible. Recite the verses again, and once more walk around the circle of letters, allowing the key to swing. When you come to a letter over which it remains still, you have found the second initial of your love.

* Replace the key in the Bible at the correct page, tie the Bible with the ribbon and place it next to your bed. You will dream of your love, and he or she will reveal their full name if you have not already guessed it.

A St Agnes eve love spell

This is one of the saints' festival love spells that were popular throughout Europe, and especially in Germany, from the eleventh century right through to the twentieth century in the UK – as well as in America, where they were taken by colonists.

Young women traditionally practised love divination and magic on St Agnes eve (January 20) or on the following night (the actual saint's day). Agnes is the patron saint of virgins and betrothed couples. She was martyred under Emperor Diocletian in the year 306 CE because she had dedicated herself to chastity and refused to compromise her faith. She, like other saints, was believed to help young women (and men) find love. Whatever your age and sex, you may like to try this spell to bring love into your life or increase the love you already have.

Before working the spell, the maidens would fast all day, a practice which would have induced light-headedness and psychic visions, but you can eat a light meal. They also often recited a Pater Noster (The Lord's Prayer) as they picked each pin from the cloth or pincushion, rather than the St Agnes blessing I have used. If you want to use The Lord's Prayer and do not already know it, you can find it in any prayer book (use the traditional version). In earlier times everyone knew the prayer in Latin because they heard it every week in church.

You will need

A pincushion or a square of folded cloth stuck with pins in neat rows; a nightdress with sleeves, or a pyjama top.

Timing

On St Agnes eve (January 20) at 10 pm.

The spell

- Put on the nightdress or pyjama top.
- Working by a dim light, preferably from outside the room, take the pincushion and pull out the pins one by one, fastening each, one at a time, to the sleeve of your nightgown or pyjama top so that they form rows. Each time you transfer a pin, say:
  St Agnes, send your blessings and bring me love / increase love.
- When all the pins are in your sleeve, carefully remove the garment and set it close to your bed. (Our hardier ancestors slept in the pin-covered nightgown, but to do so would require great care.)
- As you get into bed, recite the following verse (you can adapt the words if you are seeking a woman):
  Sweet Agnes, work thy fast.
  If ever I be to marry man
  Or ever man to marry me,
  I hope this night him to see.

You will dream of your lover or of an as yet unknown love, and before May time comes, you will know happiness.

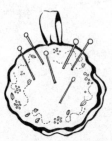

An alternative St Agnes eve ritual to meet your intended husband/wife

This version of the St Agnes eve spell comes from Scotland and the north of England. It dates from a time, before the industrial revolution of the early nineteenth century, in which people generally married partners who lived in or near their home village. The true love of the spell-caster was therefore presumed to be somebody whom she already knew, and the purpose of the spell was to kindle a psychic awareness that would enable her to recognise intuitively or acknowledge that a particular person would make her happy. In modern life, too, we sometimes know a person for a long time on a non-intimate level before eventually falling in love with them. (Perhaps we have felt reluctant to risk trying to develop a friendship into something more because we fear rejection, or because we harbour dreams of princes or millionaire footballers.) However, there is so much more movement of people in the modern world that it is also possible this ritual may bring you a true love in the form of a New York rep on business in your office, or a Spanish local you meet on a summer holiday.

Though this spell was originally written for women (since it was generally only women who would admit to using such magic), it works well for men too if the words are adapted.

You will need

A box of pins; a pincushion or folded square of cloth.

Timing

On St Agnes eve (January 20) at 10 pm.

The spell

* Take the pins one at a time from the box and pin them in horizontal rows from the bottom to the top of the pin cushion or folded cloth, saying each time you fasten a pin:

Fair St Agnes, play the part
And send to me my own sweetheart,
Not in his best nor worst array
But in the clothes he wears each day
That tomorrow I may him ken (know)
From among all other men.

If you speak softly and slowly, the words will take on a natural sleepy rhythm, and you will find yourself relaxing into a different kind of awareness, in which anything is possible.

* When you have fastened all the pins or sense that your energies are waning, position the pincushion (still stuck with the pins) to face the direction of the front door (even if you are working in your bedroom). The spell is done. When you go to bed, you may have dreams filled with love, peace, happiness or beautiful colours and fragrances. Do not change your routine the next morning unless you have a strong instinct to go to a particular place at a certain time.

A St Valentine's hemp seed ritual to find out who you will marry

Most famous of all those saints who preside over love is Valentine – I have included a number of Valentine's day spells in this chapter.

St Valentine was, according to legend, a young priest who defied an edict of the Emperor Claudius II that soldiers should not be allowed to marry as it made them poor fighters. St Valentine conducted the weddings of a number of young soldiers and was in consequence executed on 14 February 269 CE, thereafter becoming the patron saint of lovers. It is said that while he was imprisoned prior to his execution, he restored the sight of the jailer's blind daughter and that she fell in love with him. Legend adds that before he was taken to his death, he wrote on the wall a message for his love: 'Always, your Valentine'.

Many of our Valentine's day customs derive from Lupercalia, a Roman festival of love and fertility that took place on 15 February. Lupercalia was dedicated to the goddess she-wolf Lupa, who suckled the twins Romulus and Remus, later the founders of Rome. On this day, unmarried girls and single young men performed love and sex rites in the Grotto of the She-wolf in order to bring fertility to animals, land and people.

The hemp seed ritual is found throughout Europe and Scandinavia, and may be one of the oldest love rituals in existence. It can be difficult to obtain hemp seeds, but any type of seed (such as sunflower or those found in bird seed) is just as good. The birds will carry the seeds away, dropping some, which will take flower. I have a splendid sunflower crop in my garden as a result of a friend doing this spell. Traditionally, the spell-caster ran around a churchyard, but you can use a garden or any open space.

You will need
A container of hemp or other seeds.

Timing
Midnight on St Valentine's eve (13–14 February). You may need to modify the timing for safety purposes.

The spell
* Go into a churchyard (or your garden or any area of open land). Throw the seed over your shoulder, as you do so saying:

I scatter hemp seed;
Hemp seed I sow.
He that is my true love,
Come after me and mow.

* Look over your right shoulder and you will see a vision in your mind's eye of the future, with your love mowing the land where the flowers have grown from your seeds. You may recognise him or her. If not, close your eyes and let a name come into your head spontaneously. It may be someone you know.

* Go home and go to bed. You will dream of yourself and your love together in the summer.

A Valentine's day flower love charm

This is a European charm based on the coming of the first spring flowers, a time when fertility rites were traditionally performed to celebrate the awakening of the earth. The yellow crocus is the flower of St Valentine. By Christian times, wearing a crocus on Valentine's day had become a romantic gesture.

You will need

A yellow crocus or a yellow early spring flower (if you live in colder climes, you will have to use a hot-house flower).

Timing

Valentine's day (14 February), as soon as you go outdoors.

The spell

● Before you go outdoors for the first time on St Valentine's day, fasten the yellow crocus in your buttonhole or in your hair, as you do so saying three times:
St Valentine, the lover's friend,
I ask this flower my love to send.
Before the end of the day, you will have met or heard from someone who could make you happy (or through whom you will meet a new love).

A spell to discover who has sent you a Valentine's card

The practice of sending Valentine's love notes, often illustrated, began in the early Middle Ages. Hand-cut, illustrated Valentine's messages survive from as early as the 1500s. The first Valentine's card was printed in 1761.

Superstition has it that we should not attempt to find out the identity of the sender of a Valentine's card, and, indeed, it has always been considered very unlucky to write your name on a Valentine's card at all. Break either prohibition, and tradition warns that you will never marry your beloved. On the other hand, if you have received a beautiful card with words of love and want to know the identity of the sender, it would seem the waste of a good opportunity to let superstition stand in your way. And if you still need convincing, because you carry out this ritual after sunset on a day after the event, it does not count — that is, according to the nineteenth-century astrologer Zadkiel, whose works were published by the publisher of this book.

The red ink used in this spell was traditionally blood. I have made this modification because I personally have a distaste for blood in spells. It is possible to buy a magical red ink called 'pigeon blood' in more reputable New Age stores that is made entirely from plant materials. The quill pen was originally a crow's feather, but these may be hard to come by.

You will need

A quill pen or fountain pen; red ink; the anonymous Valentine's card.

Timing

Just before midnight on the first Friday after you receive the Valentine card (a week after Valentine's day itself if that falls on a Friday).

The spell

● Using the quill or fountain pen and the red ink, write on the back of the card the day, hour and year of your birth; the current year; the moon's age (i.e. the day of the current 28-day lunar cycle); and the star sign into which the sun has entered, for example Aries. You can get the latter two pieces of information from *Old Moore's Almanack*, from the astrology section of a newspaper or from the Internet.

* Rest the card on or in your left shoe and put both card and shoe under your bed, level with your heart. (The original spell suggests sleeping with the shoe under your pillow.)

* Go to bed. Lie on your left side and repeat three times:

St Valentine, pray condescend
To be this night a maiden's friend;
Let me now my lover see,
Be he of high or low degree.
By a sign his station show,
Be it weal or be it woe.
Let him come to my bedside
And my fortunes thus decide.

During the next week you will discover the identity of your secret Valentine-sender, either in a dream or in waking life.

Some St Mark's eve spells to call your love

Midnight on St Mark's eve (24 April) was another traditional time for love magic. There were a number of rituals a young girl could perform in order to call the spirit form of her future husband to visit her. One of the less aesthetic spells worked on this night was the watching of the farthing candle. A group of young men or women would steal a pig's tail, place it on the floor and light it. When the tail turned blue, each person present would see their future husband or wife. It is definitely not one I recommend.

The following are some of my favourite St Mark's spells — eager lovers might like to perform more than one. They work for either sex. If you have a developing relationship, ask your lover to carry out the rituals at the same time in his or her own home. If the relationship is new and you do not want to mention the spells, you can still use them to increase the spiritual connection between the two of you — they are a good way of increasing telepathic communication between lovers. If you are single, these spells will alert you to a potential partner.

Visions of etheric or spirit doubles, such as are induced in these spells, are a common psychic phenomenon and seem to result from an-out-of-body experience or mind travel. Such a double is an exact replica of a real person, except mistier and more ethereal. You may see it in actuality or in your mind's eye. When you next encounter in real life the person who appears in these spells, he or she may report a vivid dream of being in your house, your garden or a church — or a dream in which you appeared.

* **Spell 1:** At midnight set a supper table in silence. The etheric or spirit double of your love will sit down to dine.

* **Spell 2:** Go to a church at midnight and peer through each window in turn. The lover's face will appear through the last window.

* **Spell 3:** (This is my favourite of the spells.) Pluck 12 leaves from a red sage plant, one at each stroke of midnight. The lover will appear in spirit form.

* **Spell 4:** Scatter ash on the hearth on the first stroke of midnight. The lover's footprint will be there in the morning.

A midsummer love spell for three, five or seven women

There are several versions of this ritual, carried out on the eve of the longest day (or, in some traditions, on the evening of the longest day itself). With the sun at its height, midsummer was a natural love and fertility festival. There was fierce competition among women, maiden and married, to pick the yellow flowers of the magical St John's wort, or hypericum (see pages 52 and 98).

This spell uses sage instead of St John's wort, and works best for a small number of young women who are all looking for love or to develop an existing relationship; however, you can do the spell alone. Although most old spells are unisex, for purely practical reasons this one does not translate very well for men.

You will need

A sprig of red sage (or any other type of sage) for each woman working the spell, picked from a garden at sunset (or leave the sprigs in a vase of water outdoors – or at least outside the spell room – before the ritual); a stool; a bowl of rose water (either buy rose water from a shop or soak rose petals in water and 1 tsp vodka in a sealed jar for 24 hours, then strain – see my *Fragrant Magic*, Foulsham/Quantum, 2004 for more on making flower waters); a length of washing line or a clothes horse; 2 or 3 of each woman's prettiest undergarments or blouses; a small candle.

Timing

On the eve of the summer solstice (usually 21 June, but the date varies slightly from year to year, so consult a diary, a newspaper or *Old Moore's Almanack*), just before midnight.

The spell

* Set up a room with the washing line tied across it so that it passes over the stool, or if you are using a clothes horse, place it near the stool. Set down the bowl of rose water and place the undergarments in a pile.
* At midnight, enter the room, taking with you the sprigs of sage, and then put the sprigs into the bowl of rose water, each in turn.
* Light the candle so that you have a dim light to work by (taking care to place it safely away from the pile of undergarments.
* In silence, turn your undergarments inside-out and hang them on the washing line or clothes horse.
* Sit in a row. It is said that a few minutes after midnight, each woman's future husband will take the sage out of the rose water and sprinkle her undergarments with it. You may only see this in your mind's eye, or you may smell the sage and rose water strongly for a moment or two as the psychic connection is made.

A midsummer herb spell for an early marriage

Young girls traditionally picked St John's wort on midsummer's eve (or on the evening of midsummer's day itself) in order to attract a husband. However, this spell can be used by men as well as women. The only proviso is that you should not already be married (permanent separation counts as unmarried for the rules of this spell).

You will need

St John's wort growing either in your garden or in a pot — yellow-flowering chamomile, dill or vervain can be substituted, though St John's wort is the best.

Timing

On midsummer's eve (June 23) or the evening of midsummer's day itself, at sunset.

The spell

* Tradition has it that you should fast from sunrise; however, you can eat a light meal during the day if you like.
* At sunset gather St John's wort (or one of the substitutes), as you do so saying:

Good St John, please do me right
And let my true love come tonight
That I may see him in the face
And in my fond arms him embrace.

* Place the plant under your pillow and you will dream of your true love, known or unknown. It is said that you will be married before the year is out.

Seven short halloween love spells

There are even more love spells associated with halloween than with Valentine's day. This is because halloween, or samhain as it was called in Celtic times, was the beginning of the Celtic new year and so a natural time for looking into the future. In parts of the world where the descendants of the Celts settled — from Scotland and Ireland to America, Australia, New Zealand and South Africa — halloween fires are still lit and ancient rituals sometimes practised, especially in the more remote places.

The halloween rituals listed here have come down to us mostly through a poem written by the Scottish poet Robert Burns. They are very short and were intended to be worked in quick succession during or after gatherings on 31 October. In their original form, the first five were intended for women, and the last two for men, but all may equally well be worked by those of either sex. Although, as you will see, they are all light-hearted, you may be surprised at their effectiveness and accuracy.

Timing

On halloween (31 October), to be completed by midnight.

* **Spell I:** Go to the cabbage patch (or get out the pre-bought cabbages) and put on the blindfold as you do so saying:

Kind lover reveal thy nature and thy intent.

The amount of dirt clinging to the roots of the cabbage indicates the financial status of the prospective partner (much dirt equals much money); the shape of the cabbage foretells the appearance of the intended; the flavour and sweetness of the raw cabbage heart reveals the future husband's disposition. Put the cabbage stalk behind your front door. The first person to call in the morning or to contact you will be your future husband.

Spell 2: Find another unmarried maiden. Each of you take one end of a string threaded with raisins and say together six times, getting faster and faster:

The fruit is sweet, so is my love; first or last, at the altar meet. The spell is cast. Love do not tarry, but me marry soon.

Hold the string tight in your mouths, first chewing on the string and then eating the raisins. Whoever eats most raisins will be first married. If you eat an equal number of raisins, there will be a double wedding.

Spell 3: Place three plates in a row, one empty, one full of clean water and one full of dirty water. Put on a blindfold, turn around three times and say:

Fortune, fortune, tell me,
Am I pretty or plain,
Or am I downright ugly
And ugly to remain?
Shall I marry a gentleman?
Shall I marry a clown?
Or shall I marry old pots and pans
Shouting through the town?

Reach out with your left hand. If you touch the clean water, your future spouse will be young, attractive and unmarried. If you touch the dirty water, he or she will be older, perhaps a widow or widower, or divorced. If you touch the empty plate, you will remain single until next halloween.

Spell 4: Place four cups on a table. Place a silver coin in the first cup, a ring in the second and a sprig of heather in the third. Leave the fourth cup empty. Put on a blindfold. Twirl around three times deosil (clockwise) and three times widdershins (anticlockwise) and then reach for the cups. If you pick the cup with the ring, you will marry within the year; if you pick the cup with the heather, you will have good luck; if you pick the cup with the coin, money is coming; if you pick the empty cup, you will make your way in the world by hard work.

Spell 5: Set out a dish of mashed potato containing, hidden within, a ring, a silver coin, a sea shell, a button, a heart-shaped charm and a key. Turn off the lights and take a scoop of mash. If you find the ring, you will be happily wed; if you find the coin, you will have great wealth; if you find the button, you will have a family; if you find the heart charm, you will have a passionate love affair; if you find the shell, you will travel to far-off places; and if you find the key, you will have a new home.

Spell 6: Place a small piece of wood in a glass or bowl of water before you go to bed. You will dream of falling off a bridge into a river. Whoever rescues you will be your love.

Spell 7: Eat a roasted or raw salted herring immediately before going to sleep. Your true love will bring you a glass of water in a dream to relieve your thirst.

A St Catherine spell for a good husband (or wife)

St Catherine of Alexandria, the fourth-century patron saint of young women, inspired maidenly devotion for many centuries. On her feast day, 25 November, young unmarried women would go to her chapels and pray for a husband. Catherine died when she was only 18, and was martyred in the fourth century. She became the centre of a widespread cult in Europe in the Middle Ages, especially in connection with love. Today, her name graces the main boulevard in Montreal.

I came across this love ritual in the St Catherine's Chapel at the abbey at Abbotsbury in Dorset, England. Such a ritual was common wherever her chapel existed. I also found a more elaborate version of the same rite involving a holy well, such as is often found in the grounds of a church or cathedral. In the churchyard at the ruined abbey at Cerne Abbas in Dorset, for example, there is a sacred well above which the chapel of St Catherine formerly stood; like many such wells, it consists of a pool in a grotto, fed by a stream. Ideally, for this spell you should have access to a natural water source. There are sacred wells all over the world, many of them dating from pre-Christian times. Often they have a stream and a flat pool of water, making them ideal for water spells. It is more difficult to obtain water for rituals from the wishing type well.

If you can find a St Catherine's chapel – even a ruined one – it would make a wonderful venue for this spell, and you may be able to attend a religious service in Catherine's honour on her feast day. You could then carry out the spell outside the chapel afterwards – using a small bottle of moon water (see below) if there is no chapel well.

You will need

Access to a natural water source, or some moon water (made by leaving a bowl of still mineral water – some brands come from sacred springs – in the full moonlight).

Timing

On the morning of St Catherine's day (25 November).

The spell

* Standing next to the natural water source or bottled moon water, turn round three times deosil (clockwise), as you do so saying:
  A husband, St Catherine;
  A handsome one, St Catherine;
  A rich one, St Catherine;
  A nice one, St Catherine;
  And soon, St Catherine.

* Kneel on the ground facing the direction of the sun (even if it is cloudy) and open the bottle of water or lean over the well and draw some water out. Use the water to make a cross on your forehead, as you do so repeating the chant.

* If you can, spend the rest of the day in the open air. (If you visit the well at Cerne, you can walk through the churchyard and climb the hill to the chalk giant, a powerful fertility symbol.)

A St Andrew's eve spell for contacting a new lover telepathically or seeing your future love

Scotland has its own time of love, on St Andrew's eve (29 November) – or on the night of St Andrew's day itself. This spell and the following one travelled with Scottish emigrants to America, Australia and New Zealand. The spells work equally well for either sex.

One old version of this first spell promises you the sensation of your true love's hair in your hand, but I suspect this worked only if the lover knew his lady would be carrying out the spell and waited outside. You may, however, find a text message waiting on your phone when you have finished the spell, or you may appear in your intended's dreams.

You will need
A chiming clock (optional).

Timing
The stroke of midnight on St Andrew's eve (29 November) or St Andrew's day itself.

The spell
* Make sure you will be alone in the house at midnight.
* At the stroke of midnight, take hold of the latch of the front door and call out three times:
  Gentle love, if thou lovest me, show thyself.
* Open the door a few inches (you can leave the safety chain on), reach out into the darkness and you will touch the hair of your lover – and fleetingly see his etheric form.

A two-person St Andrew's eve spell for contacting a new lover telepathically or seeing your future love

For this spell you will need the presence of a friend of the same sex who is also seeking a partner or who is at a similar early stage in a relationship to you. The spell involves using hairs from your head, a practice that I do not generally recommend. In this case, however, the nature of their use is entirely benign.

You will need
2 small pieces of natural fabric, such as cotton, wool or silk; a small dish of dried rosemary (originally the herb 'true love', or trillium, which when rubbed on the body in the form of an infusion is said to attract love – nowadays this herb is difficult to obtain); a pair of small scissors (optional).

Timing
The stroke of midnight on St Andrew's eve (29 November) or St Andrew's day itself.

The spell
* Set the two pieces of fabric on the table side by side, together with the scissors, if you are using them, and the dish of rosemary.
* Sit down at the table with your friend and remain there in silence until one o'clock in the morning. During this time, take it in turns to cut or pull, one at a time, from your own head as many hairs as you are years old. Over-25s could perhaps take one hair for each five years. Place each hair on your piece of fabric.
* When you have finished, sprinkle a little of the rosemary in the corners of the cloth, not covering the hairs.

* As the clock strikes one, both of you should turn every hair on your cloth, one at a time, as you do so saying:

I offer this my sacrifice
To him most precious in my eyes.
I charge thee now come forth to me
That I this minute may thee see.

It is promised that the spirit of your love or the one who will make you happy will sit down at the table. To see this vision you may have to focus on the empty chair opposite, close your eyes, open them, blink and then 'see' either in the chair or in your mind's eye the image of the lover.

A Christmas eve wedding divination spell for a group of friends

Christmas has been a popular time for love spells and divinations for centuries. In pre-Christian times, a mid-winter festival was celebrated at the solstice, around 21 December. On this the shortest day, rituals were carried out to encourage the sun to rise again. In 353 CE, Pope Julius I decreed that the birth of Christ should be celebrated on 25 December (instead of the former 6 January), and gradually, over the centuries, Christmas came to eclipse the older pagan festivities. Meanwhile, in Orthodox Christian parts of the world, Christmas stayed put on 6 January.

For this lovely spell it is suggested that you work with three or more romantically uncommitted friends. However, you can also carry out the spell alone if you wish, although you may have to modify it a little. If you do not have an open fire, you could make a bonfire and work outdoors or, alternatively, scale the spell down and use a large candle in a metal bucket half filled with sand or earth. If you choose the latter, use single holly leaves (three for each person) and salt (but not oil or earth), burning the leaves one at a time in the flame.

You will need

A triple chain of (one strand each) holly, mistletoe and juniper, with an acorn or hazel nut tied between each strand — alternatively, a single long chain of holly or mistletoe; a log; some salt; some earth; some oil; a prayer book containing the wedding ceremony; an open fire.

Timing

At midnight on Christmas eve.

The spell

* If you are indoors, lock the door and hang the key over the mantelpiece.
* Wrap the chain around a log; sprinkle it with the oil, salt and earth; and burn it on the fire.
* Sit around the fire with the prayer book open at the wedding service and take it in turns to read the wedding vows over and over again until the chain has burnt. Each person will see his or her future wife or husband crossing the room.

Four short Christmas eve spells

Try these Christmas eve rituals as an antidote to the commercial aspects of Christmas, especially if love – or lack of it – is on your mind. All the spells must be completed by midnight. They are all suitable for people of either sex.

* **Spell 1:** Sew nine holly leaves to your night clothes and place a gold-coloured ring on your wedding finger before you go to bed. You will dream of your future wedding day and, as you wake, will see, momentarily, your true love standing beside you.

* **Spell 2:** Tie a sprig of holly to each of the legs of your bed and eat a baked apple before going to sleep. Your true love will speak to you in your dreams.

* **Spell 3:** Use oats, barley and water (or a cake or flapjack mix) to make a dumb cake. These are prepared in silence on Christmas eve and baked in the oven late in the evening for eating on Christmas day. At midnight the kitchen door will open and the etheric double of your true love will come and turn the cakes. Since he or she may appear only in your mind's eye, be sure to set the oven timer for five minutes after midnight to avoid having to send for the fire brigade!

* **Spell 4:** Walk upstairs backwards eating a piece of Christmas cake and place the crumbs beneath your pillow. You will dream of your true love.

A Slavic love wish ritual

It was traditionally believed that if the full moon image could be captured in either a mirror or water, then the moon would have to grant a wish in order to be released. Myesyats, the Slavic moon god, was first worshipped as a young man, until he reached maturity at the full moon. With the waning phase, Myesyats passed through old age, dying when the moon disappeared from the sky. He was reborn with the new moon three days later.

You will need
A large round mirror.

Timing
On a full moon night when it is clear enough to see the moon clearly. The two nights on either side of the full moon are also possible.

The spell
* Position the mirror so that you can catch the image of the moon within it.
* Look at the mirror in the glass and say:
  Father Moon, I would not hold you captive a moment longer than I need. Grant me one love wish and be on your way with my gratitude for your service.
* Make your wish for love, or perhaps around some specific aspect of a new relationship, and then tilt the mirror so that the moon image is gone.
* Cover the glass so that you do not accidentally capture the moon again, as then your wish would not be granted.

A nineteenth-century English love charm for a romantic lover

Love charms, especially written ones, were very popular during the Victorian period. Young people invoked Aphrodite and Venus (the ancient love goddesses of Greece and Rome) with their flowers – roses, pansies and violets – tied with pink or green ribbons. They dropped coins made of copper – the metal of Venus – wrapped in myrtle leaves, into wishing wells. They sometimes even kept white doves (the messengers of the love deities) as pets.

This charm is a good example of how ancient love icons can be used to call into our life a romantic lover or to inject a little romance into the soul of a present lover whose ideal evening is a Chinese takeaway followed by a couple of hours of TV sport.

You will need

A small square piece of blank paper; a fountain pen and black ink (or any other black pen); a beeswax candle; a small fabric purse.

Timing

At 6 pm on the next Friday after the full moon (best of all when the full moon itself is on a Friday).

The spell

* Light the candle.
* Using the fountain pen and square of paper, and writing as small as possible – so that the words run into each other – and without any capitals or punctuation, write out the following: *I, (your name), call (your lover's name or 'a lover') in the name of Aphrodite and Venus, lady of love, to come to me with tenderness, courtesy, gentleness and infinite adoration. Make me her/his god/dess that she/he may bring due tribute and worship me in word and deed for ever and a day. Lady Aphrodite, Venus of desire, I call him/her by the next full moon to my altar of love.*
* Fold the paper as small as possible and seal it with three drops of beeswax by carefully dripping the candle on to it.
* When the wax is set, put the love charm in the purse and keep it in a drawer next to your bed until the next full moon. Then, if you are in a relationship, invite your love for a romantic evening. If you are single, get dressed up in your best clothes and find a social event to attend, or invite friends for a meal and include someone you like but do not know well.

A simple mirror spell to call love

Although in the past mirror spells were often worked on significant seasonal festivals, such as midsummer, halloween or Christmas, there were also standard mirror love spells that could be carried out on more personal occasions, such as a birthday, when the first stirrings of love were felt on meeting someone new, or the betrothal of a relation or friend, when the unvoiced question arose: 'Will it ever be my turn?' This and the remaining spells in this chapter are all drawn from the folk customs of eastern and western Europe and Scandinavia, and travelled with the colonists to the New World.

This spell will work equally well for those seeking love later in life. Its repetitive form creates a semi-hypnotic state, a relaxed yet higher form of consciousness in which the barriers of time and space fade away. The spell has a dual purpose, both calling the person who will make you happy and allowing you to see in the mirror (or your mind's eye) the identity of the lover.

You will need
A mirror large enough to see your whole reflection from the waist up when you are sitting in front of the glass; a beeswax or rose-scented candle (optional); a hairbrush.

Timing
Midnight – especially potent when the moon is visible in the sky.

The spell
* Just before midnight, place the mirror so that the moonlight is reflected in it or, if there is no moonlight, light the candle so that its light is reflected in the mirror.
* At midnight sit looking into the mirror and brush your hair gently (this is not a time to tackle tangles), establishing a steady rhythm.
* Continuing to brush, count silently to 100, clearing your mind of everything except the motion of brushing, the soft light casting a glow over your face and the counting.
* When you reach 100, stop counting but continue brushing, now so that the brush only lightly touches your hair.
* Begin to whisper the old words, spoken through the centuries by those seeking love:
Come lover, come now to me,
Over river, over sea,
Over mountain, far or near;
In my glass now appear.
Repeat the verse as many times as feels right, then put down the brush.
* Touch the mirror with your lips, impregnating it with your essential essence. Behind you, reflected in the glass, you may momentarily see the face of the one who will love you in the future or who, if you have already met them, will become closer to you. The image may appear in your mind's eye instead (which is just as good). If you see nothing, still facing the mirror, shut your eyes and count to 100, fast this time. When you reach 100, shut your eyes, open them, blink and then look in the mirror. You may see an image of the guy who misses the train every morning or of your best friend's older brother who still calls you Titch. The subconscious has an amazing way of alerting us to possibilities so close to home that we miss them because we are so busy scanning the horizon (or the Internet) for Mr or Ms Perfect.

A water spell to dream of your wedding

A number of the old holy wells, for instance the one at Madron in Cornwall, Britain, had a love seat; these wells often emitted fumes that had a semi-hypnotic effect. Wells and sacred lakes were used to see visions of a future wedding. One such recorded case is that of a nineteenth-century servant girl in Yorkshire, England, who visited the Fairy's Pin Well, so named after the custom of dropping pins in the water as an offering to the fairy that lived there. The girl drank from the well, asking the fairy to bring her a dream of the man she would marry. As tradition demanded, she fell asleep by the well, whereupon she dreamt that a would-be suitor, dressed in wedding finery, brought her a wedding ring. The two were taken off to Elf-land for feasting and revelry.

This spell must be carried out near water – you can perhaps fit it into a weekend away.

You will need

A natural water source near which you can sleep or at least close your eyes for ten minutes (this could be an ancient sacred well, or a lake or river); a silver-coloured coin, earring or charm, or a bent silver-coloured pin.

Timing

If you are using a sacred well, any afternoon is suitable; if you are using a river or lake, Friday, Saturday or Sunday are appropriate, these being magical days that belong to the fairy people.

The spell

* Cast the coin, earring, charm or pin into the water as your gift to its guardian, as you do so saying six times:

  In my dreams come to me,
  A lover true that I may see.
  Lover true, do not tarry;
  Reveal the place where we shall marry.

* Make yourself comfortable and fall asleep next to the water source. In your dream (or perhaps day-dream) you may recognise the place where the wedding takes place and maybe the identity of the groom. If you do not, be patient. All will be revealed over the coming months.

A wedding ceremony dream ritual

Here is a version of my favourite love dream ritual. It is sometimes practised at one of the old love festivals, such as midsummer.

You will need

A prayer book containing the wedding ceremony (the traditional version is best); 2 red and white ribbons; a sprig of lavender or fresh rosemary, or a long-stemmed rose (remove the thorns from the stem); any plain ring.

Timing

Wednesday or Saturday, before you go to bed.

The spell

* Open the prayer book at the marriage ceremony, at the place where it says, 'With this ring I thee wed'.
* Repeat these words six times and put the ring on your wedding finger.
* Place the plant in the prayer book, close the book and bind it with the ribbons to signify union in marriage.
* Put the prayer book by the side of your bed and go to sleep picturing your wedding. You will dream of the ceremony. If you have not met anyone yet, you may also discover the identity of the groom (or bride).

A European knot ritual to increase the love between you and someone you have recently met

Throughout the ages the knot has been a symbol of true and lasting love, given by lovers as a talisman, with the words: 'So long as this knot endures so shall our love'. On page 42 I described an ancient Egyptian knot ritual. The lovers' knot also appears in runic inscriptions throughout northern Europe and may well have been linked to the Norse goddess of love and fertility, Freyja.

Woven from cords of natural fibre, the love knot was made to attract a lover or to bind an inattentive one. In the past, the knot would also include a drop of the spell-caster's own blood, together with hairs from her intended. However, these additions may be seen as a form of magical compulsion (not a good basis for a relationship or a spell), and love knots work as well without them.

You will need

Two small dolls (many ethnic stores, especially those selling Central and South American crafts, have tiny cloth or wooden dolls, or sets of worry dolls, but any small dolls will do) or alternatively 2 tiny featureless figures crafted from modelling clay (if you use children's modelling clay, you can make one pink and one green doll); a pink ribbon; a green ribbon.

Timing

On a Monday during the waxing moon, just before going to bed.

The spell

* Take the two dolls and tie them together with the two ribbons so that the ribbons entwine. Make three knots, saying as you tie each one:
Three times the lover's knot secures;
Firm be the knots, long the love endures.
* Keep the knotted dolls under your pillow for three nights.
* On the fourth morning, take the dolls outside and undo the knots one by one, shaking each cord in the air and saying:
Three times the lover's knot flies free.
The love is bound between him/her and me.
So shall it be!
* If you can hide one of the dolls in your intended's home or workplace, do so. Otherwise, leave the two dolls in a drawer in your own home, companionably entwined but not tied.

A second European knot ritual to increase the love between you and someone you have recently met

You will need

Any item of clothing from your intended (you may need the help of a sympathetic friend of his or hers to avoid accusations of grand larceny; otherwise, be patient and watch for your opportunity – an old t-shirt left at the gym, a scarf, dropped with a pile of coats on a chair at a party ... one friend of mine asked her man to donate old clothes for a charity she was supporting); an item of your own clothing; a pink ribbon; a green ribbon.

Timing

On a Monday during the waxing moon, just before going to bed.

The spell

* Take the two items of clothing and tie them together with the two ribbons so that the ribbons entwine. As with the previous spell, make three knots, saying for each knot as you tie it:

Three times the lover's knot secures;
Firm be the knots, long the love endures.

* Keep the knotted clothes under your pillow for three nights.

* On the fourth morning, go outside and undo the knots one by one, shaking each cord in the air and saying:

Three times the lover's knot flies free.
The love is bound between her/him and me.
So shall it be!

* If possible, return the item of clothing secretly to your intended. Otherwise, leave the two items in a drawer in your own home, entwined but not tied.

A hair brushing and mirror spell to call a known lover who is far away

Like the previous spell, this one relies on the mesmeric rhythmic brushing of hair to lull the mind into a meditative state. For this spell you cannot use any artificial light, so wait for moonlight to shine in through your window. If the need is urgent, you can use the reflected light of a street lamp or a landing light through a half-closed door. This is a good spell to use if you have met someone on holiday abroad, or your lover is in a different part of the country or away in the forces. It works well if you have not heard from them for a while and are starting to worry that they have lost interest. Even if the relationship does not come to fruition, the spell is a good way of resolving matters.

You will need

A large round or oval mirror; a hairbrush.

Timing

When moonlight fills your mirror (or, failing that, at 10 pm).

The spell

* Gaze into the mirror and begin gently to brush your hair. Do not count the brush strokes.

* When you have established a mesmeric rhythm, chant the lover's name (or just the word 'lover' if you do not know a name) softly and slowly three times, then recite the traditional mirror chant:

Mirror, mirror, send me
A vision pure and true
Of he who is waiting
Over seas so blue.
Beyond the tallest mountain,
Along the village street,
Come within the glass, my love,
That we therein may meet.

The image of your love may appear in the glass or in your mind, and you will feel the connection. You should receive a letter (perhaps delayed), an e-mail or a phone message within a few days.

A simple candle spell to encourage a reluctant lover

The candle was probably the first magical tool used by ordinary people, and candle spells have been practised through the ages. The candle is considered so very magical because it contains all four elements: the body of the candle represents Earth, the smoke Air, the flame Fire and the melting wax Water. In the days before coloured candles were commonplace (less than a century ago) poorer people would sometimes save the beeswax candle that they had had blessed at the Candlemas church ceremony in February and use it for special folk rituals such as this one. In this spell, the candle represents the lover. Repeat it weekly until love flows.

You will need

A tall beeswax or white candle in a deep holder.

Timing

At midnight.

The spell

- Light the candle at precisely midnight, as you do so saying:
  When this wax melts, so melts her/his heart.
- Sit in silence until the wax begins to melt (not long, because beeswax melts fast).
- As the first wax falls, say:
  The wax melts, so melts her/his heart.
  May we never part.
- Blow out the candle. When it is cool, wrap it and keep it safely.

A traditional candle and pin charm to increase the ardour of a prospective lover

This spell appears in countless places across eastern and western Europe and Scandinavia. Traditionally, pins were stuck into candles so that a reluctant lover might feel the pangs of love, while the heat of the flame kindled his or her heart with devotion. However, I am uncomfortable about the idea of sticking pins in a candle for the purpose of causing discomfort to another human, even in the cause of love. Together with the original version of this spell, I have therefore given what I consider to be a more ethically acceptable adaptation. (In another old version of the spell, two pins were stuck in a candle to represent two alternative lovers; when the candle burnt down to the correct pin, the door would open and the true lover – or at least a vision of him – would walk in.)

You do not need to be dating the subject of the spell for it to work; if you have a secret passion for someone you know but have been reluctant to reveal it, a candle love spell will carry your feelings telepathically. If the other party is receptive – consciously or unconsciously – your feelings will be acknowledged and reciprocated.

You will need

A beeswax or green candle in a deep holder (beeswax is best because it is soft, and it is therefore easy to insert pins without cracking the candle); 2 long sharp pins (hat pins are ideal); a metal tray.

Timing

On the night of new moon (i.e. two and half days before the crescent appears).

The spell (original version)

- Light the candle and, as it begins to soften, insert the two pins, pushing gently but firmly, through the centre to form a cross. The pins should pass through the wick.
- Recite the following rhyme:

'Tis not these pins I wish to burn,
But my lover's heart to turn.
May he neither sleep nor rest
Till he has granted my request.

If the pins remain in the wick after the candle has burnt past the place where they are inserted, the lover will appear at the door before the candle has completely burnt down. If the pins fall out, the lover will not make an appearance and the match is unlikely to come to fruition.

The spell (adapted version)

- Light the candle and, as it begins to soften, insert the two pins, pushing gently but firmly, through the centre to form a cross. The pins should pass through the wick.
- Recite the following rhyme:

'Tis not these pins I wish to burn
But a willing heart to turn.
As I softly speak your name,
I call you love through candle flame.

Now call your lover by speaking his name.

- Sit quietly in the candle light. If the pins remain in the wick after the candle has burnt past them, your reticent lover should contact you within a relatively short time. If the pin falls out, it does not mean that love will not come, merely that you may need a little more patience or perhaps that other areas of your life are temporarily taking priority.
- Blow out the candle, sending love and the wish that your love may come willingly.

A three-day candle spell to call a lover

Colour contains a great deal of energy for attracting what we want. By lighting a coloured candle you are animating that colour and opening the door to opportunity. In love magic you need to decide which colour candle to use. The message you send telepathically to a lover or would-be lover will depend upon the colour you choose. You might use a pink candle for new love, green to attract commitment, red for passion, silver or purple for spiritual connection and white if you feel this really is the one person for you. Rosemary has been used since Shakespearean times to recall happy love and to call lovers.

You will need
A broad candle in a flat metal holder; a jar of dried rosemary.

Timing
At dusk for three days.

The spell
* Light the candle and set it close to a window facing the direction in which your lover lives.
* Look into the flame and say:
  I call you, my love, in fire, that my love may reach you through the darkness and enflame your heart.
* When the wax around the wick begins to melt, scatter just a little rosemary into the melted wax around the flame and say:
  I call you, my love, in rosemary, that you may recall your love for me and hurry to my side.
* Blow out the candle and say:
  I call you, my love, in fire and in rosemary. Recall our love and come to me.
* Repeat the ritual on the two following nights.
* On the third night, let the candle burn through and only then say:
  I call you, my love, in fire and in rosemary. Recall our love and come to me.
* Use the intervening time to write a love letter, poem or e-mail that you can send when the spell is done.

3 SPELLS FOR COMMITMENT AND MARRIAGE

After the uncertainty and excitement of meeting someone new and becoming closer, there usually comes a point when it is desirable to make a more permanent commitment and perhaps move in together.

In a sense, our ancestors had an easier time in this respect, because the community expected marriage to follow when a couple had been walking out together for a while. Pre-marital sex was frowned upon before the 1960s – and still is in some traditional cultures – so in order to give vent to their passion, it was necessary for lovers to marry. These days, because of high housing costs and other financial constraints, a growing number of young people are continuing to live in the parental home into their late twenties or even thirties. This can mean postponing the next stage in a relationship, with the result that boyfriends and girlfriends tend to become extra family members.

I am often asked to cast or recommend spells for people who want to move on to the next, more permanent stage, in a relationship. This may be an informal acknowledgement of mutual commitment or it may be an actual wedding ceremony. In this increasingly secular age, the public – and sometimes religious – ritual of marriage can provide a vital seal on love, especially if the couple want children in the future.

The true criterion for formalising a relationship must be whether emotional commitment exists between two people. The spells in this chapter will not coerce an unwilling lover (a recipe for disaster) but will encourage a reticent, hesitant or over-comfortable lover to make the necessary leap or shuffle towards forever.

A Druidic love divination in water to chart the progress of a relationship

Druids and Druidesses were probably the first marriage guidance counsellors (and were often married themselves). Acorns are a symbol both of potential and – as the seeds of the sacred oak, itself symbolic of permanence and stability – of commitment.

Even if a relationship is going well, it can be reassuring to have your feelings confirmed by divination. It is also useful to see revealed the dynamics behind the way you and your lover react to each other, in order to create a positive basis for the future. Of course, you should not make major decisions on the basis of a divination, but the results do usually reflect underlying feelings – and sometimes worries – and can help you to plan the best strategies if commitment is what you want.

You will need
Half a dozen acorns (or champagne corks – preferably from a wedding); a large clear glass bowl, half filled with water.

Timing
Thursday, the day of Jupiter (auspicious for commitments).

The spell
❋ Place two acorns or corks in the bowl of water. Designate one for you and one for your lover.
❋ Say three times:
   Acorn to oak, leaf to tree,
   Oak so wise, I pray you guide me.
❋ Observe how the acorns move:
   • If they float instantly close or circle and then move and stay together, the relationship is moving towards commitment and you need do nothing.
   • If they float completely separately or in opposite directions, you may

have an unresolved worry about the future that you need to share with your lover, or it may be that neither of you is yet ready for a deep commitment. Be patient and go slowly, while making sure you spend time together pleasurably and without confrontation. Do not worry too much about five years hence.

• If your acorns float close, then away, then back again, your relationship is full of the normal ups and downs. It perhaps needs a little more romantic input or time away from everyday life and commitments to deepen bonds.

• If only one acorn moves, then that person is making all the effort. Ask yourself if it is worth pursuing such a course indefinitely. If it is you doing the chasing, perhaps you should pull back a little and focus on other aspects of life for a while. On the other hand, your partner may simply need extra reassurance of your love, especially if he or she is having a hard time in the world currently. Or he or she may have personal baggage, such as a past betrayal, that makes commitment hard. If this latter is the case, you need to talk things through.

• If neither acorn moves, there may be a major sticking point that has locked you both in an intractable position, or you are both scared of the next step.

❋ If there appear to be unresolved issues, one at a time add other acorns to the water, to represent those who may be influencing your relationship or your decision-making, for example prospective in-laws, children from previous relationships and ex-partners. The movements among all the acorns can be very revealing. Look especially at any acorn that floats between you and your lover – it may not be who you think. Take note of any indications that your partner is colluding, albeit unconsciously, in some other unhelpful relationship. The nicest of us can, for example, unwittingly enjoy having a partner and a parent competing for our attention.

* When you have finished, take the two main acorns (or corks) and bury them under a tree to symbolise the growth of commitment. As you work, repeat the chant. The acorns may grow, so choose a planting place that can accommodate large trees!

An autumn oak and ash commitment ritual

In this very old commitment ritual, the energies accumulate over winter, with love being cemented and commitment (hopefully) made by spring. The spell involves the symbolic union of the oak and the ash, both of which are icons of strength, growth and expansion. A good place to find these trees is an arboretum. The oak and the ash grow in many countries throughout the world, but if you live in a place where they are not native, try a botanical garden. Acorns can be used for growth and abundance spells of all kinds throughout the year, so collect them whenever you find them.

You will need
An acorn with a cup attached; a sprig of ash leaves with seeds (or keys).

Timing
A windy morning in autumn.

The spell
* Take your acorn and ash leaves out into nature – preferably somewhere where there are leaves blowing around.
* Wrap the ash leaves around the acorn and bury both, if possible between an oak and ash tree, otherwise where a clump of trees is growing. As you work, say six times:
Autumn leaves do blow away,
But my love is here to stay.
Acorn cup and ashen key,
May we long together / married be.

A windy day love-calling ritual

The wind has always been regarded as a messenger of important news. If you go to a crossroads at halloween, the wind will tell you all you need to know for the rest of the year.

You will need
Nothing.

Timing
A windy night around the time of the full moon.

The spell
* Stand below your beloved's window.
* Whisper his or her name three times into the wind and then ask:
Winds from the sea,
Bring to me
Love that will last
Till time is past.
Hear, love, and give a sign.
* Ring the doorbell or phone soon afterwards – or, if you prefer, go silently away and let the wind do its work.

A holly and ivy forever spell

This is a faster-working version of the above spell. It is suitable if you are in a long-term relationship that is not progressing. The spell is based on a Celtic belief that persisted right through to Victorian times and is expressed in the carol 'The Holly and the Ivy'. The Holly King of the waning, or declining, year (from midsummer to the winter solstice) was married to the Ivy Queen of Winter. Ivy was associated with marriage and fidelity, and was worn in bridal headdresses, before orange blossom became popular.

You will need

A piece of holly (or any prickly evergreen plant); a very long strand of ivy (or any trailing plant); some green cord (optional).

Timing

Any time of the year, but most powerful between June 22 and December 22 (or thereabouts), when the Holly King ruled. If possible, the anniversary of a significant date for the two of you.

The spell

* Bind the ivy round and round the holly in spirals, taking care not to scratch yourself. As you work, say:
  Bound to me eternally,
  And I to you, till life is through.
  Bound to me willingly,
  And I to you forever true.
* Tie the ends of the ivy in a double knot, if necessary securing with the green cord.
* Hang the holly and ivy on the wall or make it part of a greenery display in a room where you and your lover often relax together. Replace when it dies.

An Andalusian love-joining rite

Throughout the Mediterranean, and especially in southern Spain, grapes were associated with marriage and fertility. If you are still steering your lover towards commitment, this spell can be performed by you alone, but it works as well performed by a pair of lovers. The idea is to keep up a continuous rhythm of plucking a grape, speaking a line of the verse, eating the grape and picking another. If you are working with your lover, each should pluck the grape and speak before feeding it to the other. (See also the apple spell on page 74.)

You will need

A length of vine with ripened grapes still attached (or a bunch of ripe grapes).

Timing

At noon, in sunlight.

The spell

* Pick a grape and recite:
  The vine it binds ...
  Eat or feed the grape.
* Pick another grape and recite:
  Your heart to mine.
  Eat or feed the grape.
* Pick another grape and recite:
  The vine it winds.
  Eat or feed the grape.
* Pick another grape and recite:
  Our hearts entwine,
  And you are mine.
* Continue the cycle until you have eaten all the grapes or can eat no more.

A soul to soul candle-anointing spell

Whereas attraction spells rely on pinks and greens, commitment spells are better performed using rich deep reds. Save scarlet for passion (see pages 85–7).

Candles are good for all joining spells, since the wax from two candles will mingle and then harden together. Anointing candles is a good way of infusing them with power as you rub the oil in. It also makes them more flammable, so anoint them unlit and use a large metal tray underneath them.

You will need

2 dark red candles (or a red candle in the shape of entwined lovers) in low flat holders (the kind with a spike to hold the candle) – or set the candles directly on to the metal tray; a metal tray; a sharp nail, nail file, small paper knife or other object suitable for engraving a candle; a rose-fragranced anointing oil or pure virgin olive oil (buy anointing oil from a New Age or candle store, or add a single drop of rose essential oil to some olive oil); a small glass or ceramic dish; a small piece of silk.

Timing

An evening when you can see Jupiter in the sky. (Jupiter is large and bright but, unlike a star, does not twinkle.) Alternatively, any Thursday after dark.

The spell

* Pour a small quantity of the oil into the dish and gently swirl it nine times deosil (clockwise), as you do so picturing light and power pouring into the oil.

* Using the nail, nail file or paper knife, carve your name into one of the candles and your love's name into the other.

* Starting at the bottom and using an upward motion, rub oil into the candle representing your partner. Anoint the whole candle, as you do so speaking aloud words of commitment to your absent partner. You need use only a small quantity of oil, as the action is symbolic.

* Now, starting at the top and working downwards, rub oil into the candle representing you, as you work speaking aloud the words of commitment you would like your partner to say to you. (If you are using a joint candle, rub the oil upwards from the bottom to the middle as you speak your commitment, and then downwards from the top to the middle as you anticipate your partner's words.)

* Light your candle and then light your partner's from it, setting both in the holders on the tray. Repeat your own and your lover's anticipated commitment vows and allow the candles to burn through, the melted wax mingling on the tray.

* As the wax is cooling, draw a heart in it and repeat the commitment words for the final time.

* When the wax is almost cold but not hard, cut out the shape and keep it wrapped in the silk near an object you and your lover chose together or that was a gift from him or her.

A five-incense pentagram ritual for lasting love

The pentagram is a magical symbol used for attracting and uniting positive energies, which in this case takes the form of the coming together of two people in permanent union. You can carry out this ritual at any stage when you feel you are moving closer together, perhaps before an occasion when you will be discussing the future or making decisions. The ritual is also useful if one of you has to travel away a lot. Practise setting your incense stick holders in a pentagram shape in advance.

You will need

A dark red candle; 5 incense sticks in one or more of the following fragrances: rose, lavender, neroli, jasmine, mimosa; 5 separate incense stick holders; a pot or jar with a lid.

Timing

At midnight.

The spell

* Imagine the pentagram shape above impressed on your table or working area. Arrange the incense stick holders on the points of the invisible pentagram. Light the candle and place it in the centre of the pentagram.
* Light the first incense stick and say:
  Incense of love, incense of power,
  So do I empower you now at this hour.
* Set this stick in position at the top point of the pentagram, as you do so saying:
  Incense of faithfulness, incense of truth,
  Bring love that will last, in age and in youth.
  In sickness and sorrow, in health and in joy,
  In wealth and in dearth, may nothing destroy.
* Reciting the two charms, continue to light the incense sticks and set them in place, moving first to the one to the left of the top point, then to the one to the right (to form the horizontal), then to the one on the bottom left and finally to the one on the bottom right.
* Let the candle and incense burn though and then collect the ash from the incense in the pot or jar.
* Before you meet with your lover – or when you have time if you are using the spell less specifically – take the ash to an open place and scatter it to the four winds, as you do so saying:
  Go free in love and return in joy that we may be together forever.

A ring binding spell

This spell uses the same words from the Song of Solomon as the new year's eve divination on page 44. Solomon was not only a great king but also a magician, given his knowledge by the Archangel Raziel. If the lover was recognised in the new year's eve divination, this second spell was sometimes carried out on the evening of new year's day; however, it works for any relationship where there is genuine feeling but hesitation. I have found it to be especially effective where a lover has gone through a bad divorce and fears things going wrong again. He or she may be holding back or even backing off – apparently inexplicably. You will need to learn the relevant verses from the Song of Solomon before performing this spell.

You will need

6 small green candles in holders; a green scarf; a ring, borrowed from someone who is happily married (not necessarily a wedding ring) or a family ring with happy associations or any ring of your own; a traditional Bible (such as the St James's version) containing the Song of Solomon; some dried basil or rosemary (the latter is good if the partner has temporarily gone cold); a pen and some paper; an envelope.

Timing

The night of the full moon if possible, or a Thursday when the moon is shining.

The spell

* Set the candles in a circle. Place the ring on the green scarf in the centre (ensuring that the candle circle is wide enough to avoid wax dripping on the scarf or the scarf catching fire).

* Light the candles deosil (clockwise), as you do so, reciting the following words from the Song of Solomon (Chapter 8, verses 6 and 7):
Set me as a seal upon thine heart, as a seal upon thine arm, for love is as strong as death. Many waters cannot quench love, neither can floods drown it. If a man would give all the substance of his house for love, he would be contented.

* Around the outside of the wedding ring, sprinkle a deosil (clockwise) circle of dried basil or rosemary, as you do so repeating the words from the Song of Solomon.

* While the candles burn through, write a letter to your love, expressing your desire for commitment and any other feelings that are relevant (you will be sending this letter later). Put the letter in the envelope but do not seal it.

* When the candles are burnt through, add a few of the now empowered herbs to the letter. Put the ring on your heart, then on your finger and finally to your lips. Seal the envelope, then press the ring three times to the front and back of it, as you do so repeating the words from the Song of Solomon.

* Sleep with the ring on your wedding finger (or any finger it will fit). You may dream of your wedding or of your life together as a couple.

* In the morning touch the front and back of the envelope, just once, with the ring still on your finger.

* Post the letter, catching the first post if possible.

A cake spell for emotional security and stability

This spell can be especially effective if one of you comes from a broken home where there was trauma, or has past experience of an abusive relationship. It can also help if you are intending to graft children from a previous marriage onto a new permanent relationship.

You will need

The ingredients of your usual recipe for a sponge cake (or a cake mix); I tsp sugared violets or rose essence (both available from delicatessens); I tsp allspice or cinnamon; I tsp chocolate chips; I tsp dried fruit; I tsp still mineral water that has been left outside in a covered container from dawn to noon; a mixing bowl; a wooden spoon; a cake tin.

Timing

Sunday afternoon.

The spell

* Make the sponge cake batter, as you do so picturing a happy settled home with the ones(s) you love or – in the case of stepchildren – hope to grow to love.
* To the batter add, one by one, the violets or rose essence (for gentleness and tolerance), the allspice or cinnamon (for powerful positive feelings), the chocolate chips (for sweet words and kind deeds), the dried fruit (for spiritual riches) and the mineral water (for purity of intent and emotional warmth). Stir in each ingredient separately, saying:
Mix and blend our hearts as one;
Join our lives till time is run.
Merge and mingle, old sorrows leave,
Bad memories no longer grieve.
Mix and blend our hearts I pray;
Bless all who eat this food today.
* Before baking the cake, ask your partner to stir it nine times and make a wish. You can invite any children to do the same.
* When the cake is baked, recite the chant over it nine times. Allow it to cool and then share it with your loved one(s).

An ancient Egyptian fragrance love spell to bring long-distance lovers together

Sometimes long-distance commuting or homes very far apart (even in different countries) can mean that partners meet for short intense periods but never manage to set up a permanent base together. While this can be exciting and may suit some couples, others may want a proper home, especially if only one of the pair is travelling. This spell will help to bridge the gap between your two different locations.

Flowers were important in ancient Egyptian love magic, and the potency of fragrance is often referred to in ancient Egyptian poetry. It was believed that fragrance contained the essence of the gods and could call a loved one and bind them to you eternally. This ritual is one of a number based on a verse from the Papyrus of Turin, which was translated into English by Aylward M. Blackman in 1955. For another such ritual, see my *Fragrant Magic*, Quantum, 2004.

You will need

A photograph of you; a photograph of your lover; a photograph of you and your lover together; a bowl of dried hibiscus flowers, lavender heads or rose petals, or any pot pourri mix containing powerful floral fragrances.

Timing
About an hour before you and your lover normally have long-distance contact, by phone, e-mail or any other means.

The spell
- Set your own photo on a table or flat surface close to the means of communication you will use to contact or be contacted by your lover. Sprinkle a single deosil (clockwise) circle of flowers round the picture, as you do so reciting:
  I am to thee like a garden, which I have planted with flowers and with all manner of sweet-smelling herbs, my heart is satisfied with joy — because we walk together.
- Place your lover's picture so it covers yours and make a second circle of flowers on top of the first one, as you do so repeating the verse.
- Place the image of you and your lover together on top of the other two photos, scattering a third circle of flowers on top of the first two and reciting the verse again. Leave the photos surrounded by the flowers.
- Immediately before you are about to have contact with your lover, encircle the phone, computer or whatever with a deosil (clockwise) circle of flowers, as you do so repeating the verse.
- As communication takes place, inhale the floral fragrance and the right words will come to you to bring about a permanent union.

A candle ritual for the evening before a wedding or permanent commitment

The joining of the lights of two candles in a single flame is a potent symbol of unity in both formal and informal commitment ceremonies (and has become particularly popular in weddings in the USA). This version of the ritual can be carried out privately by you and your partner as a way of affirming mutual commitment. It can be very helpful if you are having a big wedding and feel that you are losing sight of the reasons for the union amidst the frantic preparations. It can also be a simple way of marking your first evening as a committed or cohabiting couple if there has been no public acknowledgement of the event. This is a good rite to repeat periodically.

You will need
A large white pillar candle; 2 smaller white candles in separate holders.

Timing
The last time you meet before the marriage ceremony, or on your first evening together as a couple.

The spell
- You and your lover each take a separate white candle and light it, as you do so saying:
  These are the qualities I offer to thee,
  As I reach forth to attain unity.
  Name the gifts you offer the other person in marriage or commitment.
- Both simultaneously light the pillar candle from each other's candle, as you do so listing qualities you most value in each other.
- Extinguish the separate candles one after the other, as you do so saying in turn:
  I am no longer separate but willingly unite in love and fidelity, in trust and in harmony.
  Henceforth we two are one.
  Leave the pillar candle to burn down.

A ring spell for a marriage proposal

This spell can be carried out before you propose or suggest living with your partner. If you are moving in together but not getting engaged, you can substitute a less formal ring as a token of commitment. You can also use a dress or signet ring if you would like to become engaged but your partner is being slow to take the hint (see the following spell).

You will need

A ring; a green candle; some dried basil.

Timing

The night before the full moon.

The spell

* Light the candle and circle the flame three times deosil (clockwise) with the ring, holding it above the flame so you do not burn yourself. As you do so, say:

Round and round the ring of truth,
Love in age and love in youth,
Love in sickness and in health,
Love in dearth and love in wealth.

* Place the ring in front of the candle and sprinkle a little basil (the herb of marriage) in the flame, as you do so saying:

Come my love, come now to me;
Come, if it is right to be.
Come my love and with me stay;
Stay for ever and a day.

* Blow out the candle and, in your mind, send the light to your love, picturing him or her wearing the ring. As you do so, say:

Come to me by dark or light.
Come by day or come by night.
Come, I ask; the time is right.

Picture yourselves living happily together.

An apple spell to get a long-term lover to propose

This is an eastern European spell that works on the principle of absorbing love through food. The spell works well when a couple have lived together for a while and one of them would like to seal the relationship in marriage (perhaps because they are planning a family). I have avoided using compulsion in this spell, relying instead on genuine affection as the driving force.

You will need

An apple divided into a red half and a green half – if possible pick it yourself (if your lover hates apples, find another fruit that you can divide in half); a silver-coloured fruit knife.

Timing

During the waning moon (also a good time for picking fruit).

The spell

* When you are alone, wash the fruit under running water, saying:

Fruit sweet, as she/he does eat,
Move (name) to married state.
Fruit sweet, as she/he does eat,
Let him/her not hesitate.
Fruit sweet, as we do eat,
No longer wait to say I do,
Me and you, our lifetime through.

* At an opportune time when you are together, cut the fruit in half and give your lover the red half. As you share the fruit, recite the words of the charm in your head three times.

* Retrieve any pips you can and bury them with other fruit trees or in a pot.

A dedication spell on marriage or moving in together

From the Mediterranean to Scandinavia and the Baltic it has been a custom since Roman times for a woman getting married to take a burning coal or piece of wood from the family hearth to kindle the fire in her new home. In this way the good fortune and happiness of her childhood home was believed to be transferred. Whether you are getting married (for the first or subsequent times) or planning to live with your partner, this spell is a good way to transfer the love and luck of your present home life into the new relationship. If children are involved in the transition, they can join in the ritual, bringing their own piece of wood or coal.

You will need

A piece of wood or coal for each person participating (coal or kindling if you have an open fire or wood-burning stove or can make a bonfire, otherwise a small piece of unvarnished wood, such as a twig, a scrap of wood from the toolshed or a piece off some broken furniture – if one of you already lives in what will become the mutual home, they should find wood from around the home or garden); a metal bucket partly filled with sand (unless you have a hearth or stove).

Timing

On your first night together in the new home.

The spell

* Light a small fire in the hearth, stove or sand-filled bucket, or make a bonfire (I have even seen the ritual done with a barbecue pit and coals, minus the cooking grill).
* First your lover lights his or her piece of wood from the fire, as it begins to smoulder casting it into the fire and saying:
Blaze fire with love and warmth from the old world to bring warmth and love to this new dwelling and relationship.
If you are using coal, your lover should cast the coal unlit.
* You then cast your piece of coal or light your piece of wood from the fire, as it smoulders casting it into the fire, close to where the first was thrown, and saying:
Blaze fire with love and warmth, to join with warmth and love what was, what is now and what ever will be.
* When the fire has burnt itself out, bury some ashes near the front of your home.

A ritual to strengthen waning commitment or to help you decide if you want to commit

There often comes a point in a long-standing relationship where you must go forward or the relationship will become a habit and wane in intensity. You may be experiencing doubts that are valid or that are linked to a feeling of frustration at the relationship not progressing. This ritual is based on the ancient Holy Grail legend, in which the cup or chalice used at Christ's Last Supper becomes a symbol of spiritual perfection — in medieval times linked with the female aspects of ideal love. The lance or spear was another sacred Grail treasure, which became linked to the male aspects of ideal love. In pre-Christian times the spear and the cauldron (the latter an early version of the chalice) were treasures belonging to the Irish father god Dagda. This is a very powerful ritual.

You will need

A brandy or large wine glass filled with dark grape juice or red wine; a small silver paper knife or ordinary slim-bladed silver knife.

Timing

After dusk

The ritual

* Hold the knife just above the glass and ask the traditional Grail question that is said to reveal the magical answer:
  Whom does the blade unite?
* Allow your mind to go blank. If your heart knows the union is right, the knife will move downwards, guided by your hand into the liquid. You then say:
  You and I united are in love and in fidelity.
* If the knife does not move, it does not mean you will never be committed; only that now is not the right time.
* You can now choose whether to give more time to rekindling the former intensity or to let matters take their course.

4 SPELLS FOR FIDELITY AND ENDURING LOVE IN AN EXISTING RELATIONSHIP

The spells in Chapter 3 aim at moving towards permanence in a relationship. In the early days of commitment, when a night apart is agony, it is hard to imagine how money, career, children, family members and chores can turn passion and adoration into discussions about leaking taps and mortgage payments. However, the reality is that few of us could permanently sustain the intensity of a new lover's complete absorption in their partner.

So this chapter is about the long haul – the happy-ever-after that most people still seek in a relationship, especially if an earlier marriage or commitment went wrong. In a good relationship, passion can be maintained or rekindled through decades. Warm companionship, fidelity and trust can carry a relationship through difficult times into the halcyon waters of later life.

For many of us, there comes a time when we ask if we should leave a marriage grown stale, particularly if we married young or if our children have just left home. At the low ebb of a long-term relationship, there will be few among us, male or female, who have not wondered whether a night of unbridled passion with a colleague on an overnight business trip, or with the plumber who comes to fix the heating and stays for one too many coffees, is really so wrong. Although I have myself suffered the hurt of betrayal, I believe that people must make up their own minds on this matter. However, I have observed that in very few cases does an extra-marital fling or a new love based on another person's hurt prove as satisfying as hoped.

This chapter therefore contains spells – new and traditional – for preserving fidelity and trust through good times and bad, as well as spells to heighten passion once the honeymoon years are past. The passion spells can be used equally well if you are uncommitted. However, in my own experience – and in the experience of many of the people I have worked magic with over the years – I have found that if you know and trust the person with whom you share erotic bliss, there is an extra dimension of spiritual as well as physical unity in sex.

A ring writing charm for ever-lasting love

In Europe during the sixteenth and seventeenth centuries, posy rings (from the French *poésie*, meaning 'poetry') were engraved inside, so that the inscription was hidden from all but the wearer. Because the ring is a perfect circle, it symbolises love without end. In this spell I have used the words engraved on an old ring that is now in the British Museum in London. It is made of gold and bears an image of clasped hands (a symbol of fidelity) on the outside.

You will need

A ring to be given to a lover/partner at a wedding or on an anniversary, alternatively your own wedding ring or eternity ring, or your partner's wedding ring; some good-quality pure white paper; a green pen or a fountain pen and green ink.

Timing

Before a wedding or anniversary, or at any time when the waxing or the full moon is in the sky, as the sun is setting.

The spell

* Set the ring in the centre of the paper. Using the green pen (the colour of fidelity) draw around it, in a circle, an image of clasped hands, followed by entwined hearts with your joint initials in the centre, followed by a knot, followed by clasped hands again, then entwined hearts – and so on until you have encircled the ring. Leave small spaces between the symbols. As you draw, silently renew the pledges you have made to your partner or speak the words you will say at a future commitment ceremony or anniversary party.

* When you have finished drawing, recite aloud the following rhyme, over and over again, touching each symbol as it is mentioned. You may like to 'speak' the words 'hands', 'hearts' and 'knots' silently in your head as you come to them, simply touching the relevant symbol (but chant the rest of the rhyme out loud):

Our hands and hearts with one consent
Have tied this knot till death prevent.

If you have been round the entire circle and touched every symbol but have not finished the last chanting of the rhyme, keep on going round, touching the symbols, until you have completed the rhyme.

* You may like to have clasped hands, entwined hearts and a knot professionally engraved inside the ring used for this spell – however, this is not necessary, because you have magically charged the ring with lasting love.

A basil mobile phone fidelity spell

This spell gives a modern twist to the herb basil, which has been used as a countryside fidelity charm since time immemorial. The spell can be used to endow your partner's phone with the power of fidelity, ensuring that loving phone calls and texts are directed in your direction only. It can also create a telepathic link between you and your partner during times when you are not together, and it will encourage a forgetful partner to keep in touch. It is particularly useful if you and your partner spend a lot of time apart, for instance travelling frequently or living away during the working week. Uncertainty and suspicion can arise between the most loving of couples if one partner fails to contact the other, even if they have a very good reason.

Imagination can run riot when you are waiting for a call that does not come, or a phone is permanently on answer mode. When the call finally does come, you may – as I know from experience – be resentful or accusatory, which only serves to drive a further wedge.

You will need

Your partner's mobile phone (if you are the one going away and your partner will be at home, you can empower the home phone as well); a jar of dried basil (the kind you use for cooking).

Timing

The night or early morning before you or your partner go away on a trip.

The spell

* Sprinkle a deosil (clockwise) circle of basil around the phone, as you do so saying:
  Be only for me, think only of me, and when we speak let it be lovingly, till you / I return faithfully.

An Odin stone ritual for fidelity

Stones with holes in are sometimes called Odin stones in lands where the Vikings invaded. This was in honour of the father god of the Vikings who turned himself into a worm in order to pass through a hole in the rock to steal the mead of poetry and inspiration that was guarded by the giantess Gonlad. However, he did marry her as compensation.

Magical as well as healing properties are attributed to Odin stones. The stones were also used as a pledge of fidelity between couples, who would join hands through the huge stone while they made their vows. In Celtic times, a couple would join at Lughnassadh, the festival of the first harvest, for a year and a day in a form of marriage which might be renewed annually. This did not mean that marriages were shorter lasting, rather that a couple willingly renewed their pledges every year.

You will need

A holed stone (if you are lucky or resourceful you may find one of the huge sacred stones *in situ*); a long red cord (optional).

Timing

July 31 is the traditional pledging day, but any early morning of a significant anniversary will serve as well.

The spell

* If you are using a sacred stone, link hands through it. With a small stone, thread the cord through the hole and hold an end of the cord each so that the stone is suspended between you.
* Make a promise for the year ahead, speaking spontaneously and from the heart. When you have finished, say one after the other:
  So I vow and so I stay faithful and true, a year and a day.
  Never false, never stray, grow love for ever and a day.
* Make a vow to return in a year and a day's time to renew the vows, or put the small holed stone safely away and make a note in your diaries of the renewal ceremony a year hence.

A spell to keep your partner faithful under temptation

Even the most devoted partner may be momentarily tempted by the office vamp or Casanova, especially if there are temporary difficulties at home. If the advance coincides with a mid-life crisis, your partner may be very flattered. You may find out that something is up when your partner reacts with embarrassment to a text message and rapidly deletes it, or when a previously open e-mail account suddenly acquires a password lock. A little gentle humour and more time together is often all that is needed to repel any threat. However, without interfering with your partner's free will, it is also possible to create psychic 'keep off' signs that will turn the would-be romancer towards another prey. If you know your partner is a flirt (other good qualities may compensate!), you can carry out this spell even when there is no specific threat – perhaps prior to a work party or a business trip.

You will need
A rich-blue candle; a red candle; a sharp metal nail, small silver-coloured screwdriver, paper knife or other sharp object to inscribe the candles; a candle snuffer.

Timing
The day after the full moon, at midnight

The spell
* Set the candles side by side, with the blue candle (to represent the enduring love of you and your partner) to the left and the red candle (representing the tempter or temptress, known or unknown) to the right.
* Inscribe the blue candle with the words 'Love forever' and the red candle with the words 'Temptation begone'.
* Light the blue candle and say:
  Love burn eternal
  Between me and you.
  Love burn forever,
  Faithful flame true.
  None come between us,
  Between me and you.
  None ever have,
  Nor ever will do.
* Light the red candle from the blue one and say:
  Be as a shield
  To take away fire.
  With this joint love
  Be quenched false desire.
* Extinguish the red candle with the snuffer and throw it away with the rubbish. Let the blue candle burn itself out. Collect any wax, engrave your own and your partner's entwined initials on it while it is soft and then place it in a sealed glass jar in the kitchen. Add the wax of any further spells to the jar.

A seven-year yarrow marriage renewal spell

Restlessness in a long-term relationship can set in at any time, but seven years (and subsequent seven-year intervals) seems to be a common time for a blip. In days when divorce was not possible for ordinary people it may be that the following ritual evolved to counteract the seven-year itch. If you and your partner have been happy, it is an effective way of ensuring that your happiness continues.

Yarrow is known as the herb of enduring love, said to keep a couple together for at least seven years, and is therefore traditionally given to newly-weds on their wedding day. A couple would keep the herb in a special sachet and replace it just before seven years was up, continuing to do so at each seven-year interval throughout their life together. Alternatively, a ring of dried yarrow was hung over the marital bed. The seven-year renewal allowed for readjustments in the relationship and served as a reminder of the underlying love and trust that brought the couple together in the first place.

You will need

A bunch of dried yarrow (dry your own by hanging a bunch of fresh yarrow leaves from the ceiling of a well ventilated sunny room, or outdoors in a sunny sheltered place where it will not get wet) or some dried powdered yarrow and a small purse; a mortar and pestle or a small dish and a wooden spoon (optional); a red cord about 25 cm/ 10 in long.

Timing

When you have just got married or moved in together. If you are married or in a permanent relationship, carry out the spell on any Friday evening.

The spell

* If you are using whole yarrow you have dried, weave it into a tight ring. If you are using powdered yarrow, mix it in the mortar or bowl and then tip it into the purse. As you work, chant the following rhyme seven times, saying as you do so:
  By seven times seven the love is cast,
  Love without question, love that will last,
  In sickness and health,
  In hard times and wealth,
  And so love is bound in yarrow.
* Secure either the yarrow ring or the purse with the cord, tying seven knots in it and repeating the chant for each knot.
* Hang the ring over the bed. If it crumbles, you may need to replace it before seven years is up, repeating the spell to charge it magically. Keep the purse hidden in the marital bedroom.
* Repeat every seven years on the anniversary of your commitment.

A flower fidelity spell for establishing trust

The best relationships are those where trust exists without fear of betrayal or abandonment. If we have suffered infidelity in past relationships or were abandoned either by a parent in childhood or by a lover in a cruel manner, we may question whether love can last even in the happiest relationships. I have known people live for decades in fear that a loving partner will be unfaithful, thus projecting their past pain into a present good relationship. Indeed, this spell is an adaptation of one that I worked with two sisters who were wracked with fear that their husbands of 30 years might leave them and so were, ironically, unable fully to enjoy the present good times. Their childhood home had been shaken by their father's constant infidelities, and the bitter quarrels when they were discovered. The spell is all about loosening the bonds of fear and possessiveness and willingly letting go, so that the love exists freely and without conditions. It involves making vows and trusting that they will be reciprocated.

On page 68 I spoke of ivy as a symbol of married love and fidelity. In the Celtic Druid tradition another trailing plant, honeysuckle, is linked with eternal love. You can use either ivy or honeysuckle, or indeed any other trailing plant in this spell.

You will need

Freshly picked fronds of ivy, honeysuckle or any other trailing plant, alternatively use green shiny ribbon; 2 tiny dolls made of cloth or wood (you can buy these in ethnic shops or make them yourself from modelling clay); a stick of jasmine or rose incense; a small undyed straw basket; some green leaves and small flowers.

Timing

At twilight.

The spell

* Using the trailing plant, bind the two dolls loosely together face to face. Take care not to break the plant fronds. If you do break them, pick some more.

* Light the incense stick and weave smoke around the dolls, creating knots of smoke to give strength to the plant. As you do so, say:
  Ivy, ivy, plant of love,
  I know my lover is true.
  With willing love myself I bind
  And thus our vows renew.

* Line the basket with the leaves and flowers. Unravel the dolls' bonds and set them, face to face, in the basket, together with the ivy. As you work, say:
  Trust needs no bonds,
  Fidelity no chains.
  Take away the ties,
  And willing love remains.

* Leave the basket until daybreak in a sheltered outdoor place or on a balcony where it cannot get wet.

* In the morning, use your fingers to weave invisible fronds of morning light and shade over the basket.

* Set the basket with the dolls on water – a running source if possible, but a pond will do. Take out the ivy and cast it into the water ahead of the basket.

* As the basket sails away, turn away and do not look back. Say:
  Go free in love and free remain.
  Together, apart, it is the same.
  Nothing I fear,
  My love is clear.
  I henceforth trust his/her heart.

A lodestone spell to link you with your partner when apart

On pages 28–30 I give lodestone and magnet rituals to attract love. A pair of lodestones, one male and one female, is also traditionally used to preserve fidelity and maintain contact between partners who must be apart, whether for a short period or for a long time, for instance when one partner has to go away to work. Lodestones have always been popular as a fidelity symbol among service personnel deployed abroad, both in peacetime and during war, when communicating by conventional means is often difficult.

If your partner wants to join in the ritual, you can adapt it, each preparing the lodestone you will give to the other and alternating words and actions. The words I have used come from Sir Philip Sidney's sixteenth-century sonnet 'My true-love hath my heart, and I have his', a poem that seems to have acquired magical significance in love spells through the centuries; however, you can substitute any love poem or song that has personal significance for you and your partner. You can also change the gender of the words. The ritual works equally well for same-sex couples.

This is one of my favourite rituals, and I have taught it successfully to a number of couples.

You will need
2 lodestones that attract; 2 small red drawstring bags and 1 larger red bag; 2 lengths of red cord; a wooden bowl; some magnetic sand or dried and finely crushed lavender; a rose, geranium or patchouli anointing oil (available from New Age stores or by mail order over the Internet); a piece of red silk.

Timing
Friday morning, the traditional time for lodestone spells.

The spell
* Place the lodestones in the bowl and roll them in the magnetic sand or lavender, as you do so reciting continuously:
My true-love hath my heart, and I have his,
By just exchange, one to the other given.
* Sprinkle the lodestones with a few drops of the anointing oil, as you do so saying:
I hold his dear, and mine he cannot miss,
There never was a better bargain driven ...
His heart in me keeps me and him in one.
* Place one lodestone in each red bag, as you do so saying:
My heart in him his thoughts and senses guide:
He loves my heart, for once it was his own ...
My true-love hath my heart and I have his.
* Tie each bag with the red cord (red is the colour of Frigg, the Scandinavian goddess of happy marriages), making six knots.
* When one of you goes away without the other, give your partner the lodestone that represents you, while you keep the one that represents him/her. Keep the bags closed while you are apart.
* When you meet again, reunite the lodestones and leave them on a piece of red silk in your bedroom the first night you are together. Keep them in the large red bag until you need to use them again.

An Earth, Air, Fire and Water spell to maintain or restore passion in an established relationship

When partners have been together many years, the sexual passion of the early days will inevitably mellow and often deepen. But over the years also, with the pressures of the external world and the effort involved in combining work and home life, spontaneous sexuality may become relegated to once a week or once a month or even cease. Some couples are happy with this. However, when I do phone-ins, I am often asked, especially by older women, how to restore the magic in an established relationship.

I demonstrated this ritual on UK television, and so enthusiastic were the presenters that the elaborate golden bed, prepared by the television crew, collapsed as they leapt onto it – to the fascination of the team working on the soap opera *Coronation Street*, who were on the other side of the wall.

To perform this spell you may need to temporarily rearrange the bedroom a little. The spell also works well for maintaining a fulfilling sexual relationship if carried out every three months.

You will need

A bowl of fresh rose petals or a rose-based pot pourri mix; a stick of cinnamon or ginger incense or any other spiced fragrance; an incense-holder that can be easily carried; a red candle in a deep heatproof holder that can be easily carried; a goblet or wine glass of still mineral water; 4 small tables or flat surfaces.

Timing

After dusk. Make sure your partner and any children or curious residents are otherwise occupied or out of the home.

The spell

* Place the bowl of rose petals on a small table at the head of the bed.
* Set the incense stick in its holder on a small table to the right of the bed as you face the bedhead, about halfway down. Light the incense.
* At the bottom of the bed set the red candle on another small table. Light the candle, making sure it is not too near the bed or any soft furnishings.
* To the left of the bed as you face the bedhead, about halfway down, place the glass of water on the fourth table.
* Go to the bedhead and take up the rose petals. Starting at the table where the petals were placed, sprinkle a deosil (clockwise) circle of them on the floor around the bed and outside the tables, as you do so chanting continuously:
I call my love with the power of Earth.
Return the rose petals to their place.
* Take up the incense stick and, starting at the table where the incense was placed, make another complete deosil (clockwise) circle of the bed, this time making a smoke trail and chanting continuously:
I call my love with the power of Air.
Return the incense to its place.
* Pick up the candle and, starting at the table where the candle was placed, make a third deosil (clockwise) circle round the outside of the bed, being careful not to drip wax and chanting:
I call my love with the power of Fire.
Return the candle to its place.
* Finally, take up the goblet or glass of water and make a fourth circle, starting at the table where the goblet or glass was placed and sprinkling water drops in a deosil (clockwise)

circle on the floor, as you do so, chanting:

I call my love with the power of Water.
Return the water to its place.

- Sit in the centre of the bed, facing the door. Enchant the bed by making circles over it with your hands, palms down, the left circling deosil (clockwise) and the right simultaneously circling widdershins (anticlockwise) – or vice versa if that feels right. As you enchant the bed, say:
Earth, Air, Water, Fire, make her/him only me desire.
Earth, Water, Fire, Air, make her/him for me only care.

Air, Water, Fire, Earth, so I ask give passion birth.
Move your hands and chant faster and faster, until your hands seem to spin.

- When the movement and chanting have reached a peak, end with the cry:
Earth, Air, Water, Fire, bring I ask this night desire!
(If you want to have a baby, you can add a third line:
Earth, Air, Fire, Water, bring to me a son or daughter.)

- Blow out the candle and call out:
Passion be, power I free.

- Leave the incense to burn out and close the door.

A Slavic spell for love and passion eternal

There are a number of Slavic love spells that address the lover's desire as though it were a person. This is an adaptation of one such ritual, passed on to me by a friend who spent time studying in Russia. However, there are many excellent Slavic folklore sites on the Internet, and I would recommend that you visit some of them for translations of complete authentic spells. This particular version is good if your lover has been away or you have both been preoccupied and you need to restore the focus to the relationship. I have written the spell to be spoken by a woman, but you can change the gender.

You will need

Petals of any kind in a large bowl.

Timing

Just before your lover comes home.

The spell

- Stand outside the house or on a balcony or at an open window. Begin to scatter the petals, continuing until all are gone. As you do so, repeat the following rhyme as many times as necessary:
Brother winds from the far islands,
I call Desire to bring my love to my arms.
I go from the door to the gateway,
From the gateway to the fields.
I call his name.
Find him, Desire, wherever he may be
Under the stars, the sun or the moon.
Tug at his garments,
Touch his heart and stir his mind.
As fish out of water, babe without mother,
Bird without nest, star without sky,
So am I without his presence.
Bring him home safe to my arms
And my waiting bed.

- Go indoors. Do not look out of the window or attempt to contact your returning love but wait, and he will return filled with longing for you.

A ritual for combining passion with tenderness

This ritual works by creating a magical atmosphere in which passion will be more readily experienced and expressed, and the underlying tenderness of an established partnership fostered. By varying the colour of the candle and the background fragrance, you can subtly alter the mood, according to whether you want to initiate unbridled passion or enjoy a slower more spiritual build-up to consummation (see also the following spell). Musk, frankincense and ylang ylang, together with a scarlet candle, are suitable for passion; jasmine and mimosa, with a delicate pink candle, for tender love. For spiritual love and gentleness, substitute a beeswax candle for the incense stick. Combine passion-inducing incense with a gentle candle, or vice versa, for a balanced night of love.

You will need

An incense stick in one of the above-mentioned fragrances or a beeswax candle; an entwined lovers candle in one of the above-mentioned fragrances (available from New Age stores, some gift shops and by mail order on Internet); a love candle anointing oil or some pure olive oil in a small dish; a metal tray or large flat metal candle-holder; your favourite bubble bath or bath oil; some small pink candles in suitable holders; some scented tea-lights.

Timing

Any evening or night when you will not be disturbed.

The spell

※ About an hour before going to bed, light the incense (or beeswax candle) in your bedroom. Trail your fingers through the smoke, being careful not to burn yourself, and say:
Incense flow,
Passion grow,
Tenderness know
This night together.

※ Half an hour before going to bed, take up the entwined lovers candle. Stroke each figure in turn with the oil, being careful not to get any on the wick. Work from the base to the centre and then from the top to the centre for the female figure. Work in the reverse direction for the male figure. As you anoint the figures, repeat as a mesmeric chant:
Candle glow,
Passion grow,
Wax flow,
Join so.
Two are one.
The spell is done.

※ Light the candle and leave it to burn in a safe place in the bedroom, on the metal tray or candle-holder.

※ Run yourself a bath, using the bubble bath or bath oil. Surround the bath tub with the pink candles and light them. As you have your bath, swirl the light where it falls on the water, as you do so repeating the candle chant. When you have finished your bath, blow out the candles and return to the bedroom.

※ If the candle in the bedroom has not burnt through, blow it out, sending desire to your partner.

※ Light the scented tea-lights and place them around the bedroom to add further fragrance.

A spell to call an overworked or overstressed partner to your bed

If your partner has been having a difficult time at work, studying hard or feeling anxious or depressed, your sex life can suffer. Sometimes sick children or relatives may preoccupy both of you at the expense of passion. While patience, understanding and hugs can compensate for prolonged lack of sexual contact, sometimes passion needs a kick-start to prevent temporary lack of interest becoming a habit (unless, of course, this is what both parties want). This spell is also a good one to work if you are the partner who has lost interest. You can even work it if all is going well to ensure that things stay that way, perhaps choosing a night or weekend away together as your time (be careful about lighting incense near the smoke alarm in your hotel room).

You will need

A large red pillar candle; a flat metal candle-holder or a metal tray; a stick of strawberry or artificial musk incense in a deep holder; some rose petals in a bowl.

Timing

If possible, the night before the full moon, but any night at about 10pm will work.

The spell

* When you are alone in the bedroom, light first the candle and then the incense from the candle, as you do so saying:

Candle of love, incense of desire,
I call my love in fragrance and in fire.

* Take a handful of rose petals in your power hand (the one you write with). Pass the closed hand three times over the flame and then three times over the incense smoke, taking care not to burn yourself. As you do so, say:

In flower and fragrance and in fire,
Three times my love I call with desire.
Once to find, once to remind,
Once to entwine him in passion and in fulfilment.

* Scatter the handful of petals, first in a deosil (clockwise) circle around the incense and then in the same direction around the candle. Use all of them and say as you scatter:

I call my lover, with fire,
With fragrance and with flower.
I send thee light, beloved;
Resist no more this hour.

* Extinguish the candle and let the incense burn through. Scoop up the rose petals and hide them beneath the mattress.

* Keep the candle and use it to repeat the spell when you next wish to kindle passion.

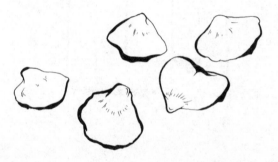

A ritual to encourage expression of love in a long-standing relationship

This is a good ritual if you or your partner find it hard to express your deeper feelings. You could adapt it for a joint ceremony when the time seems right, but at first you may choose to work alone to open the channels of deep communication.

You will need

2 small white candles of equal size and 1 larger white one; a thin taper; a small white purse filled with dried bay leaves (the culinary kind).

Timing

A significant anniversary in your relationship, not necessarily a formal one.

The spell

* Set the three candles in a row, the two smaller ones on either side of the large one. Set the purse open in front of the central candle.
* Light the left-hand candle to represent yourself and aloud make promises to your absent partner for your future life together.
* Light the right-hand candle and make the promises you would like you partner to make to you for your future life together, for example beginning:
  I ask that she/he may be true and gentle ...'
* Light the taper first from your candle and then from the flame of your partner's, as you do so saying:
  May we speak freely of our love for each other.
* Light the central candle from the taper, as you do so saying:
  We two are one, one heart, one voice. So may we speak of our love without hesitation.
* Blow out first your and then your partner's candle, saying for each:
  May words of love be exchanged that we may share what is in our hearts.
* Leave the central candle to burn for a while as you look at photographs and recall happy times with your partner.
* Blow out the central candle and put the closed purse near to or beneath the bed you share.
* When you are together, quietly relight the central candle and let the words of love flow.

5 SPELLS FOR FERTILITY

For thousands of years the fertility of human, beast and soil was inextricably linked. The cycle of seasonal festivals marked not only major events in the agricultural year but also the rising and falling levels of natural fertility that flow through humans just as through animals and land. The festival day or days when these energies were particularly strong were once dedicated to the old sun gods. With the advent of Christianity, the names were changed to those of saints, but in essence the festivals continued to celebrate the fertility of the land and its inhabitants. A traditional practice was for couples to make love in the woods or fields at times of sowing or peak growth, thus re-enacting the sacred marriage of the horned god (or sky father) and Earth mother, which symbolically fertilised the crops as well as ensuring their own fecundity.

If trying to conceive has made lovemaking stressful for you, you may find this chapter particularly useful. It does not promise miracles, but I know of a number of cases in which – whether by design or coincidence – conception has followed the performing of a fertility ritual (even where conception had been proving difficult). Perhaps this is in part because spellwork involves harmonising with natural rhythms. Ritual can also help to relax the mind and body and so increase chances of success in cases where medical intervention is necessary.

You might like to start working fertility spells three or four months before you hope to conceive, in order to strengthen or re-establish your connection with the natural fertility cycles of your own body and of the Earth. This may be especially useful if you have used the contraceptive pill for a number of years.

All the spells can be modified if you intend to conceive a child without a partner or you are hoping to adopt a child.

A traditional egg fertility spell

Eggs are a universal fertility symbol and feature in many fertility festivals. Eggs were set on the shrine of the Viking spring goddess Ostara and the Anglo Saxon Oestre (from whose name we get both 'Easter' and 'oestrogen'). This wordless spell — one of my favourites — is a version of a Polish ritual in which the first eggs of spring were painted and given at Easter in memory of the Virgin Mary, who was said to have painted eggs to delight her infant son Jesus. The symbols painted on the egg date back to Neolithic times, suggesting that the spell is very old and certainly pre-Christian.

You will need

A fresh hen's egg; paints or permanent marker pens in yellow, blue and red; some almond or olive oil in a small dish; half a coconut shell or a small straw basket; a long silver pin or paper knife.

Timing

When the crescent moon is in the sky.

The spell

* Paint or colour the shell of the egg with mother goddess symbols: spirals, butterflies, bees and birds.
* Place the finished egg on the window ledge of your bedroom and leave it there until the night of the full moon.
* On this night prick the egg very gently with the pin or paper knife, making sure you do not completely penetrate the shell. This action is a symbolic union of male and female.
* The next day, early in the morning, sprinkle the shell with a few drops of the almond or olive oil (both oils of fertility).
* Place the egg in the coconut shell (the coconut being the most potent fertility fruit) or the straw basket and set it sailing on a river, a stream or — best of all — the outgoing tide.
* Make love whenever you wish during the month, unless this is medically inadvisable because of ongoing treatment, and on the night of the full moon. Repeat the spell monthly.

A fertility spell from Turkmenistan

Fruits, flowers and trees have long been regarded as symbols of human fertility. For example, in folk wisdom making love between two fruit trees on the first day of the month at dawn is considered a good way to conceive. This spell and the five that follow are very simple nature-based fertility rites traditionally practised by women.

Timing

On the first day of spring (on or around 21 March — consult a newspaper, an ephemeris or *Old Moore's Almanack* for the exact date) or on the first day of any month (May is an especially auspicious month).

The spell

* Roll on the ground beneath an apple tree in order to become pregnant with a boy. Roll beneath a pear tree for a girl. For twins roll beneath two trees in quick succession, choosing the species of tree according to the preferred sex of the twins.

A moonstone fertility spell

Moonstones have become associated with fertility due to the fact that the moon reflects the female monthly fertility cycle. Indeed, one of the earliest deities worshipped was the moon mother, who was believed to bring fertility to people, crops and animals. When there was no artificial lighting, all women menstruated at the end of the waning moon cycle and reached peak fertility on the full moon. This pattern is still common among those peoples who do not have artificial light in their villages.

While no spell would claim to replace medical intervention, fertility spells do help the body to relax back into natural harmony and rhythms that may have been interrupted by a long period of artificial contraception, perhaps followed by anxiety when conception does not occur quickly. If medical tests and intervention are taking place, the mind can become even more anxious and the body more tense. This is why spells can be helpful during fertility treatment. You may need to carry out the spell for several months to allow your body to synchronise with lunar rhythms. You can use a moon diary, the weather section of a newspaper or *Old Moore's Almanack* to find out the current moon phase if the weather is cloudy.

You will need

A tiny perfectly round or oval white moonstone or selenite (another moon crystal); an egg, either a crystal or a wooden or cardboard decorative one that splits in half, or a hen or duck egg from which all the liquid has been extracted (by making a hole in the side) and the shell then split and the two halves washed and dried; a needle or long silver pin; a white scarf.

Timing

From when you first see the crescent moon in the sky until the night of the full moon.

The spell

* On the evening when the crescent moon appears in the sky, set your moonstone inside half of the open egg shell on the window ledge of your bedroom.
* Leave it there until the night of the full moon and during this time make love when you want rather than using an ovulation chart (you may wish to return to the ovulation method in subsequent months as well as following the spell).
* On the night of the full moon, prick the moonstone with the pin or needle and leave them together in the shell. If at all possible, make love on the night of the full moon even if you are having IVF (unless it would be medically unwise).
* In the morning, cover the egg shell, with the moonstone and needle inside it, with the other half of the egg and wrap it in the scarf. If the needle does not fit, wrap it next to the egg. Keep the egg in a covered place such as a drawer until the next crescent moon.
* Repeat monthly as necessary.

An ancient Egyptian clay image fertility spell

The ancient Egyptian goddess Hathor ruled over fertility as well as love and marriage. At her temple at Dendara thousands of clay fertility figures have been excavated, including couples making love, babies being suckled by their mothers and women with swollen breasts and belly. Such figures were also placed on ancient Egyptian domestic altars and have occasionally been found in tombs, with inscriptions such as: 'May a child be born to your daughter.'

This spell calls on the energies of the three main Egyptian mother goddesses. These were Hathor; Nut, the sky mother whose body was covered with stars and who gave birth to Ra, the sun god, each morning; and Isis (see page 144), who was the mother of Horus, the young sky god. Images of Isis holding her infant son formed a prototype for the later Christian madonna and child pictures that are popular in Europe.

You will need

A small piece of clay (modelling clay is fine) or a tiny cloth doll; 2 large palm leaves or leaves from another luxuriant green plant, such as a rubber plant; a good supply of rose incense sticks.

Timing

Between the crescent and the full moon.

The spell

* As the sun is setting, mould a baby out of the clay (if you are using clay).
Make the two leaves into a cradle and set the baby (or the doll) in it.
* Each evening, including the first evening, as near to sunset as possible, light a stick of rose incense and pass it over the cradle in deosil (clockwise) spirals, as you do so saying:
You who have been mothers, Isis, Hathor and Sky Mother Nut, mothers three, let me likewise this night be granted the blessings of a child.

If you are a Christian, you might like to pray to Mother Mary, who took over the role of Isis, or you can just focus on the powers of all mothers everywhere.
* Place the incense near the cradle and let it burn out.
* Make love when you wish during the days leading up to the full moon.
* On the evening of the full moon, recite the chant and waft the incense stick nine times over the cradle before leaving it to burn out.
* Set the doll in its cradle on the inside bedroom window ledge, facing the moon, and if possible make love.
* After the night of the full moon, roll the clay back into a ball or put the doll away in a drawer. Bury the leaves.
* Repeat the next month using the same doll or clay and fresh leaves. You may find that your cycles begin to harmonise with those of the moon and you relax into conception.

Making a moonlight fertility charm

The full moon is the phase most associated with fertility and the moon mother, and therefore offers great potency to any fertility charm charged with its power. Traditionally, such a charm would be a moon crystal such as selenite, milky quartz or, of course, moonstone (see page 91); or a silver ring, bracelet or necklace (silver being the metal of the moon).

The empowerment of a moon charm generally takes about six full moons and so can be used to accompany long-term fertility treatment or ongoing attempts to conceive by natural methods. If you need a lot of power suddenly – for example before an IVF treatment or on an evening when you instinctively feel that lovemaking will result in conception – you can give the charm an extra charge. If the moon is not full on this occasion, use a silver candle to invoke its presence. You can also use a silver candle if the night of the full moon is overcast.

You will need
A moon crystal (see page 689) or a piece of silver jewellery; a silver-coloured or clear glass bowl; some still mineral water; a silver candle (optional – see above).

Timing
On the night of the full moon if possible, or before an important event connected with fertility.

The spell
* Half fill the bowl with water and position it so that you can see the moonlight or candle light reflected in the water.
* Holding the moon crystal or jewellery in your power hand (the one you write with), splash six drops of water on it with your other hand, as you do so saying six times:
  Mother Moon, maternal might,
  Fill now my womb with fertile light.
  As you are full, so may I be;
  Let new life grow and wax in me.
* Hold your crystal or piece of jewellery high in your cupped hands so that it sparkles in the moonlight and turn it over six times, as you do so repeating the moon chant six more times.
* Wear or keep your empowered symbol close whenever you make love or discuss fertility with professionals.

An eastern European fruit tree spell

This spell is not for the squeamish!

You will need
One of your undergarments; a small, well ventilated box containing some leaves.

Timing
Just before dark.

The spell
* Climb a strong fruit-bearing tree and hang the undergarment on a branch.
* The next morning, retrieve the undergarment. If an insect or caterpillar has crawled into it, wear the garment: the fruitfulness of the tree will be transferred to you. Place the insect in the box and keep it there until evening, when the spell's work will be done.
* Return the insect to the foot of the tree where you found it and release it.

An Indian goddess spell

In northern India, coconuts are fertility symbols and are sacred to Sri, goddess of prosperity. Coconuts are kept in shrines, blessed and given by priests to women who wish to conceive. The shell represents the womb, and the milk the flow of new life.

You will need
A spade or trowel; a coconut; an implement to break open the coconut; five different types of seed.

Timing
At dawn on the first Saturday of the month.

The spell
- In your garden or another suitable space, make a small mound of soil.
- Break open the coconut. Drink the milk and eat some of the fruit, then chop up and bury the rest of the coconut in the mound of soil.
- Plant the seeds in the mound and tend them regularly.

A Yorkshire haystack spell

If you are a town-dweller, you will need to spend a long weekend in the countryside – perhaps camping, caravaning or staying in a farm B&B – in order to perform this spell.

You will need
Nothing.

Timing
On a Friday evening.

The spell
- Go to a hayrick or into the fields and pick a wheat or corn straw for every boy you want. Then pick an oat or barley straw for every girl.
- Bind the straws into a garter above your right knee.
- Wear the garter over the weekend (you can take it off to have a bath). If it is still in place on Monday, your wish will be granted and the first child will be conceived within a year. However, you must not tell your husband or lover about the spell. If the garter falls off, all is not lost. Pick up the straws and make them into a bracelet. If you can wear it on your left arm until Tuesday, the spell will be saved.

A power of stones spell

This spell should be performed, together with your partner, within an ancient stone circle or on the flat stone that served as an altar stone next to a monolith (a single pointed standing stone). Such circles and stones exist throughout western and eastern Europe and Scandinavia, many of them remote; they can be located by searching on the Internet or consulting guide books. Other lands have sacred places of their own; you may be able to find such a spot where you can perform this ritual, but take care to do so without offending indigenous sensibilities.

You will need
Nothing.

Timing
A misty morning near dawn.

The spell
* Just before dawn, go to the stone circle or monolith and make love. As you reach orgasm (simultaneously if possible), call out to be blessed with a child. You may feel a gentle breeze as the spirit of a potential child draws near.

Finding the King

Tall stones, both single pillars and members of stone circles, were used for fertility rites until the beginning of the twentieth century. In Brittany a woman who wanted a child would rub her stomach against a menhir (or single standing stone). She would give thanks by anointing the stone with a fertility substance such as honey, milk or oil. In Sardinia the Preda Frissa (meaning 'oily rock') menhir in the Barigadu region was used for the same purpose. In England, the King stone, one of the Rollright stones, near Banbury in Oxfordshire, was similarly visited on May day eve by women who wished to become pregnant. They rubbed their breasts against the stone at midnight.

You will need
Some flowers (for an offering).

Timing
Any quiet time.

The spell
* Find a tall pointed ancient stone (you may find there is one locally that has fertility legends attached).
* Go to the stone at a time when no one will be around and rub either your breasts or your stomach against the stone nine times, as you do so asking to become pregnant.
* Leave your offering of flowers.
* Make love as soon as possible afterwards, even if it is not the right time for conception in your ovulation cycle.

A spell to make a grass baby to awaken fertility

The giving of grass babies – often to a couple on their wedding day – was an old country custom. The idea was that once the grass hair had grown on the baby's head, the couple would have conceived. That was in days before reliable contraception, when every woman was expected to get pregnant soon after the wedding. In modern times a grass baby is often made at the point when a couple give up using contraception. The baby helps them to ease into the natural rhythms of the body. If one partner is resistant to the idea of having a family, a grass baby can be made by the more eager partner in order to help the other work through their reluctance and overcome any fears.

You will need

A thin cotton sock, a stocking or a small porous fabric bag; enough sawdust to almost fill the sock, stocking or bag; a handful of fast-growing grass seed; some twine; some marker pens, or some sequins or buttons and some glue (optional); a saucer.

Timing

On the day of the crescent moon if possible, as soon as you see the moon in the sky, even if this is before dark.

The spell

* Fill the sock, stocking or bag seven-eighths full of sawdust and shake well to remove all the loose pieces.
* Add the grass seed and tie the top of the sock, stocking or bag firmly so that you have a round ball. If you wish, you can add eyes, a nose and a mouth, either by drawing or sticking on buttons or sequins.
* Place the grass baby on the saucer and add water to the saucer each morning. Before the full moon your baby will be sprouting grass hair.
* When the grass is long, cut it. Continue to water and then cut until the new moon appears again in the sky.
* Make a new grass baby each month for three months to open your eagerness to have a child to the cosmos. Keep the old grass babies until they wilt and then bury them beneath a fruit tree.

Making a male potency figure

Throughout southern England, chalk figures of men or horses can be found etched into hillsides. These are widely regarded as powerful potency figures. One of the most famous is the Cerne Abbas giant. Carved into the chalk hillside near the village of Cerne in Dorset, the giant is 55 m/180 ft tall, with an 8-m/27-ft erect phallus. and may be more than 2,000 years old. Many women have attested to pregnancies conceived after making love on his huge phallus. Indeed, even his image in miniature was believed to increase potency in husbands and lovers. In pre-industrial England on the Christianised midsummer's day (24 June) or on the longest day (around 21 June) young women, married or unmarried, would make a small Cerne figure from clay or mark the outline of one in a dish of earth and plant it with fast-growing herbs or seedlings. The figure would then be left out in the open air from dawn until noon to be empowered by the masculine energies of the sun.

You will need

A small tray of earth; some very small white stones or a sharp stick to mark an outline; some seeds of a fast-growing herb or culinary plant, such as mustard and cress.

Timing

Ideally on midsummer's day or the longest day, at dawn, otherwise any Sunday at dawn.

The spell

* In the tray of earth mark the outline of a phallic figure, either with the stick or with the stones.
* Plant the figure with the seed.
* Name the man with whom you wish to conceive a child and say:
  May we be fruitful!
  Repeat the naming and the wish three times.
* Leave the tray outside from dawn to noon.
* Bring the tray indoors or keep it in a sheltered place and tend it every day, repeating the man's name and the wish three times.
* When the herbs or plant are grown, cut them and serve them as part of a meal for your man, perhaps cooking a special meal for the two of you.

Two midsummer spells for conception

In traditional folklore the Sun King reached the height of power at midsummer. His warmth made outdoor lovemaking possible, enabling lovers to connect with the fertility of the earth by coupling directly on the ground. In modern times, a camping trip can get around the problem of privacy, though if you can find a secluded field or woodland, that is even better. Midsummer fertility spells maintained their significance for hundreds of years. These two are written for women, but can be adapted if you are a male spell-caster.

* **Spell 1:** On the summer solstice (the longest day) or on the Christianised midsummer's day (24 June), make love with your partner on the earth or grass four times: once at dusk on the evening before the longest day or

midsummer's day, then once at midnight, dawn and noon of the day itself. Your lover will take on the power of the old sun god, and lovemaking will be long and fertile.

* **Spell 2:** Find a field where St John's wort grows (or plant some in your own garden earlier in the year). Alternatively, look for another yellow flowering herb, such as yellow chamomile. On midsummer's eve (23 June) at midnight, walk naked in the field or garden (wearing a light robe if the area is overlooked). Pick some St John's wort or yellow flowering herb. If possible, make love *in situ* or in the open air near where you picked the flower. Alternatively, put the herb under a pile of pillows or cushions, or under a soft rug on the floor indoors and make love on it.

A German May eve or Walpurga night spell for fertility

May eve was known to the Celts as Beltane and was the beginning of summer (Celtic festivals ran from dusk the previous night). It was one of the most important fertility festivals, and remained so well into Christian times. According to the poet Rudyard Kipling, even in Victorian times young girls and men would make love in the woods on May eve and stay out all night gathering hawthorn blossoms.

In Germany, the pagan fertility goddess of the May festival, Walpurga (or Walpurgis), was christianised as St Walpurga, sister of Saints Willibald and Wunnibald. Around the sixteenth century, her festival was introduced into Sweden (first being performed around Stockholm), and it became very popular here too. Walpurga's night was said to be a time when magic was afoot and elves and fairies roamed free. Bonfires were lit, especially on high hilltops, songs were sung around the fire, and couples made love.

This spell can be very helpful if you are undergoing IVF or having artificial insemination. It has been used successfully by lone women prior to insemination. If you cannot make a bonfire, substitute a huge red candle in a bucket of sand and burn six pieces of the same twig, burying the pieces of twig and any ashes beneath the tree from which the twig came.

You will need

A small bonfire; 6 twigs or small branches from a single tree that is not in bud, each twig/stick slightly larger than the last; a small container; 6 small moonstones.

Timing

After dark on 30 April, or when you first decide to try for a child.

The spell

* Light the bonfire.
* Hold the smallest twig in the flame so that the end chars but does not catch fire, as you do so saying:
  Fire to fire, flame and rise higher, may I give birth to my/our child before the fire is lit anew.
  (I.e. before the next Walpurga night.)
* Toss the stick into the bonfire, as you do so saying:
  Fire joined to fire, carry my blazing desire into the sky that I may give birth to my/our child before the fire is lit anew.
* Singe and then throw the next smallest twig, repeating the chants. Repeat this process with each twig or branch, working in ascending order.
* When the bonfire has burnt through and the ashes are cool, use the container to scoop up some of the ashes.
* Bury the ashes together with the six small moonstones beneath the tree from which you picked the twigs.

A Slavic dew fertility ritual

Morning dew rituals for fertility were popular on May day morning in western European traditions. Further north, summer comes later, and so dew rituals and other fertility rites were dedicated to Kupala, the Slavic, Balkan and Russian midsummer goddess. Her dew was collected on the summer solstice (around 21 June), and people would roll in it to increase their fertility.

You will need

A small fabric doll; an eye dropper (available from pharmacies); a clear glass phial or small bottle with a stopper; a pure white cloth; a dark scarf.

Timing

As early as possible in the morning, when the dew is sparkling. May day and midsummer mornings are both magical.

The spell

* Go out into the open air with the eye dropper and collect nine drops of dew from a flower or plant (rather than the ground). Store the dew in the phial or bottle.
* Using the eye dropper, drop a single drop of dew at a time onto the doll, saying as you drop each drop:
  Dew of the dawn,
  Dew of the moon,
  Dew of fertility / Kupala,
  Bring my babe soon.
* Leave the doll to dry naturally on the white cloth in the sunlight.
* When the sun sets, cover the doll with the dark scarf until the next dawn, then set the doll in your home, in a place that catches the sun.

A hazel nut fertility rite

Nuts are universal fertility symbols. In ancient Greece and Rome, brides ate stewed walnuts to ensure their fertility. At weddings in the south-west of England, the oldest woman in the congregation would give the bride a bag of hazel nuts to ensure her fertility. Even today, in parts of France, the bride and groom are showered with nuts at the altar, and the floor of the venue for the wedding breakfast is covered with nuts. This spell will help to relax rigid timetables for conception for a month or two, so restoring spontaneous joyful lovemaking. It can be useful for women who have an irregular menstrual cycle.

You will need

14 perfectly round hazel nuts or other small smooth round nuts; a silver cloth or some silver paper.

Timing

The first day of your menstrual cycle, even if this is irregular.

The spell

* On day one, as near to sunset as possible, lay the first nut on the silver cloth or paper, near the window of your bedroom.
* Each day, at the same time, add another nut until, on the 14th day, all the nuts have been added.
* The morning after the 14th day, as soon as you wake, wrap the nuts in the silver cloth or paper and leave them covered until the last day of your menstrual cycle.
* On the last day of your cycle, plant the nuts in a sheltered spot and water the soil regularly.
* Repeat the ritual, if necessary, until you relax into its rhythm. You may find that an irregular menstrual cycle becomes more harmonious.
* Buy a small nut tree for your garden, patio or indoors, to attract fertility to your home.

A beeswax fertility and potency ritual

The mother goddess was depicted as a bee in Palaeolithic times, and bees and beeswax have been associated with the fertility of both humans and the earth throughout our history. Although formal beekeeping did not begin until around 2500 BCE (in ancient Egypt), people have probably always gathered honey and beeswax from hollow trees.

Using beeswax to form a phallic-shaped candle, this spell combines symbols of both female fertility and male potency. If you can work with a partner, it will be doubly powerful. Rolling candles out of beeswax also gives you the opportunity to enfold your wishes in the candle by visualising yourself with a child. Bees are associated with St Anne, the grandmother of Christ, who conceived a child when she was very old. This spell is therefore good for older people who are trying for a baby.

You will need

A sheet of beeswax (2 sheets if you are working with your partner – available from art and craft outlets and from beeswax or honey suppliers); a wick (2 wicks if you are working with your partner) – the wick should be about 1cm/¹/₂ in longer than the candle).

Timing

Any Friday before dusk.

The spell

* Working outdoors in the sunshine if possible, place the wick at the edge of the sheet and roll the wax around it. If you are working with a partner, do this simultaneously. As you roll the wax, repeat the following rhyme to emulate the humming of bees on a summer's day:
Golden honey, magic bee,
Bring fertility/potency to me.
* When it is dark, light the candle (or candles) and make love by their light.

A spell to relieve male sexual dysfunction

For thousands of years, men suffering from temporary sexual dysfunction have used lodestones as a magical aid to increased virility. The lodestone was placed in love-inducing oil for 24 hours, and the infusion was then rubbed on the penis before making love. Our ancestors must have been very hardy, as even mild oil on the penis may cause irritation. This is an effective alternative.

You will need

A male (pointed) lodestone (see page 28); a love anointing oil, or frankincense or orange essential oil; I tbsp sunflower oil (optional); a small dish (optional).

Timing

One hour before lovemaking.

The spell

* Sprinkle the love oil, or frankincense or orange essential oil (both fragrances of potency) over your lodestone. If you have lost a great deal of confidence in your sexual performance, mix 5 drops of the love or essential oil with the sunflower oil in the dish and leave the lodestone in the dish from dusk to dusk. Turn the lodestone in the oil before you go to bed, first thing the next morning and, if possible, at noon. Rinse and dry the lodestone before you carry out the rest of the spell.
* Hold the stone in your left hand and visualise successful lovemaking.
* Place the lodestone under the mattress before making love.

6 SPELLS FOR RECONCILIATION IN LOVE

Betrayal, unkindness or coldness from our partner, are among the worst pains to endure. I have twice been deeply betrayed by men I loved, and years later the scars still run deep. I vividly remember my sense of rejection and the loss of self-esteem that resulted.

In some instances, such experiences may signal the end of the relationship (see Chapter 7 for spells to help in this situation); in other cases, however, the hurtful behaviour may have been out of character, precipitated by a mid-life crisis, too much alcohol or problems at work. Coldness or indifference may be caused by depression, the pressures of debt, exhaustion, worries about family members or conflict within the family. Long hours of commuting or spending weeks away from the family can sometimes result in separate lives developing slowly. Sailors' wives have told me that while their partner is away for several months at sea, the home starts to function without him; when he comes home on leave and tries to take over, quarrels quickly start. The same scenario can result when a female partner serves away from home. Retirement, even if longed for, can be another source of pressure when a couple who have led busy lives are suddenly together 24/7.

In such situations, given good will, tolerance and a real desire to mend or improve a relationship, reconciliation can be possible. What is more, the healing process can offer reminders of the original strength of feeling that existed before everyday life got in the way, pointing up the deep sense of connection that is born out of shared experiences, good and bad.

The following rituals may be carried out by one or both parties. None of them is about apportioning blame, punishing the guilty or wreaking vengeance upon the harpy, Lothario or over-possessive relation who encouraged division and doubt. Rather they create a magical space, untouched by third parties, where healing can begin. It does not matter which of you has strayed or behaved thoughtlessly. The spells work regardless.

There are some who would describe the spells in this chapter as 'fluffy' – the new term for sweetness-and-light spells. I would argue, however, that if a situation is bad, most of the bitter words will already have been spoken. If you want to mend things, there is no point in sending out darkness or negativity: it will just bounce back. It is never a compromise to your integrity to offer sweetness appropriately.

These spells do not minimise the pain caused by a partner's insensitive behaviour; rather they seek to enable the issues that may have contributed to tension or to a split to be tackled creatively and positively. If you love someone enough, it is never too late to try to mend the breach, if that is what you want. Sometimes, too, a reconciliation ritual will bring peace and the cessation of bitterness, together with the realisation that it may now be time to move on alone.

A candle spell to understand each other's point of view

This spell is worked together with your partner. It is based on the old practice of allowing a person to speak their mind or plead their cause uninterrupted until a lighted candle has burnt down to a designated mark. It is an excellent ritual if you and your partner have stopped listening to each other or if tempers flare quickly, whether over a specific issue or generally. This spell involves reversing roles and taking each other's part, as though acting as the other's advocate.

You will need

A beeswax or fast-burning orange candle (burning times are sometimes given on the label, otherwise ask when you buy); 2 tapers; a paper knife, sharp nail or other inscribing tool; an orange or golden crystal, such as amber or carnelian.

Timing

Late in the evening, if possible during the last days of the waning moon.

The spell

* Using the inscribing object, mark a notch about 3 cm/I¹/₂ in from the top of the candle. Mark further notches at 3-cm/I¹/₂-in intervals until you reach the base of the candle.
* Using the tapers, light the candle together with your partner, so that the two tapers join in the flame. As you do so, say:
Let the matter be settled between us in peace and in love. So are we joined in Fire and in our hearts despite disunity.
* Set the crystal so that the candle light shines on it.
* Begin to talk about your partner's grievances from his or her point of view, as if you were his or her

advocate. Continue talking until the candle burns down to the first notch. Your partner may not interrupt you. If you finish before your turn is ended, suggest positive solutions and concessions you would be prepared to make, as well as hopes for the two of you in the future once the problem is resolved.
* When your time is up, your partner should begin to speak, taking your own point of view, as if your advocate. No comment should be made about what you said on your partner's behalf.
* When the candle has burnt down to the second notch and your partner's time is through, blow out the candle together, again without making any comment on anything that has been said on behalf of either you or your partner. As you blow out the candle, say:
Let the matter rest between us in peace and in love. So are we joined in Fire and in our hearts without disunity.
Leave the candle and crystal in place.
* Listen to music or go for a late night walk together, without commenting on anything that has been said. Talk instead about happy times in your relationship. Do not refer to the matter of contention.
* The next night light the candle and give your partner the crystal, as you do so saying:
So are we joined in Fire and in our hearts to speak freely to reach unity.
* Let your partner speak first, about his or her fears and feelings. He or she should speak without accusation or blame, and you must not interrupt.
* When your partner has finished, he or she hands you the crystal so that

you can speak freely – with the same boundaries as above applying.

- Pass the crystal from one to the other and keep the words flowing until the candle has burnt down to the next notch.
- Leaving the candle and crystal in place, blow out the candle, as you do so saying:

So are we joined in Fire and in our hearts and move towards unity.

- If an argument is brewing, return to speak through the candle on subsequent nights, until the candle is burnt down.
- Dispose of the candle remnants. Wash the crystal under running water and place it where natural light will shine on it as a symbol of reconciliation. You may use the crystal again if necessary, with a new candle.

A pot pourri spell for the renewal of love

I originally devised this spell for the consummation of love after a period of celibacy or when making love for the first time. However, I have found it to be just as successful for restoring closeness when a couple have been physically separated or emotionally estranged. The spell does not have to result in lovemaking, unless that is what you desire, but it should enable you to feel comfortable together when sharing a bed or sitting close. Pot pourri is used because it is a blend of flowers, spices and herbs, and so symbolises coming together in love.

You will need

A large bowl of lavender- or rose-based pot pourri; 3 or 4 small bowls.

Timing

After a parting or when relations have been cold, in the early evening, when you are alone.

The spell

- Set out the pot pourri bowl. Fill it with love by passing your hands, palms down, a few centimetres above it, the left hand moving deosil (clockwise) and the right hand widdershins (anticlockwise). As you work, chant:

My love, I give my love to you,
Lover gentle, lover true.
This night will join our hearts as one,
Willingly till time is run.
You are my love and ever will be.
I call you, love, in love to me.

- Divide the pot pourri between the four small bowls. Set one in the hallway or near the front room, one in the main living room, one in the bedroom and one in any room where you quarrelled or have sad memories. If this is one of the rooms above, set two bowls there.

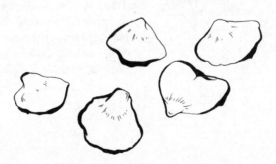

An ice reconciliation spell to renew trust or end a period of coldness or anger

This is a very gentle spell to calm hurt feelings and melt coldness or harsh words spoken out of guilt rather than malice – in an attempt to justify actions. This spell also works well after a family quarrel. Try to spend time with your partner on the night after you have carried out the spell, talking quietly by candle light. If your partner cannot be with you, write a letter to him or her, expressing only positive feelings and hopes for the future.

You will need

A small heatproof bowl or saucepan; enough ice to fill the bowl/saucepan $1/3$ full; a wooden spoon; 6 small pink candles or a small burner of the kind used in fondu sets, over which you can set the saucepan (the candles will be slow – useful if you want to sit for a while and perhaps play some music that is significant to you and your partner; if you are really in a hurry, use a low heat on a conventional stove).

Timing

During the waning moon or at any time in the hour after sunset.

The spell

* Fill the heatproof bowl or saucepan with the ice.
* Stir the ice with the spoon, not attempting to break it up but naming any resentments, fury or guilt that is bubbling inside you. Then name the positive feelings that have become frozen inside you.

* Either set the candles in a ring around the bowl or saucepan and light them, or set the bowl or saucepan on the heat source. Say three times, so softly that you are almost inaudible:
Ice go,
Water flow.
Take from me
This misery.
* Stir the ice and feel it softening as you softly repeat the chant three more times.
* Keep stirring as the ice melts, naming all the positive aspects of your partner and yourself, the situation or the relationship, however difficult this may be.
* When you have finished, sit in the candle light or the light of a soft lamp, recalling happier times – memories of shared jokes, holidays, times when you acted in unison.
* When the ice has melted, stir the water, saying quite audibly three times:
Water flow,
Sorrow go,
Leaving only harmony.
* When you have finished, pour the water down a drain, as you do so saying:
Go from me,
Flow from me,
Leave only harmony.
* Take a practical step towards improving relations, for instance making a non-confrontational phone call, cooking a favourite meal or booking a weekend away.

A candle spell for clearing the air

This is another version of the spell on page 102. It works well if a disagreement is long-standing and cannot be easily resolved. This might be over serious money problems or how to deal with a troublesome relation who cannot be abandoned. The spell uses fragrances to induce a state of relaxation and well-being if one or both parties is very tense.

You will need

A cedar or pine incense stick; a fast-burning rose-scented candle; a paper knife, sharp nail or other inscribing tool; a small dish of sea salt.

Timing

At 10 pm (the healing hour).

The spell

* Light the cedar or pine incense (for cleansing any bad feeling), as you do so saying:
  May all be cleansed and peace return.
* Using the inscribing tool, mark a notch about 3 cm/1½ in from the top of the candle. Mark a second notch a further 3 cm/1½ in down the candle.
* Working in a deosil (clockwise) direction, scatter a circle of sea salt (for cleansing) around the candle to enclose any negative feelings, as you do so repeating the words you spoke in step one.
* Light the candle and invite your partner to speak, uninterrupted, his or her feelings about the situation. He or she should avoid words of blame

or any remarks that will diminish your self-esteem. One strategy is to use 'I' statements rather than 'you' statements. Empty your mind of preconceptions and listen, for there may be grains of truth and sense in what he or she says. If your partner does not want to use all his or her candle time, sit quietly until the candle has burnt down to the notch, touching hands if you feel able and playing gentle music. Imagine any negativity being consumed by the candle flame.

* When the candle has burnt down to the notch, scatter a few grains of sea salt from the circle into the candle flame, as you do so repeating the words from step one.
* It is now your turn to speak, observing the boundaries laid down above. Speak honestly and openly but without apportioning blame or criticising, while your partner listens.
* When the second notch is reached, your partner should sprinkle a few grains of sea salt from the circle into the flame, this time saying:
  May all be cleansed and joy return.
* Let the candle burn through. Scoop up any remaining salt and tip it under running water, as you do so saying:
  Go from me,
  Flow from me.
  Anger no more
  Come to this door.
* Make a definite plan for something that will bring pleasure to both you and your partner in the coming days.

A spell to bury the bone of contention

In most relationships there are certain issues that can cause a flare-up, often linked to family, ex-partners, money, work or activities such as sports outside the home that occupy a great deal of time. Sometimes, no matter how often you discuss the matter, circumstances mean that it cannot be resolved, yet to live in its shadow can make it difficult to be positive. In this situation, resentments can harden like stone and positions become entrenched. So until time resolves the bone – or issue – of contention, it is best buried.

Burying the bone is an ancient symbolic gesture to lay an irreconcilable matter to rest once and for all. If you do not want to use an actual bone, you can substitute a bone-shaped or elongated white stone. Indeed, burying a stone engraved with the cause of the anger can be a very effective way of dissipating the weight of accumulated resentment or dread around your particular 'hot' topic.

This spell also involves planting flowers or herbs on the grave of the contention. Suitable choices might be rue for regrets, gillyflowers for renewed affection, peonies for sorrow, honesty for open communication, lilac for the promise of happiness, red roses or red carnations for lasting love, gladioli to ease pain, white carnations for new trust and affection, or white pansies for loving thoughts. A vegetable can also be a good choice, providing nourishing new growth from the buried disagreement. You could also go for a flower that has special meaning for both of you.

If you are working this spell with your partner, you can, as you are planting, decide on a key word – perhaps something humorous or the name of the flower you are planting – that can be spoken to defuse the situation if the issue arises and tempers flare again. (Even if you are working alone, when you are together with your partner and both relaxed, you could agree on a word to use when tempers rise around this matter.)

You can bury a number of bones if there are a number of key issues, perhaps concerning past mistakes that must now be laid to rest.

You will need

A spade or trowel; a bone or stone; a permanent marker or sharp knife; flowers or herbs to plant on the grave of the contention (see above).

Timing

Just before dusk (so that regrets may disappear below the horizon with the setting sun).

The spell

* With the spade or trowel, dig a hole in the earth for your bone or stone.
* Write or scratch on your bone or stone a word or symbol to represent the main problem that you are burying.
* Set the bone or stone in the ground, as you do so naming the issue and resolving to speak of it no more.
* Cover the hole with earth, and in the soil set your flowers or herbs to help more positive attitudes to grow.

A ritual for reconciliation where there has been major betrayal or separation

After any reconciliation, there may be a long period of doubt, which can all too easily end in recriminations. A simple ceremony, repeated if necessary at regular intervals, can offer a unifying force. This spell is worked together with your partner and provides a lovely way to end an evening if the two of you have met to discuss the future. It can also help you to overcome together crises on the way to reconciliation, caused perhaps by spiteful contact by an ex-lover who has contributed to the rift. This ritual works equally well for same-sex couples.

You will need

A white (or beeswax) entwined figure candle, or a silver- and a gold-coloured candle (female and male respectively), or a pink and a green candle (female and male respectively, and love and reconciliation in the alchemical tradition); a metal tray; some dried rose petals or lavender flowers; 2 tapers (optional).

Timing

At 10 pm (the healing hour).

The spell

- Place the candle (or candles) on the tray and surround it with the rose petals or lavender flowers – for cleansing old angers and reviving love.
- If you are using an entwined lovers candle, the two of you light it together, using the two tapers and as you do so saying:

So do we rekindle love, passion, trust and fidelity.

If you are using two separate candles, light your lover's candle first and then invite him to light yours, each speaking the words as you light the candle.
- If you are using an entwined lovers candle, each sprinkle a few rose petals or lavender heads into the flame, as you do so saying:

Anger, resentment, bitterness, jealousy, burn, burn away.

If you are using two separate candles, sprinkle the petals into your lover's candle first and then invite him to do the same with your candle, each speaking the words as you sprinkle the petals.
- Sit quietly in the candle light, hands joined, as the candle (or candles) burns down. Rekindle the affection between you by recalling happy times and make plans and promises for the future.

A three-day candle spell to heal a bad quarrel or rift

This is a gradual spell that sends healing energies to both the spell-caster and the subject of the spell over three successive evenings, although the results may not be felt for about a week. The magical energies can encourage a partner who has temporarily moved out to get in touch.

You will need
2 identical pink candles.

Timing
On three consecutive evenings, around 10 pm.

The spell
* Set the pink candles (the colour of reconciliation) as far apart from each other as possible on a table or flat surface. Designate one candle for yourself and one for your partner.
* Light your partner's candle and softly speak into the flame the words you would like to say if he or she were present, whether regrets or forgiveness, and some of the questions you would like to ask about what went wrong.
* Light your own candle and say:
  Return if you will, without reproach, to my arms and to my life.
* Blow out your own candle, sending a message of love to wherever your partner is. Then blow out his or her candle, repeating the words of the previous step.
* Move each candle a quarter of the way across the table, so that they are closer.
* On the second night, light your partner's candle and speak into the flame thanks for the kindnesses shown to you in the past by your partner.
* Light your own candle and into the flame express what you miss most about the relationship and would like to rekindle.
* Blow out your partner's candle, as you do so again saying the words from the third step.
* Blow out your own candle, as you do so sending positive wishes for your partner's happiness and the hope that you will soon be together again.
* Place the candles so that they are almost touching.
* On the final evening of the spell, light your partner's candle and make promises to try to be more tolerant and understanding in future, even if the quarrel was not your fault.
* Light your own candle from your partner's and repeat the words from the third step.
* Leave the candles to burn through while you sit in the candlelight looking at old photographs, reading poetry or listening to music you both enjoyed.
* When the candles are burnt through, plan a simple non-confrontational gesture of friendship – for instance, sending a postcard of a place you both visited, an e-mail recounting good news about a mutual friend or family member, or a small bunch of your partner's favourite flowers. Even if the gesture of reconciliation is refused, you have freed yourself of bitterness. If the hurt is deep, you may need to repeat the ritual several times to soften your partner's attitude.

An autumn ritual for forgiveness and acceptance of frailty

We all make mistakes, but it can be hard to realise that our idolised partner has feet of clay. Of course, serial adulterers, cheats and abusers of all kinds can turn on little-boy or little-girl charm and promise it will never happen again, but a mile down the road it always does. After one too many heartaches we learn that they are not to be trusted. A one-off mistake, on the other hand – where there has been pressure and accompanied by genuine remorse – can sometimes give way to a more grounded relationship with the real person rather than an idealised version of him or her. This ritual, ideally worked together with your partner, will help you to accept weakness, be it your own or your partner's, making a commitment to let the past go. Although originally devised as an autumn harvest ritual, it can in fact be carried out at any time of the year using berries, nuts and seeds bought from a supermarket.

You will need

2 bowls; a selection of nuts, berries or seeds (or all three mixed); some dead or dying leaves from a tree or bush, still on twigs, or leaves from dead cut flowers, or dried lavender heads – if possible still on their stems.

Timing

An autumn afternoon, or an afternoon that is misty or cloudy.

The spell

* Sit on the ground, either alone or with your lover – if the latter, with the bowls between you. Say:
  What is lost and what is gained balance out: the riches of the harvest and the dying of the leaves. As day and night are equal at the beginning of autumn, so all things now are likewise equal.
* Pick an autumn leaf from the twig and cast it on to the ground, as you do so saying:
  As leaves die, so will new ones in ripe time grow. So is it with love.
* If you are working with your lover, ask him or her to pick a berry, nut or seed and eat it, saying:
  As fruit ripens, it brings joy and takes away bitterness. So is it with love.
  If you are working alone, perform the action and speak the words yourself.
* If you are working with a lover, he or she now takes a leaf and you take a berry, nut or seed, repeating the appropriate words. Continue alternately to pluck leaves and eat, saying the words, until all the leaves, fruit, nuts and seeds are gone. If you are working alone, continue to perform both actions and speak both lines yourself.
* Leave the empty bowls and go for a walk. The leaves will blow away or remain lifeless on the ground to be swept up later and thrown away.

A sea spell for the return of a faithless lover

If your partner is unfaithful, the other man or woman cannot entirely be blamed. Infidelity is a complex issue and can have roots in a marriage where a couple have moved in opposite directions, perhaps over many years, so that all they now have in common is a house and loans. But there are men and women – I know some – to whom deliberately breaking up a perfectly happy marriage is a challenge. If you probe into the past of these real-life soap opera characters, you will usually find a whole series of broken relationships. Sadly, once their 'only true love' has given up home, family and sometimes career for them, the conquest loses its excitement and the seducer moves on to the next quarry.

Whatever the reasons for your partner's desertion, if you curse or hex your love rival, you are damaging your own karma, so waxen images and pins are definitely off limits. However, if you do want your partner back – and you may not – by the old magical laws of cause and effect, you are entitled to demand the return of a relationship that may have survived over many years and perhaps is cemented by the creation and care of children. This way you have a chance of sorting things out without the intervention of the third party – or at least of parting with less bitterness if the underlying differences are too great to be resolved.

The sea, with its powerful tides, has traditionally been invoked for the return of loved ones. In an ancient ritual the wives of sailors whose husbands were travelling across the waves would collect sea water in a bottle. When the ship was due to return, they would cast the bottle into the sea, saying: 'I return what is yours; return what is mine.' Offerings to sea deities and spirits were traditionally made in many places – and still are in ceremonies on remote islands where fishing is the main occupation. Protective sea goddesses were given different names in different cultures; for instance, the Viking goddess was known as Ran, and was said to love gold more than anything. Even in Christian times the old rituals continued, sometimes dedicated to the Virgin Mary, called Stella Maris or Star of the Sea because she guided sailors and fishermen safely across the water.

Although I have used many forms of this ritual, the plain unvarnished spell has proved by far the most effective. There are no provisos and no mention of the third party, just a 'come back and we can sort it out one way or the other'. I wish I had known this spell when I faced my own heartbreaks, as I believe it would have enabled me to be much stronger and less willing to take all the blame myself.

You will need

A bottle; a gold earring, thin gold ring or golden-coloured coin.

Timing

On an incoming tide and an outgoing tide, either on the same day or on two consecutive days.

The spell

* On the incoming tide, go to the shore – if you cannot go to the ocean or a tidal river, use any running water source – and cast the gold into the water as an offering to the benign essence of sea power.
* Wade out into the water and scoop some up in the bottle, as you do so saying:

Lady Ocean, Mother Sea,
I take of yours not willingly,
But as a token of what I lack.
I ask your help to bring him/her back.
Take the water away with you in the bottle.
* On the outgoing tide, again wade out with the bottle, this time tipping the water back into the waves and saying:

Lady Ocean, Mother Sea,
I return what is yours;
Return mine to me.
* Some people then choose to smash the bottle in a safe place where it cannot cut anyone, but I think it is more ecologically sound to recycle it – as hopefully the faithless lover will now be.

A spell to call a lost love back

If you do not know where your partner is or are not able to contact him or her for any reason, you can use the telepathic linkthat all couples share, even if it is rarely used. The herb rosemary was immortalised by Shakespeare's Ophelia, who linked it with remembrance of love and errant or uncaring lovers, in her case Hamlet. Parsley, sage, rosemary and thyme are associated with the return of lost love in the song 'Scarborough Fair', made popular by Simon and Garfunkel:

Are you going to Scarborough Fair,
Parsley, sage, rosemary and thyme?
Remember me to one who lives there.
She once was a true love of mine.

You will need

A fast-burning deep-red candle; a large-lipped holder or flat metal tray on which the candle can be placed directly to collect wax; some dried rosemary, parsley, sage and thyme; a knife; a piece of white silk.

Timing

At midnight.

The spell

* Light the red candle (for love eternal) and let it burn through while you look at old photographs, holiday brochures, letters from your love and so on, to establish the telepathic link between you. You could also listen to a piece of music that you share.
* Wait until the melted wax is no longer liquid (but still soft) and then shake and press the dried herbs into the wax in the shape of a heart, as you work saying softly and repeatedly:

Parsley, sage, rosemary, thyme,
Call back, I ask, this love of mine.

* When you have finished and the wax is cool, ease it gently off the tray with a knife and wrap it in white silk, keeping it in a drawer where your partner's clothes are or were.

A west wind bubble ritual for sending love if you parted in anger or bitterness

This ritual is particularly good for sending friendly feelings towards someone from whom you are estranged and who has moved away or is not returning your calls. It is a reminder to you both (telepathically to the absent lover) of the laughter and spontaneous fun you once shared.

You will need

A child's large bubble blower and soapy water, or a ready-made bubble set.

Timing

A bright morning, best of all with the wind blowing from the West.

The spell

* Stand in the open air or at an open window or door, facing the direction in which the person lives or in which you last saw them walking or driving.
* Blow a bubble, holding it on the bubble blower and saying:
  Grow love once more and laughter rise;
  Send my wishes to the skies.
  If the bubble does not rise spontaneously, blow it gently.
* Repeat five times, waiting until each bubble has dispersed before creating the next and repeating the chant each time.
* As the last bubble flies away, call your love's name six times and say:
  We will know joy once more;
  In spite of all, I have not closed the door.
* If you have heard nothing by the time six days have elapsed, make a simple gesture of friendship towards the estranged person, perhaps by sending a card or making a brief phone call.

7 SPELLS FOR ENDING A RELATIONSHIP

There are many reasons for a relationship ending, for example, betrayal, cruelty, or a gradual moving apart over the years or because of circumstances. We all hope that love will be forever. Even a relationship lasting only months creates deep emotional bonds that can cause intense pain on separation, whether or not the decision to part is mutual. For someone who has been married for a quarter or more of their lifetime, parting can take years to accept, let alone heal. In this chapter I have included a spell for a situation in which circumstances have forced a couple apart and a ritual I have found helpful for those whose partner has died after a long happy marriage.

These spells may need to be repeated many times, for the ending of love is much slower than the beginning. It is important to be patient with yourself and to accept that no magic, however powerful, can take away the pain of what is in effect bereavement – although magic can help to ease that pain and enable you to accept the reality of what has happened.

If your ex-partner is still alive and you are forced to see or hear of them – or must meet because of children or for business reasons – it may be very hard to grieve. Rituals can be helpful in facilitating this process, as well as enabling you to walk away with dignity and without bitterness. What is more, the power generated by spells can give you the strength to leave a destructive relationship or to end an unhappy one, and so to open yourself to the happiness you deserve in the future.

This is a very positive chapter, aimed at helping you to shed emotional luggage rather than carrying it around with you to weigh down your new separate life.

A spell to rid yourself of an unwanted admirer or would-be lover

Life has an ironic way of attracting to us an admirer whose company we dislike while we desire another or are happy being unattached. When I was divorced with two young children I seemed to attract every unhappily married man under the age of 90 and single father with children within a ten-mile radius. We may be enjoying single life, but friends and relatives will try to match us with anyone who has not yet received a centenary telegram from the Queen!

This spell does not work by banishing or using cruel means to dissuade the unwanted lover (though in Part 8 you will find spells to protect against stalkers and less benign attention). Rather it turns the would-be lover towards someone who will make him or her happy.

You will need

A small grey candle; a taller fast-burning white candle.

Timing

For three nights, beginning on a Saturday.

The spell

* Set the grey candle (representing yourself) and the white candle (representing the other person and their new beginning) close together and name each, saying:
Though you are desirable/admirable, our paths do not entwine.
* Move the white candle (only) away from yours and light it, as you do so saying:

Though you are desirable (or admirable) you cannot be mine.
* Leave your candle unlit and send good wishes for the happiness of your admirer. Then blow out the white candle, as you do so repeating the first chant.
* On the second night, again name the two candles. Move the white candle even further away from yours and light it, as you do so saying:
Send your light to s/he who will make you truly happy.
Picture your admirer walking away, towards the waiting arms of another person, whose identity you should not seek to know.
* Blow out the candle in silence.
* On the third night, move the white candle far away from yours and light it, as you do so saying:
Follow your own path in joy and no longer walk along mine.
* Let the white candle burn through, and only then light the grey candle, from a new flame, as you do so saying:
May the mists remain between us.
And so goodbye.
* When you feel ready, extinguish the grey candle and deliberately push all thoughts of the other person from your mind. Throw your candle and the wax from the white candle away.
* Gently discourage contact and, if possible, for the next week avoid places where you see your admirer, to give the spell time to work.

A spell to dampen the ardour in a one-sided relationship

If you are dating the boy next door or someone you have known since school or college, the relationship may have become a habit. Sometimes families start buying bridal magazines and everything escalates, while all you want to do is backpack to Rio or pursue a career wholeheartedly for a few years before settling down. Sometimes we drift towards a commitment we do not really want, because we are afraid of hurting the other person's feelings. This spell will help to reduce the connection in a spontaneous way – but be sure this is what you want before you work it: sometimes a person who is familiar but taken for granted may be the one who could make us happy if only we looked at him or her in a different way.

You will need

Some fresh mint, rosemary or vervain that you have picked yourself and left to dry naturally until withered; 2 seedlings or packets of seed of the same herb as above; a small bonfire or a large red candle embedded in a bucket partly filled with sand or earth.

Timing

When the moon is dark (in the nights just before the crescent moon appears).

The spell

* Light the bonfire or candle and, one by one, consign the mint, rosemary or vervain (for passion) to the fire, as you do so saying:
  What is gone or never was, let it turn to ashes by mutual consent and let new love grow, but separately.
* Leave the fire or candle to burn out.
* Plant the seedlings or seeds in different places at least 3 km/2 miles apart.

A lemon balm spell to ease the pain of parting

If you have recently parted from your partner or lover, night time can bring memories flooding back. An old remedy for the pain of such times involves lemon balm (melissa), the herb most associated with easing emotional hurt. Lemon balm grows in most climates and has a lovely delicate lemon scent.

You will need

A fresh sprig of lemon balm or some lemon balm essential oil – lavender can be substituted for either.

Timing

Before you go to bed.

The spell

* Crush one or two of the lemon balm leaves between your fingers or inhale the oil, as you do so saying:
  Be as balm to my troubled heart, my grieving spirit; bring consolation and let me sleep peacefully in your arms.
* Place the lemon balm leaves beneath your pillow or sprinkle a drop or two of the oil on to your pillow, somewhere where it will not come into contact with your eyes or mouth. As you do so, repeat the words.
* Close your eyes and picture a garden filled with flowers and fragrant herbs. Walk along the path to sleep in your mind's eye.

A spell for cutting the ties of a destructive relationship or one that is going nowhere

Ending a destructive or abusive relationship can be extremely difficult – as is waiting years for a would-be partner in an unhappy relationship to end it and commit to us. In such situations, our self-esteem and confidence may become seriously eroded, leading us to accept the blame for everything that goes wrong. If you are the person waiting for the would-be lover and they continue to hang on in their existing relationship for years, you may lose the chance of finding someone who is free and of being able to celebrate your love openly.

Even a destructive relationship is better finished gently and with dignity, as in this spell. If things are really bad, you may need to repeat the spell more than once, each time using a new and shorter cord. In this case, hold the cord so that the end is in the flame, and once it catches light, drop it on to the tray and extinguish the candle. Leave the cord to burn and then dispose of the burnt remains away from your home. The cord has become a symbol of unity in love because in the old folk custom of handfasting (or pagan marriage) bride and groom would tie their hands together with a cord.

You will need
25 cm/10 in of thin red curtain cord; a deep-blue pillar candle in a holder; a metal tray or flat metal holder.

Timing
On a Saturday, at 10 pm.

The spell
- Light the candle and place it in the holder or on the tray. Being careful not to burn yourself, hold the cord over the flame taut in both hands, so that the centre of the cord is in the flame. As you do so say:
  The cord between us is long.
  The cord between us was strong,
  But now is decaying, fraying,
  Burning, breaking.
- When the cord has burnt through, drop both halves on the tray and let the flame burn out, saying:
  The link is broken.
  The false words spoken
  Likewise have no power.
- Throw away the charred cords.

A separation spell to re-establish your own boundaries

I wrote at the beginning of this chapter about how our emotions become entwined during a long-standing relationship. When the relationship ends – especially if the ending has been sudden – the sensation can feel like ripping flesh, and many barbs may be left behind. What is more, if you lived much of your life through your partner, you may have lost sight of your own preferences and priorities. This (and the following) spell will help you slowly to rediscover and rebuild your own separate identity and boundaries so that you are no longer half of an incomplete couple but a separate person. Developing this sense of individuality can be an essential stage in the growth process. For a time in my life I rushed from one failed relationship to another, adapting myself to a new man before I had had time to rediscover – or, in my case, discover for the first time (since I married straight from my parents' home) – who I really was.

You will need

A twining or trailing plant, such as ivy or honeysuckle, in a pot; a second, smaller, plant pot; some compost; a damp cloth.

Timing

On a Tuesday morning (an auspicious day for spells for courage and confidence).

The spell

* Gently dig up the plant from its pot, as you do so saying:

  No more are we joined at our roots. We must part that I may grow again freely.

* Carefully separating out the roots, divide the plant into two. Using the compost together with just a little soil from the old pot, plant one half of the plant in the smaller pot, as you do so saying:

In new soil grow strong and tall, taking nourishment from what was good from the past to re-grow my own identity.

* Carefully wrap the other half of the plant in the damp cloth and replant it away from your house, in an open space or a park flowerbed, including some of the original soil in the planting. (It would be pointless to destroy the half of the plant representing your ex-partner, as you were once joined, and the act would reflect back on you.)

* Tend your own plant lovingly, giving it sunlight and water – and give equal care to yourself. The other plant is no longer yours to care for or worry about.

A computer spell for breaking free from a destructive or redundant relationship

Though love spells generally connote candles, herbs and flowers – and, indeed, many of the rituals in this book use these timeless materials – the tools of magic were traditionally drawn from the world in which the spell-caster lived. In the modern world, computers can therefore be a useful tool for magic. A magic circle drawn on the screen is no less potent than one created in the earth by a sword or wand.

You do not need to be a computer graphics artist to carry out this spell. The simplest images will suffice. All you need is one of the basic paint box programs, such as MSPaint for a PC or Mac Paint for a Macintosh – or a Palmtop with a marking pen. If you are not into computers, you can just as easily carry out the spell by using a notebook with plain pages, tearing out each image as you have created it and

drawing the next one on the following clean page. This method is as effective as the computer version, if less instant. Throw away all the discarded notebook images with the rubbish.

This spell can also be used as a way of distancing yourself emotionally in an abusive relationship if circumstances demand that you cannot immediately move away physically. In this case, you may need to repeat it several times.

You will need

A computer with a drawing programme; a digital image of yourself and your ex-lover, not entwined but standing side by side (optional).

Timing

After sunset on a Saturday, or any day during the latter half of the waning moon phase.

The spell

- Draw two figures on the screen, standing close but not touching. These can be very detailed or just outlines. Alternatively, get up the digital image.
- Beginning in the north of the screen, create a circle around the figures in one unbroken sweep.
- Draw a line through the circle so that a wall separates the two figures. It does not matter how thin the separating line is.
- In two unbroken sweeps, create two separate circles round the figures, one on either side of the line, drawing your own first and then your ex-lover's. Say as you create each one:

  Two joined as one; now two again, separate, complete, entire, alone.

- Use the mouse to pick up each circle in turn and move them farther apart, away from the line. If you wish, you can make the line down the middle disappear, as you no longer need it.

Keep it for extra security if you feel vulnerable.

- Thicken the line around each circle, as you do so saying:

  No more to touch, our spheres do move apart, not to impinge, intrude, invade my circle now protected.

- Continue to move your lover's circle until it has disappeared from the screen, as you do so saying:

  Go in peace; look no more to me nor think of me.

- Remove the dividing line if you have not already done so. Move your own circle into the centre of the screen.
- Make eight more concentric circles, moving outwards from your circle, as you do so saying:

  So am I enclosed within these circles of serenity. I will admit only those I choose to love.

- If your ex-lover was abusive or is persistent in trying to persuade you to return against your will and commonsense, make the outermost circle jagged – not to harm but merely to repel.

A rainy day spell for saying goodbye to a lover if the parting was not sought by you

Rain is a natural cleanser of dust and dirt, and it has always been regarded spiritually as an emotional cleanser. If a partner deserts us, for whatever reason, there is a sense of unfinished business and – as I know from experience – utter bewilderment. Like a wound that will not heal, unanswered questions and self-blame can run around in endless cycles. Desertion is undoubtedly one of the cruellest ways in which a relationship can end. I believe that the best way to deal with the pain is symbolically to wash the relationship and the faithless lover out of our mind. This may take many attempts, but it is often preferable

to trying to confront the person and perhaps facing more hurt, and definitely better than getting short-term revenge. It will enable you to take the first steps towards your own, inevitably better, future without your love rat

You will need

A large piece of black paper; a piece of white chalk or a white crayon.

Timing

When the rain is falling steadily.

The spell

- Sit indoors where you can see the rain. On the paper draw a figure walking away along a winding path.

- Scribble all over the picture the things you would like to have said, the anger, the frustration and the loss of self-esteem. Finally, write a message of farewell – affectionate, accusatory, dismissive, whatever feels right.
- Take the paper out into the rain, anchor it down with stones and stand in the rain, letting the tears flow and mingle with the rain. Wait until the letters have run and cannot be read, then leave the paper to disintegrate.
- Go indoors and surround yourself with music and light. Spend the rest of the day visiting a positive, upbeat friend or, if you do not feel like company, go to a place you have always wanted to visit.

A stone cairn or spell for leaving a lover who can never be yours

Love may not always be enough. Sometimes, after years of waiting, you realise that your would-be partner will never be free. Or perhaps you have learnt that a lover is going to live permanently far away and commitments mean you cannot follow. Or perhaps religion, culture or familial background means that you realise a relationship can never work and you have had to decide to walk away.

Stone cairns (or triangular piles of stones topped by a flat stone) are found throughout the Celtic world, dedicated to the wise crone goddess. Indeed, they are still sometimes made by visitors to natural sacred places, together with a wish to the local goddess or essence of nature. One of the most beautiful water sites in the UK is St Nectan's Glen and Waterfall, between Boscastle and Tintagel in Cornwall. At the foot of the falls are cairns in caverns, dedicated to the pre-Christian mother goddess, called locally the Lady of the Waterfall. Some stones have messages scratched on the flat surface.

For this spell you can make either a triangular stone pile, using flat stones, or a stone border along a flower bed or even round a window box. You can continue the spell for as many months as necessary, building a new cairn or border each month.

You will need
A stone for every day of the month from the date you start the spell until the same date the following month; a packet of flower or herb seeds of any kind.

Timing
If possible, the beginning of a calendar month.

The spell
- Each day place a stone and plant a few seeds around or beside it. If you are making a stone cairn, you can if you wish scratch a symbol known only to you and your partner on each stone before placing it. As you work, say:
  Today I walk without you. Today I send you love wherever you walk. We cannot be together, and so I place my stone and plant my seeds in memory of what we shared. May you and I walk in happiness.
- Make a small positive plan to be fulfilled by the next day when you place the next stone. Whenever doubts creep in, walk around your stone cairn or border or touch each of the stones, recalling how many days you have lived through since the parting and any moments of joy – however small – you have experienced. By spring the first shoots of the new life you have planted will appear.

A spell for coping with a significant event concerning the split

The months after a break-up can be traumatic, and particular milestones may need special strength. It may be the first visit to a solicitor or child welfare officer, the first weekend the children are not with you, a time when you and your ex-partner have to meet to collect belongings, or the day when official papers arrive. Or you may see your ex with a new partner, causing hurt and fury to flare within you.

This spell works by absorbing fear, panic, anger, regrets and doubts – all of which have their place in the grieving process but can get in the way of effective negotiations. As a result of working the spell, you will be calm and assertive – rather than aggressive – in the face of provocation and stress, and so will be able obtain for yourself and any children what you need and what is yours by right, without feeling intimidated or getting emotional. The spell works as well for men as for women.

You will need

A deep-purple or dark-blue candle; a reel of thin dark-blue thread; a candle snuffer; a large metal tray or square metal candle holder.

Timing

The evening before a difficult event is scheduled to happen, or as soon as possible after you have experienced a traumatic event connected with the former relationship.

The spell

* Place the purple or dark-blue candle (for quiet authority and balanced judgement) on the tray and light it.
* By the candle's light, break off pieces of thread long enough to tie a single knot in each.
* Taking one thread at a time, knot it and hold it above the flame until it ignites.
* As soon as it catches fire, drop the thread onto the tray to burn or go out, as you do so saying:
  The power to hurt and harm is done; the fear is gone. Fade in the flame or be consumed in the fire as you will; it is the same to me.
  If you wish, name fears or hurts for each thread.
* When you have burnt enough threads to feel that the fear and inner turmoil have left you, extinguish the candle with the snuffer, as you do so saying:
  No more to burn, rest in peace; let me rest likewise till tomorrow.

A candle ritual to mark a divorce or official separation

In America, and increasingly in other parts of the world, divorce ceremonies are often held to end a marriage spiritually and peacefully, especially if children are involved. Only one of the parties need be present. For many people, however, such a formal ceremony, with or without an ex-partner, would be too painful, and a private ritual, on the day the final divorce papers arrive, may be preferable. This ritual will help even if you were not officially married to your partner. You might choose to carry it out on a day when joint property is sold or you finally tie up any joint business.

The ritual is intended to be carried out by one of the parties, though if you are separating on good terms, your ex-partner can take part too. If children are involved, the ritual can help to reassure them that they still have two caring parents (even if the other partner is absent and is not actively involved in meeting their needs). While it may be difficult to perform the ritual if your ex-partner has acted callously or deserted you, or is making matters hard financially or manipulating the children, carrying it out will help to heal your own negative feelings, and even if the other person continues to behave destructively, you and any children will benefit by your positive intent.

You will need
A large beeswax or white candle; 2 smaller beeswax or white candles; a small square beeswax candle or white candle (optional: if there are children or a continuing joint business venture).

Timing
Close to the time of the decree nisi or decree absolute.

The spell
* In silence, light the large beeswax or white candle (to represent the marriage).
* From the large candle, light the two smaller ones, the first to represent your ex-partner and the second to represent yourself. Set them one on either side of the marriage candle.
* When you feel able, extinguish the marriage candle with such words as: *The flame of love grows dim, and so we go our separate ways, with regret and with thanks for the happy times we shared.*
* If you are using it, light the small square candle (to represent the family or financial security) from your ex-partner's and your own candle in turn. As you do so say: *I/we light this flame with the hope/promise that we will always be united in the love of our children.*
* Let the candles burn through in a safe place and make the rest of the day special, no matter how bad you feel.

A hand-parting spell

In a Middle Eastern custom, a person who wishes to divorce turns three times widdershins (anticlockwise), saying: 'I divorce thee, I divorce thee, I divorce thee.' Some Wiccans who separate after having been joined in a handfasting ceremony then have a hand-parting ceremony, in which they ceremonially untie the bonds that were looped between their hands and which, by custom, they will have kept. They also return their rings, which are then ritually cleansed.

This spell combines these two ideas in a very simple ritual that you can carry out alone on the day of a divorce or official separation. If you are involved in an ongoing dispute, you can also use this spell to enable you to feel free emotionally and to give you the strength to keep going and not give way to pressure or despair.

You will need

A dark-red cord about 3 m/3 yards long.

Timing

The hour before sunset.

The spell

* Find a tree – in your garden or in a park or forest. If there is no suitable tree around, you can use a washing line post, as long as you can move all around it; however, a living tree will have powerful energies.
* Wind the cord around the tree nine times and secure it with a loose knot, looping the other end over your hands.
* Slowly unwind the cord from the tree, moving in circles further and further from the tether, chanting:

Hand part
My heart;
Hand fast
Not last;
Let go;
Peace know.
It shall be so!

* With a final tug, pull the knot free and then unloop your hand, as you do so saying:

Unwind;
Knot bind
No more.

* Leave the cord on the ground and twirl around three times widdershins (anticlockwise), as you do so saying:

I divorce thee, I divorce thee, I divorce thee.
So shall it be!

* Loop the cord over the tree, securing it where it will not hurt animals, birds or children, and go indoors or home without looking back.

A four winds spell for the anniversary of a parting or divorce

The anniversary of a separation or divorce can be a time of painful reminders, even if you are at last feeling happier and more settled and perhaps have a new partner. This is a day when memories can come flooding back, sometimes together with unwarranted regrets. Separated and divorce couples do occasionally reunite when one or both has really changed or the problems dividing them have disappeared, but this event is rare. For most, this anniversary needs to be lived through as positively as possible without unrealistic hopes, simply acknowledging the memories and then allowing them to dissipate. This spell can help in the healing process (which will take years rather than months to complete, especially if you and your partner were together for many years or you gave up a promising career for the sake of the relationship). You do not need to wait for a windy day to perform it.

You will need
A paper luggage label or a long thin piece of paper with a hole punched in it and a short piece of string attached; a small silver-coloured helium balloon.

Timing
As early as possible on the day of the anniversary.

The spell
* With your wedding ring finger, trace the name of your ex-partner on the luggage label or paper, so that you leave no mark.
* Attach the label or paper to the balloon.
* Go to any open space without trees and hold the balloon, saying:
  Four winds all,
  To you I call.
  Carry from me the memories
  Brought by this anniversary.
  South, East, West and North,
  Sorrow leave me and fly forth.
* Let go of the balloon and watch it rise into the sky. With luck, it will be found by a child to whom it will bring pleasure.

An anniversary healing ritual

Because all experiences, bad as well as good, are a part of us, we cannot just wipe out an important relationship, even though it is over. We may be glad to be rid of the person who made us unhappy, but – especially if children are involved – once the wounds begin to heal it is important to acknowledge the good parts of a relationship that was once a significant part of our life. A wedding anniversary, a child's birthday or the bereavement of a mutual friend can, even years after a divorce, surface as a reminder of the happy events you shared with your ex-partner. It is no disloyalty to your new life to privately commemorate such happiness, while acknowledging that the person with whom you laughed (or cried) in those earlier days is gone from your world. If there are still lingering maintenance or property disputes with your ex-partner or you were unfairly treated, performing this ritual is also a good way of laying to rest what cannot now be resolved.

You will need
A plum, peach, pear or apple that is turning soft; some still mineral water; a plant in bud or an evergreen; a large plant pot and some compost (optional).

Timing
As the sun is rising, on the anniversary of your wedding to your ex-partner, or whenever memories of significant past events surface.

The spell
* Place the fruit in a flowerbed, large pot or window box, saying:
  The fruit decays quite naturally, yet from the old life grows the new.
* Set the plant in the earth close to the fruit and water both with the mineral water. One day the fruit will shoot new life, but until then you have a reminder of the new life that grows within you, nourished by the past from which you have taken the goodness. Now you can let the rest decay. If you have planted the fruit in a pot, you can transplant it later.

A candle bereavement ritual

Formal funerals are the public face of mourning for a partner we have lost – a chance for friends and family to celebrate his or her life. But services, however dignified and uplifting, can sometimes seem inadequate or impersonal to the person closest to the deceased. It can be hard to hold on to the essence of the person who has died and to hear their laughter in a graveyard or crematorium. Some people dream of their partner soon after the funeral or sense their presence in the home, but this does not happen to everybody – and, indeed, some would not wish it to. From my own extensive research of the afterlife, which has involved talking to many bereaved people about their experiences, I am convinced that we do survive death in a such a way that our essential self remains intact. When a couple have been deeply in love, whether for months or for 40 years, death does not instantly sever the bond: the link of love remains.

You will need

A small memento, perhaps a gift bought by one for the other of you, or an item bought on a shared holiday that evokes happy or humorous memories; a rose- or lavender-scented candle.

Timing

On the anniversary of the death, or in the days after the funeral, or at a time you regularly spent together.

The spell

* Go to a favourite place in your garden or a local park or square, taking with you the memento.
* Sit quietly in the place and let happy memories, conversations and jokes flow through your mind. Recall the familiar voice, together with any fragrances – wood smoke, tobacco, aftershave, perfume or soap – that remind you of your husband or wife.
* When you are ready go indoors and, even if it is not dark, light the candle.
* Look into the flame and speak words of love, together with any of regret
* When you have finished, blow out the candle and let the light be a link of love with the essential person who lives on in their descendants and in all the kind deeds they performed and wise words they spoke.
* You may be rewarded by a sense of peace, as well as perhaps by a fleeting shadow, a touch as light as gossamer, some words softly spoken in your partner's familiar voice or a momentary smell that you associate with your loved one. Your partner will not appear if this would trouble or frighten you, and you are not summoning a spirit. Even if you do not believe in the afterlife, you can still connect with the essential love that never dies.
* Begin a memory box, containing mementoes of your partner – for example a favourite item of jewellery, a medal, a school or trades certificate, a letter sent to you, poems or sketches he or she made, photographs of your partner's life, a holiday postcard, a wartime ration book, a passport, a pressed dried flower from the wedding bouquet, a button from a well worn coat or any newspaper cuttings in which he or she featured. Add a small sachet or purse filled with dried lavender or rose petals, fragranced on the outside with a favourite perfume, cologne or aftershave. This will not only remind you of your partner but is also an heirloom – a memento for future generations of your partner's life.

PART 2

SPELLS FOR PERSONAL HAPPINESS

his is a section often missed out in spell books — and frequently in our own priorities. Yet unless we are happy in ourselves, it is hard for us to fulfil our potential. Sensitive people all too often focus on the happiness of others and in so doing may lose sight of their own needs and dreams. They can end up following paths ordained by others, whether ambitious parents, teachers, partner or children. But it is never too late to follow your dream — and that is the dominant theme of this part of the book.

The spells in this section are concerned with attracting positive energies into our everyday world. In this way, most days can become more pleasurable and our leisure time, however short, will be fruitful as well as relaxing. What constitutes happiness varies according to our unique personality, tempered by upbringing, culture, friends, and current work and home environment. Our criteria for happiness may also change according to our age and lifestyle. For a young person bliss might be travel, for exhausted parents unbroken nights. Health is one of the greatest blessings we can have, together with loving friends and family.

Courage and self-confidence are of great help in attaining happiness, though for many — such as me — these strengths may not be fully acquired until later in life. Enough money is another significant factor (for more on this subject see Part 4). Equally vital, however, is the ability (part confidence and part application) to acquire new skills, pass tests and succeed at interviews. This ability will enable us to get what we really want, whether that is to become a merchant banker, to train in an alternative therapy or to join the local dramatic society. At some point, too, most of us desire to measure our own level of progress against that of others, or to gain admission to an organisation in which we can develop our talents. We can broaden our horizons at any age, perhaps by learning to drive, to swim or to teach a skill that we have already acquired. Through taking on such challenges we grow as a person.

Another aspect of the spells in this section involves recovering what has been lost or stolen and mending what has been broken. This applies not only to material things but also to what we have lost or broken in a spiritual or emotional sense.

The final chapter of this part of the book deals with bringing good luck into your life and making your wishes come true. This is not at all selfish. Only if we are ourselves happy and fulfilled can we make others happy.

8 SPELLS FOR GOOD HEALTH

Good health is immeasurably valuable. Spells are a powerful way of triggering the body's immune system to resist illness and balancing the metabolism to ensure sustained energy levels. The spells in this section can be cast for bringing energy and well-being to the mind, body and spirit – which even conventional medicine acknowledges are intricately linked. Healing is dealt with specifically in Part 7; here I will focus on the maintenance of health and vitality in the widest sense.

A Celtic nine-quartz crystal spell for health

This is one of the oldest spells from the Celtic tradition that was passed down orally through generations. Though originally a Druid ritual, it entered the folk tradition of lands where Celtic descendants remained, such as Wales, Scotland, Ireland, Brittany, Cornwall and the Isle of Man. Originally, the Celts used quartz pebbles found in river beds and boiled these in river water, but often today neither rivers nor stones we find are sufficiently pure. This is a modern version of the spell that I carry out once a month or when I am feeling particularly tired.

You will need

9 small smooth clear quartz crystals or, if you cannot get these, clear glass nuggets; a jug or bottle with a wide neck and a top or cover; 9 white flowers.

Timing

From dawn till noon. You can get the water ready the night before if you do not want to get up early.

The spell

* Half-fill the jug or bottle with water and into it drop the nine crystals, one at time.
* For each crystal you can make a wish about your health and well-being, for example:

One that I will have more energy, two that the cut on my hand may heal . . .

. . . and so on. You can also empower the water for someone else who is ill or especially tired or make rather more so you can use it for the whole family.
* Cover the water and crystals and surround them with a circle of white flowers.
* Leave the water from dawn until noon, either in the open air or near an open window.
* Leave the crystals in the water and put the covered jug in the fridge. Drink a little every morning for nine days.

A fruit spell for good health

Fruit is associated with good health in many lands, not just because of the physical benefits to be derived from eating it but also because of the symbolic significance of its growth from seed, increase and ripening. This is an adaptation of one of my favourite spells, which I have taught and used many times.

You will need

7 pieces of fresh fruit (they need only be small and can be all of the same type); a white cloth; a clear glass or crystal bowl; about 1 litre/1³/₄ pints of still mineral water; 9 very small clear quartz crystals or clear glass nuggets; some small glass bottles.

Timing

Sunday, from dawn till noon.

The spell

* At daybreak, set the quartz crystals in the bowl and fill it with the mineral water. Leave the bowl where it will be empowered with natural light until noon.

* At noon, set the seven pieces of fruit (one for each day of the week) on the white cloth. Sprinkle each fruit in turn with a few drops of the light- and crystal-infused water, as you do so saying:

You days of the week,
With health overflow.
With life and with healing,
Radiance show.

* Beginning on the day of the spell, eat one of the fruits each day, as you do so saying:

I take in your healing and your strength and thank you for the blessings of health.

You can refrigerate the fruit to keep it fresh.

* Pour the remaining water into the bottles so that over the coming days you can add it to baths or drinks for vitality. Splash a little on your pulse points when you feel tired.

An apple spell for health and vitality

Apples were considered a symbol of health and long life by the Celts, the Vikings, the ancient Greeks and the Romans, among others. Iduna, the golden-haired Viking Goddess, gave the gods and goddesses magical golden apples to keep them forever young and healthy. She occasionally favoured mortals with one of her golden gifts

You will need

A bowl of golden-coloured apples; a vegetable knife.

Timing

Friday, towards noon.

The spell

* Take an apple from the bowl and peel it. As you do so, chant:

Apple of youth, apple of gold,
May health and energy for me unfold.
Within this peel
Your strength I seal
And so new life in me reveal.

* Quarter the apple. Eat the quarters, with each one making a wish for the health of someone you know who is tired or unwell.

* Bury the peel and pips in the garden or in a deep tub, as you do so repeating the chant and this time asking for your own health to continue or to grow stronger.

* Give the other apples away to children, friends or family members and then replenish the bowl.

An American apple spell for health

The profusion of apple trees in the United States is credited to Johnny Appleseed, an American religious eccentric born in 1774, who for 48 years roamed the frontiers of North America with a sack of apple seeds, planting apple trees and creating orchards.

You will need

A handful of apple pips (you can save the pips over a period of time); an area of earth or large pot of soil; some water (to water the pips).

Timing

During the three days before the full moon.

The spell

* Stand on the earth or kneel over the pot and scatter the apple seeds with both hands, as you do so saying faster and louder:

Johnny Appleseed, Johnny Appleseed,
Health and power in me breed.
Like these seeds in strength I grow.
Johnny Appleseed make it so.

* Bury the pips and water them, as you do so, reciting the chant ever more slowly and quietly until it falls into silence.
* Nurture the soil and your own apple trees may one day grow.

An Italian tomato spell for good health and prosperity

Tomatoes were once called *pommes d'amour*, love apples. In Germany, they are still called *Liebesapfel*. The love connotation probably came from the well-rounded shape and the brilliant scarlet hue. Like many aphrodisiacs, the tomato is the fruit of Venus or Aphrodite. In Europe, tomatoes continued to be connected with love until the beginning of the twentieth century, when they came to be associated instead with health and abundance in every sense, including financial. This spell comes from Italy, but there are similar spells in Spain and Portugal. Since we are focusing on health here, you can consider the prosperity as a bonus.

You will need

2 large, fresh tomatoes.

Timing

As the sun rises.

The spell

* Place one of the tomatoes on the window ledge of the main living room to encourage good health. Place the second one over the fireplace or on a shelf near a source of heat to encourage prosperity.
* Replace the tomatoes when they begin to become soft or lose their colour and use them in cooking, making a wish for the health and prosperity of someone close as you stir the dish.

A rainbow spell to absorb the life force

The life force is known by different names in different cultures, for example *prana* in India and *ch'i* in China. One way to absorb this pure life energy is by eating fruit, vegetables, nuts and seeds. A perfect balance of vitality, strength and inner harmony can be attained by eating natural foods in the seven colours that make up the rainbow. These colours merge to form the pure white light that characterises the life force. For the purposes of this spell, violet and indigo have been merged into blue and purple, so giving six colours.

You will need

Fresh raw or lightly cooked foods without additives from each of the six colour groups below. Feel free to introduce appropriately coloured fruits that are not listed, choosing foods from your own location, especially when they are in season and the life force is at its most powerful.

Red: Apples, redcurrants, straw-berries, red peppers

Orange: Carrots, oranges, melons, pumpkins

Yellow: Bananas, sweetcorn, grape-fruit, yellow peppers

Green: Cucumber, pears, lettuce, spinach, grapes

Blue: Plums, blueberries, damsons

Purple: Blackcurrants, grapes, auber-gines

Timing

At dawn, when the dew is on the grass.

The spell

* Going out into the open air if possible, eat a little of the food from each colour group in turn. Say before you eat each one:

Rainbow, rainbow, force of life,
Give me vitality, bring me light.
Rainbow, rainbow, energy grow;
Within me now does radiance glow.
Thus am I renewed. I accept the life force
with thanks.

* Use any remaining food to make a meal for friends or family. If you are alone, enjoy the meal yourself. Return some life to the earth by clearing litter, helping with an environmental project or feeding the birds.

A salt spell for health

Salt has always been central to health because for early settlers around the globe it was the main preservative of food through the long winter months. The word 'salt' comes from Salus, Roman goddess of health, whom the Greeks called Hygeia. Salt was also an early antiseptic. In honour of Salus, Roman nursemaids would put a pinch of salt into the mouth of newborn infants, and salt was put into the first pail of milk from a cow that had just calved. In magic, salt represents the element of Earth, and so can be empowered for health, as in this spell, by using three different earth substances. The Three Creating Mothers appear in the mythology of many lands from Neolithic times onwards (see also page 241).

You will need

A small container with a lid; enough sea salt to fill the container $1/4$ full; a small spoon; 3 different kinds of flower petals, small green leaves or dried herbs, mixed together in a bowl; a vase of flowers or a green potted plant.

Timing

On a Wednesday, upon rising

The spell

* Fill the container about a quarter full of salt.
* Leaving the lid off, surround the container with a deosil (clockwise) circle of the petals, leaves or herbs, saying as you work:
  Earth to earth,
  By the Mothers Three
  Who gave all birth.
  Drive away sickness,
  Defend against sadness
  And bring health to me.
  So may it be,
  Mothers Three!
* Using the spoon, scoop up a tiny portion of salt and place a grain or two on the end of your tongue.
* Return the lid to the container and keep the pot of salt in your main room, together with the vase of flowers or pot plant.
* Wash the spoon and keep it aside for use in the spell.
* Repeat the spell weekly, if possible at the same time, until all the salt is gone.

A solar empowerment spell for health

This spell is traditionally carried out on the longest day (on or around 21 June) or on the Christianised midsummer's (or St John's) day, 24 June. Traditional midsummer herbs (such as sage, rosemary, chamomile, fennel, dill, thyme, ferns, trefoil/clover, St John's wort and dill) were burnt on a fire at noon as part of general celebrations when the sun reached the height of its power before beginning to decline. Friends and family can join you in this ritual, scattering herbs on the fire.

You will need

Some fresh or dried trefoil, St John's wort and dill, or a selection of the midsummer herbs listed above; a ring of small flat stones containing a bonfire or a metal bucket containing a small fire or large candle in sand (you could light a barbecue and take off the grill pan); 9 small twigs.

Timing

Midsummer's day or any sunny Sunday, at noon – have everything ready so that the fire is alight by this time.

The spell

* At noon, circle the fire nine times deosil (clockwise) outside the ring of stones, as you do so, scattering herbs on the fire and chanting continuously:
Trefoil, vervain, John's wort, dill,
Let power grow within me still.
Trefoil, vervain, John's wort, thyme,
May good health and strength be mine.
Though the sun may soon decline,
Yet shall light within me shine.
* Circle the bonfire nine times more, on each circle casting a twig into the fire and making a wish for the health and happiness of yourself and your family.

A beauty pathway spell for health and vitality

According to a Native North American legend, White Buffalo Calf Woman, a form of the creating Corn Woman, came to the Lakota nation at a time when there was a famine. She unfastened her medicine bundle, gave the women corn and root vegetables, and showed them how to make fire to cook them. She arrived among the Lakota walking along a path of light from the horizon and disappeared in the same way. This radiance can be re-created magically to give a sudden surge of energy, especially in the dark of winter, and to restore optimism and purpose. The Beauty Way is the name given to our path through life by the Native North Americans.

You will need

Some small golden-coloured glass nuggets, tiny clear quartz crystals, golden-coloured or white beads and/or pure white stones that reflect the light; mirrors, lamps, fibre optic lights and/or candles in floor or wall holders to enclose in light the path you will create in the spell; a small basket of fruits, seeds and nuts.

Timing

Just as dawn is breaking, so you can walk along the path through the door into the growing light.

The spell

* Mark the edges of your personal Beauty Way with the glass nuggets, crystals and stones, leading to the door. It need not be long and should be just wide enough to walk along.
* Illuminate the path with the lights.
* Pick up the basket and, walking very slowly and placing one foot in front of the other with great attention, begin your walk. As you walk, say over and over again:
I walk through the light on my Beauty Way. I walk to the light along the path of glory. I am the light, the light of all nature and of all creation.
* When you have finished your Beauty Walk, eat a few of the fruits, seeds and nuts – outdoors if it is fine enough – and use the rest in meals or give them to animals and birds.

A spell for boosting energy levels

Since the time of the ancient Babylonians, 6,000 years ago, untying knots has traditionally been a way of symbolically releasing energy. Until the sixteenth century, wind power was stored in knotted cords and released when a sailing ship was becalmed. If you store up energy in knots, you can release the accumulated power when you need a sudden boost or have a series of long days ahead and cannot catch up on sleep. This is a representative knot spell in which the stored energy becomes highly concentrated.

You will need

An undyed cord small enough to carry with you but long enough to tie in three knots.

Timing

If possible, on a windy morning. The day of the full moon is ideal, but any day during the waxing moon when you feel energetic will do.

The spell

* Tie one end of the cord firmly to a branch of a tree or a window handle (with the cord outside) as high up as possible. Leave the cord for an hour. If it is not a windy day, supplement with a few minutes indoors next to an electric fan.
* At the end of the hour, go outdoors or stand near an open window. Hold the cord taut in both hands in front of your face. Blow slowly and gently along the cord three times.
* Tie the first knot at the right-hand end of the cord, as you do so saying:
  May the four winds enter this knot and hold the power within.
* Tie a second knot in the middle of the cord and a third one at the left-hand end, as you do so, repeating the words.
* Blow three more times over the knotted cord, more forcefully than before, and then say:
  Knot of three,
  Till you are free
  Hold tight your power
  Until the hour
  I call thee.
* When you need a sudden increase in energy, untie one of the knots and say in your mind:
  One knot of three,
  The power's in me.
  So shall be free vitality.
* Untie the other two knots as necessary, modifying the chant to 'two knots of three' and finally 'three knots of three'. When you have used all three knots of energy, bury or burn the cord.

A de-stressing spell

Stress is one of the most common causes of a drop in energy and enthusiasm levels. Though we do need tension in our lives, too much can be bad for our health. This spell uses a shower of water to release tension. For stress that has built up over a period, a rainstorm is a good focus, but for instant results use a shower, a jacuzzi or a waterfall in a fun pool at a leisure centre. This is an old favourite spell of mine that I use regularly.

You will need

Any continuous powerful water source in which you can immerse yourself.

Timing

Rainy days or evenings, or whenever you feel stressed or overwhelmed by worries or burdens.

The spell

- If you are using a shower, turn it on before entering the shower cubicle and use tepid rather than warm water. Leave your shoes outside the bathroom and throw all your clothes in the laundry basket. If you are running out into the rain, wear a light cagoule or raincoat if you wish, but leave at least your head uncovered.
- Once you are in the water source, shake your head, hands, arms, feet, legs and whole body, repeating over and over again:

Waterfall, take stress from me;
Leave me free, in harmony.

Visualise dark water pouring from you and flowing away.

- When you feel liberated, turn off the water or come indoors and shake yourself like a dog, as you do so, repeating the chant.
- Dry yourself thoroughly and put on clean loose clothes. If it is evening, go to bed early. If it is morning, spend a minute or two away from the chaos, breathing in and out very gently, visualising a waterfall flowing over you in your mind. Recall your waterfall and the physical sensation of the water at stress points during the coming days.

A copper spell for maintaining health

Copper, sacred to the goddess Venus and before that to the Mesopotamian Queen of Heaven, has been used for thousands of years and in diverse cultures for bringing health. It is known that wearing a copper ring or bracelet reduces travel sickness and relieves arthritis and rheumatism. The effect is in part physiological, but it can be strengthened by spells. Copper should be worn on the left-hand side of the body if you are right-handed, and on the right-hand side if you are left-handed.

You will need

A copper ring or bracelet; some dried or fresh rose petals; a malachite or any other deep-green crystal (a very small one if you are using a copper ring); a copper dish; a small green cloth.

Timing

At 10 pm the night before you put on the copper ring or bracelet, and thereafter weekly at 10 pm.

The spell

- At precisely 10pm, set your copper ring or bracelet on the green cloth in the copper dish and scatter the rose petals around the jewellery, letting them fall as they will. Work in silence.
- Place the crystal in the centre of the jewellery.
- Leave the dish containing the items somewhere where air can circulate all around it, overnight.
- When you wake the next morning, put on the jewellery, take the rose petals outdoors and scatter them. Leave the crystal in the copper dish for the next empowerment.

A spell to help you keep a positive attitude to life and maintain well-being

This is another apple spell, this time to encourage a sense of ongoing positivity. A positive attitude is in itself believed to boost our immune system and encourage long-term well-being.

You will need

A small area of soil or a large deep pot of earth; 12 apple pips; a small watering can or bottle of water.

Timing

The first Friday after the beginning of the month.

The spell

* Draw up a list of 12 targets, one for each month, for example for the coming month:

   I will arrange a few days away from my routine to visit a place or people I like.

Take your time so that you have a single positive target to build into each month, be it starting a new interest, redecorating part of your home or finishing a long overdue project.

* Then set the 12 apple pips in a deosil (clockwise) circle on top of the soil.
* When the circle is in place, touch each pip, starting with the one representing the present month, naming the month and your target.
* Bury each pip as you name its focus.
* When you have finished, sprinkle water drops over the circle, naming the months one after the other, again starting from the present month. Then say:

I walk with joy and confidence into the year ahead. Unfold, you months. I welcome you all.

9 SPELLS FOR COURAGE AND SELF-CONFIDENCE

A vital part of being happy and fulfilled is having a strong identity and high self-esteem so that we are not discouraged by the criticism or negativity of others. By believing in ourselves we can maximise not only our achievements but also our opportunities, more of which will come our way if we project confidence in our abilities. The more we love ourselves, the less we are dependent on the approval of others, and so we can control our own lives and destiny.

Life and circumstances can dent our confidence, but if you can find the courage to bounce back and try again after a serious setback, then you will be unstoppable. If you lack confidence (and at 55 I still do in a personal capacity), you may need to carry out the spells in this chapter several times, but each time will be easier and will produce more rapid results.

An iron nail spell for the courage to keep a difficult resolution

Since the Iron Age, iron nails have been used both for protective purposes and for courage. Iron has been considered one of the most empowering of metals in all times, with the ability to ward off harm. Its magical association derives from the fact that it was first discovered in meteors and so was considered a gift from the gods. In the British Museum in London, there are nails from fourth-century Britain and France bearing magical inscriptions. Engraving on such a small surface is beyond the skill of most of us; this spell offers another way to use inscription magic to reinforce a resolution when your courage fails. The strength of iron will help to shore up your determination.

You will need

A long strip of paper; a red pen; a very large long nail; some red thread or wool.

Timing

Thursday (the day of the Norse thunder god Thor) or Tuesday (the day of the Roman war god Mars), during the hours of daylight.

The spell

* Using the red pen (the colour of courage), write down what you have resolved on the piece of paper.
* Wrap the paper around the nail and then tightly bind it by winding the red thread around the paper and nail, finishing it off with three knots. As you work, recite continuously:
My resolve will never fail;
It holds as firm as this iron nail.
* Put the nail and paper away somewhere private where you can look at them when your courage fails.

A horseshoe spell for overcoming seemingly impossible odds

Whether you need courage for a major life change or simply to recover from a setback, a horseshoe spell is a good way to get it. In this spell you will be invoking the power of Sleipnir, the magical steed that carried the Norse god Odin wherever he wished. Odin was an ancient deity associated with courage and strength.

You will need

A horseshoe (you can obtain an old one from a riding stable or buy an ornamental one).

Timing

Sunrise or when you wake.

The spell

* Stand facing the sunrise or the lightest point in the sky. Grip the two points of the upright horseshoe tightly and extend your arms horizontally, as though the shoe is pulling you forwards. As you do so, say:
Odin's Sleipnir carry me
To the place I want to be.
* Hang the horseshoe over your front door, inside the house, points up so that the luck does not drain away. You will see it whenever you go out into the world and will recall the spell.

A storm spell for courage

Thunder, lightning, strong winds and rain can cause destruction, but they also release a lot of power into the air. We can harness this energy if we need a burst of courage to overcome opposition or take a major step forward, maybe in the face of opposition. Many pre-Christian pantheons included thunder gods, such as the Viking Thor, who was depicted with a mighty hammer, and the ancient Greek Zeus and the Roman Jupiter, who both hurled thunderbolts when angry. Thunder deities were invoked for courage. Traditionally, this spell involved drinking rain water but I have substituted mineral water.

You will need

A glass jug with a lid; still mineral water.

Timing

During a storm.

The spell

* Fill your jug with the mineral water and take it outside. Stand with your arms raised and say five times:
  Power of the storm, you who fear none, fill me likewise with courage and invulnerability.
* Leave the jug of water, with the lid on, to be empowered by the storm.
* When the storm is over, drink a little of the water, repeating the chant five more times. Use the rest in baths and drinks, a few drops at a time, whenever you need courage.

A spell to give you the courage of your own convictions

Bead-chanting spells are an excellent way of marking ritually a determination or of building up the necessary energy to carry through a change or plan that may attract opposition. Some people use rosaries or Buddhist prayer beads, but others prefer to work with an ordinary necklace with separate chunky beads. It does not matter how many or how few beads, because you can go around the bead circle as many or as few times as necessary.

You will need

A bead necklace.

Timing

On a Tuesday, during daylight hours.

The spell

* Holding the beads between your hands, begin to walk slowly with deliberate steps in a deosil (clockwise) circle, touching each bead in deosil order on the necklace.
* As you touch the first bead say:
  I.
  As you touch the second, say:
  I have.
  As you touch the third, say:
  I have the.
  As you touch the fourth, say:
  I have the courage.
  As you touch the fifth, say:
  I have the courage of.
  As you touch the sixth, say:
  I have the courage of my.
  And as you touch the seventh, say:
  I have the courage of my convictions.
* Now reverse the direction of walking, but continue to touch the beads deosil, carrying on from where you reached in the previous chant.
* For the first bead say:
  I,
  For the second bead, say:
  I will.
  For the third bead, say:
  I will not.

For the fourth bead, say:
I will not hesitate.
For the fifth bead, say:
I will not hesitate to.
For the sixth bead, say:
I will not hesitate to speak.

And for the seventh bead, say:
I will not hesitate to speak out.

- You can repeat the walking and chanting as many times as you wish. You can also adapt the words to suit your individual circumstances.

A stone spell for helping you to endure and improve an intolerable situation

There are times when even the strongest of spells cannot change our lives because to move on would cause unbearable hurt or involve leaving someone vulnerable, perhaps an elderly relation who relies on you, a sick partner or a disabled child. You yourself may be ill or disabled and confined to the home, and know there won't be miracles.

A spell can help in two ways. Firstly, it can help to strengthen your inner resources and, more importantly, it can increase your determination to get all the help to which you are entitled. I know from my own experience how hard it is when you are worn out and vulnerable yourself.

You will need

A small, hard, round stone, such as granite; a jug of water; a deep dish; a small area of garden or a large potted plant.

Timing

Late any evening when you can first see the crescent moon in the sky.

The spell

- Sit with the rock between your hands and feel its strength. Picture your rock as part of a tall wide column or mountain, standing strong in the earth for millions of years, enduring the ravages of time, and allow the strength to pour into your body.

Repeat aloud or in your mind nine times:
Though I am flesh and bone,
mine is the strength of stone.

- When you feel ready, place your stone in the dish. Slowly pour some of the water from the jug over the stone so that it falls into the dish (do not worry about splashes). As you do so say softly:
It takes thousands of years till water breaks stone; through many lifetimes it stands strong.
Though dripping water will eventually wear away a stone, as you watch the water sliding harmlessly off the rock, remind yourself that you too can shake off the daily drip of sorrows that would wear you away.

- When the bowl is half full, remove the stone, dry it on a soft natural fabric and secure it in the soil in your garden or in the flower pot, so it is only partly buried.

- Each day, do one thing to secure extra help or resources whether making a phone call, sending an e-mail, writing a letter or asking other relatives or visiting professionals directly to help ease the situation.

- When you water the plants, watch the water rolling harmlessly off your special stone and remind yourself that you too can endure.

- Repeat monthly or until things improve.

A signet ring ritual to establish your identity and enable you to make your mark on the world

Signet rings, engraved with the image of a god or an emperor, were popular in ancient Rome. In Christian times they were renamed intaglios and bore the image of a saint. They were pressed into beeswax, sealing wax or clay and used to seal a document. Individualised seals, engraved with the family crest, a trade seal, an initial or a power animal that identified the owner, were popular up until the end of the nineteenth century for making one's mark officially. In the modern world you can use a signet ring, whether ornate or plain, as a good luck charm and as a way of symbolically stating your identity. Even if there are hundreds of rings the same, the fact that you wear yours regularly makes it uniquely your signature.

You will need

A signet ring (either your own – it need not be expensive – or one inherited from a relative); 2 beeswax or good-quality white candles; a flat metal tray or candle-holder; a pen and paper.

Timing

When your identity is under threat or your wishes disregarded.

The spell

* Set one of the candles on the metal tray or holder and light it. While it is burning, write a list of what you would like to achieve, the time scale, the strengths and assets you have, and your achievements so far in your life (however modest). If you find it hard to believe in yourself, imagine that you are listing the virtues of a friend you admire. Finally, write where you want to be in five years time in every aspect of your life.
* When you have finished writing, say:
So have I made my mark upon the world.
* When some of the candle wax has dripped on to the tray and begun to solidify, put on the signet ring and press it into the soft wax. As you lift it out, say:
So do I make my mark upon the world.
* In the wax around the mark, draw a sign of power and confidence, for example a dragon, a crown or a lion. When it is completed, say:
So will I make my mark upon the world.
* When the wax is cool, cut out a circle around the image and fold the wax seal and image inside the paper you have written on.
* Light the second candle. When the wax begins to melt, tip just a drop on to the paper to seal it.
* Keep the paper, image and seal in a drawer.

An opal or pearl spell for inner radiance

Opals and pearls have always been associated with beauty, radiance and the power to attract love. For this reason throughout the ages and in many lands from India to the Mediterranean, they have been worn or carried by women seeking love.

The black pearl is the symbol of the older woman and is said to bring love in later years. This is a traditional spell that was taught to me by a Spanish woman I met while I was researching a book on love in Andalusia in southern Spain, but I have seen similar spells posted on the Internet from the USA, Australia and the UK.

The secret is that if we can release the inner charisma we all possess that is tied up with self-esteem, then there is someone right for us with whom we will make a connection. Indeed, I believe we all have several potential partners who could make us happy, but if we feel unattractive (or maybe we have been told we are unattractive by a previous partner) we may be closed to the possibility of love coming our way.

You will need

A single opal or pearl (a black pearl if you are seeking love in later years) – it can be in a ring or any form of jewellery or a loose pearl, or if you cannot obtain these, a white moonstone or selenite; a fabric purse, preferably silk, or a small white scarf.

Timing

Before you go out socially or meet with someone you already know who could become a lover or partner.

The spell

* On the night of the full moon leave your opal or pearl where moonlight falls on it. Even if it is cloudy, the energies will fill your stone.
* In the morning, place your gem in the purse or scarf and keep it in a drawer in your bedroom until the next time you are going out on a date or to a place where you may meet other people looking for a relationship.
* When you are ready to go out, day or evening, rub the pearl or opal in small deosil (clockwise) circles in the centre of your hairline, then the centre of your brow, your throat, your inner wrists, first left then right, the palms of your hands, right and left, and finally your left and right ankle bones.
* As you do so, say over and over again in a soft whisper:
Let radiance flow through me, beauty now for all to see. I am as I am. Lovely and loving will I be.
* Take the purse and stone with you.
* Recharge it with the light of every full moon. Occasionally opals need rehydrating by wiping with a damp soft cloth.

A Heka spell for making yourself confident

To the ancient Egyptians words were powerful. When desires were spoken slowly and forcefully, the act of speaking was believed to bring the desire into being. The ancient Egyptians filled themselves with authority and confidence by speaking as if they were a god. Though we do not believe necessarily that we can assume the power of a deity, we can use the symbolism and associated power of speaking in this way to strengthen what some call the divus or diva, the god or goddess within us all.

Heka was the god who personified the concentrated, flowing, invisible power that we call magic. He represented the power by which, in one of the main Egyptian creation myths, the creator god Ptah brought the world into being – by uttering the magical word *hekau*. The charm in this spell comes from an inscription in the Cairo Museum, which was translated for me by a young Egyptologist. By reciting the words you can absorb magical power and confidence into yourself – or, in more modern terms, awaken your own higher mind power so that almost anything is possible.

You will need
Nothing.

Timing
As near to sunrise as possible.

The spell
* Go outdoors (whatever the weather) and stand facing the sunrise or the lightest point in the sky. Draw yourself up to your full height and slowly, loudly and deliberately recite three times:
I am Heka, the one who was made by the Lord of All before anything, the son of he who gave form to the universe. I am the protector of what the Lord of all has ordained to be. What I ordain so it shall be.
* Formulate any plan for the day ahead, however small, to be initiated when the rest of the world catches up.

A rainy day spell for confidence and self-esteem

When we were children, we squelched through mud and splashed through puddles and the world was ours. As adults we avoid the rain and mud, and often lack the optimism of our earlier days.

You will need
A raincoat and wellington boots or sturdy shoes.

Timing
A rainy day.

The spell
* Find a muddy area and stamp through it, as you do so saying:
I am as I am and I like what I am. I can do anything. I like and I will do what I like with pleasure.
Stamp between each phrase and continue stamping and chanting until you have left footmarks over the whole area.
* Finally, jump in a deep puddle and paddle up and down, reciting the words, until your boots are clean.

An Isis red jasper power spell for women

The symbol above represents the buckle or the girdle of the ancient Egyptian mother goddess Isis. It is still recognised as one of the most important power and fertility symbols for women when it is painted, as it has been for thousands of years, on red jasper or a blood agate or carnelian. This charm can be empowered with the traditional words of power that have passed down the ages via ancient magical papyri. It may be carried by both career women and women who are powerful in other ways, whether as mothers, carers, creators or just lovers of life. It will bring fertility in any way into their lives. It is a wonderful charm for women who lack confidence or who have been badly treated by a lover, enabling them to rediscover their self-confidence or to move on from a destructive situation. Lotus, lily and white rose are Isis's special flowers.

You will need

A red jasper or agate crystal, or another red or vibrant orange stone; a small pot of gold metallic paint; a thin brush or a permanent gold marker; 2 sticks of lotus, lily or white rose incense; a ceramic bowl filled with tap water.

Timing

When you urgently need power or a surge of fertility. It is best early in the morning, as light floods the sky.

The spell

* If possible, work outdoors in a sheltered spot. Light the incense sticks and carefully paint the design opposite on one side of the crystal.
* As you do so, chant continuously and softly, so your words almost fade into silence, the ancient words women have used for 5,000 years:
  The blood of Isis and the strength of Isis and the words of power of Isis enter this stone and enter me. The blood of Isis and the strength of Isis and the words of power of Isis empower this stone and empower me.
* When you have finished, hold an incense stick in each hand and swirl the smoke over the painted stone, as you do so repeating:
  Isis, Isis, Isis, at this hour, protect and empower this time.
  Make the words louder and louder and the movements faster and faster until you sense that the stone is filled with power.
* Plunge the sticks into the water, as you do so saying:
  Isis empower me.
* Carry the crystal with you and empower it regularly by spiralling incense sticks over it and repeating the second chant.

A seven obsidian arrows of Sekhmet spell to bring victory into your life

My own favourite protectress is the lion-headed ancient Egyptian fire and sun goddess, Sekhmet, who healed or destroyed wrong-doers and injustice. The seven obsidian arrows of Sekhmet were one of the weapons she sent out against her enemies, and they make a wonderful protective device against any form of hostility in the modern world. More importantly, the arrows can also be used to restore fortune after a setback and to bring victory, be it in the form of getting a job, passing an examination, marrying the person you love or getting a first book published. Gold and red are Sekhmet's colours.

You can buy obsidian arrows (thin, pointed blades of obsidian) from mineral stores or on the Internet by mail order. They are powerful for protection. However, you can substitute any pointed black crystals.

You will need

7 obsidian arrows or black pointed crystals; a piece of red paper; a gold pen or marker; a small drawstring bag.

Timing

At noon.

The spell

* On the paper, write in what area you need victory. Write as much or as little as you choose. Fold the paper as small as possible.
* Set the paper on a table and on top of it place the arrows or crystals, pointed ends facing outwards, in a circle. Stand behind the table and face the direction of the front entrance of your home.
* Extending your arms straight out in front of you, fingertips close together and pointing outwards as though they were arrows, say seven times:
  I, Sekhmet, send forth these arrows of victory. May they aim true and return victorious. Sekhmet, Sekhmet, Sekhmet, Sekhmet, Sekhmet, Sekhmet, Sekhmet, arrows swift send and swift return.
* Put the paper and arrows in the drawstring bag and keep the bag in a drawer.
* Recite the chant every day at noon in your head or out loud and picture the arrows flying through the air and hitting a target ringed with fire. Do this until a key event in your victory plan is due to happen (for example an examination, an interview or a marriage proposal).
* Take the arrows and the folded paper in the drawstring bag to the key event. It does not matter if you have to leave the bag in your coat in a cloakroom.
* Recite the chant in your head seven times just before the event.
* Afterwards, destroy the paper and keep the arrows for next time you need victory.

A spell for increasing self-love and self-esteem

Some spell books contain rituals to make you more beautiful or attractive. However, some of the most physically beautiful people in the world have a low self-image and agonise over every blemish or ounce of fat. In contrast, an ugly duckling may radiate charisma and confidence. Because they believe they are worthy of respect and admiration, they receive it. Most of us fall somewhere in the middle. This spell will help you to feel good and so create a good impression. Being fat and 50-plus, this is my standby for a bad hair week. Though the spell involves a pool, you do not have to be a good swimmer to perform it, as it can be carried out in the shallows. You can also adapt the spell for a bath or jacuzzi. Men can adapt the words of the chants.

You will need

Access to a swimming pool or a safe natural water pool, either with sunlight reflecting in it as pools or artificial light shining on the water.

Timing

Whenever you can find a quiet time and need a boost of self-esteem.

The spell

* Stand in the pool where there is no light reflected on the water and make widdershins (anticlockwise) circles with your arms, pushing away the water all around you. As you do so, say softly or in your head:
Doubts and dullness flow from me;
Lost in darkness may you be.
* Now swim, float or walk to a circle of light reflected in the water and make rippling deosil (clockwise) circles all around yourself with your arms. As you do so, say softly or in your head:
Light and loveliness flow to me;
Radiate on all I see.
Lovely am I and lovely I will be.
* Move from individual light pool to light pool, repeating the movements and words until you feel glowing.

A spell to make you courageous and confident whatever the obstacles

This spell comes from one of the old Egyptian Coffin Texts, engraved on the lids and sides of coffins. These were conceived as magical spells to be uttered by the deceased as they passed on their underworld journey to the Blessed Field of Reeds, to protect and empower them. The spells passed into folk tradition and were used to give power and confidence to the living. Osiris was the father, corn and resurrection god, whose main shrine was at Abydos. Re, or Ra, was the sun god. Invoking both these deities, this spell gives the power of Earth and sky.

Timing

As near to sunrise as possible.

The spell

* As soon as you wake, get up and stand facing the sunrise or lightest point in the sky. Recite with confidence:
(Name yourself), you are a god
And you shall be a god.
You shall have no enemies.
You stand with Re,
Who is in the sky,
And Osiris the great god,
Who is in Abydos.
(Name yourself), you are a god
And you shall be a god,
So long as the sun shines and the waters flow.

A tree spell for strengthening your own identity

If you are under a lot of pressure to conform to others' wishes and you know this will compromise your happiness and perhaps integrity, try this spell. It absorbs the strength of a mighty tree, such as an oak or ash, to help you to resist and maintain your independence.

You will need
A long cord or rope that will loop around the tree; a sturdy old tree.

Timing
Mid-morning.

The spell
* Tie one end of the rope or cord loosely around the trunk of the tree and then hold the other end taut, as far away as possible from the trunk.
* Slowly wind the rope deosil (clockwise) around the tree until you are touching the loop on the trunk, as you do so saying repeatedly:

Empowering tree,
Empower me,
Knot binding,

Knot finding,
Knot winding.
Preserve, I ask,
My identity.

* Touch the connection of the rope to the tree and say softly:

I would be free,
Empowered by thee.
So may it be!

* Now reverse the movements, unwinding the rope from around the trunk as fast as possible. This time chant:

Empowering tree,
Releasing me,
Knot unbinding,
Knot not finding,
Knot unwinding.
Returned is
My identity.

* With a final tug, pull the rope free, as you do so shouting:

Knot untie,
Power fly,
Fly free.
Forever be!

A daily spell for confidence and self-esteem

Over the years I have met hundreds of talented, charismatic people who have suffered at the hands of others and have come, as a result, to expect less than courteous and considerate treatment from others. Magic is not the whole answer, but it can help to reverse the spiral if others are continuing to be dismissive or discouraging.

You will need
A large mirror.

Timing
Every night before bed and every morning when you wake.

The spell
* Stand before the mirror, look at yourself and smile. Say:

Mirror, mirror on the wall,
I demand respect from all.
I am worthy of admiration;
I am worthy of consideration.
I have my place under the sun
And so I claim it.

A spell to bolster your self-esteem when it has taken a knock

If an insecure or malicious person has been bad-mouthing you, your self-esteem may have taken a knock, even if you know the accusations to be wholly unfounded. Seeing ourselves reflected negatively through the eyes of others can be very disturbing. This spell will help you to detach from these distorted impressions and regain your sense of self-worth.

You will need

A mirror; a lipstick; 2 clean, soft polishing cloths; a little glass cleaner (optional).

Timing

When light shines in the mirror.

The spell

* Using the lipstick, draw on the mirror a large doorway or gateway, so that when you look into the mirror it partly obscures your outline.

* Stand in front of the mirror and look at yourself through the doorway, as you do so saying:
I do not wish to see myself through the eyes of another any more.

* With widdershins (anticlockwise) movements, rub out the lipstick outline, if necessary using a little glass cleaner.

* When the lipstick has gone, take the second cloth and polish the mirror with deosil (clockwise) movements until it gleams.

* Now look at yourself as you are in the mirror without the obscuring outline and say:
I see myself in my true light. I am what I am and I like what I am.

* Repeat the spell when you doubt your worth, each time making the lipstick doorway smaller and smaller, so that it covers less of you.

10 SPELLS FOR happiness and harmony with family and friends

What gives you happiness, as I have said before, depends to some extent on your current lifestyle and environment. For some, happiness equates with quiet evenings and weekends spent alone after a frantic week, while for others it entails a round of invitations to parties and other social events. For yet others, happiness is a nice meal after a busy day, and an occasional night out with a partner when a babysitter is available. For most of us, happiness requires a mixture of fun, outings and moments of solitude. This chapter is a gentle and quite slow one, which will nevertheless assist you in establishing the firm foundations from which to venture forth into the world.

A blessing for a special meal

Even in the age of the microwave, the gathering of friends and family around the table to share a meal is a special time of blessing. It does not matter whether the meal is carefully home cooked or whether it is a takeaway.

When a guest broke bread together with his host in the Middle Ages, a bargain was deemed to have been struck, one of mutual respect and protection (a practice that could greatly enhance some family gatherings). The tradition of saying grace before beginning a meal has fallen out of favour in many homes, which is a pity, for as well as giving thanks for the food it also provided a few moments of quiet contemplation that united the family and set the tone for a tranquil meal. By blessing the food and the table before you eat, you can endow the meal with a spirit of gratitude and welcoming harmony. You can also suggest to family members who would be receptive that they might like to give silent thanks before beginning their meal, in view of world hunger and poverty even in affluent lands.

The blessing I use is adapted from a Celtic Christian one. It is of a type called a circling prayer, because as you speak it, you picture the person – or in this case the table and food – encircled by light. If you do not feel it appropriate to ask the blessing of God/the Goddess, you can dedicate the blessing to the Lord or Lady of Light of the Universe, or to an angel, or a more abstract benign energy pictured as cosmic white light.

You will need

A small silver- or gold-coloured bell; a dish of still mineral water.

Timing

After cooking a meal or preparing a buffet and setting the table.

The spell

● Before family or friends come to the dining table, ring the bell three times, in each of the four corners of the table. Recite at each corner after you have rung the bell:
Circle my table, Father/Mother.
Keep peace within, keep harm without.
Circle my table, Father/Mother.
Bless those who gather here, this day/night.

● Sprinkle three drops of water at each of the four corners, repeating the blessing at each one. You can, if it is easier, carry out this part of the ritual well in advance of the gathering.

● Go to the kitchen or wherever the food is waiting and, using one or two sample dishes, make a circle of water drops deosil (clockwise) around the plate or bowl, as you do so repeating the chant three times.

● Call family or friends to the table and carry the food through. As you begin to serve, picture crystalline light encircling all who are gathered around the table. In time, people will remark about the peaceful atmosphere at your meal table, even if you have young children or boisterous teenagers at gatherings.

A hospitality spell to welcome visitors and new friends into your life

This spell uses ingredients common to many cultures to attract into your life people who will enrich you with their company. It is a good spell to use if you have recently moved to live alone or do not often have the chance to meet like-minded people. As a result of the spell, you will find that new friends will appear in all kinds of unlikely situations. Old friends may also contact you after an absence or having lost touch.

You will need

Some yellow, brown or golden flowers or leaves; a small round table; a beeswax candle; a small round loaf of bread; a dish of seeds; some honey in a pottery jar with a spoon; a cup of milk; a small bowl for offerings.

Timing

Any warm day (or on a cold day work in a heated room indoors).

The spell

* Working outdoors if possible, create a circle using the yellow, brown or gold flowers or leaves. Begin the circle in the North (use a compass or make an approximation) and make it large enough to walk around. As you work, visualise the circle radiant with light.
* In the centre of the circle, on the table, place the candle and the offerings dish. To the North of the candle, on the table, set the loaf of bread. To the East of the candle place the dish of seeds. To the South place the honey. To the West place the cup of milk.
* Light the candle and say:
  Come into my life, you who will warm and cheer me, and in return share the good things that I offer.
* Starting in the North, walk round the circle deosil (clockwise), eating and drinking a little of each food. When you have tasted each food or drink, repeat the words and add a little to the offerings dish. (Add enough milk to dissolve the honey.)
* Leave the dish of offerings in front of the candle, still within the circle of flowers, while you find out about any local groups or meeting places that interest you.
* When the candle is burnt through, carry the dish to a secluded part of the garden or an open place and tip it on to the ground, as you do so repeating the words once more. Alternatively, cast the contents of the dish in to flowing water.
* Scatter the petals to the wind, repeating the words for the last time.
* Use any remaining food and drink from the ritual in cooking, or give it to wild birds or animals.

A spell for a happy family

Whether your household consists of a couple, a single parent and children, or mum and dad, children and granny, a happy family is a source of great strength. It offers a sense of security and a chance to be truly ourselves. This spell strengthens the links between all family members rather than only those in the family home, so you can include those who live far away. It will also work for friends if you live alone and have no blood family. This is one of the most effective spells I know for bringing families (and friends) closer.

You will need

Photographs of family or close friends or small objects that belong to them or symbolic objects (for example, a horse for a pony-mad child); a circle large enough in which to set the photograph/objects (use a child's hoop or create a circle from stones, glass nuggets or shells); a sage, strawberry or orange incense stick; an incense-holder; a vase of flowers or potted plant.

Timing

At a transition point (for example, the beginning of a week or year) or when you sense that family members are drifting away from one another because of work commitments or other pressures.

The spell

* Make your circle on a small table in the room where the family meet most often when at home, then set the photographs or objects within the circle, arranging them so that there are spaces between them.

* Light the incense stick and use it to make smoke spirals in the air above the photos or objects, so joining them together. As you work, say softly over and over again:
Bind invisibly in love my family/friends, that whether near or far from home, we are united still in love and harmony.

* Just above the circle itself make smoke knots at approximately the point of the four directions, North, East, South and West, saying for each:
I make this knot in the North/East/South/West, to secure the unseen love between us all. Blessings be on this family/these friends of mine.

* Leave the incense to burn through. Leave the photos or objects on the table with the circle around them. Place the vase of flowers or potted plant on the table. Arrange a get-together when practically possible.

A white candle blessing before a gathering

Whether you are entertaining friends and family for a formal dinner, or neighbours for coffee, you can infuse yourself and your guests, when they arrive, with harmony. This spell is especially good if you have been dashing around all day and don't know whether you can be bothered to entertain at all.

You will need

Several beeswax or white candles.

Timing

Before a gathering or before a visitor is due to call.

The spell

* Find the heart of your home. This may be its physical centre or it may be the room where you most usually relax and entertain. Light a candle here.

* Pass your hands, palms down, the left deosil (clockwise) and the right

widdershins (anticlockwise), on either side of the flame, taking care not to burn your hands. As you do so, repeat very softly ten times:

May blessings come our way, peace and plenty, joy and companionship. May gentle words and laughter alone hold sway. Welcome all who come in friendship and friendship take away.

⁂ Leave the candle to burn through. Keep a beeswax or white candle burning in the heart of the home until the visitors depart.

A telephone or computer spell for harmonious communications with family and friends

If you live far away from your family or have a busy work or life that makes visits difficult, phone calls and e-mails are the lifeblood of communication with friends and relatives. When we communicate through such technological means, however, subtle gestures, eye contact and the power of touch are all lost, with the result that messages may be misunderstood. If communication is of necessity brief, news and essential information may take precedence over simple words of love – or, on the other hand, a call may be fraught with emotion.

This spell will strengthen the link of distant love and ensure that even brief contact brings joy and reassurance, defusing any potential disagreements, awkwardness or misunderstandings caused by distance or infrequent contact. (It has the added bonus of making the modern nuisance of cold calls less stressful for both the recipient and the caller, whose wages depend on meeting sales targets.)

You will need

A bowl of rose- or lavender-based pot pourri; a piece of round, polished pink rose quartz or soft purple amethyst; some rose or lavender fragrance oil; a small wooden spoon.

Timing

Afternoon or early evening on a Wednesday, and thereafter whenever you answer the phone or check your e-mails.

The spell

⁂ Set the dish of pot pourri next to the phone or computer. If you use both, you can carry out the spell for each, using separate bowls of pot pourri.
⁂ Add three drops of fragrance oil to the pot pourri, stirring it in a deosil (clockwise) direction with the spoon and saying:
Blend and harmonise; melt away the distance between me and those I love.
⁂ Rest the crystal in the centre of the pot pourri.
⁂ Whenever the phone rings, you make a personal call or you switch on the computer, circle the phone or computer three times widdershins (anticlockwise) with the crystal and then three times deosil (clockwise). Hold the crystal in your receptive hand (the one you do not write with) as you talk, or set it to the right of the computer as you read and write messages. It will ensure that just the right words come and that you detect, even in hurried or stilted words, the underlying affection of the caller or e-mailer.
⁂ When you have finished speaking or e-mailing, add another drop of fragrance to the bowl, stirring three times deosil and repeating the chant. Return the crystal to the centre of the bowl for next time the phone rings.

A telephone spell to ensure that the desired caller rings

There may be many reasons why an anticipated call does not come. The friend or family member may be out of phone range, they may be occupied with a more pressing matter or they may simply have forgotten. We all know what it is like to be waiting to hear that someone has arrived safely, and we have all waited for a promised call from a person we met casually who said they would ring with details of a special social event. We may feel unsettled and afraid to go out in case we miss the call. This spell will persuade the desired person to ring. It is also helpful if family members or friends are just bad at keeping in touch.

You will need

A clear, pointed crystal quartz; a stick of frankincense, fennel, lemon or fern incense; an incense-holder.

Timing

When an expected call does not arrive and you cannot or do not wish to phone the other person.

The spell

* Light the incense stick and set it in the holder to the left-hand side of the phone.
* Hold the pointed crystal in your power hand (the one you write with) and direct the sharp end towards the phone, naming the person from whom you are expecting/hoping for a call. Say aloud:
  (Name), I await your call. I call your name that you may hear and end my waiting.
* Place the crystal on the phone table, with the sharp point touching the receiver.
* Hold the incense in your power hand and use the smoke to write in the air the words you said aloud, including the person's name.
* Leave the phone and occupy yourself while the incense burns through.
* If the call still does not come, leave the crystal in place overnight and repeat the spell nightly until you get through telepathically to your forgetful or preoccupied caller.

A spell to encourage a happy family atmosphere at an important event

Though some people associate making images with negative magic, small beeswax figures are, in fact, a very positive way of endowing the people they represent with love and light.

You will need

A beeswax candle to unroll to make the figures (this is better than using separate sheets of beeswax because the beeswax has been moulded together in the candle and so is ideal for representing a family); a second beeswax candle to light.

Timing

The evening before the important occasion.

The spell

* Unroll the first beeswax candle and break off as much wax as you need to make images of the family members who will be attending the event.
* Light the second candle and hold the unravelled piece of beeswax over the flame until it softens and you can roll it into a ball. As you do so, say:

So are we as one on this our special day.

- Begin to make figures from the ball, without features but with arms and legs. As you work, picture the event being harmonious and successful.
- As you complete each figure, hold it in your cupped hands and say:
United are we in harmony on this our special day.
- When all the figures are complete, join their hands together so they form a circle, as you do so saying:

So are we a family, in harmony and in unity, on this our special day.

- Set the figures in front of the second candle and leave the candle to burn though.
- If you can, hide the circle of figures in the room where you will gather. Otherwise leave it in sunlight.
- After the event, roll the figures back into a ball and keep the ball wrapped in fabric until next time you need it.

A triple spiral spell for personal harmony

Spirals are everywhere in nature, on shells, in finger prints, on ammonites. The triple spiral (three intertwined spirals) is a symbol of the womb of the wise, life-giving mother goddess. This shape is found engraved on many ancient stones. In modern spirituality, it is used in meditation to still the mind and restore personal harmony. Try this spell if your emotional balance and peace of mind are threatened by the quarrels or problems of others.

You will need
The image of the triple spiral above. Alternatively, scan or photocopy an enlarged version on to a sheet of white paper. You can also draw the triple spiral in white on black paper or paint it in miniature on a stone.

Timing
When your personal harmony is disturbed.

The spell
- Take your triple spiral and withdraw to a quiet place.
- With the index finger of your receptive hand (the one you do not write with), slowly trace the triple spiral, as you do so softly, slowly and continuously reciting:
Womb of the Mother, from ancient days,
Bringing rebirth in myriad ways;
Rebirth of life and hope and light,
from deepest rock to mountain height.
Dearest Mother that is all;
When you are close I cannot fall.
Womb of the Mother me embrace,
Enfold, and give me grace always.
Stop when you feel calm.

A mystic nut spell for inner stillness

Because the pace of life is so fast and stimulation constant in the modern world, it can be hard to link with your still, quiet, unchanging personal centre. Yet this is the secret of that inner calm that can help us to avoid being affected by the mood swings of others and being thrown off course by external events, good and bad. The several female mystics who lived in the period from the eleventh to the sixteenth century, discovered and shared some secrets of tranquillity. This and the following spell is based on their wisdom. I find these spells very helpful when my panic levels go through the roof.

In her book *Revelations of Divine Love,* the fourteenth-century Lady Julian of Norwich described a vision of God holding a small brown nut, which seemed so fragile and insignificant that she wondered why it did not crumble before her eyes. But she was reassured that even something as small as a nut was cared for and so she need worry about nothing. I have reproduced her words in this spell. If you often get stressed outside the home, carry the crystal for this spell with you in the purse wherever you go. Alternatively, carry a single nut with you.

You will need

A bowl of nuts or a round brown crystal (the nut-like desert rose is ideal); a small purse.

Timing

When life gets too much.

The spell

* Make an excuse to leave the stressful situation or anxiety-inducing person for a minute or two.
* Take a nut or the crystal and, holding it between your hands, focus only on that, as you do so saying over and over again (in your head or softly aloud): *God made it, God loves it, God keeps it. All shall be well, and all manner of thing shall be well.*
  You can substitute 'Goddess' for 'God' if you wish. Very soon you will feel quite calm.
* Bury the nut or wash the crystal under running water. Dry the crystal before returning it to the purse.

The Teresa of Avila walking chant

The sixteenth-century St Teresa de Avila was a joyous figure in spite of the intense austerity of her life. She likened dying to the process of a butterfly leaving the empty chrysalis behind.

Timing

When you feel control slipping.

The spell

* When you can feel tension rising, find somewhere outside where you can be alone, if only for five minutes. Ideally, it should have some greenery and paths.
* Start to walk in this place, letting your feet guide you and imagining multi-coloured butterflies all around you. As you walk, repeat as a slow soft chant (in your head if necessary):
  Let nothing disturb you,
  Nothing dismay you.
  All things pass,
  But God/the Goddess never changes.
  Walk according to the rhythm of the words and before long your mind will have slipped back into stillness and you will be able to cope with anything.

A spell to attract fun into your life

If your life seems dull or routine, use this spell to attract more social opportunities and fun into your world. Of course, you have to follow it up with action – joining a class or organisation, or going along with a friend to a place where you will meet new people. Parties do not just come knocking on your door. However, the spell will get things moving, stir up the energies around you in a positive way and send out friendly vibes.

You will need

A picture of people having a good time, perhaps in a place where you would like to be; 2 bright-red candles in suitable holders; 2 sticks of pine, orange, lemongrass or apple blossom incense and 2 separate holders; a bowl of sand or earth.

Timing

As evening falls, when you would like to be getting ready to go out.

The spell

* Light the candles and place them on either side of the picture, where wax will not fall on it.
* Light the incense from the candles and place the two sticks to complete a square around the picture. Say:

Four walls surround me,
Four walls enclose me.
I would have more.
I seek a door.

* Taking an incense stick in each hand, make large broad circles over and around the picture and the candles, as you do so saying:

Move and mingle, shake and stir;
Life rise in me, fun come to me,
Walls go from me;
I take away the door.

* Extinguish the incense in the bowl.
* Using the picture, fan the air above the candles, so that the flames dance (taking care not to ignite the paper). Say:

Flames dance;
I take a chance.
I would have more;
I take away the door.

* Blow out the candles in one breath.
* Look at the picture, then screw it into a ball and throw it as far as possible, as you do so saying:

Enough of pictures. I open the door.

Arrange to go out with a friend or relative – even if it is to a seemingly unpromising event.

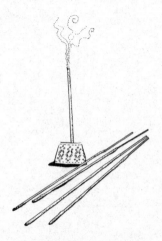

A spell for finding true happiness

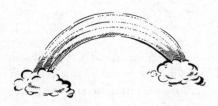

Rainbows have always been associated with happiness and wishes coming true. This is a good spell to do if your life is mostly fine, but a deep longing for moments of intense happiness and fulfilment occasionally surfaces.

You will need
A rainbow.

Timing
When you see a rainbow.

The spell
* Stop whatever you are doing and go out to see the rainbow. Face the rainbow and say:
  Rainbow magic bring to me
  What it is that now I see.
* Close your eyes, open them and you will see a vision, either externally or in your mind's eye, of how you can take the first steps to fulfilment.
* Before the rainbow fades, run, walk fast, dance in circles, sing loudly, scatter leaves, jump in a puddle and be totally, utterly spontaneous. Then arrange to do something completely out of character, however small, that you would enjoy.

11 SPELLS FOR PASSING TESTS AND LEARNING NEW SKILLS

This chapter consists of spells for boosting your natural talents and extending them into areas that have always seemed out of reach. Here you will find spells to increase your chances of passing tests and exams, spells to help you develop skills that will make your life happier and more fulfilled, spells to increase your confidence in new or longstanding abilities, and spells to focus your concentration, sharpen your memory and improve your dexterity. (For spells for interviews, see Chapter 15.)

Most importantly, these spells can help you to overcome deep-seated blocks that are preventing you from reaching your full potential. We may not even recall who first told us we were useless at mathematics, were a hopeless painter or had the voice of a grizzly bear with laryngitis. Yet negative messages can get stuck in the unconscious. Those half-forgotten voices hold us back from attempting activities that we can, with application and effort – and the help of a little magic – competently undertake.

A Bardic spell to improve your memory and concentration

Even if you are highly intelligent you can lose the skill of memorising information – particularly if you left school or formal training some years ago. This skill is often the key to success in tests and examination, as well as in mastering a new area of expertise. In the modern world, with its reliance on computers, DVDs and calculators, we use our memories less than people did even 20 years ago. In times before literacy was widespread, knowledge was memorised and passed on orally. Celtic Bards were required to learn thousands of verses by heart. This ritual comes from the modern Bardic Druid tradition.

You will need

A book of Celtic wisdom, prayer or myths (see page 708), a treasury of verse through the ages, the works of Shakespeare, a copy of the Bible, the I Ching, a sacred work from an ancient culture or a dictionary of quotations.

Timing

Daily if possible, just before going to sleep.

The spell

✳ Say:

My mind is an open book with many pages.
So do I write upon them and thus recall with
ease what I must know.

✳ Allow your mind to go blank. Picture a sky full of stars and allow them to fade one by one until there is only rich black velvet.

✳ With your eyes closed, open your chosen book of wisdom at any page and place your finger on the left- or right-hand leaf according to where your hand is drawn. Open your eyes and read the page, or if it is a continuation of a paragraph or verse, go to the previous page and begin there. You can read only a few lines or you can finish the poem or section.

✳ By reciting them over and over again out loud, commit to heart about six lines, choosing those that had the most meaning for you.

✳ Close your eyes again and see the words written in light on your dark velvet mind screen and repeat them aloud once more.

✳ The next day, repeat the spell, choosing another passage with your eyes closed, from the same or a different book of wisdom. Over the weeks your memory will speed up, and before long anything you read will imprint itself on your mind.

A spell to pass examinations or written tests

Examinations are doubly challenging because not only may questions appear on topics that you find difficult but also the test situation can make your mind freeze. Spells are a very effective means of overcoming these difficulties, because they prepare the mind in advance for the pressure. If the spell words are spoken in your head immediately before a test, they help the relevant knowledge to flow freely. The effects will last, no matter how many examinations are being taken. This spell is easy and has proved successful for examination candidates of all ages. If you like, you can repeat it the night before the exam, this time using fresh herbs and a different book. Add some of the herbs from the second spell to the purse containing the original herbs.

You will need

A small dish each of dried sage, dried rosemary and dried thyme (jars of culinary herbs are fine); the most difficult book, manual or set of notes that you have to study; a small purse.

Timing

When you begin revising and again the night before the examination.

The spell

* Set the book or notes on a table or other surface. Working with sage first (for the innermost circle), then rosemary and finally thyme, scatter a circle of each herb in turn around the book. These are the herbs of memory and concentration. As you make each circle, say:

Sage, rosemary, thyme,
Let this knowledge now be mine.
Circles three,
Memory be
Increased with speed,
So I succeed.
Sage, rosemary, thyme,
Let this knowledge now be mine.

* Gather some of the herbs into the purse and keep it with you while you study. Place it under your pillow at night so you may learn while you sleep. Take the purse to the examination with you.

A second spell to pass examinations or written tests

You can carry out this spell on your own behalf, or for a friend or family member who is having difficulty studying – perhaps because they are finding it hard to settle or are panicking so much about an examination that they are not sleeping. It is especially good for calming teenagers, as you can add a few of the empowered herbs to evening meals during the days leading up to the exam. This spell uses parsley, sage, rosemary and thyme, all herbs of concentration and memory, together with the technique of knotting, also used for memory. Not so very long ago, people would tie a knot in their handkerchief to remind them of something they needed to remember during the day. Each time they took out the handkerchief, the knot would jog their memory.

You will need

A small quantity of dried parsley, sage, rosemary and thyme (culinary herbs are fine); a mortar and pestle or a bowl and a wooden spoon; a sealable tub; a small square of yellow cloth; some yellow twine or cord.

Timing

Any Wednesday morning (Mercury's day) before school or college.

The spell

* Using the pestle and mortar or bowl and spoon, mix the four herbs together, as you do so chanting faster and faster to empower the herbs:
  Parsley, sage, rosemary, thyme,
  Make, I ask, good memory mine.
* When you can chant no faster, call:
  The power is free;
  So shall it be!
  Good memory is mine,
  By parsley, sage, rosemary and thyme.
* Scoop some of the empowered herbs into the tub to use in cooking. Tie the rest in the square of yellow cloth (yellow is the colour of Mercury, Roman god of learning), securing the cord around it with three knots and saying:
  Three, two, one,
  The spell is done.
  By knots of three,
  The power's in me.
* Keep the cloth of herbs in your study space – or, if you are working for someone else, hide it in the room where they study. Be sure to add some of the herbs to the meal the night before the examination. Take the cloth of herbs with you to the exam. If you are working for another person and they are not sceptical, offer it to them as a good luck charm on the morning of the first exam.

A spell to pass an oral test or practical examination

Oral and practical tests need a cool head so that instructions are followed exactly and the relevant information instantly accessed. A sympathetic examiner may help, but some do not have good people skills and can increase nervousness in the candidate. The following spell will encourage your creativity so that you demonstrate your competence and ability to perform under pressure.

You will need

An orange candle; a tape or CD you have recorded and are pleased with or a piece of finished work you have made.

Timing

The day before the test.

The spell

* Light the candle and gaze at the flame through half-closed eyes. Say:
  I have succeeded. I have my tape / creation (name it) as proof of my ability.
  What need I prove?
* Hold or touch your tape or creation and say:
  Yet can I prove again and again. My efforts will not be in vain.
* Place the tape or object where the light of the candle shines on it. Say:
  The power to create is still within me. Ask again and again and I will deliver what proof is needed, any time, any place, anyhow. By my creation this I vow.
* Blow out the candle and say:
  Light shine forth and show the world.
* Admire once more your achievement, perhaps playing a little of the tape or polishing the object, then put it away.
* On the morning of the test, re-light the candle and repeat:
  The power to create is still within me.
  Ask again and again and I will deliver what proof is needed, any time, any place, anyhow.
  By my creation this I vow.
* Blow out the candle in silence, touch your tape or creation and go to your test with confidence.

A bouncing ball spell to generate enthusiasm

In our busy world, the desire for learning – whether for advancement or pleasure – can get pushed aside. Tiredness and the demands of others sometimes deter us from going to the health club, to football training, to the drama group or to an evening class. As I know well, if I can drag my protesting mind and body away from the computer for a regular daily walk or to go along to a workshop not organised by myself, the benefits are almost immediate, and exhaustion is replaced by enthusiasm.

You will need
A large, multi-coloured, bouncy ball.

Timing
When you are planning on missing an activity.

The spell
* Take the ball outside and either bounce the ball up and down or kick it against a wall.
* Once you have established a rhythm, begin to chant:
One for pleasure,
Two for leisure,
Three for chores that can be left;
Four for duty,
Five for beauty,
Six for where I want to be.
Quit complaining;
Time is draining.
To pursue it
I must do it
Now.
* When you feel energised, put the ball away and go straight out to your activity, pausing only to collect any kit or books and, if necessary, to show your family where the microwave and instruction book are kept.

A spell for passing a driving test

This is a spell I am frequently asked to carry out, since nervousness in a test situation can be the downfall of many competent drivers. The spell not only calms nerves but also attracts good fortune, perhaps in the form of good driving conditions or an examiner who is in an unusually good mood – or down on his quota of pass students. The spell involves empowering a crystal to act as a talisman to be taken on the driving test and placed in the glove box or in your pocket so that you carry your confidence with you.

You will need
A map that includes the area in which the test will take place; a toy car (if possible, the model and colour of the one you will be driving); 4 bright-yellow candles in deep holders; a stick of fern, frankincense, rosemary or sage incense; an amber or carnelian crystal.

Timing
The evening before the day of the test – or, if you are working for someone else, at the time of the test.

The spell
* Lay out the map and light the four candles around the edges, about halfway along each side in approximate North, East, South and West positions. Set the toy car on the place on the map where the test will begin and set the crystal next to it.
* Light the incense stick from the northern candle, as you do so saying:
North, South, East, West,
Let me pass the driving test.

- Touch the incense stick to each of the other three candles so that it re-ignites and speak the chant again.
- Using the incense smoke, write the word 'pass' in the air over the toy car.
- Leave the candles and incense to burn through. Leave the toy car on the map until you have taken the test. Carry the crystal with you to the test.

A general study spell

It can be difficult to fit studying in with other demands, especially if you are having to work your way through college or are studying while caring for a family or working in a permanent job. For teenagers there are countless distractions, while for older people it may take longer to master new skills or information. This is a seven-day spell that builds up energies for a prolonged course of study. If you become diverted or find the going tough, you can repeat the spell monthly.

You will need
A deep-blue candle marked with 7 equally spaced notches; a lapis lazuli or deep-blue sodalite crystal (preferably more square than round); some dried mint or eyebright; a small blue purse.

Timing
When you will not be disturbed.

The spell
- Light the candle and add a small amount of the herbs (for focus and concentration) to the purse, saying:
Fill my mind with knowledge;
Let me facts recall.

Fill my mind with understanding
That I may know all.
Set the purse open in front of the candle.
- Carefully pass the crystal three times through the flame, as you do so saying:
Fill my mind with light;
Let me facts recall.
Illuminate my mind
And so understand all.
Leave the crystal in front of the candle on top of the open purse.
- While the first seventh of the candle is burning through, study hard and then blow out the candle, leaving the purse and crystal in front of it. You may wish to continue working.
- Repeat these steps each day for the next six days, adding a little more of the herbs and allowing the candle to burn down one more segment every day. On the last day, after you have blown out the final stub of candle, put the crystal into the herb purse and close it, as you do so saying:
Knowledge, illumination are combined;
Focused and eager is my mind.
- Keep the purse with your study materials until it loses its fragrance.

A spell to increase possibilities

Maybe you can't be a professional ballerina or an airline pilot, but that doesn't mean you can't learn to dance or take flying lessons. If you have a dream, you may be able to realise it, whatever your age, current financial state or health, if you are prepared to make modifications and approach it with persistence and ingenuity. People who have always been terrified of water have been known to learn to learn to swim in their seventies. Other older people become proficient in a foreign language, take a university degree or study music even though they failed at school. Getting fit need not involve tortuous sessions at the gym but can simply mean pursuing a gentle sport or taking up an active leisure interest.

You will need
A bridge, tunnel, underpass or narrow passageway that opens out on to a wide vista (find your site ahead of the spell).

Timing
When it is quiet and you can carry out the spell without attracting attention – it needs to be light enough for you to walk from the darkness in to the light.

The spell
* Enter the enclosed space and say:
  These are the limits that the discouragement of others, the circumstances of my life and my own fears have placed around me.
  Stand for a moment and let the confines surround you.
* Now walk, run or skip, as you did when you were a child, into the open air. Fling your arms as wide as possible and say:
  I walk into the light of possibility and leave behind the limits.
* As soon as you possibly can, apply for a course or book a lesson in whatever you would most like to learn. If you hesitate to go when the time comes, recall the spell in your mind's eye as you enter the building and walk into the light of possibility.

A spell to learn another language

There are any number of reasons for learning a new language. This spell takes advantage of our ability to absorb information unconsciously as well as consciously. It is the best spell I have yet found for this purpose.

You will need
An image of people in the country whose language you wish to learn; a CD or tape recording of the language; a word of greeting in the language you wish to learn.

Timing
Just before you go to sleep on three consecutive nights, and thereafter weekly.

The spell
* Sit in bed with the light on and, holding the picture in your hands, memorise the details. If you have been to the country already, you can add your own impressions of fragrances, colours, sounds and climate.
* Turn off the light and set the picture on your bedside table.
* With your eyes closed, visualise the scene as vividly as you can, as though you were still looking at it. You are now going to weave your own charm and recite it softly, using the greeting from the language you wish to learn. For example, in Swedish *hej* (pronounced *hay*) means 'hello'. My charm goes:
  Hej, I greet you,
  Hej, I meet you,
  Hej, I speak to you,
  Hej, you speak to me.
  Hej, hej, hej.
* Turn on the CD or tape very low, so that you can hardly hear the words, and go to sleep carried by the gentle sound, holding the scene in your mind.
* Before you next listen to the CD or tape during waking hours, first recite your greeting charm and look at the picture once more. Even if you generally find languages hard, you will be very receptive and learn rapidly.

A spell to master new technology

It can be disconcerting when even a relatively young child knows their way around a complex computer system while you are still struggling with the first page of the manual. People old and young do regularly become expert with new technology, however. There are numerous courses, books and magazines that offer clear guides to make you an expert. This spell has helped me, among many others, to overcome initial mental blocks and to avoid panicking when a piece of equipment does not respond as expected. Confidence is, again, the key, and – as with many spells – the psychic aspect assists the psychological.

You will need

The piece of technological equipment you have to master.

Timing

On a Wednesday morning.

The spell

* Switch on the piece of equipment and say three times:
I fear not you;
You fear not me.
Together we in harmony
Will do most wondrous wizardry.

* Follow the instructions for using the piece of equipment to the letter, without panicking or trying to take short-cuts. If things go wrong, return to the previous stage, recite the above rhyme three times, read the instructions and continue.

* When you have finished with the piece of equipment, say just once, before you switch it off:
I feared not you;
You feared not me.
Together we in harmony
Did the most wondrous wizardry.
Each time it will get easier.

A spell to improve your skill in a sport or art

You may never be a David Beckham, a Pablo Picasso or a Vladimir Ashkenazi, but there is immense pleasure in taking up or renewing an interest in a creative or sporting activity, to whatever level satisfies you. This spell can kick-start your innate talent, however modest, into action and enable you to reach your own full potential.

You will need

A video, DVD, CD or tape of the relevant sport or art; a wand or pointed crystal (see page 184).

Timing

A Wednesday morning in sunlight, or any bright day.

The spell

* Start the video, DVD, CD or tape.

* Facing the screen or the sound, hold your wand or crystal in your power hand (the one you write with) and circle it slowly nine times deosil (clockwise) in ever larger circles. Say with confidence:
May talent flow to me.
Skilled in (name the sport/art) I would be.
And so I call ability,
Three by three by three.

* Point the wand directly at the screen or source of music and say:
So I call you.

* Raise your wand so that it is vertical and say:
So I raise you.

* Bring the wand down with a cutting movement, in an arc that sweeps down to your waist and then upwards again, as you do so saying:
So I draw you to me.

12 SPELLS FOR MENDING WHAT IS BROKEN AND RECOVERING WHAT IS STOLEN

If we have lost a precious possession, whether of sentimental or monetary value, it is hard not to fret and waste time fruitlessly searching places where we have already looked 20 times. Sometimes the missing item turns up only when we have given up — and usually in a totally unexpected place. Documents, too, can disappear at a crucial moment — car registration forms, birth certificates, travel insurance policies, holiday tickets or tax forms — even when we are sure we have filed them carefully.

Having something stolen can feel even worse, as the sense of outrage compounds the loss. When the Romans were stolen from, they wrote curses on tablets of lead and cast them into the waters at Bath, in Avon in the UK, demanding that the goddess Sulis Minerva punish and unmask the thief.

Repairs can take ages to organise when a car, computer or washing machine breaks down, and these pieces of equipment are often urgently needed. If you are stranded in the middle of nowhere and out of mobile phone range or you have to get the children's school uniforms washed for the next morning or you need to send an important piece of work on a computer that has crashed, you may need a little magic. Though some men (and in my experience it is usually men) laugh at this idea, many have been grateful for their wife or girlfriend's witchery on a cold wet night when the car would not start.

There are also situations in which we need to mend a broken link or recover a person. A mother, for example, may be anxious to find a child she gave up at birth; an adult may want to trace their birth family two decades or more after the original parting; or a friend or relative may be temporarily missing and we are anxious about them. Of course, magic is not an automatic solution in any of these cases. It cannot recover papers that have been deliberately or inadvertently destroyed, and it will not recover a missing person who does not wish to be found. In many cases, however, a spell does help, not least by activating our own intuitive powers and inner radar.

Six St Anthony prayers to recover what is lost

Within the Roman Catholic Church and in the wider folk tradition of the Americas and eastern and western Europe, people pray to St Anthony to find what they have mislaid. Indeed, I know of nuns who to this day insist that St Anthony always comes to their aid in such matters. There are two Saint Anthonies, but the one referred to here is associated with Padua, in Italy, and lived from 1195–1231. He was a Franciscan monk and is also entreated for the safe return of missing persons. He is depicted in a brown habit, holding baby Jesus in one hand and a white lily in the other. In South America, San Antonio, as he is called there, is clad in blue and holds a yellow lily and a red heart.

There are many variations on the prayer to St Anthony for recovering what is lost (you will find others on the Internet). Readers from Australia to Poland and Central America have told me that these prayers really work, so they are definitely worth a try. Picture the missing object as you speak the words six times. An image may come into your head of where you left or dropped the item. The final prayer is for a missing person, and can also be used for an animal that has gone astray.

You will need:
Nothing.

Timing
Whenever something (or somebody) is lost.

> **Prayer 1:** *St Anthony, St Anthony, please come down. Something is lost and can't be found.*
>
> **Prayer 2:** *Good St Anthony, I pray bring (name item) back today.*
>
> **Prayer 3:** *Anthony, good saint, I pray return (name item) to me without delay.*
>
> **Prayer 4:** *Dear St Anthony, this I lack (name item). Haste I pray and bring it back.*
>
> **Prayer 5:** *Good St Anthony, this I lack (name item). Look around and bring it back.*
>
> **Prayer 6:** *St Anthony, to your care I commit beloved (name the person and their relationship to you). I know not where she/he may be, Keep her/him safe and return him/her in love to those who wait in love. To you we call in our sorrow, for you alone can help.*

A pendulum spell to find a small missing item, indoors or outdoors

A pendulum can enable you to tune in accurately to your automatic inner radar and locate what is missing. The unconscious movements of your hand direct the pendulum to swing in either a positive (when it is near to the missing item) or a negative direction. To work out which way your pendulum swings for positive and negative, hold the pendulum and think about a happy event. Notice how the pendulum swings: this is positive (often a clockwise circle). Now think about a sad event and notice how the pendulum swings: this is negative (often an anticlockwise circle). A pendulum may also tug down, as if pulled by gravity, and vibrate powerfully over the spot where the object is hidden. Be open to receiving either or both signals, as pendulums may circle and/or pull down at different times.

This and the following pendulum spells will increase the clairvoyant link between you and your pendulum and activate the powers within the crystal. If you are new to pendulum work, I would recommend using these spells to tune yourself in.

You will need

A clear crystal pendulum; a clear glass bowl half-filled with mineral water; a fibre optic lamp (optional).

Timing

When you are about to look for something lost. The pendulum charge will last all day.

The spell

* Before you look for the missing object, you need to charge the pendulum. To do this, hold it in the sunlight or in the light of the fibre optic lamp so that it is filled with rainbows.
* Rapidly plunge the pendulum in to the water nine times, saying on each plunge:
  Pendulum power,
  At this hour
  Find for me
  What I would see.
* Hold the pendulum to the light once more and spin it fast so that the water droplets shine, as you do so saying:
  Be as a beacon of sight and light the way to (name item).
* Describe what you are looking for, then allow your mind to go blank,

letting go of attempts to second-guess or analyse. You are handing over the problem to the pendulum.

* Hold the pendulum between the index finger and thumb of your power hand (the one you write with), allowing a length of chain that feels right – enough for the pendulum to swing freely. There are no rights or wrongs in how you do this.
* Stand in the middle of the garden, hallway or main room of your house and turn three times deosil (clockwise), three times widdershins (anticlockwise) and then three times deosil again, as you do so again saying:
  Pendulum power, at this hour
  Find for me what I would see.
* Walk straight ahead. If the pendulum begins to swing negatively, try another direction. As you get close to the missing item, the pendulum will begin to swing positively. This positive swing will increase the closer you get, and you may feel a vibration in your finger-tips. When you reach the item, the pendulum will spiral in all directions and the feeling will be intense (something like detecting a ringing mobile phone buried under a pile of papers). Alternatively, it may pull downwards.
* When you have finished using the pendulum, wash it under running water and leave it to dry naturally.

A pendulum spell to find a specific document that you need urgently

This technique can also be useful if you have put something in a drawer but cannot recall which one.

You will need

A clear crystal pendulum; a clear glass bowl half-filled with mineral water; a fibre optic lamp (optional).

Timing

When you are about to look for something lost. The pendulum charge will last all day.

The spell

* Charge the pendulum by carrying out the first three steps on page 169.
* Spread out your files and folders, and divide unsorted papers into evenly sized piles on the floor in a row.
* Walk from left to right in front of the files, folders and piles of papers, holding the pendulum above them and saying for each one:
Be as a beacon of sight and light the way to (name missing document).
* Return to the end where you started and repeat the walk, this time holding the pendulum over each file, folder or pile of papers and saying:
Is (name) in here?
The pendulum may swing positively or pull down as though tugged by gravity.
* When you have identified the correct file, folder or pile, arrange all the papers in it in a row and repeat the procedure. You do not need to repeat the chant.
* When you have finished using the pendulum, wash it under running water and leave it to dry naturally.

A pendulum spell to locate something that is missing

For this spell you will need a map, either a very detailed one of your district or a larger one of your town or an even larger area if you have lost something travelling on holiday. Once you have identified a town, for example, you can contact places you visited or stayed when you were in the area and most likely someone will be holding on to the item just in case. The pendulum works in this case by pulling downwards and vibrating over the correct spot rather than giving a positive response.

You will need

A clear crystal pendulum; a clear glass bowl half-filled with mineral water; a fibre optic lamp (if there is no natural sunlight); a map of the area where the object went missing.

Timing

When you are about to look for something lost. The charge will last all day.

The spell

* Charge the pendulum by following the first three steps on page 169.
* Hold the pendulum over each corner of the map and say:
Be as a beacon of sight and light the way to (name missing item).
* Now pass the pendulum very slowly over the map, from top to bottom, left to right, over each of the grid squares until it pulls down as though tugged by gravity over a particular spot. This indicates where the missing item can be found. You can repeat the spell with a more detailed map of the area to get a more precise location.

A pendulum spell to indicate where you might find a replacement for a broken object

If you have permanently lost or broken something of sentimental value, you may want an exact replacement. With old or unusual items, this can be difficult. This spell will help.

You will need

A clear crystal pendulum; a clear glass bowl half-filled with mineral water; a fibre optic lamp (if there is no natural sunlight); a large-scale map of the area where you intend to look for your item.

Timing

When you want a replacement for a lost or broken object.

The spell

* Using the large scale map, follow the steps for the previous spell, but when you hold the pendulum at the four corners of the map at the beginning of the spell, change the chant to:
  Be as a beacon of sight and light the way to an exact replacement for (name broken item).
* Once you have the name of the town or area, you can use the Internet or Yellow Pages to find a firm that sells what you want.

A soap and water tablet spell to recover what has been stolen

The Romans inscribed tablets made of lead (which was easy to engrave) with curses against known and unknown persons who stole property, harmed reputations or seduced wives. Some tablets demanded that the unknown perpetrator of a crime be unmasked. The tablets were then cast into the water – and thus, unbeknownst to the curse-maker, cursed all those who were poisoned by the seepage of lead, not known as harmful by the Romans. This more environmentally friendly spell uses a tablet of soap on which the stolen property is listed. It is left to karma – and hopefully the law – to punish the thief.

You will need

A large tablet of soap; a nail file, paper knife or other sharp object for inscribing the soap; a large bucket of hot water; a stick of pine, juniper or cedar incense.

Timing

After you have been burgled or mugged.

The spell

* Set the tablet of soap on a table and light the incense close by.
* Using the inscribing tool, engrave on the tablet of soap what has been stolen (or a few representative items if the list is long).
* When you have finished, pass the smoke of the incense in spirals over the tablet, listing all the items and saying:
  May they be returned undamaged before one month is through.
* Place the soap in the bucket of water and leave it to melt, adding more hot water if necessary. Busy yourself with a small improvement to your home.
* When the soap is melted, pour the soapy water down a drain and flush the drain well with a hose or with the cold tap, as you do so saying:
  May my property be returned before one month is through and may the thief know the consequences of her/his unkind actions.
* Bury the ash from the incense.

A garlic spell for restoring what has been lost or stolen, physically, financially or emotionally

Garlic has been used across cultures for banishing everything from vampires and evil spirits to ill health. Because garlic grows if the cloves are buried, it is also a very powerful symbol of the restoration of what has been lost or stolen. The effect of this spell is not immediate; it will release its energies over weeks or months and so is especially good for recovering financially or emotionally from loss. On the other hand, it will help to speed up the resolution of long-standing insurance claims where there is a dispute or unreasonable delay.

You will need
7 cloves of garlic (ideally on a string); some salt; an area of earth or a big plant pot filled with soil.

Timing
At midnight.

The spell
* Set the seven garlic cloves in a circle, cutting the string and releasing them one by one if they are joined.
* Sprinkle each clove with salt, saying:
Take away the sorrow of what is lost and cleanse the wounds that they may heal.
* Bury each clove in turn in a circle in the earth, naming it with one of the days of the week, beginning with Sunday.
* When all the cloves are covered with earth, raise your hands above them and say:
You seven days, I name you all: Sunday, Monday, Tuesday, Wednesday, Thursday, Friday, Saturday. In seven days and seven days more, restore (name what is to be restored). For seven days more keep growing, seven more and more, till all completely is restored.
* Water the area weekly, reciting the words of the previous step as you do so.

A spell to lift your mood if you can't break out of a cycle of depression

Light and sound are two of the most effective ways of enhancing mood. Mirrors have long been used magically in the Far East, especially China, both to reflect back negativity to the sender and to attract light and all manner of abundance in to the home. Wind chimes are used to break up stagnant energies and get them moving as well as to deflect harsh discordant vibes. The chant in this spell is adapted from an old American blues song. In common with other songs handed down through generations, it has a number of different forms.

You will need
A small oval swivel mirror; some metal wind chimes hanging near the door of the room where you carry out the spell, placed so that you can touch them; a silver- or gold-coloured candle.

Timing
Early morning when the light has just broken through. Repeat when necessary.

The spell
* Set the mirror and the candle on a table beneath the wind chimes.
* Light the candle.

- Chant or sing the following words to any tune:

  The sun's going to shine on my door some day;
  The wind will blow, and blow all my blues away.

  As you chant the first line, swivel the mirror to shine the candle light on the door of your room. As you say the second line, gently brush the wind chimes so that they ring.

- Repeat the chant and actions two times more, as you do so picturing the sun bringing light back in to your life and the wind sweeping away your troubles.

- Blow or snuff out the candle and, if possible, go out for a walk.

- Repeat the rhyme aloud or in your head whenever you need a little encouragement.

A spell to recover debts owed to you

We may lend money to friends or family willingly, even if the likelihood of being repaid is remote. When a borrower can afford to repay what they owe, however, we have a right to be annoyed if the money is not forthcoming, in spite of hints. Since in most such cases legal action would be heavy-handed, even if you need the money yourself, this gentle spell provides a useful alternative, reminding the borrower psychically that payment is overdue. If you are self-employed, it is an effective method of prompting payment from those who have commissioned work or ordered goods and are proving slow to pay (see also page 240).

You will need

Some green bank notes of any currency (they need be of little monetary value); a small jar or pot without a lid; a dark-green candle in a deep metal holder or on a flat metal tray; a sheet of light-green paper; a dark-green pen; an envelope (if you need to move on to the second stage of the spell).

Timing

On a Saturday morning.

The spell

- Light the candle. Fold up the money and place it in the pot, in front of the candle.

- Using the green pen, write at the top of the green paper the name of the debtor and the words:

  Please pay my money. This is a gentle reminder.

  Place the note under the pot.

- Blow out the candle and repeat the name of the debtor and the words you wrote. Leave all in place.

- The next day, light the candle and add another green currency note to the pot, repeating the previous two steps.

- Continue repeating these actions daily until the debtor contacts you or until the piece of paper is full.

- If the paper is full and the debtor still has not contacted you, burn the paper in the candle flame, saying:

  (Name), please pay my money. This is a final reminder.

- Bury the ashes and put the money in the envelope. Seal it and write the name of the debtor on it, together with the words 'final reminder'. Keep the envelope in a drawer. Usually the money will arrive the next day.

- If the money does not arrive within two days, phone, write to or e-mail the debtor, saying:

  (Name), please pay my money (specify amount owed) by (give a date a day or two ahead). I can wait no longer.

  Put the phone down or send the letter or e-mail with a brief expression of good wishes.

A candle spell to recover optimism after a series of setbacks

Based on an old rite to celebrate the rebirth of the sun on the shortest day (on or around 21 December), this spell works well at any time you have lost hope or are overwhelmed by loss, a run of bad luck or problems such as debt.

You will need

A small dark-coloured candle in a suitable holder; a large pure-white candle that will burn through the night (if you buy a church candle, the label will tell you how long it will burn for) in a suitable holder; a taper; a second white candle (optional).

Timing

Just before dusk on a Saturday (the day of Saturn and limitations).

The spell

* Place the two candles side by side and light the dark-coloured one, as you do so saying:
  Darkness go,
  Light grow,
  Hope increase,
  Despair / debt / bad luck cease.
* Sit in the candle glow until all the light has gone from the sky and let the darkness and doubts flow from you.
* When it is dark, use the taper to light the white candle from the dark one, as you do so saying:
  Light rise to the skies;
  So darkness dies.
  Farewell bad fortune, farewell sorrow;
  Life begins on the morrow.
* Blow out the dark candle and wait for it to cool down. Wrap it in a brown paper bag and throw it away before you go to bed
* Gaze into the white candle and recall happy memories, together with plans and pleasures (however small) that are still possible.
* If you wish, add the second white candle to increase the positive energies. Leave your candle(s) in a safe place until morning, when they should be burnt through.

A spell for when your car breaks down in the middle of nowhere or will not start in a remote place

None of the mechanical spells in this chapter is a substitute for regular maintenance, and you will need to effect a proper repair as soon as possible after performing them. Nor should you work these spells unless absolutely necessary, as they always fail if they are not fuelled by real need and desperation. With all cosmic repair spells, you should pay back the cosmos with a good deed to someone in need as soon as possible.

Timing
When the need arises.

The spell
* Once rudimentary mechanical efforts have failed, send any hyped-up failed mechanics or useful-suggestion back-seat passengers a few metres away.
* Leave the car to rest for about three minutes. During this time, explain to the cosmos your need to get home, and perhaps make an offer – for example that you'll phone a difficult relative for a chat or sort out some unwanted junk with a smile when the local charity comes knocking.
* Put down the bonnet and sit in the driving seat. Say:
  We must depart.
  Please will you start
  When I count three.
* Start the engine while counting to three.
* If this does not work first time, wait a minute and then repeat the chant until it works (it usually does unless your helpers have burnt out the engine).
* Once the engine is running, keep your foot down gently on the accelerator and call back the rest of the party. Insist that they sit in silence as you drive.
* Drive home or to the nearest garage, focusing on landmarks and the road and blocking out all thoughts of the car.

A spell to get home if you are almost out of petrol and there is no nearby garage

Like the spell above, this one should be used sparingly, when the expected garage is closed or your partner/offspring has emptied the tank on a previous journey. I once drove across the island where I live on an almost empty tank, in the days when there were no late-night garages, on a wet cold night with three young children in the back of the car. They still remember the occasion.

You will need
Nothing.

Timing
When you are almost out of petrol.

The spell
* Look briefly at the fuel light and say aloud – or in your head if you are among sceptics:
  Run so lightly car of mine;
  Run on air just for a time.
  Take me homeward, ever onward;
  Let the miles melt and fade away.
* Continue to chant these lines softly or silently as you drive, using the lightest touch and moderate speed. Focus on the route and resist the urge to look at the petrol gauge. You may even come across a garage open unexpectedly late.

A spell to bring a crashed or unresponsive computer temporarily back to life

When a computer breaks down, it is usually at a crucial moment, when the IT manager has just gone home or on the one occasion when you have not backed up vital files that must be sent at once. I have performed this spell with success a number of times, but make sure you don't abuse it – it only works in a dire emergency.

This spell can also be used to repair a broken washing machine or tumble dryer – just draw the crystal circles round the glass window of the machine. Make the invisible escape doorway from the highest point of the glass doorway, so that the passage leads upwards and towards the top point of the outermost invisible circle. Set the programme in advance so that you just have to switch on the power to the machine when the spell is done.

You will need

A dark pointed crystal of any kind (smoky quartz is especially effective); a pointed clear quartz crystal, or any clear white or yellow crystal.

Timing

When you are experiencing computer problems (or difficulties with any other technological equipment).

The spell

* Do not switch on the machine. Working in silence, take up the dark crystal in your receptive hand (the one you do not write with). With the pointed end, trace a square shape in the air in front of the computer, just beyond its actual outline, so that the whole machine is enclosed. Work deosil (clockwise), starting in the top left-hand corner.
* Trace a second square, around the outside of the first.
* Go on tracing ever-larger squares until you can reach no further. The squares can be close together
* Transfer the crystal to your power hand and draw a doorway midway in the top side of the squares, cutting right through them to create a passageway along which the negative forces can travel from the top of the computer screen.
* Holding the crystal above the top of the outermost square, still in your power hand, pull an imaginary long dark-grey cord from the top of the computer screen, through the passageway and out.
* In your mind's eye, wind the cord into a ball and toss it into the cosmos.
* Remove the squares by re-tracing them in reverse order and working widdershins (anticlockwise), starting at the top left corner of the outermost square moving inwards to end up where you began.
* Point the sharp end of the clear crystal at the centre of the computer screen and picture light pouring on to and illuminating the inert screen. Visualise the screen coming to life.
* At the precise moment you feel that the spell is complete, switch on the computer and speak the only word of the spell:
  Now.
* Get the machine serviced as soon as possible – psychic repairs are usually only temporary.

A spell to find a birth mother, family or child

There are now many excellent organisations worldwide for uniting birth families with children who were adopted years before. But they are not infallible, and sometimes one of the parties may be hesitating to register. I have come across many remarkable stories about people who have been inexplicably drawn to a town hundreds or even thousands of miles from their present home. Through a series of coincidences they have met the desired birth relative there. You can read more about this in my book *Mother Link*, Ulysses Press, California, 1999.

This is a subtle spell to re-open the telepathic channels of communication – which are established every time one of the parties wonders about the welfare or whereabouts of the other during the years of separation. The spell will help if you are hoping the other party will register to find you or if you are actively looking for them. It can also ease the initial awkwardness if contact is made.

You will need

Any personal item linking the two of you (for example, a baby photograph, a birth certificate or a small shoe or toy).

Timing

At a transition time, such as the beginning of a week, month, season or year, or the anniversary of the birth or adoption, on a breezy day.

The spell

* Go to a place with a flat horizon. Hold the personal item in your cupped hands and speak the following words softly into the breeze:
  Mother / Father / Son / Daughter of mine, though far away,
  I call to you in love this day.
  Wherever you are, I ask that you will try to find me.
  I send this message on the wind to wherever you may be.
* Walk for a while and then take your keepsake home. Place it indoors, somewhere where fresh air will circulate all around it.

A spell to locate a missing person

There may be many reasons why a person is missing, most of them perfectly innocuous. But the anxiety for those left wondering can be almost unendurable if days turn into weeks and weeks turn into months. This spell offers no promises, as the missing person may be unwilling or unable to get in touch. It is a tiring spell, as you are transmitting love as powerfully as you can. However, it does bring some peace of mind and may reach the missing person or at least help you to know in your heart what has happened.

You will need

A pure-white candle; some rose petals or lavender heads, fresh or dried.

Timing

A time of the day or week when you and the missing person were regularly together.

The spell

* When you are alone and quiet, light the candle and allow a picture of the missing person to come into your mind.
* Speak into the flame words of love and any positive family news. Let the words come spontaneously.
* When you have finished, say three times:
  (Name), I miss you more each day. Come back to me or send news so that I can let you live peacefully.
* Blow out the candle and, using all your strength, push the light in your mind to enfold the person in love, wherever they are.
* Repeat daily, if possible at the same time, until the candle is burnt down, then leave a day's gap before beginning again with a fresh candle. The message each day need only be short.

13 SPELLS FOR WISHES AND GOOD LUCK

"According to UK scientist Dr Richard Wiseman, we make our own luck. He concluded from his research on the subject that people who are consistently lucky have high expectations of good fortune which became self-fulfilling prophecies – or as Michael Miles (a popular television game show host in the UK) used to say: 'Think lucky and you'll be lucky.'

Dr Wiseman also came to the conclusion that lucky people took advantage of opportunities that came their way and tended to persevere when things weren't going so well, turning disadvantage into opportunity by their own efforts.

That's the psychology of good luck. But luck can be enhanced by spells, which enable us to attract fulfilment of our dearest wishes from the cosmos. According to the rules of cosmic pay-back, we then have to share that good fortune by helping others in practical ways – and, of course, it is unethical to demand an enormous win on the National Lottery.

This chapter focuses on those special wishes and dreams that we all harbour, offering a variety of spells by which you can make them come true. Of course, earthly effort will still be needed, but wish spells can help to generate the energies and the magical space in which to bring our special desires closer to reality. The things we regret most are those we never did. As I get older, I understand increasingly how important it is to seize every moment of happiness, as long as you are not hurting others by your actions.

I am not talking here about creating about a psychic shopping list but rather about finding happiness through being able to fulfil the plans that matter to us. Many of these wishes are not materialistic in nature. What is more, the happier we are, the more we can spread that happiness, inviting others to share our good fortune. Some of the richest people are deeply unhappy – and are often incredibly mean with their money.

So pick one of the spells in this chapter – some ages old, some brand new – and make a wish come true. You can also make wishes for those you love.

A holed stone wish ritual

Small, perfectly round, holed stones are used for granting wishes. It is said that the wish is heard by a benign essence or transformed into magical energies, like sparkling dust, to translate it into actuality, or at least distinct possibility. It was believed for hundreds of years (and still is by some) that you can access another dimension by looking or speaking through the 'window' in a holed stone. It is worth waiting until you find the right stone to perform this spell. Less than perfectly round stones can be used for healing and fidelity magic.

You will need

A perfectly round holed stone.

Timing

A birthday, Christmas, new year or any significant marker point in the year or your life. As the sun or moon is rising is especially magical.

The spell

* Hold the stone so that your lips enclose the hole. Whisper your wish through the hole three times and then breathe three soft breaths to carry the wishes into the cosmos.
* Tell no-one your wish and use your stone no more than three times a year.
* A wish stone is a wonderful gift for a child, but have a wish for yourself before you hand it on.

A crystal spell to fulfil your secret wish or dream

Because crystals, even small ones, contain a lot of stored energy, they are ideal for filling with power and carrying with you or wearing as a charm. When you feel the power weakening, simply wash the empowered crystal under running water and repeat the spell.

In this spell you endow your crystal first with power, using the four elements: Earth, Air, Fire and Water. Afterwards you write your wish or desire in incense over the stone so that only you know the hidden meaning of the stone. There is a sound psychological reason for this. If we tell people of our plans and dreams, some will be encouraging, while others will cast doubt or scorn. Magically, using words only you know is a way of creating extra power. For this reason the spell is conducted entirely in silence.

Suitable crystals for this spell include amber, beryl, carnelian, citrine, crystal quartz, spinel, topaz and zircon for an urgent wish, a wish involving great or sudden change, or a wish for success or prosperity. Use softer-coloured stones such as rose quartz, amethyst, fluorite and jade for love, fidelity or personal happiness. Choose your incense fragrance also according to the nature of the wish. Use a powerful fragrance such as frankincense, sage or sandalwood for a strong forceful desire. For a gentler wish choose a fragrance such as chamomile, lavender or rose.

You will need

A clear or sparkling crystal (see above); a small metal tray; a small dish of sea salt; a stick of incense (see above or use the list of incense properties on pages 695–97); a pure-white or beeswax candle; a small dish of still mineral water or flower water; a small square of cloth, a square tile or stone.

Timing

At sunset during the waxing moon. For a gentle wish, work early in the lunar cycle.

The spell

* Set up your cloth, tile or stone on a table or in your special magical place if you have created one. Place your crystal in the centre of the cloth, on the small metal tray (in case the candle drips).
* Place the salt in the North (to represent the infusion of practical Earth energies into your wish and translate it from thought to actuality).
* Place the incense, in its holder, in the East (to represent the movement of Air energies and initiate the progression of your wish from the thought plane into possibility).
* Place the candle in the South (to represent the inspiration of Fire and the impetus to break through the barrier between the thought plane and actuality).
* Place the water in the West (to represent the power of Water to endow your wish with real desire and emotion, the most vital ingredient in raising the energy to translate the dream into the pleasurable sensations of attainment).
* Light the candle and look into the flame, as you do so defining in your mind the precise wording of your wish
* Take the salt and sprinkle three deosil (clockwise) circles of salt around the crystal, as you do so reciting the wish three times in your head. Return the salt to its place
* Light the incense from the candle and as the two flames momentarily join, picture your wish coming to fruition. Make three circles of incense smoke deosil around the crystal, again reciting the wish in your head. Return the incense to its place.
* Pass the crystal three times through the candle flame, as you do so again reciting the wish in your head three times.
* Sprinkle three deosil circles of water, as you do so again reciting the wish in your head, this time once only.
* With the incense stick, write your wish in the smoke a few centimetres above the crystal and picture the words entering it.
* Dowse the incense in the water and blow out the candle, sending the light to empower the fulfilment of your desire.
* Carry the crystal with you, holding it and reciting the wish when you feel doubt.

A first star spell for a wish

Stars have always been associated with wishes, and the star rhymes we learnt as children are relics of old spells. This and all the star spells that follow should be practised outdoors. If it is cold, lie wrapped up on a sun bed so you can look directly upwards.

You will need
Nothing.

Timing
As the stars are coming out.

The spell

* Focus on the first star to come out in the sky – or if there are a number, pick one. Say three times aloud:
  Star light,
  Star bright,
  First star I see tonight,
  I wish I may,
  I wish I might
  Have the wish I wish tonight.
* Make a silent wish and tell no one.

A modern star spell

The charm in this spell was immortalised in Walt Disney's film of the book *Pinocchio*, in which it is sung by Jiminy Cricket, Pinocchio's guide.

You will need
A clear quartz crystal.

Timing
When the sky is full of stars.

The spell
* Hold the crystal in your receptive hand (the one you don't write with), look at the stars and say:

When you wish upon a star
Makes no difference who you are.
When you wish upon a star
Anything your heart desires will
Come to you.

* Hold the crystal to your lips and whisper the wish into it.
* Repeat the rhyme once more.
* Place the crystal under your pillow and leave it there for three nights.
* Each day make a small step towards fulfilling your dream and things will start to fall into place.

A Pole Star spell for achieving a dream that seems ambitious or far off in time

The Pole Star has always been considered especially magical – particularly with regard to secret ambitions and dreams that will take time, hard work and more than a little luck to fulfil. The Pole Star changes every 2,000 years. The current one is called Polaris. It marks the top of the symbolic world tree, the legendary axis of the world. Shamans – the magic men and women priest healers of many indigenous cultures in the Northern Hemisphere – use it as a focus when they ascend the world tree on their magical journeys to visit the upper realms and the wise ancestors who sit by their fires in the night sky.

You can find Polaris between the Big Dipper and the constellation of Cassiopeia. Use a sky globe or sky map to identify its position precisely. If you live in the Southern Hemisphere, you can focus on the Southern Cross.

You will need
Nothing.

Timing
A cloudless night when you can see the Pole Star.

The spell
* If possible, go to a place where there is a tree through whose branches you can look up and see the Pole Star. Otherwise, go outside and stand so that you seem to be directly below the star.
* Look upwards at the Pole star and say:
I climb through the starry sky
And carry my dream up so high.
Dreams are many, days are few;
I entrust this my wish to you.
* In your head, say what you want, no matter how impossible it seems or how distant in time.
* Sit and watch the stars and know that there are infinite possibilities that may unfold in your life if you are open to them

A meteor spell for a life-changing wish or seemingly impossible dream

For thousands of years, humans regarded the meteorites that blazed across the skies and fell to earth as gifts from the deities. Especially valued were those that contained rich deposits of iron or crystals such as olivine (peridot) or even occasionally diamonds. The vast majority of meteorites originate in the asteroid belt between Mars and Jupiter, and at certain times of the year (such as August in western Europe) there are meteor showers for two or three nights. However, you may be lucky enough to see one at any time if you are observant. Meteor spells are very potent when you have a burning desire for a major change of direction or a dream so unlikely to be fulfilled that you have never voiced it.

You will need

A small meteorite (from museum and mineral stores or by mail order); a gold-coloured candle.

Timing

When you see a meteor (or a shooting star) – carry your meteorite just in case.

Be patient and wait for just the right conditions. If the need is urgent, you can focus on the brightest star in the sky.

The spell

* Take up your meteorite (most are about 4,560 million years old) in your power hand (the one you write with). Focus on the place where you saw the meteor or shooting star.
* If you cannot be overheard, make your wish aloud. Then say three times:
  Shower me with your gifts. Fire me with power to make my wish come true, that I may blaze as glorious as you through the skies and make my mark on Earth one day.
* Leave the meteorite open to the skies all night, and in the early morning, as it becomes light, light the candle and pass the meteorite through the flame, repeating the chant.
* Leave the candle to burn through in a safe place where its light shines on the meteorite.
* Carry your meteorite as a reminder of what you can achieve.

A crescent moon spell for a gradual improvement or increase in your life

Like stars, the moon is traditionally believed to grant wishes. Moon wish spells should be cast outdoors, generally between the crescent and the full moon, after which lunar energies decrease. When the crescent first appears in the sky is an auspicious time for modest wishes that may be fulfilled over the months. This is a gentle pre-Christian version of the moon wish ritual.

You will need

A bunch of small, white, scented flowers.

Timing

When the crescent moon is in a dark sky.

The spell

* Holding the flowers, face the crescent moon. Say softly:
  I see the moon; the moon sees me.
  I bless the moon; may the moon bless me.
* Make your wish for any increase or improvement in your life or the life of loved ones.
* Separate the flowers and form them into a crescent shape on the ground, somewhere where they will not be disturbed and can fade naturally.
* When the flowers have faded, dig them back into the earth.

A crescent moon or early waxing moon three-wish spell

For this spell you should ideally be able to see the moonlight reflected in water, such as a stream, river or pond. You may need to explore possible locations near your home. A garden pond is useful for magic. If you cannot find a suitable location or the night is cloudy, use three silver-coloured floating candles in a bowl of water. This is a very old spell.

You will need
3 silver-coloured floating candles in a bowl of water (optional).

Timing
The early part of the moon cycle, after the crescent. The timing is crucial with this spell, even if you are working with a bowl and candles, so check in *Old Moore's Almanack*, a diary or the newspaper.

The spell
* Looking at the moon (or lighting the candlelight in the water), say:

  New moon, true moon,
  Moon in the stream,
  Grant my wishes in my dream.

* Make a wish, close your eyes, open them and look at the water. You may see a picture in the reflected light that indicates how and when your wish will be granted. If you are using candles, blow one of them out.
* Repeat the first two steps twice more, so that you have made three wishes in total. The wishes can be related or separate, for yourself or for those you love.
* Try not to talk to anyone for the rest of the evening. Go to bed early and look for the moon through your window, as you do so repeating the chant, even if you cannot see the moon. In your dreams you will see symbols or conceive ideas you had not thought of to bring your wishes to fruition. You may also see people who will help you. Before the moon is full, you will have a sign of how and when your wishes will come true.

A waxing moon wish spell

As the moon waxes from the crescent to the night before full and its light increases from the right, more powerful energies are available to support a more powerful wish. The closer to the full moon, the more powerful the energies.

You will need
Some small silver bells on a string; a twig from any tree that grows near water (for example, willow or alder, both moon trees) – if you like, rub this smooth, sharpen it to a point and add a small quartz crystal to the end to make a wand – alternatively use a bought wand or pointed crystal; a moonstone.

Timing
Any night from the crescent to the full moon when the moon is bright enough for you to stand in a pool of moonlight.

The spell
* Working outside on earth, sand or grass, put the moonstone in the centre of the biggest pool of moonlight you can find.
* Stand in the pool of moonlight with the wand in your power hand (the one you write with) and the string of silver bells (the metal of the moon) in your receptive hand.
* Ring the bells once and state your wish.

- Staying within the circle and not moving your feet, circle the wand nine times deosil (clockwise) and repeat the wish nine times.
- Ring the bells once more and say:
  So shall it be by the next waxing moon.
- Leave the moonstone in the centre of the pool of light and move in circles away from it, ringing the bells, circling the wand and chanting your wish as you step into other areas of light on the ground.
- When the light has faded, bury the moonstone where the centre of the main moon circle was.

A full moon wish spell

The concept of holding the full moon in water, crystal or glass is a traditional way of concentrating its energies for a wish you would like fulfilled quickly.

You will need

A clear crystal sphere or clear glass paperweight, ball or globe — it need only be small but should be kept for moon work only; a bowl of still mineral water; a soft white cloth; a bowl of dried mimosa, jasmine or any white petals.

Timing

The night of the full moon or, if the full moon night is not clear, the night after (you need shining moonlight). If the conditions are not right, use a different spell.

The spell

- Go outside in to the moonlight. Lay out the cloth (securing it with a rock if it is windy) and the bowl of water.
- Dedicate your moon globe by plunging it three times in the water in moonlight. Kneel in front of the bowl and say:
  Moon Mother, Moon Mother, Moon Mother, so I call upon your power and your benevolence to enter here.
- Dry the globe with the cloth, repeating the chant.
- Pick up the bowl of petals. Holding the globe in your receptive hand (the one you don't write with), stand up and turn round, scattering petals in a widdershins (anticlockwise) circle around you. As you turn, repeat the chant. Set the bowl of petals in the centre of the petal circle.
- Take up the globe and catch the image of the moon within it (you can work out the positioning by rehearsing this ahead of the spell). Say:
  Lady Moon, I bid you enter and rest awhile, for I would speak with you.
- As you gaze at the moon within the crystal or glass, speak your wish aloud slowly, just once, and then say:
  Lady Moon, you are a welcome visitor, but I would no longer detain you from your journey. I give you thanks for blessings soon to be received.
- Set down the globe and spiral out of the circle, scattering petals until they are all gone and saying your wish in your head over and over again.
- Tip the water in the centre of the circle. Wrap the globe in the cloth and keep it for moon magic.

A faerie dust wish spell

In the faerie lore of old Ireland, it was believed that if you found glittering faerie dust, fallen from the cloak of the beautiful Queen Oonagh, whose white gown shone with pearls and diamonds, any wish would be granted. Fortunately for us, most New Age stores now sell tiny bottles of faerie dust (or glitter). You can use any tube of silver glitter for this spell.

You will need
A small tube of silver glitter.

Timing
When the dew is still on the grass.

The spell
* Stand in any natural circle of trees or bushes, a circular patch of earth, or a clearing. If you can find a faerie ring or a natural circle of toadstools or mushrooms to work in, the spell will be doubly powerful
* Holding the tube of glitter in your power hand (the one you write with), walk round the circle edge nine times deosil (clockwise), saying the wish in your head.
* Go to the centre of the circle and call your wish out once aloud as you scatter just a little of the faerie dust.
* Thank the faeries and nature spirits and walk out of the circle. Do not look back. Save the rest of the glitter for other wishes.

A shell wish spell

There are many spells in which wishes are enclosed in two shells tied together (see page 280) or a single shell is used to carry wishes on the tide. This spell uses half a double shell. It is good for fulfilling wishes that depend in part on the good will or help of others, or are already partly fulfilled but need extra impetus to be completed. This spell should ideally be carried out by the sea or another tidal water. If you are using a non-tidal water, you will have to gently set your shell boat afloat.

You will need
A hollow half shell, preferably found on the shore before the spell; a very small, perfectly round, white stone, preferably found on the shore before the spell.

Timing
Just as the tide is reaching its height.

The spell
* Hold the stone in your cupped hands and softly speak your wish and the time scale you desire.
* Put the stone in to the shell and, holding both in cupped hands, repeat the wish.
* Leave the stone in the shell just below the high tide line, so that the sea will cover it before the tide turns. Make your wish for the third time.
* Turn away and do not look back.

A wish box spell

Wish boxes are found in many cultures. They are a bit like a cosmic suggestion box. Any box with a lid – or the kind with a small drawer in the side – can be used as a wish box. If you think your box may be touched by others, it should have a lock (unless you allow them to post a weekly wish). Use it no more than once a week (and less often if you like). In return, make a pledge to carry out some small helpful action for the good of others. This is part of the cosmic exchange. You must make only positive wishes.

You will need

A medium-sized, lidded box in any material (you must not be able to see into the box when it is shut); a small notebook with removable pages; a pen that you keep solely for your wishes.

Timing

The first Sunday in the month, and thereafter every Sunday if you like.

The spell

* The first time you use your box, hold it between your hands and say:
  May this box be used for the highest purpose and pure intent, abiding by the laws of cosmic exchange. So shall it be!
* Remove a piece of paper from the notebook. Write your wish and beneath it the pledge of help you make in return for its granting.
* Fold the paper as small as possible and place it in the box. Close the box and do not open it until the following Sunday. Do not re-read your wish.
* Try to carry out your part of the bargain before you make the next wish.
* When the box is full, burn the wishes unread and re-dedicate the box by carrying out the first step.

A kite wish spell

Kites are used in Oriental rituals to carry petitions to the deities. The wish is written either on the kite itself or on pieces of cloth or paper tied to the kite's tail. This spell can also be carried out using either a helium balloon with a design linked to your wish (there are an amazing number of different designs) or an ordinary, coloured balloon.

You will need

A children's kite in brilliant colours; some paper luggage labels or a long strip of paper (choose a colour appropriate to your wish, for example yellow for travel and happiness, red for courage, orange for health and fertility, brown or gold for money – see pages 687–90 for colour meanings); some string.

Timing

On a windy day.

The spell

* Write your wish or wishes on the labels or strip of paper. Using the string, tie the labels or paper to the kite tails, making a triple knot and saying:
  Knot tie,
  Kite fly,
  Carry my wishes to the sky.
* Make sure that the kite string itself is fastened only loosely.
* Go to an open space – a common, hilltop or expanse of flat parkland – and run with the kite until it catches the wind. Repeating your chant with increasing speed and volume, gradually let out the string so that the kite goes higher and higher. Feel the string tugging as the kite soars higher.
* Finally, the kite should break free. If it does not, let it go. Call out at this moment:
  The power is free,
  The power in me,
  That I may be (shout your wish).
* Follow the path of the kite until it is out of sight.

A bubble wish spell

This is a simple, fun spell for making a wish come true.

You will need
A children's bubble blower and some bubble mixture or washing-up liquid.

Timing
Whenever you have a wish.

The spell
* Using the bubble blower, blow a bubble. As the bubble ascends, say the first word of your wish aloud. If the bubble breaks, repeat the word.
* Do the same for the second word, and so on until you have spoken the entire wish aloud.

A bread wish spell

The practice of wishing on the making and eating of bread or buns goes back to pre-Christian times. The original hot cross buns were dedicated to the goddess of spring; the pastry cross-represented the astrological glyph for the Earth. Eating the bun symbolised absorbing the abundance of the Earth mother. Even in Christian times hot cross buns retained magical associations and were believed to protect sailors from drowning.

You will need
A bread or bun mix – or make your own.

Timing
Early, so that the bread or buns will be ready for breakfast.

The spell
* Working in silence, make the bread or buns, keeping a little dough aside.

While the dough is rising, rest in any early sunshine or sit quietly by a fire (or heater), weaving your dreams. Let pictures come into your mind of your real needs and wishes.
* When the bread or buns are proved, make a dough image (or images for buns) of what you most desire. Place it on top of the loaf or buns. Alternatively, use the dough to write the initial of your wish on the bread or buns.
* When the bread or buns are cooked, eat them while warm. As you consume the image of your wishes, remember the magical belief that eating your wishes endows you with the power to make them come true. If you have made wishes for family or friends, share the bread with them, but keep the wishes secret.

A knot wish spell

The witches of old tied up the wind in knots. This spell involves knotting a cord with nine knots in ascending order of power. Red cord is traditionally used. The power of the wish can be released at the end of the spell or over the following nine days.

You will need
Nine thin scarves of any colour or nine short cords, just long enough for a knot to be tied in each.

Timing
Traditionally with the sun shining on your back, but any time you need a wish to come true fast.

The spell
* Name your wish aloud.
* Place the nine scarves or pieces of cord on a table and slowly tie a knot

in each until they are all secured together in a circle. As you work, say with increasing intensity:

By the knot of one, the wish is spun.
By the knot of two, this wish comes true.
By the knot of three, the power's in me.
By the knot of four, I make it more.
By the knot of five, the wish is alive.
By the knot of six, the wish is fixed.
By the knot of seven, my cause is leaven.
By the knot of eight, I make my fate.
By the knot of nine, the wish is mine.

* Toss your knotted scarves or cords into the air and then spiral around, waving them and chanting:

My power renewed,
The dream is true,
The wish is free.
So shall it be!

* Gradually slow down and reduce your chant to a whisper, until you are still and silent.

* Sit and make a nine-day plan for materialising your wish. Each morning untie one of your knots as you repeat the chant.

A second knot wish spell

This spell is much slower than the last, but no less powerful. Take your time holding the cord taut and formulating your wish. I have suggested what is a very common order for tying the knots, but, if you prefer, you can tie them along the cord from left to right or from alternate ends inwards. If you have not done this before, practice tying the knots before performing the spell. An old pair of tights is useful for experimenting on.

You will need

A red cord long enough to have nine knots tied in it.

Timing

Traditionally with the sun shining on your back, but any time you need a wish to come true fast.

The spell

* Tie nine knots in the cord, following the order given in the diagram or working to your own order and re-arranging the chant accordingly. Keep on repeating the rhyme for each particular knot until that knot is tied. As you work, speak the chant more and more loudly and intensely but not faster:

Knot one renew my power.
Knot two in courage be.
And so knot three.
The power is more; I make knot four.
And so I strive within knot five.
With fate not fixed, I tie knot six.
My strength I leaven and tie knot seven.
I master fate, and so knot eight.
The wish is mine within knot nine.

* Pull the cord taut and say with confidence:

The wish is mine
Within these knots nine.
The power is free.
So I decree and it shall be!

* Either hang the knots on your wall as a talisman or undo one each day.

A suggested knot tying order

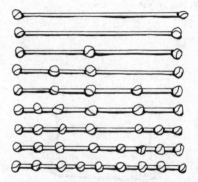

A third knot wish spell

This knot spell is useful if you need immediate fulfilment of the wish.

You will need

A scarf or cord long enough to tie nine knots in.

Timing

Whenever you urgently need a wish fulfilled.

The spell

* Take up the scarf or cord and tie nine knots in it, one on top of the other, as you do so speaking the numbered chant from the spell above.
* When you have finished tying the knots, you can if you like untie them rapidly, one after the other, as you call out the final power chant from either the spell above or the previous one (pages 188–9). (If you want to do this, tie the knots very loosely.) Otherwise, keep the knotted scarf or cord as a talisman.

A candle wish spell

This is probably one of the oldest known spells. It forms the basis not only of many of the spells in this book but also of a large number of those in general magical use. If your wish paper ignites instantly and burns steadily, then your wish will be swiftly accomplished. If it burns slowly, stops, smoulders and goes out – or begins burning again – you wish will still be granted, but it may take longer.

You will need

A large pure-white candle or a candle in a colour that corresponds to your wish (see pages 687–90); a thin strip of paper; a pen; a large deep or flat metal holder for the candle.

Timing

At midnight.

The spell

* Light the candle and look into the flame, visualising whatever you most need or desire moving into your life. Anticipate the pleasure, excitement or relief that the fulfilment of your wish will bring.
* Write the wish on the strip of paper, reading it aloud as you write.
* Repeating the wish, hold the end of the paper in the flame until it catches light.
* Drop the paper on to the metal tray and let it burn away or go out.
* Look into the candle flame once more and visualise again the wish coming true.
* Blow out the candle and whisper:
  The wish is free
  And it shall be!
* Bury the ash and any remaining paper under an evergreen or fruit tree or bush and dispose of the candle.

PART 3

Spells For Success At Work

What we achieve and how we earn our living is an important part of making our mark on the world. We may be working full-time at home, caring for children or older or sick relatives; juggling a part-time job and family commitments; pursuing a long-term career; or in the throes of changing careers mid-way in life. Some of us choose (or need) to work from home, perhaps turning an interest or talent into a money-spinner; others among us prefer the social buzz of the office.

Of course, not all of us work for money. Voluntary work can bring great satisfaction and can also provide a transition back in to paid work after a break – perhaps to have children or to study in order to change professional direction. Indeed, I am often asked to cast spells for those who are returning to work, especially after a period of unemployment or maternity leave, when self-esteem and confidence have sometimes been lost.

As we all know, work comes with its own set of potential problems. There may be setbacks to a project you have nurtured, unexpected unemployment or a lack of opportunities. Or you may find yourself working at a less than satisfactory job simply because it brings in necessary money or fits in with family demands. Jobs now are rarely for life, and the workplace has become more competitive than ever before. Spells can help with work issues in all kinds of ways – by opening doors to opportunity, increasing your profile so that you are not passed over for promotion, or offering a lucky break on the road to success.

This section of the book begins with spells for a happy workplace, a theme I return to in later chapters. Harmony at work is the single most important factor in making the workplace a happy place to be, especially if the nature of the job is demanding or stressful. Whether you work alone at the dining room table (as I do) or on a factory floor with dozens of other people, if the setting is pleasant and relaxing, and relationships between workers are good, the hours pass quickly – and productivity is high.

Some of the spells in this part of the book are from an older, slower world, but one in which there was no welfare system to fall back on. Most, however, have been created to meet the changing needs of modern life. All are aimed at bringing to the fore natural talents and expertise, and finding or shaping the kind of work environment in which you can fulfil your potential.

14 SPELLS FOR a harmonious WORKPLACE

The busiest of workplaces can be harmonious when there is an underlying supportiveness and friendliness that ensures even the most junior worker feels valued and respected. In such places production is generally high and absenteeism low, and people put in extra effort when they are able to, knowing that if there is a crisis at home or they are unwell, it is possible to be leave early without adverse comment. The size of the organisation and the splendour of the building are not relevant to the degree of satisfaction of the workers. There can be more warmth and harmony in a small scruffy unit on an industrial estate than in a state-of-the-art steel and glass architectural wonder with fountains and indoor garden areas. The key is the people rather than the places – though I have suggested in this chapter (and in others throughout the book – see pages 336–8) ways in which the energies of a building and the land it sits on can be balanced and harmonised.

Begin your harmonisation programme with your personal workspace. Like ripples spreading in a pool, gradually the harmony you create around you will reach ever wider, so that over weeks and months the atmosphere becomes lighter and tolerance levels higher. As a result, you can start to draw on these positive energies. On pages 171–8 I have suggested ways to counter spite and negativity; here we will focus on increasing what is positive in the workplace.

A crystal angst shield spell

Even in the most amicable of workplaces, things can get fraught and tempers rise. A large, round, dark crystal is ideal for absorbing angst. Unlike the usually pointed defensive crystals, this one will absorb rather than repel any bad feelings. It works as a background filter and is effective for removing any free-floating negativity or lingering anxiety from the atmosphere.

You will need

A smallish, dark obsidian, onyx, smoky quartz or blue goldstone sphere or egg (blue goldstone is dark blue with golden glints like a starry sky).

Timing

Any.

The spell

* Hold the crystal between your cupped hands. Slowly breathe on your hands three times, between each breath saying:
  Be as a shield for me, to block out negativity.
  Allow only light to pass and harmony.
* Set the crystal in your workspace, somewhere where it faces a door or an area through which people pass.
* Wash the crystal weekly under running water to remove the accumulated angst and allow it to dry naturally.

A spell for creating a rainbow of harmony

Even if the organisation is vast, you can keep energies balanced in your own particular area of the workplace by making a personal crystal rainbow. Keep this in your workspace where it can catch the light and you will find that the people around you – particularly those with whom you closely interact – also become more positive. Carry out this spell at work.

You will need

A small round crystal in each of the following colours: red, orange, yellow, green, blue, purple and white or clear – pick sparkling or vibrant shades; some sparkling mineral water in a clear glass bowl; a filter or sieve; an empty mineral water bottle.

Timing

When there is sunshine after rain.

The spell

* Wash the crystals well under pure running water.
* Drop each of the crystals, in any order, into the bowl of water, as you do so saying either in your head or aloud:
  Rainbow of harmony, shine for me;
  Sparkle and glisten like sun after rain.
  Rainbow of peace, shine for me;
  Sparkle and glisten, shed jewels of light,
  That harmonious moods remain until night.
  (Change 'until night' to 'through the night' if you are a night worker.)
* Leave the crystals in the water.
* Just before you go home, pour the crystal-infused water through the sieve or filter into the mineral water bottle and keep it at work for use in spells (see below). Leave the crystals to dry.
* The next day, place the crytals in a rainbow formation in your workspace where they will catch the light, whether natural or artificial.
* Wash and empower your crystal rainbow weekly, making a new supply of rainbow water.

A rainbow water spell for lifting the atmosphere

Rainbow water made with rainbow crystals is very powerful (see page 194 for the method). However, you can empower it further by using a real rainbow. If you see one, set the bottle of rainbow water close to the window to absorb the extra rainbow radiance. Add a few drops of this water to colleagues' drinks, perhaps before a morning meeting that you know can sometimes get fraught. This spell involves purifying the workspace with rainbow water so that all who enter are uplifted.

You will need
Some rainbow water (see page 194); a spray bottle (the kind used to water plants); some orange essential oil.

Timing
If possible, before anyone else arrives on the first day of the working week, or the first shift you do in that week.

The spell
* Transfer about half of the bottle of rainbow water to the spray bottle and add five drops of orange essential oil (sometimes called the oil of the sun) for added radiance.
* Spray around your own workspace and then in widening circles in the air as far as you can, for as long as the water lasts. As you spray, picture sunbeams and rainbow lights spreading through the air.
* Add a little more rainbow water to the spray bottle and keep it to spray when the mood dips.
* Repeat the ritual weekly, when you make new rainbow water.

A hand washing ritual

This is a quick and easy ritual that can be performed at any time.

What you need
Nothing.

Timing
Whenever things get tense.

The spell
* Make your excuses if necessary and go and wash your hands. Use soap and wash them well, as you do so saying in your head over and over again:

Away from here,
Stay from here,
Stress and disruption.
To peace and to calm
Let there be no interruption.

* Rinse your hands under running water, repeating the chant.
* When you have finished, shake your hands dry, thus symbolically shaking off any residual stress, and say:
Now I am calm again.
Return to work, stress free.

A crystal sphere vitality spell

In feng shui, placing a clear crystal sphere (known as 'the essence of the dragon' in the Orient) near a telephone or on top of a computer or fax machine brings in advantageous business calls. Set near the centre of a workspace it will also attract positive health-giving energies, vitality and positivity. The crystal used in this spell is a complement to the one in the crystal angst shield spell on page 194. Work this spell under a skylight, a glass dome or in the open air, so that the light falls directly downwards onto the crystal. Find the right place in advance.

You will need

A smallish clear crystal sphere (real crystal rather than glass).

Timing

When there is bright sunlight.

The spell

* Go to your chosen spot and hold the sphere between cupped hands so that the light filters down in to it, activating it with the life force.
* Keeping your hands still, picture the light, amplified by the crystal, passing into you and filling you with light and vitality. Say:
  Be to me the key; be to me the light that whether rain falls or clouds blacken the sky, you fill me still with pure vitality.
* Hold the crystal for a while as it fills with light, then carry it – if possible in a raised position – to the centre of your work space. Here it will cast its positive energies around you whenever you feel that you are being depressed by a heavy or negative atmosphere.

An oil harmony spell

Certain essential oils are natural harmonisers and can be introduced into the workplace to create a calm atmosphere. Aside from their recognised aromatherapy qualities, they can be empowered to release tranquillity no matter how high the pressure of the job or how fraught the situation. If the moon is not shining on the night you carry out this spell, you should light a silver-coloured candle.

You will need

A bottle of essential oil in a harmonising fragrance such as lemon verbena, orange, neroli (orange blossom), rosewood or melissa (lemon balm); a wand (be it a pointed crystal, a wand you have purchased from a New Age store or a twig – see page 184); a silver-coloured candle (optional).

Timing

The night of the full moon.

The spell

* Go out into the moonlight (or if it is a cloudy night work indoors by the light of the candle). Hold the unopened bottle of oil in your receptive hand (the one you do not write with) and the wand in your power hand.
* Point to the moon (or the ceiling) with the wand, as you do so saying:
  By Lady Moon I call down peace into this wand, if right it is to be.
* Circle the oil bottle with the wand three times deosil (clockwise) and say:
  By Lady Moon I call down harmony into this wand, if right it is to be.
* Circle the oil bottle with the wand three times widdershins (anticlockwise). Say:

By Lady Moon I call tranquillity into this wand, if right it is to be.

* Tap the lid of the oil three times with the wand and say:
  By Lady Moon I banish here anxiety, stress, disharmony, for it is right to be.
* Leave the sealed bottle with the wand in front of it in the moonlight (or in front of the candle until it has burnt down).
* The next morning, take the bottle with you to work, add a couple of drops of oil to a cup of warm water and place it on your desk or workbench. If you sit near a radiator, you can balance a saucer of oil-in-water on top of it, or soak a cotton wool ball with the oil and put that on the radiator. A sense of background tranquillity will emanate.
* Top up as necessary. You can empower different fragrances in the same way at each full moon.

Making a harmony spell bag for the workplace

Spell bags are the eastern and western European equivalent of the Afro-American mojo bag. They usually contain symbolic items, such as metal, a crystal, a natural object and fragrance. Once filled, they are empowered and closed.

You will need
A pale-blue drawstring bag or purse; some pale-blue cord; an unbroken silver chain bracelet or necklace; a blue lace agate crystal; some crushed and dried lavender heads; a small blue candle (optional).

Timing
At 10 pm on a Monday.

The spell
* Assemble all you will need. Place the chain or bracelet, crystal and lavender heads one by one into the bag or purse, working by a very dim lamp or the light of the small blue candle. Work in total silence.
* Close the bag or purse by winding the cord around it and sealing it with three knots.
* Now speak the empowerment by forming the words with your lips but making no sound. State the name of the workplace the spell bag is for, the purpose and any people who especially need the calm. Say silently:
  I made it; only I can empower it, and so I do.
* Touch the centre of your brow, between and just above your eyes. This is the site of the third, or psychic, eye. Now, with a flick, push the energy from the third eye into the bag. Speak aloud, saying:
  Enter here, the power of peace; empower, bless and protect all.
* Keep the harmony spell bag not in your drawer but somewhere else in the workplace, where it will not be found.
* Check the spell bag every two or three weeks. When it has lost its fragrance, it must be dismantled, the contents buried, the bag burnt and a new spell bag made.

A tapping spell for keeping the balance

This is an almost instant spell you can use to restore balance, first your own and then – gradually – that of the people around you. The more you practise office spells, the quicker they are to activate and the more wide-ranging are the results.

You will need

A distinctive pen to use for nothing but this spell; an amethyst; a dark scarf.

Timing

Any time on a Friday.

The spell

* Either at home or at work (if you can be alone), start to tap the pen on a surface gently and rhythmically.
* Once you have a rhythm, chant softly aloud as you tap:
  Nought harm,
  All calm.
  Tension cease;
  Be at peace.
* Tap and chant the words aloud about 50 times (you need not count precisely).
* Keep the pen in your workspace, but out of sight, where it cannot be borrowed. Whenever you start to feel unbalanced or the emotional temperature in the workplace rises, get out the pen and start tapping the rhythm very softly, so as not to increase irritation in others. Chant the words in your head, over and over again, until you feel the stress levels falling.
* Once a week wrap your pen in the dark scarf together with the amethyst and leave it overnight to recharge it. Wash the amethyst in the morning.

A screen saver spell

There are many screen savers available. Find one that captures for you the essence of utmost tranquillity, whether a rainforest, an ocean, a starry galaxy or a holiday photograph.

You will need

Your favourite screen saver.

Timing

Whenever you get tense.

The spell

* Call up your screen saver. Using your two index fingers, point directly at the screen, so that they almost touch a particular image within the screen saver. Allow your fingers rather than your conscious mind to select the image.
* Raise your arms over your head, as though stretching, and then return your hands to your sides, all the time focusing on that one image.
* Count slowly from nought to ten and then say in your head:
  Take me there where I would be.
  Here is not the place for me.
* Keep focusing on the image, so that you can smell, feel, hear and taste the sensations of being there. Make the image grow larger and larger in your mind until it enfolds you.
* When you are ready – usually after no more than a minute, although you may feel as if you have been away forever – count back slowly from ten to nought. Stretch again and switch back to work mode, exchanging your screen saver for the business in hand.
* Next time you feel tense, return to the same place on the screen saver or to another aspect of the scene. Eventually, you will be able to switch into altered consciousness just by looking at the screen saver.

A radiant flower spell

On page 131 I write about the importance of the life force (called *prana* in India and *ch'i* in China) to health and well-being. Prana is also central to a sense of harmony. If you work where there is no fresh air coming in through windows, only air conditioning, or if the nature of the work generates a lot of tension (perhaps at times when there are urgent deadlines), your workplace may from time to time suffer from pranic deficiency. The colour and fragrance of flowers is a good transmitter of this energy and will restore your personal calm as well as spreading pranic energy around your workplace. If you prefer, you can exhale through your nose for the breathing part of this spell.

You will need

A growing, flowering, scented plant or a vase of brightly coloured scented flowers — alternatively a dish of aromatic fruit such as oranges, lemons or limes, pierced to release the smell.

Timing

When you start to feel stagnant and notice other people getting fidgety.

The spell

- Focus on the plant, vase of flowers or fruit, inhaling the fragrance slowly. Let your abdomen and then your chest fill with breath. Picture this breath as the same colour as the plant, flowers or fruit.
- Slowly exhale any stagnation or tension through your mouth as if sighing (silently if necessary). You can visualise this as a dark mist.
- Carry on breathing in this way, aiming to establish a regular slow rhythm.
- Now for the magic bit. When you feel full of fragrance and light, mentally project your out-breath so that you can see in your mind's eye the aura of its colour spreading over the whole room and bringing a sense of peace. Others may comment on how intense the fragrance of the flowers has become. This is the point at which you know the magic has worked.

A spell to counter a disruptive office member or factions

White sugar is second to none for an instant sweetening spell. When someone at work is being sour or you can sense backbiting, empowered sugar will sweeten the culprits almost instantly. If the people concerned drink sweetened tea or coffee, so much the better.

You will need

Some boiling water; a jug; some white sugar; a teaspoon.

Timing

During a natural break in the day.

The spell

* Pour a small quantity of the boiling water in to the jug. Add to it a teaspoonful of sugar for each of the difficult people.
* Stir enthusiastically widdershins (anticlockwise), saying in your head:

Dissolve, be sweeter;
Acid tongues be still.
Words be of honey;
Be there good will!

* Stir until the sugar is dissolved.
* Pour the sugar water down the plughole, as you do so saying:

Flow and grow sweet.
When we do meet,
Your sugary smile
Will last a while
And maintain this harmony.

* If the difficult people take sugar, stir their drinks widdershins as you add sugar or sweetener and recite the chant. If they do not take sugar, briefly touch the bottom of their cup or mug with the unwashed spoon you used for the spell. This will magically transfer the sweetening energies.

A herb spell to create a happy workplace

A very old method of transforming disharmony into peace was to get those who entered a dwelling to walk across or through a specially empowered peace substance. Both this and the following spell work by transferring the harmonious essence of herbs to both the workplace and the people who walk across the floor.

You will need

4 tbsp unscented baby powder; some rosewood or lemon verbena essential oil; 2 tsp crushed chamomile flowers or lavender heads; a mortar and pestle, or a ceramic bowl and small wooden or glass spoon; a stick of rose or strawberry incense; a strong envelope.

Timing

At dusk on a Sunday evening if possible – otherwise, any evening at dusk.

The spell

* Light the incense stick and place it near the mortar or bowl – somewhere where the ash will not fall in.
* Put the powder in the bowl, add the crushed flowers and then add eight drops of the oil, mixing all well together and chanting:

Peace and calm and harmony
Within this mix. Blessed be!

* When you have finished mixing, write the chant just once in incense smoke in the air over the bowl, then leave the incense to burn through.
* Put the mix in the envelope or padded bag and take it with you to work. Each morning put just a pinch outside the entrance to the workplace, so that the good vibes will enter as people walk in.

A second herb spell to create a happy workplace

Though simpler, this spell works on the same principle as the preceding one.

You will need
A few lavender heads or some dried rose petals or some grains of culinary sage — alternatively a commercial lavender- or rose-scented floor freshening powder.

Timing
On the last day of the week you work, before you go home.

The spell
* Offer to sweep or vacuum your room or work area.
* Scatter the lavender heads, rose petals, sage or floor freshening powder on the floor, from your workspace to the door. (You may have to wait until everyone has gone home.)
* Sweep or vacuum in widdershins (anticlockwise) circles, as you do so imagining all the dark vibes being absorbed and leaving an invisible carpet of flowers.
* Repeat monthly to keep the office psychically sweet.

A happy outing, workplace party or training weekend bean spell

Socialising with people who work with you, as opposed to those you count as friends, can be difficult. There may be generational differences, as well as the thought that the person to whom you told hilarious jokes about the managing director under the influence of more bottles of wine than were good for you heads the promotions board. This spell will ensure that everyone gets on well with one another and that you create the right impression. (If someone you would like to know better will be at the event, place two of the beans in a pink purse and take it along, keeping it with you all evening.)

You will need
A packet of dried butter beans or kidney beans; a strong fabric drawstring bag (the larger the workforce, the bigger the bag).

Timing
The evening before the social or training event.

The spell
* Take a bean for each person attending the event, including yourself. If there are a lot of people, you can take an approximate representative number.
* Add the beans to the bag one by one, saying for each:
  You are welcome. I am welcome. Let us enjoy each other's company without fear or favour and good times savour.
* When you have added all the beans, close the bag tightly and shake it vigorously ten times, as you do so saying:
  Mingle and mix,
  Join and blend.
  For this one night / day
  Shall differences end.
  Be of good cheer,
  Be of good company,
  For this one night / day,
  Friends we shall be.
* Just before you leave for the event, shake the bag and repeat both chants.

An office jungle filter spell

Green plants are a good filter for any negativity at work. They can also defend against any negative land energies beneath the workplace. However, workplace plants can get tired and so fail to flourish. Use this simple spell to enable your workplace plants retain their health and vitality and thus to shield you.

You will need

One of the following Bach Flower Remedies: Impatiens, Rock Rose, Star of Bethlehem or Five Flower Rescue Remedy – alternatively choose any Remedy that works for you.

Timing

When a workplace plant starts to wilt or there has been a lot of stress in the workplace – otherwise, every week or so.

The spell

* Take the Bach Flower Remedy bottle to work and leave it somewhere where light falls on it all day.
* Just before you go home, hold the bottle between your hands and say:
  Empowered be this essence, sister to the plants who call upon your strength, brother of all green things here who bring protecting calm and harmony. Blessed be by the mother of all nature and by me!
* Add a single drop of the essence to the soil, near the roots of the plant.

An amethyst weekly cleaning spell

On page 198 I give an amethyst spell for cleansing a home or workplace of negative earth energies. This is a simple weekly maintenance spell to filter out any negativity that may be left behind to sour the atmosphere over a weekend or holiday.

You will need

A pointed amethyst crystal.

Timing

Before the building will be empty for a period or when you feel that the atmosphere is heavy.

The spell

* As you leave your workplace to go home, turn around and point the sharp end of the amethyst towards the building (you can stand a distance away if there are people around).
* Visualise rows of dark grey dots being drawn from the building and converging around the point of the amethyst. You may feel a pull like that of a magnet. Say:
  Dust and debris from the earth, stagnation and sourness transform and be filled with light.
* Holding the crystal tightly, turn round widdershins (anticlockwise), as you do so flicking any remaining negativity off the amethyst and saying:
  Crystal be clear and filled with light.
* When you get home, wash the amethyst under running water and keep it in a dark cloth until you next need it.

An office elemental spell for harmony and balance

In the Westernised world, elemental balancing can work better than feng shui, which was created for Far Eastern spaces. Ideally, there should be an elemental balance, with all four elements represented. This spell will ensure that all is in harmony.

You will need

A compass; one item from each of the following elemental groups:

Earth: Herbs, flowers, miniature trees, coins, fruit, nuts and seeds, pot pourri, pot plants, wood, clay, fabrics, ceramics, cushions, mosaics, paper, account files and books of all kinds, anything green or brown.

Air: Feathery grasses, stainless steel and chrome, paper clips and knives, fans, pencils and pens, pins, scissors, all technological equipment including computers and phones, tools or instruments, ceiling mobiles, wind chimes, keys, fragrances and fragrance sprays, anything yellow or grey.

Fire: Lights of all kinds, especially fibre optic lamps, sun catchers, crystal spheres of all kinds, essential oils, natural sunshine, rainbows, oranges and all orange fruit, sunflowers and all golden or orange flowers, gold foil, anything made of glass, radiators, dragon images, gold jewellery, anything gold, orange or red.

Water: Milk, water, tea, coffee, juices, sea shells, water features, vases and all containers, nets or webs of any kind, dream catchers, fish in tanks, sea creature and dolphin images, silk scarves, silver bells on cords, Tibetan singing bowls, anything made of silver or copper, silver foil, anything blue or silver.

Timing

When you feel the need for balance at work.

The spell

* Use the compass to find the directions.
* Set an Earth item in the North of your workspace, an Air item in the East, a Fire item in the South and a Water item in the West. If possible, do the same in the room or area where you yourself work.
* Face each of the four directions in turn, saying at each (in your head if necessary):

Earth, Air, Water, Fire,
Bring the balance I desire.
Air, Water, Fire, Earth,
Bring harmony and peace to birth.
I seek a peaceful workplace.

A spell to bring more Earth into the workplace

If you, your colleagues or your seniors in the workspace are being unusually critical, sarcastic or witty at the expense of others, there is an excess of Air and you need more Earth. Other symptoms of this imbalance include gossiping, being liberal with the truth and losing data or forgetting appointments.

You will need

An item from the Earth list above.

Timing

When you sense an imbalance as above.

The spell

* Introduce the Earth item into your workplace – if possible into the room where you work, as you do so saying in your head:

Earth, add stability and bring peace.

A spell to bring more Air into the workplace

If you notice that you or those around you are being unusually unenthusiastic, sluggish, obsessed with details, pessimistic, fussy about neatness or possessive about property, there may be an excess of Earth around.

You will need

An item from the Air list on page 203

Timing

When you sense an imbalance as above.

The spell

* Introduce the Air item into your workplace – if possible to the room where you work, as you do so saying in your head:

Air, add lightness and bring peace.

A spell to bring more Water into the workplace

If you notice that you or those around you are being unusually irritable and impatient, throwing temper tantrums, flirting excessively, forcing an unrealistic pace of work on self and others or becoming increasingly accident-prone, there may be an excess of Fire.

You will need

An item from the Water list on page 203.

Timing

When you sense an imbalance as above.

The spell

* Add the Water item to your workplace – if possible to the room where you work, as you do so saying in your head:

Water, add empathy and bring peace.

A spell to bring more Fire into the workplace

If you notice that you or those around you are becoming over-emotional about a professional matter, being manipulative, playing favourites, instigating rivalries or being over-sensitive to constructive advice, there may be an excess of Water.

You will need

An item from the Fire list on page 203.

Timing

When you sense an imbalance as above.

The spell

* Add the Fire symbol to your workplace – if possible to the room where you work, as you do so saying in your head:

Fire, add illumination and bring peace.

15 SPELLS FOR FINDING A NEW JOB

I am frequently asked to cast or recommend spells for finding the right job, be it a first job after school or college, a second step on a planned career ladder or a return to work after an absence. Finding a job may prove difficult because of high unemployment in the area where you live or because a redundancy, illness or personal crisis has robbed you of confidence. In any of these cases a spell can give you the determination, together with the opportunity, to get back into the workplace and succeed.

While ultimately it is your own talent and charisma that will land you the position you want and ensure that you do well, a spell can help to make your application form or CV stand out from the pile and will ensure that you shine at an interview. It can also provide that crucial initial impetus that gets the plane off the tarmac and you into the job market.

A spell to boost your confidence before an interview

If you value your strengths and talents, your sense of confidence will permeate both your applications and your performance at interviews. This spell involves making a featureless clay image of yourself and endowing it with power. The power resides partly in the fact that you have made the image yourself.

You will need
Natural clay (available from craft shops) or modelling clay made from plain flour, water and cooking oil (knead it to make it soft); some salt; a stick of pine, lemon or cedar incense; some sparkling mineral water or bubbling tap water; some clear glass nuggets; some gold-coloured nuggets.

Timing
A sunny day if possible.

The spell
* If possible, work outside barefoot on grass, sand or soil, so that your feet touch the earth as you work. Mould the clay into a featureless image of yourself, as you do so picturing yourself working successfully in the job of your choice.
* Sprinkle the figure with a little salt, pass the incense stick over it, hold it to the light and finally sprinkle it with the water. Say:
  Through Earth, Air, Water and Fire
  Comes the job I most desire.
* Press the clear and gold-coloured nuggets over the figure, as you do so saying:
  So do I shine bright and so my true worth is recognised.
* Keep the figure on a window ledge in your bedroom, where sun, moon and stars can shine on it. Set it before you when you fill in application forms and touch it before going for an interview or to post an application, reciting both chants and feeling the power enter you. Recite the chants before any interview. You will find that interviews go well and doors begin to open.

A spell to overcome a lack of confidence

If you are looking for your first job or you have suffered a series of rejections, you may lack faith in yourself. This can make it harder to apply for posts and may also instil your applications and interviews with a sense of self-defeat. This spell uses the power of the air to blow away doubt and get the energies moving.

You will need
A feather you have found; some very fine thread.

Timing
A windy day.

The spell
* Find a tree or bush on top of a hill or in an exposed space. Hawthorn is especially powerful.
* Tie the feather very loosely to the end of a branch, as high as you can reach. As you do so say:
  Fly high, let me succeed, be freed from doubt and fear, that I may hear good news.
* Walk away without looking back.
* When you get home, apply for a job or read the situations vacant section of a newspaper. Once the feather pulls free, your confidence will soar and opportunities will come as a result.

A quick candle spell before filling in an application form

Among a pile of applications, it is easy for some to get overlooked. This is an effective way of getting yourself to the top of the pile.

You will need
A bright orange candle in a deep holder; some salt; the application form; the pen you will use to fill it in.

Timing
Before filling in an application.

The spell
❋ Light the candle and set in front of it the blank application form and pen.
❋ Look into the candle flame, sprinkle a little salt into it, and as it sparkles say:
So may I shine that you will notice me favourably, whatever applications there may be.
❋ Blow out the candle and say:
Sparkle and shine, notice me favourably.
❋ As you fill in the application form, picture it on top of the pile.
❋ Repeat the chants when you post or e-mail the application.

A candle spell before phoning to enquire about a vacancy or fix an interview

It can be nerve-wracking to phone about a job – especially if you have to ring repeatedly because the relevant person is not available or is too busy to talk. Yet a phone call is an ideal opportunity to make a favourable first impression. This spell will help you to get through to the right person and will ensure a positive response.

You will need
A yellow candle; the advertisement or piece of paper with the phone number.

Timing
Just before phoning about a job – you can have the phone ready and speed-dial.

The spell
❋ Using a well ventilated room, if possible close to the phone, light the candle and read the advertisement or contact details aloud.
❋ Gently blow on the candle so that it flickers but does not go out.
❋ Address the person you are calling out loud by name, as though you were actually speaking to them. Say:
May I speak to you about this job. I am just the person you are looking for.
❋ Blow out the candle and say:
I will call now. Please answer me.
❋ Phone as soon as you can after the spell. If the number is engaged, keep trying and persist until you reach the person you need to talk to.

A nine-day spell to find a job in a location of high unemployment or in an area of expertise where there is a lot of competition

If you are up against much competition for a job, you can raise your own profile in the application process by performing this spell.

You will need

A dark-blue candle; a bright-blue candle; a success candle-dressing oil (available from New Age stores or by mail order on the Internet) or some pure olive oil in a small dish; a nail file, small paper knife or other inscribing tool.

Timing

At the same time each night if possible, starting on a Thursday.

The spell

* On the side of the dark-blue candle inscribe the words 'new job be mine'.
* Working widdershins (anticlockwise) from the bottom to the centre of the candle and deosil (clockwise) downwards from the top to the centre, rub the candle with the oil, as you do so, focusing on getting an interview and starting in the job and repeating over and over again:
New job be mine!
* Light the candle, remembering to be careful, as candles are more flammable when dressed with oil. Look into the flame and say:

Let me get a job before (time).
* Blow out the candle and say:
New job be mine!
* Repeat these steps for three more days.
* On the fifth day, inscribe and rub with oil (as above) the bright-blue candle.
* Light the dark-blue candle and say:
Doubt fade away; renewed be as certainty!
* Light the bright-blue candle from the dark-blue one and extinguish the darker candle, as you do so saying:
Doubt fade away; renewed be as certainty!
* On the final four nights, light only the bright-blue candle and, gazing into the flame, say:
New job be mine!
* Blow out the candle, as you do so repeating:
Doubt fade away; renewed be as certainty!
* On the final night, light the candle and repeat the words:
New job be mine!
* Let the candle burn through.
* Dispose of the wax saying:
Doubt fade away; renewed be as certainty!
* The next morning make a massive effort to scour every source of potential jobs, even ones that have been unfruitful in the past.

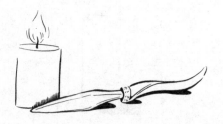

Five St Joseph employment prayers

St Joseph the carpenter, earthly father of Jesus, is invoked by Roman Catholics and non-Catholics alike for getting a job. He has been called on in times of mass unemployment and also by individuals seeking reassurance and help when mortal efforts fail. He is also asked to grant permanent employment if only temporary or part-time jobs are on offer. Joseph is pictured at a carpenter's bench or holding the baby Jesus.

Prayer 1: Found on an old prayer card with a picture of St Joseph, given by nuns to my late grandfather during the early 1920s, when he walked from the Midlands to Wales to try to get work in the mines:

*Dear St Joseph, you provided for your family
with your own hands. May I like you earn
bread to feed my family and not be forced to beg
it.*

Prayer 2: From the rosary recited in honour of St Joseph. Recite it nine times while waking slowly in a circle until you have finished. You can add your personal request for work after the prayer:

*Hail Joseph, the Carpenter of Nazareth.
The Lord is with Thee.
Blessed art Thou among all workmen.
And blessed is Jesus, the Carpenter's Son.*

Prayer 3: Again, state your specific need after the prayer:

*Remember, loving St Joseph, ... that no one ever
had recourse to your protection, implored your
help, or sought your intercession and was left
forsaken. Filled therefore with confidence in your
goodness ... I ask you graciously hear and grant
my petition.*

Prayer 4: To be written six times on white paper in black ink, folded and set in front of a pure-white candle:

*St Joseph the Worker, that the unemployed may
find work, I/we beseech you, hear me/us.*

Leave the candle to burn through and keep the paper in a drawer or box until you get work, when you should burn it.

Prayer 5: This is the prayer for employment most commonly associated with St Joseph – it is my favourite.

*Dear Saint Joseph, you were yourself once faced
with the responsibility of providing the necessities
of life for Jesus and Mary. Look down with
fatherly compassion upon me in my anxiety over
my present inability to support myself/my
family. Please help me to find gainful
employment very soon, that I am soon able to
provide for myself/those whom God has
entrusted to my care. Help me to guard against
bitterness and discouragement, so that I may
emerge from this trial spiritually enriched and
with even greater blessings from God. Amen.*

A salt spell to do well in a interview

In the Afro-American tradition, empowered salt was sprinkled in an interview room when no one is looking to gain the admiration of the interviewer. Obviously, this is very difficult to pull off in practice. However, it may be possible to leave a silver foil twist of empowered salt in the waiting room, in your coat or carry it in your bag or pocket into the interview. The ingenuity comes in leaving the twist in the building afterwards without causing a security alert.

You will need

Some sea salt; a dish; 10 thin brass curtain rings; a string of bells; some silver foil.

Timing

Five, ten, 15 or 20 hours before the interview, according to which is most practical.

The spell

* Put one of the rings on each of your fingers and place the salt in the dish.

* Hold the silver bells over the salt and ring them, as you do so saying:
  Silver bell and golden ring,
  Good fortune to me bring.
  Salt of wealth and health and power,
  Bring success to me this hour (name the hour of the interview).

* Place the string of bells in a circle around the bowl of salt and drop the rings from your fingers, one by one, to form an outer circle around the bells. Then repeat the chant.

* Leave the salt in the circles until an hour before you leave for the interview.

* Using the foil, make three twists of salt.

* Put one foil twist in the lowest place in the house and another in the highest place in the house, to represent your ascent in fortune. Take the remaining foil twist to the interview.

* Wash the rest of the salt away under flowing water (such as a tap) to set the energies moving.

A spell to obtain good references

References can sometimes be a worry, especially if you have been out of work for a while or parted on less than friendly terms with your previous employer. Even if you have passed the interview and are sure your referees will be positive, waiting for confirmation that all is well and the desired job is yours can be anxiety-provoking. Use this spell to ensure that all goes smoothly and the references are glowing.

You will need

A photograph of yourself looking happy; some olive, ivy, laurel (bay) or other large evergreen leaves on pliant stalks or fronds; some copper wire cut to form a circle to fit the top of your head; a purple candle.

Timing

The brightest part of the day.

The spell

* Plait the evergreen fronds around the circle of copper wire to make a crown. If necessary, secure the edges with twine. (Victors in a number of cultures, including the Roman, wore laurel crowns.) As you work, picture yourself receiving praise for good work at your new job, even though you may have been offered the position subject to references.
* Put on the circlet, name your referees as though you were addressing them and say:
  Think highly of me,
  Speak highly of me,
  That I may victory see
  In this job I so greatly desire.
* Set the circlet around the photograph of yourself and repeat the chant.
* Light the purple candle and let the colour of victory and of rightful acclaim shine down.
* Leave the candle to burn through and put the photo where it will remind you of good times past and promise even better times ahead.

A candle spell for preparing a CV

A good CV can be crucial in determining whether we get to the interview stage in the job application process. However carefully your CV is prepared, there is an element of luck involved in determining whether it is read and how favourably it is received.

You will need

A photocopy or print-out of your CV; a green candle in a heatproof holder; a metal tray.

Timing

Before you post or e-mail your CV.

The spell

* Place the candle in its holder on the metal tray, and your copy CV in front of the candle (also on the metal tray).
* Light the candle so that the light shines on the CV. Say:
  May I be reflected in the most positive light
  and my good qualities shine through.
* Carefully drip wax on each of the four corners of the CV. When the wax is set, fold the corners inwards and drip more wax to seal the paper. Say:
  So I set a seal upon my fortune.
* Blow out the candle, as you do so repeating:
  May I be reflected in the most positive light
  and my good qualities shine through.
* Post the fair copy of your CV. Keep the wax-sealed copy where it will not be touched but the daylight can shine on it.

A three-day spell to find the job of your dreams

This is a general spell that works for all employment-seeking situations. However, it is especially effective for obtaining a particular job you have always wanted or for gaining an opening in a new field that interests you. The spell is a slightly more complex version of the previous one.

You will need

An advertisement for the job you would like, or paper and pen to write you own job advert; 3 deep-blue candles in broad-based holders; a metal tray large enough for all 3 candles.

Timing

If possible, three consecutive nights during the waxing moon – best of all the two nights leading up to the full moon and the night of the full moon itself.

The spell

* Set the candles, in the holders, in a row on the tray.
* Light the left-hand candle.
* Read the job advert aloud or write an advert for your ideal job by the light of the candle and then read it aloud. Say:
I ask for this job;
This job is for me.
Bring it closer,
And ever closer be.
* Place the paper on the tray in front of the lighted candle. Blow out the candle and leave the job advert there.
* On the second day, light the left-hand and the central candle. Read the job description aloud again and repeat the rhyme above.
* Place the job description in front of the middle candle. Blow out both candles in reverse order of lighting and leave the job advert there.
* On the third day, light all three candles – first the left-hand one, then the middle one and finally the right-hand one. Read the job advert aloud for a third time, repeat the chant and place the advert beneath the right-hand candle.
* Roll the job advert into a taper shape and hold it briefly in all three flames in turn so that the paper just catches alight, moving from left to right and being careful not to burn yourself.
* Drop the taper on the tray (not too near the candles). When it is burnt, crush the ashes.
* Leave the candles to burn through and scatter the ashes to the wind.

An instant spell for making the right job appear

You may know the job you want and have the right experience and qualifications, but it seems that wherever you look there are no suitable vacancies in your field. This spell will open possibilities of finding your position through sources you had not considered, as well as attracting opportunities.

You will need

5 flat stones; a body of water.

Timing

At any time you are searching for a job.

The spell

* Say aloud the kind of the job you want.
* One at a time, skim the stones over the water, saying each time a stone hits the water:
Fly over the water and send what I desire to me.
* Repeat every day for a week.

A second instant spell for making the right job appear

If you don't live near a body of water (required for the spell on page 212), try this spell.

You will need
Nothing.

Timing
At any time you are searching for a job.

The spell
* Name aloud the kind of job you want.
* Go to a hill, stand on top of it and call out ten times:
  Find me, hire me; I am right for your vacancy.
* Run or walk down the hill as fast as you can, repeating the words.

A spell to get a first job or to return to work after an interval away

I originally devised this spell as a general employment one, but feedback from readers suggests that it works especially well for school or college leavers and for people returning to work after an absence of weeks or months.

You will need
A large deep-blue or white pillar candle on a very broad metal holder or tray; a strip of white paper and a pen (optional); a brown paper bag; a pot of mint (optional).

Timing
The morning the newspaper with suitable jobs is published or before a visit to a Job Centre or careers office.

The spell
* Find an advertisement for a job you have seen and would like, or use the paper and pen to make up an advertisement for your ideal job.
* Light the candle.
* Read the advertisement aloud three times and then form it into a taper and slowly burn it in the candle flame, allowing the ash to fall on the candle-holder or tray.
* When the taper is burnt, gather the ash in a small brown paper bag. (If the taper goes out, it simply means you may have to be extra persistent in your attempts to land the job you desire.)
* Bury the ash from the paper beneath a power tree such as an oak or ash. If you cannot find a suitable tree, bury the ash in a pot of mint (a powerful energiser).

A Celtic spell for an active approach to job hunting

You may have decided it is time to move on from your present job to something more fulfilling, stimulating, better paid or just less stressful. This spell works well for job changes of all kinds and will give you impetus to keep trying if previous efforts to gain employment have failed. In the Celtic world, Cernunnos, the antlered god, was father of winter, animals and the hunt. He was invoked in order that the huntsmen might catch their prey. Other cultures have their own horned gods, including Svantovit in the Slavic tradition and Pan in ancient Greece. If you are a poor shot, practise in advance so that the spell goes smoothly. If you like, you can carry out the spell at an archery range (even beginners can pick up the skill of archery with half an hour's instruction).

You will need

A paper and pen; a bow, arrows and a target (a children's archery set is fine) or a dartboard and darts.

Timing

Whenever there is clear light.

The spell

- On the piece of paper write down exactly what you are aiming for career-wise. Assess the time it will take in weeks (or even months for a long-term objective) and devise a game plan.
- Pin the paper to the centre of the target or dartboard.
- Take three arrows or darts and shoot them one at a time towards the centre of the paper, saying for each:
  My aim is true; my goal is set. Cernunnos, I hunt for my success.
- Take your time and focus on getting the arrow or dart as near as you can to the centre of the paper. If any arrows fall to the floor or miss the target, you can repeat the exercise.

16 SPELLS FOR IMPROVING YOUR CAREER AND GAINING PROMOTION

The career ladder is not for everybody. Some people are happy in a low-paid or relatively unchallenging job as long as the atmosphere is good and the work not stressful. Career issues may also take a back seat during a phase in our life when other aspects predominate – perhaps because we have young children or because we are pursuing an interest. If this is the case for you, this chapter will be of only passing interest. If you are happy with your current work situation, you should not feel pressurised to be more ambitious – job satisfaction is worth a great deal. Others, though, do want a job with more responsibility, greater opportunities and perhaps the chance to take further qualifications or get training.

The spells in this chapter focus on gaining tangible recognition for your efforts at work. This may be in the form of a salary increase or promotion, or it may entail doors opening to wider opportunity and the possibility of greater job satisfaction – whether or not that involves a high-flying career. For spells regarding career changes, have a look at Chapter 18. You may also find some of the spells in Part 6, Spells for Changes and Transitions, useful in this connection.

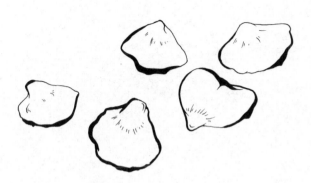

A yellow crystal sun spell to get your talents recognised

The sun is associated with success and the flowering of talent, as well as financial rewards. If you work hard and get results but are passed over for promotion, or you are labelled as reliable but unexciting, a sun spell will make sure you shine.

You will need

Any small sparkling yellow crystal, such as a topaz, citrine or spinel, or alternatively a clear quartz crystal

Timing

In early morning sunlight or natural light on a Monday.

The spell

* Hold the crystal up to the light in your power hand (the one you write with) and say:

Sun enter and empower me that I may likewise shine.

* Lift the stone to your mouth and blow slowly three times on to the crystal to endow it with your essence.
* Wear or carry the crystal. When you get to work, set it where the light will continue to fall on it right through until 3 pm (you may have to use artificial light on a dark day or in a dark workplace).
* Repeat the first two steps at 9 am, 12 pm and 3 pm (or as close to these times as you can), each time returning the crystal to where it can absorb light.
* Take the crystal home with you after work and repeat the ritual each day, right through your working week.

A gold candle recognition spell for darker days

Gold is the colour associated with career advancement, especially if advancement involves a significant salary rise. This spell is a good alternative to the previous one if the weather is dull or you work nights.

You will need

A large gold-coloured candle; an item of gold or gold-coloured jewellery; a small yellow or gold-coloured heatproof dish; a long pin (such as a hat pin).

Timing

When you hear that promotions or salary increases are likely at work, if possible before the start of a shift.

The spell

* Using the pin, write invisibly along the side of the candle the words 'recognition, promotion, reward'.
* Place the jewellery in the dish and set it in front of the candle. Light the candle.
* Write in the air, over the jewellery: 'recognition, promotion, reward'.
* Lift the dish so that it is above the flame but not too close and say aloud: *So do I rise. Flare flame and carry me to success. Recognition, promotion, reward are mine.*
* Return the dish to its place in front of the candle and say three times: *Recognition, promotion, reward are mine.*
* Blow out the candle and wear or carry the jewellery with you to work.

An instant sun water spell to ask for advancement

You will have to wait your moment for this spell.

You will need

A bottle of unopened sparkling mineral water.

Timing

When you want to ask for a promotion or salary increase but feel too shy.

The spell

* Take the bottle of mineral water to work and keep it somewhere in your work area where sunlight at times shines in to the water. (Experiment to find the best place.)
* Whenever the water is filled with sunlight, drink a gulp of the water, then e-mail, write a memo or speak to the relevant person, asking them for what you want.

An orange and lemon spell for better opportunities

This spell will help to clear any stagnation that has hit your career path. It is also useful when promised opportunities do not materialise because of management inertia.

You will need

Some bergamot (lemon) or lemongrass essential oil (or fragrance burning oil); some neroli (orange blossom) or orange essential oil (or fragrance burning oil); an oil burner; a tea-light.

Timing

An evening after work.

The spell

※ Fill the bowl of the oil burner about one-third full and add five drops of lemon essential oil and five drops of orange essential oil (or fill one-third full with neat fragrance oils).

※ Light the burner. As the fragrance spreads through the room, waft the sweet-smelling air with your hands as though covering yourself with it (do not get too near the burner in case you knock it over). As you immerse yourself in the fragrance, softly chant:
Stir energies and carry me.
Beyond this impasse may I pass,
To where I want to be.

※ When you feel filled with new determination, blow out the tea-light under the burner.

※ Take the orange and lemon oils to work with you the next day and add a few drops to a cup of hot water to inhale as you work.

※ Actively explore in-house training and advancement programmes, ask for a career review and, if necessary, be prepared to move on.

A bicycle spell for increasing your prospects

This is a good spell to use when you feel that you are struggling to advance yourself in your career.

You will need

A bicycle or adult's scooter.

Timing

A day off from work in fine weather.

The spell

※ Find a not-too-steep hill and either push your bicycle or ride slowly uphill, focusing on the struggle you have experienced or are experiencing in moving upwards in your career.

※ When you reach the top of the hill, rest a few moments and then get back on the bicycle, as you do so saying:
Doors will open and I shall pass through them rapidly very soon.

※ At the word 'soon', freewheel down the hill, enjoying the sensation.

※ At work the next day, state what you would like to get out of your job and what you can offer in return.

A telescope spell for when a promotion or salary increase seems far away

You will need

A telescope.

Timing

When you despair of ever receiving a promotion or salary increase.

The spell

⁕ Look through the wrong end of the telescope and say:

Promotion / advancement seem so far away.

⁕ Turn the telescope around and look through the right end. Say:

Promotion / advancement is in my grasp. I reach out and seize the moment.

⁕ Explore all opportunities as soon as possible with a senior manager. Also look for similar positions beyond the horizon of your current employer.

A spell to get a leadership position

You may hesitate to apply for a promotion that would involve leading a team, even though you may have done this informally on a number of occasions. Others may take your hesitancy as a lack of interest in the position. To increase your confidence and your profile, try this spell.

You will need

A garden or open space lit by streetlights or artificial lights such as fairy lights (string a set of outdoor fairy lights on a tree, using the outdoor socket for lawn mowers etc. – check first that the voltage is the same); a tube of gold glitter.

Timing

When a leadership vacancy arises, after dark.

The spell

⁕ Stand where there is no light and say:

I do not like the shadows of obscurity. I take my place in the light.

⁕ Move to where the lights shine all over you and say:

I welcome the chance to shine. Success be mine.

⁕ Sprinkle glitter all around you, letting it fall on your clothes and in your hair. Say:

Let the light shine all around me, on me and within me. I seize this opportunity.

⁕ Turn round very fast until you become slightly dizzy. As you steady yourself you will see the lights moving towards you (a physiological phenomenon that you can use psychically). Say:

The light is within me. I cannot fail.

⁕ Stay in the garden a while, and the next morning make it known that you are interested in the position.

A spell for moving your career upwards

Perhaps you have worked at the same place for ages, or you have started a new job, but the promised promotion or pay rise hasn't materialised and someone who does less work is being better rewarded. Or you may have been passed over for more interesting, better-paid positions even though you have the relevant qualifications, simply because you are so good at your present job and the idea of replacing you is unthinkable. If polite requests or formal applications for an increased salary or a better job fail, you may need to create a high-profile aura, or energy field, around yourself.

You will need

A large round mirror; 3 gold-coloured candles or a golden fibre optic lamp.

Timing

As the morning light floods your house, close to the night of the full moon.

The spell

* Place the mirror so that natural light shimmers around it. Light the candles around the mirror, or switch on the lamp, so that the mirror is filled with artificial light.
* Stand in front of the mirror. Stretching out your arms, make an arch over your head and then bring your arms down in front of your body, as you do so saying:
I am pure gold.
* Repeat these movements and words eight more times, visualising the gold entering the psychic energy field all around your body and flowing through your heart, your throat, your stomach, and down your arms and legs into your hands and feet.
* Close your eyes, open them, blink and you will be dazzled by the momentary radiance. If you shake your fingers, you may feel them tingling and see this psychically as sparks of gold.
* Blow out the candles or switch off the lamp and get ready for work. You will find that people seek your opinion more often than usual and listen to what you say. Before long you should receive a pay rise or promotion.

A career success spell bag

This is a personal spell bag. Keep it with you during any meetings or opportunities to impress others in your career. When the bag is not in use, lock it in a drawer or locker at your workplace. Leave it there when you are on holiday or off duty to continue to spread its powers.

You will need

A dark-blue candle; a deep-blue drawstring bag or purse; a deep-blue cord; a lapis lazuli or turquoise crystal; a small gold item; some cinnamon; some dried eyebright, rue or sage.

Timing

On a Thursday evening.

The spell

* Light the candle.
* Add the crystal, gold item, cinnamon and herb, one by one, to the bag or purse, saying for each:
Bring success to me.
* When all are inside the bag, close it and tie it with the cord, making three knots and saying:
One for the making,
Two for increasing,
Three for achieving what I do seek.
Work for me every day of the week.
* Pass the bag over the candle flame, not too close, and repeat the chant. The bag is ready for use.

An Oriental success cord spell

Bells and red cords or ribbons are a sign of success and prosperity in China and Hong Kong, and are hung behind doors or from the ceiling to attract positive energies. Promotion is, at least in part, affected by profile and image. If you are competent and talented but tend to be modest about your achievements, make yourself a success cord as a reminder to yourself and others of your potential.

You will need

A string of gold-coloured bells (Tibetan ones are ideal); a hook (to hang the bells from); a length of red ribbon cut into five equal pieces, each of which should be long enough to tie into a bow.

Timing

On the first day of the month, when you wake.

The spell

* Find a place to hang the bells where natural light will shine on them. Choose somewhere where you can reach them easily.
* When you have hung the bells, ring them and say:
So I increase my profile and my prospects of promotion.
* Starting at the top and working down to the bottom of the string, tie the lengths of ribbon in five bows at regular intervals between each bell, repeating the chant after each ribbon is fastened.
* Leave the bells hanging on the wall until you go to work, then remove them and take them with you.
* Hang the bells behind your door or in your locker and ring them whenever you doubt yourself.

A stepping stone spell to long-term success

This is such a good spell that it is worth seeking out stepping stones over a stream to do it. Possible locations include parks, water gardens, seafront gardens, garden centres, stately homes and theme parks. My own favourite stepping stones are at Dovedale in Derbyshire, in the UK, over a flowing river, set among the hills – a beautiful area to visit.

You will need

Some stepping stones over water; a round white stone, preferably found near the stepping stones.

Timing

Whenever you find the stepping stones.

The spell

* Holding the white stone, list the steps you need take to achieve success.
* Still holding the white stone, begin crossing the stepping stones, stopping on each one and saying:
So I take a step towards success.
* When you reach the middle stone, cast the white stone in to the water, as you do so saying:
I cast my fortune in to the waters. Success flow back to me, increased immeasurably by your power.
* Continue to walk across the stepping stones, stopping on each one and saying:
So I take a step towards success.
* When you have reached the other side, allow ideas to flow spontaneously into your mind about how you will achieve your ambitions.
* Try to find another route back across the water.

An ancient Egyptian fire spell for gradual increase in personal power and success

To the ancient Egyptians the sun and the sun god, Ra or Re, were a source of power and success. Equally important was Ra's shadow, or alter ego, Osiris — the corn and resurrection god. Osiris empowered Ra to be born each morning at dawn. Clay figures of Osiris were filled with seeds and buried as a symbol of the growth of power and of life. This spell is good for long-term career ambitions, especially if you have suffered a setback or a loss of confidence. If it is a dark day, work the spell indoors, lighting four gold-coloured candles, one at each corner of the cloth.

You will need

A cloth; a dish of seeds, such as sunflower, poppy, cumin or caraway; a ball of natural clay; 4 gold-coloured candles (optional); 4 large red flowers; a yellow cloth.

Timing

Outdoors in sunlight (or see above), preferably at noon.

The spell

⚜ Set the cloth on grass or on a large rock (if you are working indoors, use a table).

⚜ Place the four red flowers one in each corner of the cloth (in front of the candles if you are working indoors), saying for each:
So blooms the desert flower. So blossoms my life. So shall I reap the harvest even in desert places.

⚜ Place the clay and the seeds in the centre of the cloth.

⚜ Sit facing South. Taking the clay, hollow out the shape of a featureless figure, just deep enough to contain the seeds. Say:
Grow, be fertile, Osiris of clay, you who are to be reborn.

⚜ Set the seeds within the figure, as you do so saying:
I have within me also the seeds of the harvest. I take in the power to be born anew in the certainty of success.

⚜ Leave the clay figure, the seeds and the four flowers in position on the cloth until the sun fades (or the candles burn through). Meanwhile, busy yourself with plans, perhaps looking on the Internet for opportunities for further qualifications or openings.

⚜ Bury the figure when the sun has gone, and tend the ground regularly. Even if the seeds do not flourish, the symbolism of the planting remains. Put the flowers in water, and when they die, bury them near the figure.

A candle attraction spell for a promotion or pay rise

This spell is helpful for any career advancement, but especially good if you are contemplating seeking your promotion with another organisation. One bonus is that a few days after the spell your present firm may offer similar (or better) terms to those of the post you are applying for. This spell was originally devised for job hunting, and it works well for finding any new job.

You will need

An orange candle; a pen and paper, or an advert for the kind of job (if relevant, including the salary level) you are thinking of applying for; some olive oil or candle oil containing cinnamon, patchouli or peppermint.

Timing

Thursday evening, at sunset.

The spell

* By the light of a small lamp, write your job requirements on the piece of paper or silently read the advert.
* Read the advert or list of requirements out loud.
* Rub the oil into the candle, working from the top down to the centre, and then from the bottom up to the centre. As you work, imagine the candle as a magnet and either name the job you want over and over again or say:

Bring to me a salary of (amount).

* Switch off the lamp and light the candle. Look in to the candle flame, visualising the moment when you are offered the job or the pay rise, hearing the words, feeling the handshake, perhaps even smelling the particular fragrances of the workplace. Also feel your own sense of satisfaction. (The more multi-sensory a visualisation, the more powerful it is.)
* Run through the experience in increasing detail two or three times and then blow out the candle, as you do so saying:

So shall it be as I decree!
All shall end happily!

* Sit in the darkness and visualise the successful outcome once more.

A spell for performing well in an interview

Even if you are well qualified for the job on offer, a promotion interview or test can be nerve-wracking. Under pressure we can sometimes forget what we were going to say – or we may appear too eager. Performing a spell on the morning of an interview is a good way of increasing your professional desirability aura (or psychic energy vibes) and creating a calm, confident centre inside you that radiates outwards.

You will need

A glass bowl half filled with sparkling mineral water; 9 tiny clear quartz or yellow citrine crystals (or 9 yellow or clear glass nuggets); some gold-coloured foil; a gold-coloured drawstring bag or purse.

Timing

Start on the day before the interview, and complete the spell as dawn breaks on the day of the interview, so that the morning light will flood the bowl.

The spell

* The morning before the interview, place the nine crystals or glass nuggets in the bowl of water. Leave the bowl somewhere where it will absorb the sun power during the hours of daylight (preferably outside).
* At dusk (or as near as you can manage) cover the bowl with the gold foil and, if you can, leave it outside again (otherwise place it near a window).
* At dawn on the morning of the interview, take the foil off the bowl and place it by the bowl's side. Work outdoors or by a window where the first light will shine in on the water.
* With your fingers, ripple the surface of the water, as you do so, whispering mesmerically:
  Gold of the sun, flow within me
  That my talents all will see.
* Take the crystals or nuggets out of the water and leave them to dry on the foil, as you do so saying:
  I will succeed, by the power of the sun.
* Have a bath or shower, adding the sun-infused water from the bowl to the hot water. Visualise the empowered water entering you and filling you with sparkling gold.
* Put the crystals or nuggets in the golden bag or purse and take them with you to the interview. If you panic while waiting to be called, touch each of them and recite the chants of the spell in your head.

A spell to achieve a major career ambition or get the job of your dreams

This is a very old spell used in lands from Scandinavia to Brazil. In the Western magical tradition, the four elements of Water, Air, Earth and Fire are combined by making a fire below the high-water mark, to be surrounded by and eventually consumed by the sea. You can perform this spell by any body of water, but it is best worked by the sea or a tidal inlet or river. Because it is such a powerful spell, however, it is worth waiting until you have exactly the right conditions, perhaps when you are on holiday. The spell is particularly effective if the job of your dreams is in another country.

You will need

Enough stones to make a circle to enclose a small fire; enough kindling or driftwood to make a small fire; some rosemary or thyme (the culinary kind is fine); a gold earring or gold-coloured coin; a torch (optional); a bucket (optional).

Timing
If possible, at night under a bright full moon that sheds light over the beach and water. Otherwise, use a powerful torch. Work just before high tide (use a tide table to check when this is).

The spell
* Use the kindling and driftwood to build a small fire of dry wood on stones just below the high-tide line.
* Light the fire and sprinkle some thyme or rosemary on it, as you do so saying:

Burn bright
That the height
Of my ambition
I may achieve.

* Cast the coin or earring into the water as an offering and ask for what you desire, saying afterwards:
Lady Ocean, Mistress Sea,
I bring you gold;
Bring success to me.

* Sit and watch as the water of high tide meets the fire and carries it away. If you are working with non-tidal water, scoop up a bucketful of the water to dowse the fire, still using the chant above. Bury your offering.

A Viking Runic full moon and sun ritual for a burst of power in your career

On the day of the full moon, you can see the moon rising in the East as the sun is still in the sky in the West. This is the most powerful time of the month, and one when you can take a huge leap forward. By using your own body to make Algiz, the Runic sign of your own essential power, you can absorb the solar and lunar power and fill yourself with energy none can ignore.

You will need
A place where you can see both the moon and the sun at the same time.

Timing
As soon as you can see the full moon and the setting sun together in the sky (check in *Old Moore's Almanack*, a diary or the weather section of a newspaper for precise times).

The spell
* Extend your arms upwards. Point to the moon with one hand and the sun with the other, so that your arms form a V. Place your feet together and your body will complete the Rune. Say:
In me meet the sun and moon. Algiz fill me with your radiance.

* As the sun fades, or when you are tired, relax your body.
* Create an Algiz somewhere in your workspace – on your computer, on the front of a file, on a workbench – as a reminder of your new-found power.

A summer ritual for success

This spell is traditionally associated with midsummer and long sunny days. It acts on the principle of giving out willingly so that you may receive back three-fold. In this case, you are symbolically sending out your search-and-find energies for advancement in the best way possible in your career. The spell is useful if you are uncertain of the best way to proceed in your work life, and often attracts benefits from outside your immediate workplace.

You will need

A hilltop or high ground, or a wide open space; 6 gold-coloured coins.

Timing

Close to noon on a sunny or bright day.

The spell

* Stand on the hilltop and face the sun, holding three of the coins in each hand.
* Cast the coins high into the air so that they scatter, as you do so saying:
  So I send out my gifts to the world. May they be returned in kind and opportunity.
* Walk on the hillside, absorbing the light and the power. Within a few days or weeks, a new opportunity should come into your life. If pursued it will resolve any issues about your career prospects.

A computer spell for attracting success in any way you need it in your career

You will need

A computer and a drawing programme.

Timing

Whenever you need career confidence or a quick burst of energy to push yourself forward at work.

The spell

* In the centre of the computer screen, write a word or phrase to represent what you want to attract into your career or general life plan. Alternatively, draw an image, or choose one from clip art, to represent what you want to attract. You can also use a digital photograph.
* Create a mantra to express your need, for example:
  Power of fortune, increase see;
  On television may I be!
* Repeat the mantra over and over again, in your head or aloud, getting faster and faster and feeling the sensation of power and excitement rising within you. As you chant, gradually increase the size of the image or word on screen until finally it fills the whole screen.
* When you cannot enlarge the word or image any more, end the spell by saying:
  The power is mine,
  As I count nine:
  One, two, three, four, five, six, seven, eight, nine.
* On the count of nine, press the print button so that the image will emerge in a tangible form that you can pin on the wall as a reminder of your coming success when you get discouraged.

An elemental computer spell to draw success

This is a more complex version of the spell on page 226.

You will need
A computer and a drawing programme.

Timing
Whenever you need career confidence or a quick burst of energy to push yourself forward at work.

The spell
* Draw a circle on the screen and label it with the four cardinal points and their elements: North/Earth, East/Air, South/Fire and West/Water. Draw a cauldron in the North, a sword in the East, a candle in the South, and a chalice in the West.

* Choose a word, phrase or image to represent what you need or desire, and place it in the centre of the circle. Use the mouse to move the word, phrase or image to the North/cauldron, as you do so, chanting an appropriate chant, for example:
I call my television career with the power of Earth.
* Next move the word, phrase or image to the East/sword and add to the chant, for example:
I call my television career with the power of Earth. I call my television career with the power of Air.
* Move the word, phrase or image next to Fire/candle and then to West/chalice, at each point elaborating the chant
* Repeat the chant louder and louder and faster and faster, and increase the size of the word, phrase or image, until finally it covers the four marked directions and the circle.
* Erase the circle, as you do so saying:
The power is free:
The power's in me.
Earth, Air, Water, Fire,
Let nothing stop what I desire.
* Wipe out the image – the power is within you. Repeat the spell when necessary as you take steps towards fulfilling your dream.

A water spell for fulfilling career plans after a setback

In the modern job market, a senior executive is as vulnerable to redundancy as a newly employed teenager, and may be faced with the problem of meeting significant outgoings with no income, while at the same time having to deal with a huge loss of self-esteem. If you have lost your job after becoming established in your career, the power of water – great for getting things moving – can be especially useful (see also page 146). This spell is performed in a swimming pool, but you do not need to be able to swim to do it; the shallow end of the pool is fine.

You will need
A swimming pool.

Timing
When the pool is quiet and, preferably, lit by either natural sunlight rippling on the water or poolside lights.

The spell
* Stand in the water in a circle of sunlight or artificial light. Stretch out your arms in front of you and slowly circle them away from each other and around your body until they meet behind your back. Clasp your hands there. The circle you have drawn marks your outer limits at present.
* With your arms outstretched, bend your knees, press down on the bottom of the pool and push yourself up as high as you can, remaining within the invisible circle you have drawn. Say in your head or aloud:
I will rise higher and higher; I will succeed again, even better than last time.
* Repeat the bouncing action and the words eight more times, each time bending your knees and pressing your feet more strongly on the bottom of the pool, so that you push yourself further and further out of the water. As you bounce and chant, feel any resistance melting away and focus on a specific goal or on an area in which you can and will succeed.
* Starting with your arms outstretched behind you and fingers clasped, reverse the drawing of the water circle, so that you finish with your hands before you.
* Keeping your hands outstretched, look into the future with renewed optimism. Say:
I push back the limits. The restrictions are gone. I can succeed once more.
* Swim around the pool or walk around the edges to mark your new-found confidence.
* When you return home, explore a new avenue of opportunity, perhaps one you thought you were not ready to try or had rejected as beyond your scope.

17 SPELLS FOR SELF-EMPLOYMENT AND WORKING FROM HOME

This is a chapter close to my heart since I have, for the past 15 years, worked from the dining room table, assisted – or more usually interrupted – by children and cats with their demands, variously, for food, money, taxiing, petting, and fixing wounded egos and battered hearts. But there are consolations – a walk on a sunny day, the freedom to work until midnight if a project is interesting and then snatch an afternoon nap on a cold grey afternoon.

Some people begin a small business from their front room that grows into an empire, finding a niche in the market and working all hours to keep down overheads until the magical profit signs appear. Dressmaking, accountancy, graphic design ... there is apparently no end to the skills that can be turned into a mobile or home-based business – and with high technology it is becoming increasingly possible to run even a complex global business from home (see also Chapter 18).

If you have young children, it may be more practical for you to work from home, so that you can accommodate unexpected illnesses, school closures and holidays – though, as I can attest, this is not necessarily as easy an option as it may appear. Nevertheless, many women (in particular) balance the baby on one knee and the mouse mat on the other.

Many home-based jobs, though vital, are modestly or not at all paid: caring for children (your own or other people's), looking after sick or elderly relatives and home-making. Others, such as farmed-out factory work, may be mundane bread-and-butter jobs, providing essential income to enable a family to get by financially.

This, then, is a varied chapter. Although the spells given are for setting up a business, they can also be used to great effect to improve an existing business or venture. A cleansing or empowering premises spell, for instance, can clear the psychic dust that has gathered over years and open the way for new outlets and renewed interest in products or services.

A spell for setting up a business from home or new premises

If you are planning to work from an area of your house or from outbuildings at home, this spell can be a great help in transforming gentle domestic energies into more dynamic success- and money-generating ones. You can also use this spell to dedicate a small industrial unit. I have cast this and the following spell several times for business people setting up alone, with good results. Before you perform the spell, you may need to switch off smoke alarms temporarily. (See the handsel spell on page 233 for another spell to bless a business.)

You will need

A CD of gentle ocean, rainforest or meditation harmonies; a blue candle in a deep holder or on a metal tray; a compass; I brown, I yellow, I orange and I green candle, each in a holder; some allspice or cinnamon (the culinary kind is fine); 12 unused coins of any denomination (you can get these from a bank or post office); a yellow cloth.

Timing

After dusk, a day or two before you start your venture.

The spell

* Set the CD to play softly.
* Dedicate your main work area by lighting the blue candle and placing it in the holder or on the tray, in the centre of the room. If necessary, drop a little hot wax on the tray to secure the candle.
* Use the compass to find the four cardinal points, North, South, East and West.
* Light the brown candle and place it half way along the northern wall of the room, to represent the practical aspects of the business, including the paperwork.

* Light the yellow candle and place it half way along the eastern wall of the room, to symbolise technical expertise and – if you are working in the field of alternative medicine – healing powers.
* Light the orange candle and place it half way along the southern wall of the room, to symbolise powers of communication and publicity.
* Light the green candle and place it half way along the western wall, to symbolise gradual financial growth, as well as environmental concerns.
* Sit in the centre of the room facing the blue candle and looking North.
* Place the twelve coins (one for each month) in a circle around the blue candle.
* Drop a few grains of allspice or cinnamon in to the flame of the blue candle and say:
  Flame and flare, rise and grow, that my business may be profitable to me and of benefit to others.
* As the wax begins to melt and falls on the coins, say nine times, as a soft rhythmic chant:
  Flow and increase; bring success, prosperity and fulfilment to my forthcoming venture.
* Sit with half-closed eyes, allowing the music and the light to flow around and within you and the room. This will make it an oasis of calm and harmony in the coming days, no matter how frantic things may get.
* When the candle is burnt through, drop some more spice in the hot wax.
* Allow the wax to cool, and then cut a circle of wax containing the coins and the spice. Wrap it in the yellow cloth and keep it in a drawer in your new premises, until it crumbles.
* Throw away the wax from the other candles when they have burnt down.

A spell for making business premises your own

If you are moving into an existing shop or unit, you need to cleanse the old energies away and bring in new life – especially if the previous business closed down. You can also use this spell to cleanse an area of your home if you are converting it into business space.

You will need
A new broom; half a bucket of hot water and a scrubbing brush; some pine, juniper or tea tree essential oil; a mop (optional); some salt and pepper; a string of silver bells; a convex mirror.

Timing
The morning before you move equipment into your premises.

The spell
* Add nine drops of the essential oil to the bucket of hot water and scrub the back door step. Throw the dirty water over the back yard or down a drain.
* Come in and shut the back door. Open all windows.
* Starting at the back of the premises, use the broom to sweep any dust and litter out of the front door and then into the gutter – or collect it in a sack outside the front door and dispose of it. This will remove any bad financial luck that is lingering.
* Vigorously scrub or mop the main areas, again working from the back outwards, using a bucket of clean hot water with nine more drops of the essential oil added.
* When you get to the front door, scrub or mop the front step and then tip the water down an outside drain.
* When you go back inside, sprinkle the front step with a pinch of salt, followed by a pinch of pepper, to prevent any negativity entering.
* Go to the centre of the premises and ring the bells – the power of sound will clear any stagnant energies.
* Again standing in the centre of the premises, hold the mirror facing outwards and move it deosil (clockwise) around you, to illuminate any dark corners. Then hang the mirror over the front door, facing outwards on to the street. Alternatively, hang it inside on a wall facing the front door.

A spell for cleansing any equipment you inherit or buy

You can use hyssop, a herb that has been used for purification since early Hebrew times, to cleanse any equipment you take over or buy. By psychically purifying equipment you can make your own mark on it, cleansing it of the vibes of those who sold it to you, handled it, packed it, used it before you and – if it was cheap – maybe failed with it.

You will need

Some hyssop (available from herbal stores and by mail order – hyssop is by far the best, but if you can't get it, use another purification herb, such as mint); a glass measuring jug or bowl with a cover, or a small teapot with a lid; a teaspoon.

Timing

Whenever you inherit or buy a piece of equipment.

The spell

* Make an infusion of hyssop in the measuring jug or teapot by placing one teaspoon of the dried herbs or three teaspoonfuls of fresh herbs in a cup and pouring on about a cupful of boiling water. For larger pieces of equipment use 30 g/ I oz of the dried herb or 90 g/ 3 oz of the fresh herb to 600 ml/ I¹/₄ pints of water.
* Stir the infusion, chanting continuously to empower the herbs:
  Hyssop, hyssop, purify and make all new.
* Let the solution stand for five to ten minutes, stirring occasionally, then strain the infusion.
* Use the liquid to sprinkle three widdershins (anticlockwise) circles around items (or groups of small items) of equipment, as you do so repeating the chant.
* Pour the rest of the infusion down an outside drain near the front door.

A handsel spell to make your business profitable

The first paper money or cheque received by a business should be framed and displayed facing the front door. This practice is called handsel (from an Anglo-Saxon word) and will bring into play the sympathetic magic principle of like attracting like. If the first cheque is for a large amount, cash it and when you draw some of the money out of the cashpoint, frame the receipt instead, or frame the bank statement showing that the cheque has been paid in. You can also keep a copy of the first invoice you send or first order your receive. Place it in a sealed envelope in the first folder in your filing cabinet. Always put the first coin or note of each day in your pocket if you are running a market stall or selling goods or services at a trade fair.

You will need

The first cheque your business has received.

Timing

When you receive your first cheque.

The spell

* Hold the cheque in your power hand (the one you write with) and say five times very fast:
  May there be more
  And more by the score,
  Till it pours through the door.

A Celtic blessing spell for a workplace or business venture in the early days

This is a good blessing to use in the early days if orders are slow and you have few customers. It can be frightening to realise that you will only get a salary if you earn it. If you are frozen by panic when you should be looking for new outlets, try using this blessing to centre yourself. In Celtic times, a stone was placed on a cairn or pile as an offering each time the blessing was recited. This was a tribute to the ancient Scottish crone goddess the Cailleach, who protected the family and all who toiled.

You will need

A small glass dish; a tub of gold-coloured glass nuggets; a tall glass jar with a lid (a cookware jar will do).

Timing

Every morning before you start work, turn on your computer or open the post.

The spell

* If possible, go outdoors and face the rising sun. Say:

  May there always be work for my hands to do,
  May my purse always hold a coin or two,
  May the sun always shine on my windowpane,
  And may a rainbow be certain to follow each rain.

* Every time you make a sale or order, however small, place a nugget in the dish.

* Before long the dish will be full and you can transfer the nuggets to the jar and start again.

A metal and wind spell for long-term success

Having an empowered charm in the background is a good way of keeping positive energies flowing when you are so busy you do not have time to make a cup of tea, let alone cast a spell. This spell uses metal and wind, originally ingredients of Oriental folk belief, but which have entered popular Western magic.

You will need

3 coins with holes in the centre (for example, Chinese divinatory coins or the old Spanish 25-peseta coin; a thin red cord; some metal wind chimes.

Timing

On a Wednesday morning.

The spell

* Tie the three coins to the cord, knot the cord top and bottom and attach it to the wind chimes.

* Hang the wind chimes near a window or near the entrance to the room or premises where you work.

* Set the wind chimes in motion by blowing on them three times, saying between each breath:

  Whensoever you chime, spread good fortune and success throughout my workplace and my endeavours.

* The wind will re-empower the chimes.

A crystal pathway spell to bring customers and prosperity to your shop or business premises

Sometimes I am asked by people I know if I will help to bring prosperity to their business premises, especially if they rely on passing trade and perhaps are sited slightly off the main way or if they are just starting up. One method is to create a crystal arrow pathway at floor level to guide customers into and around the shop, ending at the cash till. This is not in any way compelling people to buy, merely directing them inwards to the shop and then around the displays so that the merchandise appears in its best light. The crystals should be hidden from the view of the customers – but if you are working the spell for someone else, you should tell them where the crystals are located.

Cerridwen, Brighid (pronounced 'Breed' and Rhiannon, referred to in the chant, are three Celtic goddesses associated with abundance. Cerridwen and Brighid had magic cauldrons of nourishment and regeneration.

You will need

Depending on the size of the premises, about 15 crystal points (clear quartz crystals with a point at one end); a heatproof bowl; a loose sagebrush smudge stick or stick of cedar, myrrh, frankincense, or sandalwood incense.

Timing

On a Wednesday (the day of commerce), before the business opens for the day.

The spell

* Slightly angle two crystal points, one in each corner of the display window, points facing inwards, so that you are guiding the customer's view psychically inwards.
* Set a crystal point on either side of the doorway at about a 45-degree angle, points facing into the shop.
* Continue placing the crystals at strategic points, like direction arrows, to guide the customer around the premises. Use as many or few as you need. Adapt the positioning according to the premises, moving furniture to create an ongoing pathway to avoid doubling back.
* Set a final pair of crystals on either side of the cash register or pay-order point.
* When all the crystals are in place, empower the shop by lighting the smudge stick in the small heatproof bowl or holding a lit incense stick in each hand and standing in the approximate centre of the shop or premises. If there is more than one room or section, you can empower each, starting with the one nearest the entrance door and working inwards.
* Turn round three times deosil (clockwise), three times widdershins (anticlockwise) and then three times deosil again, as you do so chanting:
Cerridwen, Brighid, Rhiannon, Mothers all,
By Earth, sea and sky to you I call.
Let abundance on this place now fall,
Here and hereafter,
Cerridwen, Brighid, Rhiannon, Mothers all.
* Re-empower the premises monthly.

Making a business success mojo

Unlike a spellbag, a mojo is not empowered. Whereas it is not crucial for a spellbag to remain hidden (although, obviously, you would not go waving one around), a mojo should be concealed. Mojos always contain an odd number of items. They tend to be more powerful than spellbags for bringing success to a business.

You will need

A green candle; a green drawstring bag in a natural fabric; a green cord; a root of high John the Conqueror (or low John the Conqueror) – available from herbal stores or by mail order over the Internet; a sugar lump or twist of sugar in foil; a silver dollar (or any silver coin); a little powdered ginger; a small open padlock without a key; a little whisky or bourbon.

Timing

At midnight.

The spell

* Light the green candle (the colour of business success) and work in silence by its light.

* Place into the bag the root of high John the Conqueror (this is poisonous, so handle it with care and keep it well away from children) – very effective for attracting business and overcoming slumps. Add the sugar, for sweetening customers; the silver dollar, for attracting money; a sprinkling of the ginger, for speeding up business and bringing prosperity; and the padlock, for opening doors of opportunity. Finally, sprinkle a few drops of the whisky into the bag.

* Use the cord to secure the bag, fastening it with six knots.

* Hide the bag near the front door of your house (if you work at home) or the door to your workspace, or conceal it in a locked drawer, where no one will find it. If they do, the bag must be thrown away and a new one made.

* Replace the bag every two or three months, when you sense that its power is waning. Dispose of the ingredients (be careful where you put the Conqueror root) and burn or throw away the bag.

A smudging spell for working at markets, fairs or festivals

Setting up a stall at a trade fair, market or festival is an excellent way both to make fast money and to attract future customers. However, even New Age fairs can generate a fair amount of competitiveness – and the inevitable anxiety that no one will visit your stall can actually create a barrier to potential customers. If you are involved in any kind of therapeutic work, you may pick up a lot of negative energy and – whatever your line of work – by the end of a day full of questions and sometimes complaints, you can feel like a wet dish rag. This spell will ensure that all remains tranquil and positive. It is especially good if you are attending a two-day event, at which you will need to pace yourself.

You will need

A large sagebrush or cedar smudge stick; a feather (optional).

Timing

Immediately before you set up your stall – on both days if it is a two-day festival.

The spell

* Put all your equipment and boxes to be unpacked on or around any table.
* Light one end of the smudge stick, blow out the flame and gently blow on the tip until it glows red.
* Hold the smudge in your power hand (the one you write with) and, using either the feather or your other hand, waft spirals of smoke in three deosil (clockwise) circles around the objects, as you do so saying:
May only good enter here, and I and those who visit me share a profitable exchange of energies.
* End by wafting the smoke up and down in deosil spirals around you, letting it find its own pathways, as you repeat the above words.
* At the end of the day, make three large widdershins (anticlockwise) circles round the area of your stall, as you do so saying:
May peace only remain and positive energies of exchange.
* Finally, waft widdershins up and down yourself, repeating the chant. You should now be able to relax on the drive home or during your overnight stay.

An instant spell for when you need a sudden burst of positive energy

This spell is great if you are just about to try to win an order or meet your bank manager. It also works well if you simply feel dispirited with all the responsibilities of running a business.

You will need

2 clear pointed quartz crystals (cheap and easy to buy).

Timing

When you need a sudden burst of energy.

The spell

* Hold a crystal in each hand, with the points facing outwards.
* Cross the crystals over your head and around your body, moving faster and faster and saying:
Power glow in me, show instantly.
* When you have finished, blink and you will be able to detect a glow of energy round yourself.
* Plunge the crystals under a running tap, allowing the water to splash you.

A honey candle spell to win orders or bookings

No matter how good the service you offer, there will probably be times when you need to sweeten potentially important clients, financiers, the media or planning officers — without losing your integrity. This simple honey spell will enable you to keep smiling no matter how awkward clients are or how unhelpful official sources are proving.

You will need

A beeswax candle (substitutes will not do for this spell); a honey pot (preferably the old-fashioned kind with bees on it); an unopened jar of honey, if possible containing honeycomb; a jam, tea- or honey spoon.

Timing

On a Sunday evening, or the evening before you open for the week, or before an important meeting. 24/7 people should stick to Sunday evening.

The spell

* Light the candle.
* Spoon a full spoonful of honey in to the honey pot, holding and twisting the spoon so that as much as possible goes in. As you do so, name a person or situation you need to sweeten and say:

By the power of the honey bee,
May my words fall persuasively,
May you respond favourably
And all conclude amicably,
By the power of the honey bee.

* Spoon another spoonful of honey into the honey pot, lick the spoon and repeat the chant.
* Eat a small honey sandwich the next morning, using the honey in the pot. This will transfer the power of the spell to you.
* Top up the pot when it is empty, using this spell to empower the new honey.

A lodestone spell to draw business

The lodestone works especially well for the self-employed, whether they are sole traders or employ a number of workers. Even if you use lodestones in other forms of magic, keep a special one for employment spells. You can carry out this spell at home before work or in your workplace.

You will need

A very pointed lodestone; a red bag; some magnetic sand or iron filings (obtainable from hardware, New Age and crystal stores); a piece of brown paper (use a small paper bag cut in half without the seams); a red pen; a white china plate; patchouli essential oil (you can buy special success or business oils, but patchouli is cheap and just as effective).

Timing

On a Friday morning.

The spell

* Write on the paper the precise purpose of the spell.
* Place the lodestone on the plate and place the plate on top of the paper. The paper should not overlap the plate.
* Anoint each of the corners of the paper with a single drop of patchouli oil, for each drop stating the purpose, using the precise words you wrote.
* Sprinkle just a little magnetic sand on the lodestone, stating your purpose once more in the same words.
* Leave the paper and the lodestone on the plate and each day sprinkle it with a little more magnetic sand, repeating your purpose in the same words.
* The following Friday, if possible at the same time, sprinkle the lodestone once more with magnetic sand, state your purpose and place the lodestone in the red bag.
* Dispose of the paper and wash the plate in very hot water. Keep the red bag at work with the lodestone inside, facing inwards towards the premises.
* Put the lodestone on the plate and sprinkle it with magnetic sand every Friday, repeating your purpose in the same words. Wash the plate afterwards.
* If your need changes, do the spell again, from the beginning.

A herbal spell to attract business

Whether your custom comes through cyber space or the local community, traditional herbs such as basil and mint are excellent for attracting business, working as they did for cottage industries centuries earlier.

You will need

One unopened jar each of dried basil and dried mint (the culinary kind is fine); a bowl that has been washed in very hot water and dried with a new white dish cloth; a small paper bag (not plastic).

Timing

When you see the crescent moon in the sky. If it is cloudy, wait until the next day.

The spell

* Open the basil and mint and tip a small quantity of each into the bowl, making sure you do not touch the herbs.
* Mix the herbs by turning and swirling the bowl, saying softly as you do so:
  Mint and basil, draw to me
  All that is good to be.
* Don't worry if any spills out, but do not try to put it back.
* Carefully tip the contents of the bowl into the bag, again without touching the herbs.
* The next morning, sprinkle a little of the herb mix from the bag outside the main entrance or door to your workplace. Use the rest in cooking to empower yourself and your family.

A spell to make a lucky knot cord

If you are self-employed in any field, a green silk knot cord will encourage the steady flow of work so that you have plenty of opportunities but do not get overwhelmed. This, like the metal and wind spell on page 233, is a background charm, re-empowering itself as the air circulates around (until you need to use the power tied in one of the knots).

You will need

A green silk cord long enough to reach more than half way down a door when it is tied with 9 knots; a green candle.

Timing

At midnight.

The spell

* Light the candle and work only by that light.
* Pass each end of the cord in turn through the flame very fast, so it does not catch light, and say:

So enter power. Flow constantly, gradually and easily towards my prosperity.

* Working slowly, tie nine knots in the cord, as you tie each one, reciting the appropriate line from the chant below. Knot the cord in what feels a natural order and include two end knots in your total of nine:
  With the knot of one, success begun,
  With the knot of two, much work to do,
  With the knot of three, increase be,
  With the knot of four, open every door,
  With the knot of five, let business thrive,
  With the knot of six, contracts are fixed,
  With the knot of seven, new work is given,
  By knot of eight, my future's great,
  By knot of nine, all can be mine.
* Hang the knot cord behind the door of your workplace and only undo a knot if things at work are stagnant. If you undo a knot, repeat the spell so that all nine knots are restored.

A gold and spice spell for when you have a temporary cash-flow crisis

This spell works best with gold you have bought yourself. If you do not have any, buy the cheapest gold-plated earrings or collar stud you can find. I use this spell when no one has paid me; cheques tend to appear within a day or two as a result.

You will need

A small piece of real gold; some powdered ginger, saffron or cinnamon cooking spice in a tub with a shaker in the top; a small gold-coloured purse.

Timing

At noon.

The spell

* Put the gold in the purse.
* Shake a little spice into the purse. Say:
  Gold and silver have I none;
  To my life good fortune come
  Now please.
* Close the purse and shake it three times, as you do so saying:
  The wolf is coming to the door;
  Fortune, I can wait no more.
  Come now please.
* Keep the purse with the financial records for your business or, if you are owed a lot, with your unpaid invoices.

A spell to combat dispirited feelings if you are self-employed and working from home

Setting up your own business can be very exciting, but it can also be incredibly hard work and very lonely, especially if you work from home. In the early days you need a lot of stamina and optimism if you cannot afford to employ anyone to help you. Increasing numbers of women, in particular, are combining working from home with bringing up a family – a situation in which a very active positive spell can come in handy. The computer version of the spell is simple enough for even IT beginners to handle.

You will need

A computer or several sheets of white paper and a black pen.

Timing

When you feel dispirited.

The spell

* Write your name in the centre of the computer screen or a piece of paper. As you do so, name yourself aloud and state what you do or make. For example:
  I am Cassandra and I am an author.
* If you are using a computer, make the name larger on the screen. If you are using pen and paper, write it again on a second sheet of paper, larger this time and still in the centre. Repeat your name and what you do aloud, twice this time.
* Go on increasing the size of your name, each time repeating the words an extra time, until by the seventh or eight increase your name fills the screen or paper. At this point say:
  So shall my business grow and prosper and increase. As I write, it shall be so!
* Print out the largest name, or use the last piece of paper you wrote on, and pin it behind the door of your workspace, so that you can see it as you work.
* If you hit problems, write your name again, very large, over the printed or written name and repeat:
  So shall my business grow and prosper and increase. As I write, it shall be so!

A spell to help home-based mothers and fathers cope

For a number of years I stayed at home looking after five small children. You may be at home full-time, combining taking care of the family with part-time work or study, or pursuing a full-time career from home while you look after children. Whatever your situation, a series of childhood illnesses and sleepless nights can make you feel like giving up. For single parents especially, as I know, there can be little relief. This spell, based on a very common Celtic blessing, links you with mothers throughout the ages who have sat by the fire or a child's bedside late into the night half hallucinating. The Sacred Three originally referred to the threefold goddess who was seen as three sisters or three mothers. The three separate goddess figures were portrayed in Roman Celtic sculptures, sitting in a row holding children, pets and bread or fruit. In the Christian Celtic tradition, the Sacred Three were the Holy Trinity. Personally, I like the concept of the protective mothers.

You will need
A white candle.

Timing
When the house is finally quiet.

The spell
* Light the candle and sit for a few minutes letting the cares of the day fade. (You would probably not be able to sleep straightaway in any case.)
* Softly recite, as a mesmeric chant, over and over again:
  The Sacred Three,
  My fortress be,
  Encircling me.
  Come and be round
  My hearth, my home.
  Fend Thou my kin
  And every sleeping thing within,
  Thy care our peace
  Through mid of night
  To light's release.
* When you feel relaxed, blow out the candle, sending love to your child/ren and wishes for a peaceful night's sleep, then go to bed.

A spell for carers

As people live longer and, in many countries, state welfare support decreases, you may find yourself either having to give up work to care for an elderly or disabled relative or combining caring with a job. Even in retirement you may find yourself with responsibility for a sick partner. The most difficult time can be the evenings, when you are tired and see the days stretching endlessly ahead. This blessing from the Celtic tradition will not only remind you of your own life at a time in the more distant future but it will also help you to break through the tiredness and fight for the help you need from the authorities and from charities. Brighid (pronounced Breed), or St Brigit as she became in Christian times, was a patroness of the hearth and home and of all who care for others there.

You will need
A white candle.

Timing
During the evening, when you are sitting down.

The spell
* Find a routine task that occupies your hands and leaves your mind free, for example mending, knitting, embroidering, making a clay model, painting areas of colour in a picture you started earlier or polishing a small item. As you work, recite three times, very slowly and softly:
Brighid of the Mantle, encompass us;
Lady of the Lambs, protect us;
Keeper of the Hearth, kindle us;
Beneath your mantle, gather us.
Mothers of our mother,
Guide our hands in yours
To kindle the light,
Both day and night.
From dawn till dark,
From dark till dawn.
* Just for tonight, leave undone anything that does not have to be done. Blow out the candle, sending the light to yourself.

A spell for home-makers

This Celtic blessing is for anyone who works in the home, making it a welcoming place, whether you live alone or have a large family.

You will need
Some old-fashioned lavender polish and a cloth, even if you usually use spray or furniture wipes.

Timing
When the house is full of natural daylight and is quiet.

The spell
* Choose a piece of furniture near the centre of the main living room and slowly polish it, as you do so, saying as a continuous chant:
May God be with you and bless you.
May you see your children's children.
May you be poor in misfortune, rich in blessings.
May you know nothing but happiness
From this day forward.
* Visitors or even in-rushing family may stop when they enter and comment on how peaceful the house feels.
* Repeat weekly if you have time.

18 SPELLS FOR SECOND CAREERS AND TURNING AN INTEREST INTO PROFIT

This is another chapter dear to my heart, because I did not begin a writing career until I was 40, though it had always been my ambition. It has taken me a further 15 years to get anywhere near established. But in spite of the difficulties in the early days, the career change has been well worth the effort. I would encourage anyone, whether a would-be novelist, an amateur jewellery designer or a musician, to give it a try. You may not reach the top. I certainly failed in my original dream to be a bestselling novelist – I still get rejection slips by the score for my fiction work. But to see your paintings on sale in a local gallery or your name in a magazine is a tremendous buzz and can become a source of extra income.

Many people who have worked successfully – and perhaps lucratively – for years, often in a profession for which they trained when they were young, subsequently move into a second career in alternative therapy work or the caring professions. Others turn an existing interest into a new career. I know of one person who successfully turned amateur DIY expertise into a new avenue of work abroad, leading to a whole new life. In most of these scenarios, the transition involves a difficult period in which you are working at your day job and either studying or practising your second career on the side, in the hope that one day its income will support you.

Working as a volunteer may offer training and a way into other fields, while if you have retired, are at home for a while or have cut down on other career commitments, there is great satisfaction to be gained from supporting a charity and helping it to fulfil its function.

The spells in this chapter are all about having faith in your talents and the perseverance to overcome setbacks. Many involve fire and light as a metaphysical means of amplifying your gifts and gaining recognition for them. You will also find spells here for attracting that elusive moment of good fortune when everything comes together to make success.

A spell for turning a talent into expertise

Practice and perseverance are vital to success, but not magic in themselves. To succeed in turning an interest into a career, it is necessary to break the barrier between being a talented amateur and someone who can command a market for their gifts. The barrier is not so very great and here magic can help. Practised two or three nights a week, either in a sink or a bowl or while you are having a bath, this spell builds up the magical energies to ease the transition. Combining the spell with a bath is a good way of relaxing your mind and body and opening yourself to the positive energies that make absolutely anything possible.

You will need

A sink, bowl or bath and suds or bubbles; 10 small white or gold-coloured tea-lights in holders.

Timing

An evening after you have been practising or working on your project.

The spell

* Light the room where you will be working with the tea-lights.
* Fill the sink, bowl or bath and add the bubbles.
* Using both hands, carefully scoop up a large bubble and gently blow it so it rises.
* Name your talent and say:
  So would I rise to recognition. I break through the barrier between me and success.
* Go on scooping up bubbles and chanting the words until you have floated ten bubbles and repeated the words ten times. You may need to blow gently into some of the bubbles to enlarge them. If one bubble breaks, try another.
* If you are working in the bath, dry yourself; otherwise, dry your hands. One by one, blow out all but one of the tea-lights, as you do so naming your talent and repeating the above chant for each one.
* When only one final tea-light remains alight, say:
  The final step. Luck is with me. I am waiting for your call.
* Let the tea-light burn down, in recognition of the intangible luck factor involved in success, which may need patience as well as perseverance.
* In the morning get up early and light just one of the unfinished tea-lights. As it burns, do something small but positive towards furthering your dream, if necessary before getting ready for work.
* If the tea-light is still burning when you finish, blow it out and make a wish for future success.

Lightning magic for a lucky break

The lightning flash has for thousands of years been regarded as the fire of the deities. It can be used for bringing a sudden spark of opportunity when you feel you can't do any more to get your talent recognised.

You will need

Any tree in your garden, or one you can see from a window (the oak and the ash are traditionally considered the most magical trees because they attract lightning).

Timing

When there is forked lightning. For this spell you have to wait for the weather.

The spell

* When the storm breaks, stand so that you can see the tree with the lightning illuminating it. You can be either indoors looking through the widow or in a sheltered place outdoors.
* Count from one to three between the lightning flash and the thunderclap, raising your arms as though conducting the power. At the precise moment the lightning next appears, chant:

Mighty tree, cleave;
Path leave clear for me.
Mighty tree, cleave.
In lightning see the way ahead
That I shall tread to victory.

* At the second 'cleave' bring your arms down together on to a surface as though you were the lightning slicing the tree in two. As the lightning strikes, picture it splitting the tree, clearing a path for you to move towards your goal.
* As the storm gets nearer and the lightning more frequent, repeat the words and actions, increasing the speed of the chant and the vigour of your movements until, when the storm reaches its peak, you shout the chant and bring your hands down with a final bang.
* As the storm recedes, make definite plans for an all-out effort to get your work accepted professionally.
* In the morning, take a small twig from your lightning tree, or one similar, and keep it with your work materials as a reminder.

A flashlight spell before sending off a letter or samples of your work

We can spend far too much time editing a typescript or cassette and never get around to sending it for scrutiny. Many excellent artists and writers have very acceptable examples of their work that they never offer. Years later they may end up regretting their indecision. My late father-in-law was a first-rate artist and those pictures he did submit to galleries sold almost instantly. But he had a whole roomful of paintings that the world never saw. I fear that after his death they were simply disposed of unrecognised.

You will need

A large flashlight on which you can increase the intensity of the beam and the length of the flash.

Timing

At night, when it is pitch-black.

The spell

* Switch on the flashlight with the flash infrequent and the beam weak. Say:
  I send my work into the unknown. Yet do I fear rejection.
* Gradually, increase the speed and intensity of the beam, as you do so saying repeatedly:
  The light radiates ever further. So increases my effect upon the world.
* Set the flashlight to its full intensity and say:
  Carry my creation(s) and be radiant. Why should I fear?
* Turn round faster and faster deosil (clockwise), with the full beam illuminating the darkness, as you do so saying repeatedly:
  The light is all around. So I walk to light and to acceptance.
* If you are outside, go indoors. Switch on the lights and prepare something for sale.

A torch and two-mirror spell to find the right outlets for your talents

Sometimes rejections come because what we offer is not reaching the people who would value it. Even if you have a contact name, the person you need to speak to may be away from the workplace for a while or preoccupied – or the market may suddenly change. Success may often result from an intuition that prompts you to take your designs for children's wear to a manufacturer on the very day they have a rush order and their usual supplier is unable to fulfil the contract.

You will need

2 large mirrors; a wide-beamed torch.

Timing

At night, when it is pitch-black.

The spell

* Set up the mirrors facing each other and far enough apart for you to stand between them and shine the torch in the mirror in front of you.
* Switch on the torch and make the beam dance in one of the mirrors, so that you can see the beam and its reflection.
* Look into the mirror at the reflection of the mirror behind you. You will see not only the reflection of the torch beam, and maybe the reflection of the reflection, but also a flash of brilliance. (If you do not see this, adjust the angle of the torch. It may take some experimenting before you are able to see it.) Hold the torch steady so that the brilliance also steadies. Do not look directly at the intense light, as it will hurt your eyes. Say:

Give me likewise brilliance of vision that I may know the right place and the right time for acceptance. Mirror tell me.

* Stare ahead into the mirror, close your eyes, open them, blink and you may see as an image or hear as words the place and time you should submit work. This awareness may come in symbols. For example, an arrow might mean that you should submit your manuscript to a publisher called Arrow Books; a maypole might mean that I May is the time to submit, or that you should take a stall at a local May market. The awareness may also emerge less tangibly, as impressions or images triggered by the mirror experience.
* Switch off the torch and, by the faint gleam of the mirror, let your ideas formulate. Try to allow your wise unconscious mind to make more connections. These may appear in your dreams.

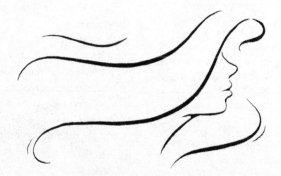

A fire spell for making a leap into a new or second career

You may already have started training in an alternative career or you may be working in two fields at once, hoping to drop one and focus on your real passion. This spell will help to speed and ease the transition.

You will need

About a dozen outdoor torches (the kind that burn with a real flame rather than the battery-operated variety).

Timing

After dark on a clear night when the stars are shining.

The spell

* Make a circle of the torches, with an entrance so that you can walk into the middle and move around without getting burnt.

* Light the torches and enter the circle of fire.

* Starting at the entrance, dance or walk around widdershins (anti-clockwise) three times, ending back at the entrance.

* Stop and say:
  I change direction. My new life moves forward from here. There is no going back.

* Walk or dance around three more times deosil (clockwise).

* Leave the fire ring and say:
  I take your power.
  This is the path I choose from this hour.

* Let the torches burn through while you star-gaze.

* The next day begin to further your second career, perhaps reducing the hours you spend in your other job or taking extra training in the evenings.

A second fire spell for making a leap into a new or second career

You will need

An outdoor fire of some kind (a bonfire, a fire in a pit of stones on earth or sand, a brazier, an incinerator or a garden chiminea – the Spanish/Mexican outdoor stove with a chimney, on sale at many garden centres); 3 sticks long enough to hold in the fire without burning yourself.

Timing

At a natural decision point regarding the change, after dark.

The spell

* Light the fire. When it is burning, take the first of your sticks and hold it in the fire, as you do so saying:
  There is no going back. I burn the old without regret.

* As the stick catches light, cast it as far as you can into the fire, as you do so saying:
  Flame and fire, my desire is for the new. Past, success and failure alike, I consign you to the fire without regret.

* Burn the remaining two sticks in the same way, repeating the chants.

* Use the bonfire to burn any old wood from the garden or the chiminea to cook something – so that the fire has a purpose.

A herb spell for encouragement when you find it hard to keep going

If you are still working full-time at a day job, it can be hard to come home and concentrate on designing your website, sewing intricate designs for a trade fair or practising chords, while everyone else is having fun. Parsley is an important success herb, traditionally planted on Good Friday, the only day the devil has no power, according to folklore. It is also a herb of strength and so will give you stamina.

You will need

A parsley infusion made with dried culinary parsley (see page 232 for instructions on making an infusion); some parsley growing in a pot.

Timing

Any Friday, especially Good Friday.

The spell

* Sprinkle drops of the parsley infusion in deosil (clockwise) circles radiating outwards around tools, books or equipment you use for your second career.
* Beginning and ending at the door to the place where you work on your second career, sprinkle the infusion around the edges of windows and walls.
* Place the pot of parsley where it will get the light. Use sprigs in cooking to empower you.

A spell for the success of a major project

The first published book, professionally recorded song or design commission is generally the hardest to achieve. This spell will give you the initial impetus to launch your project and the drive to carry it through to completion, especially if risks are involved. It is also effective if you work for someone else and suddenly have a chance to take responsibility for a big project.

You will need

A stream, lake or river (not a weed-choked one) with a bridge; 5 blue flowers.

Timing

If possible, just before the full moon, when the sun and moon are both visible in the sky, the sun sinking towards the West and the moon rising in the East.

The spell

* Stand on the bridge holding the five flowers. Raise them first to the sun and then to the moon, as you do so saying:

Moon power, sun power,
At this hour,
Moon power, sun power,
Fill each flower,
That I may fulfil my venture.

* Cast the flowers one at a time from the bridge upstream into the down-flow, as you do so saying:

Grow as the river,
Flow to the sea,
Fulfil my venture
Successfully.

* As you may have done when you were a child, watch your wish come through the bridge and sail off. If any flowers get caught on the bank, see if you can rescue them. If more than two flowers get caught or sink, repeat the spell another day until they do sail away.
* Buy some blue flowers for your work room.

A honey ritual to make profit from an interest or hobby

Honey rituals have been popular in many cultures and ages because honey was the first sweetener and preserver and thus became associated with wealth and abundance. *Melissa* is the Greek word for 'bee'. Aphrodite, Greek goddess of love, was worshipped at a honeycomb-shaped shrine at Mount Eryx. Her priestesses were known as *Melissae.*

You will need

A hive-shaped honey pot, containing honey (often to be found going cheap at garage sales); a honey spoon; a beeswax candle (one with bees on it would be especially appropriate); a small bowl of hot water.

Timing

On a sunny day if possible – use an extra beeswax candle in winter or on a dark day.

The spell

* Light the candle and say:
  Melissa, Lady, Mother Bee,
  Ever shine your light on me.
* Take the lid off the honey pot and put some honey on the spoon. Hold it up to the light and say:
  Melissa, Mother Honey Bee, take your own
  as tribute.
* Eat a little honey from the spoon, as you do so, saying:
  Melissa, Mother Honey Bee, for promised
  abundance in my life I give thanks.
* Return the lid to the honey and wash the spoon in the hot water, as you do so saying:
  Abundance flow and grow in my life.
* Leave the candle to burn down next to the honey pot.
* Pour the honey water away under flowing water and keep the spoon for use only with that honey pot.
* Eat some of your empowered honey before taking or offering goods or services for sale.

A spell to sell yourself in your new role at an interview or meeting

This spell will attract opportunities to you and help you to create the right impression at an interview. It began (and works well as) a general employment and promotion spell, but it has proved especially potent for turning an interest into a career.

You will need

2 identical pieces of white paper; a red pen; a red cord about 30 cm/1 ft long.

Timing

Eight days before a major interview or opportunity, in daylight – preferably morning light.

The spell

* On the first piece of paper, write down your five-year plan as a series of bullet points, including any training you hope to take and contracts you hope to be offered. Take as long as you like to formulate the plan and be as ambitious as you like.
* On the second piece of paper, write down all your assets and talents and what you have achieved so far. All you have to do now is magically fit what you want with what you can offer and send the energies out into the cosmos to connect and return the two fused as opportunities or openings.
* Roll the two pieces of paper together and tie them with the long red cord, knotting it seven times into separate knots. As you tie each knot, say:
  With seven knots, I will succeed;
  Success will come as knots are freed.
* Each morning undo one of the knots and repeat the rhyme. Remind yourself, in your mind or out loud, of your strengths and what you are aiming for.
* After untying each knot, take a practical step towards preparing yourself for the meeting or interview.
* On the eighth day, after untying the last knot, re-read the papers, out loud. Chant seven times:
  With seven knots, I will succeed;
  Success will come, and the knots are freed.
* Take the cord with you to the meeting or interview.

A spell for increasing self-confidence

Sometimes other people can dent your confidence in your talents or discourage you from taking what they see as a risk. Those close to us can resist any change in us that will perhaps change the way they perceive or wish to perceive us. But the things I regret most in my life are the opportunities I did not take. This spell started life as a general confidence one but has proved to work well in connection with alternative career dreams.

You will need

5 small purple candles or tea-lights; rose essential oil; ylang ylang essential oil; a pink rose quartz or purple amethyst crystal; a green aventurine or amazonite crystal.

Timing

Whenever your self-confidence takes a knock.

The spell

* Place the purple candles around the bathroom so that they will cast light-pools on the water when you fill the bath (making sure you choose safe places).
* Light the candles and run a bath.

- When the bath is ready, add five drops each of the rose and ylang ylang essential oils, dropping them into the pools of light.
- Place first the rose quartz or amethyst (for self-esteem and self-approval) and then the aventurine or amazonite crystal (for strengthened resolve) in the water.
- Get in the bath and lie in the water swirling each of the light-pools in turn and making an affirmation for each one, for example:
I believe in myself and my talents (name them). I value myself, and others value what I have to offer. I am complete in myself. I treasure what I have and what I am, as I am right now. I will succeed in my new life path.
- Continue to swirl the light, visualising it flowing within you, making you powerful and confident.
- When you are ready, get out of the bath, wrap yourself in a soft towel or robe and take out the plug, as you do so saying:
Doubts and sorrow, flow from me.
What I wish, I can be.
- Carry the candles into your bedroom or living room and spend the rest of the evening not working but reading a special book, listening to music or just dreaming of golden tomorrows as you gaze into the light.

A sun spell for a new path, whatever the weather or time of year

Even when we cannot see the sun, its power is there. We often most need cheering when the days are dark or cold. This spell will encourage you.

You will need
A circle of yellow or orange paper; a black pen; a red candle; a square of orange or yellow paper; an envelope.

Timing
Between noon and 3 pm, at any time of year (and in any weather).

The spell
- Make a large black dot in the centre of the paper circle to represent the sun. (A circle with a dot in the centre is the astrological glyph for the sun.)
- Place the yellow circle in front of the candle, far enough away that wax will not fall on it. Light the candle.
- On the square of paper, write your goal, as briefly or in as much detail as you wish, as long as you can fit it on the two sides of the paper.
- Fold the square of paper, put it in the envelope and seal the envelope.
- Set the envelope on the paper circle so that it covers the dot in the centre of the circle.
- Let the candle burn through.
- Fold the yellow circle around the envelope and put it away in a drawer.
- Open the envelope and read your goal in two months time. If you have not fulfilled any part of it, repeat the spell.

A spell to make a power charm

Ceramic, glass, crystal and metal charms were used by the ancient Egyptians. It was believed that the symbol contained the essence of what it represented. When the charm was empowered, its energies would be transferred into the wearer's life. You can choose a charm that will directly symbolise your new path, for example a musical instrument, a book, a hand (for healing), a heart (for counselling), a tool, a hat (for clothes design), a tennis racquet and so on. There is a vast array of charms on the market, and you can be ingenious about fitting one to your chosen field. Alternatively, you can empower a crystal. Crystals can represent a quality or strength you need to succeed, for example orange carnelian for courage, amber for ancient knowledge, lapis lazuli for passing an examination or succeeding in training, and so on. You can adapt the charm or crystal by naming specific qualities when you empower it.

You will need

An appropriate charm (see above); a stick of frankincense, sandalwood or myrrh incense.

Timing

A cloudy night when the moon cannot be seen. Midsummer's eve (23 June) is the best night of all.

The spell

* Hold your charm or crystal in cupped hands and, speaking slowly and quietly, name what you want the charm or crystal to represent. You can be as specific and detailed as you wish.

* Light the frankincense, sandalwood or myrrh incense. (These are regarded as ceremonial incenses and so are traditionally used for the empowerment of charms.) Summarise in one word the power that your charm or crystal represents, and use the incense to write it all around the charm or crystal, as though you were weaving a smoke web.

* When you have finished, write in smoke over the area of the smoke web your own name and the name of any company you want to start or have recently started. Then say:

  It is done. I carry my power and the power of the skies with me. Smoke rise and carry my wishes ever upwards.

* Leave the incense to burn through.

* Carry or wear your charm day and night and it will grow ever more powerful. If you sense it weakening, re-empower it by wrapping it in cotton wool and enclosing it with an amethyst in a dark silk scarf for 48 hours.

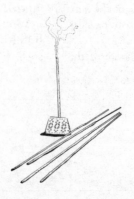

A spell for a high-profile career

If you have a talent such as dancing, singing, talking to people, telling jokes, making music, writing or acting, you may well dream of breaking into the big time. You may have left school or college and gone into a safe career but kept up your talent in an amateur capacity. Whether you are working on hospital radio, dancing in the chorus at the local pantomime or writing a novel far into the night, dreams do come true. People can become stars at any age and unexpected opportunities do arise, especially in the days of reality television!

You will need

A crystal with inclusions, such as golden rutilated quartz with golden needles inside, an amber containing a fossilised piece of plant, or a milky white quartz with streaks within it – phantom quartz, sometimes clear white with a green chlorite phantom crystal inside, is especially powerful.

Timing

When the stars are visible in the sky.

The spell

* Hold the crystal in your power hand (the one you write with), point it towards the stars and say:

  Star of fortune, shine on me;
  Famous I would wish to be.
  Star, like you, I would shine;
  Star of fortune, make stardom mine.

* Under the stars, dance, sing, hum, tell jokes, introduce your favourite television or radio show, or recite the first lines of your novel.

* Ignore anyone who stares at you oddly. You are going to be a star.

* Keep the crystal beneath your pillow. Each night before you go to sleep, hold the crystal and repeat the chant.

* Take the crystal to any auditions or performances. It will not need re-empowering.

A spell to find the right position in the voluntary sector

It seems as if it should be easy to turn a passionate concern for the environment or children who are sick into a career, especially if you do not want to be paid – or at least not paid much. However, voluntary sector organisations place restrictions on who can help them in what way. Some of these are quite justifiable, intended to protect the vulnerable, as well as those would-be helpers who imagine they can sail off to save a village on the other side of the world after a week's training. But if you don't get a positive response to your offers, whether to fundraise, to help with selling products or to work abroad in the field, don't give up. There may be all kinds of reasons for the apparent rejection – organisers may be rushed off their feet, the organisation may not be efficiently run or, on occasion, a local branch of the charity may be territorial and cliquey. Nevertheless, help is always desperately needed in charitable concerns at all levels. A spell can help to match your enthusiasm and talents with an urgent need or vacancy that you may have not been linked with in your original enquiries.

You will need
A large picture of your favourite charity in action; a small globe of the world (available cheaply in children's toy stores) or a small blue or green crystal sphere.

Timing
On a Monday morning, when people are stirring.

The spell
* Put the picture on a table, and the globe or sphere in the centre of the picture.
* Spin the globe or sphere very fast, saying quickly until it stops spinning:
  North, South, East and West,
  Where will I help the best?
  Nearest town or furthest coast,
  Send me where I will help the most.
* Write a letter, send an e-mail or phone the head office of your chosen organisation.
* Repeat the spell each morning until you get a response. If the organisation is unhelpful, try a similar organisation that may be more eager to take advantage of your talents.

PART 4

SPELLS FOR
MONEY AND PROSPERITY

The previous section of this book included spells to generate money through your talents and efforts. This section is about generating money and ensuring prosperity in the widest sense.

I am sometimes asked if it is right to cast spells for instant money and longer-lasting prosperity. Certainly I do not advocate a psychic bank account at which we have a limitless overdraft. But many people do ask me for spells for money. They are not greedy would-be Lottery winners but ordinary men and women struggling to pay bills, buy new tyres for the car or afford a family holiday. Under the traditional rules of magic we can ask for enough for our needs and a little more. That precludes Lottery wins that we do not need – and if everyone did a Lottery spell, each person's winnings would be minimal. However, it is quite justifiable to cast spells for either an immediate specific sum of money genuinely needed or for a general increase in prosperity.that would make life easier and more pleasurable. There is nothing immoral about having money in itself; it is the misuse of money or the acquisition of money for its own sake that is wrong.

It is difficult to cast spells for the well-being of the planet or for the welfare of caged animals if you are worried sick about paying the mortgage. Many people have come to rely on credit not through greed or stupidity but because there is no other way to pay living expenses or help a child through college. The spiral of debt drains energy, pleasure and peace of mind. Spells – together with more practical help – can unfreeze the sense of helplessness that debt may generate and can sometimes create avenues to resolve an acute or ongoing crisis. We should not feel guilty about using spells to ask for money to get us on track.

So this section of the book does include spells to win competitions and to speculate wisely. The most successful business people often rely on an intuitive sixth sense to know when to bid, to buy and to sell, when to back a seemingly promising venture and when to pull back from what seems on paper a sure-fire winner. As you begin to cast money spells, this innate intuitive radar will become activated in you too. You will start to see money-generating opportunities around you and will be able to sense when a purchase or investment is unwise.

This section of the book includes a chapter on abundance. Abundance is, of course, about having a sense of plenty in our lives not just financially but in every way; however, long-term prosperity is an important part of this plenty. Just as our ancestors cast spells for an abundant harvest on the seasonal change points, so we can work to generate enough for everyone. For me, working for abundance is like throwing a pebble into a pool and watching the ripples spread. It is about generating and generously spreading the resources created or attracted, using them wisely for the good of self, family, friends and the wider world.

For some people abundance will be a well filled larder and a comfortable home, little debt, and enough money left over for holidays and a reliable family vehicle. For young people it may mean enough money to pay their way through college and get a foot on the housing ladder. For others abundance may be not dreading the arrival of the postman and the household bills. Abundance can also mean generating vast amounts of money in order to set up a healing foundation or charitable organisation, or the creation of more modest wealth in order to have the freedom to retire early and live in the sun.

If you have money, you should under the laws of cosmic payback, do something positive to ease the burdens of those who have little, whether by helping a struggling family member or supporting a charity. In return for the fruits of a money spell, give something to those around you. This may not necessarily be in money terms but could also be in time or practical help. That is cosmic balance. Those who only take, whether through earthly or magical means, will find that money does not bring happiness, only loneliness and an emotionally and spiritually arid life.

So this is intrinsically a chapter about exchange of energies and balance. It is about seeing the constant outflow of money slowly reversing and the inflow of money freeing up energies for other positive aspects of living.

19 SPELLS FOR BRINGING IN MONEY QUICKLY

One of the most common and useful forms of money magic is for bringing an instant or very rapid infusion of money for a specific purpose. This money will not usually hang around long in your bank account, but it may enable you to keep afloat until pay day, to get an urgent repair done on the car or to buy a new pair of trainers for a child. Money spells of this kind tend to be successful because they are infused with urgency and emotion. Of course, they are not a substitute for budgeting, and if you call on the cosmos too often to bail you out, the spells will lose the edge of urgency and will be less effective.

Under the laws of cosmic payback, when you ask for money to meet an urgent need, whether for yourself, a friend or a family member, you should try to repay the cosmic pot within a week or so. This could be by visiting or contacting a difficult family member, helping a new colleague who is having trouble with office equipment or putting up a birdtable in the garden. Choose something that will involve some effort. That way you are investing positive energies for when you need to ask again.

In time you will probably adopt – and maybe adapt – one or two money spells that work especially well for you to use in a hurry. I have found that the simplest spells often work the best. Sometimes the money you need will come in the form of an expected but delayed payment, a gift, a rebate, a commission, a bonus, a small prize, the offer of an extra shift or the chance to sell something you no longer need for a good price.

Collect a supply of coins for working money spells, for example small change from trips abroad that you cannot change at a bank and coins that are no longer legal tender. It is usually the colour of the coins rather than their value that is of importance in money spells. Green bank notes are also useful. I have a number from Egypt that are almost valueless in money terms but excellent magically.

A money pot or jar spell for money within eight days

Generally, money jar or pot spells are used for ensuring that a steady flow of money comes into the home (see page 285). However, you can also use a money jar or pot for a seven-day spell when you know that you will have a demand for money or will need to settle a bill within eight days and you don't have sufficient funds – perhaps because a promised payment has not arrived or pay-day is a fortnight away. If the money comes before the spell is complete, discontinue the spell but still bury all the bay leaves and give the coins to charity. I did this spell once when I had to pay my caravan site fees by the end of the week or lose the pitch. Within three days a totally unexpected foreign royalty cheque arrived.

You will need

A brown pottery jar with a lid (I use an old honey jar I bought at the roadside in Spain); 7 coins (copper for a modest sum, silver or gold for larger amounts – the denomination of the currency does not matter); 7 dried bay leaves (the culinary kind).

Timing

Seven days before the day you need money.

The spell

* Open the pot and encircle it with the coins and bay leaves, set alternately.
* Drop the first coin you set in the circle into the pot, as you do so naming precisely the amount of money you need and what you need it for.
* Drop the first bay leaf you set in the circle into the pot, as you do so saying:
May the money be found within seven days.
This I ask and this I firmly believe will come to pass.
* Replace the lid.
* The next day, repeat these steps, but this time adding the second coin (to the right) that you set in the circle and then the second bay leaf.
* Each day for another five days repeat these steps, every day moving around the circle one place to the right when you pick up the coin and bay leaf.
* On the eighth day, take out the bay leaves and bury them. Give the coins to a charity (or donate as much as you can afford if the coins are not legal tender).

A seven-day tea-light money spell

This is another good seven-day spell when you need money to pay a looming bill or demand. It does not need coins.

You will need

7 white or red tea-lights (around Christmas time you can buy spice fragranced ones), ideal for fast money; 7 saucers or a heatproof tray; the offending bill or bank statement, or a piece of paper with the amount you need written on it.

Timing

Seven days before the day the money is needed.

The spell

❋ Set the tea-lights on the saucers or heatproof tray in a circle around the bill, bank statement or piece of paper.
❋ Light the first tea-light and say:
Gold and silver I have none;
Spell of increase, money come
By (name the day you need the money).

❋ Recite the day you need the money, what you need it for and how much you need, then blow out the tea-light. Say:
Money come by (name date).
I send light
To make it right.
❋ On the second day repeat these steps, lighting the first tea-light again and then the second. Blow out the tea-lights in reverse order of lighting and repeat the final chant after blowing out each one.
❋ Each day light an extra tea-light, so that by the seventh day all are burning. If any are burnt through before the end of the spell or will not light, replace the individual tea-light. It will not affect the spell. By the eighth day, if not before, your money should arrive.

A basil pathway spell for money needed urgently

Basil is a traditional herb for drawing money. At one time people would line the path to their door with basil plants. Basil is fast-acting and can be used when you need money quickly. You do not have to specify the amount in this spell and the results often come in a number of small money infusions, usually from unexpected sources, within two or three days. If you have a front path, use that. If not, work from your front door outwards. If you have a shared entrance hall, you can sweep up the basil afterwards but place a pot of basil outside the front door to guide the money to you.

You will need

2 jars of culinary basil, with a shaker lid.

Timing

When you need an urgent infusion of cash.

The spell

❋ Take five paces from your front door, making the strides as long as possible. If there are flower beds or earth on either side of the path, scatter some of the basil there as you walk.
❋ When you have made five paces, turn and walk back along the same path, scattering a basil trail along the path and saying continuously:
A basil pathway to my door,
Bringing wealth and so much more.
Wealth and joy, prosperity,
But, first, money swift to me.

A sage smudge or incense spell for when you or a family member need money for something special

You can carry out money spells on behalf of friends or family members as well as yourself. This spell is designed for when you or someone you know need to find money for a special event, such as a holiday, a birthday party or a celebration dinner. There is nothing wrong with casting money spells to bring pleasure into your own life and the lives of the people close to you, as long as the aim is realistic. In other words, the spell is more likely to work if you are planning a celebratory buffet in a local wine bar than if you go for a three-course sit-down meal for 50 in a five-star hotel. Similarly, a spell for a week caravanning or a package holiday is more likely to be effective than one for a month-long luxury cruise. Nevertheless, a spell cast for modest pleasures can sometimes result in an unexpected upgrade or last-minute bargain when you visit the travel agent. If possible, work this spell outdoors; otherwise, make sure the room is well ventilated and work in an uncarpeted area, away from soft furnishings.

You will need

A brochure with prices for the event you are planning, or a piece of white paper with what you desire and an estimated cost written on it; a sagebrush smudge stick or a stick of sage incense (or use cedar); a large metal tray (optional).

Timing

At noon.

The spell

* Set the brochure or paper on the ground – on the metal tray if you are working indoors.
* Light the smudge stick (see page 331) or incense stick. (Sage is excellent for attracting money, and cedar is another money-bringer.)
* Being careful not to drop sparks, waft pound, dollar or euro signs (whatever is your currency) in deosil (clockwise) smoke rings around the brochure. As you smudge, say:

So I draw you, so I call you,
Far away or near,
That I may buy, that I may try
To have what I hold dear.

(Or substitute the name of the person for whom the spell is cast.)

* Finish by making a large smoke currency sign over the brochure or paper and saying:

May this (name what you want) be possible
before (name time scale) is through. Cosmos,
I hand this to you.

A golden tiger's eye prosperity ritual

Golden and yellow crystals are symbols of prosperity in a number of cultures. Under the like attracts like principle, called more formally sympathetic magic, they are believed to draw prosperity into your life and home. On the whole, tiger's eye tends to bring a slow but regular infusion of money and to reduce the outflow of financial resources. If you need prosperity more urgently, go for yellow sparkling citrine. The earth or sand used in this spell offers a solid foundation. Beeswax candles are wonderful for prosperity magic, as bees have always been associated with wealth. You can find brown pebbles on riverbanks, on hillsides and in forests – or buy brown agate or jasper crystals. Four and eight are the numbers of security, and the square represents stability. Under the cosmic law of exchange, try to do something helpful every day of the spell, perhaps by giving time or encouragement where needed.

You will need

4 tiger's eye crystals; a square tray or tin filled with earth or sand; a gold-coloured or beeswax candle; a dish of 8 brown pebbles or crystals.

Timing

On a Saturday for slowly accumulating wealth or a Wednesday for a faster influx, as it is getting dark.

The spell

* Set the candle in the earth or sand so that the wax will melt into it, symbolically planting the candle.

* Light the candle and state the purpose of the ritual into the candle, naming what you need prosperity for. Speak for as long as you wish. Endowing the candle quietly but clearly with your financial needs may serve to clarify matters for you.

* Take up a tiger's eye crystal. Hold it in the flat of your power hand (the one you write with) so that light shines on it. Say:
  Grow safe and secure. I set one cornerstone of prosperity. So shall it be!

* Face the candle and set the tiger's eye to form the top left-hand corner of an invisible square.

* Create three more corners with the remaining tiger's eyes, setting the top right-hand first, then the bottom right-hand and finally the bottom left-hand crystal. Repeat the chant for each tiger's eye.

* Blow out the candle and say:
  I send out light. Light grow that I may prosper.

* Each subsequent night when possible, re-light the candle and add a single pebble to the sides of the invisible square, starting with the top side and moving deosil (clockwise) around the square. Continue until there are two pebbles on each side of the square, blowing out the candle and repeating the second chant each night.

* By the tenth day, you may have received a sign of how the prosperity will come, together with some good ideas and unexpected help.

A gold and silver glass nugget abundance exchange spell

Gold and silver are colours of abundance. Gold- and silver-coloured glass nuggets can be bought very cheaply, as also can sparkling ones – making them ideal for spells where you need a lot of 'crystals'. There are times when we need abundance to flow into our lives, not necessarily financially but perhaps in terms of happiness, security or good health. This spell should help to bring it. It is a fast spell that requires you to speak spontaneously, so allowing your subconscious to get in the driving seat, revealing factors and desires of which your conscious mind may up until now have been unaware.

You will need

A large, deep glass bowl half filled with water; at least 10 gold- and 10 silver-coloured (or sparkling) glass nuggets in separate bowls; two or three white, silver- or gold-coloured floating candles (one of each if you prefer).

Timing

On a Wednesday evening (good for energy exchange spells).

The spell

* Place the floating candles in the bowl of water and light them.
* Take a gold nugget and, without thinking about it, drop it into the bowl, as you do so asking for the abundance you need.
* Without pausing, drop a silver nugget into the bowl and offer a blessing on animals, birds, people or places.
* Continue picking a gold nugget and asking, and picking a silver nugget and blessing until there are no nuggets left or you have run out of abundance wishes and blessings.
* Look at the candles making patterns on the water and the gleaming nuggets beneath. You may see images or conceive ideas that will help you to bring abundance into your life.
* Sit quietly and just watch the candle light on the water until the candles go out.
* The next day, try to do something, however small, to further abundance in one of the areas you named.

A gold and wax money spell

Gold and silver, both the colours and the metals, form the focus of many money spells. This spell can be used for large sums of money that are urgently needed and for longer-term prosperity. The result will probably take about a month and may manifest as, for instance, a win, an unexpected inheritance, a dividend or bonus, a forgotten insurance policy, a loan on favourable terms or a job offer with a greatly increased salary.

You will need

A gold-coloured candle (one that is not dipped, in other words the colour goes all the way through and is not just on the surface of the candle); a large flat metal holder or tray; 3 silver coins; a paper knife, small silver screwdriver or other inscribing tool; some waxed paper.

Timing

On the full moon.

The spell

* Light the candle and, looking into the flame, say:

  Within this flame I seek to turn
  Money towards me.
  Burn, flame, burn;
  Fortune turn
  Your face and smile on me.

* While the candle is burning, go around the house and collect anything that is gold in colour, from fruit to jewellery, and place it around the edge of the tray. Say for each item: *Gold by gold increases, so comes money into my life. Fortune turn your face and smile on me.*

* When the candle is melted, press the silver coins into the wax.

* Using the paper knife or other inscribing tool, draw a deosil (clockwise) circle of currency signs in the wax. Cut a circle of wax to include the coins and the currency signs, but do not remove it. Leave the wax with the gold objects around it until the day after the full moon.

* On the day after the full moon, return the empowered gold objects to their places around the home to draw prosperity.

* Lift out the small wax circle you cut and keep it wrapped in waxed paper in a drawer until the next full moon. By this time you should have received good news of a financial nature and can dispose of the wax circle. Otherwise, keep the wax circle until news arrives, and then dispose of the circle.

A wishing well spell to carry out at home

If you do not have a local wishing well and have a sudden pressing need for money for yourself or family members, you can create your own wishing well at home.

You will need

A large clear glass bowl; 3 gold-coloured floating candles; 3 silver-coloured coins; a pointed clear crystal.

Timing

At 9 pm on a Sunday.

The spell

* Fill the bowl about half full and light the candles.
* Push them gently to start them moving over the surface of the water and extinguish all other lights in the room.
* Drop a coin into a light-pool in the water, as you do so saying:

  Flowing gold, flow now to me;
  In-flowing money would I see.
* Drop the other two coins in to different pools of light, repeating the chant.
* Stir the water three times deosil (clockwise) with the crystal, as you do so saying:

  One for silver,
  Two for gold,
  Secrets now to me unfold.
* Close your eyes, count to three, open them and look into the bowl. In the patterns of light and water you may see an image of how you can acquire the money or how it will come to you. Some people do not see images in the water but in their mind, which is just as good. You may, alternatively, receive impressions and ideas that will hold the key.
* Gaze into the water and allow more images and ideas to form spontaneously.
* When you are ready, blow out the candles, making a wish for each one.
* Sit in the darkness, banishing anxiety and knowing that all will be well.

An instant money spell

This is the spell to cast when you have three hours to find £50. Keep matches by the candle in readiness and don't doubt, don't panic. This simple money spell is one of the most powerful I know. It should therefore be used only sparingly. You need to be specific about the amount you actually need – the more precise you are, the better the spell will work.

You will need

A money candle – either a beeswax candle with a coin pressed into the soft wax about three-quarters of the way down or a large square Chinese candle with a lucky coin inside it.

Timing

When the need is very urgent.

The spell

* Light the candle and gaze into the flame, saying quickly six times (or nine times if things are really dire):

  Five hundred pounds (or what you need),
  It surrounds . . .
  It compounds . . .
  It astounds me.
* At the end of the final chant, blow out the candle and call out the amount of money you need.
* Then do nothing. Push away concerns about the money and do not repeat the spell for at least a fortnight.

A wishing well money spell

The wishing well tradition goes back to Neolithic times, when people would throw coins and charms down wells and into water sources as a tribute to the water deities. In return they would ask for blessings. Wishing wells can be found in all kinds of places. If you have a local one, you can use it to ask for immediate financial assistance as well as more lasting prosperity. Even modern wells acquire magical significance through the power of those who have wished there over a period of months or years, especially if the money is collected in a mesh and given to charity.

You will need

3 coins.

Timing

Just as the sun rises is the customary time for well rituals, but any time during the morning will do, especially as the sun breaks through the clouds.

The spell

* Throw the first coin down the well, as you do so, naming your need, the precise amount of money you require and the time frame.
* Repeat this with the other two coins, in quick succession.
* In return you must do something positive connected with water and water creatures – anything from feeding ducks to helping a dolphin charity or campaigning for local wetlands. This mutual water connection is especially important if you intend to use the wishing well again in the future.

A brass wish spell for slowing expenditure until you can cope

Brass is not just a substitute for gold but has its own magical tradition of attracting wealth and also offering protection. It is good for spell-casting if you cannot pay a bill you are being pressurised about or if a lot of expenses occur one right after the other (see also page 271).

You will need

Any brass object (you can pick them up for almost nothing at garage sales); a soft yellow cloth.

Timing

By moonlight, sunlight or the light of a yellow candle.

The spell

* Polish the brass, as you do so slowly and continuously whispering:
  Brass restore all;
  Let me not fall.
* When the brass is gleaming, place it on top of the bills or demands for 24 hours. Either some assistance will come or you will have the confidence to deal with the problems and stop the pressure.

A moon spell for improving finances

On pages 183–4 I suggested ways of working with the crescent moon for wishes. The crescent moon is also associated with the increase of money. This spell and the following one are traditional crescent moon money spells. This spell is based on the idea of turning silver over three times and bowing to the crescent moon. It originated in ancient Egypt, where the three times was in honour of Osiris, the father god; Isis, the mother; and Horus, their son, the young sky god. As the moon increased in size, so it was believed money would flow in in increasing quantities.

You will need
A silver-coloured coin.

Timing
During the crescent moon, when the moon is visible in the sky. If it is cloudy, wait for a break in the cloud.

The spell
* Stand in an open space, facing the moon and holding the coin in your receptive hand (the one you don't write with).
* Bow three times to the moon and then turn the money over three times with your power hand, while keeping your gaze on the moon.
* Whisper the financial help you need to the moon and then bow three times more.
* Bury the coin as close as you can to where you are standing.

A second moon spell for improving finances

This spell is worked at the time of the crescent moon for a financial improvement by the time the full moon appears (about two weeks later).

You will need
A silver-coloured coin.

Timing
During the early days of the crescent moon.

The spell
* Stand in an open space, facing the crescent moon and holding the coin in your open power hand (the one you write with). Say three times slowly:
  New moon, true moon, moon in the sky,
  Bring me money before you ride high.
* After the third chant throw the coin over your left shoulder, still looking at the moon, and walk away in the direction of the moon without looking back.

A salt ritual to get money flowing in fast

This is a good spell to use if you have been owed money for too long or if you need a fast infusion of money, either for a specific purpose or to ease finances generally. Salt is associated with money as well as with health. It was traded for treasures by the Celts, and the Roman sometimes paid their soldiers in sacks of salt because it was such a valuable commodity.

You will need
A tub of sea salt; a piece of stiff card; 4 gold-coloured candles; a glass bowl half filled with water.

Timing
At night during the crescent moon.

The spell
* Form a cone of sea salt on the piece of card. Around it, at regular intervals, place the gold candles – making sure the wax will not fall on the salt.
* Light the candles and leave them to burn through. Spend the time listing your assets and skills, mailing or phoning contacts, preparing anything you have to sell (on-line auctions such as eBay can bring in fast money) and planning any other money-spinning schemes you have thought of but never tried. Write and send invoices, together with reminders to anyone who owes you money. Draw up a game plan. The magical energies you are generating will inspire you.
* As soon as the candles have burnt away, fold up the ends of the card and tip the salt cone into the water.
* Stir the water with the index finger of your power hand (the one you write with) until the salt is all dissolved – add more water if necessary.
* Go outdoors and hold the bowl up to the crescent moon (or the sky if it is cloudy) and say:
May what is due and what deserved come to me swiftly before the moon is full.
* Pour the salt water into flowing water, for example a drain with a tap running or the spray of a garden hose.
* The next morning choose an idea from your game plan. Keep trying ideas until something hits. You may find that people start paying what is owed almost at once, or help comes from unexpected sources.

A moon money spell

Whereas the crescent is good for increase, the full or nearly full moon gives the impetus for a sudden surge of power if the need is almost instant or the amount required large. If it is cloudy, position tall silver candles so that they shine on the water. This spell is easily carried out.

You will need

A deep glass bowl half filled with water; a silver coin; a small hand mirror.

Timing

The night of the full moon or the nights immediately before and after.

The spell

* Position the bowl so that the moon shines in to the water (or, if you are working indoors, the candlelight shines in to the water).
* Hold the coin in your power hand (the one you write with) and the mirror in your receptive one.
* Angle the mirror so that it makes a flash and then throw the coin, aiming for the centre of the brightness.
* As the coin falls into the water, say:
  Fill my hands with magic gold.
  I gather all that I can hold.
* Plunge your hands three times into the silver water, as you do so saying:
  So I take not with greed,
  But to solve my urgent need.
* Hold your hands above the bowl and shake them so that silver droplets cascade from your fingers.
* Dip the mirror into the water and say:
  Come to me prosperity;
  Give to me all I can see.
* Look into the shimmering mirror, shake it and leave it to dry naturally.
* Tip the water and the coin outdoors on to earth, grass or a paved area and leave the coin to be picked up by someone else.

A second moon money spell

This spell needs special conditions but is well worth carrying out when you are near a body of tidal water since it can bring long-term prosperity.

You will need

6 small silver coins; the sea or a tidal water, when the tide has gone out, leaving pools; a large flashlight (if it is dark when you work).

Timing

At full moon or the nights on either side, when the moon is bright enough to light up the rock pools.

The spell

* Walk in the moonlight on the shore, holding the coins and allowing the power and beauty to fill you with optimism.
* Identify five small rock pools leading down to the water.
* Begin to walk, casting a coin in each pool and saying:
  Moon water, moon light,
  Bring money power to me this night.
* When you reach the water's edge, cast the final coin as far as you can into the water, as you do so saying:
  Return threefold on the tide and threefold more, as five tides roar and fortune brings anew.

A sunshine and rain money spell

If you live inland, this spell makes a good alternative to the previous one. It works with the power of the sun, which can also bring money quickly or in large quantities. This is a strange little spell, but I have used it for years and have found that it does work.

You will need

6 coins; some puddles.

Timing

When there are puddles in sunlight, preferably as the rain is easing.

The spell

* Go outside and walk about, casting your six coins into six puddles filled with light. For every coin you throw, say very fast:
Sun be sunny;
Bring me money.
* When you have cast the final coin, splash in the puddles in reverse order of casting the coins, reciting the chant just once as you stamp in each.
* Leave the coins in the puddles and do something for fun, even if it is just for an hour.

A Viking Rune spell for winning through financially when things look dire

In this spell the power is released by etching the Rune on a candle and reciting the Rune's name. The Runic sign for prosperity is *fehu*. This referred to the cattle the Vikings herded before them on their travels and sometimes took in boats to lands they colonised. Fehu is the first rune in the set, and so has special power. This is an excellent spell for overcoming financial difficulties and pulling the magical rabbit – or in Viking terms hare – out of the bag to save the day.

You will need

A red candle and a deep holder; a paper knife, long sharp nail or other inscribing tool.

Timing

On a Thursday, day of the thunder god Thor, after dusk.

The spell

* On one side of the red candle (Viking colour of power and courage) inscribe the Rune fehu, as you do so saying its name (pronounced *fayhoo*) slowly eight times.

* Light the candle and recite the power Rune eight more times slowly.
* Chant 'fehu' faster and faster until you can feel the power has reached its height. Then blow out the candle with a final cry:
Fehu empower and enrich me!
* Light the candle when you rise the next morning, repeating the cry eight times with confidence.
* Blow out the candle.
* At dusk, light the candle and repeat the chant, then blow out the candle.
* Continue repeating the process in the morning and at dusk until the desired result materialises or the candle will light no more. In either case dispose of the rest of the candle.
* Repeat the spell if the problem is obstinate and the obstacles great.

A hair spell for getting something you really want

In general, I do not like the idea of using nail clippings, hair and so on in spells. However, since in this spell hair is used as a symbol of your innate power and right to use resources to make yourself and others happy, it feels all right to me. You can use thin pieces of brown or orange sewing silk if you prefer or your hair is very short. This is a spell to be used only occasionally, but you should not feel guilty about seeking to further your own career or your own happiness magically as well as practically.

You will need

8 of your own hairs (cut or pull them from your head, or take them from your hairbrush or comb); a silver or gold ring belonging to you; some thread (optional); brochures or images of what you really want.

Timing

On a Friday, as close to sunset as possible, so you can work in fading natural light

The spell

* Bind the eight hairs around the ring (eight is the number of material security), knotting or plaiting them together. If necessary, use thread to fix them. Say:
  I bind my strength, I wind my strength
  Round circle clear and true.
  I bind my strength, I wind my strength
  And power thus renew.
* Put the ring on the finger on which you usually wear it and say:
  I bind my strength, I wind my strength,
  I wear it in my heart.
  I wind my strength, I bind my strength
  And so my dream I start.
* Place the ring on top of the brochures or images and say:
  I bind my strength, I wind my strength;
  This dream shall come to me.
  I bind my strength, I wind my strength;
  Follow prosperity.
  This is my dearest wish.
* Leave the ring on the brochures or images for seven days and nights. Put it on whenever you make a phone call, write a letter or send an e-mail about your plans or apply for funding or finance. Return the ring to the top of the brochures or images immediately afterwards, checking that the hairs are still bound. Retie or replace them if necessary. On each of the seven days of the spell, do something small but helpful for someone inside or outside the home or for a good cause.
* Unwind the hairs and burn them, as you do so saying:
  My dearest wish come true. I claim this right and will repay in due time.

A moon cycle spell for making money come into your life if you have many outgoings or many people make demands on your resources

This is a long-term spell that is effective if there are too many people or demands for your income to go around. If you carry the spell out once every season (spring, summer, autumn and winter), it will keep money gently rolling in in the required amounts for everyone to have at least a thin slice of the financial cake.

You will need

A supply of small squat bright-yellow candles; a candle-holder; a metal tray; 28 or 29 very small equal-sized pieces of paper, depending on whether the moon cycle you are working with has 28 or 29 days – pages from a small notebook are ideal; a silver pen; an old lidded pot or jar, such as a coffee jar.

Timing

Work from full moon to full moon, choosing a moon cycle in the middle of each season.

The spell

* On the night of the full moon, write on each of the pieces of paper whatever you see as the solution to your financial difficulties, for example, 'increased income', 'more financial input' or 'extra income sources'. You can write the same phrase on each paper or use different phrases. Write only one phrase on each piece of paper.
* On each of the 28 or 29 days of the spell, whenever you have time during the evening, light a yellow candle. Use the same candle until it will light no more and then replace it with another.
* Pick a piece of paper and read the phrase written on it aloud.
* Make the paper in to a taper and burn it in the candle, as you do so repeating the phrase. Once the paper has caught alight, drop it on to the metal tray to burn through. It does not matter if it only partially burns.
* Blow out the candle and say:
  Money come to me and stay.
* When cool, tip any ash into the pot and put the lid back on.
* When all the papers are burnt, let the final candle burn through.
* When the wax is cool, crumble it and add it to the pot.
* On the day after the next full moon, throw away the jar.

A spell to help build up your resources quickly or help you make the best use of what you have

For spells in which the aim is to build up or maximise resources quickly, children's building blocks that clip together, such as Lego bricks, are ideal. Yellow candles, the colour of Mercury – the planet of speculation and money lenders as well as of healing and learning – add fast, animated colour to money-making plans. The essence of this fun spell is speed.

You will need
A box of brightly coloured children's bricks that fit together; 3 small yellow candles.

Timing
On a Wednesday morning.

The spell
* Arrange the candles in a triangle, the geometric shape of increase.
* Make a square of four bricks. This will be the foundation of a tower of bricks.
* On the square, begin to assemble the tower as fast as possible, as you do so chanting continuously:
Two becomes four, accumulate more.
Four into eight, speculate.
So grows my fortune to great height.
When foundations are firm, results will be right.
* When the tower will go no higher without toppling over, repeat the chant, this time more and more slowly, until eventually the words fade into silence.
* Leave the candles to burn through around the tower while you make calculations or financial plans.
* When the candles go out, slowly dismantle the tower and return the bricks to the box.
* Repeat the spell weekly or when you need a boost to your determination or enthusiasm.

20 SPELLS FOR ABUNDANCE AND PROSPERITY

Long-term financial security is a pretty much universal goal. While money spells for immediate needs are a valuable tool during temporary cash-flow problems, by increasing our general prosperity we can make the need for such spells a rare occurrence.

There are many ways to increase our prosperity, for example through career advancement, wise investment, saving and cutting down debt. All of these practical measures are dealt with in this part of the book, for we can always use some magical impetus to fuel our earthly effort. Prosperity is like a magnet – or a psychic snowball. If we emit prosperity vibes, all manner of good things may come to us, from opportunities to sell our talents, to promotion, to money from unexpected sources. The main focus of this chapter is on making ourselves psychically prosperous so that material prosperity is attracted, as day follows the night.

Prosperity's twin sister, abundance, is that ripple caused by casting the stone of prosperity into the pond. For the spells suggested in this chapter are not geared to greed or acquisitiveness. Abundance is created when prosperity is shared – through cooking a meal for friends and family, giving a gift, organising an outing, filling our environment with beautiful things that are not necessarily expensive, and so on. These are simple expressions of abundance and generate happiness that we can pass on, thus creating memories that sustain us through the years. What is more, abundance can be shared in the form of practical talents and work exchanged even when money does not change hands.

The good harvest of our rural ancestors filtered down to all levels of society. Wealth should not be like a cake that is finite but like a stew that becomes more nourishing the more that is added to the pot. As long as we become more generous and spread the pleasures of a better lifestyle rather than clutching them to us, prosperity magic is both positive and creative. As I said in the previous chapter, if you are always worried about the future, then it is hard to give freely of time and energy to others. Even our ability to give to those in need is potentially enhanced by our own prosperity.

This chapter contains spells for both personal and family abundance. In repayment for the magic, make a small donation to a charity, organise a treat for the family or do a good deed for a person known or unknown.

A spell to make an abundance basket

This spell and the three that follow it may sound more like practical tips than magic, but in fact if you carry out any of these practical measures regularly, you will attract all manner of good things in to your life. I can only explain this as the stirring-up of the abundance energies, which then circulate freely, bringing the generosity of others in to your world. A dear friend of mine from Chile gave me a painted wooden abundance basket filled with wooden fruit and grains. For a while I hung it from a tree in the middle of my garden and lent it to people who needed good things in their life. You can make your own living abundance basket and keep it in the heart of your home, to be shared by visitors and family members alike.

You will need

A wicker or straw basket; a yellow cloth inside; some golden-coloured fruit; some tiny orange and golden-coloured crystals such as carnelian and citrine; skeins of orange, red and gold-coloured ribbon; some individual packs of nuts, dried golden-coloured fruits and seeds (organic grocers stock environmentally friendly packets); small packets or miniature jars of sun herbs such as sage, rosemary and chamomile; some olives; a vase of fresh flowers or golden-coloured dried grasses and corn.

Timing

Any.

The spell

* Line the basket with the yellow cloth and fill it with the other ingredients (except for the flowers or grasses). Set it near the centre of your home or the place where visitors most often congregate, with the flowers or grasses arranged beside it.
* Keep the contents fresh and topped up, and invite visitors to take something home with them from your abundance basket, so spreading the abundance.

A spell to share an abundance meal

You will need

Some good natural food to offer, for example homemade breads and cakes, cheese, golden-coloured fruits, nuts, seeds, salad, roasted or baked potatoes and root vegetables, homemade golden-coloured soup, fruit juices and barley wine; a small wrapped gift made of natural materials such as wood, clay, undyed fabric, seeds, etc.; a pot plant.

Timing

Once a month, at any time.

The spell

* Invite friends and family for a bring-and-share meal of natural produce. Ask everyone to bring a very small gift made from natural materials (put a limit on the price) and a pot plant.
* During the meal, have an abundance hour when everyone shares a good experience that occurred during the previous month and describes an event or plan they are looking forward to completing.
* After the meal, invite everyone to choose a small wrapped present and a plant to take home.

A spell to start an abundance talent exchange

Our reliance on expertise in every field, together with the trend for frequent house moves, has eroded the traditional neighbourhood exchange of skills. However, this is re-emerging in some communities. When I was a single mother, I traded Latin and English lessons for babysitting. Of course, there is always someone who will exploit these kinds of exchange, but on the whole they create a lot of good will. With e-mail and text phones, these days little organisation is needed.

You will need
Nothing.

Timing
Any.

The spell

* Get to know the skills of your friends and neighbours and their families. Now if you need electrical sockets replaced, you can trade it for sewing labels on school clothes, typing up correspondence, accounting or decorating. You can also offer emergency cover (a dress for the school play urgently needed) for a later payback.

A spell to organise an abundant goods exchange

When my children were young and I attended Quaker meetings regularly, I was the recipient of excellent hand-me-down clothes for my five offspring, together with unwanted toys, bicycles and so on. In return I was able to hand on things I no longer needed or my family had outgrown. It may seem a chore to give rather than just throw away fashion mistakes, unused perfume, jewellery, games and so on, but these things are sometimes someone else's joy, and they spread abundance rather than consumerism. On the other hand, giving away perfectly serviceable furniture to someone setting up a first home may be a lot easier than selling it second-hand, and good things will come back to you.

You will need
Nothing.

Timing
Any.

The spell

* Either formally or informally, initiate not garage or car-boot sales but exchanges. The idea is that you exchange something you do not need any more for something you do – for example, a printer and scanner for a games console, a computer for a stereo deck. Start in a small way with friends and family and the trend may spread.

A Viking Runic spell for abundance

In the Runic divinatory, gebo – the rune for the gift – represents general abundance. In the Viking tradition a gift given required one in return. Indeed, hospitality and altruism were greatly valued as qualities by the northern peoples. Gebo also forms the sign of the ancient Earth mother.

You will need

An area of open land, grass, sand or earth on which you can mark gebo with a stick or outline it with stones and then walk around your Rune.

Timing

Just after sunrise.

The spell

* Find a stick and draw gebo in the earth, enclosing it in a circle. Alternatively, make gebo and the circle from stones.
* Walk around the circle deosil (clockwise) and then walk to the centre of gebo down any of its arms.
* Stand at the centre of gebo, face the direction of the newly risen sun and say:

Abundance is free and without restrictions, given and received and given again. I open the way to abundance.

* Rub out the circle or remove the stones directly ahead of where you are standing, to create a pathway through which the sun can enter.
* Walk straight out of the pathway and say:

I welcome abundance given and received and given freely again. Welcome the morning.

* Leave the gebo sign as a tribute to the Earth.
* Invite a friend or someone you know is lonely to share a meal with you in the near future.

A cinnamon, oat and ginger abundance spell

The first fruits of any harvest were traditionally offered to the Earth mother, and later the Virgin Mary, in thanks for abundance received. If your family really hates spices, you can substitute raisins or sultanas for the cinnamon and ginger in this spell.

You will need

A biscuit jar or cake tin; some cinnamon or ginger oat biscuits or cakes (bought or homemade).

Timing

On the first of the month, in the morning.

The spell

* Take the first of the batch of freshly baked cinnamon or ginger oat biscuits or cakes (both spices attract good things into your life) or the first one from the packet. Take it in to the garden or an open space and crumble it on to the earth or a bird table, as you do so saying:

Mother Earth, I offer thanks and tribute for the blessings and abundance you bring into my life and to those I love. Abundance give and abundance receive.

* Put the biscuits or cakes in the jar or tin and offer or eat them as you wish. Every month, or when the tin is empty, bake or buy fresh biscuits or cakes and repeat the previous step in the same spot. Crumble any remaining biscuits from the last batch on to the ground when each month is up.

A general spell to attract prosperity and financial security into your life

This is a spell for increasing the prosperity vibes flowing towards you. It is especially good if you are recovering from a period of financial uncertainty or are worried about future finances.

You will need
6 small, squat green candles; a shiny, circular metal tray; 9 gold-coloured coins; some dried basil (the culinary kind is fine); a piece of green silk.

Timing
Any evening during the waxing moon, preferably when the moon is visible.

The spell
* Working where you can see the moon through the window (forget superstitions about seeing the moon through glass) or in a sheltered outdoor place, set the candles in a tight circle on the tray, so that they are almost touching.
* Light the candle to the North, (estimate the direction) and then the other five, moving deosil (clockwise) and saying for each:
  Light of increase,
  Shower on me
  Money and security.
  Bring, I ask, prosperity.
* Allow the candles to burn down.
* While the wax is still warm, press the coins into the centre of the candle circle, one in front of where each candle was and three in a triangle formation in the centre, repeating the chant as you set each. The triangle is a symbol of expansion.
* Sprinkle basil between the coins, as you do so, repeating the chant.
* When the wax is hardened, cut out a disc containing the nine coins. Leave your coin amulet on a window ledge indoors where it can catch any light (day or night) until the night after the full moon.
* On the day after the full moon wrap the disc in the piece of silk and put it in a drawer.
* On the next crescent moon get the disc out again. When you see the crescent, turn the disc over and repeat the chant three times.
* Leave the disc on the window ledge until the day after the full moon, when you should wrap it again.
* When the wax begins to crumble, dispose of the disc and bury the coins under a fruit tree.

A basil and candle prosperity-growing spell

Basil is one of the best prosperity and long-lasting financial security herbs – as well as a fast money-generating one (see Chapter 19). It can be planted near your front door, either in the earth or in a pot, so that as it spreads and grows, your prosperity will increase. You can also use it in cooking to empower yourself for any major financial thrust.

You will need

A small healthy potted basil plant; a green candle in a holder; 8 small green crystals (jade, or tree or moss agate are excellent for growth).

Timing

Any of the three days before the full moon, traditionally the best time for planting herbs.

The spell

* Set the crystals in a square formation around the basil plant, two on each side, to indicate financial security.
* Place the candle next to the basil plant and within the square, taking care to choose a spot where wax will not fall on the plant or the crystals.
* Light the candle and pass both your hands slowly deosil (clockwise) nine times over the candle, being careful not to burn yourself or catch your sleeves in the flame. Say:
  Grow security, grow stability, into lasting prosperity.
* Now hold your hands above the plant, this time moving them widdershins (anticlockwise) to download the power from the candle. Repeat the chant.
* Blow out the candle, as you do so saying:
  Bring prosperity.
* Plant the basil by moonlight, placing one of the crystals in the soil. Carry another with you for luck and keep the rest with your magic things to empower them.

A kelp and whisky spell

This is a traditional ongoing spell to ensure continuing prosperity.

You will need

A piece of dried kelp (available from health food stores) or a piece of seaweed you gathered yourself; a glass jar with a lid; some whisky.

Timing

The night before the full moon.

The spell

* Place the kelp or seaweed in the jar and pour in the whisky until it covers the seaweed. Seal the jar.
* Place the jar on a window ledge and prosperity will always flow in to your life.
* Every new year's eve, throw away the whisky and kelp before midnight, replacing them after midnight on new year's day.

A money tree spell

'Money doesn't grow on trees,' my late mother used to say, but many magic spells do involve growing money symbolically in the soil around a money-bringing tree.

You will need

A bay, palm or orange tree – or any other ornamental tree or bush with 3 extra ribbons added to it (you can buy miniature potted bay, palms, orange and kumquat trees all over the world); a gold-coloured coin; a silver-coloured coin; a copper-coloured coin; 3 gold-coloured ribbons.

Timing

After the crescent moon, the earlier in the moon cycle the better.

The spell

❋ Bury first the copper coin, then the silver one and finally the gold one in the soil around the tree. Gold, the metal of the sun, promises money; silver, the metal of the moon, promises that money will continue to flow throughout your life; and copper, the metal of Venus, promises that it will bring happiness to you and to those you love.

❋ Tie the three ribbons loosely to the tree's branches, saying as you hang each:

Money tree, money tree,
Grow for me.
Gifts I bring;
Gold for gold,
Money tree, your gifts unfold.

❋ Tend the tree regularly, replacing the ribbons if they become frayed.

A fenugreek seed growth pot spell

This is a very old spell popular in many lands. Fenugreek was introduced into Britain and northern Europe from Mediterranean regions via trade routes. It has been associated with prosperity since Roman times.

You will need

A tub of fenugreek seeds (or substitute cumin or coriander); an open pot or jar.

Timing

At the new moon (about two and a half days before the crescent moon appears – check *Old Moore's Almanack*, a diary or the weather page of a newspaper for the exact date. The glyph is a filled-in circle.)

The spell

❋ Put a few seeds of fenugreek in the open pot or jar and place it on a kitchen shelf or in the hearth.

❋ Add a sprinkling of seeds each day until the jar is full.

❋ Empty the jar and plant the seeds – to ensure the money supply will continue to grow – and then begin a new jar of seeds.

A spell to open you to inflowing possibilities for prosperity and abundance from all around you

Parsley, basil, sage and mint are all linked with prosperity. If you want a quick infusion of abundance and prosperity in your life, candle power is a good way to stir the energies. Melting wax represents the flow of good things. This spell attracts riches and blessings from unexpected places that may prove a regular source of income or long-term positive input in your life.

You will need

A small, very waxy, rough-textured beeswax or red candle; a broad metal candle-holder; some kitchen paper or a plate; a jar of dried parsley, sage, basil or mint (the culinary kind is fine).

Timing

At noon.

The spell

* Sprinkle a generous amount of herbs on the paper or plate and roll the candle in the herbs, as you do so saying:

May I attract the abundance and prosperity of the universe into my life.

* When some herbs have stuck to the candle (it need not be many) light the candle and say:

May abundance and prosperity flow through my life continuously as the years pass.

* Blow out the candle and say:

I draw you, light, within; may fortune smile continually.

* Repeat the spell weekly or monthly, rolling the candle in more herbs, until the candle is used up or will light no more.

A second spell to open you to inflowing possibilities for prosperity and abundance from all around you

You will need

A candle in a glass container scented with spice, fruit or a woody fragrance (available from large supermarkets); a jar of dried parsley, sage, basil or mint (the culinary kind is fine).

Timing

On a Thursday evening.

The spell

* Light the candle in the room you use for sorting out finances.
* When the wax has melted and the centre of the candle is hot liquid, carefully shake a few herbs into the melted wax as the candle burns. Say:

Within me are the seeds of prosperity. Burn ever brighter, prosperity; enclose me in your universal benevolence.

* Blow out the candle. The wax containing the herbs will harden. This is a good time to sort out papers, fill in forms, balance books and so on.
* Light the candle for a few minutes every Thursday and repeat the chant. When the wick will no longer light or the wax and glass get sooty, replace the candle.

A tiger's eye spell for restoring wealth

After a major financial setback, this spell will help you to rebuild your finances far faster than you anticipate.

You will need

A golden-brown candle; a packet of any kind of seeds; a golden tiger's eye crystal; 3 sticks of frankincense or sandalwood incense; a brown purse.

Timing

On three consecutive days.

The spell

* At dawn on the first day, light the candle and one incense stick. Pass the crystal around the flame of the candle three times in a deosil (clockwise) direction, as you do so saying:
  Let my true light once more shine through.
  Success return, good times renew.
* Blow out the candle, picturing gold and silver coins cascading towards you and filling your hands. Leave the incense to burn through.
* At noon on the second day, light the candle and another incense stick. Pass the crystal around the flame a further three times (building up the positive energies) and repeat the chant.
* Blow out the candle, this time saying:
  I bind to me the power of fire,
  That I may release at my desire.
* Leave the incense to burn through.
* At dusk on the third day, light the candle and the third incense stick. Repeat the first chant as you pass the crystal again three times deosil around the flame.
* Place the crystal in front of the candle and leave the candle to burn through.
* Write in the air in incense smoke, 'Prosperity return once more,/Even better than before', then leave the incense to burn through.
* Place the crystal in the brown purse and carry it with you to attract prosperity. Repeat the spell monthly to keep the crystal charged with wealth-generating power.

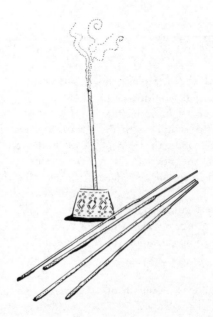

A three day candle spell for abundance and prosperity

Abundance rituals using light are often associated with mid-winter festivals — still celebrated in a number of cultures, including those of India and Israel (as well as Hebrew communities all over the world). You can, however, use candles to attract money and resources to the home at any time of the year. Seasonal or personal transition points are particularly appropriate — or work the spell when you are hoping for a major influx of money.

You will need

3 gold-coloured candles, each of different height; 3 candle-holders; symbols of abundance and increase, such as ears of corn, golden-coloured vegetables, gold jewellery, gold-coloured coins and yellow or orange crystals (for example agates, amber, carnelians, citrine and jasper; a gold- or silver-coloured tray, or any tray covered with foil; three gold-coloured fruits; 2 handfuls of nuts; a few seeds; a pottery jar.

Timing

At dusk.

The spell

* In the centre of the tray place the three candles (in holders) in ascending order of height from left to right. Encircle the candles with the symbols of abundance, the golden-coloured fruits, the nuts and the seeds, placing them around the edges of the tray.
* Light the smallest gold candle and, visualising your prosperity increasing and good things showering upon you, say nine times:
Light grow.
* Eat one of the golden-coloured fruits to absorb the magical energies.

* Extinguish the candle, sending the golden light into your life and to those you love, with the wish that it attract riches and joy in every way.
* At dusk on the second day, re-light the smallest candle, reciting, once only:
Light grow.
* Light the second candle, again visualising your prosperity increasing and good things showering upon you and this time saying nine times:
Light grow,
Increase show.
* Eat a golden-coloured fruit and a handful of nuts.
* Extinguish the larger golden candle, then the smaller, sending the light from both golden candles to all who are in need of abundance, near and far, not forgetting yourself and your nearest and dearest.
* At dusk on the third day, light the smallest golden candle, saying once:
Light grow.
* Light the second candle, saying once:
Increase show.
* Light the third candle, saying nine times:
Light grow,
Increase show,
Joy to know.
* Eat the remaining golden-coloured fruit, the second handful of nuts and the seeds.
* Leave the three candles to burn through on the tray, still encircled by the symbols of abundance.
* Over the ensuing days eat what can be consumed from your store of abundance and keep the coins and crystals in the pottery jar near a source of warmth where they can incubate.

A prosperity mojo for increased financial security

As this is a hard-working mojo, you will need to fill it quite full.

You will need

A white or undyed cream-coloured bag; some gold-coloured ribbon; 3 small dark-green peridots or lighter-green olivines; a twist of wheat germ in foil; a twist of dried kelp in foil or a small piece of dried seaweed; 3 almonds; a copper ring; a credit card cut up diagonally to give four pieces, or a receipt for a paid bill cut in the same way; a little bourbon, barley wine or wheat beer.

Timing

Late on a Thursday evening – finish by midnight.

The spell

* Working in silence, fill the bag with the crystals, wheat germ, kelp or seaweed, almonds, copper ring and credit card or bill. Add a few drops of bourbon, barley wine or wheat beer.
* Use the gold ribbon to close the bag, tying it with three knots.
* Hide the mojo somewhere where the air will circulate around it, as high in the house as possible.
* Replace it every three months.

A garden gnome money-attracting ritual

Garden gnomes are not at all like Disney's *Snow White* characters. They are older, browner and more taciturn even than Grumpy in the film. They are the creatures of the element of Earth and renowned for accumulating treasure. Though you may not see your garden gnome, you can still ask for his or her help with problems or questions about financial security – gnomes' speciality. In gnome magic, accumulating the desired wealth requires a lot of ordinary earthly effort.

You will need

A model garden gnome (available from garden centres, or make your own from an old tree stump – you can often find pieces of wood that already possess features and just need a little smoothing down; alternatively, make a clay gnome, drawing in his features and firing him in a kiln or oven); a square piece of orange paper; a gold pen; a silver- or gold-coloured coin; a dish of water; some seeds.

Timing

Just before sunset, when the garden is quiet.

The spell

* Using the gold pen, write what you most need for financial security on the piece of orange paper.
* Wrap the paper around the coin and bury it at the feet of the gnome just as the sun is setting.
* Place the dish of water next to the gnome, together with the seeds (for him to share with the birds).
* After five days you should be given the answer to your problem, perhaps from an unexpected source. If not, repeat the ritual every five days – in case your gnome is a slow thinker.

A money spell for the regular flow of money or the gradual increase of prosperity

This is a more complex version of the salt spell given on page 267 and is good for ensuring a long-term flow of money into your life.

You will need

A rich-brown candle in a holder; some salt; a metal tray; a small spoon; 12 coins; a jug or bowl half filled with water; a small pot or jar with a lid; a green candle (optional).

Timing

During the crescent moon.

The spell

* Make a small pile of salt in the centre of the metal tray and surround it with a circle of coins.
* Light the candle and set it in its holder on the tray so that the light shines on the salt and the coins. Say:

Money grow,
Light flow.
Bring to me
Prosperity.

* Repeat the chant 11 more times, faster and faster, and then blow out the candle, sending the light into the salt and coins.
* Re-light the candle, gather up the coins and set them in the pot, without its lid, in front of the candle.

* Scoop up the salt, spoonful by spoonful, and tip it into the jug or bowl of water, stirring it until it dissolves.
* Pour the salt water down the sink or in to a drain under running water, as you do so saying:

Money flow free,
Flow to me,
From the rivers
And the sea,
Bringing me
Prosperity.

* Leave the candle to burn through.
* Put the lid on the money pot and then place the pot, with the coins inside, in a warm place in the kitchen or a sunny part of the house.
* Each day add a single coin, as you do so saying:

Money grow,
Money flow.
Bring to me
Prosperity.

* If you hit a temporary glitch, burn a green candle over the pot. When it is full, buy a small treat for the family or give the money to charity and repeat the spell.

An empowered coin charm spell

Traditionally, on both sides of the Atlantic, the kitchen copper jar, made of brown pottery with a lid, is kept on a shelf or by the hearth. (See page 258 for a variation on this spell.)

You will need

A brown pottery pot with a lid; some copper-coloured or real copper coins (coins minted during a leap year are especially fortunate); a small purse.

Timing

During the waxing moon.

The spell

* Every day add a copper coin to the pot, keeping the pot, with the lid on, in the kitchen or somewhere warm.
* On the first day of the crescent moon, take the pot outside. Take the lid off and remove nine coins, turning over the ninth one three times and then bowing to the moon (or the sky if it is cloudy) three times.
* Place the coin in the purse and replace the others in the pot. Whenever you are going out on a venture that involves worldly matters, take the coin in the purse with you and turn it over nine times before the encounter or transaction.
* On each new moon repeat the second step, picking a fresh ninth coin from the pot for your money purse and replacing the old coin in the pot (this will increase the strength of the money pot).
* When the pot is full, tip the coins out and start again.

An incense spell for promoting prosperity

This spell uses Air power to circulate money energies around your life. Carry it out in a well ventilated room or sheltered place outdoors.

You will need

6 sticks of incense in one or a mixture of the following: cinnamon, ginger, basil, rosemary, mint, sage; a tall metal vase or pot to hold the incense sticks; 12 silver- or gold-coloured coins.

Timing

On a Sunday evening.

The spell

* Working deosil (clockwise), surround the container with a circle of coins, with each coin touching its neighbours.
* Light the incense sticks and, taking each in turn, name its fragrance together with your desire and make a deosil smoke circle round the coins. So, for example, you might say:
  Cinnamon, I ask of thee,
  Bring to me prosperity.
  Make each smoke circle outside the previous one, so that the circles radiate outwards. You can name the same or a different desire for different sticks of incense.
* Take the incense sticks outside to burn down where their energies can rise to the cosmos.
* Use the coins for a small treat or give them to charity.

A spell to help give you the willpower to save

Finding the incentive to save can be difficult, especially when there are so many demands on your resources and counter-incentives to spend. However, even a small amount saved regularly can, over months, amount to a reasonable investment. What is more, this spell will attract saving opportunities on a larger scale by setting in motion accumulation energies in your life.

For the spell

A large money box in the shape of an animal (a pig is traditional); a coin purse (only use the purse for the money collected for this spell).

Timing

Whenever you are given change from a transaction.

The spell

* As soon as you are given change, put one coin of a reasonable value into the coin purse.
* When you get home, set the coin purse in front of the money box. Say to the animal:

This is for you.
* Pop the coin into the money box. Turn the money box round nine times deosil (clockwise), as you do so saying nine times:

May more follow more and like follow like.
* When you can afford to, add two coins from your change to the purse.
* As you add each coin to the money box, turn it nine times and again say:

This is for you.
* Once a month or once a week, on pay day, add three coins, repeating the words and the actions.
* When the money box is full, make time – on the same day if possible – to bank the money in a special savings account.
* Turn the empty money box nine times, this time widdershins (anticlockwise), as you do so saying:

May more follow and like follow like.
You shall not stay empty.
* Begin the spell again and keep it going.

21 SPELLS FOR SPECULATION, SAVINGS AND LUCK WITH MONEY

There are other ways to accumulate money apart from earning it. Some are spectacular one-offs, such as winning a competition or making an unexpectedly lucrative investment. Others are more mundane and steady, such as saving regularly.

When I was a little girl almost everybody had a post office savings account book, but the habit of saving in this way has all but died out. This is sad, because there can be great satisfaction in saving for something you really want or putting spare money in what used to be called the rainy day pot for emergencies and special occasions. When you save even a very small amount regularly, not only does the money build up but also the psychic vibes make money more available for savings.

Speculation can be a fast and effective way to increase assets. Some people, with or without financial advice, have an uncanny knack of knowing when what looks like a piece of junk at a car boot sale is in fact valuable. Others know precisely the right moment to bid for items in an auction, when property values are about to soar, or where there is a niche in the market ripe to be filled. Some people are gifted at winning competitions, even those that do not rely on skill.

While gambling can be destructive if it becomes an addiction, betting in the office sweepstake on a horse whose name seems significant, or following a sudden urge to buy a Lottery ticket and enter certain specific numbers, may draw on a deep intuitive foreknowledge. In my observation, this does not work for huge Lottery wins, but at the more modest level you may be tuning in to the prevailing energies.

In all these instances, spells can be used to tap into the energies of good fortune and accumulation, and can help to turn the occasional lucky investment or win into a more regular source of income.

A picking up money spell

As I walked upstairs to fetch my laptop this morning, I found the usual scattering of small coins en route. My younger daughter has also accumulated a considerable sum of money in abandoned change, which she has put in her savings account. While a family may yield a treasure trove, it is surprising what you find will find even if you live alone or with just one other person. Try looking on tables, on the floor, in the car and in pockets before you put clothes into the washing machine.

You will need

A glass jar for each denomination of money.

Timing

Whenever you see an abandoned coin around the home.

The spell

* Pick up the coin, hold it in your cupped hand and say:
  Find a penny, pick it up
  And all day you'll have good luck.
  A penny found
  Is worth a pound.
  (You can adapt the rhyme to the coinage of your own country.)
* Put the coin in the appropriate jar and repeat the rhyme. You will be surprised how fast the jars fill up. Save the money for a family outing.

A spell to help savings to accumulate

On page 258 I mentioned the custom of incubating money in a pot. This is a traditional spell to ensure that your money pot brings a regular inflow of money that will accumulate slowly and gradually over the years. It can also magically increase your saving potential.

You will need

A brown pottery pot with a lid; a coin you have found (around the house is fine); a green candle.

Timing

Any, but the waxing moon period will give you a good start.

The spell

* Begin by warming the jar and then lighting the candle over it.
* Place the coin in the jar, as you do so saying:
  Accumulate, make more;
  Two turn into four.
  Accumulate and speculate;
  Four soon will become eight.
* Put the lid on the money jar and leave it in a warm place in the kitchen or living room.
* Once a day add a coin to the pot, repeating the chant.
* When the jar is full, bank the money in a special savings account so that it will accumulate interest over the months.
* Start the next pot with another found coin, and repeat the spell.

A fern or golden flower spell to increase your savings

Ferns, especially around midsummer, are associated with the increase of wealth and finding treasure. This and the following two spells work well with any golden fern frond or flower. In fact, the golden fern flowers that bloom in legend at midsummer are probably bracken, a form of fern that turns yellow and red at the height of summer. Another theory has it that the legendary ferns are those species with yellow fibrous hairs at the root. Fern spores, sometimes referred to as seeds, are an ingredient of many of the old traditional spells.

You will need

A golden-coloured dried fern.

Timing

Any.

The spell

* Keep the fern with your savings books or dividend certificates and replace it when it crumbles. This will ensure that savings or dividends continue to accumulate.

A Russian midsummer's eve spell to find treasure

In the original spell, a golden fern was used as a dowsing tool to lead you to treasure. The following version is not an infallible method but it is a good way of getting in touch with your own unconscious wisdom and with the powerful energies of midsummer, which are good for prophecy.

You will need

A piece of paper; the stalk of any golden-coloured fern (break off the fronds).

Timing

Just before midnight, on midsummer's eve.

The spell

* Divide the piece of paper into squares. In each square write an option for future savings or investment plans for the year ahead.
* Let your mind go blank and hold the stalk over each option in turn, as you do so saying:
  Midsummer fern, tell to me
  If this venture profit see.
* Note the options over which the stalk vibrates or you get good feelings.

A Bohemian midsummer's eve treasure spell

For this spell, you need to go to a hill or high place. According to tradition, you will find gold on the hill once the spell has been performed.

You will need
A golden fern or a golden flower that blooms at midsummer, picked on midsummer's eve.

Timing
As the sun is setting.

The spell
* Holding your golden flower or fern, climb to a high place as the sun is setting.
* Cast the flower or fern towards the sunset, as you do so saying:
Golden fern, show to me
How my fortune increased may be.
* Pick up the first small stone you see and take it home.
* Be in bed by midnight, with the stone by your bedside. Repeat the chant five times and you will dream of a wise investment or an opportunity to make money.

An olive oil spell to increase your saving potential

Olive oil has always been associated with wealth and increased assets, and a bottle of empowered olive oil on an open shelf in your kitchen will attract money into the home. As you use the oil in cooking or salad dressings, its energies will attract money-making opportunities into your life and encourage money to stay with you.

You will need
An unopened bottle of extra-virgin olive oil; 10 small olivine crystals (quite common and relatively inexpensive); a carton of cherry tomatoes.

Timing
At noon.

The spell
* Place the bottle of olive oil on the kitchen table or a work surface. Make a triangle of olivines around the bottle, with the apex at the top. (The triangle is a shape of increase.)
* Enclose the triangle in a circle of cherry tomatoes (a natural prosperity bringer – see page 130).
* Place your hands loosely and gently around the bottle and, keeping it within the triangle, shake it nine times, as you do so saying:
Three by three the increase be,
Money coming soon to me.
Money stay and money grow,
Profit in this oil to show.
* Leave the bottle of oil surrounded by the olivines and tomatoes until sunset.
* Put the olivines in a purse to bring you luck in any investment, potentially profitable new venture or speculation. Use the cherry tomatoes in a meal as soon as possible. Return the olive oil to the shelf.
* Throw away the bottle of olive oil when there is just a tiny bit of oil left (do not empty it) and empower the next bottle using this spell.

A green olive increase spell

Olives, especially the golden-green kind, are natural wealth attracters and make another good addition to an open kitchen shelf (see the previous spell). This is an adaptation of a spell I learned in Spain. It releases energies slowly every day, ensuring that even if increase is modest, an ongoing positive upturn in fortunes is created.

You will need

A dish full of golden-green olives with stones; a small dish for the stones.

Timing

On a Thursday morning.

The spell

* Set the dish of olives on a table. Hold your hands, palms down, about 15 cm/6 in above the dish and circle your hands together deosil (clockwise), as you do so saying nine times:
  Fruit of increase may you be,
  That increased profit I do see.
  As you grow and ripen slow,
  Shall my money likewise grow.
* Put the dish of olives where visitors and family may eat them in passing, with the dish for the stones next to it.
* When the bowl is empty, top it up and repeat the enchantment. Wash the stones and plant them, repeating the words of the charm.

An olive tree spell

In the Mediterranean and the Near and Middle East, olive trees are an annual source of income and so have come to signify continuing prosperity. With global warming, olive trees now grow further north. I have one that is thriving in my garden on the Isle of Wight, in the south of England.

You will need

2 olive trees for planting outside, or 2 miniature indoor or patio olive trees.

Timing

Any.

The spell

* Plant one of the olive trees facing (or just inside if it is a miniature version) your front door or a street-facing window to draw money in.
* Plant the other tree facing (or just inside) your back door to reflect prosperity back into the house whenever anyone opens the back door.

A seed spell for casting your net to attract assets and good investment

Casting seeds over a wide area of land and seeing which take root is a concept that comes from the Bible. It is a good way of casting forth your energies and allowing the cosmos to bounce them back as increased profitability, whether with regard to an existing venture or to a new investment or money-spinning plan.

You will need

As many sunflower seeds or wild bird seeds as there are days in the current month; a tall tin or jar with a lid; a large area of earth, preferably unplanted (for example, a local wasteland, an area of parkland or a nature garden that has been left wild).

Timing

The first day of any month, early.

The spell

* Place your sunflower seeds (associated with wealth) or bird seeds in the tin or jar and put on the lid.
* Take your tin or jar of seeds to the open space and shake the tin the same number of times as there are seeds, as you do so saying:
  Seeds increase and multiply;
  Power of wealth intensify;
  Grow from the earth to the sky.
* Take off the lid and walk around scattering seeds until they are all gone.
* Maximise an existing scheme or plan a new money-increasing venture.

A spice spell for profit through speculation

Traded both to preserve food and to improve its flavour in the days before refrigeration, spices have been associated with fabulous wealth for thousands of years. The hotter the spice, the greater its magical power to attract profit, especially through speculation. All kinds of ground spices can be bought in glass jars for cooking. These are ideal both for speculation and for acquiring money from unexpected sources over a period of time.

You will need

A spice rack with at least six different spices, such as saffron, chilli (hot and mild), curry powders, ginger, allspice, cinnamon, cloves, turmeric and nutmeg; a small red candle in a holder for each spice jar.

Timing

After cooking, when the kitchen is still warm.

The spell

* Working on the kitchen table or a work surface, place your spice jars in a circle and around them set a circle of red candles, so that each candle is in front of a spice jar.
* Light the candle furthest away from you, naming its spice and stating what you would like it to bring you, for example:
  Ginger, burn with fire, for I desire prosperity, by speculation or accumulation. I ask only security in the years ahead.
* Working deosil (clockwise), light the next candle, name its spice and state what you would like it to bring to you.
* Continue working around the circle until all the candles are lit.
* Leave the candles to burn through and return the spices to their rack. Use them in meals.
* When you empty a jar, light a red candle and repeat the empowerment.

A spice sachet for speculation

If you wish to carry the spice power with you when you have a meeting connected with investments or speculation, or you are attending a sale where there may be bargains, make yourself a small spice sachet.

You will need

A mortar and pestle or a bowl and wooden or ceramic spoon; at least three different spices, best of all from jars empowered by the previous spell; orange or frankincense essential oil; a small red fabric purse.

Timing

On a Wednesday morning – a good time to work for any investment or speculation where there is uncertainty of outcome.

The spell

* Shake a little of each spice into the bowl.

* Add one drop of essential oil for each spice, naming the oil and the spices and chanting an appropriate chant, for example:

  Frankincense I would empower,
  Nutmeg, ginger,
  Saffron at this hour.
  Fill them with fortune
  That I may know
  Where best a profit soonest show.

* Continue to chant faster and faster as you mix the spices and oil until you feel that the power has built up.

* Plunge the spoon into the bowl, as you do so saying:

  Speculate,
  Accumulate,
  Do not hesitate.

* Scoop the spices into the purse.

* Open the purse and inhale the fragrance just before making a purchase or concluding a deal.

A 12-month spell to accumulate money

In all the chapters on money, gold has featured for attracting both instant and long-lasting prosperity. A gold-coloured dish full of golden items will, if you add to it monthly, encourage wealth to accumulate whether through saving, investment or speculation.

You will need

A gold-coloured dish; a gold item of sentimental value; 11 small golden items (for example, chains, earrings, charms – you can pick these up cheaply at garage sales); a box with a lid.

Timing

The beginning of any month, at noon.

The spell

* Set the gold-coloured dish where it can catch the noon daylight through a window and add the gold item of sentimental value, as you do so saying:

  From small grow greater;
  From modest beginnings does fortune grow.
  As months become years,
  I ask it shall be ever more so.

* Hold up the dish to the light and repeat the chant.

* On the first day of each month, add another gold item to the dish and repeat the charm. Keep the unused items in the closed box and add to your collection regularly so that the spell can be ongoing from year to year.

* When necessary, buy a larger dish.

A spell to make a speculation mojo

Speculation mojos, worn hidden around the waist or slung around the neck, have always been very popular among gamblers. They work well for all potentially money-making situations, from competitions, lotteries, and games of chance to auctions and sales where a purchase may yield profit when renovated or quickly resold. The mojo can also be hidden near a telephone or computer if that is where you do a lot of buying or selling, for example on eBay. Hide one also in a car, boat or house that you hope to sell for fast profit. Usually mojos are made in silence, but this one involves a chant.

You will need

A lucky hand root (see the spell below); a ten of diamonds playing card taken from a miniature pack; some white sage; a silver dollar, a token from a games arcade, a gambling chip (from a home casino game) or a metal Monopoly counter; a green aventurine or amazonite crystal; a white drawstring bag made out of a natural fabric, or a leather purse or bag of any colour; a little whisky, sherry, port or malt wine; a white cord.

Timing

Early on a Wednesday morning.

The spell

* Working in the first light, place the lucky hand root, the ten of diamonds, the sage, the dollar (or alternative), the gambling chip and the crystal in the bag or purse. Add a drop or two of alcohol.
* Close the bag or purse with the cord, tying it with three knots and saying:
  Rich I'll be,
  For luck's with me.
  Fortune, I ask,
  Favour me.
* Replace the bag every two months, or sooner if the mojo has been working hard.

A spell to make a game of chance charm

The lucky hand root, the root of a rare kind of orchid, is considered to be the single luckiest gambling or game of chance charm. Sometimes shaped like a hand and the size of an average button, they can be bought from large herbalists and New Age stores, and by mail order over the Internet.

You will need

A lucky hand root; some good luck oil (available from New Age stores) or patchouli oil; a tiny leather or undyed fabric bag or purse.

Timing

Any.

The spell

* Sprinkle the lucky hand root with a drop or two of the oil and place it in the bag or purse. Carry it with you whenever you take part in any game or competition, and put the bag on top of entry forms before posting them.

An amazonite and aventurine spell to win money or rewards

This is another charm for good luck when there is a random element involved in a transaction or when you are taking a chance that your input or investment will be increased rapidly. Amazonite and aventurine are both lucky crystals for money-making, games of chance and all forms of speculation or risk with money. Vetivert is a lucky gambling herb.

You will need

A green aventurine or amazonite crystal; a stick of sage or vetivert incense; an incense holder; an emerald-green scarf or square of cloth.

Timing

On a Wednesday, any time after dawn.

The spell

* Place the crystal on the green cloth.
* Light the incense and, moving around the outside edges of the cloth (so you do not get ash on the cloth), write continuously in the smoke the word 'win'. Leave no spaces between the words.
* Leave the incense to burn in the holder near the cloth.
* When the incense is burnt through and cool, sprinkle a pinch of the ash on the cloth and bind the cloth tightly around the crystal, knotting it like a bundle in the scarf and saying seven times as you tie it:
  Win.
* When you need luck with a money venture or competition, undo only as much of the bundle as you need to take out the crystal. Holding the crystal in cupped hands, recite:
  Win.
* After use, wash the crystal under running water, allow it to dry naturally and return it to the bundle, as you tie it, reciting seven times:
  Win.
* After seven uses, re-empower the crystal by repeating the spell (using a fresh incense stick).

A spell to win competitions

Some people have amazing luck with competitions, winning not necessarily the star prizes but weekends away, cases of wine or free admission to cinemas. As well as skill, in most competitions there is an element of chance. Cloves and juniper are both money attracters.

You will need

A money crystal, such as a tiger's eye or the kind of iron pyrites that looks like a piece of gold, alternatively a small gold lucky charm; 3 gold-coloured candles; a small, clear glass dish filled with cloves or dried juniper berries and with enough space in the centre of the dish for the crystal.

Timing

The day of the full moon, if possible at noon.

The spell

* Make a triangle of candles around the dish of cloves or juniper. Light each one, as you do so saying:
  Gold of fortune increased be;
  Lady Luck smile down on me.

* Circle the crystal three times around each candle flame in order of lighting, for each candle repeating the chant.
* Place the crystal right in the centre of the dish, as you do so saying:
  Gold of fortune, fill with power;
  Lady Luck, this crystal shower.
* Taking one candle carefully in each hand (the ones nearest to you), swirl the light around the dish in spirals, so that the light dances over the glass dish, as you do so chanting:
  Light of gold, intensify;
  Power of luck, multiply.
  Nothing now can me deny.
  Good fortune come;
  The spell is done.
* Extinguish all three candles in order of lighting and leave in place the glass dish with the cloves or juniper and the crystal in it through the day and night. By the next noon the crystal will be filled with power.
* Place the crystal on any competition forms or carry it in a purse with seven of the empowered cloves or juniper berries whenever you compete or speculate.

A popcorn spell for extra good luck

Popcorn is associated with light-heartedness and pleasure. If you relax when bidding at an auction, competing or bargaining, your intuitive awareness will take over and act as a wise guide. A good mood also attracts good fortune.

You will need

Some uncooked popcorn; an airtight container.

Timing

Any.

The spell

* While cooking the popcorn or heating it in a microwave, chant:

Pop, pop,
Don't stop;
Popcorn by the score.
Make a lot
And eat a pot
And you will win your corn.

* Eat some of the hot corn to take the good luck within you and save the rest in an airtight container.
* Eat just a little empowered popcorn and chant the rhyme ten times fast before making a bid or playing a game of chance. You can also hand out your popcorn as a snack during family games of chance. It will keep the mood light and stop people cheating

A spell to double your money or investment

You will need

A new banknote and another new note worth double the first (they need not be large amounts); a white resealable envelope; some dried white sage, basil or vetivert; a red pen.

Timing

The day before the full moon, in the evening.

The spell

* Put the smaller value banknote in the envelope and write on the front: 'double your money'.
* Sprinkle a little of the herb on the front of the envelope, as you do so saying:
  Double your money overnight.
  If the will is good,
  The spell is right.
* In the morning open the envelope, take out the money and repeat the charm.
* Replace the bank note in the envelope, together with the larger one, and reseal the envelope. Write again on the front: 'double your money'.
* Sprinkle a little of the herb on the front of the envelope and repeat the chant.
* The next morning open the envelope and take out the money. Invest the smaller note in a safe way, for example in a savings account, or spend it on a necessity. Repeat the chant and return the larger note to the envelope.
* Put the envelope, with the larger note still inside, in a drawer and keep it for when you need to invest or buy an item you think will bring a profitable return. Repeat the chant before using the note.

A kitchen or hearth spell for keeping money in the home

You will need

A crystal.

Timing

Any.

The spell

* Go at least a mile from your home and look for a perfectly round white stone. When you find one, pick it up and take it home, leaving the crystal as a payment to the earth.
* Wash the stone well and leave it to dry naturally.
* Place the stone either on the hearth or near your stove and leave it for exactly a year to ensure that money flows in.
* When the year is up, return the stone to the place where you found it and select another one, from the same place if possible.

A spell to ensure that items you are selling fetch a good price

Carry out this spell before sending items to an auction, antique shop or specialist dealer, or before selling them yourself. It works even for online sales and auctions.

You will need

Your wand, a smooth twig with a pointed end or a pointed clear quartz crystal.

Timing

Before a sale or auction.

The spell

* Stand facing the items to be sold. Hold the wand, twig or crystal in your power hand (the one you write with). If you are using a crystal, hold the blunt end.
* Point the wand, twig or crystal and the index finger of your other hand directly towards the items and say firmly:

You. You will sell well and be a credit to me. All who see will be impressed. Many will want you; only one may have you. Find your new owner.

* With your wand and finger still pointing ahead, turn around nine times and say:

One for money,
Two for wealth,
Three for plenty,
Four for riches to myself,
Five for luck,
Six for pleasure,
Seven, eight, nine
For undreamed treasure.

* Take the item to be sold or call the dealer or agent.

22 SPELLS FOR REDUCING DEBT AND STOPPING THE OUTFLOW OF MONEY

In the modern world debt is becoming an increasingly serious problem. Even a relatively small amount owed can become significant as spiralling interest charges lead to more borrowing. Those who get into debt are usually responsible people who have hit a patch of bad luck – perhaps a job loss, an illness, a relationship break-up or a business failure. Debtors may also have been given bad advice or tried to borrow their way out of trouble.

In most countries there are organisations to help those in trouble with debt, offering practical advice as well as support. (The Citizens' Advice Bureau is the first port of call in the UK.) Spells can also help in slowing the outflow of money from our lives, as well as galvanising our own energies not only to economise and change the spending patterns encouraged by advertising campaigns but also to come up with creative money-spinning ideas to reduce the burden of debt.

A scales spell for balancing the books

If you know how much money you need to live and your incomings do not match it, even after you have economised, a spell can help boost your income to match your expenditure. While you may not be able to save, at least you should be able to survive, and perhaps slowly pay off some of your debts.

You will need

A pair of scales (the kind with a pan on either side); a box of clear glass nuggets; 2 glass jars.

Timing

A day or two after the full moon, at dusk.

The spell

* Tip the nuggets into the two pans of the scales so that there is about a third more in one pan than the other. Say:

The scales are out of balance, yet can all be righted.

* Take some nuggets out of the heavy side and put them in the lighter side, as you do so repeating the chant.
* Continue to move nuggets until both sides balance. Say:

So shall all be righted. I welcome balance into my life.

* Put the nuggets in the two jars, roughly in proportion to what you owe and what you have coming in.
* Each time a small bonus comes into your life, as a result of earthly effort and/or the positive vibes awakened by the spell, take a nugget from the heavy jar and put it in the light one, reciting both chants. If you persevere, one day you will be able to balance the scales.

A radio spell to reverse a run of bad financial luck

Sometimes one bad deal follows another or it seems that half the household appliances breakdown in the same week. What is happening is that one or two random pieces of bad luck have made us jittery, and so we are more likely to be receptive to bad luck than to good. Bad luck is like being tuned into a radio station you do not like: it is easily changed.

You will need

A radio.

Timing

Late at night.

The spell

* Run through the radio stations until you find one you do not like or you can't understand. Say:

You do not do. You are not what I want to hear. I do not want to sing to your tune.

* Turn down the volume until you can hardly hear the words or music. Say:
You fade from my life, and now I seek the happy songs that bring light and sunshine to my world.
* Run through the dial until you can faintly hear a station that plays your favourite music. Say:
I would hear more of your music.
* Turn up the volume and sing along or even dance as your financial good fortune is restored.
* If you start to feel jittery about money, play your favourite radio station very loud to remind you that you don't have to listen to the old bad sounds.

A seven-day spell for turning loss into profit

You will need

7 sheets of white paper; a black pen; a clip to hold the papers together.

Timing

The morning of the first day of the working week.

The spell

❋ Write on the first sheet of paper a list of any unpaid bills or things you need to buy within the next week. Read it aloud and then say:

I ask for need and not from greed that all these needs may be met swiftly.

❋ Put the list on the bottom of the pile of blank sheets of paper and clip the pile together. Leave it in a place where the paper will catch the light. Do not re-read or even think about the list.

❋ On the second day take the top sheet of paper and write the list again, deleting anything paid and adding any new demands or needs, but only those that must be paid within the original week defined on the first day.

❋ Read aloud the new list, repeat the chant and put the paper at the bottom of the pile, clipping the papers back together. Again do not re-read or think about the list during the day.

❋ Continue following the same steps each day. By the seventh day you will have filled in each piece of paper. Read the final list and put it on the top of the pile of paper, repeating the chant.

❋ In the evening, cut or shred the papers without reading them and throw them away.

❋ Repeat the spell for a different week using fresh paper if the cosmos is slow to respond. However, you should find that the inflow of resources and opportunities for you to make money does increase, even when you have ceased the spell.

A candle spell for balancing the books

You will need

A fast-burning yellow candle; a broad metal holder; a long sharp pin, nail, thin screwdriver or other inscribing tool; a jar of dried basil (the culinary kind is fine); a dark jar.

Timing

On a Wednesday, at dusk.

The spell

❋ Using the inscribing tool, scratch on one side of the candle the approximate annual total of your expenses. On the other side scratch your total income (including any bonuses or extras).

❋ Light the candle and say:

Flow together, balance, blend and be resolved.

❋ Leave the candle in a safe place to burn through, so that both sides of the candle melt into one.

❋ Into the warm wax sprinkle some basil (for prosperity).

❋ When the wax is cool, chop or grate it into fine pieces, put it in the dark jar, add more dried basil and keep it in the highest part of the house, so that your fortunes will rise and your debts will sink.

A spell to stop money flowing out too quickly

We all have those months when money flows out faster than it comes in. The car unexpectedly breaks down or the children need new trainers way before you had budgeted for their shoes to wear out. The following spell should be carried out regularly throughout the year – especially if you have a family. It is also good if you have built up a lot of debt. It will enable you to meet your financial commitments by slowing unexpected expenditure.

You will need
A bath or sink tap.

Timing
On a Saturday, after dusk.

The spell
* Turn on the cold tap in the sink or bath, leaving the plug out.
* As the water flows away, say:
  Flowing and going, going and flowing, stop the tide.
* Slow the flow of water and put in the plug, as you do so saying:
  Slowing the flowing, slowing the going. Stay money, stay.
* Pull out the plug and let the water flow away.
* Turn the tap on again, this time even more slowly, so that it is not much more than a drip, and leave the plug in, saying:
  Money flow slowly,
  Inwards and stay.
  Money flow slowly;
  Do not flow away.
* When the bath or sink is half full, turn off the tap and leave the water with the plug in for at least ten minutes before letting out the water for the final time.
* Repeat weekly, each time leaving the final sink or bath of water an extra five minutes before emptying.

A sand and sea spell to reduce debt

When you were a child, you may have made sandcastles below the high tide line and then watched the sea wash them away. This is a powerful way of letting the sea wash out of your life whatever is making you unhappy, in this case debt. As a result you will not only feel more positive but you will have stirred up positive energies in your life that will help gradually to erode the debt mountain.

You will need
A child's spade; some shells or stones found on the beach (optional).

Timing
Just before tide turns.

The spell
* Make a castle or mountain of sand, as simple or elaborate as you wish.
* Using the shells or stones, or with the end of your spade, write on the castle: 'reduce debt'.
* Watch the tide wash away the castle or, if you wish, paddle into the incoming tide and demolish the castle by jumping on it. Say:
  You grow small. Diminish and disappear by the power of the tide. No more abide with me.
* Leave the shore and for this day do not worry.

A spell to stop money flowing out of your life

You will need

A long blue cord or ribbon; a small padlock and chain (an old one will do); an old box; a deep-blue candle.

Timing

During the waning moon, after dusk.

The spell

* Light the candle and singe both ends of the cord in the flame, as you do so saying:
  Cut off the flow;
  Money no more outward go.
* Tie a knot about a quarter of the way down the cord, as you do so saying:
  Knot one I make; the flow I break.
  Thus I bind;
  Money find
  Within this knot.
* Tie a second knot about halfway down the cord, as you do so saying:
  Knot two I make;
  The flow I break.
  Thus I bind;
  Money find
  Within this knot.
* Tie a third knot about three-quarters of the way down the cord, as you do so saying:
  Knot three I make;
  The flow I break.
  Thus I bind;
  Money find
  Within this knot.
* Tie the two ends of the cord together, as you do so saying:
  Knot four, the last;
  Bad luck is past.
  Money bound tight;
  All shall be right.
* Place the knotted cord inside the box and secure the box with the padlock and chain. Throw away the key.
* Keep the box in the place where you usually work out your finances or sign cheques to pay bills. Leave the candle to burn through and throw away the wax.

A spell to help you or a family member with debt problems

Debts can accumulate because we have had to borrow to live. It is all too easy to end up in a spiral of interest payments, borrowing more to pay what we already owe. Magic won't make the debts disappear but it can help you to galvanise your survival energies and to draw a little help from the cosmos.

You will need

A child's blackboard; a piece of white chalk; a blackboard rubber or soft cloth.

Timing

During the waning moon, after dark.

The spell

* Write all over the board in chalk the word 'debt', forwards, backwards, sideways, top to bottom, diagonally, in spirals, so you can hardly see the separate words.
* One by one, rub the words out, saying softly over and over again:
  Overcome, I overcome, I overcome debt, debt I overcome, overcome, debt is overcome.
* When the blackboard is clean, write in huge letters across it: 'solvency'.
* Leave the board where you can see it as you tackle one debt, however small compared with others.

A sea spell to turn the tide on debt

The ebbing tide is very effective for taking away not only debt but also the helplessness it causes, which sometimes freezes us into inaction. You can work with tidal water or any flowing water, but the sea is the best. A day trip to the ocean is enough in itself to restore your energies and get you feeling positive again; that combined with this spell may turn the personal tide of financial fortune for you.

You will need

A joined double shell; a coin small enough to fit inside the shell; some twine or seaweed to tie the shell together.

Timing

During the ebb tide.

The spell

* Place the coin inside the shell and hold the shell in your cupped hands, saying:
  I consign my troubles to you, Lady Sea.
  Accept my tribute and my need.
* Bind the shell with the twine or seaweed, as you do so saying:
  So I bind my troubles, Lady Sea. Wind up my worries, shut away the fears.
* Wade into the shallows and cast your shell on the seventh wave, as you do so saying:
  Carry my troubles on the waves, Lady Sea, away on the ebb, to be transformed on the incoming tide as new hope and new prosperity.
* If you can, stay at the seaside until the next incoming tide. Collect a shell or white stone washed up by the tide and take it home as a lucky charm to keep with your financial papers.

A dark and light candle spell to reverse a run of bad financial luck

Dark and light candle spells work well for financial problems if you are starting to feel jinxed, because they will help you to reduce your fears as well as your misfortune. Furthermore, you will kindle within yourself the impetus to start reversing bad times and experiences and build up your financial status again. The grey intermediate candle helps to absorb the impact of debts and create a transition between your present position and a much brighter future. Where debts are concerned, it is not usually possible just to shed them overnight, black to white; the process is more gradual.

You will need

A tall white candle in a broad-based holder; a medium-sized grey candle in a broad-based holder; a short black candle in a broad-based holder; a metal tray; a paper knife, long sharp pin or other inscribing tool; 2 paper bags; a piece of white silk.

Timing

On the last day of the month.

The spell

* Light the black candle and say:
  Debt and dark luck, burn away;
  Debt and dark luck, no longer stay.
* Light the grey candle from the black candle and say:
  Be absorbed in grey;
  Debt melt slowly away
  That I may rise above you and see the light again.
* Light the white candle from the grey one and say:

Good luck, bright luck, come to me,
Happier days ahead to see.
Good luck, bright luck, fill my life.
No more debt, no more strife.

* When the black candle is burnt through and the wax beginning to harden, using the inscribing tool, mark a cross straight through the wax. Let it cool and then break it into pieces, as you do so saying:
  Debt and dark luck burnt away;
  Bad luck, debt gone away.
* Put the wax in a paper bag and throw it in the rubbish.

* When the grey candle is burnt through, let it cool and then dispose of the wax in the same way. (Do not break it before throwing it away.)
* When the white candle is burnt through and the wax beginning to harden, carefully cut out a circle of wax. On it write your initials surrounded by pound signs or the currency of your country.
* When the white wax circle is cool, wrap it in the silk and keep it as a good luck charm in a drawer near your financial papers.

A rainy day spell to wipe the slate clean

The rain, like the sea, has the wonderful ability symbolically to wash away debt and all its associated negative emotions. This spell works on the idea of wiping the slate clean metaphorically, and then working towards that state in actuality.

You will need
A small blackboard; a piece of white chalk.

Timing
On a rainy day.

The spell
* Write on the blackboard a representative amount you owe, or the words: 'debts to be reduced'.
* Hold the blackboard and say:
  Rain, rain, wash away
  Debts that I cannot pay.
  Rain, rain, wash away
  Fears that haunt me night and day.
  Rain, rain, wash away
  What must no longer stay.
* Go out into the rain, reciting your rhyme, and leave the blackboard in the rain to be wiped clean.
* Stand for a moment getting wet and repeating the rhyme. Then say:
  The slate is wiped clean.

A spell to call in what you are owed or to get more money from an employer

It can be hard to insist on more money, especially if you enjoy your job and your firm is more like a family. If you are a freelance you will probably be all too well aware that others may be willing to do a job cheaply to get a foothold in the market. Sometimes, though, even a relatively modest salary increase or bonus would make all the difference in managing monthly bills. This spell diverts necessary funds by freeing up the energies so that resources are more evenly shared and the employer feels good about his or her sudden and seemingly inexplicable generosity. Goldfish are a symbol of wealth.

You will need

A fish tank with goldfish, or a pool with fish you are allowed to feed (try a park or zoo – trout are often very amenable to rising up or even leaping for food); some fish food.

Timing

When light shines on the water (if you are working indoors, switch on the light in the fish tank).

The spell

✷ Cast the fish food into the water, as you do so, picturing your employer handing you a bonus or offering you a salary increase. Say to him or her across the distance:

Towards me may money go;
From you to me does it now flow,
Given by you willingly,
Received as gratefully by me.

✷ As the fish eat the food, the bargain is sealed.

A cobweb spell for clearing financial chaos

It is all too easy for chaos to occur if you have a busy life. Financial matters may remain not dealt with. You may be paying higher than necessary interest rates on loans because of lack of time to find better ones. You may be fined because you have not had time to fill in tax papers. (More than a million people in the UK failed to send in tax forms on time in January 2004.) It is partly a question of changing priorities and making time for damage limitation. A spell is wonderful for clearing the web of tangled finances so that you can make a start on spring cleaning them, whatever the time of year. While spiders – especially the small ones known as money spiders – are lucky, webs indoors are not.

You will need

At least one abandoned indoor spider's web (always ask the spider's permission first); a long broom or duster.

Timing

Any Monday morning (a traditional cleaning day in an age when many women did not go out to work).

The spell

✷ Carefully dismantle the web or webs with the broom or duster, saying for each:

Away with you, web of chaos;
Untangle disorder and unbind
That I may find,
As I unwind,
The thread of solvency.
So may it be!

✷ Shake the broom or duster well outdoors, as you do so repeating the chant.

✷ Sit down and for half an hour devote yourself to the most pressing financial matter.

A credit card spell to reduce plastic borrowings

Though credit cards are very useful (it is difficult to book tickets or hotels without them) their costs are often the first thing to get out of control. Some of mine are not due for clearing at the present rate for 30 years. This spell works by symbolically reducing the cards' power and then picking them off in reality, one by one, highest interest card first.

You will need

Your current credit cards; a small box with a lid; 2 sticks of incense in such fragrances as patchouli, sage, frank-incense, mint and orange (use one fragrance or mix them) and 2 suitable holders.

Timing

Saturday afternoon after shopping – a good time for the reality factor to kick in.

The spell

* Arrange your credit cards in a circle or a row, depending on how many you have. Light the incense sticks and place one on either side of the cards, where ash will not fall on the cards.
* Take an incense stick in each hand and spiral the sticks widdershins (anticlockwise) at either side of the row or circle of cards. Chant the following rhyme, adapting the numbers according to the number of credit cards you have:

Ten expensive credit cards standing in a line,
One got paid off then there were nine.
Nine expensive credit cards, payment always late,
One got cut up then there were eight.
Eight expensive credit cards, payments never done,
Shut them tight up in the box, then there are none.

* Put down the incense and one by one place the cards in the box and put on the lid.
* Spiral the incense again widdershins, this time around the closed box, as you do so saying:

Your power is gone. I will pay you off and then I will have won.

* Work out which is the most expensive card and start to minimise your use of it. Cut down on your use of the others too, if possible, keeping them in the box in a safe place when not needed.
* Repeat the spell monthly. Its energies become faster and you will find unexpected sources of income – maybe small – to help pay your card debts off faster than you expected.

A spell for spending wisely

With more access to credit and increased advertising, it is very easy to buy items we do not really need. We may also buy things for our children simply because they are subject to peer pressure to conform to the latest fashion. If, like me, you are a shopaholic because you enjoy shopping and not as a result of a deep-seated trauma, it can help to do a mild binding spell on yourself and anyone else whose purchases you will be financing before you go out on a spree.

You will need

Your credit and debit cards, cheque book, purse and so on; a deep-purple ribbon; 6 purple or blue flowers (silk or dried are fine, or use a purple pot pourri mix).

Timing

At twilight on the evening before your shopping spree. The waning moon is especially good for binding spells of any kind.

The spell

* Make a pile of the credit cards, cheque books, purse and so on.

* In the ebbing light, encircle the pile with the flowers, as you do so saying quietly and calmly over and over again until you are totally relaxed:
Wisely spend and slow;
Moderation show.
Spending is a pleasure;
Spending slowly is the treasure.

* Taking up the ribbon, equally slowly and calmly bind the pile of cards quite loosely together, as you do so saying:
Wisely spend and well.
Power of binding spell,
Bind my impulsivity.
Spend thoughtfully and sparingly.

* Leave the cards and so on in the circle of flowers in the darkness overnight.

* In the morning gently unbind the ribbon and say:
Thus unbound, but powerful still,
Go I with my own free will,
Free in heart and soul and mind;
Recklessness I leave behind.

* Tie the ribbon inside your bag as a calming influence and touch it if you feel that you are about to make a wild and totally unsuitable purchase.

A misty day spell

You need the right conditions for this spell, but it is worth waiting for.

You will need

Nothing.

Timing

On a misty day with the sun just breaking through.

The spell

* Stand in the mist and start to walk towards the light.
* Shake your hands and fingers, symbolically removing all the unnecessary expenditure that is clinging to you.

* Once you reach sunlight, open your arms upwards and outwards and enclose in them a piece of light as you bring them together. Say:
Be my inspiration and my guide.
* Enjoy the sunshine, however briefly.
* In the evening look at bank statements and records of expenditure and find five small ways to save money (for example, cancelling unnecessary mobile phone insurance and other covers that companies sometimes sneak through when we do not bother to check.)

A misty bathroom spell

This is a version of the previous spell that can be carried out at any time, although it is not quite as magical. However, you can repeat it regularly, so it is useful for budgeting updates.

You will need

A steamy bathroom; a soft cloth.

Timing

When you have five spare minutes and will not be interrupted.

The spell

* Turn on the hot taps so that the bathroom fills with steam.
* When the bathroom is steamy, write on the bathroom mirror with your index finger either 'unnecessary expenditure' or 'money wasted'.
* Open the window to let out the steam.
* Rub out the words with the soft cloth and polish the mirror.
* When you have time, find small painless ways to economise, such as not buying an expensive glossy magazine that you hardly read or cancelling a subscription to a special offer that has gone on long after your interest, or that of a family member, has waned.

A longer-acting shopaholic spell

This is a very helpful spell that releases its powers over weeks rather than days. The key is restoring balance so that the craving to spend is reduced when you are in a store.

You will need

A vibrant-orange crystal, such as an amber or carnelian; an orange banded agate in muted tones; a vibrant-brown or gold tiger's eye or a gleaming golden polished iron pyrites or a copper nugget; a muted-brown or sandy-coloured agate.

Timing

When you go shopping.

The spell

* Put the vibrant-orange and vibrant-brown stones in a pocket or purse on the power side of your body (the side of the hand you write with).
* Put the muted-orange and muted-brown stones on the receptive side of your body. (You could also keep them in appropriate compartments of a small money belt.)
* After a week or so, you may find that the urge to spend recklessly is decreasing. If so, carry just the orange stones on their respective sides of the body.
* When your impulsivity has been dampened down even further, use just the brown stones, on their respective sides of the body.
* Finally, you may be able to dispense with the crystals altogether.
* If the urges come back, return to carrying all four stones for a while.

A spell to deal with unpleasant demands

No-one has a right to intimidate or threaten you, no matter how much you owe. You should, of course, approach the police and a debt advice organisation to stop the hassling, but you can also return the unpleasantness symbolically to the sender. This does not involve curses or dark magic. A spell will make you feel more powerful and therefore more able to stand up for your rights and settle the matter in an appropriate and assertive way. You can also use this spell this if a firm is repeatedly hassling you by telephone or with house calls when you have made a reasonable offer to pay what you owe.

You will need

A photocopy of a threatening letter (not a court summons as those must be dealt with through due legal process) or a list of phone calls and visits; a red pen; a brown envelope; an incinerator or outdoor fire.

Timing

The evening after the threatening letter is received.

The spell

* Cross through the photocopied letter or list with the red pen.
* Write on the envelope in red pen the name and, if you know it, the address of the person or firm that sent the unpleasant message.
* Put the photocopy of the letter or the list in the envelope and seal it.
* Burn the envelope outside the house to remove the bad energies from your home, as you do so saying:
  Take back the pain.
  Do not call like this again.
* You are not attacking individuals who may be following instructions but the company that has ruthless collection policies.
* Take the actual letter to the advice bureau for them to help you resolve the matter on an earthly level.

PART 5

Spells for Protection

Protection spells have always formed part of human defence against the dangers of life, both the normal and the paranormal. In earlier times, perils included wild animals, invading tribes, fire, whirlwind and flood. In the modern world the dangers are different but no less acute. Though most of us do not fear predatory beasts, nevertheless we suffer the effects of natural disasters — which are becoming more prevalent as global warming increases. The threat of burglary or personal attack, especially in cities late at night, can also create a feeling of vulnerability, particularly as more of us live alone or isolated from extended families and familiar neighbourhoods. Bullying is a problem, not just for children but also for adults as the workplace becomes increasingly pressurised and competitive. Since September 11, travel has been perceived as more hazardous, provoking anxieties even in seasoned travellers.

Though we no longer think of psychic attack in terms of demons or evil spirits, nevertheless those who wish us harm can consciously or unconsciously transmit negative feelings that leave us jittery or apprehensive. Night-time magnifies such fears, and for children night terrors can loom large, increased by images on television of attacks and disasters. Whether or not you believe in ghosts, certain places can seem cold or unpleasant, and areas in a home may feel spooky or dark, even on summer days. One explanation is that the earth energies have become blocked or soured, whether by unhappy events long ago that have left impressions, or by emissions from electricity pylons, old mine workings, nearby construction works or radio masts.

Protective spells work on two levels, The first is by repelling danger or fears of harm, whether actual or perceived — sometimes through the empowerment of a protective amulet, which we can carry with us into hazardous situations. On a more subtle level they enable us to build up a psychological and psychic shield so that we are less vulnerable to spite and other negative influences. This can be helpful in enabling sensitive children and adolescents to develop coping strategies.

You will probably find that one or two of the spells in this section work especially well for you, in which case you can adapt them to guard you in any situation. When you feel secure and confident, most problems can be resolved and opportunities explored without fear.

23 SPELLS FOR PHYSICAL PROTECTION OF SELF AND LOVED ONES

We live in dangerous times. Although, naturally, we should take precautions not to expose ourselves to unnecessary risk, it is important not to curtail our own freedom or worry excessively when loved ones are away or late home. This is where magic can help. Magical spells have traditionally been used to protect, be it at home, at work, when out travelling or when having a good time. You will find spells for protecting children, protection when travelling and protection at work in separate chapters of this book. Here, I will concentrate on spells that prevent harm and reduce anxiety. I have also included one or two spells for establishing protective boundaries so that you can become less obviously a target for those who would wish to do you or loved ones ill.

A protective dragon spell for cutting ties that may endanger you or a family member

The killing of dragons is usually associated with St George or St Michael. But there is a gentler dragon slayer, St Martha, patron saint of housewives, cooks and servants, who in the Gospel of St Luke is described as cooking and tending to Jesus's needs while her sister sat listening. After the crucifixion, she crossed the Mediterranean and went to France, where she killed a dragon that was threatening the people she had promised to protect – using holy water rather than a sword. It is said that if you light a candle and pray to Martha on nine consecutive Tuesdays, she will grant any petition, no matter how difficult, by the ninth Tuesday.

Sometimes what constitutes a threat to yourself or a family member can seem attractive to the 'dragon' involved – for example, a dangerous new hobby or an unnecessary but adrenaline-boosting risk. Alternatively, your dragon may encourage a lifestyle extravagant beyond your means or advocate dubious money-making schemes. It is not just young people who can fall under the thrall of undesirable influences. A colleague may persuade a partner to spend longer and longer in the pub after work, leading to heavy drinking. A new friend may persuade an impressionable or unhappy family member to experiment with drugs or to gamble recklessly. We cannot interfere with the free will of the person taking the risks and nor should we attempt to harm the tempter or temptress, no matter how much disruption they are causing. However, this spell will lessen the bad influence and help to turn the family member back towards the family.

You will need

A bowl of still mineral water; a small dish of salt; a silver paper knife or long thin pointed clear crystal; a black pen; old broken costume jewellery, glittery buttons, sequins, or anything small and gaudy, even old Christmas tinsel; a scarf or cloth large enough to enclose the items and knot at the top; a pink candle that will last for the nine Tuesdays of the spell.

Timing

On nine consecutive Tuesdays, after dusk.

The spell

* On the first Tuesday, light the candle.
* Add three pinches of salt to the water and, using the knife or crystal, make the sign of the cross – either the Christian equal-armed upright cross or the pre-Christian diagonal one – in the water. Say:
  Mother Martha who slew the dragon with gentleness, bless this water with love and with good influence that (name) may turn towards the family love and protection once more.
* Set the glittery items on the scarf, on a table where the candle light will shine on them.
* Using your power hand (the one you write with), scatter around the scarf a single circle of water droplets. Say:
  Bright and sparkling, not of worth, glittering gaudy, dazzle and grow dim, separated from (name) by this sacred water.
* Wrap the items in the scarf and knot it tightly at the top.
* Blow out the candle, sending through it love to call the straying person back into the family fold.
* Sprinkle a few drops of the water on the floor around the influenced

person's favourite chair, bed and anywhere he or she works or spends time in the home.

* Pour the rest of the water away down a drain and keep the scarf hidden near the possessions of the family member.
* Repeat the first eight steps on the next seven Tuesdays, using the same glittery objects, candle and scarf but taking a few of the objects away each time and disposing of them so that by the ninth Tuesday only one object is in the scarf when you open it.
* On the ninth Tuesday, repeat the first eight steps again and throw away the final object. Blow out the candle and thank St Martha for blessings received (even if the 'dragon' is still around).
* Dispose of any remaining candle and wash the scarf.
* If the dangerous influence is still around, repeat the spell with the washed scarf, starting on the following Tuesday.

A Celtic blessing for protection throughout the day and throughout life

Though the Celts were a fierce people, they valued their home life and cherished their kinfolk. It was an absolute rule that those welcomed under one's roof would be protected from harm. Likewise, visitors were under a charge not to do harm by word or deed to their host and their host's family. This blessing is equally effective for family members who no longer live at home. It can also be directed towards special friends. The blessing is quite long, so at first you will need to read the words, but in time you will find they come naturally. Once you know the blessing you can focus on the image of family members as you recite the words.

You will need
Photographs of yourself and family members and friends you wish to protect – a group portrait is excellent.

Timing
On a Sunday, or any other day when you have time to focus on the individual family members, in morning light.

The spell
* Set the photographs so that the morning light shines on them. Touch each of the pictures in turn and then recite:

May the blessing of light be with you – light outside and within.

May the sunlight shine upon you and warm your heart till it glows like a great peat fire, so that the stranger may come and warm himself by it.

May a blessed light shine out of your two eyes like a candle set in two windows of a house bidding the wanderer to come in out of the storm.

May you ever give a kindly greeting to those whom you pass as you go along the roads.

May the blessing of rain – the sweet, soft rain – fall upon you so that little flowers may spring up to shed their sweetness in the air.

May the blessings of the earth – the good, rich earth – be with you.

May the earth be soft under you when you rest upon it, tired at the end of the day.

A protective Celtic blessing for the family

This is among my favourite Celtic blessings. It is especially good if you have to be away from the family temporarily or if the family are widespread. It also sends strength to individual family members at times when they need protection. You might like to perform this blessing regularly, making it a special centring time first thing in the morning before you go about your day – if you are busy, once a week or once a month is fine. I think of it as my 'chicken's call', sending protection to all my chicks, especially if I am away. There are many versions of this blessing; this is one I heard on the Isle of Skye, in Scotland.

You will need

A candle, a fire or a wood-burning stove (in a hotel you can improvise with a lamp).

Timing

When you get up in the morning.

The spell

⁕ Light the candle, fire or stove.

⁕ Facing the source of light or heat, name those you wish to protect, focusing on any who are currently in special need of protection, for example:

Alison on her first day at college.

⁕ Recite three times:

I kindle my fire this morning with this good peat, without fear or envy of any who walk beneath the good sun this day.

I kindle this flame in my hearth and my heart for food on my table, health in my home and a gentle parting when my days are ended.

I kindle in my heart this morning a flame of love to my neighbour, my foe and my kindred and God over all protecting.

May you be protected.

⁕ If you are using a candle, blow out the flame, sending light to the family. If you are using a fire or stove, add a small piece of fuel.

⁕ Before you rush into the day, send a few special words to anyone among your friends you feel might be in special need.

A wax amulet spell to keep you or a family member safe from spite

The Celtic goddess Brighid was associated with the serpent, symbol of feminine wisdom and fertility. This link continued when Brighid was absorbed into the Christian saint called Bridget or Brigit in Ireland and Bride in Wales in the late fifth century CE. St Bridget's day also took over the pagan goddess's festival at the beginning of February. Some say that Bridget was a converted Druidess made a saint to attract pagan worshippers into Christianity. On St Bridget's day, a prayer was said for protection against snake bites. This prayer is equally effective against human serpents that make your life or that of a family member difficult. The spell does not harm the 'serpent' but may throw them off balance. The wax amulet is made from beeswax, sacred to the pre-Christian goddess and later to the Virgin Mary and her mother, St Anne. You can use extra candles if you want to make more than one amulet at the same time for different people.

You will need

A small squat beeswax candle or a pure-white fast-burning candle; a flat metal holder without a spike; a nail file, paper knife or other inscribing tool; a piece of paper; a pen; a white cloth.

Timing

Whenever you need protection, if possible just before it gets light.

The spell

* Light the candle. Name the person for whom the spell is being cast (yourself if you are working for your own safety) and the human serpent, together with his or her main form of attack.
* Recite three times aloud:
  Today is the Day of Bride;
  The serpent shall come from the hole.
  I will not molest the serpent,
  Nor will the serpent molest me.
* While the candle is burning through, practise drawing on paper a design of a protective serpent that will keep away the human one. You will be engraving this design into the melted candle wax. Also devise some private protective words you will say (in your head) to empower the amulet.
* When the candle is burnt through and the wax is cool but still soft, use the inscribing tool to engrave your protective serpent in the cooling wax and then draw three deosil (clockwise) circles around it.
* Repeat the chant three times more, and then say in your head your secret protective words three times.
* Cut around the outermost circle and allow the amulet to cool and harden fully.
* Wrap the amulet in the white cloth. Keep it safely out of sight or give it to the person under threat to keep at home, but do not tell them the secret words.
* When the threat appears or when you know your family member or friend will be under stress from the serpent, recite the Bride rhyme and the secret words in your head just once and picture the candle flame.

A nail charm for stopping threatened legal or official action against you or a family member

There are all kinds of reasons why law-abiding people find themselves embroiled in legal action. You may have become involved in a boundary dispute with a hostile neighbour, committed a minor traffic offence, been wrongly accused of shoplifting or become caught up in an incident with friends. Of course, you should get as much help as possible from both a solicitor and any charitable organisations working in the area of your particular problem. Sometimes a family member may be ashamed to mention a debt problem or a motoring offence, and it is only when a Court Order or the bailiffs arrive that you learn of the problem – which may have escalated from a relatively small debt or an unpaid parking fine. This spell is a good way of directing your energies, especially if – like most of us – you are sent into a panic by a brush with the law. It will usually bring a positive and helpful response.

The charm used in this and the following spell dates back to medieval Europe. Many such old charms used religious terms to give them power; this was not intended to be blasphemous. Rather, medieval spell-workers recognised that we sometimes need a bit of higher help, whatever we call that higher source. In the original spell, the devil (representing the hostile action) was nailed to the post. I think both this and the following version are more appropriate in the modern world.

You will need
3 old nails; 3 new nails; an upright post.

Timing
Immediately after you have received an unwelcome legal communication or your home has been visited by the police or bailiffs.

The spell
* Working upwards, hammer the nails into the post in a vertical row, as you do so, reciting over and over again:
  Father, Son and Holy Ghost,
  Nail this dispute to the post.
* Once you have finished, take immediate practical action.

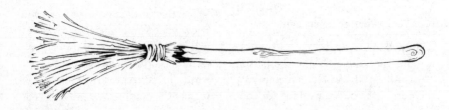

A second nail charm for stopping threatened legal or official action against you or a family member

In religion and folklore, St Jude is the patron saint of hopeless causes and can be called on for help when there are problems of any kind. He is especially effective in legal or official disputes. Dressed in green and white robes, he is portrayed with a small flame on top of his head. Advertisements are often placed in the personal columns of newspapers with the message, 'Thanks, St Jude, for blessings received'.

You will need
3 old nails; 3 new nails; an upright post.

Timing
Immediately after you have received an unwelcome legal communication or your home has been visited by the police or bailiffs.

The spell
❋ As in the previous spell, working upwards, hammer the nails into the post in a vertical row, as you do so in this spell reciting over and over again:
Good St Jude I trust the most,
Nail this dispute to the post.
❋ Once you have finished, take immediate practical action.

A year's turning spell for keeping yourself and loved ones safe

This is an annual ritual, traditionally carried out at halloween, once a time when the spirits of the family ancestors were welcomed at the hearth. In the Celtic calendar, halloween was called samhain (which means 'summer's end') and was the beginning of the new year. The spell works equally well when carried out on new year's eve or the night of 1 January. However, if you prefer to work it at halloween, it is a wonderful antidote to plastic skeletons and ghosts in white sheets. If you have a hearth in your home, perform the spell there. Otherwise, create a hearth for the purpose of the spell with a circle of bricks or stones, or buy a hearth surround at a DIY store and set it against a wall indoors or out. You can carry out the spell alone or with any family members or close friends who will not feel uneasy.

You will need
A small dish of salt; a stick of sage, cypress, cedar or any other woody incense in a holder; a purple candle in a deep or enclosed holder; a small dish of mineral water, in which a smoky quartz or any other dark crystal has been soaked for 12 hours – leave the crystal in the water if you wish.

Timing
At halloween, on new year's eve or on 1 January. Alternatively, cast the spell at the beginning of any month and repeat either a year later or on the next halloween or new year's eve/day. Work in the evening, before supper.

The spell
❋ Either alone or with family members or close friends, sit or kneel around the hearth. You are going to regard the back of the hearth as symbolic North.

* Place the salt (for the protection of Earth) at the centre back of the hearth to represent North. Place the incense stick (for the protection of Air) to the right of the salt to represent East. Place the candle (for the protection of Fire) at the centre front to represent South. Place the dish of water (for the protection of Water) to the left of the candle to represent West. You have now created an elemental square of protection.
* Take up the salt and, beginning at the back of the hearth and continuing around yourself and any loved ones, scatter a circle deosil (clockwise), finishing where the salt dish was. As you do so say:
  Within this circle of protection, let none harm you, by thought, word or deed, by the power of this salt, substance of Mother Earth, who casts her mantle over all.
* Return the salt to the hearth.
* Take up the incense and make a similar circle, starting at the back of the hearth, surrounding any loved ones and ending behind the dish of salt, and saying as you do so:
  Within this circle of protection, let none harm you by thought, word or deed, by the power of this incense, substance of Father Sky, whose thunderbolts and mighty winds drive away all that may do hurt.
* Return the incense to the hearth.
* Take up the candle, lifting it in the holder. Picture a circle of light in the air around your loved ones and say:
  Within this circle of protection, let none harm you by thought, word or deed, by the power of this fire, substance of Brother Sun, who shines light and warmth upon this circle of love
* Return the candle to the hearth.
* Take up the water, and sprinkle a circle deosil from the back of the hearth, around the family and to the back of the hearth again, as you do so saying:
  Within this circle of protection, let none harm you by thought, word or deed, by the power of Sister Water, who encloses you on her magical island of security.
* Return the water to the hearth.
* Touch each of the elements in turn, and say for each:
  Earth (Air / Fire / Water), cast your circle of protection wherever my loved ones are, be it across the room or over oceans. I ask in love and in love may it be.
* Leave the candle and the incense to burn through while you have supper.
* Clear away any wax and ash and leave the ritual objects in place. Keep the hearth or circle of bricks well-tended, perhaps decorating it with flowers, evergreens and fruit in the centre. If you or a family member face an uncertain or hazardous situation, the night before light a candle and a stick of incense in the hearth.

A smoke spell to protect yourself and loved ones from physical harm

Smudge sticks (tied bundles of dried herbs, usually sagebrush or cedar) come from the Native North American tradition – though these days smudging is becoming popular in many different lands and spiritual systems. The herbs are ones of healing and offer protection to those who use them or are blessed by their smudge smoke. Traditionally, the smoke is wafted around an individual, a group of people or symbols representing people to build up a shield of spiritual protection. You can smudge a large number of people by working with their photographs. If an individual member of the family or one or two people close to you needs protection, you can smudge them directly. You can also smudge homes (see page 331).

Smudging is a powerful way to give and receive lasting protection from harm of all kinds. It can lower your profile if there is risk of attack, and also shields against accidents. Smudge sticks, large and small, can be bought from New Age and health food stores, as well as by mail order over the Internet. However, if you cannot get hold of any, you can use a sage, cedar or pine incense stick. Work in the open air or in an uncarpeted and well ventilated area away from soft furnishings.

You will need

A smudge stick; a feather or fan (optional); a candle; photographs of loved ones (optional).

Timing

At sunrise or sunset.

The spell

⁂ Light the candle. If you are smudging pictures, assemble them in a small circle. Otherwise, stand facing the person or people you are going to smudge. (You can, of course, smudge yourself for personal protection.)

⁂ Light the tip of the smudge stick from the candle, allowing the flame to die down and then gently blowing or fanning the tip until you see red sparks and a steady flow of smoke.

⁂ Holding the smudge stick in your power hand (the one you write with) and the feather or fan (if you are using one) in your receptive hand, turn to face each of the four cardinal directions in turn, beginning in the East. Then point the smudge stick or fan the smoke downwards to the Earth and finally upwards to the sky. This is called greeting the six directions.

⁂ Using the feather, the fan or your hand to direct the smoke, smudge yourself, each person or each photograph upwards from the feet using widdershins (anti-clockwise) and deosil (clockwise) spirals alternately – to keep away negativity and to draw protection respectively. Follow the contours of the body so that you enclose the person within the smoke. When you have worked from the feet to the crown, work downwards from the crown to the feet, and then back up to the crown again, ending with three deosil circles just above the head. If there is more than one person, you can if you like create one large spiralling sphere upwards, downwards and then upwards again to enclose all those being smudged within it. End with three deosil spirals at the top of the sphere. If you are smudging a circle of objects, work up and down and then up again, creating a cone of smoke over and around them. Make the final deosil circles at the point of the cone. The secret is to allow your body to find a natural rhythm, like a slow gyrating dance. Keep moving and let your body, not your mind, be your guide. As you work, chant in a slow mesmeric rhythm:

Mother Earth, Father Sky,
Protect, guard and sanctify.
Guard from danger,
Hostile stranger.
Mother Earth, Father Sky,
Bless, guard and sanctify.

* Repeat the spell weekly or monthly, according to the extent of pressures from external negativity.

A spell to guard you or family members against accidents, misfortune or attack

Accidents and other mishaps can happen to us while playing a sport, crossing the road, fixing the car or doing just about any other activity. Some people seem to be especially prone to accidents or to losing possessions. Misfortune can also strike in the form of mugging, which in the modern world may occur for the sake of a few pounds or a mobile phone. This spell works on the very old principle of wrapping sharp objects as a symbolic way of turning away harm from those we love. Polynesian women practised a similar spell for their menfolk when they went away hunting or fishing.

You will need

A blunt or rusty knife, pair of scissors, razor, nail or anything once sharp that has now become useless; some cotton wool or bubble wrap; a padded bag or layers of thick brown paper and tape.

Timing

Around the night of the full moon, a time notorious for accidents.

The spell

* Take the blunt and rusty objects and wrap them together in the cotton wool or bubble wrap, as you do so saying:
Danger be blunted, perils lose your edge. Rust, sharp blade, turn from (name yourself and as many family members/close friends as you wish) that we/they may be safe from harm for three years times three. Steel pierce not (name anyone facing a particular hazard/ who is accident-prone). So I ask and so shall it be three years times three.

* Place the cotton wool parcel in the padded bag or wrap it in the brown paper and seal it, as you do so repeating the words.

* Put the parcel on a high shelf in an inaccessible place.

* Repeat the spell every nine years, throwing away the blunt and rusted objects somewhere where they can harm no one.

A candle ring spell for personal protection

Whatever the hazards facing you, a candle ring sets up a barrier of protection by creating a circle of light around you. You give yourself the ability to activate this protection instantly whenever you need it by establishing a psychic short-cut during the spell.

You will need

8 small white candles or tea-lights in holders (you can improvise tea-light-holders from old bottles, jars or saucers – they need to be stable enough to stand freely on the floor); a compass (optional).

Timing

Ideally at noon, so that the sun amplifies the candle power. If it is a dull day, use more or brighter candles, or lamps around the room.

The spell

* Set the candles or tea-lights in a circle large enough for you to sit in the centre. If you can arrange the candles around a pool of sunlight, the spell will be very potent.
* Sit in the circle, facing South, the direction of the noonday sun.
* Beginning in the South and moving deosil (clockwise) around the circle, light each candle in turn. (Estimate the directions or use a compass.) As you light each candle, say:

Burn bright, candle light;

Drive away all danger.
Protect me as I work and live
From false friend and stranger.

* Stand in the centre of the circle of light and carefully turn deosil nine times, as you do so repeating the invocation.
* Sit once more facing South in the centre of the circle of light. Picture the circle forming a sphere around you and then hardening like a transparent, golden crystal shield. Extend your hands so you can feel its edges.
* To establish the activation mechanism for times when you cannot light a circle of candles, touch your psychic third eye (or pineal gland), on your brow, between and just above your physical eyes. As you do so, say:

When I touch my third eye in times of need, I activate my candle circle of safety.

* Blow out the candles widdershins (anti-clockwise), beginning with the one immediately to the right of the southern-most candle, so that the last candle alight is the first one you ignited. See the physical light fade, but know that the spiritual light remains.
* Repeat the spell whenever you feel the protection getting weaker, especially if you have activated the protective shield a number of times.

An Eye of Horus blue crystal spell to stop a particular person envying you

The Eye of Horus, the ancient Egyptian sky god, has been a symbol of protection against envy in the Middle East and eastern Mediterranean lands for thousands of years. Such envy was called 'the evil eye' because it was believed that if a person gazed enviously on your family or property, harm might befall through jealousy. The Eye of Horus was made of blue glass or faience (a blue glass and ceramic mix), or painted on a blue stone such as lapis lazuli, sodalite or falcon's eye (the blue form of tiger's eye) – this latter because Horus was depicted as a falcon-headed deity (see also page 381). The protective image was worn on a necklace or carried as a charm.

You will need

A round, flat, blue crystal; a small pot of acrylic or modelling paint and a thin brush, or a fine-line permanent ink marker in a colour that will show clearly on your chosen crystal.

Timing

During the waning moon, after sunset.

The spell

* Draw or paint the Eye of Horus (as shown above) on the blue crystal, as you do so, picturing the envious person surrounded in gentle blue light and turning away from you
* When you have finished painting, enchant your crystal by moving your hands nine times over it, palms downwards, the left hand circling widdershins (anti-clockwise) and the right hand simultaneously circling deosil (clockwise). As you move your hands, chant:

Eye bright,
By day and night
Turn the sight
Of (name envious person) from me
And on them light
Bright blessings.

(If you can send blessings to an ill-wisher, you will be doubly blessed yourself.)

* Keep the eye charm somewhere between you and the envious person.
* When the paint chips or fades, it is time to replace the charm (but this may never become necessary).

24 SPELLS FOR PROTECTION OF THE HOME

Protection of the home has always been one of the key reasons for spell-casting among ordinary people. Though dangers change and most of us no longer have cause to fear fierce wild animals at the door, nevertheless attacks on the home and domestic robbery are a major modern problem in both town and country. We may also face the negativity that comes from outside pressures or family quarrels, as well as from ill-wishers who project envy or malice onto our home life. Whether your problem is a ghost, an unwelcome earthly visitor or a neighbourhood where there is a high risk of vandalism and break-ins, in this chapter of spells drawn from around the world you will find a spell to enable you to sleep safe and sound in your bed at night.

A crystal guardian spell for your home

Working a crystal spell is an easy but effective way of protecting your home. Traditionally, crystals were thought to contain individual protective angels or spirit essences. If you look into a dark, misty or richly coloured semi-transparent crystal that contains inclusions, you will see how such beliefs arose. It takes only a minute or so once a month to set your sentinel crystals on each window ledge at the same time that you lock the doors for the night. Children may appreciate a crystal guardian at the window in their bedroom at night (see also pages 352 and 353).

You will need

A crystal for each window ledge (it need only be small) chosen from the following: amber, amethyst, Apache tears/obsidian, smoky quartz, purple and green fluorite, rutilated quartz, watermelon tourmaline; a bowl big enough to contain all your crystals; 2 sticks of cedar, frankincense, myrrh, pine or sandalwood incense and a suitable holder(s).

Timing

As dusk is falling – a windy night is especially good.

The spell

* Working in the open air or near an open window to absorb the power of the night, set the crystals gently in the bowl, taking care not to scratch them.
* Light the incense sticks and, holding one in each hand, slowly weave a spiralling web of smoke over the bowl (taking care not to drop ash on the crystals). As you work, chant softly:
  As the sun sets, power of dark,
  Kindle this protective spark.
  Weave your web of dark and light,
  Guardian spirits of the night.
* When you sense that the power has entered the crystals, slow down the movement of your hands and the chant until all is still and silent.
* Leave the incense to burn through in holders next to the crystal bowl.
* Just before you lock up for the night, set one crystal on each window ledge.
* Collect the crystals once a month, just before dark, and re-empower them.

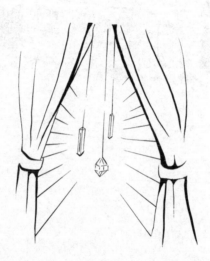

A spell to activate a guardian stone

An early tradition involved placing a small monolith (a single pillar stone) as a sentinel for the home. Huge ceremonial monoliths (a single massive column-like stone structure) may first have appeared in western Europe as early as 5000 BCE. Like all ancient sacred stones, the monolith marks and enhances the power of the place in which it is set. A smaller, homelier domestic monolith can bring protection and power into your life, albeit in a less dramatic way.

Look for a small pillar-shaped stone on a seashore, plain, moor or hillside. It need be no larger than 15 cm/6 in high, as it is the symbolic strength that is important. Carry a small rucksack or backpack to transport it. I certainly do not advocate plundering a sacred site, but you may find just the right stone, discarded or ignored, close to your special sacred place or on the old processional route to a long barrow. If a stone feels unusually heavy or cold, leave it and choose another. If possible, avoid the environs of more commercialised sites. Alternatively, explore craft outlets in an area famed for its local stone. Amidst all the carvings, you may discover a small, unadorned pillar. A garden centre close to a sacred site may have stones used for garden boundaries that come from the same source of local unhewn rock that formed the boundaries of the holy enclosure. It doesn't matter if your pillar is slightly squat. While ideally the stone should be positioned at the front of the house (to the side of the front door), you can also place it indoors near the entrance in a large pot filled with earth.

You will need

Your chosen stone; a few drops of any Bach Flower Essence or patchouli, tea tree or mimosa essential oil; a few fresh or dried herbs of any kind; some herb or flower seeds or seedlings, or a small pot of flowers.

Timing

Early on a Saturday morning.

The spell

* Set the stone in position, if necessary hollowing out a little earth so that it fits snugly.
* Scatter the herbs over the stone, as you do so saying:
  Guardian spirit of the stone, bless and protect my home by day and night. I ask this favour and I pay honour.
* Sprinkle a few drops of the Flower Essence or essential oil over the stone, as you do so repeating the chant.
* Plant the herb or flower seeds or seedlings around the stone, or place the pot of flowers near it.
* Scatter herbs and sprinkle oil over the stone monthly, as you do so repeating the chant. If you ever sense that the stone wants to go home, its work is done and you should return it to as close to the original site as possible. Wait and another stone will come naturally into your life.

Making a protective witch bottle

Protective witch bottles, some dating from before Roman times and others from as late as the beginning of the twentieth century, may be seen in museums around the world. There are fine examples in the small and eccentric but fabulous Pitt Rivers Museum in Oxford, UK. Witch bottles usually consisted of a sealed stone or bellaramine jar, filled with bent iron nails and pins, and buried under the entrance of a house. Iron is considered the most protective metal against all kinds of harm. Although the old witch bottles were often designed to guard against witches, the modern ones are used to repel any form of malevolence or bad feeling that may enter the home.

You will need

A dark glass or stone bottle with a cork or tight lid (the kind used for cider is ideal); some sealing wax (optional); enough old rusty nails and pins to half fill the bottle; enough cheap or sour red wine or vinegar to almost fill the bottle; 2 or 3 sprigs of fresh rosemary or 2–3 tsp dried rosemary.

Timing

At around 10 pm when the moon is no longer visible in the sky.

The spell

* Working in a dim light, rinse the bottle under a tap.
* Place the rusty nails and pins in the bottle, bending them if you can to form a horseshoe shape.
* Add the rosemary and then enough wine to cover the nails (the original protective fluid was urine, but this is not suitable for modern witch bottles!).
* Close the bottle and, if you choose, seal it with sealing wax (the traditional method).
* Shake the bottle nine times, as you do so saying:
  Keep away harm,
  Keep away danger,
  Keep from my door
  False friend and stranger.
  Drive away malice,
  Drive away spite,
  Guard this my dwelling
  By day and by night.
* Either bury the bottle in deep earth near the front or back door or keep it on a high shelf in a basement or cellar. Alternatively, place it high as possible in the house, where it cannot be seen.

A witch bottle spell for those who live in a potentially dangerous area or live alone and feel nervous of intruders

This spell is more active than the previous one. It is the only spell I have ever come across that uses thyme (protective against all harm), here added to the traditional rosemary. The spell was taught to me by Annie, an old lady I met in Aberdeen, in the north-east of Scotland. When Annie was a teenager, her great-grandmother told her she had buried a witch bottle in a corner of her remote croft. She shared the recipe so that, when married, Annie could do the same. The shiny needles and pins substituted for the more usual rusty nails make the bottle extra powerful. It was intended to be buried as far away as possible from the home but within the land boundaries.

You will need

A small dark-green or brown glass bottle with a lid or cork (an old beer bottle of the type used by traditional breweries is ideal; a dark beeswax or brown candle (one with colour that goes all the way through the candle – i.e. not dipped); enough sharp shiny needles and pins (in about equal numbers) to one-third fill the bottle; 3 tsp dried thyme (the culinary kind is fine); a heatproof jug; 3 or 4 sprigs of fresh rosemary (or 3 tsp dried rosemary if you cannot get fresh).

Timing

As near to the dark moon as possible, when the moon cannot be seen.

The spell

* Rinse and dry the bottle and then light the candle.
* One by one, add the pins and needles alternately to the bottle, bending each into a horseshoe shape before you put it in.
* Place the thyme in the jug and add about three cups of boiling water. Stir three time deosil (clockwise), cover the jug and leave it for ten minutes.
* Strain the liquid and pour it into the bottle while it is still warm (but not hot). It should just cover the pins and needles.
* Add the rosemary to the bottle and press it down, so that it absorbs some of the liquid.
* Carefully shake the uncorked bottle, as you do so saying:
  Needles and pins, rosemary, thyme,
  Guard thou my home, witch bottle of mine;
  Not to harm but to drive far away
  All who would harm it by night or by day.
* Put in the cork or screw on the bottle, and then drip on some wax from the candle to seal it, taking care not to burn yourself.
* When the wax is set, hide the bottle secretly; either buried at the end of your garden or, if you live in a apartment, at the top of a store cupboard or in any loft or basement space.

A nature spell to keep your home and possessions safe from harm

In pre-industrial times, when most people lived in the countryside, home boundaries were often made of hawthorn bushes. With its long sharp thorns, the hawthorn offered a physical deterrent as well as a magical power of protection. Nettles also formed both a physical and a psychic defence against intrusion. In some modern gardens, both hawthorn and nettles are grown near a boundary wall. In hotter climates, a large cactus was placed against each of the four boundary corners indoors or outdoors, to mark the limit beyond which anyone with ill intent would feel reluctant to enter. Even if you do not have a garden, you can still use protective plants to create a psychic force field to deter potential wrong-doers. While you must, of course, take all the usual earthly precautions too, a psychic barrier can lower the profile of your home, thus making it less of a target, by creating an invisible but powerful force field around it.

You will need

4 of the following trees, bushes and herbs (miniature potted trees are just as effective as full-sized ones): bay, palm, cactus, juniper, rowan, basil, cumin, wild garlic, parsley, rosemary, sage, thyme, vetivert; a small silver bell, some Tibetan bells on a string, a small wind chime, or Tibetan bell music on CD/tape and a headset; 4 small wind chimes or hanging bells (optional); a few caraway or coriander seeds (optional); some clingfilm/plastic wrap (optional).

Timing

The first night of the waning moon.

The spell

* You are going to walk the boundaries of your property. In psychic terms, these are defined as the furthest extent of your property in all four directions from the centre of your home. The boundaries will have four corners and four sides. Work at ground level (or the lowest floor if you live in an apartment). First of all choose your starting place.

* Ringing the bells or chimes, or listening to the Tibetan music begin to walk the boundaries deosil (clockwise). As you walk, picture the sound forming a shimmering barrier that extends up to the roof and encloses your property. Be sure to visit each of the four corners of the boundary, if you wish setting one of the small wind chimes or hanging bells in each of them.

* Walk around the boundaries once more, this time placing a tree, bush or herb as a plant guardian at each of the four corners.

* Walk around the boundaries one more time, this time enchanting each of the plant guardians by passing your hands very slowly a few centimetres above or in front of it with your palms downwards and the left hand moving widdershins (anti-clockwise) and the right hand simultaneously moving deosil (clockwise). As you move your hands, say:

One from theft,
Two from storm,
Three from sickness and from harm,
Four from fire and careless stranger,
Five from foe and unseen danger,
Six from malice,
Seven from pain,
Eight from flood and ceaseless rain,
Nine from all who come for gain.
Nine eight, seven, six, five, four, three, two, one,

May this spell last through moon and sun.
So shall it be as I count three:
One, two, three. Protect!

- At the word 'protect', raise your hands and push harm away.
- If you have any items that are particularly valuable, whether in financial or personal terms (for example your car, your computer, the tools of your trade, special jewellery), roll some of the caraway or coriander seeds in a piece of the clingfilm and hide or tape them in the item.
- Repeat the spell every few months or if you have a spate of burglaries in your area.

A home and garden smudging protection ritual

Smudge sticks come from the Native North American tradition and are long slender bundles of herbs, usually sagebrush or cedar, tied together with thread. They are lit at one end and the smoke used for cleansing and purifying people, places and artefacts. This spell marks out the boundaries of your home and any land to declare harm and negativity off limits. The smoke acts as a protective barrier that remains long after the physical smoke has dispersed. For smudging communal walls indoors, open windows and keep the smudge smoke away from children, pets or anyone with chronic lung problems.

You will need
A candle; a small sagebrush or cedar smudge stick (available from New Age stores and by mail order over the Internet), or a large stick of juniper, sage, cedar or pine incense; a feather (optional).

Timing
Early morning, after it is light.

The spell
- Light the tip of the smudge or incense stick from the candle (taking care not to get wax on the smudge). When the smudge flares, blow out the flame and gently blow on and fan the tip until there is a steady stream of smoke and the tip is glowing red.
- You are now going to smudge all the boundaries of your home. If you are able to walk all the way around the outside of your home, this is easy, and you can use walls and garden fences, gates and hedges, as the perimeter markers. Otherwise, where your home has a communal wall or walls smudge indoors to complete the protective enclosure. Hold the smudge almost vertically in your power hand (the one you write with) and fan the smoke with the other (or with the feather), wafting it in spirals and allowing your power hand to dictate the course. You may find that you enter a natural rhythmic half-mesmeric state. Smudge at waist or shoulder height. Start at the front doorstep, as you smudge saying:

Light, life, laughter and loveliness enter here.
Hope and joy will banish fear.
Sorrow and anger, disease and danger,
Remain a stranger
To my home.

- Working deosil (clockwise), continue smudging around your house or garden boundaries. For extra security smudge the external house walls themselves as well. Include the step of the back door and the external walls of the entrance to any outhouse, pet homes or garage.
- Finally, smudge any communal walls or fences to mark the limits of your private safe territory.
- Repeat monthly or when you feel your home is especially vulnerable.

A seed charm to keep malevolent or spiteful people from entering your home

Seeds such as caraway, cumin and coriander have long been used for preventing theft and repelling malevolence and spite. Other protective seeds include sesame, sunflower and pumpkin. Originally, the seeds would have been kept in a narrow phial, like a test tube. Should the protective power of the seeds fail and an ill-wisher (in more superstitious times a witch) enter the house, the seeds would spill and the hostile visitor would be forced by magic to count every seed before proceeding. By this time, of course, they would be either exhausted or discovered by the householder. At one time such seed charms were given as Christmas, new year and Easter presents, and would be hung over a doorway.

You will need

A selection of caraway, cumin, coriander, sesame, sunflower and pumpkin seeds (wild bird seed often contains a number of different seeds, including some of the above); a long tube you can suspend above the door, or a seed net or very finely meshed bird feeder of the kind you hang on trees, or a clear plastic or glass tube with a stopper (such as glitter is bought in).

Timing

On a Sunday or on Good Friday, when no evil-doer dare venture abroad.

The spell

* Fill the tube or mesh with the seeds. (If one of your children is nervous of strangers coming to the door, he or she can help you.)
* Seal the mesh or tube, as you do so saying nine times in rapid succession:
  Count the seeds, never the same.
  Count the seeds or leave in shame.

A Middle Eastern hand spell to keep all harm away from your home

All over the Middle East and in some parts of Asia, a hand with an outward-facing palm, and sometimes the fingers splayed, forms a protective device painted over doorways, embroidered on clothes and made as a magical gesture during ritual. This symbol gives powerful protection of the home, be it an apartment or a house with land all around. If you live in a neighbourhood where there has been a number of burglaries or if you live alone and feel vulnerable, this spell can help to give you a sense of security.

You will need

A lipstick or whiteboard pen; a permanent marker or some paint and a brush (optional).

Timing

Whenever the house is quiet and you will not be disturbed.

The spell

* Beginning near the front door, go into every room and place your palm in the centre of the window, as you do so saying:
  Harm and hardship, come not here;
  Darkness, danger retreat in fear.
  The hand repels all bad intent;
  Hostile forces far are sent.
* When you have visited every room, go to a downstairs window that faces the street, place your palm on the glass and, using the lipstick or whiteboard pen, draw around your hand.
* Leave the drawing there until the

morning light has shined upon it, then rub it away, polishing the window until it shines.

* If you wish, use the paint or marker to draw a small protective hand somewhere near the door of your house, where it will not be seen – perhaps on the inside of a hall cupboard, on the inside of an outhouse door or on a coat rack in the hall.

A spell to invoke the protective guardians of your home after dark

In Iceland and parts of Scandinavia it is still is accepted that land and homes are protected at night by land wights, tall shadowy guardians who watch over boundaries and stand where roads or paths meet, keeping away ill-wishers, both earthly and paranormal. This belief was once upheld throughout northern and eastern Europe and Russia. In Iceland offerings are left for these spirits in fields sacred to them. No one will build on this land. If you live in a place that is lonely or where vandalism often occurs after dark, try this spell. You don't need to believe in land wights; just think of the protection as symbolic and psychological. The spell will also protect against evening phone calls or visits from anyone who makes you unhappy and perhaps pressurises you. Alternatively, you can send the protection to the home of a relative or friend whom you know feels vulnerable at night.

You will need

3 tall white candles; 3 candle-holders or a three-candle holder in which the candles are at different heights, the tallest in the middle; a mirror (optional).

Timing

After dark, whenever you feel your home needs extra protection.

The spell

* Place the candles in a row in a darkened room, facing an uncurtained window that does not have a streetlight directly outside, so that when you light the candles, you can see the flames reflected in the window. If you have no such window, place the candles before a mirror.

* Light the candles one by one, for each candle saying:
  Be thou the guardian of my (or name the person to whose house you are sending the protection) home.
  Roam far and near,
  Turn back the phantoms of the night,
  So all is calm till day returns as light.

* Each candle now represents a guardian. Give each one a secret name. These may be, for example, the names of angels or deities, or they may be names of your own making.

* Blow out each candle in turn, as you do so, naming the guardian and saying:
  Go peacefully, (name), and in peace return.

* Replace the candles regularly but keep the same names.

A spell for protection of your home and possessions from burglars

Like the witch bottle spells on pages 328–9, this spell uses the magical protection properties of metal. Even in well secured homes, the fear of theft can be great, whether you live in an urban or a rural setting. What makes a burglar choose a particular home to rob is sometimes hard to fathom. Ancient peoples believed that it was possible to create a protective atmosphere around a home to deter such intruders. I first came across the original version of this spell when on a childhood holiday in Wales, more than 40 years ago. I have since discovered similar spells in Scandinavia. The spell as given here is something of a composite.

You will need

An iron or tin box (search garage sales, gift shops and hardware stores), alternatively a large biscuit tin; an obsolete key from a lock somewhere in the home; small metal household or personal items such as old teaspoons, buckles, chains or earrings; an old padlock without a key (you can throw the key away before the spell); a length of old chain, preferably rusty; 4 dark round stones.

Timing

During the waning moon, on a very cloudy night.

The spell

* Put a stone in each corner of the box to weigh it down. Place the key in the box, together with the symbolic household and personal items.
* Slam the box shut, wrap the chain around it and secure it with the padlock. Say:
  Key of my home, of all I love,
  Binds with iron chains from burglary
  The treasures of my family.
  Turn away all with ill intent;
  Empty-handed be you sent.
* If possible, bury the box in a deep hole in the garden. Otherwise, put it with junk at the back of a garden shed or cupboard where it will not be disturbed. If the box is found, no harm will come, but the spell will need to be repeated.

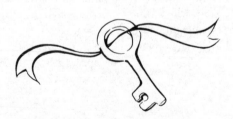

A spell to create shadow guardians to protect you in your home after dark or on dull days

In China and other parts of the Far East, stone lions are used to guard official buildings and important residences. The ancient Egyptians had their sphinxes, lions with a human face (often that of one of the Pharaohs), while medieval churches and cathedrals typically had winged griffons or hideous gargoyles carved over entrances to keep away evil spirits. Our ancestors believed that the essence of these stone representations would patrol the area at night, driving away potential attackers as well as paranormal forces of the night. I have a big ceramic cat, a representation of the ancient Egyptian cat-headed goddess Bastet (Bast is her cat form) that I use for protection. Bastet or Bast was said to care especially for women and children, as though they were her kittens.

This can be a reassuring spell if you hear noises outside at night or feel generally jittery in your home. You are not animating spirit forms, merely psychologically and psychically activating benign protective energies. You can use any animal or bird statue, one of your favourite deities from any culture, an angel of the night (Gabriel is especially good) or a saint. I have also used this spell to reassure children who are afraid of night-time intruders.

You will need

1 or more protective statues set against a light-coloured wall on a shelf or table; a candle that is shorter than the statue, in a glass holder.

Timing

After dark or on a very dull day whenever you feel afraid in your home.

The spell

* Light the candle. Place it before the statue or statues so that they appear to dance in the flickering light. Watch them moving in the light and say:
  Turn back harm, turn away danger, keep all safe within that I/we may sleep secure and peacefully.
* Blow out the candles before you go to sleep, picturing in your mind the dancing forms enclosing you protectively.

A salt and pepper spell for scrubbing away negativity

In the homes of descendants of African and West Indian cultures – and recently in American homes more generally – salt and pepper are central to magical domestic cleansing rituals, since they represent both protection and life-enhancing energies (see also the following spell). In one ritual, salt and black pepper are sprinkled on the floor and then swept up and burnt (or vacuumed up) to keep away ill-wishers and time-wasters who come to the door or, in more recent times, phone. Another very popular ritual forms the basis of this spell. According to custom, the back and front door steps (or the nearest parts of the home to the outside world) were scrubbed with a mixture of black pepper and sea salt dissolved in warm water before sunrise. This mixture will not give you the instant gleaming white of commercial products, but it will help you to cleanse away negativity. As any feng shui expert will tell you, the act of scrubbing is a good way of shedding the personal bad vibes that can accumulate if you have had a few fraught days at home or at work.

You will need

Some sea salt and black ground pepper; a bucket three-quarters filled with warm water; a scrubbing brush or mop; a stick to stir the water (optional); peppermint, lemon, geranium or tea tree essential oil (optional).

Timing

Begin about 15 minutes before sunrise, pouring the water away, if possible, at dawn (more easily done in winter, when dawn is later).

The spell

* To the bucket of warm water add ten pinches of salt and ten pinches of pepper (or if the tubs have a shaker, add ten shakes). Add ten drops of the essential oil if you are using it. As you add these ingredients either count each pinch (or drop) or chant the following old rhyme:

Father, Son and Holy Ghost,
Bless home and those I love the most.

* Stir the water with the stick or the mop until all is dissolved.
* Set to work, scrubbing first in widdershins (anti-clockwise) and then in deosil (clockwise) circles, beginning with the doorsteps, front and back. Scrub any uncarpeted areas, adding more water as necessary. As you work, sing to establish the cleansing rhythm. Traditionally, spirituals such as 'Swing Low Sweet Chariot' were sung, but choose any rhythmic melody, repeating the refrains over and over until you have finished. If any family members want to help, the effect on domestic positivity is really powerful.
* As dawn lights the sky, pour the water away down a drain or a paved front path that slopes away.
* Open all the windows and doors for a few minutes to let the day flood in.

A herb spell for cleansing your home of unhappiness and protecting it from negativity

A traditional way to restore equilibrium to the home and remove lingering negative words or feelings is to wash floors, patios and yards with a protective infusion of herbs in hot water. Herbal cleansing is also a helpful ritual after a quarrelsome person or someone who was creating a bad atmosphere has moved out or stopped calling or telephoning. This spell is gentler than the previous one. Instead of making an infusion, you can also add eight or nine drops of a cleansing essential oil such as lemon, eucalyptus or tea tree essential oil to a medium-sized bucket of warm water.

You will need

40 g/2 oz of any one or two of the following dried herbs: chamomile, fennel, juniper, lavender, mint, parsley, pine, rosemary, thyme; a metal bucket with a lid; a long wooden spoon or stick; a second bucket of any kind; an old-fashioned floor mop (if possible).

Timing

Very potent in spring, especially at the spring equinox, in the morning.

The spell

❋ Infuse the dried herbs in the metal bucket with the lid, using 600 ml/ 1 pint of boiling water for each 40 g/2 oz of herb.

❋ Using the wooden spoon or stick, stir the infusion nine times deosil (clockwise), as you do so, reciting the following traditional protective cleansing chant (which I have found in several folk traditions):

One for joy,
Two for gladness,
Three and four to banish sadness,
Five and six flee useless anger,
Seven, eight, nine, linger no longer.

❋ Put the lid on the bucket and leave for five to ten minutes; then strain off the herbs, transferring the infusion to the second bucket.

❋ Stir the infusion nine times widdershins (anti-clockwise), as you do so saying:

Nine, eight, seven, six, five, four, three, two one,
What is not welcome now be gone!

❋ Cleanse your home with the infusion, picturing angry words and negative thoughts flowing into the water. If you like, you can sprinkle a little of the infusion in to the corners of rooms that you cannot mop.

❋ When you have finished, pour the dirty water down any external drain to allow the negativity to flow away, adding personal words of banishment as the water disappears.

A fragrance house-cleansing ritual after a bad quarrel has occurred

Occasionally, an ordinary quarrel can spill over into something more bitter — perhaps because a family member is under stress or teenage hormonal swings meet those of the menopause. Even after the quarrel is mended, there may be a sour atmosphere in the house. The most effective way to cleanse such bad vibes is with a fragrance. Fragrances have the power to sweeten and heal even the bitterest of words.

You will need

A pump-action spray bottle (the kind used for watering plants); essential oil in a harmonising fragrance, such as chamomile, lavender, melissa (lemon balm), neroli (orange blossom) or rosewood.

Timing

At first light.

The spell

* Mix ten to 15 drops of essential oil to half a litre/1 pint of water in the spray bottle.
* Shake the mixture, as you do so saying:
Darkness, sorrow, anger, be no longer at rest in my home. Stir yourselves and depart with the morning light.

* Chanting the above words continuously and visualising negative energies flowing towards the nearest exit point, spray each room by standing at the entrance and exit points of each individual room and spraying with the doors open. Start at the top of the house and work downwards. Open the windows briefly and spray outwards. Also spray plug holes, waste pipes, sinks, toilets and even chimneys. Leave any corridors and hallways until you have finished the rooms. Spray down the stairs from the top (but upwards from any cellars or basements).
* Any residual energy will collect at external doorways, so open the back door, chant and spray outwards, then close the door.
* Spray out of the front door, as you do so saying:
Away, do not stay,
Linger no longer;
My power is stronger.
Be gone and do not return.
* Slam the front door closed.

A salt ritual to drive away ghosts, poltergeists and dark influences, normal and paranormal

Most negativity in the home is caused by the stresses of daily life, minor quarrels, everyday worries or petty rivalries. However, you may become aware of an invisible presence or unfriendly atmosphere in a particular room that makes you uneasy. This may not be a ghost in the accepted sense, but rather sad impressions left from the past, perhaps of someone who lived in the house or, if the house is new, on the land (see also page 349). Things may start breaking, seemingly without reason. Poltergeist activity has been linked to human mind power where one or more family members are in conflict, but the cause is less important than easing the atmosphere, especially if it is making a child nervous or unable to sleep. This ritual can be very reassuring for them.

Salt is still used in the preparation of Holy Water. A symbol of life, it has for countless years been considered the most effective way of removing negative energies and feelings from a place.

You will need

A lemon or pine-scented candle; a small dish of sea salt; a white or clear glass bowl of still mineral water or rain water that has not touched the ground (caught in a barrel or dish on a low roof); a silver paper knife or thin stainless steel bladed knife (the more ornamental the better).

Timing

On a Sunday morning.

The spell

* Light the candle in a safe place in the centre of the room where you or the family spend most leisure time
* In the same room, drop three pinches of salt into the bowl of water and use the knife to make the sign of the cross three times on the surface of the water – either the Christian cross or the diagonal cross that is the old sign of the Earth Mother.
* As you make each cross, say:
  By salt and water, purify this home and all within.
* Beginning in the room where the candle is placed, sprinkle a few drops of the salt water in the four corners of each room, repeating the above words in each corner in turn. If you sense a paranormal presence in any rooms, or there have been a lot of minor accidents and quarrels there, sprinkle three ever-widening circles of water drops there, as you do so saying:
  Friend, if it be right, depart in peace or remain as guardian of our home and friend.
* When the candle is burnt through, open the windows and doors in every room for a few minutes.

A spell to fill your home with protective light

There are many reasons why our homes – or certain rooms in them – can seem dark and unfriendly (see the previous spell and the one on page 349), even in summer. A quick solution is an infusion of spiritual (as well as physical) light. This is a Victorian 'light in the darkness' spell, a type of spell that was sometimes a part of evening prayers in more formal households. Try it on a dark winter days or when sadness seems to fill the house. You might then like to hang sun-catchers, crystals on strings or glass nugget mobiles at windows to direct light inwards.

You will need

A pure white or vanilla-scented candle in a holder.

Timing

Whenever your home is – or feels – dark.

The spell

* Light the candle in the middle of the dark room, or in the centre of the house if the whole home seems gloomy.
* Gazing into the candle flame, repeat four times:
  Light of angels, cleanse this room,
  Lift the all-pervading gloom.
  Michael, Gabriel, Raphael, Uriel, Archangels four,
  Protect and bless this home and light restore.
* Leave the candle to burn, repeating the chant when it is almost burnt through.

A mirror spell to reflect back negativity and attract abundance

Mirrors feature in both Eastern and Western spells as a means of deflecting any negativity or hostility from the home. For this reason, they are often set facing entrance doors or windows looking out on to a street. In China and Hong Kong, special mirrors are set above a gateway or doorway outside the home. Garden mirrors are becoming increasingly popular in the West to make small gardens and patios seem larger, but they also have a potent psychic defence purpose. Nervous children may enjoy empowering a small protective mirror to hang facing the door or window of their bedroom to keep away night fears.

You will need

A mirror (large or small); a soft yellow or golden-coloured cloth.

Timing

At noon or in the early afternoon.

The spell

* Set the mirror in a secure place at an angle, so that it will catch the light.
* Hold the back of the mirror with one hand, and with the other hand begin polishing small sections of the mirror, using deosil (clockwise) circles and whispering in a soft continuous chant:
  Sun-white brightness enter here;
  Sun-bright lightness banish fear.
  Send back with your radiance clear
  Dark and sorrow, doubt and fear.
* If you like, silently endow the mirror with a private wish for your own safety or for that of a family member.
* Hang the mirror in its special place and re-polish it if it becomes dull.

A Viking ritual for protection

For many years, I have been interested in Runes and the Vikings who used them – not only for divination but also for protection and victory. In central Sweden, in the old red wooden farmhouses in the forest, protective metal or wooden runic protection symbols can still sometimes be seen at the top of external walls. The houses are not much more than 150 years old. The two most popular runic protective symbols are Thurisaz (which represents the mighty hammer of the thunder god Thor) and Ingwaz (symbol of the ancient fertility and earth god Ing, also known as Frey). The diamond shape is also considered protective throughout the Middle and Far East. Work this spell away from flammable materials, preferably outside.

You will need

A small square of white paper; a red pencil; a deep, metal fireproof tray or container (an old saucepan will do) with sand or earth in the bottom; a small dish.

Timing

Thursday (Thor's day), before dusk

The spell

* On the paper, draw in red (the traditional colour for Runes) both of the above Runic symbols. If you wish, you can weave them into a pattern or intricate design (called a bind Rune). This will be doubly powerful.
* Fold the paper, set it alight and drop it into the fireproof container.
* When the paper is burnt through, collect the cooled ash in the dish. Scatter the ash to the winds, as you do so saying:

  By the power of Thor and Ingwaz, sword and hammer, plough and scythe, send protection from North, East, South and West. Banish to realms of fire and ice the harsh words and inhospitable deeds of all who ill-wish or would harm my home and those that dwell therein. Thor, Thor, Thor and Lord Ing, mighty and true.

A spell to protect a brand-new property or one which has had major renovations or building work

Until the seventeenth or eighteenth century – and later in remote places – a shoe was placed in the foundations or in a supporting wall or chimney of a new house in order to protect it and its inhabitants. Mummified cats and even human remains are a reminder of a more barbaric past, when the protective spirit of the home was thought to demand a living tribute.

If you are moving into a property that is still being built, it may be possible to insert a herb-filled shoe beneath an unconcreted driveway or in an area dug for lawn. This spell is also effective after renovations. I found this out when builders took over my home for six months to fix subsidence and left both house and garden totally unrecognisable. I carried out a re-dedication ceremony and hid an old small herb-filled shoe belonging to one of my children. Whether your home is new or renovated, look around for a good place to conceal a shoe perma-nently. You may be able to find a hiding hole in a crevice or piece of loose brickwork. Tuck the shoe in and seal.

You will need

A small soft shoe; some dried bay leaves, basil, dill and vervain (all four if possible, but any one or two will suffice).

Timing

On a starry night.

The spell

* Working with as little light as possible, fill the inside of the shoe as tightly as you can with the dried herbs, as you work saying softly and repetitively:
  Bay, basil, vervain, dill,
  Keep out evil at your will.
  Dill, vervain, basil, bay,
  Protect forever and a day.
* Hide the shoe in silence and tell no-one where it is. Make a private blessing on all who live in the house now and will in the future.

A horseshoe ritual for protecting a new home against illness and mishaps

Traditionally, horseshoes that are found are ten times luckier than those that are bought. However, any horseshoe is lucky. It should be nailed over the entrance or fireplace of the main room, with the open end pointing upwards, so that the luck does not run out. If you are moving in to your first home, set the horseshoe in place before moving in the furniture. Whenever you move house, take your lucky horseshoe with you and set it over the new front door or hearth. If you were unlucky in your old home, it may be time for a new horseshoe to replace the old overworked one. In this case, take the old one down before you leave and dispose of it in the rubbish.

You will need

A horseshoe; a hammer and nails to secure the horseshoe on the wall or lintel.

Timing

When you move to a home.

The spell

* Using the hammer and nails, secure the horseshoe, reciting continuously as you hammer:
  Power of the horseshoe charm,
  Keep my home safe from harm.

A spell for transferring protection and happiness from one house to another

Young Roman women moving from their family home to the new marital one would take with them burning embers from the family hearth to transfer its protection and good fortune to their new life. Whether you are moving into your first home away from the family or simply moving house, take with you as part of your hand luggage something small that is connected with the land or house itself. This could be a pot of soil containing a favourite garden plant, a rug or an ornament that has sentimental value connected with the old property (perhaps the first gift on moving in or an item from your childhood bedroom that you have treasured since you were very young).

You will need

A special item from your own home (carry it in your hand luggage, so that it can be the first item to be unpacked); a key from your old home; a spare key for your new home; a red cord.

Timing
On the day you move.

The spell

* When you reach the new home, set the special item as near to the centre of the house as possible and leave it there until the evening, when you should have time to carry out the spell.
* When all is quiet, place the item in its new corner.
* Using the red cord, tie the old and new door keys together, making three knots and saying for each key:

Golden days will increase,
Home of joy and house of peace.
Old and new
And what is through
Join in blessing
This new dwelling.

* Keep the keys on the cord underneath the special item until the first anniversary of the move or until you move again. Then you can dispose of the old key – or if members of your family will be living in the old house, keep it in a safe place.

A three-horseshoe protection rite to keep sickness and poverty from the home

Iron is protective against all harm, preventing sickness and misfortune from entering a dwelling. It gained this reputation because it was first discovered in meteorites, and so considered a gift from the gods. Most protective is the lucky iron horseshoe associated with St Dunstan, patron saint of blacksmiths, who nailed the devil to the smithy wall and refused to set him free until he promised never to enter a house or a forge with a horseshoe nailed to the wall.

This spell is medieval but comes from the Anglo Saxon tradition. It invokes three deities. 'Wod' is short for 'Woden', the Anglo Saxon father god. The modern expression 'one for luck' is a corruption of the spell chant, 'one for Lok', intended to appease Loki, god of mischief and change. The use of the name of the Christian God indicates how pagan and Christian ideas co-existed quite happily in the folklore of western Europe and Scandinavia for centuries. In the old versions of this spell, an iron hammer representing the hammer of Thor, Norse god of thunder, would be nailed horizontally across the three horseshoes, specifically to drive away illness.

You will need

3 small iron horseshoes or 3 long iron nails bent into a horseshoe shape; a piece of wood or a beam or lintel over the front door or fireplace; a hammer (for symbolic purposes); suitable nails, hammer and/or drill for the site of your horseshoes (if the DIY seems too daunting, set the horseshoes in a row on the hearth or a focal point of your living room); another ornamental hammer (optional).

Timing

Wednesday (Woden's day), in the afternoon.

The spell

* Prepare the place where you are going to hang or place the horseshoes, with the equipment you will need ready and waiting.
* Lay the three horseshoes or horseshoe-shaped nails in a row and, using the symbolic hammer, gently tap the centre of each in turn three times, saying for each tap:
  One for God, One for Wod and one for Lok.
  Hammer of Thor, hammer true.
  Sickness, poverty pass not through
  This barrier of protection.
* Set each horseshoe in place, repeating the chant for each shoe.
* Leave the symbolic hammer, head uppermost, either on the hearth or behind a cupboard door, or hang the ornamental hammer on the wall with the horseshoes.

A candle spell to guard the home against natural disasters such as fire, high winds and flood

In Christian times, the blessed candles used in the Candlemas services at church at the beginning of February were taken home by chosen members of the congregation and preserved as a charm against natural domestic disasters such as fire, flood, earthquakes and storms. This custom (like the festival itself) derives from the earlier festival of light on the same date dedicated to the Celtic Brighid, the maiden goddess of early spring, who was Christianised as St Bride (see page 317). The spell also offers some protection against disasters caused by human error, such as bathroom floods.

You will need

2 beeswax or tall white candles (do not use oil-based candles); a tall metal canister half filled with water.

Timing

At the end of January or the beginning of February, or when you move into a new home, as dusk is falling.

The spell

* Light one of the beeswax or white candles (sacred to Brighid, St Bride and later the Virgin Mary and her mother St Anne), as you do so reciting the following adaptation of an old protective and healing spell common in Europe during the Middle Ages (see page 469):
  Two angels came from East and West. One brought fire and one brought frost. Out fire, in frost.
* Plunge the candle into the water. The flame will hiss and go out, representing triumph over fire and lightning.
* Pour the water away and light the second candle, as you do so saying:
  Two angels came from East and West. One brought frost and one brought fire. Out frost, flame fire.
  This will create a balance of fire and water in your home.
* Allow the candle to burn for a minute and then blow it out, sending the light to defend against any particular natural forces that are prevalent where you live and stating, for example:
  Out whirlwind and out storm. Do not harm. Angels bring calm.
* Keep the partly used candles on your hearth or in an open ornamental vase until next Candlemas or a year after the first house moving ceremony.
* Light either of the candles if, for example, there is a severe weather warning in your area, picturing your home protected by golden light. Blow out the candle, naming the hazard and saying:
  Do not harm. Angels bring calm.

A kitchen spell to prevent accidents and bring prosperity to your home

In the Oriental tradition, every kitchen has a shrine. A picture of the god of the stove or hearth, Tsao-Wang, is placed in a small wooden temple over the hearth, facing south. Pictured next to him, his wife Tsao Wang nai-nai carries the sayings of the women of the household to the Jade Emperor in the heavens. Each morning, three incense sticks are burnt before this domestic shrine, and offerings of food, flowers and drink are made. Over the years I have devised a number of protective and enriching kitchen shrine spells, based around a small protective area that can be accommodated in even the tiniest kitchen. Within a week or so you will notice an increased sense of calm and a reduction in the number of spills and accidents. This is my favourite kitchen spell and one that I know works well.

You will need

A small shelf in the kitchen; 2 or 3 soft watery crystals (more if you wish), such as jade, rose quartz, amethyst or fluorite; a small green fern or feathery plant; a small dish (for a daily offering of water); a small pot of sea salt, with a lid; another, larger, pot with a lid (for a daily offering of a coin); a tiny statue of the Buddha, the Madonna, an angel or a fairy (optional); a small flat dish (for a daily offering of food); a lemon, an orange and a lilac incense stick in a suitable holder or holders (or substitute orange, carnation, or rose); some tiny fruits, seeds or flowers.

Timing

Day time, when the kitchen is quiet and cool.

The spell

* Using the items above (but keeping back the fruits, seeds or flowers), set up your kitchen shrine. You can add any other items that seem right to you. The incense sticks should be placed in a triangle formation at the centre of the shrine.

* Light the first incense stick, as you do so saying:

The first I light, asking the wise guardians to keep safe this kitchen and my home from fire, explosion, accident and injury. Bless all who dwell here and those who come as welcome visitors.

* Light the second incense stick, as you do so saying:

The second I light, asking the wise guardian for abundance, that the needs of the family and those who shelter within these walls for food, fuel, clothing and money may be met realistically.

* Light the third incense stick, as you do so saying:

The third for happiness. I ask the wise guardians of the shrine, shine radiance on us as we cook, eat, clean and go about our work, and make this a place of joy, comfort and harmony.

* Now for your part in the bargain. Fill the small dish with water and the offerings dish with the fruits, seeds or flowers. These you will replace regularly, keeping the shrine well tended. As you set out the offerings, say:

I pledge my own devotion to the essences of protection, abundance and joy, that I will welcome all who seek my hospitality and share the blessings I am given.

* Leave the incense to burn through. A fitting end to the spell would to be to cook a good meal for friends or family.

* Light three incense sticks every month or so to re-empower the shrine.

A protective spell-bag charm from the Viking culture and Europe

Herbs, dried corn or wheat ears and salt have been used in the home from time immemorial for protection, sometimes made into empowered domestic charm bags. Dried dill seed heads, for example, were hung over doorways and above cradles or scattered around the boundaries of a home for protection from all malevolence, especially envy. Protective charm sachets have been found in both eastern and western Europe, areas of Viking settlement, Russia, the Mediterranean and the Caribbean. Until Victorian times, country folk would, on moving to a new home or setting up home for the first time, fill a little red bag with symbols of love, health, wealth and happiness to protect home and family from any misfortune or hardship.

You will need

A small red drawstring bag; a pinch of salt; a piece of cloth; a tiny lump of coal or wood; a silver heart or a piece of silk cut into the shape of a heart; a silver coin; a dried ear of corn, wheat or barley (or use caraway or coriander seeds in a twist of silver foil); a white or natural-coloured cloth; some red thread; a needle (optional).

Timing

Traditionally, on new year's eve, to be finished by midnight.

The spell

* Assemble all that you need on the cloth.
* Into the bag put each of the items (except the red thread and needle), in the order listed.
* Pull the drawstring tight and either knot or sew the bag shut with the red thread, as you do so saying nine times:
  This bag this night I make for me
  And also for my family.
  Let it keep through every day
  Trouble, ills and strife away.
  Flags, flax, food and Frey.
* The last line refers to flagstones for a safe home, flax for enough clothing, and food for a full larder. Frey was the old pagan god of fertility in northern Europe, who under his other name, Ingwaz (see page 341), guarded homes from harm.
* Keep the bag in a drawer in the kitchen.
* Make a new bag next new year's eve.

A five herb spell-bag charm from Europe

The contents of this spell bag vary according to the land in which it is found, but the principle is the same. So, for example, in Spain and Portugal it would contain orange, lemon and olive blossom or leaves, plus hibiscus, Spanish sage and soil. This is a fairly common version found in a number of lands, and may be a relic of quite an old rite because of the reference to the Earth mother.

You will need

A pinch each of dried basil, coriander and mustard seeds; a few bay leaves; 5 elder flowers or berries; a white drawstring bag made of a strong natural fabric; a tiny quantity of soil.

Timing

On a Saturday (the day of the cautious Saturn), at around sunset.

The spell

* Place the herbs and flowers or berries in the bag, as you do so saying:
  From theft and bad weather, sickness, dearth,
  Protect our home, dear Mistress Earth.
* Sprinkle the soil into the bag and fasten it tight.
* Hang the bag in a sheltered place outside the home, as high up as possible, until the bag splits or rots, when a new bag should be made and empowered.

A protective home mojo from the Hoodoo tradition

Mojos are small bags containing an odd number of symbols (one to 13) associated with particular energies. Protective mojos are good if you live in a high-crime or lonely area, or you have a difficult ex-partner who seeks constant access to your home. For more about mojos see page 399.

You will need

A small drawstring bag of red flannel (the traditional mojo fabric) or brown material (suitable for domestic protection; a piece of angelica root or some dried angelica (available from herbal stores); some salt and pepper; waxed paper (the kind used in cake making); some patchouli oil or brandy.

Timing

After dark.

The spell

* Place the angelica root directly into the bag or twist some dried angelica in a piece of waxed paper and put it in.
* Twist some salt in a piece of waxed paper and add it to the bag.
* Twist some pepper in a piece of waxed paper and add it to the bag.
* Add a few drops of the patchouli oil or brandy to the bag.
* Draw the string tight and say:
  May protection last till one (or two) moons
  are past.
* Keep the bag somewhere near the front door, out of sight. (Mojos lose their power if seen.)

An amethyst house cleansing spell to remove negative earth energies

Some houses feel dark and unfriendly even on the sunniest of days. The inhabitants may suffer from a lot of minor illnesses or there may be a lot of quarrels in a particular room. The cause may be blocked earth energies beneath the building – these can have an effect even several floors above ground level. Such soured energies may be the result of unhappy events that occurred perhaps hundreds of years earlier on the land. Alternatively, they may be due to major rebuilding works, especially if these involve the uprooting of trees or hedgerows. Mobile phone masts or even an excess of electricity pylons can also cause subterranean earth energies to become blocked. The remedy is simple. Amethyst points (pointed amethyst crystals) are powerful cleansers of earth energies, restoring light and harmony to your home. You can also use this spell to cleanse your workplace. If it would be difficult to carry out the spell *in situ*, draw a rough plan of the building (or just of your particular floor) and work with the dish of water in the centre of the plan. When you have finished the spell, keep the plan, with the amethysts placed upon it, in a safe place at home.

You will need

6 small amethyst points or amethyst crystals with one end more pointed than the other; a small dish of sea salt; a small dish of still mineral water.

Timing

When your home is quiet.

The spell

* Set the dish of water as near to the centre of your home as possible and sprinkle into it a few grains of salt.
* Stir the water three times with the pointed end of each of the crystals in turn, saying for each:
Salt and water purify
This place of negativity.
Cleanse and clear what I hold dear;
Let energy flow once more clear.
* Place an amethyst point either under the carpet or on a surface in each of the four corners of your home. Set one also on either side of the main entrance to your home.
* About once a month, or when you sense negativity returning, wash the crystals under running water and repeat the spell.

A simple spell to protect your home against fire

The discovery of fire was the greatest gift to humans – for warmth, cooking, light and keeping away predators – but with it came domestic fires and accidents. Even the modern home, with its safety precautions and inflammable materials, can be hazardous. Since candles have come back in to fashion as decoration, house fires have increased.

You will need

A candle, a deep candle-holder and a candle-snuffer (available from stores that stock ornamental candles), alternatively a large candle and a metal bucket with a lid.

Timing

At sunset.

The spell

* Light the candle (in the bucket if you are using one) and say:

  Fire burn bright,
  Warm and light;
  Cook and comfort,
  Keep harm far this night.

* Picture your home bathed in warmth and light that illuminates the darkness around and the family safe inside.

* Snuff out the candle or cover the bucket to cut off the air supply, as you do so saying:

  Fire, do not burn when not kindled; sleep silently till summoned. Do not harm nor roam my home unchecked.

25 SPELLS FOR THE PROTECTION OF CHILDREN

Children have always been the focus of spells because they are naturally vulnerable and also find the world strange and sometimes frightening. Spells for children are remarkably easy to carry out because the power resides in the love and natural protectiveness of the spell-caster towards his or her own child or to children who are close emotionally.

Many telepathic experiences occur as a result of this natural bond between children of all ages and their parents. Spells are an effective way of organising and directing these energies at specific times for particular needs, most importantly the desire to protect the child, whatever the age, from harm and unkind people or from accidents and misfortune.

As well as protective spells for adults to carry out alone or with their children I have included a few spells devised by children themselves. These are not Harry Potter type wizardry but remarkably sensible ways of taking control in situations that worry or frighten the young spell-caster.

A holed stone spell to drive away a child's nightmares and fears of the dark

Even with the presence of a night-light, some sensitive children are afraid of darkness and may be plagued by nightmares and night terrors (when the child wakes screaming and in half-sleep may point at some phantom left over from their dream). In earlier times parents or guardians would empower a holed stone with starlight and hang it over the child's bed to catch any moonlight entering. Stones with three holes were considered especially protective. A cord was tied through each hole, and the three cords were joined together at the top. (See Chapter 41 for spells for ridding children of nightmares and night terrors.)

You will need

A holed stone; a red or silver cord.

Timing

When there is bright starlight.

The spell

* Go outdoors with the child and the holed stone. Ask the child to look through the hole and choose one star or group of stars. You may be able to identify the star(s) from a star map or computer program, but it is not important.
* Ask the child to picture the guardian of the star, who might look like an angel or fairy, and to recite the following charm with you three times:
  Star light, star bright,
  Star friend I choose tonight,
  Guard my bed as I sleep tight,
  Till I wake at morning light.
* Take the stone indoors and use the cord to suspend it from the ceiling, somewhere where the child can see it as they lie in bed. Tell the child that the star guardian is there even in the darkness and that if they close their eyes they will see the brightness again, even in the darkest night. Encourage them to repeat the rhyme if they wake in the dark.

A mother Earth spell for when you know a child has a difficult day ahead

This is a traditional spell found in many lands and used to endow a child of any age with the protection of mother Earth. It is one that I still carry out when my over-sized baby birds venture out into the world. You need to be subtle about carrying it out; however, it can be very effective if you know that the child is not looking forward to the day, but you cannot go along with them to the difficult event.

You will need

Earth from the garden or, if you do not have a garden, from a large plant pot placed near the front door.

Timing

When a child of any age leaves the house without you and is apprehensive.

The spell

* As the child walks down the path or steps, or through the front gate, throw a handful of earth after them and say:
  May the peace of mother Earth protect and bless you till you return. My love goes with you.

A mother of pearl spell to protect your child's bedroom

In south-east Asia and parts of the Middle East, mother of pearl buttons are attached to the clothes of young children (and also brides) for protection. Wishes for safety are spoken as the buttons are sewn on (see also page 354). Mother of pearl is associated with protection from sea goddesses throughout the world, as well as with the Virgin Mary, who is called Stella Maris or 'Star of the Sea'. A westernised version of this practice involves empowering a small jar of pearl buttons and keeping it either downstairs in an area below a child's bedroom or, if you live in an apartment or bungalow, within sight of the child's room. If your child is small, keep the jar in their bedroom, in a place where they cannot reach it.

You will need
7 mother of pearl buttons or beads; a small clear jar with a lid; a white or silver-coloured candle.

Timing
The first Monday after the full moon, any time after sunset.

The spell
* Light the candle and place the jar where the candle light shines on it.
* Pass each of the seven buttons or beads around the candle flame, for the first one reciting 'Monday', for the second 'Monday, Tuesday', for the third 'Monday, Tuesday, Wednesday', until with the seventh button or bead you name all seven days in turn. After you have empowered each one, place it in the jar.
* Put the lid on the jar and shake it vigorously seven times, saying for each shake:
  Monday, Tuesday, every day,
  Guard my precious child for me.
  So I ask and so I say.
  With these pearls protected be!
* Let the candle burn through and then put the jar in the chosen place.

A Celtic blessing spell for a child upon a journey

Though this is a general blessing for loved ones who are going travelling, I find it especially appropriate for children (of any age) who are going away, be it on the school bus for the first time, on a school journey, to stay with a parent who lives elsewhere, backpacking, or driving away to their first own home.

You will need
Nothing.

Timing
At any parting, short or long.

The spell
* As you wave the child or young adult goodbye and once they are out of earshot, recite just once:
  May the road rise up to meet you.
  May the wind be always be at your back.
  May the sun shine warm upon your face,
  The rain fall soft upon the fields, and until
  we meet again
  May God / the Goddess / goodness hold you in
  the palm of His / Her / its hand.

A sewing spell for protection of children when they are outside the home

Sewing spells were practised by Viking women, who spun threads with amber and quartz spindles to protect their husbands, brothers and sons while they were away fighting or voyaging to discover new lands. As they spun the thread and sewed garments, they chanted protective charms so that the wearer would remain safe from harm and return victorious.

You can sew similar power into your own clothes or those of loved ones. A sewing spell is an excellent way of giving a child protection in situations where you can't be with them, such as a first day at school or a first camp, and then as they go out into the world as young adults. Choose a coat, school uniform or garment that will be worn when they go out socially. You may wish to empower more than one garment if your child is having a difficult time in the world or is timid. You need not tell the wearer and nor need you be a seamstress. Even if, like me, you can barely sew on a button, you can make a few stitches in a lining or on a washing instructions tag to equal effect. The spell will work as well with hand or machine sewing.

You will need

A garment belonging to the child or young adult you wish to protect; some gold or yellow metallic thread; a silver-coloured needle; a gold-coloured candle and mirrors (optional).

Timing

At noon, preferably in sunlight.

The spell

* Take the garment and sit in a pool of sunlight, or if the day is dark use the gold candle and mirrors to reflect light on to the garment.
* Thread the needle (silver for the moon), using the gold or yellow metallic thread (for the power of the sun), and begin sewing. You need do only nine stitches hidden inside the lining, on a tag or on a hem. If you are making the whole garment, you add the nine magical stitches towards the end. As you sew the magical stitches, chant:

I sew for thee tranquillity;
I sew for thee protectively;
I sew for thee most lovingly.
Joy and protection I decree,
For days and nights passed peacefully.

* Leave the garment in the sunlight until the light fades or the candle burns through.

A spell to protect a child from any form of abuse

Even the most benign of witches gets angry at the idea of people harming children. Some go so far as to say that it is justifiable to hex or curse someone who has abused a child. This is a very grey ethical area. I personally worry that once you open the floodgates in terms of punishing wrong-doers or potential wrong-doers, you are assuming the role of judge and jury. It is all too easy then to slip into a habit of using magic to punish others of whose lifestyles you disapprove, thus tainting white magic with negativity. This spell uses light in darkness to enclose your child (or children) in beams of protection. Of course, you should also educate your child about potential dangers and take practical measures to keep him or her safe. If your child has expressed anxiety, he or she can join in the spell, holding one of the torches.

You will need
2 torches.

Timing
After dark.

The spell

* If you have stairs and a landing in your home, work there. If not, choose passageways and the entrance hall. Work in the dark.

* Go to the highest point you can reach in the house and switch on both torches, creating light beams on the ceiling and walls.

* Begin to move down through the house, pausing and spiralling the lights on your child's (or children's) bedroom door, and then continuing downwards until at last the beams are joined over the main front door. As you work, chant:
I light you on your way (name child or children). Child of mine, this beam light your safe journey through the world. May none pass who mean you ill, rather cast themselves into the dark and there remain till light illumines their heart.

* As you recite the last line, switch off the torches and stand in the darkness.

* Switch on the torches once more with a final flourish of light and say:
Blessed be and protected till you return safe to me!

A spell to protect against bullying

Bullying, physical and emotional, is an increasingly serious problem in schools. Though there is a growing awareness of the issue, parents can sometimes feel helpless, especially if the school is slow to help victims. Being a poor scholarship girl at a college for wealthy girls, I suffered a great deal of emotional bullying, and three of my five children have also experienced difficulties, bad enough to make them unwilling to attend classes. On a practical level, you need to work in cooperation with the school to ensure that the bullying is stopped or does not become an issue in the first place; however, a spell can help to shield your child from the notice of bullies and can also give off signals that deter threats and intimidation.

You will need

Some garlic granules; some dried sage (the culinary kind is fine); some dried and chopped nettles (available from health food stores and old-fashioned grocers); a large square of paper; a black pen; a gold pen; a tall, lidded ceramic pot.

Timing

When you suspect that bullying is going on.

The spell

* Using the black pen, draw a picture of your home and the school, including the playground, on the paper. Mark between them the route your child will take to school, plus a picture of any public transport they use. Also mark any shops or parks your child visits en route.
* Using the gold pen, draw a jagged continuous square around the edge of the paper, as you do so saying:
So shall (name child) be safe within this field
of protection from spite, attack, teasing and malice. Within these limits shall there be no fear, intimidation or threats.
* Make a square of garlic granules round the edge of the paper (garlic is a very protective substance), as you do so saying:
Within this square of garlic, walk safe and travel freely. Work freely, speak freely and play without interference from any.
* Make a square of protective sage just outside the square of garlic, as you do so saying:
Within this square of sage, walk safe and travel freely. Work freely, speak freely and play without interference from any.
* Make a square of nettles just outside the square of sage (nettles are fiercely defensive against mental or physical harm), as you do so saying:
Within this square of nettles, walk safe and travel freely. Work freely, speak freely and play without interference from any.
* Scoop up some of the herbs and place them in the pot. Then fold up the paper very small and place that also in the pot.
* Sprinkle a little of the herb from each of the jars into the pot. Put the lid on the pot and keep it in the kitchen, where it will be warm.
* Scatter the rest of the herb squares to the winds.
* Each morning when your child sets off for school, add a small quantity of each of the three herbs to the pot, as you do so saying:
By the power of these herbs, shall (name child) walk safe and travel freely, work freely, speak freely and play without interference from any.
* When the pot is full, bury the contents and repeat the spell with new paper.

A computer spell to help a child to overcome bullying or teasing

As I mentioned in connection with the spell above, you should insist that problems with bullies are taken seriously by your child's school. Carrying out this spell with a bullied or teased child, especially a younger one, will help the child to feel more in control of the situation.

You will need

A computer with a drawing program.

Timing

When the child is relaxed.

The spell

❋ Ask the child to draw the outline of a bully, as ugly or fearsome or funny as they wish. You can help if necessary.

❋ In the figure or underneath, write a list of all the nasty things a bully does. (This can be very revealing if the child has been reticent in talking about the problem.)

❋ Enclose the bully and the words in a circle and expand their size until the circle fills the screen. Say:

You do not frighten me. I am going to cut you down to size.

❋ First remove the words representing the nastiness, one by one, saying for each:

Go, be gone, away, never come back.

❋ Then reduce the size of the bully and the circle bit by bit, saying as you do so:

Be small, shrink and disappear.
Now you are the one who feels the fear.

❋ When the figure and circle are very tiny, ask the child to press the delete button and say:

I cannot see you. So how can I fear you?

❋ Repeat the spell as often as necessary, each time making the bully figure smaller once it has been drawn, until eventually you start with a tiny figure. You can also reduce the list of nasty things the bully does as the child becomes more powerful and less vulnerable.

A drawing spell to help a child to overcome bullying or teasing

If you do not have a computer and so cannot do the spell above, try this version using paper and pens. This is a good spell for very young children who are having trouble with a particular child who makes fun of them or excludes them.

You will need

A pad of plain A4 paper; some felt-tip pens.

Timing

When the child is relaxed.

The spell

❋ Ask the child to draw the outline of a bully to fill a piece of paper. Help the child to write all the nasty things a bully does or says, scribbled across the figure.

❋ Now say:

We will get rid of that bully.

❋ Ask the child to draw a big cross through the figure. Then he or she can block out the words one by one.

❋ When all the words are gone, the child can screw the paper up into a ball and throw it into a bin, putting on the lid and saying:

Stay in there bully till you can be nice to me.

A Cornish spell to protect young children at night if they are afraid of strange noises and shadows

This is a folk spell that works very well with both young and sensitive older children and will often make them laugh. You can tell the child to recite the words if they wake in the night and feel scared. (See Chapter 41 for spells for ridding children of nightmares and night terrors.)

You will need
A bedside lamp.

Timing
Before the child goes to sleep.

The spell
* Spend some time talking with your child about the different sounds of the night — pipes clanking, owls hooting, distant traffic — and how shadows can seem to make faces but really are just night pictures.
* Switch off all lights except the small lamp and recite faster and faster:

From ghouls and ghosties and long-legged beasties,
From scaries and hairies and bad-tempered faeries,
Good Lord protect us.

* Encourage the child to join in and add his or her fears — creaking floorboards, the branches of a tree banging against a window ... It does not matter how long the list is.
* When the child is settled, switch off the lamp, leaving maybe an electrical night-plug glowing or a landing light switched on for reassurance. Tell the child that if he or she wakes in the night and feels scared, they should switch on the lamp and say the rhyme faster and faster until they are tired. Then they can turn off the light and recite the words with their eyes closed until they fall asleep.

A chant to protect children at night

When I was a child there was an ancient rhyme or prayer that I believe comes from Cornwall and was spoken by the men who worked in the dark, dangerous tin mines. I think my mother must have taught it to me, although it seems as if I always knew it. Before going in to a dark place (and one of our bedrooms did not have electricity), I would spin around, chanting the rhyme. It makes an excellent clapping spell that is good for children of all ages before they settle at bedtime. In spite of the spooky words, like the chant of the previous spell, this one can help the child to laugh at their fears and relax.

You will need
Nothing.

Timing
Just before the child gets ready for bed.

The spell
* Encourage the child to clap along as you recite the following rhyme, six times. Older children may like to join in. Keep the rhythm brisk:
  Creatures of darkness, fiend and foe,
  Shades and spectres high and low,
  Father, Son and Holy Ghost,
  Save me from what I fear the most:
  Caverns and mines, boggits wailing,
  Dark in their mines forever calling.
  Protect me from what I fear the most,
  Father, Son and Holy Ghost.
* When the child is in bed, recite the rhyme six more times, making each slower and slower and the clapping slower and quieter until you and the child end in silence and stillness.
* If the child wakes in the night, tell him or her to clap six times and the protection of the chant will drive away anything that frightens them, whether noisy central heating or a bird flapping outside the window.

A toy spell to protect a shy or nervous child day and night

If you need to leave your child at daycare or with relatives overnight, you can use a favourite toy to send reassurance, empowering it so that it reduces the child's anxiety and endows the child with your love.

You will need
The child's favourite toy; a fibre optic lamp or twinkling fairylights.

Timing
After dark, the night before you need to leave the child with another carer.

The spell
* Wait until the child is sitting holding the toy and then switch on the fibre optic lamp or the twinkling lights (if the latter, perhaps draped around a tall pot plant) so that the light shines on the toy and the child.
* Tell the child that the magic of the light will help the toy to take care of them.
* Inhale the sparkle with your in-breath and then softly blow it through your mouth towards the child and the toy, picturing the toy becoming brighter and the child also surrounded by a halo of sparkling light.
* When you leave the child, tell him or her that if they need you, they should hold the toy and think of the lights and they will be able to feel you with them, even when you are not there. Tell them that the toy will keep them safe until you are able to come back.

Six spells by children for children

While many parents are concerned by the kind of magic portrayed in such cult series as *Buffy the Vampire Slayer*, simple spells devised by children are really no different from playground rhymes. What is more, they are an effective way of empowering a child and can serve as a basis for practical steps, which you can discuss as you help your child to create the spell. All of these spells have been used by my children or children I know well at various times in their lives.

A spell to make a bad tempered teacher nice

✻ Walk in a circle shaking a packet of dried macaroni or rice (make sure the packet is sealed tight, or put some in a sealable plastic box). As you walk, say the following rhyme at least three times:

Macaroni, spaghetti, tapioca, rice,
Please make (name teacher), my teacher, nice.

✻ Work hard all next day at school and don't poke anyone with your pencil.

A spell to stop other children being nasty

✻ When you see the bully or bullies heading your way, cross your fingers behind your back and say in your head three times (definitely not out loud):
Bully, woolly,
Chips for tea,
Pick your nose,
Don't pick on me.

✻ Walk straight past him or her and say hello to another friend or go and join in a game.

A spell to make a new friend

✻ Use a skipping rope or bounce a ball as you say the following verse two or three times – in your head if you are at school:
Shiny shoes, new socks,
Striped, red or grey,
Make my new friend (say the name of the person you would like to be friends with)
Play with me/talk to me today.

✻ If you are at home, call the person you like on the phone or go and knock on their door. Otherwise say hello in the park, street, playground or supermarket, but not at a quiet time in class or you will have a cross teacher again.

A spell to stop a run of bad luck

✻ Find a round white shell or stone and write 'good luck' all over it in black marker pen. Carry it in your pocket and as you walk along say to yourself:
Black cats, horseshoes,
Four leafed-clover,
Bring me good luck,
When I turn the stone over.

✻ When you next see the moon, turn your stone over three times and make a wish. But remember, every time you have good luck, do something nice for someone else.

A spell to drive away bad dreams

* Find a small, perfectly round, white stone. At bedtime walk around your bed three times clockwise with it and say:

Boggits, bogey men,
Scaries and hairies,
Out of my bedroom
And away with the fairies.

Even if you do not believe in fairies, scary things do, so you will be safe all night.

A spell to make the dark friendly

* Find a small, perfectly round, white stone. Before you get into bed, put the stone under your pillow, slip your hand under the pillow and say:

Old moon, new moon,
You're not very clear.
Try some new batteries,
And shine them down here.

* Dash for the light, turn it off, jump into bed and check your stone is there. Shut your eyes and imagine the moon and stars coming out in the sky. If you wake in the night, touch your stone and fall asleep again.

A Celtic blessing spell for when a child is abroad and has not contacted you

Sometimes adult children who are travelling abroad or working a long way from home forget to phone home, oblivious to the fact that you may be frantic about their safety. As I found when my son Jack was travelling in Europe, imagination can run riot. When I received his charge card bill, I realised I had probably been paying for every other young traveller in Europe as well as Jack to phone home, perhaps as a result of their anxious mothers carrying out this spell!

You will need

A photograph or symbol of the absent child (perhaps something belonging to them); a map of the widest area the child could be in.

Timing

At teatime, when adult children seem to think of home, even in different time zones.

The spell

* Place the picture or symbol on top of the place name on the map where you last heard from your child.
* Call the child's name six times and then recite the blessing from the spell on page 353 six times.
* Call the name six times once more and picture the child picking up a phone and dialling your number.
* Leave the map and picture as close to the phone as possible.
* Repeat daily till the call comes.

A spell to protect an adult child in times of difficulty

Parents know that when a grown-up child leaves home, their problems do not. Frantic phone calls, depressed e-mails or, worse still, worrying silences may indicate that your over-sized baby bird needs protection – and usually practical help. The practical help is generally straightforward, if often expensive. While writing this section of the book, I have bought one of my grown-up children new shoes, replaced three balding tyres on the car of another, and done a major grocery shop for an independent but impoverished offspring. Emotional support can be much more difficult, and sometimes all we can do as parents is stand back and wait to pick up the inevitable pieces of a shattered heart or career blip. A spell is also a good way of transmitting strength and emotional support when distance or a child's pride separates us from a troubled offspring.

You will need

A white or beeswax candle in a deep holder or on a metal tray; a dish of salt; a small present for the adult child, for example a box of their favourite sweets or biscuits, a miniature bottle of cologne or a voucher for cinema tickets – even a postcard of their favourite holiday location or work of art will make the link.

Timing

When the house is quiet and you know your child will also be sitting quietly.

The spell

* Light the candle and set the gift so that the candle light shines on it.
* Carefully sprinkle a few grains of salt in to the flame so that it sparks, as you do so saying:
I send my love to you. Though no longer young, you are my child. Right or wrong you may be. I am here to help, comfort you and support you even if I do not approve of your actions.
* Put a few more grains in the flame, as you do so saying:
I send this gift in love. Within it lies my unconditional care and my affection waiting should you need me, now or in future times.
* Leave the candle to burn down and write your child a simple note with positive news and a reminder that you are always there.
* When the candle is burnt down, seal the note with a single drop of the melted wax. When the wax has hardened, wrap the gift, enclosing the note.
* Scatter a circle of salt around the parcel and leave it overnight.
* Post the parcel the next morning. You may receive a phone call or e-mail from your offspring even before the gift arrives.

26 SPELLS FOR PROTECTION WHILE TRAVELLING

Human beings have always been great travellers. The ancient Egyptians, Vikings, Greeks and Romans crossed vast oceans in wooden ships. Indeed, the Vikings, led by Leif, son of the famed Erik the Red, reached America in about 992 CE, centuries before Christopher Columbus.

These days we rely on planes and high-speed freeways for our travel – usually for a holiday or business rather than conquest. Of course, the hazards remain, though of a different kind from the wild beasts and bandits of earlier periods. As traffic becomes heavier both on the road and in the skies, so the dangers become more acute. Robbery from stationary cars in a traffic jam is a new and nasty crime. With an increased threat of terrorism, many of us also more feel nervous of flying. And even if a journey is not fraught with danger, it may be filled with frustration. Road works, cancelled trains, overcrowded buses ... all of these can contribute to the stress of travel.

Ever since humans first left their caves to explore the wider world, magical rituals have been performed for a safe journey and return. Magical protection is still a supplement to more mundane precautions and can help to keep you safe when you run into an unexpected hazard. Many of the oldest surviving travel charms are linked with Christian saints but have become part of a wider protective tradition.

A Celtic blessing for travel across seas

This is my personal favourite travel protection spell, whether I am travelling by boat or plane. It is used by Breton fishermen, who return to harbour at first light in their small wooden fishing craft. You can substitute the word 'plane' or 'car' for 'boat' if you wish, though I prefer to keep to the original words. The spell is also helpful if you encounter bad weather on a cruise ship or turbulence in a plane.

You will need
Nothing.

Timing
Before boarding the boat or plane and whenever you feel nervous or encounter bad weather during the journey.

The spell
* Before beginning the journey, recite slowly six times, either aloud or silently:

   Protect me, O Lord, for my boat is so small.
   My boat is so small, and your ocean is so wide.
   Protect me, O Lord.

A St Patrick spell for protecting travellers in remote or hazardous places

St Patrick converted Ireland to Christianity in 431 CE. It is told that when St Patrick and his men were travelling to the king's court, he discovered that the Druids had prepared an ambush for him. As the saint and his followers walked, they chanted the sacred Lorica, or Deer's Cry – later known as St Patrick's Breastplate Prayer. When the party passed the ambush, the Druids saw only a gentle doe crossing the horizon, followed by 20 fawns. The prayer has become part of the folk tradition for protecting travellers in lonely places or when they feel alone and afraid. More recently it has been adopted by people who arrive alone or with a young family in an unfamiliar city, especially if promised transport is not waiting. This is an abridged version of just one of the many versions of the prayer. You can find the full prayer and the variations on the Internet.

You will need
Nothing.

Timing
When you feel vulnerable or uncertain about the safety of those travelling with you.

The spell
* Still your mind, letting go of any anger or panic, and recite silently just once:

   I arise today
   Through the strength of heaven,
   The light of the sun,
   The radiance of the moon,
   The splendour of fire,
   The fierceness of lightning,
   The swiftness of wind,
   The depth of the sea,
   The firmness of earth
   And the hardness of rock.
   Through the creator of creation.
* Picture a protective shield around yourself and loved ones, and a thick mist concealing you from danger.
* Imagine the mist slowly clearing. A solution or some help will almost certainly emerge within a short time.

A St Christopher spell for a safe journey or holiday

Most famous of all talismans for travel is the St Christopher medallion that is worn or carried by people on journeys, especially motorists and seafarers, in many parts of the world. The legends surrounding St Christopher (whose name means 'Christ-bearer') have endowed his medallion with magical as well as strictly religious symbolism, and it is worn by Christians and non-Christians alike.

According to legend, Christopher was a giant-like man who vowed to serve only the most powerful master. Converted to Christianity, he met a hermit who told him to live a solitary life next to a deep ford and carry travellers across the fast-flowing river on his back. One day a small child asked Christopher to carry him across the river. To Christopher's surprise, the child became heavier and heavier until halfway across Christopher feared that they might both drown. He asked the child why he was so heavy. The child revealed that he was Christ, struggling beneath the weight of the sins of the world. Immediately the burden was lightened. Christ told Christopher to plant his staff as they reached land and the next day it would bear flowers and golden leaves as a token of God's forgiveness to the world.

Before he died, St Christopher asked God to protect from pestilence, plague and other dangers any place where his image was placed. He also vowed that none who looked upon his image should die. His feast day, 25 July, is a particularly fortunate day on which to travel or begin a journey.

You can make a St Christopher medallion even more powerful with the following spell, perhaps giving it to a family member before they go travelling or backpacking. The spell is also protective against road rage.

You will need
A St Christopher medallion; 3 silver-coloured candles; a tiny drawstring bag or purse, or a chain for the medallion.

Timing
The night before travel, after dusk.

The spell
* Arrange the candles in a triangular formation – this is a very protective and also empowering shape. Set the St Christopher medallion in the centre of the triangle, on top of the purse or bag or encircled by the chain.
* Light the candles, beginning with the single one at the point and then moving from left to right at the base of the triangle, saying for each candle:
Protective light, keep me/my child/my friend/my partner safe upon this journey. Good St Christopher, stand sentinel and let no harm befall me/him/her.
* Pass the St Christopher amulet over each of the three candles in turn, as you do so saying:
Light of Christopher, enter this amulet of protection. Guide through bad weather, dangerous roads, skies and seas, guard from thoughtless friend or angry stranger and bring me/him/her safely home again.
* Place the St Christopher medallion inside the purse or bag or on the chain.
* Leave the candles to burn through while you make preparations for your own or your loved one's journey.
* The medallion can be worn round the neck or the purse containing it kept in luggage or the glove compartment of a car.

A Scottish spell for protection when travelling

The charm in this spell was recited in parts of Scotland to enable a person to pass safely through hostile or lonely places by transforming him or herself into an animal. You can still hear versions of the charm at ceilidhs. When I worked as a teacher in a school in Fife, more than 25 years ago, the children used one version as a skipping game. *Yen, twa, shree* is 'one, two, three' in local dialect. This may be an old reference to the triple goddess of the Celts. The charm is very effective if you are travelling by car with children and get lost or break down in a strange or deserted place. It relaxes the children and usually summons help or produces a signpost. I have also recited it in my head when lost in an unfamiliar airport or station abroad. By the time the spell has caused the panic to subside, the relevant sign has appeared or an announcement been made – or a friendly stranger has appeared as though by magic.

You will need
Nothing.

Timing
When you hit a hazard and panic while travelling.

The spell
* Recite the following charm six times with your eyes closed, getting faster and faster. If you stumble over the words, begin again. Children can join in:

  A magic cloud, a magic cloud,
  From dog to cat,
  From mouse to house,
  Hide the man, hide the maid,
  Hide the bairns from harm.
  Yen, twa, shree,
  And off you go to help me.

* Open your eyes, blink and the answer or aid will come – or a child in your party may instantly spot the missing direction post hidden behind an overgrown branch.

A Druid spell to enclose you in safety if travelling becomes hazardous

I am a Druidess, but this blessing can be used by anyone who believes in a benign force of protection, whatever name they give to this energy. However well we plan, the unexpected can happen – a drunk who looks as if he may get violent can get into your otherwise empty railway carriage, a group of revellers in a town square where you are waiting for a taxi can turn nasty, or a side street in a foreign resort may turn into a dark and possibly dangerous alleyway. The words of the charm in this spell are not only calming but also create a bubble of psychic protection around you.

You will need
Nothing.

Timing
When you are in a potentially dangerous situation or feel under threat.

The spell
* Picture yourself enclosed by a high wall of white light. Recite the following charm continuously in your head until you feel calm:

  Grant, O God/Goddess/Spirit, thy
  protection,
  And in protection, strength,
  And in strength, understanding,
  And in understanding, knowledge,

And in knowledge, the knowledge of justice,
And in the knowledge of justice, the love of it,
And in the love of it, the love of all existences,
And in the love of all existences,
The love of God/Goddess/Spirit and all
goodness.

* Usually the hazard diminishes or other supportive people arrive. You may, in addition, now have a quiet authority that deters any who would bother you.

A three realms Earth, Sea and Sky travelling spell

In Celtic magic, the three realms of Earth, Sea and Sky were represented by a three-armed symbol called the triskele. This is a triangle opened out to spread its power and takes the form of a rounded spiral with three arms radiating from a central point, turning widdershins (anticlockwise). The triskele was engraved for protection on chariot axles and jewellery during the second and third centuries. It would seem that it was also drawn in earth or sand or marked out in stones and walked to endow a traveller with the protection of the three realms before he or she set off on a journey. If you travel a lot, you could have a permanent triskele made of small stones in your garden. Otherwise draw a temporary one to walk before a major trip, especially if you are going somewhere unfamiliar – practise drawing it in advance. You can walk the triskele on behalf of a friend or relative, adapting the words of the spell accordingly.

You will need

An area of smooth sand or soil and a long stick (a large child's sandbox is ideal), or some chalk and a paved area, or a permanent triskele marked out with stones on grass, just large enough to walk around, or a triskele painted on the floor indoors (perhaps underneath a rug).

Timing

At sunset the night before a major trip.

The spell

* Go to your triskele, or create one if it is to be temporary.
* Stand at any one of the ends of the spirals and allow your feet to guide you as you walk all three realms in turn. You will visit the centre twice and exit via the last spiral you walk.
* As you walk, picture the successful conclusion of the journey, both outwards and return, and say:
  Earth, Sky and Sea, protect, I ask, your child. Enclose me in your spiral womb. Lovingly, gently, quietly, carry me over Earth, Sky, Sea and safely home again.
* At times of need when you are travelling, 'draw' the triskele sign in the palm of your power hand (the one you write with) with the index finger of the opposite hand to gather protection round you.

Making a magical protection amulet for long-term or long-distance travel

If you travel a lot, be it commuting long distances to work, flying or driving regularly on business trips, visiting friends or family abroad, or going backpacking around the world, you need a long-lasting spell, rather like ongoing travel insurance.

A traditional and effective form of protection dates from the Middle Ages and involves writing a magical word square. Word squares were often created by medieval magicians, and sometimes their apprentices, using corruptions of Latin words from ceremonial magic. The words are written forwards, backwards, upwards and downwards. Though we do not know the significance of some of the letter squares, they have acquired power through usage over the centuries. One of the most common protective word squares, the SATOR, was written on parchment or wax and worn round the neck in a red flax bag (the colour and fabric associated with the Norse mother goddess Frigg). Some researchers have dated this square back to Pompeii, but it may well be a mediaeval construction. The square looks like this:

SATOR
AREPO
TENET
OPERA
ROTAS

It can be translated as, 'Arepo the sower holds the wheels with his work.' Sator is 'sower'; arepo is 'plough'; tenet is 'he/she/it holds'; opera are 'works' or 'tasks'; and rotas is 'wheels'. One of the many uses of this square was to offer protection while travelling. You can make the square for yourself or for someone close to you.

You will need

A long narrow strip of high-quality paper (traditionally parchment but this is hard to write on); a fountain pen and black ink or a black pen; some red wool; a red fabric bag, or a metal tube in which to roll the word square, and a neck-chain on which to hang it (if you use the latter, you will need to write very small).

Timing

On a Saturday, in natural light.

The spell

* Using the black pen or ink, write the letters of the square on the strip of paper. Work in silence and unobserved, even by the person for whom you are making the charm. In accordance with tradition, make all the letters of the same size, work from left to right and top to bottom, and as you work do not let your shadow fall on what you have written – otherwise you must start again.
* Still working in silence, roll the amulet into a scroll and secure it with the red wool, making three knots.
* Place the scroll in the bag or tube and either carry it or wear it around your neck when you travel. If the square is for someone else, tell them not to open the bag or tube.
* Replace the amulet every midsummer's eve just before sunset, burning the old rolled scroll.

A spell to make a triskele travel amulet

A triskele (see page 367) amulet is good in times when travel by plane or boat has become more worrying, perhaps because of fear of terrorism. It protects also on car journeys when traffic is fast and furious, and some drivers aggressive. You could also embroider or use a laundry marker to draw a triskele in the lining of a child's coat if he or she has to travel alone to school on public transport. It will guard against stranger danger and problems with bullies while travelling. In this case carry out a shortened form of the spell, holding the garment up to the noon light and reciting the rhyme 12 times (once for each month). Alternatively, paint or draw the triskele on a crystal using acrylic paint or a permanent marker. Before you carry out the spell, practise engraving or painting the triskele until you can complete it in sweeping widdershins (anti-clockwise) movements from the centre without taking your pen off the paper.

You will need

A wooden disk on which to draw or etch the triskele; a suitable marking pen or engraving tool; a flowering plant in a pot.

Timing

At sunset.

The spell

* Using the wooden disk and engraving tool (or any of the alternative materials suggested above), engrave your triskele..
* Place the triskele on top of the soil of the flowering plant and put the pot somewhere where the sun, moon and stars will shine on it for 28 days. Remove the triskele only (if necesssary) to water the plant, leaving the patch of soil that the triskele rests on dry.
* On the 29th day at around noon, hold the triskele up to the light and say:
  Earth, Sea and Sky, enclose me, (name), with your blessings and your strength that I may not fear, but return safely to those I hold dear.
* Repeat the spell when the triskele fades or if you have a series of major or hazardous trips.

A spell for safe holidays, in your own country or abroad

Aside from the journey itself, there are many potentially risky situations that can arise on a holiday – you may hire a car abroad, explore difficult terrain by foot, play a new sport, try new foods or drink more alcohol than usual. Most problems are avoidable with sensible precautions, but a protective charm can help you to relax and enjoy yourself, particularly if you are a nervous traveller. You can also make a charm for any family member who is going on holiday, either with you or independently. Adapt the chants accordingly. If the family member is sceptical, keep the charm yourself and wear it for them while they are away. Almost every culture has a tradition of protective knot bracelets, but they are particularly popular in India and Africa. Street vendors in Rome also make them – and then sell them to tourists at extortionate prices. This is a very old spell that has been modernised to accommodate more modern dangers.

You will need

I yellow, I blue and I green cord or piece of wool, each long enough to fit around your wrist loosely;

Timing

Just before you are about to go on holiday.

The spell

* Weave or plait together the yellow, blue and green cords or lengths of wool (to represent sky, sea and earth, or safe travel in all its aspects). As you work, say:
  Bind and wind protection in;
  Keep me safe as thus I weave –
  Safe from harm and safe from danger,
  From accident or threat of stranger.
* Tie the ends of the cords or wool together with seven knots, one after the other, as you do so saying:
  Seven times the knot I tie,
  Safe on earth, on sea and sky.
  Seven, six, five, four, three, two, one.
  The spell is done.
  Bound is the power, protection won.
* Wear the bracelet until the end of the holiday, except when swimming or in the shower. If the bracelet breaks, it does not mean the protection has gone. Retie the seven knots at the place where the cords have snapped, as you do so repeating the two chants.

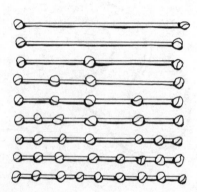

A spell for safe and smooth daily journeys to and from work or when ferrying passengers

Car accidents tend to be more common on short journeys, especially through towns and in bad weather during the winter months. It can be helpful to keep an empowered charm in the glove compartment of your car or fixed to the dashboard to assist you to cruise relatively effortlessly through hazards. The spell will also help to prevent your car being stolen or attacked and will protect against the new problem of road rage. The presence of the crystal charm will guard vulnerable passengers, such as babies, the very old and the nervous, the crystal calming them and encouraging cheerful or at least quieter reactions — even on the school run.

You will need

One of the following crystals: turquoise, kunzite, sugilite, jet, smoky quartz, garnet, bloodstone (or moonstone if you frequently travel at night); a bowl of water; a purple candle; a blue candle; a small purse or pouch.

Timing

Monthly on the first Saturday of the month, if possible the hour after sunset.

The spell

* Light the candles and switch off any other lights.
* Drop the crystal into the bowl of water, as you do so saying:
  I drive in hope and in confidence that all shall be well and my journey uneventful. This is my token of safety I cast forth.
* Imagine driving on a sunny day on quiet roads with passengers who resemble the Brady Bunch rather than the Simpsons.
* As the ripples spread outwards, take a candle in each hand and drop a little wax into the water from each candle, so that the wax hisses and sets on the surface (representing safe travel and safe arrival at the destination). Say:
  In the midst of danger, so do I remain secure, my car an oasis of calm in a fast-moving world. All within is tranquil, insulated from chaos beyond and quarrels within.
* Picture the miles passing by with no breakdowns or roadworks.
* Blow out one of the candles and let the smoke travel upwards. Say:
  So do I rise above the anger and frustrations of others who share the roads, above delays and distractions, irritations and pressures to take risks.
* Visualise yourself close to the destination in half the usual time.
* Take the protective crystal from the water, dry it and place it in the purse, as you do so saying:
  I (and my precious passengers) reach the destination without hazard, hassle or harm. I keep you with me as a token of security.
* Imagine yourself arriving at your destination full of energy after a perfect journey, with the most cantankerous relative you ever have to drive smiling — or at least waking up from a sleep that has lasted for the whole journey.
* Keep the purse with the crystal in the glove compartment of your car or secured beneath the dashboard, where no-one is able to touch it between empowerments.

A spell for when unexpected delays or problems arise while travelling

Even the best planned journeys can go wrong due to circumstances beyond your control. I devised this spell when my late-evening plane from Aberdeen, in north-east Scotland, was suddenly cancelled mid-air and landed in Newcastle, about 150 km (250 miles) north of my destination, Southampton. I was cold, tired and hungry after a long weekend working and needed to get home because my babysitter was due to leave that night. Even spells cannot produce a plane out of thin air, but they can galvanise your energies and get those responsible to sort out the crisis quickly for you, unexpectedly finding themselves glad to help.

You will need

A watch.

Timing

As soon as you realise things are not happening according to plan.

The spell

* Stop your watch and say in your head:
  Time stand still. I will backtrack to right the lack of natural progression.
* Then put the watch back to the approximate time when things started to go wrong, usually marked by a public announcement. Say:
  And now in quick succession we will put this lack back on track again.
* Now put the watch on to the actual time, as you do so saying:
  Continue now, anyhow, for life is back on track and I am on my way again.
* Without hesitating, find the most senior official and explain why you have to get on the move as fast as possible. Ask calmly how they are able to put you back on track. If the official blusters, is dismissive or makes excuses, touch your watch, recall the spell and doors will open.

A spell to avoid losing possessions or becoming a victim of theft while on holiday or in transit

One of the worst things about losing possessions on holiday, either in transit or during the stay, is the problem of getting replacements. If you lose a young child's favourite toy, the result may be sleepless nights or a frantic search to find a replacement for a chewed bear with one ear, smelling of chocolate. In some parts of the world, especially in large cities or major tourist resorts where there is much local poverty, theft may be quite common. The following spell is well worth trying to make sure that you and your possessions remain united. This spell appeared in one of my earlier collections. I have changed it only slightly, because it works so well.

You will need

Your luggage; your travel documents and foreign currency; a wallet or small bag that you can wear.

Timing

The evening before you travel.

The spell

* When all your luggage is packed, arrange the bags in a circle. Put your travel documents and currency in the wallet or bag and either put the wallet in your pocket or wear the bag.

* Stand in the centre of the circle of luggage and turn around very slowly three times, as you do so holding your hands palm down and moving your right hand deosil (clockwise) and your left hand simultaneously widdershins (anticlockwise) at waist height. This will bind your possessions magically to you. As you turn, say slowly, mesmerically and continuously:

Stay with me; do not stray.
Let no-one take you away.

* When you have made your three turns, whisper:

Three, two, one,
The spell is done.
So may it be!

* While waiting at the station or at the airport to check in, repeat the first chant in your head, picturing waves of protective light binding your luggage to you.

A spell to reduce your profile at hazardous times, or when you want to be left alone on holiday or while travelling

Some people seem to attract nuisances and bores – and sometimes more sinister attention – while travelling. If you are a sociable, kind person, you probably have a very open aura, or psychic energy field, around you. There are times, perhaps late at night or if you are lost in an unfamiliar city, when you do not want to attract unwanted attention. This spell will help you temporarily to lower your profile, thus reducing the chance of your being targeted by pickpockets, lecherous locals with roving hands or overly persistent street traders. It is also helpful if you are tired and really do not want to talk to anyone. Carry out the spell in advance and activate its power at the moment of danger or insecurity. Renew it every few months.

You will need

A small sage or cedar smudge stick, or a stick of lavender or sage incense; a holder for the smudge or incense stick; some silver candles in appropriate holders (optional).

Timing

During the waning moon, as dusk falls.

The spell

* Working in the open air or in a well ventilated room away from soft furnishings, extend your arms straight above your head, lower them to the side and sweep them down to the floor (the extent of an average aura and the area you are going to obscure from view with the spell).
* Light the smudge or incense stick and hold it at approximately a 45-degree angle.
* Turn to the North and waft spirals of smoke, allowing the smudge or incense stick to dictate the smoke's direction and saying:
May blessings and protection surround and enfold me from the North. So shall it be!
* Turn to the East and waft spirals of smoke, as you do so saying:
May blessings and protection surround and enfold me from the North and the East. So shall it be!
* Turn to the South and waft spirals of smoke, as you do so saying:
May blessings and protection surround and enfold me from the North, the East and the South. So shall it be!
* Turn to the West and waft spirals of smoke, as you do so saying:
May blessings and protection surround and enfold me from the North, the East, the South and the West. So shall it be!
* Face North again and point the smudge downwards and then upwards towards the sky. Waft the smoke in spirals, as you do so saying:
May blessings and protection surround and enfold me from Mother Earth and Father Sky.
* Now you are going to cast a cloak of invisibility around yourself. Beginning at ground level and in front of your body, swirl the smudge upwards from side to side, when you reach your face being careful not to get so close that you choke. Smudge over your head and around your back. As you swirl the smoke, move rhythmically so that your aura blends with the smoke. Allow your hand movement to dictate the pathway of the smoke. As you smudge, chant:
Grey of smoke, hide sight of me
From those who come in enmity.
Let me fade and disappear,
That my foes may come not near.
Free from harm, quiet and calm.

- When you have finished, leave the smudge or incense in the holder to burn down, and sit quietly, allowing yourself to let go in to the twilight.
- When you are ready, touch your heart with your right hand and say:
  When I make this sign, I will draw around myself the cloak of invisibility.

- Switch on the light or light the silver candles and shake yourself like a dog, including your fingers and toes, to restore the brightness to your aura. Your cloak of invisibility can be activated at any time by touching your heart.

A spell to overcome the fear of flying

Even people who do not have an out-and-out phobia about flying can be very apprehensive about take-off and landing. After so many security alerts at airports in recent months, more of us need extra courage. You can carry out this spell before travelling and repeat part of it when you are on the plane. I have used it for years and recommended it to many nervous flyers. This is the most effective of several versions. If heightened security prevents you from taking the bottle on board, leave it in your luggage and drink mineral water during the flight while holding the crystal in your receptive hand (the one you do not write with). Say the spell words in your head whenever you become nervous.

You will need

A dark-blue sodalite crystal (the best for fear of flying) or a dark-purple amethyst; some dried basil (the culinary kind is fine); a small dark plastic bottle or phial of still mineral water with a lid; a small deep-blue cloth or flannel; a waterproof bag.

Timing

At dusk, the day before you travel.

The spell

- Half fill the bottle with still mineral water and place the crystal in it.
- Surround the bottle with a circle of basil (the most helpful herb for fear of flying) and say:
  Fly high through the sky, plane.
  Fear do not remain.
  Plane land safe and smooth.
  Anxiety thus I remove.
- Leave the crystal in the water until the morning.
- Remove the crystal from the water and put the lid on the bottle. Dry the crystal and keep it in your hand luggage, along with the bottle of water and the flannel, in a waterproof bag.
- Just before take-off, moisten the flannel with the crystal water and rub it on your temples and your wrists while reciting the spell in your head. Repeat if you encounter any turbulence and before landing.
- Empower some more water with the crystal before the return trip.

A ritual for creating a safe path when walking alone

While we may take every precaution to avoid walking alone late at night or in unfamiliar places, there may be a time when it is unavoidable. Even if there is no danger, this spell is very reassuring should you feel nervous. I have used it many times after late-night radio work, when I have to return to a hotel in the early hours of the morning. I have also used it on autumn evenings when I am visiting the small caravan I own near the sea and the site is deserted. It works, too, if you get lost down a side-street as dusk is falling (my own speciality when exploring new places). The more you carry your crystal, the more protective it will become. If you need your crystal but do not have it with you, picture its light enclosing you.

You will need

A round protective turquoise or smoky quartz crystal.

Timing

When you find yourself in a dark or unfriendly place.

The spell

* Hold the crystal and imagine it casting a dark shadow around your outline.
* Walk towards your desired destination, seeing it quite clearly in your mind's eye just ahead, along a clear path of golden light – the kind that extends across the sea to the sun at sunset. It doesn't matter if your destination is in reality out of sight. (Alternatively, imagine a taxi drawing up just ahead to let out a passenger.)
* Visualise steep crystal walls around your path. You may find that your footsteps seem unusually silent. This is part of the protective magical aura you are creating.
* Keep to the clear, bright, narrow passage you have made and carry on moving towards the widening opening of light. The crystal walls will close behind you to deter unfriendly followers and you will reach your destination or see a taxi far sooner than you anticipated.

27 SPELLS FOR PROTECTION AT WORK

Because many people spend a lot of time at work, a happy atmosphere can make all the difference not only to productivity but also to health and well-being. Whether you are an employer or an employee, a positive upbeat workplace is the key to success. However, problems can arise through pressure of work, personality clashes or undue competition caused by a ruthless corporate system or fears of redundancies.

Magic works in the background, both protecting you personally from spite and malice and also cleansing the workplace of the negative energies that can build up over the months, especially if there has been a crisis or a period of uncertainty. You can carry out most of these spells at home and then take an empowered charm or crystal in to work to protect and uplift you during the day.

A spell for a happy and harmonious workplace

This spell is a basic smudging or incense smoke spell that can be cast at home. It is very effective whether there is a sarcastic and over-competitive atmosphere at work or constant negativity and lethargy so that enthusiasm and energy drain away. Because it is not easy to cleanse an office with smudge or incense without attracting unwanted comment and setting off smoke alarms, work at home by the principle of sympathetic (or attracting) magic, using a plan of the key features of the workplace.

You will need

A large tray of sand or an area of smooth earth (you can put some in a large metal or wooden tray); a candle; a taper; a smudge stick (a bundle of sagebrush or cedar tied together in a wand, available from New Age stores and by mail order), or a firm stick of sage or cedar incense; a feather (optional); a stick.

Timing

At sunrise or sunset.

The spell

* Working outdoors in a sheltered location or in a well ventilated room, draw an approximation of your workplace in the sand or earth, using the stick. Draw different floors side by side as adjoining boxes. Draw in any key areas, such as where you sit, and also any particularly significant people who cause problems or are always discouraging.
* Light the candle and then use the taper to light the tip of the smudge or the incense from the candle. Let the flame die down and then blow gently on the tip of the smudge stick until it glows red. If the smudge goes out at any point, re-light it and continue with a loop where you stopped smudging – in order to join the energies.
* Kneel or sit before the plan, so that you can reach right over it. Holding the smudge or incense in your power hand (the one you write with) and fanning the smoke with your other hand or the feather, pass the smudge or incense around the edges of the plan widdershins (anti-clockwise), creating small widdershins smoke circles.
* Hold the smudge or incense about 10 cm/4 in above the plan and spiral it widdershins over the whole plan, paying special attention to your work area and to the work areas of those people who are problematic. Allow the smudge to find its own rhythms and pathway. As you smudge, create a mantra or continuous chant that becomes mesmeric. One of my own favourites is:

Nothing harm;
Peace calm.
Troubles cease;
Live in peace.

You may find yourself swaying as you smudge. Picture the actual setting, with everyone who works there relaxed and harmonious.

* Now smudge the plan and chant again, this time moving deosil (clockwise) and making deosil smoke circles around and over the plan. This will infuse the workplace with positive energies – for you must always replace what you have taken out, so leaving no space for the old stagnation or hostility to return.
* Destroy the plan after smudging by rubbing it out.

A blue light spell for relieving a bad atmosphere at work

This spell is quite similar to the previous one and can also be cast at home. Even business premises have an aura, or psychic energy field, that can become clogged as a result of quarrels, spite or just pressure of work. In time, the bad atmosphere slows productivity and leads to inertia and even stress-related absenteeism. This spell will strengthen your own protective shield and often has a surprisingly positive effect on your colleagues.

You will need

A square of white paper, large enough to draw a detailed plan of your workplace; some different coloured marker pens; a small soft-blue crystal or glass nugget to represent each of the key people with whom you work or liaise; a larger blue crystal for yourself (for example, blue lace agate); a blue candle in a deep holder; a small green plant.

Timing

During the waxing moon.

The spell

* Using the marker pens, draw a plan of your workplace. If there is more than one floor, draw it in another square or rectangle. Include yourself on both floors if you visit both. Mark with small circles the places where key people (positive and negative) sit, and with small squares any areas such as photocopiers or coffee machines where staff congregate.
* Set a blue crystal or glass nugget on each of the circles to represent the other workers, and place the green plant in the centre of the plan.
* Light the candle near the plan, somewhere where its light will shine

on the paper but wax will not drip on it. As you do so, say:

Light of blue,
Aura of blue,
Send your peace on all we do.
Aura of blue,
Light of calm,
Keep all within
Safe from harm.

* Breathe in the candlelight slowly and deeply through your nose and imagine yourself being filled with soft blue light. On each out-breath, with a sigh through your mouth, gently blow the light all over the plan, picturing it extending over your actual workplace and those who share it with you. Visualise the blue light also entering the green plant and mingling with its natural energies.
* Repeat the chant and blow out the candle, sending its light to all who share your workplace.
* The next day take the plant to work and put it in your workspace, encircled by the crystals or glass nuggets. You can place your own crystal in the centre of the pot, next to the plant.
* Whenever things seem fraught or tensions set to rise, breathe in the blue of the crystals and the green light of the plant and gently blow it on to the circle of crystals, naming in your head each key person they represent and sending them blessings, even if they are being difficult.
* Wash the crystals under a tap at work to restore their energies and remember to take great care of your hard-working plant.

A spell for stopping gossip or a whispering campaign, or for clearing away secrecy at work

Gossip behind your back or rumours spread about you by a source you cannot identify is perhaps one of the worst forms of unpleasantness. The perpetrator may be someone who is jealous of you or who resents what they see as your idyllic life. Or they may have insecurities about their own abilities or job security and have chosen you as a victim to divert them from their own weakness. Others who may not generally be unpleasant, can be swept along by gossip. This spell avoids hexing the source of malice (which would be unethical) but works by exposing the gossip or rumour-monger for what they really are. You are attacking the gossip rather than the gossiper. Try to carry out the spell before work.

You will need

A grey candle on a flat, wide metal holder or tray; a white candle, also on a metal holder; dark-grey cord about 25 cm/10 in long; a dark-handled knife or dark-coloured scissors.

Timing

When you are the victim of gossip or rumour.

The spell

* Light the grey candle and encircle it with the grey cord.
* Take up one end of the cord in each hand. Sear one end of the cord in the candle, so that it flares and goes out, then drop it on the holder or tray. As it burns, say:

Burn through this secrecy.
Let there be clarity.

* When the burnt end is cool, cut the cord in half, as you do so saying:

So I cut through secrecy.
Let there be clarity.

* Discard the half that has the seared end.
* Light the white candle from the grey candle and repeat the first chant.
* Blow out the grey candle.
* Sear one end of the remaining half of the cord in the white candle flame, as you do so repeating the first chant.
* Blow out the white candle, as you do so saying:

Let all be revealed now to me.

* In the aura around the candle flame or in your mind's eye you will see images or a scene and may even hear words in your head that will either give you the information you need or identify the source of malice. If it is all hazy, the person will reveal him- or herself inadvertently at work or an unexpected ally will come to your defence.
* Bury the discarded half of the cord under a dying tree or in a compost heap, or dispose of it in the rubbish.
* When cool, hang the cord seared in the white candle over a window through which the morning light shines.
* Take the cord with you to work and leave it on your desk when you go out of the room.

A Hathor mirror spell for businesswomen under threat

Even in the modern world, women in business can sometimes fall foul of a workplace where chauvinistic attitudes are entrenched. Though legislation exists to counter discrimination, many women suffer in silence because the job fits in with their childcare arrangements or because there is high unemployment in the area. Other people may be too embarrassed to report sexual harassment. The ancient Egyptian goddess Hathor has become the natural protectress of businesswomen – and indeed of all working women – in the modern world, specifically because of her symbolic mirror, through which it is said we can see ourselves and others in their true light. A tiny mirror can act as an amulet against malice and also physical threat. Men who are harassed at work by the opposite sex can also use this spell.

You will need

A small mirror, such as a make-up mirror (or an object with a shiny surface, such as a highly polished gold medallion or a stainless steel pen holder); a sharp pin, thin sharp blade or other engraving tool – or a small piece of paper, a pen and some glue; an orange or red candle; a rose incense stick; a small dish of water containing a few grains of salt and a few drops of olive oil.

Timing

At sunset (Hathor's time).

The spell

* Either scratch on the back of the mirror or shiny object or draw on the piece of paper the protective eye of Horus (the Egyptian sky god), sometimes called the eye of Ra (in later myth the two gods sometimes merged). If you are using paper and pen, use the glue to stick the image on to the back of the mirror or shiny object. (You could alternatively ask a jeweller or silversmith to engrave the image for you.)
* Light the red or orange candle and the rose incense (the colours and fragrance of Hathor) and empower your protective mirror or object by first passing it over the flame and saying:
  May he/she who seeks to harm or slander me see reflected back his/her own weakness and malice. Look on thy true self and depart in peace.
* Pass the mirror or object through the incense smoke, as you do so repeating the chant.
* Sprinkle the mirror or object with a little of the salt and oil water, as you do so again repeating the chant.
* When the person who causes you problems at work comes towards your work space, hold the mirror or shiny object so that the eye is facing you and the shiny surface is facing outwards and repeat the chant silently until the person moves away.

A spell to repel nastiness and bullying at work

It is not just children who suffer from bullying; adults get bullied too. Bullying may take a subtle form, such as criticism or sarcasm whenever you speak and may be a result of cliquishness at work. However, bullying can also be openly vicious. Although in some cases it may be possible to seek redress through the courts, if you are working in a prestigious job that you don't want to lose, or you cannot afford to be unemployed for the duration of a legal battle, it can be hard to take a stand. This spell is stronger than the previous one. If you wish, you can empower the shiny or reflective object as in the previous spell, without drawing the Eye of Horus on it.

You will need
A shiny or reflective object such as a small mirror or a spare pair of spectacles.

Timing
When under attack at work.

The spell
* As the bully comes towards you, place the shiny object in front of you and say in your head:
  Come not here in malice.
* If the person begins or continues a tirade, look full into their eyes and say in your head:
  Take back what you inflict on me, with all its barbs, and feel the hurt.
* You are not cursing them, just sending back the negativity that rightly belongs to them and emanates from some inadequacy in their make-up that causes them to off-load unpleasantness.
* As soon as possible, splash water on the shiny or reflective object.

A visualisation spell for protecting or recovering self-esteem

A run of bad luck – a bad sales month, a series of rejections for projects, negative feedback from an boss who is going through a stressful period – can hit the best of workers. Confidence may plummet, and even ordinary banter can feel like sarcasm. Less friendly colleagues may take the temporary glitch as an excuse to make you feel even more inadequate. This is an adaptation of a spell I have used and taught for years. It has helped bosses and employees alike to overcome a temporary crisis of confidence and get back on track.

You will need
2 small mirrors (for a sunny day) or 2 small torches (for a dark one).

Timing
Before anyone else arrives at work.

The spell
* Stand in your workspace. Holding a mirror in each hand if it is a bright day or a torch in each hand if it is dull, make an arch of light over your head and then down by your sides, sweeping towards the floor.
* Continue to do this very fast, saying either in your head or aloud:
  Light surround me,
  Light compound me,
  Give me power within.
  Sunbeams shine,
  Make this day mine.
  What was darkness now be gone,
  Transformed to light beams by the sun.

- Put down the mirrors or torches and picture any doubts, failures, unfair remarks, bad sales figures or rejection slips swirling around in front of you until they form a dark-grey wispy ball.
- Take the invisible ball and cast it towards the light outside the window, as you do so repeating the chant. If you look out of the window, you will see a shimmering, even on the greyest day, as your negative vibes get transformed into pure sunlight.
- You may need to repeat the spell two or three days running, but before long you will be back on track.

A metal spell for when you are never given a chance to speak at meetings or offered new opportunities

Lack of experience or expertise is only one reason why our efforts to succeed may be blocked. In other cases a stone wall may be put up because, for example, a boss has taken an unfair dislike to us, or senior colleagues are entrenched in their attitudes. If the reason is prejudice rather than merit, a spell can be effective. This one uses metal to symbolically cut through the barriers that stand in our way. It is a new version of an old favourite spell. I have adapted it according to the suggestions of readers.

You will need
An aluminium foil dish or a piece of foil; 2 stainless steel knives; gold and silver glitter.

Timing
If possible, the six days leading up to the full moon and the night of the full moon itself.

The spell
- Using as a base the aluminium foil or dish (for the clear communication of Mercury), set the stainless steel knives (for cutting through the fear of speaking out and severing the tangle of frustrated opportunity) crossed upon it, as you do so saying:
  Crossed at every turn, yet shall my voice be heard.
- Sprinkle first gold and then silver glitter (for the positive energy and confidence of the sun and the more subtle hidden power of the moon) over the knives, as you do so saying:
  So shall I break through the barriers of prejudice and inertia and make my mark.
- Uncross the knives and place them side by side on the foil, as you do so saying:
  No longer crossed, but equal shall I speak and shall be heard. So must it be!
- Leave the foil or dish, the knives and the glitter where they can catch both sunlight and moonlight, adding more glitter every night and repeating all the chants.
- On the night after the full moon, wash the knives and throw away the foil or dish and glitter.
- Repeat monthly if necessary.

A spell to protect you from unfair criticism of your work and from theft of your ideas

Some bosses and senior colleagues can diminish self-confidence in others by belittling their ideas or criticising every suggestion or piece of work submitted. Even worse, they may later present the ideas they ridiculed as their own. This spell works in either or both cases.

You will need

Some unscented baby powder; rose essential oil; orange or neroli essential oil; rosemary essential oil; an orange candle; a ceramic bowl and wooden spoon or a mortar and pestle; a small purse or drawstring bag; a sealed jar.

Timing

Tuesday (the day of Mars, for courage and defence), after dark.

The spell

* Light the candle and hold your palms upright in front of it (not too near) as though warming your hands. Say:
I absorb courage and confidence. I fear none, least of all (name the unkind person).
* Set the bowl where the candle light will fall on it. Add enough talcum powder to the bowl to fill the purse, and shake in a few drops of orange essential oil (for self-confidence). Stir the powder three times deosil (clockwise), saying for each stir:
I believe in myself and in my work.
* Add a few drops of the rosemary essential oil (for self-esteem and defence of your work) and again stir three times deosil, saying for each stir:
I defend myself and my ideas from all who would deny their worth and/or take them for their own.
* Add a few drops of rose oil (for justice without malice) and again stir three times deosil, saying for each stir:
Let there be justice without malice for (name) that I receive credit for what is rightly of worth and what is rightly mine.
* Stir the mix three more times deosil, as you do so repeating the first chant.
* Hold your hands once more in front of the candle and say:
So shall all be resolved amicably but with justice.
* Blow out the candle and picture yourself enveloped in rich orange light.
* Scoop the powder and oil mix into the purse or bag and seal it, keeping any left over mix in a sealed jar for future use.
* Take the purse to work and keep it there. Take it to any meetings where your work or performance may be questioned.
* Replace when the powder loses its fragrance.

An eastern European sun spell to drive away spite at work

If you sit near a window at work, you can use this spell at any time of the year; otherwise, wait for a hot sunny day. You can also do the spell at home and carry the effect with you to work. There are a number of similar spells that use the burning power of the sun, not to harm the spiteful person but rather to destroy their spite.

You will need

A shallow saucer or flat dish (an old one in case it cracks); some tap water; a small quantity of water left overnight any time during the waxing moon (prepare in advance, bottle and store in the fridge).

Timing

On a hot sunny day, or at any time where sun shines through a window or there is a hot radiator close by.

The spell

* Put a small quantity of tap water into the saucer or dish and set it where the sun will shine or near a source of heat. Say aloud if possible, otherwise in your head:

Sun of power, parch the harsh words of (name); dry up their spiteful deeds and unkind utterances.

* When all the water in the saucer has evaporated, offer some tea, coffee or juice to the spiteful colleague. If they refuse, make some for yourself, saying aloud or in your head as you prepare the drink:

When (name) must drink, may only the waters of gentleness slake their thirst.

A spell to recover from redundancy or unfair dismissal

There may be all kinds of reasons why things go wrong at work, from the malice of a colleague, to an insecure boss, to a slump in orders, to a major takeover. Even if you are given more than the minimum redundancy or win an unfair dismissal case at a tribunal, you may still have to face the destruction of self-belief, the niggling fear that you were somehow to blame or the difficulty of challenging a company through the legal system. We have experienced both forced redundancy and unfair dismissal recently in my family, so I can appreciate the heartache and the financial problems these situations bring. Combined with practical measures, magic can help to overcome fear of failure and self-defeat at a time when we need every bit of will power and confidence to climb back in to the employment market. This spell is also good for the relations of the victim (as I discovered myself). Family members can suffer just as much, but need to keep up a confident, encouraging front, even when they are panicking inside. Because this spell has proved so effective I have not changed it at all from the version I originally devised.

You will need

A small area of damp earth (water it beforehand if necessary); thick-soled shoes or boots; a deep plant pot; a spade; some seedlings of thyme, rosemary, sage or any fast-growing greenery.

Timing

In the early morning.

The spell

* Stand in the soil with your legs apart and press down with your feet until you have made a strong impression with both your feet in the earth. Say three times:

I am myself; I am complete.
Failure is earth beneath my feet.

* Walk around the plot of earth widdershins (anticlockwise), stamping hard to make footprints and saying:

Out with anger, out with pain;
I am myself, myself remain.

* Reverse your path and walk deosil (clockwise) until the area is filled with your mingled footprints. Say as you tread:

I am myself; I make my mark,
And I will fight back, though all seems dark.

* Using the spade, fill the plant pot with footprinted soil and plant the

herbs or greenery in it, saying:
From dark to light,
Grow to great height.
So I shall rise
And touch the skies.

* Keep the plant where it gets plenty of light and repeat the words of the spell over it whenever you become despondent.

A fire spell for surviving in an unfriendly atmosphere

At some time we all encounter unwarranted hostility at work, whether as a newcomer to a firm who got the job promised to an internal candidate or because the atmosphere is poisoned by ruthless corporate management or impossible targets. Leaving may be the best solution, but you have to survive while working out notice or maybe finding another job to go to. This is quite a powerful spell, so try to carry it out in as positive a frame of mind as possible. You may even find you can survive without leaving.

You will need

A small iron or stainless steel pan; a cooking or camping stove with a flame; a glass bowl filled with rain water that has fallen directly into the bowl without touching any roofs or guttering, or with spring water; a wooden spoon; some dried mint.

Timing

On a day when you are not working, at around noon.

The spell

* Fill the iron or stainless steel pan (for the courage of Mars) about one-sixth full with the rain water and set it on the stove. Do not turn on the ring yet.

* Add about ten pinches of dried mint to the water, as you do so saying:
May coldness, ruthlessness and indifference melt away (name any particular perpetrators by adding 'between me and —'). So I say and so may it be!

* Turn on the ring and heat the water, stirring it constantly with the spoon and saying over and over again:
Warm and welcome, fires of friendship, fires of compassion, fires of kindness, fan and flame into this cold unfeeling place. So I say and so it can be!

* When the water is boiling, turn down the heat, stop stirring and allow the water to boil almost away, as it does so, saying over and over:
Simmer and sear;
Leave only goodness here.

* Turn off the heat, as you do so saying:
Enough! So I say and it should be!

* Drain the herbs, as you do so saying:
Water of fire, water of flame,
Bring acceptance to my name.

* Dry the herbs naturally or, for quickness, place the damp herbs in the microwave for a few seconds.

* Bury the herbs, as you do so saying:
Enough! So I say and it shall be! Fire, I claim immunity.

28 SPELLS FOR PROTECTION AGAINST BAD NEIGHBOURS

Bad neighbours are perhaps one of the most challenging of domestic problems. Unless we live in a house surrounded by many acres (and even then there can be problems with boundary disputes), we are affected by those whose homes surround our own. This is especially true if you live in an apartment or a modern house with thin walls.

While the advantage of having the support and friendship of neighbours generally outweighs the irritations, when things go wrong, stress levels can soar. Problems can range from noise levels that prevent sleep, parking disputes, complaints about children playing and quarrels over the maintenance of fences to threats and even violence.

These days there are many organisations offering formal and informal conciliatory processes for resolving neighbourhood disputes, and most local councils in the UK have noise enforcement officers to deal with unreasonable levels of noise. Our ancestors had none of these avenues. They used magical means to establish boundaries and deter less than friendly visitations. Working a spell can help us to overcome a sense of helplessness in the face of nuisance or persecution from our neighbours, and can enable us to protest effectively without confrontation.

A spell to rid yourself of the effects of negative neighbours

You can't do spells to compel your neighbours to move – although there is a spell on page 392 for sending psychic suggestions of places where they might be happier. This spell works on a cosmic exchange principle and encourages the growth of more positive, or at least quieter, interactions between you and noisy or troublesome neighbours.

You will need

A large whisky, brandy or wine glass or goblet, one-quarter filled with wine or dark fruit juice; an offerings bowl (optional).

Timing

On a Friday, as soon as possible after first light.

The spell

* Stand outdoors as near possible to the neighbours' fence, or in a shared entrance in an apartment block, or next to any adjoining indoor wall.
* Hold the glass in both hands and raise it slowly until it is above your head and in front of you, then lower it to chest level. Raise it to your lips, take a sip and say:

I drink to quieter times and happier days between our households. I ask that (name two or three activities by your neighbours that make your life especially difficult) cease.

* Raise the glass towards the fence, wall or neighbours' door and say:

I offer you in return greater understanding/ tolerance/respect.

(Even if your neighbours are truly awful, try to think of positive things you can bargain in return for their improved attitude.)

* As close to the boundary as possible, raise the glass skywards again and tip the rest of the wine or juice into the earth. If you do not have outdoor space, pour the contents of the glass into an offerings bowl and then tip it away after the ritual. Say:

I make this offering to you, Mother Earth. Accept and sanctify this exchange between me and (name neighbours). Blessed be!

A spell to mark your boundaries

In warmer lands, bamboo was used to mark the limits beyond which strangers could not pass. I have noticed that in supermarkets and garden centres in the UK, leafy bamboo plants are now widely available, as well as the more conventional green bamboo shoots. These make excellent barriers, keeping even the most persistent neighbours on their own side of the fence unless invited over on to yours. This spell also works well if you suffer from nosy or interfering neighbours.

You will need

I small bamboo plant in a pot for each end of all adjoining walls, upstairs and down (or use cacti, aloe vera or ferns); a red cord or ribbon for each plant.

Timing

At the beginning of the month, in the morning.

The spell

* Set the pots of bamboo in a circle and walk deosil (clockwise) around the outside, beginning at an approximate East. Touch each plant as you pass it and say:

Mark now my limits. Keep firm my boundaries.

* When you have completed the circle, go round again, this time attaching a

red cord or ribbon to each plant and saying for each:
Protect against intrusion, guard from interference.

* Put each plant in place at the end of the party walls, upstairs first and then down, as you do so saying:
Stand sentinel for noise, disturbance and interruption.

* Open the front door and say:
Welcome to those who come by invitation or with moderation. Blessed be!

A spell to deter a gossiping or trouble-making neighbour

Most streets have one ... a person who smells trouble or sorrow on the wind and can't wait to knock at your door to tell you of the latest scandal about the people who live two doors down. You can be certain that at the next port of call highly coloured versions of your comments will be broadcast to the rest of the street. I call this spell 'enough and no more', because the minute the gossip heads towards your door your psychic fence is activated and causes a change in route. Garlic is a very protective herb, especially when strung. It is traditionally hung from two nails in the kitchen.

You will need

A string of garlic; 4 very small scented yellow candles or tea-lights (citronella, lemon and grapefruit are good for repelling gossip).

Timing

On a rainy or cloudy day.

The spell

* Place the string of garlic on a kitchen table or surface and light the tea-lights in a square around it, moving widdershins (anti-clockwise). As you light each candle, say:
Enough and no more.
Your gossip does bore me,
So if you have no good to say,
I bind you now to stay away.

* Leave the candles to burn through while you busy yourself in the kitchen. Sorting out drawers or cleaning out the fridge are just two activities that stir up your active protective energies.

* When the candles are burnt through, hang the ends of the string of garlic from a beam or two nails over the kitchen window. Recite the rhyme again.

* If your neighbour's visits do not decrease, light a citronella, lemon or grapefruit candle in the kitchen every time you receive a visit and recite the chant very fast three times in your head.

* Bury the garlic every three months and replace it, repeating the spell for ongoing protection.

An instant method to purify a bad atmosphere that stems from a quarrel or dispute with neighbours

If there have been angry words or slammed doors between neighbours, the fall-out can last for days. When conventional methods of damage limitation fail, you may want to cleanse and seal your home psychically. This spell will cool the situation and stop any further protests or threats of action against you. The method is called 'asperging' and is traditionally used for cleansing an area to be used for a magical circle.

You will need
A medium-sized bowl of warm water; tea tree, eucalyptus, pine or lemon essential oil; a small springy twig.

Timing
In the morning.

The spell
* Add five drops of essential oil to the bowl of warm water and, using the twig, stir the water nine times deosil (clockwise), as you do so saying:
Power of light, power of life,
Banish anger, drive out strife.

* Beginning outside, and repeating the chant as you work, use the twig to sprinkle a few drops of the oil water from any back gate, along the boundary fence in the back garden, then on to the back doorstep, along adjoining internal walls and in to the centre of every room, passageway and staircase, in the natural order for walking progressively through your home. As a general rule, work from back to front and top to bottom, so that you end at the front door step. Asperge this, any front boundary fence and finally the front gate. If you have difficult neighbours on both sides, you can sprinkle the water along the boundaries on both sides, outside and in.

* Empty any remaining water outside the front door.
* Break the twig in tiny pieces, casting it out and saying:
So breaks the negativity and all shall be well.

A spell for quietening noisy neighbours

If you live next door to someone with a drum kit, a blasting sound system or a barking dog (see page 550), it can be hard not to feel under siege. Or you may, as I have in the past, live next door to someone who regularly hammers and drills the adjoining wall. If friendly overtures have failed, you may need to have recourse to official channels. In the meantime, this spell will help to psychically insulate the noise source so that the activities become muted. This spell was taught to me by my dear friend, a healer called Lilian. This is the version that seems to work best. The spell involves creating images of your neighbours. This is not for any malicious purpose but in order to project suggestions for a more tranquil life without attempting to harm the perpetrator in any way.

You will need

Some cotton wool; some pink wool; a pink candle; some green or pink dough (mix flour and water with a teaspoon of cooking oil, a little food colouring and a pinch of salt, then mix well) or children's soft play clay; a soft towel or woolly scarf.

Timing

Late in the evening, whenever the neighbours are temporarily quiet, so that quietness and harmony can flow in their dreams, resulting in a lowering of their personal volume during waking hours.

The spell

* Light the pink candle.
* Create small featureless figures and/or animals from the dough to represent the sources of noise, as you do so saying softly as a chant:
Live in peace close to me;
Softly move and quietly.
* Wrap a layer of cotton wool around the figure(s), as you do so saying:
From the sea of tranquillity
Come waves of rest and harmony.
Float this night and blessed be.
* Tie the layer of cotton wool very loosely with three pink wool knots, as you do so saying:
Gently held, floating free,
On the sea of tranquillity.
* Whisper softly the improvements in noise level you would like, ending with:
Wake in peace, but quietly.
Speak soft, washed with tranquillity.
Blessings do I send to thee.
* Continue with the layers, the knots and the chant according to how bad the problem is.
* Wrap the bundle in the towel or scarf and place it in a drawer near to the wall through which the noise comes. Blow out the candle and send the soft pink light around your home as insulation.
* After a week, free the figures, even if the neighbours are still being noisy, as you do so saying:
Go free and in tranquillity.
* Re-roll the figures into a ball and dispose of them.
* Create new figures weekly until the problem improves.

A spell to encourage difficult neighbours to move on

You may have had really good neighbours for years, and then new ones move in. Problems or disputes start from the first encounter, and their behaviour is anti-social. It can get so bad that you contemplate moving yourself. Before you take that step, cast this spell. While I am certainly not advocating using magic to drive away your neighbours, you can carry out a very positive spell to encourage them to think of moving on to an alternative location where they would be happy. Always visualise them in a better setting so that they gain from the possible move.

You will need

Pictures cut from an estate agent advertisement in the newspaper of nice houses not too far away that would make your neighbours happy – choose ones that are slightly upmarket and take account of any interests or hobbies (a big workshop if they have a collection of old cars that they park in front of your home, a big garden for their huge noisy dog ...); a box or bowl of gold and clear glass nuggets or small bright crystals; 5 very small gold- and 5 very small silver-coloured candles, or 10 white tea-lights

Timing

At 10 pm (the healing hour).

The spell

* Arrange the house pictures in a pile, with the most attractive on the top.
* Create a straight pathway of alternate gold and silver candles leading from the pile of pictures, saying as you set each candle:

Find a home where you can be
Secure, content; live happily.

* Light each candle in turn, beginning with the one on the left-hand side furthest from the pictures, then the one on the right-hand side, then left, then right, moving towards the pictures. Say for each candle:

I light your way that you may see
Your perfect home, if right to be.

* Now, working from right to left, beginning at the pile of pictures and working outwards, create a pathway of alternately coloured gold and clear glass nuggets or crystals within the candle path, taking care not to burn yourself. As you set the nuggets or crystals, repeat the second chant.
* Leave the candles to burn through and collect up the nuggets or crystals and return them to the box.
* Keep the picture collection in a small folder with the box of nuggets on top. Regularly add any new pictures you find of suitable houses.

A spell to stop a neighbour constantly complaining

Most streets have a complaining neighbour who monitors other people's lawns, hedges, cats, children and parking habits and is always at your door or phoning you with one complaint after another. However reasonable you are, you may feel that your home is not your own. This spell is very good for deterring such over-zealous neighbourhood policing.

You will need

A metal tin with a lid (a storage jar is fine), half-filled with dried beans or peas.

Timing

Immediately after a complaint and at any time thereafter when the neighbour complains.

The spell

* Make sure the lid is tightly on the tin and then shake the tin nine times, as you do so saying:
  Fuss and fluster, moan and groan,
  Nag no more upon my phone.
  As I do shake, complain no more;
  Bang no more upon this door.
* Keep the tin in the hallway ready.

A spell to bury the hatchet

The phrase 'burying the hatchet' is these days metaphorical, but it has its roots in an old European practice for settling disagreements between neighbours. It travelled to the Mid-West of America, where it was used to resolve disputes over boundaries and water rights as land was colonised and farmed. The concept is suitable for resolving any form of dispute, especially an ongoing one that you are tired of and would like just to let drop. Though in the original practice both parties buried the hatchet, or axe, together, you can carry out the spell alone on your side of the boundary.

You will need

A small hatchet, hammer or screwdriver; a new bush or sapling – or, if you have to work indoors, a large plant pot with an indoor plant (use a very small tool).

Timing

Traditionally on a Sunday morning before church, but any morning when you feel calm.

The spell

* Hold the hatchet and say:
  Let the matter between (name neighbour) and myself concerning (name dispute) be once and for all laid to rest.
* Dig a hole in the earth and bury the hatchet. Close to it, plant the sapling or bush. Say:
  I have buried the hatchet once and for all. Let us now move forward amicably.
* Make a small gesture of reconciliation and avoid thinking about or discussing the contentious issue unless pressed.
* If the neighbours still will not let go, at least you have distanced yourself and can deal with the problem more dispassionately.

A spell to stop legal or official threats by a neighbour

It may be that no matter how reasonable you are, a neighbour persists in threatening to report you to the local authorities or take you to court. However trivial the matter or how right you know you are, you may want to avoid the hassle and expense of solicitors. This is quite a strong spell, but it binds the threat, not the person who is making it, so it is not counter to magical ethics.

You will need

A freezer or the freezer compartment of a fridge; a small square piece of paper; a waterproof pen; a foil container with a lid or a plastic lidded box.

Timing

Before going to bed, so the spell can work overnight.

The spell

* On the paper write the threatened action continuously, over and over again, until the paper is full.
* Draw a cross through the writing, fold the paper as small as possible and sprinkle enough water on it to dampen it.
* Put the paper in the container, seal it and place it in the coldest part of the freezer.
* Leave it there until you next defrost the freezer.

A spell to deter a neighbour who keeps borrowing and never returns your property

Most people are happy to lend tools, ingredients for cooking, crockery and garden chairs for a party as part of a neighbourly mutual exchange system. Some neighbours, however, never return either the favour or what has been borrowed, and can become offended if reminded. Carry out the following spell for even small items, in order to break the pattern.

You will need

An egg timer bought especially for the spell.

Timing

As soon as the neighbour has left the house or garden with one of your possessions.

The spell

* The moment the neighbour leaves, start the sand running through the timer and say ten times very fast:
  Borrow with pleasure,
  Return it at leisure,
  But it is my treasure,
  So please bring it back.
* Leave the sand to run through and put the egg timer away somewhere where it will not be used for any other purpose.
* If the item does not come back within what you would consider a reasonable period, take out the timer and repeat the spell once a day until the neighbour's memory is jogged.

29 SPELLS FOR PROTECTION AGAINST PSYCHIC ATTACK

Psychological attacks can be just as nasty as physical ones, whether the attacker is an abusive relative who is always sarcastic and dismissive or an acquaintance who repeatedly speaks ill of us. There is no doubt that the effects of malicious intent can penetrate our minds even over a distance. This is so whether the malevolent thoughts or wishes are deliberately sent our way as a psychic attack or unconsciously projected by someone lying awake at night fretting over a remark we made or envying our life or happiness. When my ex-husband was having an affair, even though I was unaware of his infidelity, I would be suddenly and struck down by heart palpitations, panic attacks and muscle weakness. It was only later that I was able to piece together the times and dates and learnt that his mistress was obsessed with me and would rage about my perceived inadequacies.

The spells in this chapter work by creating a shield against negativity, whatever its nature and source. Don't worry about being the recipient of a curse. Not only do curses rebound on the sender with three times the force but also you don't have to accept a curse. On page 396 I suggest a way you can return a curse – as you would any other unwelcome offering.

A spell to repel ill wishes, or remove a curse from yourself or those you love

I spend a lot of time reassuring people who have been warned by an unscrupulous fortune teller, vicious relative or so-called friend of possible harm or even death to a child or themselves because of some omission or seeming slight. Sometimes these ill-wishers will say, 'God will strike you down (or take that baby) if ...' There may be no reason for these malicious and quite inaccurate predictions, just a desire for power and to frighten a person when they may be vulnerable. If this happens to you, use this spell and then forget all about the ill wish.

You will need
Nothing.

Timing
At sunset.

The spell
* Stand facing an open window or door and carefully press your vertical palms outwards, straight in front of you, in the air.
* Quietly call the ill-wisher and say just once:
  I return the pain;
  Send it not again.
* Shut the window or door firmly.

A spell to create a psychic electric fence around yourself

If you are a kind, sensitive person, you may experience more than your fair share of spite and malice. In time this can cause you to feel constantly anxious and exhausted because you are unable to relax. You may feel spooked at night (even though you are not), because nasty remarks, sarcasm and belittling words attach themselves to your aura (the invisible psychic energy field that surrounds each of us). By creating a protective psychic fence you can shed the negativity that others have imposed on you and prevent further attacks on your psyche.

You will need
A fibre optic lamp or two torches.

Timing
Just after dark.

The spell
* Holding a torch in each hand, shine light all over your body with whirling movements, or stand in the glow of the moving fibre optic light. Picture the light forming sparks around your outline.
* Put down the torches (but leave them shining towards you) and shake yourself like a dog who has been in water to dislodge any lingering negativity from your aura.
* Shake your hands and arch them over your head, picturing a gentle golden glow spreading around you like a golden sphere. Say:
  When I shake my hands I will activate the
  force field round me so none can harm me
  with word or malicious thought.
* The imagined light will fade, but it will remain in the background for whenever you need protection.

A spell to leave negativity at the door

Bad moods are infectious, especially those caused by the negative or bitchy remarks or the inconsiderate actions of others. It can be hard to leave this negativity at the front door, but to carry it home with you can sour interactions with family members or friends who call. Even if you live alone, you can sit fretting about injustices or spite received during the day, so compounding the hostile vibes, going to bed unsettled and waking troubled. On both sides of the Atlantic and in Russia and Scandinavia, the knot pot was once a feature of many homes. Before a cross or dismissive remark was made, a piece of wool was knotted and the unkindness tangled up and put in the sealed pot. By this time, the unkind remark was usually defused and remained unspoken. Other family members can also use the knot pot.

You will need

A dark jar with a sealable lid; a basket full of dark wool, cut into lengths just long enough for a knot to be tied in each.

Timing

As soon as you come through the front door after a bad day.

The spell

* If you are stressed or someone has been unfriendly or malicious, take a thread from the basket, summarise the incident either in your mind or aloud and tie a knot in the thread, as you do so saying:
Tangle the anger,
Tangle the bane.
By this knot
Make me free again.
* Remove the lid from the pot and place the knot inside, as you do so saying:
It is gone,
It is done.
Peace come.
* Replace the lid, unless you still have negativity to shed, in which case, repeat the knot tying and chants as many times as necessary and only then close the pot.
* When the pot is full, throw it away and start a new one.

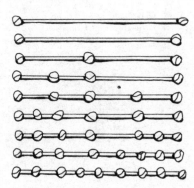

A spell to stop persistent psychic or psychological attack against you or your loved ones

This is a very powerful spell to use if someone is constantly sending you bad vibes, for whatever reason. The person may be jealous of you or soured by life and personal disappointment, or they may want something you have. Over the years I have been sent a lot of negative vibes and have also encountered nastiness that, even in my fifties, has left me totally on the floor. The spell is based on a very ancient but effective method of protection: making and empowering an anti-venom bottle. It will deflect negativity almost instantly. However, you should reserve it for when you or loved ones are being viciously attacked emotionally or your good name slandered. Keep in mind that you are getting rid of the venom, not getting rid of the person.

You will need

A small bottle with a cork or lid; enough sour milk to half fill the bottle; a little dried ginger powder or allspice; a few drops of eucalyptus essential oil, or a bath foam or shampoo containing eucalyptus.

Timing

As close to the end of the waning moon cycle as possible, but any time if the need is urgent.

The spell

- Half fill the bottle with the sour milk, as you do so saying:
Venom and spite, sourness and viciousness, cease and lose your sting.

- Add a few pinches of ginger or allspice, cork the bottle and shake it vigorously, as you do so saying:
Venom and viciousness, sourness and spite, be gone from my sight.

- Turn the bottle nine times widdershins (anti-clockwise) as you do so saying:
Turn away your malice and malevolence and mischievous uttering, your unkind mutterings.

- Uncork the bottle and, under a running tap, pour away the contents, as you do so saying:
Trouble not me. Transformed be to healing rain.

- Wash out the bottle and the sink with hot water and a little of the eucalyptus until both are quite cleansed.

- Dispose of the bottle where it can be recycled. Though you did not target your persecutor by name, you will find that suddenly you are left in peace.

Making a psychic protection mojo

Mojos are small bags containing between one and 13 symbolic objects – but always an odd number. They are associated with particular energies and are always kept hidden, whether worn or left in a room. Mojos come from the Hoodoo tradition, a form of folk magic very popular in the USA today. It draws upon the African tradition but also incorporates Native North American and European magic.

A protective Mojo hidden near the door of the bedroom or the hallway, or worn round the waist, will keep away all negative influences (normal and paranormal) at night. It is a good device if you live alone and have become unsettled, whether by silent phone calls, prejudice in your community or spirit energies (which sensitive people sometimes detect if unhappy events happened in their house or on the land years before – see also pages 339 and 349). Night time is always the worst, so this bag is geared specifically for night-time protection. Though mojos are usually made in silence, in this case a chant helps to bind in the power.

You will need
A dark-grey or purple fabric drawstring bag; some angelica root or rosemary; some salt and pepper in twists of silver foil; an animal or bird bone, or if you prefer 7 black beads; a dark-green thread or ribbon; a few drops of brandy or barley wine.

Timing
Any time when you are alone.

The spell
* Place the angelica or rosemary, salt and pepper, bone or beads and thread or ribbon one by one into the bag. As you add each, say:
  While you remain hidden within, keep safe without.
* In silence, sprinkle two or three drops of the alcohol over the contents, close the bag and hide it.
* The bag should be replaced every two months, when you should bury it and its contents separately under a dead tree.

A candle spell for keeping psychic or psychological attack away from yourself or your family at night

Candle light has always been regarded as protective against hostile psychic forces, though in the modern world we realise that living minds, rather than spirits or demons, cause these bad vibes. Nevertheless the methods of defending against them are the same. If you know the source of the bad feelings, you can name the perpetrator; if not, you can be less specific.

You will need
A dark-coloured candle (beeswax is especially potent).

Timing
As darkness falls.

The spell
* As the room darkens, do not switch on the light but light the candle.
* Look into the candle flame and say:
  I hold thee, (name if known),
  Wherever you may be,
  From harm this night.
  May angels bright
  Guard over me/us
  Till morning light.

A spell to defend yourself from people who are playing mind or power games with you or loved ones

Some people seem to exert a hypnotic effect, especially over those who are young or vulnerable, and can bring about a change of character in a usually loving and responsible person. You may yourself have experienced a sense of helplessness as someone overrides your will, whether an abusive family member or a 'friend'. Though they make us unhappy, we cannot break the tie.

You will need

A dark-blue candle; some dried parsley, rosemary and nettles (the latter available from health food stores or specialist food outlets) – or just use one or two of the herbs; a small dish; a small cauldron (available from many New Age stores and by mail order over the Internet, but check that the one you choose is cast-iron and fireproof) or cast-iron cookware pot

Timing

At midnight.

The spell

* Half fill the cauldron or pot with water, light the candle and place it so that the light shines in the water.
* Mix the herbs in the dish and sprinkle them, pinch by pinch, on to the surface of the water, as you do so saying:

With light I cast your influence away.
I break your hold on my/(name's) mind.
When these herbs are gone,
No longer will you bind.

* Keep chanting until all the herbs are in the water.
* Blow out the candle, as you do so saying:

The power is gone;
Your day is done
To hold me/(name) against my/her/his will.
You must be gone.
I wish you no ill.

* Tip the herb water on to soil or into a large pot of earth.
* Repeat weekly if necessary.

A mirror spell to banish the effects of emotional blackmail

There are a number of protective mirror spells, derived from many cultures, in this book, because a mirror is the single most effective way of repelling any form of psychic or psychological attack. Mirrors are very good against emotional blackmail – manipulation through the use of guilt or sentiment – which holds a lot of people in thrall. The emotional blackmailer may not be a bad person, just lonely or very insecure. He or she may be frail physically, an elderly relative we cannot abandon. For that reason, this is a gentle spell that

nevertheless helps to remove the barbs stuck in our flesh in the name of love.

You will need

A very-pale-pink candle; a large hand mirror (a dark witch's mirror – like a black polished tile, obtainable from New Age stores – is ideal).

Timing

Before and after you meet the person who pressurises you emotionally.

The spell

* Light the candle. Hold the mirror in your receptive hand (the one you don't write with) positioned so that

when you look into the mirror you see the reflection of the candle rather than yourself.

* Still holding the mirror in your receptive hand, use the other hand to cast three deosil (clockwise) circles in the air round the mirror, as you do so, saying:
As mirror reflects back light, so may your guilt and intense emotions, your binding words of obligation, be reflected back from me and not penetrate my mind.

* Blow out the candle and say:
I extinguish this light with kindness and gentleness. May you find what you need within yourself.

* Repeat the spell after the meeting and whenever needed.

A blessing to banish any negativity that weighs you down

Sometimes when we are in contact with negative unenthusiastic people or those who will not help themselves, we become infected by their inertia and hopelessness. Though this is not a deliberate attack, the effects are the same. If we are not careful, we too start to have negative reactions and display a lack of enthusiasm and openness to life. This spell comes from India.

You will need
A wild or garden flower.

Timing
In the late morning.

The spell
* Stand in an open space, holding the flower, and say softly three times:
May my life be like a wild flower, growing freely in the beauty and joy of each day.

* Leave the flower where someone may find it and share its beauty.

A dark of the moon spell against psychic attack

Some practitioners regard the dark moon as the first two and a half days of the new moon (before the crescent appears – marked in diaries and newspapers as a black circle); others consider it to be the three last three days of the waning moon. Choose which feels right for you.

You will need
A dark candle on a deep metal dish or tray, or set in sand in a cauldron; a dark cord; any perfume or fragrance you regularly use.

Timing
As soon as it gets dark.

The spell
* Light the candle and make sure there is no other light.

* Hold the cord so that it is completely taut and the middle is just in the candle flame. Say:
I break the link from you to me. No more can you reach my mind. I am gone beyond your sight.

* When the cord breaks, leave it to burn out on the tray or in the sand.

* Anoint your brow with fragrance, just between and above your eyes, where your third eye resides. Say:
With this fragrance I seal the entrance to my spirit.

* Blow out the candle and sit in the darkness, inhaling the fragrance.

* Anoint your brow with fragrance whenever you feel under attack, and repeat the second chant if you feel that the person is trying to reach your mind.

A cutting and binding ritual against psychic or emotional attack

If you only bind a person, known or unknown, from harming you or someone you love, they may still have their energies tangled with yours and so you may not feel free. This ritual is very effective against emotional blackmail where the person knows exactly what they are doing and is playing a power game. It can also be used in combination with another spell.

You will need

Some grey clay or modelling dough; some red wool; a pair of scissors.

Timing

When you wake.

The spell

* Make a small featureless figure in clay.
* Loop three pieces of red wool around the figure and around three fingers of your left hand, so that the image remains on a table or on the floor.
* Cut the loops one by one from your fingers, as you do so saying:
  Ties that bind,
  Cut, unwind.
  Leave me free.
  So shall it be!
* Tie the three pieces of wool around the image, making nine knots and saying:
  Bind from harm.
  All is calm.
  Think not of me,
  Not to see, nor to send.
  The link must end.
* If possible, bury the figure on the shore or by a tidal river below the tide line. Otherwise, bury it in a very deep hole beneath a tree, away from your home. If you see the person, greet them politely but avoid eye contact or personal conversation where possible.
* Repeat the ritual as many times as necessary, making the loops on your fingers looser and the knots tighter.

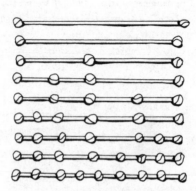

PART 6

SPELLS FOR CHANGES AND TRANSITIONS

Nowhere is magic more necessary and more exciting than at change points in our life. We start to encounter these from the first moment we become aware we are separate from our mother, and exploration of the infinitely fascinating, if sometimes dangerous, world beckons.

If, on the journey through life, we have had good experience of changes, together with plenty of encouragement to make them, we will probably associate change with positive energy and welcome it as an adventure. If, on the other hand, our experience has been less favourable and we have not received this kind of support, we may have come to fear facing new experiences – or, conversely, we may be constantly trying new things in order to find an ever more elusive dream. Whatever your personal experience of changes and transitions, magic can get the energies moving and ease us from one natural stage to the next – or maybe on to a new path. It can also make us aware of new opportunities and may bring people or situations into our lives that will set us on a totally unexpected road to happiness.

Some cultures regard change as constant and unavoidable. The Chinese, for example, believe that we are in a never-ending state of change, with nothing remaining the same from one moment to the next, and that we need to ride on the wave of opportunity rather than resisting it, otherwise we will be submerged. The Vikings believed that the web of our fate was constantly being rewoven and that how a person responded to a change point on their web would determine their future destiny (at least for a while).

New beginnings and starting over again after a setback form the first – and core – chapter of this section. Following on is a chapter of magic to ease changes in family life, be it the birth of a baby, new people coming into the family through marriage or adoption, or a child leaving home. Most such changes entail huge disruption but bring immense blessing. We then move on to changes involving travel – moving to a different country, going backpacking and travelling on business overseas. Whereas Chapter 26 deals with protection while travelling, this chapter focuses on seeking opportunity and maximising every moment. In Chapter 33 we look at changes in residence. Selling or buying a house comes high in the stress stakes, as does major renovation – and moving from one rented property to another brings its fair share of problems too. However, such changes may also represent acquiring the house of our dreams, perhaps swapping town for countryside or vice versa. Finally, we look at change in the workplace, from starting a new job, to shifting career, to redundancy, to retirement (less an ending than a transition that may open whole new worlds.

This is, then, a very positive chapter. It will enable you to use spells to ride that wave safely to shore – or wherever you wish it to carry you.

30 SPELLS FOR NEW BEGINNINGS

In most cases, a new beginning is a cause for excitement. Starting a new phase in our life, visiting a place we have never been to, taking a path we have never before explored – all are gloriously full of potential. Of course, a new beginning can also be frightening, be it our first day at school, our first day in a home away from the parental nest, or our first day of retirement. I have written in detail about some of these transitions in later chapters; here I focus on spells to make those first steps into the unknown.

For those starting over again, a new beginning is a chance to wipe the slate clean, to take what has been learnt and fashion it into something better than the old. The page is blank, and we can write our destiny anew. Of course, it may not be quite as simple as that in reality, but new beginnings do open wide the horizon.

Points of transition, such as new year and birthdays, are also new beginnings. New year offers a collective surge of energy. As the year turns, the new one promises another chance to get it right. A birthday is a more personal affirmation of a new year – and sometimes of a magical transition, especially at the key ages of 18 and 21, at changes of decade and at the age of retirement. Seasonal change points are also significant. I talk about these on pages 674–7.

Magic can add a little extra impetus to launch you out on to the tide of the future, whatever the transition, with confidence and the promise of good fortune in the months ahead.

A playing card spell for a new start

Playing cards have long been associated with life situations and with good luck, as evinced by sayings such as: 'I was dealt a bad hand' or 'I have to make the best of the cards I was given.' But life is more than a chance deal of the cards. We can refuse to accept the limitations seemingly imposed by fortune or fate. This spell is very empowering if you have lived by other people's rules for a long time. Juniper, a possible ingredient in this spell, has been used in Scotland for many years for new year cleansing ceremonies (see page 412).

You will need

A stick of pine, rosemary or juniper incense, or alternatively a candle in one of these fragrances; an old pack of cards or a very cheap new one; a piece of silk.

Timing

At any natural transition, such as the new moon; at the beginning of a new week, month or year; or in the early morning.

The spell

* Take the Jokers out of the pack and shuffle the cards. Place the Jokers on top of the pack.
* Light the incense or candle.
* Pick up the cards (holding them face down) and take the Jokers away, placing them face down and saying:
  I discard unwise actions from the past and with them the guilt and regrets for what was lost as a result.
* Still holding the pack face down, say:
  As these cards I turn,
  New ways shall I learn.
  If I must start again,
  I can bear the pain.
  Though the road is long,
  I shall still be strong.
  Though the pathway stings,
  I shall walk with kings.

* You are now going to deal the cards until they are sorted into their four suits, in ascending order from Ace to King. The cards must be set down consecutively, so, for example, a three of Spades must be set in its row before you can add the four of Spades, and so on. In order to start each suit, deal until you find its Ace. Place the rejected cards in a central pile face down. When you have worked through the pack once, take up the pile of rejects and deal them again. Continue with this process until all the cards are sorted in correct order. The first suit to be completed will indicate the initial best way forward. Diamonds represent a step-by-step progress from small beginnings, so that you change the current situation bit by bit. Hearts represent going with the flow, taking any opportunities and following the path you truly want to take. Clubs represent inspiration, the totally new and unexpected go-for-broke opportunity that will arise and which you should seize, even if it seems out of character for you to do so. Spades represent the powers of logic and the ability finally to cut any old destructive ties.
* When you have dealt out all the cards, repeat the chant and put all the cards except for the four Aces and the four Kings back in the pack – these represent the beginning and the end of the road.
* Set the Aces and Kings in a circle around the incense or candle and leave them there until it is burnt through.
* Throw away the Jokers but keep the rest of the pack wrapped in silk until your change is successfully accomplished.

A spell for following a new path when the road ahead seems hard

We often start out on a new project full of confidence and enthusiasm – it's like the first day in a new job or the first day at school, when anything seems possible. Yet in a very short time that wonderful journey we planned may become frustrating. Mirror pathway spells are an old and very effective method of breaking through the barriers that can trip up a venture almost before it starts. They work by showing the end of the road attained.

You will need

A large mirror of any shape, positioned so that you can see your head and shoulders in the glass when you sit down; 4 white candles.

Timing

After dark, during the waxing moon.

The spell

* Arrange the candles diagonally on a table so that they form a pathway leading into the mirror and continue the pathway within the mirror. You may need to experiment to create the pathway effect.
* Sit behind the candle that is furthest from the mirror, so that in the reflected image you are at the end of the candle pathway.
* Light the candle nearest to you and extinguish any other lights in the room. Say:

The path is clear,
The way is bright.
Though it seems dark,
The end's in sight.

* Light the other three candles, working your way towards the mirror and repeating the chant as you light each one.
* In your mind, walk the pathway of candles into the mirror. When you reach the one closest to the mirror, breathe slowly in through your nose, then hold your breath, in your head counting 'one and two and three' and picturing yourself moving through the mirror.
* Sigh your breath out through your mouth, again counting 'one and two and three', and picture yourself continuing to walk towards where you can see your reflection at the end of the road.
* Look at your reflection in the mirror and see yourself at the end of the pathway, looking back on what you have achieved.
* Slowly extinguish the candles, beginning with the one nearest the mirror and continuing until only the candle nearest to you (the one representing the end of the candle road in the glass) is still alight. Say:
I take in the light at the end of the road and so move forward with hope and with joy.
* Blow out the final candle.

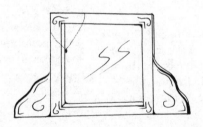

An earth empowerment spell for a new beginning

Whatever the new beginning, there is always a moment when you have to put the grand plan in to practice. This is one of my favourite earth spells for launching a new venture.

You will need

A place where you can stand barefoot and touch the earth, soil, sand or grass (for example, your garden, the park, a beach); a dark-brown pebble or brown crystal such as smoky quartz or any of the brown or sandy-coloured banded agates.

Timing

At sunrise.

The spell

❋ Go to your chosen place and stand barefoot watching the sun rise.

❋ Take up the stone or crystal in your power hand (the one you write with) and say:

I have the power to make this work, and I will.

❋ Circle the stone or crystal deosil (clockwise) around yourself, as you do so feeling each bone and each muscle warmed and renewed by the symbolic strength of the earth.

❋ Feel the sun warming your body and your own root energies rising from deep within you, giving you the stamina for the venture ahead. Repeat the chant once again.

❋ Go for an early morning walk, pick up another brown stone or pebble and take it home. Place it, together with the crystal or stone you used to work the spell, in your garden or in a large plant pot indoors. If you like, you can make it the beginning of a small circle of stones or the edging for a path.

❋ Each time you make a new step, add another stone, as you do so repeating the chant.

A herb and stone empowerment spell for a new beginning

This is another spell that uses the strength of the earth to launch you on a new path.

You will need

A bowl; enough dried tarragon or sage to fill it one-quarter full; a pointed stone found on a walk the previous day.

Timing

The morning of the new beginning.

The spell

❋ Whether you are working indoors or out, face the light. Shake enough of the tarragon (the dragon herb of courage) or sage (another power herb) into the bowl to one-quarter fill it.

❋ Pound the herbs with the stone, as you do so, saying over and over confidently:
Earth to earth,
Give this plan birth.

❋ When you feel that both you and the herbs are endowed with power, plunge the stone down once into the herbs, as you do so saying:
Earth enter me, empower me and give me strength this day for my new beginning.

❋ Tip the herbs on to soil and set the stone, point upright, as a marker of your determination to make this new beginning work.

A dragon spell for a new start under difficult circumstances

Dragons, living in caves beneath the earth and frequently guarding fabulous treasures, are an ancient and universal symbol of Earth energies. European dragons are primarily guardians of gold, while in the East they watch over gems and pearls. Pearls are said to bring courage and wisdom to humans who find them, scattered after rain. Whether your new beginning excites or scares you, the dragon is an excellent symbol of courage.

You will need

Materials to make or draw a two- or three-dimensional dragon (for example, clay, wood, newspaper and glue, thin copper wire, different papers, paints, a computer drawing program); a small dish of dried tarragon.

Timing

Two or three days before the new venture begins.

The spell

* Create your power dragon, giving it huge wings so that you can soar high in the clouds to launch your new venture.
* Set out your dragon and place next to it the dish of tarragon (herb of dragon courage). Say:
  I have the power, I have the courage, I have the dragon gold. How can I fail?
* Keep your dragon somewhere where you can see it, repeating the chant last thing at night and first thing in the morning in the days before your launch. If possible, add tarragon to meals.
* Buy a tiny ceramic or silver dragon to carry with you for your new beginning.

A snake power spell for a new start

The ability of the snake to shed its skin led to the belief that snakes did not die but were reborn each time their old skin fell off. Thus the snake became a magical symbol of renewal. It is an excellent symbol to work with just before a new beginning, especially if you have a lot of old fears, inhibitions or doubts to shed. Though this spell is suitable for anyone, women in later life may find it especially empowering

You will need

A stick or twig shaped like a serpent; a small chisel, plane or penknife; brightly coloured paints or wood varnish (optional).

Timing

The evening before your new beginning.

The spell

* Take up your wooden snake and, as you touch the bark, name what you wish to shed and what you wish to carry forward in to your new beginning.
* Using the chisel, plane or penknife, scrape away the bark of the stick so that only smooth wood remains.
* Hold the smooth wooden snake and say:
  The old is gone and done. I move forward in hope and freedom, having shed the past.
* If you wish, paint the snake in bright colours, using a pattern of spirals, or varnish the unadorned wood.
* Place your snake where you will see her as soon as you wake. On waking every morning, repeat the chant as you open your eyes.

A seed spell for new beginnings

Seeds are, of course, another symbol of new beginnings, especially if the beginning is a small one or will take time to reach fruition. This spell was originally associated with the beginning of February, called Oimelc or the Feast of Ewe's Milk in the pre-Christian calendar. It was sacred to the goddess Brighid in her form as the maiden and marked the time when fresh milk again became available after a long winter. In Christian times the festival was linked to St Brigit and to Candlemas.

You will need

A dish of edible seeds, such as sunflower, sesame or pumpkin; a small container of milk; 8 small pink or blue candles or tea-lights.

Timing

The evening before the new beginning.

The spell

* Place the candles in a ring, and in the centre set the milk and seeds.
* Light the candle furthest away from you, then dip a seed into the container of milk and eat it, as you do so saying:
  So do I take the first step on this new road.
  Though the path may be long, yet will it bring happiness.
* Working deosil (clockwise) around the circle, repeat the previous step until all eight candles are alight.
* Blow out the candles in reverse order of lighting, making a wish on each concerning your new beginning.
* Bury any remaining seeds and give the leftover milk to an animal or pour it into the earth, as a tribute to the Earth mother.

A toy boat spell

When you were a child, you may have sailed a toy boat on a pond. If the boat sank, you probably just fished it out and set it sailing again. When we face a new start in adult life, especially after a lot of sorrow or pressure, we may need to regain that childhood sense of optimism and trust.

You will need

A toy boat with a string; a pair of scissors or a knife; a pond or small boating lake.

Timing

In the early morning.

The spell

* Set the boat carefully in the water and hold the string. Say:
  I launch you in hope that you will make my fortune.
* When the boat is a little way out, cut the string, as you do so saying:
  There are no guarantees, no safety nets or assurances. Yet I trust all shall be well.
* Walk away from the pond and do not look back. With luck, the boat will come to shore and be found by a child to whom it will give pleasure.

A four-feather wind spell for a new beginning

In Native North American spirituality four main feathers are used in feather magic: the eagle feather in the East, the hawk feather in the South, the raven feather in the West, and the owl feather in the North. In Westernised magic, colours are substituted for feathers – yellow for the eagle, red for the hawk, black for the raven and white for the owl. This is a good spell to use if your new beginning is slow to materialise

You will need
4 feathers (sometimes available in the appropriate colours from fabric shops or New Age stores, but any four feathers will do).

Timing
On a windy day.

The spell
* Stand in the wind and turn to the East (an approximate East is good enough). Release the eagle feather and say:
  Eagle, fly far and swift and bring my new beginning.
* Turn to the South, release the hawk feather and say:
  Hawk, fly far and swift and bring my new beginning.
* Turn to the West, release the raven feather and say:
  Raven, fly far and swift and bring my new beginning.
* Turn to the North, release the owl feather and say:
  Owl, fly far and swift and bring my new beginning.
* Watch the feathers fly away and then do something to help speed your own venture.

A smudging or garden incense spell

This is another spell to stir the Air energies around you, giving you a flying start. It is also good if you want to travel (see Chapter 32).

You will need
2 sagebrush or cedar smudge sticks, or two large sticks of pine, citronella or lemon garden incense (the kind that stands in the ground); 2 containers (if using smudge sticks).

Timing
In the morning.

The spell
* Go to an open space, such as your garden, the park or a beach. Light the smudge or incense sticks and hold one in each hand, using them to make large swirls and spirals in all directions as you move around and chant the following:
  Up, down, to the ground
  And all around
  Power surround
  And carry me to where I would wish to be.
* Name your new beginning and let the wind carry your words.
* Leave the smudge or incense sticks (the former in the containers) in a safe, sheltered outdoor place to burn through and carry the positive energies upwards.

Five short new year spells

New year marks a time of new beginnings, a time to wipe the slate clean and to make resolutions. Although the year begins at different times in different cultures, the significance is the same. When societies first began to measure time, the new year was often made to correspond with the spring equinox (around 21 March in the Northern Hemisphere), when the sun rises due East and new life buds. In mainland Europe, new year only moved from the equinox to its present date when the Gregorian calendar was introduced, in 1582. In Protestant England the new calendar was not adopted until 1752. The Celtic new year began on 1 November (the modern halloween being the Celtic new year's eve). In the Isle of Man, a mummers' hogmanay dance at halloween recalls this earlier connection. The name 'hogmanay' comes from the old solar hero giant of the North, Hogmagog.

Spell 1: On new year's eve, clear out all your old clutter, dust away any cobwebs and sweep last year's luck out of the front door. Put all rubbish outside before midnight. Do not sweep on New year's day or put out the rubbish from your new year's eve party or you will put out the good fortune of the new year. Do not wash your clothes on new year's day either, or you will wash your luck away.

Spell 2: Before midnight on new year's eve, post invoices asking for any outstanding payments or refunds owing to you. Post any payments owed for outstanding bills (or a letter giving the date when you can pay). Do not lend any money on new year's day (give children any money they will need the day before). Do not use an ATM or fill in any loan forms or you will be giving out money and needing to borrow all year.

Spell 3: On new year's morning in Scotland, all exits are sealed and juniper berries are burnt until everyone is coughing heartily. The home is thereby purified by fire for the coming year. Good fortune will follow. Much better is to light a single stick of juniper incense and, entering by the front door, carry it through every room from the top to the bottom of the house. If the weather is fine, go out the back door and around as many of the external walls and fences as possible, and then back in through the front door again. Leave the incense to burn out in the hallway. Bury the ash in the garden.

Spell 4: The first water drawn from a well on new year's morning was said to bring great fortune and happiness. The person who got 'the cream of the well' sprinkled hay or petals near the well to let others know the well had been deflowered. A modern version of this custom is to turn on the cold tap in the sink as soon as you rise, running it fast so that the water bubbles. Use a brand-new glass to drink a glass of water straight down and without speaking. Surround the glass with a circle of petals or seeds and do not wash it until 2 January.

Spell 5: Make sure you are laughing at midnight on new year's eve, as what you are doing when the year turns will influence your happiness and moods for the year. In the morning dance around the nearest tree to your house 12 times deosil (clockwise), naming a month for each circuit. You will have happiness, luck and prosperity all the coming year.

A new year spell for a good year ahead

In places influenced by Celtic, Scandinavian and Teutonic customs, all the doors of a dwelling are opened by the head of the household just before midnight on new year's eve to let out the bad luck. Then they are closed. A dark-haired man, representing the new year, knocks at the front door on the stroke of midnight. When this first footer is admitted by the head of the house, he offers bread to ensure food for the household all year, a piece of coal for warmth and a coin for prosperity. He then leaves by the back door without speaking and re-enters by the front door to a chorus of 'Happy new year!' There are many variations on this ceremony. In Dundee and other fishing communities in Scotland, a herring is given to the first footer.

An older Scottish first footing custom harks back even more clearly to ancient horned god ceremonies. A young man covered in a cow hide runs round the outside of the house, while his fellow revellers bang sticks on the walls. On being granted entry to the house, the leader of the bovine revellers chants: 'May Hogmagog bless the house and all that belongs to it, cattle, kin and timbers. In meat, clothes and health of all therein, may fortune abound.'

This and the following spell are modern variations on the old first footing rituals. If you are celebrating outdoors, you can substitute fire-crackers for the white candle and noisy objects in this spell. Light them at midnight. You can also burn the whole calendar in the fire. You will not need the dark-coloured candle.

You will need
A dark-coloured candle; a deep metal tray; a small calendar for the year that is about to pass; some red wool; a white candle; noisy objects such as bells, wind chimes, saucepan lids, etc.

Timing
Five minutes before midnight.

The spell
* Light the candle on the tray.
* Using the red wool, tie up the calendar, making nine knots to fasten it.
* Tear a corner off the calendar and burn it in the candle flame, as you do so saying:
  Old year turn,
  Old year burn.
  Bad luck, do not return.
* Put the rest of the calendar in the bin.
* Light the white candle from the black one and count down to midnight.
* On the first stroke of midnight, blow out the black candle and shout:
  Happy new year!
* Bang and rattle the noisy objects to get the new year luck energies flowing in your home.

A new year's eve spell to bring luck into your home

You will need

A dark-coloured candle; a small bag containing a copper, a silver and a gold coin, sweets, dried fruits and nuts, symbols of your trade (such as a pen, a tiny calculator or a small tool) and a pinch of 2 or 3 herbs (such as basil, juniper berries, pine needles, sage or thyme); a bowl of water; a light-coloured candle; 3 coins or gold-coloured or clear glass nuggets for each person present.

Timing

A few minutes before midnight.

The spell

* Designate someone to be the new-year-bringer (traditionally a dark-haired male, but a person of either sex in dark clothing is fine). Give them the bag and the light-coloured candle and send them outside until midnight strikes.
* Place the dark-coloured candle (to represent the old year) on the hearth or in a warm place and light it. Place the bowl of water next to it.
* As midnight strikes, the person or people within shout:
Come in, New Year. New Year, you are welcome.
* The first footer enters by the front door, with the bag, shuts the door and goes out of the back door, saying:
Out you go, Old Year. Your time is past.
* Then the first footer comes back in through the back door and shuts it, walks up to the top of the house and then comes back down again, shouting:
Happy new year!
* He or she deposits the bag on the hearth (or in the warm place), lights the light-coloured candle (representing the new year) from the dark-coloured one and then blows out the dark candle of the old year.
* Each person present then throws their three coins or nuggets in to the bowl of water, making a silent wish for each.
* Do not throw the water away until 2 January.

A birthday candle spell

The first birthday candles were lit on moon-shaped cakes dedicated to the ancient Greek moon goddess Artemis on her annual festival. Her devotees would make a wish and blow out the candle, asking that Artemis would accept and grant their wishes. Some birthdays are more significant than others, perhaps because they mark a personal transition or the opening of a new decade. This ritual is a private celebration just for you. It is especially good if you are alone or away from home on your birthday – or if everyone is busy and does not have time to mark the occasion properly. The giving to yourself in this spell is important, even if you get lots of presents from other people.

You will need

A golden-coloured candle and a flat metal holder; a metal tray; gifts and cards received from family members or friends, plus small gifts bought for yourself (tiny crystals, flowers, bath oils, a book or CD you especially want); a photograph of yourself when young; a photograph of you as you are now; a small piece of white wool for each year of your age, including the new one.

Timing

A quiet moment on your birthday, either in the morning or just before you go to bed.

The spell

- Light the candle, as you do so saying:
I welcome this my birthday. I welcome the turning of the year and the new opportunities it brings.
- Encircle the candle with any gifts or cards you have received from others and open the ones you have bought for yourself.
- Place the photographs on either side of the candle, the younger one to the left.
- One by one, singe one end of each piece of wool in the candle and then drop it on to the tray, as you do so, looking from the younger you to the older one and saying:
What is lost and what is gained by age, they balance. I walk into the future and a new beginning. Come what may, it starts today.
- Leave the candle to burn through as you plan a personal treat, either an outing for your birthday or for your next free day. Choose something you will enjoy as opposed to something that will make others happy.
- When the candle is burnt through and the wax is soft but not liquid, push the wool strands in a circle into the melted wax so that they look like the rays of the sun.
- Leave the wax to harden and then cut out the wax circle. Keep it until you have made the first beginning of your personal new year.

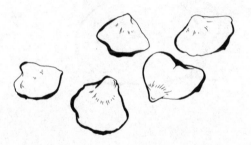

A spell for starting a new job or school, or moving in a new direction

New beginnings require an in-rush of motion to carry the new beginning successfully into being. The physical movement in this spell symbolises the more general movement coming into your life.

You will need

A place you have never been to before (it can be local but should be outdoors); a small yellow purse or drawstring bag; a small yellow crystal or stone.

Timing

The morning of the day before the new experience.

The spell

* Place the crystals in the purse and take it to the new place. Stand in the open air facing the direction of the sun or, if it is cloudy, approximately east.
* Hold the crystal in your power hand (the one you write with), and the purse in your receptive hand. Raise the crystal towards the light and say: *This is new. This is good. Tomorrow will be good and the days after will be good till new becomes familiar.*
* Put the crystal back in the purse and close it.
* Find or buy something tiny in the new place: a flower, a stone, a tiny piece of twig, or anything small enough to go in the purse.
* Standing in the same spot as before, hold the new item in your power hand and the closed purse in your receptive hand. Offer the new item to the sky and repeat the words.
* Put the new item in the purse with the crystal.
* When you are ready, go home. Keep the purse near an East-facing window (the direction of new beginnings) overnight.
* In the morning, carry it with you or give it to the person experiencing the new beginning as a lucky talisman.

31 SPELLS FOR CHANGES WITHIN THE FAMILY

Families change over the years. New babies are born, grandparents die and new members enter or leave the family circle as a result of divorce, re-marriage, fostering and adoption. A family may be large and complex or it may consist of just you and a child, you and a partner or you and a parent. Your nuclear family may be involved with a number of other family units either immediately related to you or whom you see regularly.

Before the Industrial Revolution, most families would have lived in the same village for hundreds of years, usually marrying people they had known since childhood. Even up until the time of the First World War, relocation was much less common than it is nowadays, and families tended to go on living close together in the same area, and still in the 1950s it was not unusual for several generations to share the same house or to live in adjoining houses in the same street. Children grew up with cousins and with grandparents who shared their daily lives.

The nature of personal relationships began to change in the 1960s, with many families establishing themselves without legal ties, and divorce and re-marriage becoming more common, so that the family circle might often be joined by new in-laws and step-relations. While some would see this shift as indicative of a lack of stability in modern families, change does not necessarily equate with unhappiness. Indeed, some of the happiest and most secure families I know are headed by single parents. (My own family is one of them.)

When legal and geographical family ties are less strong, magic can help to form the glue for holding diverse people together in positive and loving ways. Because the extended family may meet only at transition points, such as a christening or a wedding, these rites of passage may be doubly important for reaffirming the family bond (rather than renewing rivalries). Spells can help to lower potential tensions on such occasions and bring shared happiness.

Within the smaller, immediate family circle there will be many changes and transitions. Children start school, begin a first job and leave home. Individuals must grow into the role of parent or grandparent, and then, as the children grow up, adapt again. All of these changes are significant and can be marked by rituals to affirm their importance, so marking — formally or informally — the way to the next stage. This is perhaps the chief role of spells for family change.

A spell for becoming keeper of the family records

Four or five generations ago, an older member of the family would have kept a family Bible or a scroll in which family births, marriages and deaths were carefully recorded in copper plate handwriting. In the UK, official records have only been kept since the 1830s. You don't have to be the most senior member of the family to take on the task of record keeper; you just need to be persevering enough to track down past generations and set up a family tree. On to this you can graft more recent events – family births; marriages, re-marriages and permanent unions; deaths; and adoptions. Once your record is as complete as you can make it, take it along to family occasions and ask those who are celebrating to record any recent family changes. It does not matter if there are gaps. Over time, other family members may help to fill them in. In creating a book, you are symbolically creating the heart of a family, perhaps one that is geographically separated.

You will need

A large book or scroll; a pen and ink; a beeswax candle; photographs of any older deceased family members and any family pictures past or present, such as a group at a wedding or christening; I small dish each of dried rosemary, sage and thyme; some fresh flowers, such as lilies.

Timing

On a Friday, at sunset.

The spell

* Light the beeswax candle and set any photographs you have around it.
* By the light of the candle, carefully write at the front of the book the main family surname and say:
  May I be a wise keeper of these memories.
* If you have done any research into the family past, record it in the book or on the scroll. If not, list the different branches of the family, together with current and past permanent partners, for they all form part of the changing story.
* When you have finished writing, sprinkle a circle of dried rosemary around the open book. Then sprinkle a circle of sage outside the rosemary. Finally, sprinkle a circle of thyme outside the sage. As you make the circles, say:
  Rosemary for fond memories, sage that these events may not be forgotten and thyme for fond thoughts of family, past, present and future.
* Sprinkle three similar concentric circles around the photographs and then around the candle, as you work repeating the chant.
* Allow the candle to burn through, then close the book, as you do so saying once again:
  May I be a wise keeper of these memories.
* Keep the book or scroll, together with the three dishes of herbs and the flowers, on a table where the early evening sunlight will fall on it.

A memory box ritual for when a relation has departed

When a friend or family member dies, especially if they lived alone, many of their old trinkets and photographs can get cleared out in the hurry to resolve matters. This is a pity, because sorting through old papers, knick-knacks and photographs can provide a sense of connection that is often missing at funerals, which can be sad or awkward events at which the essence of the deceased person seems absent. Before you clear out all your relative's possessions, try doing this ritual to celebrate their life and create a permanent memorial to them.

You will need
A wooden box with a lid; a sachet of dried lavender.

Timing
When a relation has died.

The spell
* Look through your deceased relative's possessions for special mementoes of them. You may find a ration book, a brooch given to the deceased person as a birthday present, a wartime photograph, a medal from a sporting triumph, general letters of family news or perhaps a poem they wrote.
* Ask friends and relatives of your departed loved one to donate a small memento of their relationship – for example, a souvenir or postcard from a holiday, a favourite recipe, a cinema ticket from a film they enjoyed. Alternatively, each person can write a few lines about the deceased person, perhaps including a fond memory. Even children can usually think of a shared joke.
* After the funeral, fill the wooden box with the mementoes and read aloud the memories before also putting them in the box.
* Put the sachet of dried lavender in to the box and close the lid. The box can be kept in the deceased's family home or, if they lived alone, a friend or family member can act as caretaker.

A spell to create a living family tree

If you have a garden or an area where you keep pot plants, you can plant small herbs, flowers or bushes for each family member. In this way, the family will grow symbolically together.

You will need
A herb, flower or bush for each family member; a suitable flower bed or potting materials; some labels.

Timing
Any.

The spell
* Plant your herbs, flowers or bushes, dedicating each one to a particular family member and making a private blessing, even if you find the particular family member difficult or do not approve of a relationship.
* Label each herb, flower or bush with the name of the family member it is dedicated to.
* Tend the plants, adding a new one whenever a new member comes into the family. If someone leaves the family permanently, perhaps because of divorce, transplant their plant a little way off, so that they are separate but still come under your care.

A christening or naming ritual for a new baby

The naming of a baby has always been a special occasion. In earlier times the baby's name was not spoken until the ceremony. Whatever faith the ceremony belongs to, it marks the baby's transition from being part of the mother to a separate individual. This ritual is intended to be performed by the mother or father. Perform it alone or together with the other parent, each taking it in turns to pour the water and offer blessings.

You will need

A rose quartz or jade crystal; a jug of cold sparkling mineral water.

Timing

On the day of the Christening or other naming ceremony, when you can get five minutes to be alone.

The spell

* Take the crystal (to represent the baby) and the jug of water into the garden or to where you have a large green plant.

* Hold the crystal over the earth, pour a little water on to it and name a gift or blessing you wish for the baby. (The custom of pouring water over a sacred object goes back to ancient Egyptian times.) Then, as the water falls on the earth, say:
  Mother Earth, bless and protect my child as she/he walks your paths through life.

* Continue to pour and ask for blessings, remembering to ask for those things you really consider important (rather than just worldly success), and each time you pour, asking the blessing of mother Earth.

* When the jug is empty, go indoors and dry the crystal. If there is to be a Christening feast, set the crystal in the centre of the table. Otherwise, keep it safely in a drawer.

* On each of your child's birthdays, re-dedicate the crystal by pouring water over it and on to the earth, and add new blessings.

A candle ceremony for the birth of a baby

This spell is intended to be performed by a close relation or friend of the mother and infant, or perhaps a person chosen to be a godmother or godfather. (See Chapter 39 for more spells for pregnancy and childbirth.)

You will need

12 white or beeswax candles of the same shape and size.

Timing

When the mother goes into labour, and thereafter on the child's birthday.

The spell

* When the labour starts, light one of the candles in your home to ease the passage of the unborn infant into the world.

* Light another candle after the birth, endowing it with all your hopes for the little one and for the welfare of the parents.

* On each of the child's next ten birthdays, light one of the candles, either as part of the birthday celebration or at your home, and send love and light to the child.

* When the child is ready to leave home, buy a special candlestick for his or her new home, together with a supply of candles.

A spell for going to school for the first time, changing schools or leaving home

As I mentioned on page 354, Viking women would chant protective spells as they sewed the garments of their warrior husbands. Even if you are not an expert seamstress, you can still sew your love into a garment that will be regularly worn by your child. This spell works by empowering the thread rather than the garment. If you empower a reel of thread for each of your children, when they go away without you (on holiday, for instance), you can give them a mini emergency sewing kit with a little of the thread wrapped around a strip of card. Although the child probably won't use it, the protection is there. (You can empower several reels of thread at the same time.) Alternatively, you can sew a few stitches in a garment your child will be wearing at night or in a sleeping bag. When your child leaves home to go to college or start a job, put their special thread in to a box of useful items or sew a stitch or two in a duvet or pillowcase to transfer the protection.

You will need

A ball of thread for each of your children; 6 small green and/or pink candles (or tea-lights); a stick of rose or lavender incense.

Timing

On a Friday, after dusk.

The spell

* Place the candles in a circle, with the reel or reels of thread inside. Light the candles, starting with the one furthest away from you and moving deosil (clockwise). Say:
  Air and Fire enter this thread. Protect my child from danger, stranger, malice, malevolence and the consequences of her/his own thoughtless actions.

* Light the incense and pass it in deosil spirals over each reel of thread, as you do so repeating the above chant continuously.

* Blow out the candles in reverse order of lighting, in your head sending the light in to the thread. Leave the incense to burn out.

* Keep the empowered thread in a special drawer. Use it to sew a small loop or a few stitches in an item that will be used at bedtime, so that the protection can be absorbed during sleep. Repeat the chant as you sew – and if you are really worried, light a green or pink candle as you work. Pack the thread in your child's luggage when he or she goes away.

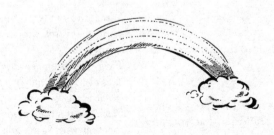

A spell for when a child first goes into the outside world (daycare, nursery or school)

Even though you know your little one will be well cared for and have a wonderful time, the first day with a childminder, at nursery or at school is still a big change for both child and parents. This spell will ease the transition, enabling you to give out relaxed vibes at the temporary parting. This is also a good spell if your child is very nervous about starting school.

You will need

One of the children's first soft shoes or a garment from babyhood; a shoe or garment that the child will be wearing at daycare, nursery or school; a pink rose quartz crystal.

Timing

On the two nights before the first day away from home.

The spell

* On the first night, wrap the rose quartz crystal in the baby clothes or place it in the shoe, as you do so saying:
Safe in my arms
That all may be calm.
Take this protection
Whatever direction
You follow.
Let nought be of harm
Until back in my arms.
* The next evening, transfer the rose quartz crystal to the shoe or garment the child will be wearing outside the home and repeat the chant.
* On the morning of the adventure, help your child to dress and leave the rose quartz crystal in the child's room until the happy return.

A spell for saying bon voyage to a family member

If a family member is going overseas or moving in with a partner, carry out this spell. If possible, work outdoors on a large flat-topped stone, tree stump or picnic table. Otherwise, find a place in the house from which you can see the rising sun or that faces approximately east.

You will need

A symbol or photograph of the family member; a length of white ribbon; some dried rose petals or rose pot pourri; a small box.

Timing

A day or two before the departure, at dawn.

The spell

* Set all the materials for the spell on a flat surface. Stand so that you are facing the direction of the rising sun with the items in front of you.
* Hold the photo or symbol in the air, between your hands, and offer it to the East, as you do so saying:
Though I may no longer share the days with you, yet will my love, constantly renewed with the morning light, go with you.
* Scatter a circle of rose petals or pot pourri around the symbol, as you do so saying:
Though I may no longer hear your voice each day, yet will your memory also be renewed with each rising sun, in my heart and in my mind.
* Wrap the white ribbon around the symbol several times, as you do so saying:
Though I cannot walk with you each step of the way, yet do I willingly enfold you in my love and memory.
* Place the symbol or photo in the box, together with some of the rose petals or pot pourri, and keep it with your personal treasures.

A spell for getting on well with in-laws and step-relations

Both in-law- and step-relationships can be hazardous, especially at first, since you are suddenly thrust into close proximity emotionally and physically with people who are virtual strangers and who may have a very different lifestyle from your own. Where re-marriage is involved, the ghost of previous partners can need much tact and tolerance to overcome, especially if the previous daughter- or son-in-law was very close to your new partner's family. If one of your children is re-marrying, you may acquire a whole new family, with their own divided loyalties, almost overnight. The key is to meet on an area of common ground.

You will need

2 small hoops or circles made out of wire or raffia (the kind baskets are woven from); some modelling clay or dough; some rose or lavender water or any floral cologne water; a large fabric bag.

Timing

Before a family occasion, on a Friday morning.

The spell

* Arrange the two hoops so that there is a large overlapping area between them.
* Using the clay or dough, mould featureless figures to represent each member of the two families to be joined, marking each with an initial to identify them. Begin with yourself and the person connecting you with the new family.
* Place yourself and the person linking you to the other family in the overlapping part of the two hoops. Join the hands of these two figures to avoid divisions caused by the family upheaval. Say:

Those whom love joins let none put asunder.

* Set the other figures in their respective family circles.
* Beginning with the other family, take one of the figures and set it in the overlapping circle. Sprinkle it with a few drops of the flower water and repeat the chant.
* Now move one of your own family figures to the centre, repeating the actions and words.
* Continue to move the figures alternately, sprinkling them and chanting, until all the figures are in the overlapping part of the hoops.
* Remove the hoops and sprinkle a deosil (clockwise) circle of flower water around the figures, as you do so repeating the chant.
* Keep the figures hidden in the fabric bag in the place where the meeting will take place (or in your car outside).
* When the figures crumble, you can dispose of them. Hopefully the work will be done. If not, repeat the spell.

A spell for becoming a parent for the first time

Whether a baby is planned or a surprise, your life will never be the same again. On pages 510–11 I write about getting to know your unborn child. This spell is about a couple acknowledging and preparing for what will be a huge life change, no matter how much the pregnancy was hoped for and anticipated. You can carry out this spell with your partner or alone.

You will need

An item you have bought for the baby or the baby's room; a mobile or hanging crystals.

Timing

Whenever what will be the baby's room catches light through the window.

The spell

* Set the items in what will be the baby's room, no matter if it is currently empty or furnished for another purpose.
* Walk in through the door and close it behind you, as you do so saying:
Behind me lies my old life. I walk through the door willingly into parenthood and responsibility.

* Put the baby item roughly where it will be when the baby is born and with your power hand (the one you write with) touch your heart. Place your other hand on the baby item and say:
Come into my heart, come into my life. I am ready to care for you, to cherish you and if necessary lay down my life for you.
(You can leave out the last part if it seems inappropriate, but many parents do feel that way.)
* Hang the mobile or crystals at the window and open the window slightly, as you do so saying:
No longer one but two. I open my mind to the joys and the uncertainties, the pleasures and the responsibilities.
(Adapt the words if you are working with a partner.)
* Wait until the mobile is moved by the breeze (or if it is a windless day, shake it gently). This symbolises the child entering your life.
* Close the window and leave the room with the door open.

A spell to adjust to becoming a grandparent

Grandparenting brings many pleasures, not least being able to enjoy grandchildren and hand them back to the parents at the end of the day. Most grandparents develop close bonds with their grandchildren, although they may themselves be working full-time, caring for their own parents or pursuing (at long last) personal dreams. The first grandchild represents a huge change point, requiring adjustments in the way the new grandparents react to their own children (now parents) and in their perception of themselves as suddenly part of the older generation. This spell will help to ease the transition and open a new path to joy.

You will need

Sticky-backed loops of different coloured or gold and silver paper (for making paper chains).

Timing

On a Sunday afternoon.

The spell

* Using the loops of paper, make a long paper chain, as you do so reciting:

  Chain, we are part of a chain,
  Linked by our history,
  Yours shrouded in mystery
  Of good things to come.
  I have much I would share with you,
  Wonders to show to you,
  Long days to know you.

  My history goes back as yours lies ahead.
  We are part of a chain that ever will spread.
  Chains, we are chains,
  And the link runs right through.
  Grandchild of mine,
  So I welcome you.

* Keep the paper chains until the baby is born and then use them to decorate a welcome home banner for your new grandchild.

A spell for welcoming new younger members into the family

If a divorced parent marries again, their child will acquire not only a new step-parent but also step-grandparents, aunts, uncles and cousins. Children tend to be less good than adults at masking feelings of uncertainty, divided loyalties and resentment. This spell will enable a new younger member of the family to feel welcome and help them to bridge the transition. You can carry out the spell alone, or if you know the children well enough, ask them to help you.

You will need

Enough white tea-lights or small candles to represent the new young family member(s) and the existing family members; a selection of dried scented flower petals, such as rose, chamomile, lavender, lily, violet and any others you can acquire (available from craft stores or florists – keep them in a large container with a lid until the spell); a wide clear glass jar with a lid; orange essential oil.

Timing

After dark.

The spell

* Arrange the tea-lights or candles in a circle. Working deosil (clockwise), light them, naming a family member out loud for each one (beginning with yourself and including the new young additions) and saying:

  May they be blessed and bring blessings.

* When all the lights have been kindled, open the box of flowers and add a few flowers to the glass jar for each person, again naming the family member, new or old, and repeating the above blessing. If the children are working with you, they can help add the flowers.

* When all have been named and blessed, add three drops of the orange essential oil to the flowers in the jar and repeat the blessing.

* Put the lid on the clear glass jar and shake it once for each family member (old and new), saying for each shake:

  So are we one, blended with affection, joined willingly to live now as family. You are all welcome.

* Leave the jar of flowers in the middle of the candles until they have burnt down. Put the blessed petals in a bowl in the main living room. Keep the sealed container for when you need to empower more flowers, perhaps before a family occasion.

A spell for holding families together in times of upheaval

Family splits can occur for all kinds of reasons: marriage to a partner whom the rest of the family dislikes or distrusts, divorce, an old rivalry that suddenly comes to a head, the death of the person who holds the family together, quarrels over an inheritance, or part of the family moving far away. This is a good spell also for a crisis within the immediate family – perhaps an adult child moving in with a partner you feel sure will make them unhappy or a teenager suddenly moving out to live with unreliable friends and quitting school or college. As with any upheaval, the effects can cause the family to become fragmented or cease to function as a unit. A spell can help to bring together the 'missing' as well as the 'surviving' family members and offer the space for the dust to settle and a new direction to be found.

You will need

Fronds of greenery from a number of different plants, ferns or trees; a vase or pot to hold the fronds; your favourite Bach Flower Remedy (good ones are Red Chestnut/Cerrato, Chestnut Bud and Water Violet) or rose or lavender water.

Timing

The three days before the full moon, just before twilight.

The spell

* Partly fill the vase with water and place it in the centre of your workspace.
* Add a few drops of Flower Remedy or lavender or rose water to the vase, as you do so saying:
Essence of joy and kindliness, let only goodness flow and grow within the family as we change and evolve and find a new pattern of living.
* Take a frond of greenery and name it for the family member undergoing the most change, as you do so sprinkling a few drops of the Flower Remedy or lavender or rose water over it and saying:
Kindly be and filled with understanding.
Set the frond in the vase.
* Repeat the previous step for each family member, including yourself.
* Place the vase of greenery near the centre of the main room of the house, as you do so saying:
Be close and comforting, tolerant and welcoming.
* When the greenery dies, bury it or put it on the compost heap and let time take its course.

A spell for coping with family troubles caused by unwelcome change

This spell is very good if a family member has suddenly experienced a personality change or mood swings and is disrupting family life. It is a good supplement to dealing with the problem practically and emotionally, and can ease tensions.

You will need

A pot of bubble mixture with a blower, or a lidded container filled with very soapy water and a piece of wire twisted in to a small circle with a handle.

Timing

Any clear morning.

The spell

* Go to an open space and look directly upwards at a clear patch of sky.

* Shake the bubble container nine times and say:
  Above, below and all around,
  From highest sky to lowest ground,
  So I blow these troubles away.

* Slowly blow your first bubble. As it ascends, name the first or main disruption and its effects, adding:
  Take this away.
  No more stay
  To bring sorrow to my family.

* Blow as many bubbles as you wish, for each either repeating the main disruption or naming other related worries and chanting the chant.

* When you have finished, walk away without looking back.

* Make one more effort with the person, trying to arrange something you both enjoy.

A spell to welcome an older family member into your home or to assist you in moving into theirs

For financial or health reasons, it may be practical for an older family member to move in to your home or for you to share theirs. This can work extremely well, but there may be territory disputes until you are settled in the new lifestyle. Conversely, both parties may be on their best behaviour and unable to relax. A spell can help to bring the two households or individuals into closer harmony. This spell is also good if you move into a new partner's home, maybe with your children, and feel like a visitor (or vice versa).

You will need

A pair of your shoes or slippers; a pair of shoes or slippers belonging to the person with whom you now share living space.

Timing

When the house is quiet.

The spell

* Exchange a shoe or slipper from each pair, so that you have two pairs of odd shoes.

* Sit or kneel on the floor and pick up the first odd pair of shoes, holding the other person's shoe in your power hand (the one you write with). Say:
  May I walk in your shoes for a mile or more.
  May you walk in mine. May we walk together in harmony.

* Repeat the previous step with the other pair of odd shoes, this time holding your own shoe in your power hand as you chant.

* Leave the shoes side by side overnight.

A spell to persuade overgrown baby birds to fly the nest

Because of high housing costs, these days children may stay at home until they are in their late-twenties or early-thirties. Sometimes an adult child returns home after a partnership split or a job loss. This may not be a problem, and it can be good to have someone to share expenses and chores, and provide pleasant company. But if you can never get into your own bathroom and thirty-something overnight visitors of your children start telling you that you have run out of their favourite cereal, it may be time for a gentle magical rattling of the coop.

You will need

An old box or cage with a wire-mesh door (for example, a cat box, hamster cage or birdcage).

Timing

On the first of the month, in the early morning.

The spell

* Open the door of the cage or box and gently rattle the bars, as you do so saying softly over and over again:
  Fly, baby chickens,
  High baby chickens,
  For you are too large for the coop.
* Leave the door of the cage or box open until sunset.
* Repeat on the first of every month until your adult child has decided to move on.

32 SPELLS FOR TRAVEL

Travel is generally a very positive form of change. It may entail enjoying a weekend break, planning the adventure of a lifetime or going abroad for business. You may be intending to live or work abroad for a time, perhaps buying a second home in the sun, or you may be relocating permanently, maybe opting for a slower lifestyle (see also pages 445 and 446).

Chapter 26 deals with spells for protection while travelling. This chapter focuses on spells to make travel more likely if you want to broaden your physical horizons and to ensure that whatever travel plans you make go smoothly. Of course, there is some overlap, since spells for happy travel inevitably include an element of protection. Try mixing and matching the spells to allay fear, minimise hazards and make sure that even a mundane trip is pleasurable.

A Lady of Guadelupe travel charm

The Virgin of Guadelupe, or La Malinche, is a Christianised version of the old Mexican mother goddess and is the patron saint of Mexico. She is pictured dark-skinned, very beautiful, wearing red or orange and green robes and surrounded by roses. Her image is everywhere in Mexico, including roadside shrines, buses and trucks, so she is an excellent travellers' icon. She offers protection especially to those who travel many miles a year and will ensure you are comfortable and find good, safe places to stay. She will also help if you are in an unfamiliar country. Carry her image on a medallion or in a tiny prayer wallet (available over the Internet). I use this spell when I am driving and unexpectedly need to find somewhere to spend the night (usually because I have been delayed and missed the last ferry home). On most occasions, before I have gone a mile or two more, I see either a motel sign or a direction off the main road to a friendly inn with a vacancy.

You will need

Nothing.

Timing

When you or a family member have travelled many miles in a day and are getting tired.

The spell

* Recite the following prayer:

Lady Mother, you who once turned a bare hillside into fragrant roses, I am tired and am far from home. Before the road gets longer and the night darker, send me a place to rest my head, a soft bed, a warm hearth and a welcoming smile.

A St Julian the Hospitaller prayer for a friend or family member who is backpacking

St Julian is the patron saint of ferrymen, innkeepers, long-distance and impoverished travellers, wandering musicians and circus people. In penance for killing his parents by mistake, Julian built a hospice for the poor near a wide river that he would ferry travellers across. One night he took in a leper who was close to death and gave him his own bed. The man turned out to be an angel and told Julian he was blessed. Although Julian's medallions and images are less common than those of St Christopher, he is a much-loved protector, especially in the Netherlands. You may find his talisman of use if a friend or a member of your family is undertaking a lengthy or budget-cost journey. I used it when my 18-year-old son, Jack, was travelling through Europe with a friend for three months.

You will need

Nothing.

Timing

Nightly, when a friend or family member is on a lengthy journey or travelling cheaply abroad.

The spell

* Recite the following prayer:

My child/brother/sister/friend sleeps this night I know not where. Grant them kind lodging, or if they are under the stars, make their bed soft, their sleep peaceful and watch them until the morning.

* Repeat the prayer nightly while the traveller is away.

A mojo bag for a regular traveller

This mojo is ideal for hiding in a car beneath the spare wheel compartment or in a pocket of a case that you do not open. Given levels of airport security, you should not take the mojo on a plane journey, since if you have to open the bag, it will lose its power. Mojos must be kept hidden. If you are travelling by air, leave the mojo at home in your bed and while you are away recite the words of the 23rd Psalm each night before you go to bed. Take the Psalm paper with you, tied up with white thread, rather than placing it in the bag, and add a little of the cooled candle wax to the bag so that it contains the necessary odd number of items for a mojo (see page 399). This mojo is not only protective but will also add all manner of good things to your holiday or journey, ensuring that you find a good place to stay and that everyone is helpful.

You will need

A yellow candle; a comfrey root; frankincense essential oil or specially prepared travel fragrance oil (available from New Age stores); a piece of white paper; a black pen; a St Christopher medallion; some dried mint; a turquoise crystal; a drawstring bag made out of yellow flannel or a natural fabric; a length of white or yellow cord.

Timing

The night before you travel.

The spell

* Light the yellow candle to work by.
* Pour three drops of the frankincense or travel oil on to the comfrey root.
* Using the black pen, write the 23rd Psalm on the paper:
  The Lord is my Shepherd;
  I shall not want.
  He maketh me to lie down
  In green pastures;
  He leadeth me beside the still waters.
  He restoreth my soul.
  He leadeth me in the paths
  Of righteousness for His name's sake.
  Thou preparest a table before me
  In the presence of my enemies;
  Thou anointest my head with oil.
  My cup runneth over;
  Surely goodness and mercy shall follow me
  All the days of my life;
  And I will dwell
  In the house of the Lord forever.
* Fold the paper around the comfrey root and place it in the bag.
* Add the St Christopher medallion, dried mint and turquoise to the bag.
* Leave the candle to burn down.
* When the candle has burnt down, close the bag and tie it with the cord, as you do so, again reciting the 23rd Psalm. The mojo will last for about two months.

A spell for a perfect day

You will need

Nothing.

Timing

At or around sunrise just before a journey.

The spell

* Wherever you are, stop and face the light. Say slowly three times:

  This then is my perfect day.
* Shake your hands vigorously and repeat the words faster three more times, letting any fears or frustrations drop away.
* Repeat at noon and sunset if you are still travelling, and again when you finally reach your destination.

A smudge ritual for a safe and happy journey and holiday

This is one of the easiest rituals I know for overall holiday happiness. It involves smudging the luggage. You might like to carry it out together with the spell on page 373 to prevent belongings getting lost. I do not know the origins of the Native North American version of the Lord's Prayer used in this ritual, but it is very beautiful and I would love to be able to credit the source in future editions of this book if any reader knows it.

You will need

A sagebrush or cedar smudge stick.

Timing

When all is ready, the evening or morning before you travel.

The spell

* Set all your suitcases and travel documents in a circle formation on the floor.
* Light the smudge stick and hold it in your power hand (the one you write with). Blow gently on the tip until it glows and, fanning the smoke with your other hand, walk in a wide deosil (clockwise) circle around the luggage, smudging it with deosil smoke spirals and reciting softly and continuously the following lines from the Native North American version of the Lord's Prayer:

The Great Spirit above a shepherd Chief is. He ... draws me to where the grass is green and the water not dangerous, and I eat and lie down and am satisfied. He gives me a staff to lean upon. He spreads a table before me with all kinds of foods. He puts His hand upon my head and all the tiredness is gone. My cup He fills until it runs over ... And afterwards I will go to live in the Big Tepee and sit down with the Shepherd Chief forever.

* Make a widdershins (anti-clockwise) circle around the luggage, this time smudging it with widdershins smoke spirals as you recite the prayer.
* Make a third deosil circle around the luggage, smudging it with deosil smoke spirals and reciting the prayer.

A Chinese happy travel charm

Kwan Yin was one of the ancient protective mother goddesses of China. She is associated with compassion, protection and good fortune, especially while travelling. She is also considered to be one of the enlightened ones in the Tibetan Buddhist tradition. Kwan Yin gold stickers are put in cars in Hong Kong and mainland China to prevent accidents. In the West, statuettes of Kwan Yin are now widely available in New Age stores and by mail order – or try the Chinatown area of a large city.

You will need

A shiny brass Kwan Yin statue; a dish; some red, yellow or golden-coloured flowers or a pot plant.

Timing

The night before you travel.

The spell

* Set out your Kwan Yin statue and place the flowers or pot plant close by as a tribute to her.
* Place any travel tickets, hotel passes or car keys in the dish in front of the Kwan Yin statue and leave them there to charge overnight.

A spell for a good holiday

This spell will help to increase good vibes so that your journey flows smoothly and your holiday – be it a weekend away or your main trip of the year – is free of hazards and frustration.

You will need

A photograph of your main holiday mode of transport (or example, a car or a plane); a photograph of where you will be staying (cut from a brochure) or the name of the hotel written in red on white paper; a photograph of yourself and whoever will be travelling with you; 4 green candles.

Timing

When you have a spare half-hour on the day before you travel.

The spell

* Place all three photographs in a pile, with the transport on top, the location in the middle and yourself and fellow travellers on the bottom.
* Set the four green candles in a square formation around the pile of photographs.
* Light the candle furthest away from you (to represent the journey). Look into the candle flame and say:
  An easy journey I would see.
  So I ask and it shall be.
* Moving deosil (clockwise) around the square, light the second candle (to represent the holiday itself). Look into the flame and say:
  A good apartment / villa / hotel I would see.
  So I ask and it shall be.
* Still moving deosil, light the third candle (to represent the people with you on holiday, the other guests at the hotel, those who will look after you and maybe someone special you will meet). Look into the flame and say:
  Good company I would see.
  So I ask and it shall be.
* Light the final candle (to represent the fulfilment of all the previous candle requests and that indefinable extra that makes a holiday perfect). Look into the flame and say:
  Bring me memories to treasure,
  Of happy days and nights of pleasure.
  So I ask and it shall be.
* Leave the candles to burn down.
* Put the three photographs in your hand luggage. When you arrive at your destination, set them in a pile near a window where they will absorb light.
* When you get home, keep the photographs, together with any souvenirs and photos of the holiday.

A 23rd Psalm ritual for when you are taking children on holiday

This is a wonderful spell if you are travelling with young children, especially if you are going away alone or to an unfamiliar place. I used it when travelling with two young children as a single parent. I have also found it a good way of smoothing arrangements with older children, so that all goes well and you can relax in the knowledge that they are having a good time.

You will need

A necklace with chunky beads (at least 10) – a crystal necklace will add extra energies.

Timing

Nightly, beginning the night before the holiday.

The spell

* Hold the beads in your receptive hand (the one you don't write with) and with your power hand touch each bead in turn, turning the necklace so that the bead you touch is always at the top. As you touch the beads, recite the 23rd Psalm softly and continuously three times (see page 431 for the words).
* Put on the necklace and repeat the Psalm again.

A spell for a happy holiday even if things go wrong

Sometimes the holidays we remember most fondly are those involving setbacks that became part of the family folklore – collapsing beds, a surly hotel owner or getting totally lost and later finding you were within a stone's throw of the hotel all the time. A spell that can be activated every morning is a good way of releasing positive vibes so that any unavoidable setbacks can become part of the fun and not a dampener on the holiday.

You will need

A sparkling citrine, amber, clear quartz or any other sparkling crystal; 4 blue candles; 4 sticks of lavender or fern incense; 4 separate incense-holders.

Timing

The day before your holiday, in the morning if possible.

The spell

* Place the candles in a circular formation, with one at each of the four compass points (these can be approximate) and the incense-holders equidistant between each. Set the crystal in the centre of the circle.
* Beginning with the candle in the North, light each candle in turn, as you do so, saying for each:
  Light of laughter, follow me
  Over land and over sea.
  This I ask that it shall be.
* Beginning in the north-east, one by one light the lavender or fern incense sticks (fern is the incense of travel), saying for each:
  Words of happiness follow me
  Over land and over sea.
  This I ask and it shall be.
* Take up the north-east and south-west incense sticks, one in each hand, and weave patterns over the candles and the crystal, as you do so saying:
  Weave in hope for happy days,
  Sunshine, joy and tranquil ways.
  This I ask and it shall be.
* Return the incense sticks to their holders and take up the remaining two sticks, repeating the weaving action and the words.
* Leave the candles and incense to burn through, with the crystal still in the centre of the circle.
* Place the crystal in your hand luggage. When you arrive at your holiday destination, set it outdoors in the sunshine for an hour.
* Place the crystal in the middle of the breakfast table each morning and take it with you on trips. Whenever a setback looms, hold the crystal, repeat all the words of the spell in your head and you will be able to turn the situation into an adventure.
* While you are away, re-empower the crystal by placing it outdoors in the light for an hour a day.

A spell for a smooth journey and good business trip

Although this spell was originally devised for general trips, it works especially well for business travel.

You will need

A turquoise or garnet crystal (you can buy unpolished garnets cheaply – they are just as powerful as their polished cousins); a glass bowl half filled with water; a yellow candle; a silk scarf or handkerchief.

Timing

About 12 hours before you leave on the trip.

The spell

* Working in a quiet place, for example a garden or a well-loved room, drop the turquoise or garnet (both protective and empowering crystals) into the bowl of water.
* As the ripples spread outwards, light the candle (for a swift, pleasurable journey).
* Drop a little candle wax into the water, so that it hisses and sets on the surface, forming an island (to represent your safe arrival on terra firma). You may find that the wax has made the shape of the country you will be visiting or your mode of transport. (You can do this even if you are not going abroad.)
* Blow out the candle and let the smoke travel upwards, symbolically carrying you above any minor setbacks and irritations to the success – and hopefully pleasure – derived from your trip.
* Take the crystal from the water, dry it and wrap it in the silk scarf or handkerchief to travel with your in your hand luggage.

An incense air ritual to make a dream of long-distance or long-term travel possible

Whether you want to winter in a warm country or visit relatives on the other side of the world, this spell will open to you all kinds of unexpected opportunities, bringing cheap offers into your sphere or unexpected money and invitations to travel.

You will need

A bowl of fresh rose petals (or any fresh perfumed petals); a map or sketch map you have drawn showing where you are now and where you want to be.

Timing

At dawn or in the early morning, as early in the month as possible.

The spell

* Working outdoors, fill your hands with rose petals from the bowl and scatter them across the map, following the route you will take to your chosen destination. As you scatter, say faster and faster:
Carry me from here to there,
When and how I do not care,
But make it soon,
Within three moons.
* Dip into the bowl of petals and fill your hands once more. Turn round and round in circles, repeating the chant and scattering the petals.
* When you start to feel dizzy, steady yourself, pick up the map and shake it, so that the pathway of petals flies free, and shout the chant at the top of your voice.

A spell for the destination of your dreams

This spell works for any destination, be it a holiday home in France or an expedition HQ in the Arctic Circle.

You will need
Photocopies of a picture of your dream destination.

Timing
Any.

The spell
* Put the photocopies up absolutely everywhere at home – on the backs of doors, on the front of the fridge, on your bedroom wall, inside books, as a screen saver on your computer, by the telephone, on your desk at work, in the garage, in the shed.
* Every time you see your dream destination, stop, face it and touch the image, as you do so saying:
Coming through,
Coming soon.
Loud and clear,
I shall be here.
Unexpected opportunities will arise to further your dream.

A computer drawing spell to fulfil a travel dream

If you are not very computer-literate, go on a day course to find out how to use a computer drawing program – or ask a child. Children are all computer experts.

You will need
A computer and a computer drawing program.

Timing
Any.

The spell
* Download a picture of where you want to be and insert a digicam picture of yourself or a clip art figure to represent you into the scene.
* Make the picture (with you in it) your screen saver, so that every time you start up the computer you see yourself in the place where you want to be.

A dandelion clock travel spell

You will need
Nothing.

Timing
Whenever you find a dandelion clock.

The spell
* When you find a dandelion, name your travel dream and say:
Make it true by ...
* Blow the dandelion as hard as you can, and keep on blowing until all the spores are gone. Count each blow, starting with the month after the present one. You now have a target date for the materialisation of your travel dream.

A second dandelion clock travel spell

You will need

Four dandelion clocks; a small neck or waist pouch to carry them in; a compass (optional).

Timing

On a Wednesday morning.

The spell

* Taking your dandelions, climb to the top of a hill.
* By estimating or using the compass, find the direction of your chosen destination. Face it and say:

North, South, East, West,
Take me where I love the best: (name the place).

* Spin round nine times deosil (clockwise), as you do so saying:

Far from home
May I roam,
Far to fly,
O'er sea or sky.

* Take the dandelion clocks out of the purse and, starting with your chosen direction, blow one for each direction, as you do so saying:

Fly far, fly free,
Cross land and sea.
With you I go.
Let it be so.

* Run or walk fast down the hill, as you go reciting your chosen destination as a mantra.
* When you get home, make a step, however small, towards planning your desired trip.

A toy spell to go where you want to go

This is another spell that gets the travel energies going in your life.

You will need

A toy plane, boat, train or car to represent your mode of transport; a small flag of the country you want to visit (sometimes included in packs of toy soldiers); brightly coloured beads, glass nuggets or tiny crystals; a map that includes your home and your desti-nation; a box with a lid.

Timing

On a Thursday morning.

The spell

* Set the means of transport on your home town on the map, or on the nearest airport or ferry port, pointing towards your destination. Place the toy flag on the destination.
* Make a ring of beads, glass nuggets or crystals around the mode of transport.
* Leave all in place for 24 hours and in the meantime do anything you can to advance your travel plans in the real world.
* After 24 hours, put the map; beads, glass nuggets or crystals; and means of transport in the box. Do not talk or think about the project until the next Thursday, when you should repeat the spell. Each Thursday think of some new way of advancing your trip. The spell will make this easier.

A spell for travel tickets

Whether you're on standby for a plane ticket or need to change a coach, train or ferry booking, a spell will increase the likelihood that a ticket is waiting or comes onto the system, maybe as a result of a last-minute cancellation. You may have to be adaptable, perhaps changing your route slightly or waiting an hour extra at an airport en route, but this is worth it if the need is urgent. If you carry a green aventurine crystal with tickets regularly, it will be already tuned in to your travel needs.

You will need

A green aventurine crystal.

Timing

When you urgently need to book or change a travel ticket.

The spell

* Hold the crystal in your power hand (the one you write with) as you wait for your call to connect or stand in the queue at the ticket desk. If you already have a ticket that you want to change, hold it in your receptive hand. Look at the ticket desk or picture the call centre.
* Still looking at the ticket desk or picturing the call centre, rotate the aventurine in your hand ten times widdershins (anti-clockwise) to

mentally cancel the old booking, as you do so saying:

New for old is what I need,
Not in silver or in gold,
But a ticket I can hold,
To take me to (name destination)
At (name time of departure).
I ask in need
And not in greed.

* Still looking at the ticket desk or picturing the call centre, rotate the aventurine ten times deosil (clockwise) to obtain a new booking, as you do so repeating the chant.
* If you have a ticket to exchange, look down at it, otherwise visualise a ticket, in either case picturing the new time and travel details on it.
* When you get through on the phone or reach the desk, put the aventurine in a bag or pocket on your power side. Looking into or imagining the person's eyes, smile and ask confidently for what you need.
* While the ticket clerk is checking availability, repeat the chant in your head and, if possible, touch the aventurine.
* Thank the ticket clerk and wish him or her a nice day. In return, vow in future to cancel any reservations you don't need as early as possible.

A spell for an adventure

We all have different ideas of what constitutes an adventure. For me it was a holiday totally alone in Bruges, Belgium. Although I travel a lot with my work, I had never been on holiday alone. For others it will be riding the Orient Express, cycling through Mexico or white-water rafting in the Rockies.

You will need

A special notebook (perhaps with a starry cover); a pen.

Timing

Any.

The spell

* Every single day, as soon as you wake, write in your notebook: 'I am going to ...' and name the place.
* Every time you fill a page, collect more details about your adventure, so that it keeps becoming more real. Before you have filled the book you will have made it happen.

33 SPELLS FOR MOVING HOUSE OR RENOVATING A HOME

House moving is among the most stressful of activities, ranking with divorce and giving birth. But it can also be very worthwhile, whether you are renting your first apartment, buying your first home, upgrading to a house you really like, downsizing or moving to another part of the country.

A spell can help to bring the right house into your sphere, perhaps in the form of a for sale board that you notice when you get lost out driving or your dream house coming on to the market the minute you walk in to the estate agents. A spell can also help with house sales, ensuring that a buyer who has already sold their house or can offer cash payment snaps up your home. Together with a lot of hard work, magic will help to give your house a saleability factor, making it appear warm, light and welcoming to valuers and potential buyers alike.

Magic can be very helpful in easing the transition if you are moving abroad, perhaps to satisfy a desire for a slower or more fulfilling way of life, to pursue a career or as a result of a relationship with someone from a different country. If your move is only for the duration of the winter months or for an extended summer break, again magic can help to smooth the way. Many people in colder climates now rent apartments or buy second homes in the sun.

And finally, for those who are starting out anew in the same home, this chapter includes spells for renovation and redecoration. Doing up a home can be fun or a nightmare — and is usually a mixture of the two. Spells can help to ease tensions, calm tempers, steady hands and create a pool of ingenuity for turning unexpected obstacles into desirable features.

Spells are all about making dreams come true, albeit sometimes in modified form. This is a chapter of wide horizons.

A spell to find a home to rent

This is a spell for finding your first rented accommodation, finding rented accommodation in a hurry or putting you ahead when a number of people want to rent the same property.

You will need

A box of Lego bricks; a stick of fern or frankincense incense.

Timing

An hour before the local newspaper with the to let adverts appears in the shops, or before you check Internet to let pages or phone an accommodation bureau.

The spell

* Light the incense stick and build a Lego house to represent the materialisation of your new accommodation.
* Take up the incense stick and write three times in incense smoke over the house (each time overwriting your previous words): 'No vacancy. Rented to me.'
* Leave the incense to burn through. When you find a property, put the Lego house on top of the advert (or next to the computer or phone) and repeat three times:
  No vacancy. Rented to me.
* Apply at once.

A spell for selling your home and buying a new one

Carry out this spell before each major stage in the buying and selling process. If you are buying for the first time, omit the selling symbols or adapt them, perhaps working instead towards getting a mortgage.

You will need

A picture of your current home; a picture of the property you are buying or of the kind of property you would like to buy; a tube of gold or silver glitter; a very light glue pen; a metal tray.

Timing

Early on a Wednesday morning.

The spell

* Arrange the pictures side by side on the metal tray.

* Rub a little glue over the pictures and scatter glitter on them, as you do so saying:
  Make bright this day, make glorious, bring my move closer with each dawn.
* When the glue is dry, turn the pictures over and shake any loose glitter on to the tray, as you do so repeating the chant.
* Carefully glue the two pieces of paper together, back to back, glitter outwards, as you do so saying:
  Be joined and move harmoniously to a speedy and satisfactory conclusion for everyone involved.
* When dry, keep the glued papers in your house move file or folder.

A crystal spell for attracting good energies for a possible house purchase or rental

This is a good spell to use if you are trying to rent, especially if you face a shortage of suitable apartments in the area you want. It is also effective if you are buying a house on a tight budget and cannot afford to make a high offer.

You will need

A citrine or yellow jasper crystal if you are looking to rent, or a lapis lazuli or sodalite crystal if you are looking to buy; a newspaper containing an advert for the house you want to rent or buy, or details from an estate agent.

Timing

Just before you make an appointment to view a property.

The spell

* Set out the advertisement and point the crystal downwards so that it touches the centre of the advert or picture of the house. Say three times:
  Be for me.
  Keep for me
  This property.
  So shall it be!

* Leave the crystal on the paper while you are making the appointment to view, and repeat the chant three times before you actually dial or e-mail.
* Take the crystal to the viewing in your pocket or bag. Touch the front door with it before knocking and say the chant in your head three times.
* In each room of the property, touch the crystal, point down, to a piece of furniture (keeping it in your power hand if possible). As you do so, recite the chant in your head three times. As you talk to the property owner or agent, picture the coloured light of the crystal surrounding him or her.
* When you get home, place the crystal on top of the advertisement and repeat the chant three more times. Leave the crystal on the advertisement until you hear from the vendor or agent.

A spell to secure a property that you have viewed and like

Do this spell in no more than three prospective homes.

You will need

A small stone or piece of twig from your present garden, or a small crystal or ornamental stone, not new but that has been kept in your old home.

Timing

Whenever you view a property that you like.

The spell

* When you go to view a house or apartment, take with you the small stone or twig from your present garden, or the small crystal or ornamental stone.
* If you like the property you are viewing, drop the stone or twig in the garden or leave the crystal in the hall. (You may need to be ingenious.) This will transfer something of your essence to the house and get the energies moving in your direction.
* If you visit one of the properties again, transfer another stone, twig or crystal. Continue to do so each time you visit.

A sun and moon spell for finding the right house

If you are selling as well as buying, do this spell followed by the one below.

You will need

A model house (a toy or china house, or one taken from a Monopoly set) or a tiny picture of a house (of the size and kind you would like to buy) cut from an advertisement; a road map of the area you want to move to (or if you don't have a preference, a map of the whole country); a door key from your present home; a small piece of brick; a clothes peg; a box of matches; a bath or sink plug.

Timing

At dawn, three days before the full moon.

The spell

* Place the model house on the map, on the place where you would like to live. If you don't have a preference, revolve the map nine times deosil (clockwise) and put the house down without looking. Pay attention to where the house lands. Even if the location seems unlikely, it is possible that it could enable an improvement in your life.
* Place the key underneath the model house and say:

I close the door. My new home waits. May I find it soon, before this moon is through.

* To the north of the model house place the small piece of brick (to represent the bricks and mortar of the new house) and repeat the chant.
* To the east of the house place the clothes peg (to represent washing and drying your clothes in your new garden – or on your new balcony) and repeat the chant.
* To the south of the house place the box of matches (to represent warmth or cooking in your new home) and repeat the chant.
* To the west of the house, place the plug (to represent the water in your new home) and repeat the chant.
* Leave all in place until the full moon. Each day when you wake during this period, touch the house, the key beneath it and the four symbols in order of placing them, and repeat the chant.
* On the day after the full moon, put the symbols away but continue to repeat the chant each morning when you wake. By the end of the lunar month you should have seen a house you like, perhaps quite by chance. If not, repeat the spell during the next month, beginning on the fourth day before the full moon.

A spell for selling your house

This spell can be worked in tandem with the one above.

You will need

A model house (a toy or china house, or one taken from a Monopoly set) or a tiny picture of a house (of the size and kind you would like to buy) cut from an advertisement; a map of the country; a box of pins; a magnet; a door key from your present home.

Timing

During the waning moon, at dusk.

The spell

* Set the model house on the map and rest the key on top of it (so that someone can symbolically pick it up).
* Scatter the pins over the map and say:

Come from near,
Come from far,
Come by bus and train and car.
Come over hill and across sea,
But come and buy my house from me.
I call you now.

At the word 'now', hold the magnet over the map and revolve it until you have gathered all the pins. Go on repeating the chant until all the pins are gathered and back in the box.

* Place the map, key, pins, magnet and model house on an inside window ledge until the crescent moon, by which time buyers should have arrived. If not, repeat monthly, extending the area and number of your pins.

A spell for ensuring that a house-buying chain does not break

Most house sales depend on the people above you and below you in a chain of buyers and sellers. If one party is moving too slowly, encounters financial or legal difficulties, or pulls out, everything can grind to a halt. This spell should keep things moving.

You will need

A bead with a large hole to represent each member of the chain; a cord on which to thread the beads; some cotton wool.

Timing

When you enter a house-buying chain.

The spell

* Thread the beads on the cord, as you do so saying continuously:

Round and round dependently;
Your success relies on me;
My success depends on you.
Together we will all win through.

* Tie the ends of the cord to form a circle and touch each bead on the cord, as you do so repeating the chant.
* Wrap the bead circle in the cotton wool and leave it somewhere out of sight until the new house is yours.
* Hang the beads in your new home as a charm.

A spell for when a house-buying chain breaks or stalls

This spell can be used if the preceding one fails. Should a random event or a change of mind on the part of someone in the chain threaten to break it apart, this spell will attract a new buyer to replace the missing link quickly. It will also get things moving again if there is a temporary delay.

You will need
A white candle; a bead circle made by doing the previous spell.

Timing
If someone pulls out of the chain or there is a temporary delay.

The spell
* Light the candle.
* Unknot the necklace and remove from one end the same number of beads as the number of vendors or buyers who have pulled out or are causing delays (whether or not it is their fault).
* Pass each of these beads carefully over the candle flame and say:
Be cleansed and restored that the circle of continuity may be resumed once more.
* Return the beads to the necklace and re-knot the cord, repeating the chant.
* Touch each bead on the renewed chain, as you do so saying:
Round and round dependently;
Your success relies on me;
My success depends on you.
Together we will all win through.
* Return the necklace to the cotton wool in which it is kept.

A magnet and pin spell to speed slow-moving legal matters

Even when all is going well with a house sale or purchase, paperwork, local land searches and solicitors' negotiations can cause frustrating delays. This is a speeding-up spell.

You will need
10 pins in a box; a magnet; a piece of paper; a pen; a pot of marigolds.

Timing
When progress is slow in a property sale or purchase.

The spell
* Using the paper and pen, draw a plan of your current home and a plan of the one you hope to buy, side by side. Write the name or address of each house beneath it.
* Place a straight line of pins between the two houses.
* Taking the magnet in your power hand (the one you write with), say:
Move closer, home of mine, step by step, day by day, until within your walls I live contentedly.
* Using the magnet, pick up the pin furthest away from your present home and drop it into the box, as you do so repeating the chant.
* Continue to pick up the pins and chant, working inwards towards your present home, until the pathway has gone.
* Set the marigolds (a flower associated with the positive resolution of legal matters) by the box of pins.
* Each day throw away a pin and repeat the chant. When all the pins are gone, things should be moving speedily to a positive resolution.

A spell for moving to the countryside or seaside – or from the countryside to the city

Home moves can involve a change of lifestyle. Much as you want to get away from the town – or conversely to live near theatres, shops and museums – the change may be more stressful than moving within the same environment. Magic can help to ease the transition. This is a more complex version of the spell to secure a property on page 441.

You will need

One of the following: a brown candle (for a move to the city), a blue candle (for a move to the sea), a green candle (for a move to the countryside); 2 very small identical turquoise or lapis lazuli crystals.

Timing

On the first of the month, before noon.

The spell

* Light the candle and say:

Far or near, I carry my home in my heart.
Though different now my life will be,
I carry all I need with me.

* Take up a turquoise or lapis lazuli (both empowering and protective crystals) in either hand and pass them simultaneously around the candle in circling movements, both deosil (clockwise) and widdershins (anti-clockwise), as your hands weave the pattern reciting the chant softly.

* When you next visit the new area in which you are going to live, take one of the crystals with you and bury it somewhere beautiful. Even in the centre of cities there are wildlife gardens and squares. As you do so, recite the chant.

* When you leave your old home for good, bury the second crystal in your old garden or somewhere near the house as a symbol of the memories you carry in your heart. As you do so, recite the chant for the last time.

A spell to downsize your property

There are many reasons for moving to a smaller or cheaper home: because children have left home, because we need to free up money for travel or a second home abroad, or because financial problems or a divorce require that we start again. This is a spell filled with hope. It works on the basis that we can fill our home with joy and security no matter how modest (or lavish) it is.

You will need

2 golden-brown candles; a small picture of your present home; a brown drawstring bag; some dried leaves or petals from your present garden or a potted plant you will be leaving; an agate in sandy-brown; an agate in soft-brown; a tiny dish of salt; a tray.

Timing

On a Saturday evening, before you move.

The spell

* Working in the kitchen, light one of the candles. Place it on the tray and set around it the other spell ingredients.

* Place a pinch of salt (for protection and abundance in your new home) in the bag, and then fill the bag with the picture, the leaves or petals and the agate.

* When you have finished, say:

I made my home a special place, haven and sanctuary.

* Close the sachet and pass it once deosil (clockwise) around the candle flame, as you do so saying:
I have packed all I need, for I must travel light of heart and mind.
* Leave the candles to burn down.
* When you pack to move, make the sachet and the tray the last items in a box or bag that will be unpacked first at your new home.
* As soon as you can after you have arrived at your new home, light the other brown candle in your new kitchen. Tip the contents of the brown bag out onto the tray and say:
I make my new home a special place, haven and sanctuary.
* Except for the picture, bury the contents of the bag in the new garden, as you do so saying:
I have packed all I need.
I have travelled light of heart and mind,
And peace now find.
Keep the picture as a memento.

A spell to find a permanent holiday apartment or home overseas

Moving abroad permanently or even for part of the year is a very big step. However, many people do find a slower or more fulfilling lifestyle hundreds or even thousands of miles from their original home. This spell will help you find the impetus to move the horizons of possibility and turn a fortnight in the sun into a whole winter or even a lifetime there.

You will need

4 incense sticks in one or more citrus fragrances, such as orange, lemon, lime or grapefruit (or, if you are planning to live somewhere cool, apple blossom or strawberry); incense-holders you can stand on the floor; a bowl of fresh petals or freshly chopped herbs (from your garden if possible); a bowl of water.

Timing

On a cloudy afternoon.

The spell

* If possible, push the furniture away from the walls of the room you are working in.
* Set an incense stick in a holder midway along each wall.
* Put the bowl of petals and the bowl of water in the centre of the room.
* Light the incense sticks, starting with the one furthest away from you, as you light each stick saying:
May the winds of change blow away stagnation and carry me to fulfilment.
* Take the first incense stick you lit out of the holder and plunge it into the bowl of water in the centre of the room, as you do so saying:
I remove one wall that divides me from the fulfilment of my dream.
* Scatter petals along the whole wall where the first incense stick stood, as you do so saying:
I walk the path to happiness.
* Repeat the previous two steps with the three other incense sticks.
* Each evening for a week, light a single incense stick and repeat all the spell chants in order. This will keep the energies moving.

A spell for the renovation and redecoration of your home

Whether you are having major renovations done by a team of builders or you are imprinting your personal style on your first home, building and decorating can be both exciting and fraught. Magic can help to enhance your creativity and to create calm and positive vibes so that spills and minor accidents are avoided and the work becomes a pleasure — or at least bearable. If possible, avoid decorating during the waning moon, when we are naturally more irritable and accident-prone. Instead, start work near the beginning of the moon cycle for a less hyperactive and more creative approach.

You will need

Chamomile or rosewood essential oil and an oil-burner, or a stick of lilac, strawberry or rose incense; 5 small grey candles; a small hand mirror.

Timing

The night before the work begins (preferably near the beginning of the moon cycle).

The spell

❁ Sit in the first room or area that is to be redecorated or renovated and light the oil burner or incense. Place the candles in a circle in the centre of the room and light them.

❁ Use the mirror to reflect the beams of the candle over the walls and on to the ceiling, as you do so saying:
Nought harm,
Peace calm.
We will make new from old,
Our gifts unfold
And silver beams turn into gold.

❁ Extinguish the candles and sit quietly in the darkness, breathing in the fragrance of the oil or incense until it is burnt through.

A spell to bring lasting luck to a home that is being renovated or redecorated

This spell is an age-old tradition.

You will need

A little paint in a colour that can be painted over, or a penknife or other engraving tool.

Timing

When the walls have been stripped.

The spell

❁ Using the paint, write your family name on the bare walls. Alternatively, if furniture is being assembled, scratch your family name underneath one of the legs or drawers to bring fortune to the redecorated room.

A spell to bless your new home

When you have moved into a new house it may not feel like yours, even with your furniture in place. This is because it is still imprinted with the lives of the people who lived there before or, if new, with the imprint of the builders and decorators. You can make the home yours by carrying out this simple imprinting ritual.

You will need

A sage or cedar smudge stick or a large stick of sage or cedar incense; 4 items of sentimental value; one item bought specially for the new house.

Timing

The day after you move in, in the morning.

The spell

* Place one of the items of sentimental value in each of the four corners of your home saying at each:

May this home be blessed and become my/our home and a place of happiness and tranquillity.

* Set the new item as close to the centre of the house as possible and repeat the chant.
* Light the incense or smudge stick and, beginning outside the back door, go into each hallway, corridor and room in turn and stand in the centre. In incense smoke in each place, write your name or the family one in the air, as you do so repeating the chant. End at the front door.
* Take the smudge outdoors and extinguish it in the earth or in a pot of soil or sand.
* You can adapt the ritual if you have only one external entrance, beginning and ending at the same place.

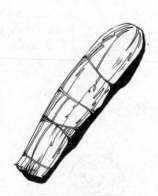

34 SPELLS FOR CHANGES AT WORK AND RETIREMENT

A career path, from first job to retirement, may follow a gentle upward trajectory with gentle natural transitions. In other cases, however, the route may be marked by a spectacular early rise to success, by several false starts or by a career change half way.

If you lose your job, whether through redundancy or dismissal, your self-esteem may plummet, and it can be hard to get back in to the job market, especially if you are fighting an unfair dismissal case. Spells can give you the confidence and stamina to make a successful recovery after reversal. They can also open you to all kinds of positive energies, thus helping you to adapt to small changes as well as major ones and enabling you to follow the path you choose rather than one imposed by others.

Part 3 of this book consists of spells for success at work. The spells in this chapter focus on changes and transitions within the career path, including career breaks and retraining.

A spell for a first or new job

No matter how experienced you are, starting a new job can be stressful. We have probably all experienced the feeling of walking into an unfamiliar setting where all eyes seem to be on us. A first job or a return to work after a career break or dismissal needs an extra boost of self-confidence. A little magic will help you to sail through the first and subsequent days. This spell is effective for all new beginnings career-wise.

You will need
A new item of clothing (with a sales tag still attached) that you will wear to work on the first day (it need only be small, for example a pair of gloves); a pair of scissors.

Timing
The morning of your first day at work.

The spell
* Cut the tag off the item of clothing and say:
  On with the new, off with the old.
  This day I know will be pure gold.
  Off with the old, on with the new.
  This job I know I can do.
* Put on the clothing and recite the rhyme three more times.

A spell for a child's first job or work experience

A child's first job can be as stressful for the parent as for the suddenly grown-up child, and advice may only make the child more nervous. This spell ensures they carry your positive energies with them, even though you cannot be there.

You will need
Shoe cleaning materials; the shoes the child will be wearing for work.

Timing
The night before the first day at work.

The spell
* Polish the shoes, saying softly and repetitively as you rub:
  Tomorrow you will shine, my child.
  The day will turn out right, my child.
  Your future will be bright.
  And so my care I send to you
  Until the day is through.

A spell for starting a new job in the same workplace

If you win promotion within your company or get moved to another department, it may be hard for people to accept your new role at first — especially if you have to give orders to friends and former co-workers and assess their work. A spell can help to alter the aura, or psychic energy, around you so that you slip naturally into the new position. It is bit like overwriting a computer file: you keep the essence but change the format and emphasis.

You will need
A green candle; a grey candle; a blue candle; a lapis lazuli, turquoise or blue goldstone (blue with golden glittery lights like stars in the night sky) crystal.

Timing
After dusk on the day you start your new job.

The spell
* Light the green candle (for how you were). Light the grey candle (for transition) from the green one and place it to the right of the green candle. Light the blue candle (for your new work persona) from the grey one, and place it in the centre of the other two candles. As you light the candles, say:

One, two, three,
You can't see me
As I was once before.
Two, three, four,
You know the score.
What I can be
Is what you see.

* Pass the crystal slowly in a straight line over each of the candles in turn, as you do so repeating the words.
* Blow out the green candle, then the grey one and leave the blue one to burn through, with the crystal placed in front of it.
* Take the crystal to work and keep it in your workspace. If you encounter problems, hold the crystal and recite the words in your head.

A wind balloon spell for going back to work after a career break

Whether you have been at home bringing up a family, studying, off sick or unemployed, this spell will give you the impetus to enter the workplace once more with enthusiasm and confidence.

You will need
3 silver helium balloons.

Timing
When the wind is blowing, preferably from the East.

The spell
* Go to a high or open place and let the wind blow all around you, so that it fills your clothes.
* Hold the balloons in your power hand (the one you write with) and feel them tugging eagerly to be away. As you resist the pull, say:

Go into the world,
Your power unfurled.
May I too rise towards the skies
So I can be me,
But gloriously.

* Release each balloon one after the other, pausing only to shout the words into the wind as you let go of each balloon.
* Stand for a while and let the wind power fill you.

A spell for learning new skills in the workplace

On page 166 I give a spell for learning new technology. This spell will help if the nature of your job suddenly changes. This may be because a computer system replaces manual forms of data processing, because an automated phone system is introduced or because a more up-to-date till is installed. This spell will also help if you have to retrain completely because your job has suddenly disappeared or changed radically.

You will need
A silver candle; a silver pendant or piece of jewellery you can wear at work.

Timing
The night before your training starts. (Wear the jewellery for 24 hours before you perform the spell.)

The spell
* Light the candle and face it, holding the silver jewellery in your power hand (the one you write with).
* Breathe in the silver candle light, slowly and audibly drawing in breath through your nose. Pause a moment and then blow the 'silver' breath out over the jewellery.
* Repeat the previous step twice more, making the in- and out-breaths even slower and the pause between them longer.
* Hold the jewellery up so that the candle light sparkles on it and say three times:
  So shines my new ability within me and from me for all to see. I welcome this change confidently.
* Leave the jewellery in front of the candle until the candle is burnt down.
* Put on the jewellery and wear it continuously for as long as you are training. Touch it and repeat the chant in your head before beginning each lesson.
* Repeat the spell at any time you doubt your ability.

A spell for coping with a takeover or new management

Takeovers can bring welcome new practices and profitability to a stagnant or ailing workplace. But inevitably there will be fears of job losses or unwelcome changes, especially if you have worked for the old firm for a number of years. This spell will help you to flow with the tide and seize new opportunities.

You will need
The sea, a jacuzzi or a swimming pool with a wave machine (or stand close to one of the water outlets).

Timing
At a weekend, during the month before the takeover.

The spell
* Stand or sit where you can feel the movement of the water but it does not threaten to knock you over.
* Ripple your hands and feet in the waves and say ten times:
  I move with the times and yet remain secure.
* Shift yourself so that the water pressure on you increases a little and then repeat the chant. Do this ten times, so that you gradually become accustomed to more movement, remaining within your own safe limits.
* After the tenth repetition, say:
  I did not fall under pressure. Come one, come all, for I will cope and thrive.
* Enjoy yourself in the water.

A spell to bring about change in the workplace

Whether you own the company or are the most junior worker, you may want changes, whether to your own particular working conditions, salary and opportunities or as part of a more organised expression of dissatisfaction among the workforce. Try doing this spell before a personal interview or union meeting to change pay or conditions or to put right an injustice. Practise using the remote control car before you do the spell, in order to avoid any collisions.

You will need

A child's remote control car.

Timing

For the three days before the interview or negotiations.

The spell

* Stand in the middle of a room and drive the car slowly towards the wall, as you do so saying:

Towards the wall
Do matters fall,
Course set for collision.
Yet paths can turn, minds can learn
To mend these false divisions.
The matter shall be resolved amicably and
favourably to me/us.
So shall it be!

* Turn the car away from the wall and move it in circles, as you do so saying:
Round in circles, arguing, getting nowhere fast.
Better to negotiate and move ahead at last.
The matter shall be resolved amicably and
favourably to me/us.
So shall it be!

* Take the car outdoors and move it around in all directions, avoiding any obstacles.

* Repeat the preceding steps on the two following days. Say the chants in your head before any negotiations.

A spell to move on from redundancy or unfair dismissal

On pages 385–6 I gave a spell for overcoming a lack of confidence caused by unfair dismissal or redundancy. This spell is for the next stage: fighting your case or getting back out into the job marketplace.

You will need

A large dried galangal or lovage root; a kitchen knife; a small purple bag; the Justice card from a tarot pack if there is a legal or union dispute, or the Hierophant or Pope card if you are trying to get a new job.

Timing

In the late evening, when you want to get a job or fight your case.

The spell

* Working by a dim light or an outside street light, chop the root up into small pieces and set it in a deosil (clockwise) circle around the tarot card, as you do so saying:
Be as advocate to me, that I may see justice
and reparation/restoration) ask for both if
you want both).

* Put one piece of root, together with the tarot card, in the purple bag and keep it somewhere dark.

* Each evening, add another piece of root to the bag, until all are used or the matter is progressing.

* Take the bag, carefully hidden, to any official hearing, solicitor's meeting or job interview.

A spell for making the transition into a career break

People give up work, either temporarily or permanently, for many reasons — illness, a return to college, parenthood or the growing dependency of a relative. Others give up work because of stress or because they hate their job so much they would prefer to be unemployed. Some younger people have a number of intervals between jobs before finding their niche. Career breaks involve both loss and liberation, so a rite of passage spell can be helpful in dealing with the change.

You will need

A quiet place where there is long grass and trees.

Timing

In the early afternoon.

The spell

* Begin to pick grass stalks, for each one saying a line of the following chant before you cast the stalk away. Go on picking stalks until you have spoken the whole chant:
  Loss and liberation,
  Freedom and regret.
  I cast away loss and regret
  And hold to me freedom and liberation from my former world.
  As I stand at the doors of change,
  I open the doors and enter willingly.
  So shall it be until I return,
  Be I a month, a year
  Or evermore away.
* Pick up nine small stones or tiny twigs, one for each line of the chant. Take them home and keep them as a symbol of what has been gained by the change.

A spell for a happy retirement

Retirement can be a shock, not only for the retired person but also for their partner. However, with people staying healthier much longer, retirement can also be the beginning of the best part of life. This spell will help you to switch from a work to a personal time frame.

You will need

An alarm clock; a watch, mobile phone or calculator with a bleeper.

Timing

On the evening after your last day at work and the first morning of your retirement.

The spell

* On the evening after your last day of work, set the alarm to go off at the usual work time, but turn off the ringer.
* When you wake up (naturally) the next morning say:
  I do not live by work time. I make my own time now.
* Set the bleeper on the watch, mobile phone or calculator to go off at regular intervals during the day. Each time it bleeps, repeat the chant and for this one day do something you really want to do until the next bleep (if what you really want to do is nothing, that's fine).
* Set your alarm clock to ring at the time you used to leave work. When it goes off, let it ring and ring.
* When the alarm clock finally stops ringing, repeat the chant and put the clock away in a drawer until it is needed to wake you for a personal or second career venture.

A spell for early retirement

Early retirement is an option sometimes taken by people in their fifties who may have worked for the same company all their lives and now want to do something different while they are still young enough. Companies also use it as an incentive for older staff to leave with a smaller assured pension, so that compulsory redundancies can be avoided in difficult times. This is a very optimistic spell, designed to reduce fears about the future, especially if the retirement was only half-willing. It will help you to avoid feeling regretful and sidelined. You will need to find the right place in advance of doing this spell, so that you can go there on a sunny day. Castles, stately homes and formal gardens often have the kind of path you need, or you may find one in a local area of woodland.

You will need

A straight path along a tree-lined avenue, leading to bright sunlight.

Timing

In bright sunlight.

The spell

* Walk along the pathway towards the light and say:
  The way opens without sorrow.
  I look for joy in tomorrow.
* When you reach the light at the end of the trees, turn deosil (clockwise) three times, as you do so repeating the chant.
* Look back, only once, and say:
  I need go no more there. Mine is the open horizon of endless possibility. I embrace it welcomingly.
* Symbolically push the darkness back down the path with your hands, palms vertical and facing outwards. Then turn to face the sun again.
* Walk as far as you can ahead before hitting a barrier or enclosed or dark area. Go back a different way so you do not walk along the original path.
* Try to stay in open areas unless it is too hot. Enjoy the rest of the day in the sun, and when you get home plan a pleasurable trip for the day after you officially retire.

A spell to cope with a company closure

If you are unlucky enough to have your company, or even industry, close or radically shed staff, this spell will help to get you out from under the cloud and moving towards a new job as fast as possible.

You will need

A box of children's coloured bricks.

Timing

As soon as you get notice of the closure.

The spell

* Build a very unsteady tower of bricks.
* Give the tower a push and as it falls snatch a single brick. Hold it in your hands and say:
  It could not last. Yet did I not fall with it.
* Build a new tower, this time of double thickness, with the salvaged brick forming part of the foundations. Say:
  So I rise again anew and climb towards security.
* Prepare your CV and find out about possible openings so that you are ahead of the crowd when the firm you work for closes.

A spell to give confidence to a mother returning to the workplace

Being a mother is probably the hardest job of all. It involves not only many skills but also infinite patience, stamina and the ability to carry out several tasks at once. This is why mothers make such good workers. However, as I know from personal experience, it is all too easy to lose confidence in your abilities while you are caring for children and not in paid employment. Mothering is given a low status in our society, and women may fear that they will not be able to cope with a child or children plus a job away from the home. This spell will help to boost your confidence, giving you a much more realistic view of your own, incredible value and talent.

You will need

Paper and a pen.

Timing

Every morning for a week before returning to work.

The spell

* On the first morning of the spell, as close as possible to the time you will begin work, write down all the things you did in the previous 24 hours.
* Read the list aloud and say:
  I coped yesterday and I will cope today. I can cope with anything.
* Tear the list into tiny pieces and throw it away, saying nine times:
  I can cope with anything.
* Repeat for five more mornings.
* On the morning before you go to work, write the list and then, before reading it, cross out all the chores or childcare you will not be doing while you are at work.
* Read out only the remaining items and say:
  I coped yesterday and I will cope today. Tomorrow I can cope with anything.
* Keep this list and pin it where the daylight will shine on it.
* Next day, as you are leaving for work, put the list unread at the bottom of your bag and say:
  I can cope with anything.
* If you feel especially nervous at work, read the list and see how many things you crossed off. Say to yourself nine times:
  I can cope with anything.
* Just before going home, tear the list up and throw it away at work, as you do so saying to yourself:
  I coped.

PART 7

Spells for Health and Healing

Throughout the ages, spiritual healing and magic have been closely entwined, with healers making use of ritual and ceremony to draw down power from higher sources to trigger the patient's own self-healing powers. Few witches would claim to heal solely by their own powers; rather they would say that they work with goddess/god energies, amplified by the powers of nature.

It is only in the modern world that spiritual healing has become a specialised art. In fact, anyone who rubs a child's hurt knee better, soothes a family member's brow when it is aching or offers a friend a hug in consolation is transmitting healing energies. For me, a spiritual healer is someone who practises positive healing work, and it doesn't matter whether they call themselves a Witch, a Druid, a Christian Scientist or adopt no title at all.

Modern research in America would seem to validate the effectiveness of magical healing. Dr Herbert Benson, a Harvard Medical School professor and founder of the Mind/Body Medical Institute at Deaconess Hospital in Boston, started his research 30 years ago. He comments:

> By repeating prayers, words or sounds and passively disregarding other thoughts, many people are able to trigger a specific set of physiological changes. Invoking prayers or mantras over and over can lower the rate of breathing and brain wave activity, sometimes healing what ails you and averting the need for invasive surgery or expensive medicine.

The spells in this section are taken from a variety of cultures and have all proved powerful. But the key to both face-to-face and absent healing is a genuine desire to help and a willingness to offer your time and energies to channel health-giving powers from the natural world and whoever you call your God/Goddess.

35 SPELLS FOR HEALING YOURSELF, YOUR FAMILY AND YOUR FRIENDS

Most of the spells in this chapter involve contact healing. This does not necessarily mean that they involve touching the patient, be it with hands or with a crystal, rather that the patient is present during the healing and interacts with you. Unless you know a person well, it is probably preferable not touch them, or to touch only non-intimate parts of the body (I include the face and stomach in the intimate category), although some people do enjoy gentle touches to the back, head or hands. For these spells ordinary indoor clothing is always worn and you can stand or sit several centimetres or more away from the patient if they are sensitive about personal space.

Some of the tools suggested in this chapter, for example pyramids and pendulums, also appear in Chapter 36, on absent healing, because they are so effective for healing of all kinds. I have written about healing animals and birds in Chapter 43 and about healing plants in Chapter 38, but in practice you can just as well use the spells in this chapter – and vice versa.

Some of the spells in this chapter are intended for use on yourself, while others require the interaction of two people. Whatever the nature of the spell, however, it will involve a degree of self-healing. Indeed, activating your own inner healing powers to heal yourself is what this chapter is really all about. Many professional healers first discovered their powers when healing themselves and only then went on to take formal training.

An opaque crystal pyramid spell to absorb a pain or relieve backache, rheumatism or arthritis

Much healing magic derives from ancient Egyptian times. While it therefore carries the authority of history, like all good magic it has evolved to fit the changing needs of different generations.

Both the actual pyramids and the scale models, especially of the squat Pyramid of Cheops built at Giza, near Cairo, around 2500 BCE, have been shown in experiments to reduce stress, anxiety, insomnia, and cigarette and alcohol dependency in adults, as well as hyperactivity in children. They also mitigate pain, relieve sore throats, speed the healing of wounds and cuts, aid digestion, reduce the intensity and frequency of migraines, and lessen PMS and menstrual problems. But despite research by such bodies as the University of St Petersburg in Russia, no-one can fully explain the source of this power. Try the pyramid spells in this and the other chapters in this section with an open mind. You may be surprised at the results.

This is quite a modern spell, although the ideas and myths behind it are very old. It is effective for healing yourself, a friend or a relative and will relieve a single area of pain or more general discomfort. The chant refers to the blue phoenix-like Benu bird, a form of the creator God Atum, who rose from the pyramid-shaped mound that emerged from the primal waters at the first dawn. Nut, the sky mother, absorbed Ra, the sun god, nightly in to her womb, to be reborn the next day. Pyramids were a replica of this first mound. Pyramid spells often trigger spontaneous words, especially when used for direct healing, so feel free to change the formula I have suggested for this and other pyramid spells.

You will need
A set of small opaque squat pyramids with a square base (often sold in sets of three, made of black basalt, calcite or soapstone and available from gift shops and museum shops); a dark-grey or brown candle, or – if you can get one – a dark beeswax candle (traditional and very magical); a stick of lotus, lily, rose, sandalwood or hibiscus incense; a deep bowl of water.

Timing
Before sleep or bed rest.

The spell
* Arrange the pyramids in a triangle around the candle, so that the largest pyramid forms the apex. (The triangle is sacred to the Osiris, the Egyptian father god; Isis, the mother goddess; and Horus their sky god son.)
* Light the candle and from it the lotus, lily, rose, sandalwood or hibiscus incense stick (all ancient Egyptian fragrances).
* Working around the pyramids, use the incense smoke to trace the outline of a triangle three times, as you do so, saying:
  Pyramid power at this hour, take away pain.
  Pain, rise to the skies like the Benu bird on the first dawn from the first pyramid mound.
  Pain, rise with the smoke and be gone into the night womb of Mother Nut, to be restored in the morn as strength and vitality.
* Plunge the incense stick into the water (representing the primal waters that existed before creation), as you do so saying:
  Pain, return to the waters of forgetfulness, there also to rest.

- Place the three pyramids under the bed, if the pain is general in a triangular formation with the largest pyramid beneath the bedhead and the other two pyramids at the edges of the bed. If there is a particular area of pain, place the pyramids in a small triangle pointing upwards at the painful spot. If the patient is up and sitting in a chair during the day, place the pyramids beneath the chair.
- Wash the pyramids weekly for continuing effect and re-empower them when you sense that it is necessary.

A spell to help you keep a positive attitude in illness and thereby encourage healing

A daily spell can help you to focus your own self-healing powers and will act as a reminder that you are still yourself and not the illness.

You will need
Sheets of white paper; a selection of crayons in rainbow colours; a black pencil.

Timing
Every day of the illness, when you get up.

The spell
- On day one, draw an outline of a figure and cover it with black dots.
- Crayon over the dots with different colours. When you have finished, say six times:
  Today I will feel better, and tomorrow I will recover even more.
- Throw away the paper.
- Each day, draw fewer and fainter black dots and make the colours brighter and more intense. Repeat the chant six times and throw away the paper.
- When, after a number of days, you have no more dots to draw, just colour the figure and repeat the words six times. The spell is done.

A clear crystal pyramid spell for healing a specific illness or pain in another person

If it is not a bright day when you do this spell, hang crystal mobiles from the windows and light four golden-coloured candles in a semi-circle behind the crystal pyramid, so that their light falls on it.

You will need

A squat pyramid of the kind found at Giza (see illustration below), made of crystal, glass or any transparent or semi-transparent material.

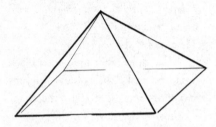

Timing

If possible, when there is bright sunlight.

The spell

* Place the pyramid in the sunlight (but make sure it does not get too hot, as crystals can concentrate light enough to set fire to paper).
* Sit side by side with the person you are healing, both of you facing the source of light and the pyramid, so that your healing energy as well as that of the sun passes through the pyramid.
* Place the index finger of your receptive hand (the one you don't write with) on or close to the point of the pyramid. The person to be healed should do likewise with the index finger of their power hand. Alternatively, each place your index finger on opposite sloping sides. Join your power hand to the patient's receptive hand to create a circuit.
* Begin to speak spontaneously – the words will flow, even if you are normally shy. Ask that higher healing energies may flow in to and through you and the crystal, and then in to the patient, enabling healing to occur. Name the patient and his or her problem. Allow words to come as they will. You may find yourself talking about crystalline pyramids, spheres of sunlight, brilliant blue skies, the blue Nile and the yellow desert stretching endlessly. Healers who have never been to Egypt often create vivid pictures of the country, maybe from some ancient memory. Your patient may add images of his or her own, and the pyramid may seem to fill with light.
* As you sense the power ebbing, allow your words likewise to trail into silence. Sit quietly, and when you are ready gently remove your finger from the crystal. Your patient will do the same in his or her own time.
* Make time to talk with the patient about the experience.
* Wash the crystal under running water, splashing water on your hands, wrists and temples to purify yourself of any negative energy that you may have picked up from the illness or sorrow.

A crystal pyramid spell for reducing personal stress levels or alleviating anxiety that is making a medical condition worse

Although this spell is primarily intended to be worked on yourself, I have found that it will also help a child who is hyperactive or has Asperger's Syndrome to settle if you share the pathway with them, describing the path and the scenes in a slow mesmeric voice. You can invite the child to trace the outline of the path to the pyramid with a finger – you may be surprised at how gentle they are with the crystal (but help them to support the crystal in case their concentration lapses). This is also a good spell for banishing phobias and irrational fears.

You will need
A semi-transparent crystal pyramid (it need only be small); a fibre optic or lava lamp (don't use the latter with a child as lava lamps can get very hot).

Timing
As the light fades from the sky.

The spell
* Hold the pyramid between your hands (or ask the child to do so). Looking at it through half-closed eyes, turn it to catch different angles of light, as you do so identifying a pathway within and in your head following it. (You can describe the pathway and the scenes around it to a child, encouraging them to add their own vision.) As you walk along the path, say:
I carry my burden along the road towards the door. I walk slowly. It is heavy but soon it will be gone and I will walk lightly home.
* Picture a door in the centre of the pyramid opening to reveal the inside, with beautiful pictures on the wall of Pharaohs hunting, feasts, white temples, huge cattle ploughing the green strips of fields and the blue Nile fringed by reeds. Say:
I open the door but do not enter. I have my own world. I leave my burden at the door. It is gone.
* Name the burdens you are leaving – for example, stressful people or situations that bring on a migraine, compulsions, obsessions and fears triggered by situations that seem out of control. A child may name things like noise, bright lights, fighting, Dad shouting. You can help him or her to identify burdens.
* When you have finished, see the light fading and hands taking the burdens inside. The door closes and you walk back down the, now star-lit, crystalline path in peace.
* You may need to repeat the spell several times. Each time the burden will become lighter to carry.

An ancient Egyptian water spell to heal yourself or others of skin irritations and allergies, cuts, burns, wounds and internal lesions or inflammation

Most famous of the many ancient Egyptian spells and rituals that have passed down into modern magic is one originally centred on stelae, ornamental stone tablets showing the young sky god Horus trampling on crocodiles. At the base of each stela, was a bowl that caught the water that was ritually poured over the figure of Horus. In each hand Horus held fierce creatures such as crocodiles, scorpions and lions.

Though originally intended to cure snake and scorpion stings, the power of the Horus water healing extended to any injury or accident, skin problems, wounds, burns and allergies. The invalid drank or bathed in the water that had flowed over the stela, thus absorbing the magical power. Healing spells were written on the back of the stelae, which were spoken to activate the magic as the water was poured. The words in this spell come from a healing tablet dating from about 300 BCE, though the spell has been adapted for modern use.

This spell is also effective for healing inner stings and wounds that have been inflicted by other people and that have left us feeling hurt or devastated. There are human scorpions in many people's lives – or you may carry old wounds, for instance from parental coldness or a cruel lover, that have never fully healed. Horus is also represented in Egyptian magic by a falcon or hawk, so you could use a small model of one to do this spell – or draw the image of a bird of prey on a stone. The spell is lovely performed outdoors under trees.

You will need

A small statue of Horus or a favourite deity from any culture, or a stone – use the picture on page 324 to trace Horus on to it; a shallow stone or ceramic dish, broad enough to stand your statue or stone in; a large jug filled with still mineral water.

Timing

In the early morning.

The spell

* Place the statue or stone in the dish and stand it on the ground.
* Pour the water from the jug over the statue, as you do so, naming the illness or the physical or emotional pain and saying seven times:

Horus (or the name of the deity you are using), protect me against the wild creatures of the desert, the crocodiles of the river, the snakes and scorpions, the insects that sting fiercely with their tail and reptiles waiting in their holes to strike.

If you face regular spite or hostility (be it at work, from neighbours or from family members) that causes you ongoing mental distress or triggers stress-related illnesses or allergies, add the following final line to the chant:

May my heel be bronze and the ball of my foot ivory.

(The idea is that if your heel is bronze and your foot ivory, stings cannot harm you whether from human or more conventional scorpions.)

* Sprinkle a little of the water on your brow and your wrists and, if it is not too painful, close to the area of pain or discomfort. If it is an inner sorrow, anoint the centre of your forehead with the water. Visualise Horus and a flock of fierce birds driving away your hurt.
* Pour the rest of the water on plants in your garden or elsewhere.

A spell for healing a child

Children are very easy to heal, because they are so open to healing energies. If they join in the spell, they usually rapidly trigger off their own innate self-healing powers. This spell can also be useful before a hospital stay or tests. You can take the crystal with you and gently massage the child with it if they become anxious. When healing a baby, you can dispense with the crystal and use the power from your own fingertips, touching the baby's heart and visualising the rays passing to the painful or unsettled part of their body.

You will need

A round smooth rose quartz, yellow or green calcite or fluorite crystal; a candle the same colour as the crystal, in an enclosed holder filled with sand.

Timing

Before the child's bedtime, so that the healing process can continue while the child sleeps.

The spell

* Set the crystal where the child can see it and light the candle so that the light reflects within the crystal.
* With your palms downwards, move the fingers of each of your hands very fast over the crystal until you can feel the light entering your fingertips. Work with both hands simultaneously.
* Touch the child's heart very gently with the fingertips of both your hands and ask the child to picture the rays of warm light moving in to his or her heart.
* Remove your fingers and ask the child to place his or her fingers on their heart and then to shake the fingertips and imagine sparks of crystal light all around them.
* Now invite the child to gently touch any parts of their body that are hurting or feel unwell, and let the light from their fingertips flow into that place.
* Blow out the candle together and send any remaining light back into the crystal.
* Leave the crystal at the child's bedside to continue to transmit healing rays during the night.
* In the morning, wash the crystal under running water and, if necessary, use the candle to recharge it the next night at bedtime.

A pendulum spell to heal yourself using the forces of nature

A crystal pendulum is an excellent tool to incorporate into healing spells. When moved over a troublesome or painful area or passed over the whole body it will tune into energy blockages, places where vitality has drained away, and tangles of pain and tension. By moving the pendulum widdershins (anti-clockwise) you can remove the obstruction or pain, and by moving it clockwise get the life force flowing again. A spell works in conjunction with the pendulum by tuning the mind and spirit into the powers all around (in this case the powers of the natural world) that amplify our own innate healing ability. Indeed, these powers are themselves strengthened by the action of the pendulum.

According to both feng shui and Western geomancy, currents of energy are all around us, some negative and some positive. By using your pendulum to tune into positive forces emanating from trees, flowers or flowing surface water, you can receive an amplified form of the life force that is present in all living matter. The early medieval mystic Hildegard von Bingen described this force as 'the greening power'.

Though this is a self-healing spell, you can use it to heal others by circling their bodies with the pendulum after filling it with power. This method works well with people to whom you are physically and emotionally close and is especially effective against exhaustion or depression. It can also cleanse the system of negative build-up if you or the patient has to work in a polluted, noisy or high-tech atmosphere. Perform the spell in a green, open space, preferably deep in the countryside and near a stream. Alternatively, work in your garden, a town square or a park – especially good if there is a pool whose water flows in and out.

You will need
A crystal pendulum (available from New Age stores).

Timing
During daylight.

The spell
* As you stand in the green open space, identify in your head your most urgent health need. Then identify other, less pressing but still significant, concerns about your well-being and energy levels.
* Holding the pendulum in your power hand (the one you write with) and in front of you in any way that feels comfortable, circle a tree, bush or flowerbed. Allow the pendulum to swing in its own way, and say:

Greening power,
Greening shower,
Power of flower,
Leaf and tree,
Greening power,
Greening shower,
As I turn,
Your light on me.

As you speak the last line, hold the pendulum higher so that the light catches it.
* Now stand with your feet still and twirl the pendulum around your head and up and down your body in spirals, again allowing it to move in its own way. Move and turn your body and repeat the chant continuously until you can feel your body pulsating with vitality and health. You may experience a tingling feeling or a sensation like warm liquid running through the pendulum into your arm

and from there to the part of the body that needs a boost from nature, then onwards throughout your whole system.

* Gradually allow your rhythm and the

pendulum to slow until you are silent and the pendulum is still.

* Sit for a minute or two among the greenery before going back to the waiting world.

A water spell to remove warts, verruccas, viruses of any kind, fungal infections and gall or kidney stones

This spell is a based on the ancient idea of giving away or selling a viral infection, an allergy or a hormonally triggered problem such as PMS. To our modern sensibility, it seems unfair to pass on your illness to whoever who may find it (one old version of the spell involved leaving a bag of the same number of stones as you had warts at the crossroads for a curious stranger to pick up), so I have included water to cleanse the symbol of the disease once it has served its purpose.

You will need
A single golden-coloured coin or any coin with a hole (such as a Chinese divinatory coin or an old Spanish 25-peseta coin) – if the problem is warts or gall or kidney stones, use 2 or 3 coins; a flowing water source such as a stream, a river or the sea.

Timing
On an ebb tide.

The spell
* Stand by the water source and rub the coin or coins nine times widdershins (anti-clockwise) either directly on the affected part of your body or on your clothes above the relevant area. For a widespread debility or a virus, choose a token part of the body. As you rub, say nine times for each coin:
Leave me, affliction. Pass into this coin as token of my need to part from you.

* Cast the coins one at a time, on to successive waves or into an eddy in a river (perhaps from a bridge). As each coin hits the water, say:
I sell this affliction to the healing waters that it may be transformed to rise as health-giving moisture and fall to earth again as fertilising rain. I ask no return.

* Leave the water source and do not look back.

A self-healing spell using stone water

For centuries the standing stones at Stonehenge in Wiltshire, England, were used for healing. They were washed with water, which was then poured into baths for the sick to bathe in. Healing properties continued to be attributed to the stones in to the seventeenth and eighteenth centuries. This practice was also carried out at less well known stone circles throughout Western Europe and Scandinavia. Sadly, most stones in circles today are so dirty that you could not use the water for healing, but you can endow a bottle of mineral water with the power of the stones. Drink it, add it to your bath or splash it on pulse points when you feel exhausted or unwell. You can also send a tiny bottle of the empowered water to anyone who needs healing or energy.

To perform this spell you will need to visit a stone circle, single standing stone or ancient rock formation with a sacred association. You could also try a ruined abbey. These are often built on ley lines, the psychic lines of power beneath the earth. Alternatively, use the cloisters of an old cathedral. Ancient churches were often built on or close to pre-Christian sacred sites and so have powerful Earth energies. Stone circles were sometimes torn down and the stone used to build the church. Delve into local history and you will find a spot. If you live in a country in which Christians were more recent colonists, you may discover an early church built on an indigenous sacred site. Wherever you choose, the stone or stones should have free access. (There is no access to the stones at Stonehenge except by prior arrangement), but the stone circle at Avebury – only about 20 miles away – is entirely accessible.)

You will need

A wide-necked bottle or flask of mineral water, if possible from a sacred spring (many commercial brands are); a red crystal such as jasper, garnet or carnelian, small enough to fit through the neck of the bottle/flask; a clear quartz crystal, small enough to fit through the neck of the bottle/flask.

Timing

If possible, at dawn, noon or sunset, all times of solar power.

The spell

* Stand close to an ancient stone and unscrew the bottle or flask of water.
* In the bottle place first the red crystal (for Earth power), then the clear crystal (for sky power) and replace the lid.
* Shake the bottle slowly three times and set it at the base of the stone or, if the stone is flat, on the top.
* Face the stone and say:
  Guardian of the stones, who has stood watch for countless centuries, bless and empower this water I ask.
* Name any particular purpose for which you want the water and say:
  Earth Mother, Father of the Skies, bless and empower this water with the stone.
  Again name the purpose.
* Picture red light rising from the stone and white light pouring down from the sky to join within the water.
* Sit quietly, leaning against the stone, until you feel that the power has entered the bottle – which may be a few minutes or half an hour. You may sense a slowing of power through the stone or a sudden chill in the air that indicates it is time to go.
* Thank the guardian of the stone, Mother Earth and Father Sky; drink a few drops of the water and spend some time walking around the area.

An ancient charm for reducing the pain of a burn, scald, inflammation or rash

This spell contains one of the oldest surviving Christian folk chants (see also page 345). I have found reference to it in Germany and the Netherlands, as well as in the East and the Midlands of England. It is good for calming children's infectious diseases, such as chickenpox, and also helps with eczema in adults and children alike. Lotions or creams applied immediately after the spell will often seem more soothing than they usually do. I am convinced that these old charms work because so many people over the centuries have endowed them with power as they recited them in love.

You will need

A thin red candle in a deep holder; a small, deep metal pitcher (or use a wine cooler, small ornamental metal bucket or deep metal vase) filled with melted ice or very cold water (get it from the fridge or freezer before the spell and put it in the room where you will be working).

Timing

When the irritation or pain is troublesome or a child is fretful.

The spell

* Light the candle and recite three times softly:

    There came three angels out of the East;
    One brought fire and two brought frost.
    Out fire and in frost!
    In the name of the Father, Son and Holy
    Ghost. Amen.

* Knock on the door of the room three times and then open it, as you do so reciting the chant more loudly.

* Plunge the candle into the cold water so that it hisses and goes out. Recite the rhyme three further times, more and more softly so that the final 'amen' disappears into silence. If the patient is a child, they can join in with the rhyme if they like.

A salt, water and candle spell for helping the body to fight an illness or to prepare for an operation or medical intervention

It is well known that a positive attitude makes recovery and responsiveness to treatment easier. However, if you or a loved one have been ill for a while or are worried about the effects of the illness on your life, work and maybe finances, it is almost certain that anxiety and the exhaustion of trying to carry on normally will take their toll. This spell can be used for yourself or for a partner, friend or family member. It draws on the powers of the sun and the moon, the seas and the Earth to restore strength and resistance. These natural powers offer strength to assist self-healing powers, speeding recovery with the help of whatever medical intervention or treatment is being used. This spell is also good when a person has become totally exhausted or dispirited by a run of bad luck.

The spell is written to be performed for yourself. If you are working it on behalf of someone else, the patient can alternate with you in lighting candles, sprinkling water and burning salt. This will make the spell doubly effective. You can run through the format together in advance, deciding how you will divide up the words and actions.

You will need

A gold-coloured candle; a silver-coloured candle; a blue candle; a green candle; 4 broad candle-holders; a dish of sea salt; a dish of water.

Timing

If possible, when the sun and moon are in the sky at the same time (check *Old Moore's Almanack*, a diary or a newspaper for times and dates – there are several such days) or when the need is acute.

The spell

* Place the candles in a square formation, with the green one (representing the Earth) in the approximate North, the silver one (representing the moon) in the East, the gold one (representing the sun) in the South and the blue one (representing water) in the West. If you are working on a square surface, you can set the candles in the middle of each of the sides.

* Light the green candle and say:
  Powers of the Earth, let me draw strength and stamina from your rich soil as I walk your pathways in hope of healing.

* Light the silver candle and say:
  Powers of the moon, uplift me and help me to flow with the natural tides to healing.

* Light the gold candle and say:
  Powers of the sun, warm, energise and empower me as you pour down light of healing.

* Light the blue candle and say:
  Powers of the waters, wash away sickness and weakness that I may likewise flow to healing.

* Sprinkle three grains of salt into each flame in turn, saying for each:
  Bring life and new vitality.
  So shall it be with salt grains three.

* Sprinkle a circle of water drops deosil (clockwise) around the base of each candle and then a large circle of water drops to enclose them all, saying for each circle:
  Flow and grow that I may thrive
  And feel alive with circles five.

* Set the dishes of salt and water in the centre of the square and leave the candles to burn down while you or your patient make positive plans for when recovered.

A spell for burning away an illness, fever or addiction that is weakening a loved one

If someone you love is not getting better, seems unable to fight back against a virus or an addiction, or is unable to slow their mind down, try this simple spell. It was once practised by an open fire in bedrooms in Scandinavia and eastern Europe to relieve fevers. However, it works just as well with a candle. You can also use the spell to relieve an addiction of your own.

You will need
A dark-red candle.

Timing
On the last night of the waning moon for an addiction, and thereafter monthly; at 10 pm on any night for illnesses, and thereafter nightly if necessary.

The spell
* Light the candle, look into the flame and say nine times, getting faster and faster:
  Burn away, turn away,
  Fever of intensity.
  No longer grieve me.
  Leave (name) free.
  If the other person is well enough, they can chant alternately with you. Chant the last chant together.
* Blow out the candle, as you do so saying:
  Burn no more. Away.
* To repeat the spell, re-light the same candle. When the problem or illness is resolved, dispose of what is left.

A garlic spell to bury an illness

Burying an illness is an almost universal magical means of removing an illness or infection. In years gone by, burying a bag of stones at a crossroads was, for instance, a common folk remedy for warts. There is no restriction on the kind of illness or distress you can bury – and the symbolic act will sometimes trigger the body's fight-back mechanisms. Children can join in a burying spell, either preparing the item to be buried and watching from a window as you bury it, or burying it themselves if they are well enough and wrapped up warm against the cold. Some people, on the other hand, prefer not to know where you have buried their illness. The spell can be used as many times as needed and can, of course, be worked for yourself.

You will need
A clove of garlic; a few grains of salt; a plant pot filled with earth (optional).

Timing
After dark, if possible on a Saturday.

The spell
* Gently crush the garlic clove between your hands, so that it does not crumble.
* Sprinkle a few grains of salt on the garlic and bury it in the garden or in the pot of earth (if the latter, set it outside the front door).

An onion spell to bury an illness

You will need

An onion, a vegetable knife or pen knife; a plant pot filled with earth (optional).

Timing

After dark, if possible on a Saturday.

The spell

- Peel the brown outer skin off the onion.
- With the knife, scratch the name of the illness or distress on the onion.
- Bury the onion in the garden or in the pot of soil (if the latter, set it outside the front door).

A stone spell to bury a headache or pain

I keep a collection of pebbles in a dish in the fireplace to do this spell – I use it a lot.

You will need

A perfectly round, washed pebble found on a walk or in the garden.

Timing

After dark, if possible on a Saturday.

The spell

- Rub the stone very gently widdershins (anti-clockwise) over the main centre of pain.
- Bury the stone in the garden or in a potted plant indoors.

An egg spell to bury a menstrual or reproductive problem

This spell is good for all gynaecological problems, including PMS and menstrual disorders. It will also help with infertility and disorders of the reproductive system in either sex.

You will need

An egg; a few seeds.

Timing

After dark, if possible on a Saturday.

The spell

- Using your index finger, carefully write on the egg shell: 'Take away (name problem) bring (name desired result)'.
- Dig a hole in some earth and crack the egg into it, dropping in the shell and saying:
  Into the ground,
  Earth surround
  And make new.
- Scatter a few seeds in the hole and then fill it in.

An Anglo Saxon rusty nail spell to bury migraines, sore throats or any sharp pain

Wayland was the Anglo Saxon smith god. A Neolithic stone barrow dedicated to him and known as Wayland's Smithy may be seen along the Ridgeway close to Uffingham and the White Horse near Wantage, in Berkshire, England. It is said that Wayland still shoes travellers' horses while they sleep, in return for a penny, left on the stones. Keep a jar of rusty nails especially for this spell. If you know someone who rides horses or is connected with a stable or blacksmith, see if you can get a supply of discarded horseshoe nails – these were originally used for the spell.

You will need
A few rusty nails.

Timing
After dark, if possible on a Saturday.

The spell
* Take a nail or two or three, according to the intensity of the pain, and bury it in the ground, saying for each nail:
  Wayland, Wayland,
  Metal loose
  From horse's hoof.
  Wayland, Wayland,
  Take from my brain
  The nails of pain
  To rust away
  Until your day
  Returns.

A spell to slow blood flow, to relieve anaemia and blood disorders, and to lower high blood pressure

This is a spell I found in Polish and Baltic folklore, but American friends have told me they can remember the charm being chanted as a childhood rhyme when someone fell over and cut themselves. You can use the spell for yourself or on behalf of others, who can join in the chant or drum. It is good for women who suffer from excessive menstrual flow and also seems to guard accident-prone children.

You will need
A small drum or tambourine to keep the rhythm – a child's one is fine (optional).

Timing
Traditionally recited on Easter morning to keep accidents away for the coming year. Dawn is a good time, but use whenever the need arises.

The spell
* Establish a gentle rhythm with the drum or tambourine or by clapping.
* When you are ready, chant 12 times (one for each Apostle):
  Christ was born in Bethlehem,
  Baptised by John in Jordaen (pronounced 'Jord-eye-en').
  There he digged himself a well
  And turned the water from the hill.
  12, 11, ten, nine,
  Eight, seven, six, divine,
  Five, four, three, the Trinity,
  Two, and then the Holy One.
  Blood stand still!
  Flow begone!

A three Marys rain chant spell

This spell was traditionally used for healing very old and very young people. However, it works well for anyone who is feeling frail emotionally or physically. It is also helpful for people who develop infections during healing (for example around the site of an operation) or secondary problems connected with an earlier disorder in the body. The three Marys were probably Mary Jacobe, the mother of the disciple James; Mary Salome, her daughter; and Mary Magdalene, the patron saint of repentant sinners – and some legends say the wife of Jesus. According to the Apocrypha, the three travelled to Provence, in France, after the Crucifixion, carrying the relics of St Anne, the grandmother of Christ, as well as perhaps the Holy Grail, the chalice used at the Last Supper. However, other sources identify the three Marys as the Virgin Mary, Mary Magdalene and Mary Jacobe, who all kept vigil after Jesus' death. It does not matter which trinity you use, as the idea is simply to send love. In an even earlier tradition, the three women in the spell would have been the three Madrones, or Celtic mother goddesses. The sick person need not go out in the rain but can watch from indoors, at the same time reciting the rhyme.

You will need
A bowl of water (optional).

Timing
If possible, on a rainy day, in the late afternoon.

The spell
* Go outdoors in to the rain (taking the bowl of water if there is no rain).
* Turn three times deosil (clockwise), then three times widdershins (anti-clockwise), then three times deosil again. If you are using the bowl of water, scatter water droplets as you turn. Recite once for each turn (nine times in all):

By the power of Marys three,
I call to thee:
Take away pain
As healing rain.
By the power of three,
So shall it be!

36 SPELLS FOR ABSENT HEALING

Absent healing involves sending positive energies across a distance to a person, animal or place that needs them — a friend who is sick or unhappy, an animal that is wounded, a place that is polluted or a land where there is war and famine. You can do this through the focus of a crystal, a candle, a photograph or some herbs, or by thought power alone. This chapter concentrates on sending absent healing to people (see Chapter 43 for healing animals and Chapter 38 for healing plants). However, the principle is the same whether you are healing a small child or a country.

How does absent healing work? We do not really know, but even conventional medical practitioners are becoming increasingly aware that the mind and spirit have important roles in healing. In research in America, a group of people in hospital as a result of a heart attack were prayed for (without their knowledge). They recovered significantly better than a control group who were not prayed for.

If you as an individual (or part of a group) send healing energies to an absent friend, a family member or even a stranger, you are giving them strength they can unconsciously draw on. Of course, we cannot expect or demand miracles. We do not understand why perfectly good kind people get sick and die or babies fail to survive. If a friend or family member dies in spite of conventional medical care, prayers and rituals carried out on their behalf, it does not mean we have failed as healers. Rather, a stronger law was in operation than we could affect, and we were swimming against a tide of cosmic energies carrying the person in the opposite direction.

That does not mean we should not try to heal, but rather that we must accept that, although we can sometimes channel higher energies, we are not God or the Goddess and cannot promise cures. For this reason I have included a spell in this chapter to ease the passing of a beloved friend or family member who may be in hospital, in a hospice or at home but with whom we cannot be for whatever reason.

A basic absent healing spell

This is a very general absent healing spell that you can adapt for almost any purpose or occasion. Calcite, the crystal I recommend for the spell, is a natural balancer of energies in body, mind and spirit, and so is good for restoring harmony even if you are not certain of the dynamics of the illness or problem.

You will need

A large piece of uncut, unpolished calcite in milky yellow, peach, green, cloudy white or icy blue – alternatively, a large piece of semi-transparent or unpolished rose quartz or amethyst; a pink or lilac-scented candle.

Timing

As twilight falls. If you live near the sea, work when the tide is ebbing.

The spell

* Light the candle and place it so that the light shines into the crystal.
* Face the direction in which the person lives or will be at the time of healing and visualise him or her in a particular place in a room or garden. If you have not met the person and do not know what they look like, visualise the outline of a figure surrounded by the colour of the crystal.
* Holding the crystal in both hands, picture dark rays coming from the patient and entering the crystal, where they are transformed into circles of crystalline colour. The circles float like bubbles into the candle, where they are taken back as light. Say three times:

Pain and sorrow, sickness, sadness and distress, be refined, transformed and blessed by the power of this crystal and this flame.

* Place the crystal on the table and hold your hands over it but not quite touching it. You should feel your hands tingling.
* Picture streams of coloured crystalline light entering your fingers, flowing up through your heart and circulating down your arms into your hands.
* When the power is buzzing in your fingers, hold your hands vertically, palms outwards, at waist height, and say:

Light, find your place to heal and warm, ease and relieve, by the power of the crystal and flame and the benign powers of healing present here.

Name a particular deity, guide or angel if you wish.

* Gently push the visualised light towards the person to be healed until your arms are fully outstretched, with your palms still vertical.
* Return your hands to the crystal to absorb more light and then gently push it into the cosmos, repeating the second chant. Continue this cycle of actions until you feel the power of the crystal slowing down and your own energies ebbing. The healing is now complete.
* Wash the crystal in running water and leave it to dry naturally.

A crystal ball moon healing spell

Clear quartz crystal balls have been used for thousands of years, from ancient Egypt to China, for healing rituals involving sunlight (see page 530). However, they can also be a very effective tool for directing full moon energies towards an area of chronic pain in your body. Moonlight is gentler than sunlight and in my experience works especially well for digestive and bone problems, for emotional trauma and where a long illness or a period of stress has left the body exhausted.

You will need

A clear crystal sphere (it can be very small); a fibre optic lamp (if you are working when there is no moonlight).

Timing

If possible, at the full moon or just before.

The spell

* Go out in to the open air and hold the crystal sphere so that the moon is reflected within it. If there is no moonlight, work indoors and use the light of the fibre optic lamp. Say:
Fill the sphere with healing light,
Mother Moon I ask tonight,
To bring me/(name) relief from pain.
Within the glass your power remains,
Moon Mother.

* Direct the light towards the pain or in the direction in which the sick person lives or is being cared for. Do not worry if the moon disappears from the sphere as you move it, as the power is still within.

* Leave the sphere in the moonlight overnight to re-charge its energy. You may find that the sphere retains healing moon power throughout the following days.

A spell to send love and light through a pendulum

Even if you are not confident about sending healing, you can transmit love and light to a person who is ill or unhappy or whom you know is under intense pressure. The easiest and most powerful tool for this is a crystal pendulum (see also page 466). It will amplify and transmit your own positive feelings and wishes, even if you have never tried healing before.

You will need

A white or purple candle; a clear quartz or amethyst crystal pendulum (even a small one works well).

Timing

At last light.

The spell

* If possible facing the sunset, light the candle.

* Hold the pendulum in front of the candle so that the light shines on it.

* Spin the pendulum gently so that the candle light reflects through it. As you look at the spiralling light, project into the pendulum (as if you were looking through a window) an image of the person you are sending love and light to.

* Speak, either aloud or in your head, the words you would like the person to hear, and visualise him or her smiling in response and perhaps holding out a hand.

* Spin the pendulum even faster, so that the colour blurs.

* When the pendulum spontaneously reverses direction, blow out the candle, using your own words to send the love and light to the face in the crystal.

A holed stone spell for absent healing

Large round or diamond-shaped monoliths with a natural hole in the centre have traditionally been associated with healing. Their healing powers were used well in to Christian times, in spite of official church opposition. Many have now been destroyed, often through the indifference of a landowner, but still surviving is the round Men an Tol, near Madron in Cornwall, England, which has a guardian monolith at either side. Even now visitors still come in search of its healing powers. Traditionally, adults would crawl though the hole to relieve back, neck and limb problems. Children suffering from bone problems such as rickets (an illness that causes defective bone growth) and infectious diseases were passed three or nine times through the hole widdershins (anticlockwise).

Even a very small holed stone is effective for healing. Look for one by the seashore or on a river bank and wear it on a red cord tied around your neck with three knots – or keep it in a fabric purse. Though it is possible, with the right tools, to drill a hole in a stone, wait until you find one with a natural hole (or buy one at a mineral store), setting aside this spell until then.

You will need
A holed stone.

Timing
At noon or in the light of the full moon.

The spell
* Hold the stone up so that the light shines through the hole (never look directly at the sun, as this is dangerous for your eyes and can cause blindness).
* Visualise the face of the person, animal or place that needs healing as though it were superimposed in miniature on the light within the frame of the hole.
* Bring the hole close to your lips (it does not matter if the light temporarily disappears) and speak a private message of blessing and healing.
* Breathe through the hole three times, exhaling through your mouth, as if blowing the light and the message to its target.
* Hold the stone once more to the light and picture the rays reaching the intended recipient. Repeat the blessing in your head.

An eight-candle spell for someone undergoing an operation or beginning a difficult course of treatment

If a friend, family member or even a child you read about in a newspaper is undergoing surgical or medical intervention, spiritual healing can create positive energies, to strengthen both the skill of the surgeon or doctor and the patient's own ability to recover. I used to worry about sending healing without permission, but I now cannot see how sending love, strength and good wishes could ever be harmful.

You will need
8 small yellow or gold-coloured candles or tea-lights; a compass (optional); a pen, paper, envelope and stamp.

Timing
At the time of the medical intervention.

The spell
* Using the compass if you have one, work out the eight directions (North, north-east, East, south-east, South,

south-west, West, north-west). If you do not have a compass, find an approximate North (orienting yourself by a place you know to be to the north of the room) and work out the remaining directions on that basis. Set a candle at each direction point and light it.

* Sit or stand in the centre of the candles and, using the index finger of your power hand (the one you write with), point to the candle in the North, as you do so saying:

Light of the North send healing light to (name) as she/he undergoes (name treatment). Blessings be!

* Go through the same procedure, substituting the name of the relevant direction in the chant, for the other seven directions.

* Sit facing north and write a letter of encouragement and positive news to the person for whom you are carrying out the spell.

* When you have finished, blow out each candle, beginning with the one in the north-west and moving widdershins (anticlockwise) and saying for each:

Blessings be on (name), love and light and healing.

* Go out and post the letter.

A gentle pyramid healing spell

On page 460 I described the healing powers of pyramids, especially the squat ones based on the pyramid of King Cheops, which is more than 4,000 years old. Crystal pyramids are especially powerful for absent healing, since the magical power of the perfect geometrical form is amplified by the crystalline energies. Amethyst, fluorite, rose quartz and calcite pyramids provide a very gentle form of healing and so are especially good for treating children and very sick or frail people. They also work well for chronic conditions and emotional problems. Clear quartz, amber and citrine pyramids will speed the healing of acute conditions and restore energy after an illness or trauma.

You will need

A clear squat rose quartz, amethyst, fluorite or calcite pyramid (calcite ones are very cheap and easily obtainable – your pyramid need only be small); a silver-coloured candle; a photograph of the person to be healed or their name written on a piece of paper; a white cloth; a vase of fresh flowers.

Timing

In moonlight.

The spell

* Light the silver candle and set the pyramid in the pool of light. If you are lucky enough to have a pool of natural moonlight to work in, use that.

* Place the photograph or paper with the name beneath the pyramid, so that the light reflects downwards on to the paper.

* Enclose your hands around the pyramid and say:

I ask for healing for (name), who is suffering from (problem). Sacred pyramid, whose powers are truly known only to the priests of old, pass now beyond this crystal to (name) that illness/sorrow will retreat into the dark chambers of your inner places and rise no more.

* Close your eyes and picture the light growing brighter and more powerful and flowing towards the person you have named.

* When you feel that the power is diminishing, loosen your hold on the pyramid.

- Leave the photo or paper with the name beneath the pyramid until the candle is burnt down (or the pool of moonlight disappears), then leave it for a further eight hours.
- Wash the crystal. Wrap the photo or named paper in the white cloth and leave it near the vase of flowers for three days.
- Repeat the healing weekly until the problem resolves itself. If the issue is ongoing, after three or four weeks continue the healing monthly or whenever you have time.

A spell to direct crystalline pyramid energy towards someone suffering from an acute illness or an illness that is not responding to treatment

This is a more powerful version of the previous spell.

You will need
A small squat clear quartz, amber or citrine pyramid; a gold-coloured candle or fibre optic lamp (optional).

Timing
In sunlight.

The spell
- Set the pyramid so it is within a pool of sunlight. If necessary, supplement the light by using the gold-coloured candle or fibre optic lamp.
- Pointing your index fingers downwards and holding them as close together as possible, touch the point of the pyramid.
- Mentally draw the light upwards from the pyramid, picturing straight beams of light entering your index fingers and your fingers becoming like crystalline wands. Say:

Power of the desert sands, of magical pyramids and secret wisdom, let your healing power flow through me to heal (name).

- When your fingers are tingling, hold your hands outstretched and jab both your index fingers simultaneously forwards, as though you were thrusting a sword to destroy the illness. Repeat this movement several times, saying for each thrust:

Go swiftly, go true and bring healing.
Pyramid penetrate through sickness and pain and bring regeneration.

- When you have finished, wash your hands and then the pyramid under cold running water.
- Rest for a while, as this is a tiring spell to cast.

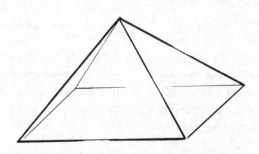

A dark and light absent healing spell for debilitating conditions and viruses

This spell is very effective for debilitating conditions, viruses and illnesses that resist treatment and recurring syndromes. It is also helpful for depression and phobias, and works well with those who are very old and sick. The spell is carried out in silence.

You will need

A piece of non-transparent unpolished amethyst, calcite or rose quartz crystal; a clear crystal or selenite sphere (the sphere need only be small – these are relatively inexpensive, especially if with imperfections), alternatively a clear glass paperweight or a paperweight with a tiny angel statue within; a pink or lilac scented candle; a pure-white candle, preferably scented with vanilla.

Timing

At dusk.

The spell

* Place the two crystals side by side on a table. It does not matter if the crystal sphere is much smaller, as its power will be more concentrated.
* Place the pink or lilac candle behind the coloured crystal and light it.
* Face the direction in which the person lives or is in hospital or a care home, visualising him or her in a particular place in a room or garden.
* Take up the coloured crystal in both hands, holding it so that the candle light continues to shine on it, and visualise dark rays coming from the sick or distressed person and entering the crystal.
* Now imagine the rays being transformed into circles of crystalline colour and floating like bubbles into the candle, where they are taken back as light.
* When this stage feels complete and the crystal seems duller and heavier, return the crystal to the table.
* Light the white candle from the coloured one and place it behind the clear sphere.
* Take up the clear crystal in both hands, holding it so that the candle light continues to shine on it, and visualise the light passing from the candle through the crystal.
* Imagine the light forming a prism, travelling as a rainbow to the sick person, entering through the crown of their head and filling their whole body with brilliance.
* Return the clear crystal to the table. Leave the candles to burn behind the two crystals, so that the light from both will continue to filter gently for several hours towards the person you are healing.

A monthly absent healing ceremony using a healing book

Many healers and healing groups have a healing book in which they write the name of anyone they know who is sick, unhappy or afflicted, whether person, animal or place. Once a week or month they read the names out by candle light and send healing. This is a good ongoing ritual and will build up your own store of healing energies as well as sending positive vibes towards those who need them. Carry out the ritual alone or make it part of a quiet family time or meeting with friends. If more than one person is present, each can light a small white candle from the central one placed behind the book, setting the candles on the floor behind the seats to create a protective circle of light. You can also take it in turns to read from the healing book, passing it around in a circle to the person on the right. Each person can speak a blessing before handing on the book.

You will need

A blank notebook – a loose-leafed book is good because you can then remove names of people who have recovered or moved out of your sphere and group the names according to categories; a white or beeswax pillar candle in a deep holder; a vase of fresh flowers.

Timing

Once a week or once a month, at 10 pm, the healing hour. Wednesdays and Fridays are especially potent.

The ritual

* Place the healing book, closed, on a low table, with the vase of fresh flowers and the candle behind the book.
* Light the candle so that the light shines on the book.
* Take up the book and add any new names to the list. Give thanks for any who have recovered. (You can make notes between sessions.) Slowly read through all the names in the book, together with the person's problem.
* Speak your own blessing, prayer or mantra to God, the Goddess, an Archangel such as Raphael or Cassiel (see pages 681 and 682) or to the benign powers of light and love if this seems more meaningful to you.
* Close the ritual with a private blessing or empowerment and extinguish the candle.
* Keep the book, candle and fresh flowers permanently in place. Light the candle for a few minutes at 10 pm whenever you can, opening the book at random. Close the book when you extinguish the candle.

A druid mistletoe healing rite on the sixth day of the moon

The Keltria Order of Druids celebrate their mistletoe rite on the sixth day of each moon cycle, focusing their ceremonies on healing and balancing energies. Private rites of healing are also potent on this evening, whether or not you follow the Druid path. Though mistletoe berries are poisonous, and you have to be a very experienced herbalist to use the other parts medically, in conventional medicine the uses of this plant include shrinking tumours, relieving heart conditions and leukaemia, reducing blood pressure and internal bleeding, boosting the immune system and increasing fertility.

You can find mistletoe growing in many parts of the world and on a variety of trees. You could, like the Druids and Druidesses of old, deliberately introduce mistletoe to an oak tree – the most magical situation of all. However, you can use any species of tree. (Be careful if you have children.) Talk to your local garden centre or botanical garden, or buy spores by mail order. If you cannot obtain real mistletoe, you can use honeysuckle (another magical Druid plant – but, again, take care if you have children, because the berries are poisonous) or any other trailing greenery.

This ritual can be carried out alone or in company. You should prepare a healing book in advance (follow the instructions in the spell above), working on the night of the new moon. This is the part of the lunar cycle when the moon has disappeared from the sky (and will not reappear for at least two and a half days). Set the book on a white silk square on a table where it will not be disturbed. Circle it with sprigs of mistletoe, honeysuckle or another trailing plant, or with pots of healing herbs such dill, fennel, rosemary, sage and thyme (see pages 691–3).

You will need
Your healing book; a long strand of mistletoe, honeysuckle or another trailing plant, plus several smaller sprigs (or small pots of healing herbs – listed above; a beeswax or pure-white candle; a silver- or gold-coloured paper knife; some small silver candles (optional).

Timing
On the sixth night of the moon cycle.

The spell
* If possible, work where you can see the waxing moon. If it is cloudy, set the silver candles around the room, light them and visualise the growing crescent in the sky.
* Light the white or beeswax candle behind the healing book.
* Open the book and read the names slowly, one at a time, together with the nature of the illness or problem.
* For every page, cut a tiny sprig of mistletoe (using the paper knife) and place it in the page, saying:
  Blessings be! Healing of the moon I ask and send in love and in humility, healing for those whose names lie within the mistletoe boughs.
* When you have read all the names, close the book, still containing the mistletoe, and allow the candle to burn down.
* The next morning, remove the mistletoe from the book and bury the mistletoe.
* Keep the book updated during the following month, adding new names and taking out the names of people who have recovered or moved beyond your personal sphere of influence.

A healing herb ritual using a cloth doll, or poppet

The modern world erroneously associates the creation of poppets with voodoo and pricking waxen images with pins. Much of this misperception is due to sensationalist films. In fact, cloth poppets (rough featureless images in green, blue or undyed cream cloth) have been used from early times in the north European folk tradition as a focus for healing. You can make a poppet to represent a sick person, as you make it endowing it with healing. If you can't face sewing, unpick the corner of a fabric toy, take out a little of the stuffing and add the dried herbs.

You will need

A rectangle of pink, green or natural fabric (the doll need only be tiny); pink or green thread; a needle; a pair of scissors; a selection of dried healing herbs (for example, chamomile for digestion and respiratory problems, lavender for high blood pressure, wounds and burns, lemon balm for anxiety, lily of the valley for heart problems, marigold for skin disorders, passionflower for asthma and phobias, peppermint for sickness and headaches, parsley for kidney and bladder problems, rosemary for circulation, depression, fertility and the liver, rose for viruses and infections, sage for all health troubles and especially lungs and exhaustion, and violet for eczema and dizzy spells (see pages 691–3 for a full list).

Timing

Just before sunset.

The spell

* Using the template opposite, cut out the front and back of the doll, as you do so seeing in your mind the sick person entirely well again. Do not think of the illness but the person as he or she was and will be again. As you cut, say:
I create this image of (name) in love and in healing. May she/he be healed by the dark, gentle womb of Mother Earth and so restored to health once more.
* Repeat the chant, then sew the doll together, leaving an opening at the top of the head. As you work, picture each stitch filled with healing light.
* Repeat the chant again and then stuff the poppet with the herbs, saying:
Herbs of healing, herbs of gentleness, fill (name) with your life-giving and restoring powers.
* Sew up the head, repeating both chants either silently or out loud.
* If you know the sick person would like the doll, send it with an explanation of how it was made. If you feel that the person might be spooked, keep the doll wrapped in very soft cloth with a few leftover herbs. Once a week, unwrap the doll, sprinkle it with a few grains of salt (for health) and repeat the two chants. If the sickness is chronic or slow to heal, every 28 days send a new doll to the sick person or replace the herbs in the wrapped poppet.
* When the person recovers, the poppet will lose any connection with them, so you can safely unpick it and dispose of the herbs and cloth.

An incense absent healing spell for a person who is far away or refuses help

Incense is better used for absent rather than contact healing because the smoke can disturb a person who is unwell. It works well if the subject of the spell is far away, especially if they are shutting themselves away from the support of friends and family or have no one physically on hand to care for them. If you perform this spell outdoors, work with the incense smoke curling against the colours of the sky. If you perform it indoors, ventilate the room well.

You will need

2 sticks of rosemary, orange or sage incense; 2 sticks of juniper, lemon or pine incense; a photograph of, or a letter or e-mail from, the person you wish to heal, or another symbol of them (perhaps a small gift they sent you).

Timing

At sunset.

The spell

* Set the photo, letter, e-mail or symbol in the centre of the table you are working on.
* Place the incense sticks at the four compass points around the photo – rosemary, orange or sage in the East and West; and juniper, lemon or pine in the North and South.
* Working deosil (clockwise), light each of the incense sticks in turn, beginning in the approximate direction that the person lives. For the rosemary, orange or sage say:
Rosemary / orange / sage for healing.
For distress relief send.
Better times remembering,
Sorrow soon to end.
For the juniper, lemon or pine say:
Juniper / lemon / pine remove all ills;
Energies restore.
Over land or over sea,
Bring health and joy once more.
* Focus on the photograph, letter, e-mail or symbol and visualise the fragrance enfolding the sick person and restoring them to health and well-being.
* When the incense has burnt through, silently or out loud speak a few words of love.
* Try to make contact with the sick person within 24 hours.

A ritual to ease the passing of a friend or family member

If you know that a friend or family member is dying, you can send them love to ease their passing. Even if you are able to visit the bedside, the ritual can still help, carried out privately at home after the visit.

The candle, burning for its allotted time, illuminating the darkness and, once dimmed, being replaced by another, is a very old symbol for human life. Candles, also known as corpse-candles or corpse-lights, are also a part of death. In many cultures throughout the ages, people have reported seeing lights circling the sick room as a person dies. These are said to be the soul leaving the body after death. Others have reported seeing a series of lights floating towards the dying person. These are believed to be the essences of departed relatives coming to welcome the newly deceased person and encourage them not to be afraid. In my own research I have come across many accounts of lights being seen in a dark room as a relative is dying in a hospital miles away. It is as though the soul has come to say goodbye.

Having undertaken my own extensive research, which has involved reading or hearing accounts from hundreds of sensible intelligent people, I now believe that the essential self survives death. But even if you do not believe in an afterlife, rites of passage can be very comforting, and, I am convinced, transmit love to the dying person.

You will need

A few brown or dark-golden flowers such as chrysanthemums, wallflowers or carnations; a vase of water; 3 purple candles in descending order of size and 3 flat metal holders; a candle snuffer; a piece of dark silk; a picture of the departing person (optional).

Timing

In the last days or hours of a loved one's life.

The spell

* Set the candles in a row, with the tallest on the left and the shortest on the right.
* Light the tallest candle and arrange the flowers in the vase close by.
* Take a single petal from one of the flowers and say:
  The earthly light is fading, but perpetual light shines just beyond the veil. Dear friend (or name family member), when you are ready, walk through the door into the light to see your waiting relations coming to greet you. I will miss you, but if you are ready to move on, I would not hold you back because of my own need of your company.

* Burn the petal in the candle and drop it on to the metal holder, as you do so speaking private words of affection, thanks, regrets and farewell.
* Light the second, middle-sized, candle from the first and then snuff out the first candle in silence.
* Take a single petal from another flower, as you do so saying:
  All business is finished between us, all old accounts settled and differences healed. Only the love remains, and that will never die. Go in peace and I likewise shall remain, treasuring your memory and your life.
* Burn the petal in the second candle and drop it on to the metal holder.
* Light the third candle from the second and then snuff out the second candle in silence.
* Take a petal from a third flower and set it in front of the third candle. Say:
  You must choose your own time to leave us, be it long or short. I celebrate your life and send you light and healing as the earthly light fades.
* Blow out the candle (do not snuff it). When it is cool, wrap it in the silk, together with the picture (if you have one), and put it away in a box or drawer.
* Release the petal to the winds, as you do so whispering:
  Be free when you will. You may walk with your head high into tomorrow and eternity.
* When the flowers die, bury them. If the friend or family member still lives, replace the flowers (but not the candles).
* When news comes of the death, light the final candle again. Set the picture beside it and buy fresh flowers for the vase, this time yellow ones. Let the candle burn through.

37 SPELLS FOR HEALING QUARRELS AND BITTERNESS

Quarrels and coldness can arise with family and friends for all sorts of reasons. Many quarrels are resolved quickly and can clear the air of unspoken resentments. But others remain and harden over the years. A family feud, sometimes spanning generations, can stem from a cause so trivial it has been forgotten, but the ill-feelings remain. Inter-generational differences and old rivalries between siblings, in-laws or friends can also escalate, leading to a loss of contact that may be regretted on both sides.

Sometimes, however, when a cold or critical friend or relation has no intention of softening their attitude, all we can do is walk away without bitterness or beating ourselves up because, for instance, we are the least favourite grandchild and have been for 30 years or more.

This chapter is aimed at putting right what can advantageously be resolved and letting go of any bitterness that is holding us back.

A bridge reconciliation spell

Bridges have traditionally been a symbolic meeting place for those who have differences and need to find common ground. The chant in this spell comes from an excellent CD produced by the Witchcraft Museum in Boscastle, Cornwall, England. I have tried adapting and abridging this chant, but I find that the whole thing is more effective for bringing peace between family or friends. Its original meaning is much wider. This spell works well if there has been coldness or a period of silence for many years.

You will need

A bridge over any body of water; a flower with a number of petals.

Timing

At around noon. The longer the estrangement, the closer to noon you should work.

The spell

* Stand in the centre of the bridge, facing upstream and holding the flower.
* Pluck the petals from the flower one by one, casting each in to the water, so that it is carried beneath the bridge and downstream. As you do so, chant rhythmically:

Building bridges between our division.
I reach out to you and you reach out to me.
All of our voices and all of our visions.
Brother / sister we could make such sweet harmony.
Brother / Sister we could make such sweet harmony.

* When all the petals have been carried downstream, turn around to face downstream and, either aloud or in your head, send a message of reconciliation.
* If appropriate, make a small gesture of warmth to the estranged person. Trust the water to do the rest.

A Celtic blessing for peace in the family

There are numerous prayers and blessings in the Celtic tradition, some surviving in their original form. Much has been passed on orally, preserved over the centuries by Celtic bards and minstrels and recorded by Christian monks from the eighth to thirteenth centuries. Celtic myths and poetry were collected even later as folklore in areas where Celtic descendants remained, and even today new Celtic literature is emerging from its living roots.

I came across a number of Celtic prayers and blessings when I worked in Scotland during the 1970s and also more recently, lecturing at healing festivals in Scotland. I tend to learn more from the people who talk to me than they do from me. A Scottish lady whose grandmother lived in Sutherland taught me this blessing. It was used when a family quarrel was getting bad. She said it was part of a longer poem, but I have not been able to trace the rest of it.

This is one of my standbys when I know I will erupt and fear I may say what I will regret. I wish I had known it years ago, as the repetition has the ability to calm me in confrontational situations. If possible try to get two or three minutes alone to recite the words, but if this is impossible, say them in your head.

You will need

A long dark cord or piece of wool.

Timing

When domestic conflict is brewing or you feel your temper rising under provocation.

The spell

- When you feel yourself becoming angry, tie knots in any way you like in the cord or wool. As you do so, recite slowly and continuously, aloud or in your head:

I weave a silence on my lips.
I weave a silence in my mind.
I weave the silence in my heart.

- When the cord is full of knots, throw it away, pushing it deep in to a rubbish bin.
- If you are still stressed, fill another knot cord and continue reciting the rhyme. Let people wait for answers. Sometimes the lack of instant reaction will make them go away or cool down.

A Celtic spell to prevent yourself being manipulated in other people's quarrels or power games

If you are a nice person, you may find yourself drawn to defend a loved one against, for example, a critical parent or two adult siblings who are arguing viciously, only to find you suddenly have both parties attacking you. Your loved one may have been playing these power games for years. I have many emotional scars gained from such attempts. The charm in this spell is the motto of the Fianns, the semi-divine Celtic warriors who have been likened to King Arthur's knights. Their leader was Fionn Mac Cumhal. It was collected by John and Caitlin Matthews (experts in this field) and appears in their *Little Book of Celtic Wisdom*, Vega Books, 2002. Because they come from such a long tradition, the words will help to give you the space and the authority to stop your home being turned into a bear garden and to remain detached.

You will need

Low-hanging wind chimes or Tibetan bells.

Timing

When you feel that you are about to intervene inappropriately.

The spell

- Touch the wind chimes (if necessary, pretend to do so accidentally) so that they ring.
- Stand still and recite nine times in your head:
  Truth in our hearts,
  Strength in our hands,
  Consistency in our tongues.
- State your opinion quietly but firmly and suggest that the combatants quarrel elsewhere.
- If they persist or turn on you, ring the chimes again and walk out of the room, reciting the words aloud or in your head until you are calm.
- Do not go back until there is silence.

A snow or ice reconciliation spell

Many ice spells come from cold northern lands where snow may persist until May. If you live somewhere warmer, however, you can just as well use ice cubes from the fridge or ice from the freezer. Because this is a slow-acting spell, aimed at gradually thawing entrenched attitudes, prejudices or long-standing family feuds, you should allow the ice to melt naturally rather than heating it. If the sun is shining, work the spell outdoors.

You will need

A glass bowl; some ice or snow; a wooden spoon; a small potted flower of a kind the estranged person likes.

Timing

From 11 am onwards (as the day warms).

The spell

* Fill the bowl one-third full with ice.
* Hold the bowl and say:

   As ice melts, so softens the heart of (name); as ice turns to healing water, so anger and bitterness flow away; as cold gives way to warmth, let fond feelings once more grow.

* Stir the ice with the wooden spoon three times widdershins (anti-clockwise), as you do so repeating the words.
* While the ice is melting, use the time to clear clutter, sort out paperwork, weed the garden or do some other useful task. Recall any good memories you have of the estranged person and set any negative feelings aside. Every ten or 15 minutes, hold the bowl, say the words and stir the melting ice three times widdershins, repeating the words again.
* Once the ice is melted, stir the bowl three times deosil (clockwise) and say: *So softens the heart of (name). Anger and bitterness flow away, fond feelings once more grow.*
* Pour a little of the melted ice into the soil of the potted plant, so that it is just moistened.
* If appropriate, send the plant to the estranged person. Otherwise, nurture it yourself and repeat the spell weekly, each time adding a little of the melted ice to the plant pot. After a few weeks a chance should arise for you to meet or at least attempt positive contact.

A spell to reunite family or friends divided

Clay or dough is a natural medium for reuniting spells. You can use it to symbolically mould together broken pieces of the family. Because the pieces can be joined seamlessly, the resulting energies seem to encourage natural opportunities for reunion, for example an unexpected celebration. If possible, work outdoors, but if the weather is bad, use small lamps and work on a table near a window.

You will need

A large ball of clay or children's modelling dough; some clear glass nuggets or very small clear quartz crystals; some pink glass nuggets or very small rose quartz crystals.

Timing

On the anniversary of an occasion when you met together happily in the past, or alternatively on a sunny day when you can work outdoors.

The spell

* Break the clay ball into as many pieces as there are people connected with the estrangement (including yourself) and keep a small central piece of clay to represent the united family. As you break up the clay, say:
  The friendship/family tie is broken, severed, separated. Yet shall all be mended.
* Beginning with the family ball, roll it so that it is smooth, as you do so saying softly over and over again:
  Smooth away discord, shape disharmony to unity. So shall it be!
* Repeat this procedure with each of the individual clay balls. Name the person it represents and say:
  May sharp words soften, wounds heal. What was said or not said, omitted or committed thoughtlessly, return to the mix of family good will and unity. So shall it be!
* When all the balls are smooth, set the balls representing individuals in a circle around the family ball.
* One by one, blend the individuals' balls into the family ball, in whatever order seems appropriate. For each ball name the person and say:
  What was broken is now mended; the friendship/family ties once severed are now joined once more in unity. So shall it be!
* When you have moulded all the balls in to the family clay, press the glass nuggets or crystals all over the surface, as you do so, repeating the chant from the above step.
* Place the family clay somewhere where it will catch the light, and leave it there until it crumbles.
* In the meantime, if an occasion does not arise spontaneously for a get-together, engineer some kind of celebration. Hide the family ball somewhere in the room in which you gather. Otherwise, send a friendly letter about your current life to all the estranged people and ask them to send you news for a communal e-mail or printed newsletter you are creating.
* Repeat the spell as necessary.

A spell for a togetherness cake

On page 721 I give a spell for making a cake for emotional stability and security in a relationship. This variation works well if there is a lot of bitchiness or rivalry when family or friends get together or if certain family members are finding it hard to fit in. Invite everyone over and arrange to be mixing the cake when they arrive. Ask them in to the kitchen to chat while you finish. If you know certain people would object to joining in, make the cake before they arrive.

You will need

Ingredients for a sponge cake or a large packet mix; a large mixing bowl; a wooden spoon; a tub of sugar hearts or silver balls.

Timing

When a number of friends or family members visit your home.

The spell

※ Prepare the basic mix, as you do so saying continuously:

Be bound in kinship, forged in friendship, willingly in togetherness within this mix.

※ When people arrive, ask each to stir the mix nine times deosil (clockwise) and recall a happy memory from the past, such as a family outing, holiday or celebration. Even the most sullen teenager can usually dredge up some moment when life was not unremittingly grey. If they say there is nothing positive, ask them to stir in silence, and as they do so recite the chant in your head.

※ Pour the cake in to the tin, as you do so repeating the chant in your head.

※ Close the oven and keep the conversation as upbeat as possible while the cake is cooking.

※ When the cake is cool, ice it and ask everyone present to set a sugar heart or silver ball on top, as they do so making a positive wish for the person sitting to their left.

※ Share the cake and the happiness.

A blue lace agate spell for gentleness if a critical or trouble-making family member or friend is present

Some family members or friends make our hearts sink when they phone or call, although they may be basically good people. Half an hour in their company leaves us exhausted and depressed, but we may not wish to – or be able to – shut them out of our lives. Sometimes a friend or relative who is very old, has emotional difficulties or is going through a crisis may have no idea of the hurt they cause. This spell uses blue lace agate, the gentlest of crystals and one that softens tongues and encourages positivity. I keep a dish of blue lace agates near the phone for sensitive and upbeat communication, and another one on the dining table to ensure harmonious mealtimes.

You will need

6 small blue lace agates (or green/blue aquamarine, dark-blue sodalite, pale-blue chalcedony, angelite or celestite); a large jug of still mineral water; a dish of small blue crystals, including blue lace agate if possible.

Timing

A night when you anticipate a visit from a difficult friend or relative the next day.

The spell

* Place the six blue lace agate crystals (for Venus and harmony) one at a time in the jug of water. As you drop each crystal in, say:
  Words gentle and actions kind,
  Within this water thus I bind.
* Cover the jug and leave it overnight.
* In the morning, place the dish of blue crystals in the room where you will entertain your visitor (they will create a gentle atmosphere).
* When the visitor calls, use the blue lace agate water from the jug to make tea, coffee or a cold drink.
* After the visit, wash the crystals in the dish under running water to remove any negativity and leave them to dry naturally. You may like to keep them in the room permanently.
* Bottle any remaining blue lace agate water and drink a little or splash some on your pulse points whenever you have to make a phone call to a critical or negative relation.

A honey spell to soften critical or outspoken relatives or friends

Most of us have a blunt 'I speak as I find' person in our lives whose good deeds are soured by a total lack of tact. This can be very hurtful to children or adolescents. As well as attempting to temper their outbursts, try a little magic to supplement your efforts. This is not interfering with their free will, because you can limit the spell to the effects of their tactlessness on your own family circle (or any particular family member who is being hurt). You are binding the words, not the person.

Honey has been associated with healing goddesses from Neolithic times, as well as with family happiness in many traditions. In a very old Hindu custom that survives to this day, a father feeds his young child honey while asking Parvati, the gentle mother goddess and symbol of the happy family, that the child may live to see a 100 autumns.

You will need

A small half-eaten jar of honey (the kind with honeycomb in it is best; a piece of paper cut into the shape of a tongue; a gold pen.

Timing

Any beginning day, such as the first day of the week, month or year.

The spell

* Remove the lid from the jar of honey
* Using the gold pen, write across the paper tongue: 'Bind (name) from wounding (name)/the family with vicious words for 365 days (366 if a leap year). Bless (name of vicious person) and let them know gentleness in their words.' Set the tongue in front of the honey.
* Eat a spoonful of honey from the jar and then recite the words you wrote on the paper.
* Put the lid back on the honey and place the paper tongue beneath the jar. Leave it in the light until dusk, then place the jar, with the tongue beneath it, at the back of a high cupboard where it will not be disturbed.
* Before the tactless person visits, give any vulnerable family member a teaspoonful of the honey, as you do so reciting the words written on the paper tongue. Incorporate honey into sandwiches and cakes to be served when the sharp-tongued visitor arrives, and use honey to sweeten their drinks.
* After the visit, throw the tongue away. Keep the jar of honey for a year (it will keep for a very long time if sealed), then throw it away. Hopefully, you will not need to replace it.

A ritual for harmony when a family member or friend is constantly intruding or interfering in your life, but you do not want to hurt their feelings

This spell is very successful if you have dropped hints to a friend or family member about one too many phone calls or visits at inconvenient moments. Possessiveness may not be malicious but often stems from loneliness in a friend, relation, child or even partner. This spell is much kinder than a traditional binding spell, as it preserves the positive aspects of the relationship and encourages the possessive person to become less reliant. This over-reliance may be holding them back from widening their horizons. The spell is also effective against interfering neighbours and colleagues.

You will need

A stick of lavender or rose incense; an orange candle wedged in to a metal pot or bucket with sand or soil; a long piece of grey wool or thread; a paper knife.

Timing

Towards the end of the moon cycle, in the early evening.

The spell

* Light the orange candle (the colour of independence) and from it the lavender or rose incense (for gentleness).

* Tie the wool or thread loosely around the sides of the pot, fastening it with nine knots and saying as you tie:
Bonds that stifle, tangle, twine, bind me unwillingly to you.

* Using the paper knife, cut through the knots one at a time, saying for each:
Ties so binding,
Sever through;
Loving you,
Not what you do.

* Burn the broken threads in the candle, allowing them to drop in the sand and saying for each:
Light of friendship, light so kind,
Free in heart and soul and mind,
Free to live in harmony,
Caring still, but separately.

* Fix a definite date a few days ahead to meet the person, maybe outside your home, and perhaps suggest ways in which they can meet more people and fill their days.

A spell to hear news of a relation or friend who has entirely cut off contact

Inevitably, some friends and relations move out of our life, perhaps because of a life change or because of a growing gulf between them and ourself. Often there is no reason to keep in touch. But then suddenly you may think of the person and want to know how they are, or even to re-establish links if your own life circumstances have changed. I lost a dear friend because her husband wanted to cut her off from her past when they married. After we both divorced, I was able to re-establish contact with her through her mother. This spell will not work if the other person deliberately shuts down barriers when you come into their thoughts suddenly, but you may nevertheless hear reassuring news from a third party. The spell can also be used if you have relatives or friends who are far away and not very good at keeping in touch and letting you know that they are safe and well.

You will need

3 yellow candles of the same size; a three-branched candlestick (or 3 separate holders); a twig that has been polished and shaped to a point or a magic wand or a crystal pointed at one end.

Timing

On a Wednesday morning.

The spell

* Set the yellow candles (for seeking news from afar) in the candelabra or in a row.
* Light the one to the left, and circle it three times deosil (clockwise) with the twig, wand or crystal, saying for each circle:
One to seek, one to find,
One to call into her/his mind.
* Light the second candle from the first. Circle each of the two candles three times deosil with the twig, wand or crystal, as you do so repeating the words (so that you have made six circles in all).
* Light the third candle from the second. Circle each of the candles three times deosil with the twig, wand or crystal, as you do so repeating the words (so that you have made nine circles in all).
* Set the twig, wand or crystal in front of the candles and leave the candles to burn through.
* Before you make any attempt to trace the missing person, circle the computer, phone or writing pad three times deosil with the twig, wand or crystal, as you do so repeating the words three times.

38 SPELLS FOR healing plants

Centuries ago, the well-being and fertility of plants was closely entwined with that of animals and humans. In the Netherlands and in East Anglia, in England, offerings of milk and honey were regularly made at field entrances in hollow stones known as 'dobby stones'. These offerings were intended for the guardians of the land, to ensure the health of what was grown in the field. In the West Country of England, fruit trees were doused with cider and wassailing songs sung on 5 January (the old Christmas eve) to encourage a healthy crop of fruit. ('Wassail' is from the Old English word for 'good health'.) Seeds were sown and crops harvested during particular moon phases, and on seasonal festivals people made love in fields and carried flaming torches around field and garden boundaries to bring fertility and call the power of the sun to ripen the crops. Harvest celebrations go back to the earliest farmers, who offered the finest of the grain and fruits to the deities as thanks.

Despite the fact that when harvest festival comes around modern children may take a tin of baked beans to put on the festival table, these strong connections between humans and the benign forces that foster healthy growth have not disappeared. The fertility of the land remains essential to the survival of us all, even if we live in a city and in the course of our daily lives never see a field of corn or an apple orchard.

While some laugh at Britain's Prince Charles for talking to plants, experiments show that plants respond to human contact, both positive and negative. In the US in the 1960s and 70s, Clive Backster and other researchers hooked plants up to polygraph equipment. They discovered that not only do plants respond to experiences in their environment but they also seem to be able to pick up on people's thoughts. The strongest readings obtained were in reaction to the destruction of living cells, whether of plant, animal or human. A threat to another plant caused intense electromagnetic reactions in the plants being measured.

Whether you have a tiny balcony or a vast acreage, the old spells and rituals are a good supplement to the necessary practical effort and skill required to maintain plant health and restore ailing plants. This chapter will show you how to use magic for the optimum well-being of your garden, tubs and pot plants.

A spell for a healthy and beautiful garden

Some people have natural green fingers and can make a beautiful garden out of a wilderness. There is an increasing awareness these days, too, of higher nature essences that can help us to create areas of natural beauty and tranquillity even in an urban setting. The most dramatic example of this co-operation between human and natural powers comes from Findhorn, in Morayshire, north-east Scotland, where a beautiful garden has been created on what was considered barren soil. Peter Caddy, a former officer in the Royal Air Force; his wife, Eileen; their three sons; and a colleague, Dorothy, created the Findhorn garden in 1962, with, they believe, the help of devas (or higher nature essences), who instructed Peter on its planting and care. Vegetables far larger than normal size grew in soil where previously even weeds had not survived.

This is a good spell to use whenever you plant a number of flowers or herbs, especially if plants have been dying in the garden or the weather has been unseasonably cold or wet.

You will need

13 small jade or moss agate crystals; a large glass jug of still mineral water; herbs and/or flowers to be planted out.

Timing

Any of three days before the full moon. (Bulbs should be planted just after the full moon, when you can repeat the relevant parts of the spell.)

The spell

* At dawn (or as early as you wake) on the day before planting, place nine of the jade or moss agate crystals (known as the gardener's crystals) in the jug of water. Take the jug outside and leave it there for 24 hours. The crystals will imbue the water with pure life force, and during the 24-hour cycle the water will absorb sunlight and moonlight, even if the weather is cloudy.

* While the water is charging, set the remaining four crystals in the four corners of the garden. If you are planting in tubs, place them in four tubs in the corners of the area you are working in. (If you are planting a single tub, use only one crystal.)

* On the morning of planting, set the flowers or herbs you are going to plant, still in their tiny pots, in a circle.

* Scatter a few drops of the empowered water on each plant, as you do so saying:
  Be filled with light and life to unfold growth. Grow tall and strong, thrive and blossom each in your time.

* Dig holes to plant the flowers or herbs, sprinkling a little of the empowered water into each, as you do so saying:
  Root deep in Mother Earth that you may live long and when you are done seed new life and so live on.

* Plant the first herb or flower, as you cover its roots, saying:
  Grow from earth to sky, breathe your green life and purify and make beautiful the world.

* Sprinkle a little more of the empowered water on the soil around the plant, as you do so saying:
  Light to life, so life continues.

* Plant the remaining flowers or herbs in this way, repeating the chants.

* Every time you water your plants, add a few drops of the remaining empowered water to your watering can. If growth seems slow at any time, make more empowered water during the waxing moon and use it to water the plants.

An offerings spell for the health of plants

The best offerings to the benign essences of nature are, I believe, to wild birds. Birds may peck at precious seeds, but they also keep destructive insects down naturally and can pollinate seeds. In my own experience, the more you welcome wildlife into the garden, the more you are blessed with healthy growth. Should you not want birds in your garden, however, you can use a small jug of milk and some bread-crumbs for this spell, holding each in turn upwards to receive the light and then placing them in an offerings bowl (using the chants below). Eat a few of the crumbs and a tiny quantity of the milk to link your offering to yourself. I do this spell every morning, as soon as it is light.

You will need

A dish of bird seed; a jug of water; a small raised bird table, piece of wood on a pole, or nut or seed feeder; a raised bird bath or dish, or a small bowl in a high place.

Timing

Whenever you have the time.

The spell

* Take the dish of bird seed and jug of water into the garden.
* Hold the seeds high to catch any light and say:
  Light enter this garden this day. Health and healing flourish that all may thrive and grow. I make this offering to the essences of the garden with thanks.
* Put the seeds on the bird table or in the feeder, as you do so saying:
  Life enter this garden this day. Health and healing flourish that all may thrive and grow. I make this offering to the essences of the garden with thanks.
* Hold the water high to catch any light and repeat the first chant.
* Fill the bird bath or bowl with water (sprinkling any remaining water on the earth) and repeat the second chant.
* Restock the bird table or feeder and bird bath or bowl each morning, repeating the chants.

A bonfire fertility and healing ritual for your garden

Traditionally, a ritual fire was lit on the ancient fertility festivals. The ashes were then scattered on fields and gardens to transfer the fertilising powers to the plants. These celebrations were held at the spring equinox; on May day eve (30 April); at the summer solstice; at Lammas (or Lughnassadh), the first harvest eve (31 July); and on twelfth night (January 6) or the evening before. You can adapt these dates or pick significant days in your own seasonal or family calendar for celebratory fires. Alternatively, use any impromptu bonfires (for the burning of wood or leaf matter) to top up your garden's magical power. If you live in an apartment, you can burn some dead leaves or flowers in the flame of a large candle placed in a metal bucket filled with sand. Bury a few of the burnt leaves in the pot of a new pot plant. Take any unburnt leaves outside and allow them to blow away.

You will need

A bonfire fuelled with wood or garden waste; a small trowel; a new plant.

Timing

On one of the old festivals, on a significant date in your seasonal or family calendar, or when you have a bonfire.

The spell

* Light the bonfire.
* When the bonfire is burning, throw some wood or dead vegetation on it, as you do so saying:
  From old life comes new. The essence of the past feeds the future. Life flames anew.
* Allow the bonfire to burn down and leave the ashes overnight.
* In the morning, scoop up a few ashes with the trowel.
* Plant the new plant, adding a few of the ashes to the soil and repeating the chant. Allow the rest of the ashes to blow away.

A ritual to make a garden grow under difficult circumstances

This spell works for either a whole garden or a problem area. There are many reasons why you may need to restore health to a garden. You may have bought a new house outside which the builders have left a sea of clay – or an old one surrounded by impersonal lawns or a junk yard. Or you may have suffered bad storm damage. If it is raining, carry out the ritual indoors, somewhere where you can see the garden, and plant the seedlings as soon as the weather improves. You can also use this ritual if you are helping with a community project such as a children's play area.

You will need

A green glass bowl or wide-necked bottle half filled with still mineral water that has been left outside for a full 24 hours with a jade crystal in it all the while; 9 small jade or moss agate crystals; 9 small seedlings in pots.

Timing

Early on a Friday or Saturday morning (both Earth days).

The spell

● Place the pots of seedlings in a circle, interspersed with the nine small jade or moss agate crystals
● Sit in the centre of the circle facing North and, beginning in the East (for the rising day), pick up the seedlings one by one and sprinkle nine drops of the mineral water over each seedling, saying for each:
From darkness to light bring healing, restoration and beauty.
● Dig a small hole for each seedling, pouring into each hole a further nine drops of water and saying:
From darkness to light flourish, reach upwards and reach fullness.
● Plant each seedling in turn, as you do so saying:
From darkness to light, may warm sun and gentle rain sustain you.
● Take the jade crystal out of the bottle or bowl and place it in a flower bed near the seedlings.

A flower essence spell to heal a sick indoor or outdoor special plant

However well cared for, a particular flower or plant may not thrive. If it was expensive or given as a present, its potential loss can be especially upsetting. As well as feeding it and making sure it gets enough light, giving it a single drop of Dr Bach's Rescue (or Five Flower) Remedy, made up of Cherry Plum, Clematis, Impatiens, Star of Bethlehem and Rock Rose, has an amazing effect on even the most dejected of plants. By using Rescue Remedy – or indeed any of your favourite flower essences (there are now hundreds of different varieties available throughout the world) – as part of a spell, you can amplify both the energy of the Remedy and the self-regenerative powers of the plant.

You will need

A small bottle of Rescue Remedy (or another Remedy of your choice); a healthy plant, preferably of the same species as the sick one.

Timing

During the lightest part of the day, preferably in sunlight.

The spell

* Holding the bottle of Remedy in your receptive hand (the one you don't write with), pass it in three widdershins (anti-clockwise) circles over the top of the healthy plant. At the same time, move your power hand deosil (clockwise) above your receptive hand, so that it passes directly above the bottle, creating a three-layer vortex of power rising from the healthy plant. As you move your hands, say three times:

Rise healing force. Share your abundant source of goodness, for life is multiplied by blessings shared.

* Using your receptive hand, pass the Remedy bottle in three deosil circles over the sick plant. At the same time, move your power hand above your receptive hand in three widdershins circles. This reverses the vortex of power so that the healing passes downwards into the sick plant. As you move your hands, say three times:

Fall healing force. Share your abundant source of goodness, for life is multiplied by blessings shared.

* Add a single drop of the Remedy to the soil of both plants, close to the base of the stem.
* Put a drop of the empowered Remedy in to the soil of the failing plant daily until it shows signs of recovery.

A spell to strengthen a weak plant or group of plants

Like humans, plants are believed to have an aura, or psychic energy field, resembling a halo around them. Kirlian photography, a method of capturing aura images, has shown that when part of a plant is cut off, the aura of the missing part remains like a ghostly image. Plants that are kept in an office, that get scratched or bitten by pets or tugged at by children, or that are surrounded by of a lot of cigarette smoke can become depleted of vitality. Slowly the plant wilts and eventually dies. One of the easiest ways to strengthen a plant and compensate for any torn or missing leaves is by using a crystal pendulum. Work this spell outdoors if possible.

You will need

A crystal pendulum.

Timing

On a Tuesday (which is an excellent strengthening day), during the brightest part of the day.

The spell

※ Holding the pendulum about 2.5 cm/ I in from the plant, move it slowly deosil (clockwise) around the plant, spiralling it close in to the plant and then out again, as though you were weaving a web with threads of light. (You are infusing the aura of the plant with light and movement.) As you weave, say softly, over and over again:

Thread of healing, thread so bright,
Weave a web of health and light.

※ When you sense the plant becoming more alive, move the pendulum slowly away, as though you were casting off and tying a knot in the invisible thread.

※ Use the pendulum to create nine deosil circles of light above the plant, one on top of the other, the innermost circle about 6 cm/$2^1/_2$ in away from the plant. This will seal in the new energy. For each circle say:

Three by three,
Restored now be

A three-candle spell for a wilting plant

This spell is very effective for indoor plants or those that have been adversely affected by a sudden frost. Patchouli oil is an Earth fragrance that is very healing for both the environment and the health of individual plants.

You will need

3 small, squat, green candles in deep holders; patchouli essential oil.

Timing

When necessary, but noon is an appropriately energy-filled time.

The spell

※ Set the candles in a triangle formation with the apex at the top. Place the ailing plant in the centre of the triangle.

※ Light the candles, beginning with the one at the apex, then moving to the one on the left and finally to the one on the right.

※ When the wax has formed a pool around the wick, picture the plant growing tall and luxuriant.

※ Taking care not to get oil on the wick, place a single drop of patchouli in the melted wax of each candle, working in the order of lighting. (If you are worried about adding oil to a lighted candle, blow the candle out first, drop the oil in to the pool of wax and then re-light it. This will not affect the spell, as you will always have two candles burning.) Say for each drop:

Restored to life and radiance. So shall it be in candles three. This healing drop from Mother Earth will bring rebirth, and you will thrive anew.

※ Leave the candles around the plant to burn through.

A spell for when a new or transplanted flower or tree fails to thrive in its new location

We have probably all at some time bought a plant that looked splendid in the garden centre but that refuses to thrive in its new home. The same thing can happen when we try to move a favourite plant to a new home or transplant a bush because it has become too big for its pot. The important thing is to increase the plant's connection to its new location. I have a raised flower box especially for intensive care in my garden, where I have restored many displaced plants, including a kumquat tree that was reduced to a stick and that now has rich green leaves and firm orange fruit. A once stringy basil plant is now also luxuriant and wonderfully fragrant. This is a good spell to use when you need to transplant a bush or tree. Prepare your crystal in advance by leaving it first in sunlight, then in rain and then in a gentle breeze. (If it does not rain, you can run it under water.)

You will need

A soft-green jade, rich-green amazonite or rose quartz crystal (jade and rose quartz are sometimes available in heart shapes, which are ideal for this spell); a trowel.

Timing

On a Friday (a good day for gentle growth).

The spell

* Standing facing the plant, hold the crystal in your open cupped hands and breathe on it three times slowly. After each breath say softly:
  Breathe life into this plant that it may live.
* Holding the crystal in your power hand (the one you write with) touch it three times to your heart and say:
  Give heart back to this plant that it may thrive.
* Dig a small hole as near to the centre of the plant stem as you can, if necessary burrowing down between the leaves.
* Place the crystal in the hole. Breathe in deeply and on the out-breath push the crystal deep in to the earth, as you do so saying:
  May roots go deep that it may find its home.
* Breathe and push the crystal deeply in to the earth twice more.
* Fill in the hole, as you do so saying:
  Rest here content and in contentment grow. It shall be so.

A pyramid spell for healing plants

On page 460 I write about pyramids and their ability to heal humans. Pyramids have also been shown to bring about accelerated growth in plants. Indeed, plant growers have reported increases in growth rate of over 150 per cent when a plant is placed under a pyramid. In experiments with different greenhouse shapes, plants grew up to 20 cm/8 in a day in summer under a pyramid – and even in freezing winter weather continued to grow under a pyramid frame. Tomato seeds also sprouted earlier when exposed to pyramid energy. Most remarkably of all, watering with pyramid water (water left beneath a pyramid shape overnight) had the same effect on plant growth as keeping plants under a pyramid. By using a spell you can amplify these effects still further. Pyramid water will revive plants that are ailing or are failing to grow, and even seems to reverse frost damage.

You will need

A squat crystal pyramid, or a pyramid frame made from copper (the best material and very pliable), wood or cardboard tubes and in proportion to the Great Pyramid of Cheops, which is 147 m/481 ft high and has four sides, each measuring 230 m/755 ft at the base (the model should be big enough to cover a large bowl of water); a large bowl of water.

Timing

At night, when the stars can be seen in the sky. (Prepare the pyramid water in advance – see the first step below.)

The spell

* During the day before the spell, prepare the pyramid water by setting the crystal pyramid in the bowl of water or setting the bowl of water under the pyramid frame (either indoors or outdoors) and saying:
The days of drought are ended. Water of the first creation, rise and bring fertility.

* When the stars come out, carry the water to the sickly or inert plant and, using both hands, scatter droplets of water from the bowl over the plant, as you do so saying:
Sirius rises anew. The fertile waters of the Nile flow forth. Strong shall you grow towards the stars.

* Keep any remaining water somewhere cool and repeat the sprinkling and the Sirius chant every night that the stars are shining until the water is gone. You should see a great improvement, even in a few days.

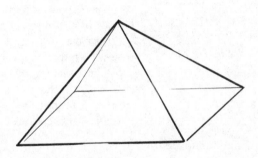

A spell for making a witch ball to keep harm away from a garden

Witch balls – which look like huge silver, green or blue Christmas baubles – are popular for gardens on either side of the Atlantic. They are hung from a tree in the centre of the garden in order to keep safe and healthy all that is reflected within them. The distorted images are intended to frighten away anything that might damage the garden and, of course, its owners. The original witch balls were probably glass fishing floats. These are widely available in department and gift stores as well as fishing shops and antique fairs. I have several secured right in the middle of my garden, surrounding my witch ball. They reflect images from all angles. If you cannot find a witch ball in the shops, you can make your own by painting a large, ornamental, clear glass sphere with metallic paint. Alternatively, use large convex mirrors suspended from branches on different sides of a central tree or sturdy bush. You can also hang a witch ball in a conservatory or on a balcony. In this case, use a regular-sized incense or smudge stick to perform the spell.

You will need

A witch ball or witch ball substitute; tea-lights, outdoor oil torches or outdoor fairylights to illuminate the garden; a large stick of citronella, cedar or pine outdoor incense (of the kind that stands in the soil), alternatively a large sage or cedar smudge stick in a safe holder in the ground.

Timing

After dark.

The spell

* As the day fades, illuminate the garden with the tea-lights, torches or fairylights.

* At first darkness hang your witch ball, as you do so saying:
Be guardian to this garden. Be guardian of all who shelter here: birds, frogs, lizards, creatures of the night, moths and butterflies, herbs, flowers, trees (adapt the list to fit your own garden and its inhabitants). Protected all!

* Either twirl the witch ball or yourself turn in deosil circles, moving from mirror to mirror and saying:
All within the glass keep safe from blight and frost and flood and drought. Serene, secure, tranquil, green, safe will be and safe remain.

* Light the incense or smudge stick and move round the garden, making smoke swirls in all directions and saying:
Shield and bless, guard and nurture, beloved garden, haven, home and sanctuary. Glass, stand sentinel and be ever vigilant. Protect the smallest ant and tallest tree.

* Move the incense or smudge smoke fast in an arch in front of the ball and spin the ball, so that the images likewise revolve. (If you are using mirrors, make arches above, below and around each one.) Say:
Hide from harm, deflect from danger; grow here in peace, fragrance-filled. Garden be healed, garden be healing; all be sealed within this magic ball.

* Look into the witch ball and spin it again (or turn rapidly and gaze into one of the mirrors). You may see an image that will answer a question that has been troubling you.

* If it is warm enough, spend the evening in the garden with family or friends until the tea-lights or torches and incense are burnt away.

39 SPELLS FOR a healThy PREGnancy and childBiRTh

Magic has always been associated with childbirth. In traditional cultures, women who are pregnant women or in labour are considered to touch another dimension, especially as and just after the child comes into the world. In Greenland until fairly recently, for example, new mothers were credited with the ability to raise winds and control storms. They had only to go out in to the wind, fill their mouths with air, come back into the house and blow it out again.

In any society a woman can feel very vulnerable during a pregnancy, especially if it is her first one. I was a competent and very self-assured teacher when, aged 30, I conceived my first child, but pregnancy left me feeling totally lost and petrified. The spells in this chapter will help to connect you with the wisdom of other women who are pregnant or in labour, endowing you with their strength. Expectant fathers can also benefit from using these spells, especially if they are feeling isolated or redundant in the process of pregnancy and birth.

The spells in this chapter come from a number of lands and ages. They will also work if you are waiting to adopt or foster a child of any age, whether you are a first-time adoptive parent or have welcomed many children into your home and heart.

A spell to discover the sex of an unborn baby

Though scans (if you choose to have them) can sometimes reveal the sex of your baby, at other times they are indeterminate (and are not guaranteed accurate). You may, of course, prefer not to know the sex of your unborn child, but if you do want to find out, try this or one of the following age-old magical methods common to a number of cultures. By connecting with the natural intuition of the mother, they are able to predict the sex of the baby with a high rate of success. Pregnant women often do know intuitively – and other women who have given birth may also be uncannily accurate about the sex of friends' or relatives' unborn infants. Using a spell enhances this intuition. This spell comes from the West Midlands of England and may originate among the canal people from whom I am descended, a number of whom are linked with an ancient water witch tradition. Originally, the pregnant woman would have stood in the middle of a circle of female relatives, who would take it in turns to whirl her round widdershins (anticlockwise) nine times in all.

You will need

A needle or pin attached to a 15-cm/ 6-in length of thread, or your wedding ring (or the ring of a woman who has given birth) tied to a piece of thread as above or a long strand of your hair.

Timing

When the moon is bright in the sky, any time after the pregnancy has been confirmed.

The spell

* Loop the needle or pin over your receptive wrist (the one belonging to the hand you do not write with) so that it is suspended or hold the thread of the wedding ring between the first and second fingers of your receptive hand.
* Turn around on the spot nine times widdershins (anti-clockwise), as you do so saying:
Widdershins, follow the moon,
Widdershins, tell me soon,
Boy or girl, speak now to me;
Show your true identity.
Boy, girl, boy, girl, boy, girl,
Boy, girl, as now I whirl.
* Stop turning and, while your head is still spinning, allow the needle, pin or ring suspended from your wrist to steady its rhythm. (If you prefer, you can hold it over your stomach.) If you are using a needle or pin, it will swing backwards and forwards if the baby is a boy and twirl in circles if the baby is a girl. If it makes both movements in succession, you may have twins, one of each sex. If you are using a ring, it will rotate widdershins for a boy and deosil (clockwise) for a girl.

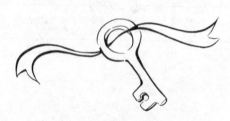

A Romany gypsy spell to discover the sex of an unborn child

In order to discover the sex of their unborn child, at the full moon Romany women would go to a forest where wild red and white roses were growing together. They would twirl around and pick a rose. Its colour would indicate the sex of the baby.

You will need

One red- and one white-flowering rose bush both close together, or tubs of white and red roses – alternatively a vase of red and a vase of white roses.

Timing

The first full moon after pregnancy is confirmed.

The spell

* With your eyes closed, spin around 11 times widdershins (anti-clockwise), as you do so saying:

  Red or white?
  I ask this night.

  Delightful child,
  In roses wild,
  Reveal your kind:
  Red or white,
  And in my mind
  Your name.

* Using both hands, reach out for a single flower. If you pick a red rose, the child will be a boy; if you pick a white rose, it will be a girl. A double-headed flower is especially fortunate, indicating an easy birth and possibly twins. A child's name may come into your mind – perhaps one that you would not necessarily have chosen but that will prove appropriate.

* When the child is born, plant a red or white rose bush. (Traditionally, a cutting was carried in a pot of earth in the caravan until the birth and then planted wherever the family found themselves.)

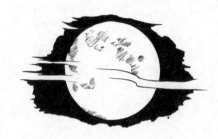

A spell to connect with the unborn infant

With modern technology playing an increasingly important role in the care of expectant mothers, pregnancy can involve much medical care and advice but leave the spirit out. If you work until close to the birth or already have a small child to look after, it can be hard to find quiet time for getting to know the baby in the womb. Some fathers will enjoy sharing this spell – and, indeed, baby time does make family bonding easier once the baby is born. If you do the spell regularly, the natural connection will be amplified. Try doing it also if you get tired and dispirited. The crystal will form the bridge between you and your unborn infant. If possible, choose a crystal from a selection of similar crystals so you can use your instinct to feel the one that is right. If you are buying by mail order, send for two or three crystals and hold each one in turn. (You can use the others as protective crystals in the nursery if you like.)

You will need

A large crystal chosen specially for this spell – unpolished amethyst, blue calcite and rose quartz can be bought quite cheaply; a soft light or fibre optic lamp (optional).

Timing

Once you feel the little one kicking (though some people may want to make the psychic connection earlier or later in the pregnancy), in soft morning or afternoon light.

The spell

* If the day is dull, work by the light of a soft light or fibre optic lamp. If possible, work in a soft morning or afternoon light. Sit where light falls on the womb, but not intense sunlight. Rest the crystal on your stomach and clasp your hands around the crystal. Your partner can put his hands over yours.

* Speak or sing softly to the infant. If you or your partner have a musical gift, however modest, play a gentle harmonious tune for the baby (scientists tell us that a baby's hearing develops early and the sounds that soothe in the womb will be recognised and equally soothing after birth). In response you may even receive a flutter, a wriggle or a kick, while you yourself may experience a flood of love and a sense of connection.

* End the spell by saying:
  Blessings, little one. I welcome you into my life and my home as I carry you now and always within my heart.
  (Adapt the words if your partner is sharing the ritual.)

* After the birth you may find you can soothe the baby by holding the crystal to the light and repeating phrases, songs or music from when your infant was in the womb.

A spell to help a first-time mother tap into the universal experience of motherhood

In earlier times, older female relatives would share their expertise with a pregnant woman, surrounding her with reassurance. But increasingly today women live away from everyday family support. Older women have careers of their own and so are not as instantly available for advice and support. The following spell taps into the universal experiences of mothers everywhere and will help you to connect spiritually as well as physically with the unborn child. Your partner may like to share the spell with you, but try it alone first to make the connection.

You will need
A comfortable chair or bed.

Timing
When you will not be disturbed and are feeling sleepy but not exhausted

The spell
* Lie or sit, resting both your hands lightly on your stomach. Say:
  You are new to being my child. I am new to being your mother. Together will we grow in love and in tenderness.
* Keep your hands on your stomach and picture pink spirals of light moving to and from the womb, enclosing you in a soft haze of warmth and contentment.
* Now place your hands flat against your stomach and say:
  I will teach you and you will teach me. One day our hands will touch and we will remember this moment when we first met in love.
* Sit in silence, sending words of love from your mind to your unborn infant.
* Repeat the ritual regularly.
* When the baby is born, enclose his or her tiny hands in yours and say:
  I will teach you and you will teach me. Our hands touch. Remember the moment when we first met in love.
* Look into your child's face and you will sense a flicker of recognition and know that the two of you can get through anything together.

A Celtic St Bridget s spell to overcome fears in pregnancy and of giving birth

St Bridget, or Bride, is the Christianised version of the ancient Irish triple goddess Brighid, so this is a prayer that has been used by women of Celtic descent over many centuries before and during labour. An American friend sent it to me. In legend, Bridget was regarded as the midwife of Christ, although in fact she lived five centuries later. However, it may be some early Middle Eastern woman did take this role and the myth was transferred. Take a small phial of the water with you when you go into labour if you wish, or simply recite the words of the charm whenever you need them.

You will need

A bottle of still mineral water; a glass bowl; some sea salt; a small silver-coloured knife; some small, lidded glass bottles.

Timing

Whenever you feel afraid.

The spell

* Place the mineral water in the bowl and add three pinches of sea salt, as you do so saying:

Come to my help,
Mary fair and Bride,
As Anna bore Mary,
As Mary bore Christ,
As Eile bore John the Baptist
Without flaw in him.
Aid thou in my unbearing.
Aid me, O Bride.

(Eile refers to Elizabeth, the cousin of Mary, who six months before Mary gave birth to Jesus, herself gave birth to John the Baptist. She was long past childbearing age, so the birth was regarded as a miracle.)

* Stir the water deosil (clockwise) with the knife and then make either the Celtic Christian equal-armed cross or the Earth Mother's diagonal cross three times in the water with the knife, as you do so repeating the chant.
* Pour the water into the bottles and keep them cool.
* Whenever you feel uncertain or experience a problem (such as early contractions) or perhaps have a scan or tests, place three drops of the water on your forehead, repeating the words for each drop.

A spell to empower a crystal birth angel to take to the birth

One of the most precious childbirth aids is a small crystal angel. I have seen many on sale in a variety of stores. They are made out of purple and green fluorite or pink rose quartz, both wonderful birth crystals. Alternatively, choose a round blue angelite, celestite or golden rutilated quartz crystal, all said to attract angels. Other possibilities are green or purple fluorite, watermelon (pink and green) tourmaline or purple amethyst. Buy the angel or crystal early in the pregnancy and carry it with you whenever you go to see a midwife or doctor or go to the hospital. Make time regularly to sit quietly by the light of a pink or beeswax candle, resting the angel on your womb and asking its protection for you and the baby.

The words of the spell refer to three mothers helped by the Archangel Gabriel: Elizabeth and Mary, mentioned in the previous spell, and Anne, grandmother of Christ, who conceived the Virgin Mary long after her childbearing years were over. They have passed into the folk tradition, sometimes replacing the Madrones, the pre-Christian three mothers. Anne and Elizabeth are the particular helpers of older mothers. Beeswax is sacred to the Virgin Mary and St Anne.

You will need

Your birth angel or crystal; 3 beeswax candles.

Timing

About three months before the due date.

The ritual

* Set the candles in a row and place the angel or crystal in front of the first candle on the left. Sit facing the candles.
* Light the first candle. Hold the angel or crystal in your cupped hands and say:
  Archangel Gabriel who helped Elizabeth, Mary and Anne during the hours of birth, send your healing strength through this angel/crystal to lead me and my unborn child likewise safely into birth. May I, when the time is right, hold my beloved child in my arms and like Elizabeth and Mary and Anne know joy in being a mother.
* Leave the candle burning, using the time to make preparations for the arrival of the baby or listening to music. Just before the candle goes out, light the middle candle from it. (If it goes out prematurely, light the second candle from a taper – it is not a bad omen, merely the composition of the candle.)
* Set the angel or crystal in front of the second candle and repeat the words.
* Again, leave the candle to almost burn down and then light the third candle from it.
* Set the angel or crystal in front of the third candle and repeat the words, then leave it to burn out and afterwards dispose of the wax.
* In the days leading up to the birth, keep the angel or crystal by your bedside when you rest. When you go into labour, whether at home or in hospital, hold the angel or set it where you can see it and say the words in your head, drawing on the strength of the mothers.
* Keep the angel near you and the baby, and when your child is old enough, you can make him or her a present of the angel or crystal.

A childbirth knot spell

In a number of cultures, midwives would carry out knot spells to ease labour magically, symbolically unknotting the cervix and so releasing the infant. The idea of birth knots has remained in some remote communities. Even with modern technological birth practices, a pre-labour knot spell can be a good way of focusing your natural birthing energies. I have known mothers carry out the ritual before a Caesarean birth in order to ease the infant's transition. Indeed, if you have an epidural or spinal block and remain awake, as I did for my third Caesarean, you will feel a gentle pushing as the baby is born. You can then recite the knot chant in your head (or even hold the unknotted cord).

You will need

A red cord 15–20 cm/6–8 in long; a natural fabric drawstring bag.

Timing

Around your due date or when you sense that labour may be about to begin – or the day before you go in to hospital for a Caesarean birth.

The spell

* Tie three loose knots in the cord, saying for each:
Babe, keep safe until your time to come into the world, and then come easily.
* Place the knotted cord in the bag, as you close it repeating the chant three times.
* Keep the bag in your hospital bag or with your birth equipment if you are having a home birth.
* When labour begins or when you go into hospital for a Caesarian birth, untie the first knot, as you do so saying:
Babe, your time has come to enter the world. Come easily and safely to me/your waiting family.
* Untie the second knot at a suitable time and then the final one as close to the birth as possible.
* Fasten the unknotted cord loosely round your wrist or keep it near you, reciting the chant in your head when you feel the need.
* If the labour is unduly slow, tie one large loose knot in the cord and then untie it, as you do so saying softly:
Babe, come safe into the world and easily.
* After the birth, loop the cord over the head of your bed and keep it there until it frays.

A power of Hathor spell for labour

According to the Papyrus Leyden, ritual played an important role in childbirth in ancient Egypt, even though gynaecological knowledge at the time was surprisingly advanced. Seven red knots, one for each of the daughters of the goddess Hathor, were tied before the beginning of labour. They were untied one at a time to help the passage of the child and the opening of the womb (see spell on page 514). This and the following spell are adaptations of ancient Egyptian birth rituals that you may find helpful before and during labour.

This spell is an alternative to the crystal birth angel spell on page 513. It may suit women who like a stronger icon. During labour in ancient Egypt, a birth attendant would tell a woman, 'I am Hathor, come to give birth for thee' or, 'Hathor will lay her hand on thee with an amulet of healing.' When the labouring woman appeared to be tiring, the attendant would touch her gently on the brow and give her a tiny statue of Hathor, thus transmitting soothing and sustaining energies. If you cannot find a statue of Hathor, you can craft yourself (or ask your birth partner to craft you) one from wood or clay. Form your chosen material in to a small pillar shape and use the image below to paint or etch Hathor on the front. You can

also use Hathor's animal icon, the cow, in the form of a silver, ceramic or hand-made charm, small enough to hold in your hand.

You will need

A small statue or charm of Hathor (available from museum shops throughout the world or by mail order); a stick of rose incense; a red candle; a purse or drawstring bag.

Timing

A few days before birth is due, during the hour before sunset (Hathor's hour).

The spell

* Light the red candle (Hathor's colour) and set the image of Hathor in front of it. Light the rose incense (Hathor's fragrance) from the candle.
* Take up the incense and weave in smoke spirals in front of the image the words: 'I am Hathor come to give birth for thee.' Then return the incense to its holder.
* Pick up the image and touch the centre of your brow with it, as you do so saying softly:
  Hathor will lay her hand on thee with an amulet of healing.
* Return the image to its place in front of the candle and, taking up the incense once more, write in smoke spirals around the image the words: 'I am Hathor come to give birth for thee.'
* Leave the incense and candle to burn down.
* Keep the image in the purse or drawstring bag until you go into labour.
* If you become tired during labour, ask your birth partner to touch your brow with the image and give it to you to hold. You can repeat the two chants in your head as often as you wish.

A Mother Isis spell for giving birth

In ancient Egypt, the story was often told of how Mother Isis gave birth to her son Horus in the papyrus marshes. Isis was assisted by Nephthys, her sister, supporting her from behind, and the scorpion goddess Serqet, or Selk, delivering. With this help, according to the Westcar Papyrus, 'the infant rushed forth from Isis, his limbs strong'.

There are any number of Egyptian goddesses whose energies protect during birth. I have experimented with many of them in work with pregnant women and have found the best combination to be gentle Isis standing in front and encouraging, with the fierce and beautiful golden Serqet standing behind and protecting from all harm. But look through any illustrated book about ancient Egypt and you may find other goddesses whose energies seem right for you. Hathor is another popular choice. (You will find more ideas in my *Ancient Egyptian Magic*, Vega, 2003.) This spell is carried out before the birth so that you can visualise the protective goddesses assisting during your actual labour, and perhaps repeat the words. If you are giving birth in an informal situation, it may be possible to light two small candles. You can repeat the ritual any number of times.

You will need

2 large beeswax or white pillar candles.

Timing

Any late afternoon or early evening in late pregnancy.

The spell

* Turn to the South (a direction sacred to Isis). Visualise Isis standing in front of you, dressed in gold, with golden wings and a sun disk between her horns. Say:
  Before me, Isis, Mother, you who gave birth to your son in the papyrus marshes. Encourage and guide me likewise that I may give birth like you, safely and easily.
* Picture Isis enfolding you in her beautiful wings, easing you through labour.
* Turn to the North and see Serqet, also dressed in gold, with a scorpion headdress and golden wings. Say:
  Behind me Serqet, Lady of the Quicksilver Scorpions. As you guarded Isis in the marshes, protect me likewise from pains and from difficulty that I may give birth safely and easily.
* Picture Serqet enfolding you in her golden wings.
* Turn back to the South and say:
  Isis, Mother, be midwife unto me and deliver me at my due time safely and easily.
* Turn back to the North and say:
  Serqet, Sister, be midwife unto me and deliver me at my due time safely and easily.
* Light a candle in the South, in the position in which you visualised Isis, repeating the two Isis chants and picturing the goddess in the flame.
* Light a candle in the North, in the position in which you visualised Serqet, repeating the two Serqet chants and picturing the goddess in the flame.
* Leave the candles to burn through.
* If you have a chance during labour, light two beeswax candles and repeat the chants; if there is no opportunity use any focal lights and imagine them as your lovely goddesses.

A Celtic birth spell

Roughly sculpted figures of a woman in the act of giving birth are one of the most powerful fertility and childbirth icons and are used by modern pagan women in childbirth, as hundreds of years ago, no doubt, they were used by women labouring. Such figures have been discovered independently in different parts of the world, but they bear remarkable resemblance to one another. In Mesoamerica, for example, small hand-held statues of Tlazoltcotl, the Aztec birthing goddess, were made (often in green apatite or jadeite) up until the Spanish Conquest at the beginning of the sixteenth century. The head of the baby can be seen emerging from the goddess. In Ireland and England the Sheelagh-na-gig is carved on churches. She is a hag-like female form, depicted squatting and holding her vulva open, as though she is about to give birth. Small Sheelagh statues were traditionally used in Celtic lands by women in labour. One would be handed down through the generations, kept locked away except when a family member was giving birth. Some Wiccan mothers I know carry on the tradition. You may find this idea a total turn-off, but Sheelagh figures are incredibly powerful, and if you are anticipating birth complications, such as a multiple or breech birth, or you are very nervous about the birth, this age-old symbol can be remarkably comforting. The chant in this spell refers to the Modrana or Madrones, the Celtic midwife goddesses who protected women in childbirth and their infants.

You will need

A Sheelagh-na-gig figurine (or another round-bellied full-breasted ancient birth mother figure, available from New Age or ethnic goods stores); a deep bowl of water, large enough to immerse the figurine in; a soft cloth.

Timing

As light breaks, when you are awake and are restless, or at sunset in the last weeks of pregnancy.

The spell

* Fill the bowl with water and immerse the figure in it three times in succession, at each immersion saying:
  Mother midwives of the night,
  Take my fears with the light.
  Sheelagh, open safe my womb
  From waters warm to welcoming room.
  Midwives, mothers of the night,
  Bring, I ask, bring forth new life.
* Carefully dry the figure and keep her covered with a soft cloth until the day you go into labour.
* Take the figure with you to the hospital or keep her near you if you are giving birth at home. Hold her if you feel anxious, repeating the chant in your head.
* Keep the figurine wrapped for subsequent pregnancies. Later, you may like to give it to your own child, or your child's partner, as an icon of safe birth.

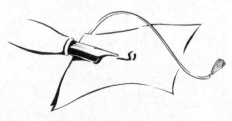

Four easy childbirth spells that can be carried out by waiting relatives

Unless you can be present at the birth, waiting while the mother is in labour can seem endless. If the mother is giving birth for the first time or the labour is long, you may feel totally helpless. The following are traditional spells from different cultures to send strength to the mother and the birth partner.

Spell 1: A Scottish locks and door spell: If labour seems slow, undo any locks on drawers and doors, and every half hour open the windows and doors (close them again after about five minutes), as you do so saying:

Open wide. Be bound no more.

If you have any cats or dogs, send them out into the garden. This way you are symbolically releasing any blockages in the birth process.

Spell 2: A West African birth ritual: The oldest woman present says:

The child is still bound in the womb, but we will release her/him.

The youngest woman present fetches a long strand of trailing plant and give it to the oldest woman, who chops it into pieces with a sharp knife, saying:

I cut through the bonds. I release the womb and the child. Come into the world, where we wait to greet you.

Spell 3: A Slovakian birth ritual: If birth is slow, the father fetches water from where two streams converge and moistens the labouring woman's forehead with it. (A woman can do this if male relatives are reluctant.) Use any converging water device, for example a mixer tap or shower attachment. Collect a cupful every hour and pour it as slowly as possible into the earth, saying:

Mother Earth, bring birth and relief to (name) as the waters flow.

Spell 4: A candle spell: Light a pure-white or beeswax candle when you first hear that the mother is in labour. As the wax melts, say:

So melts away pain and resistance. Flow new life into the world as the candle burns away.

Light another white or beeswax candle before the first is completely burnt down and repeat the words. If a candle goes out it is not a bad omen, just the result of a breeze or the composition of the candle.

A Celtic or Baisteadh Breith birth celebration

Traditionally, a Celtic midwife placed three drops of sacred water on the newborn infant's head to represent the powers of Earth, sea and sky. This ritual was said to have been first carried out by St Bridget when Christ was born. This can be a lovely ritual if you have experienced a prolonged or high-tech birth or if you are in an impersonal hospital ward. You can share it with your partner or carry it out alone.

You will need
Nothing.

Timing
When you have some peaceful time, perhaps when everyone else is asleep.

The spell
* Hold the child in your arms and say the old Celtic birth baptism words:

  To aid thee from the fays,
  To guard thee from the host,
  To aid thee from the gnome,
  To shield thee from the spectre,
  To keep thee for the three,
  To shield thee and surround thee.

(The fays are harmful faeries; the host was the Slaugh, a host of dark spirits believed to ride through the air; and the three were the triple goddess – later, in Christian times, the Father, Son and Holy Spirit.)

* Kiss the baby very lightly in the centre of the forehead for the protection of the Earth and name three earthly practical blessings for the child, for example health, abundance and common sense.
* Kiss the child a second time for the protection of the sky and name three intellectual or spiritual blessings, for example knowledge, mental ability and spiritual gifts.
* Kiss the child a third time for the protection of the sea and name three emotional blessings, for example sympathy with others, compassion and a rich imagination.
* Talk softly to the baby about her or his home, family and future life until it is time for you both to sleep.

A coming home ritual

Traditionally, the midwife would carry a baby to the top of a hill in order that it should rise in the world. If you are too tired, a relative can carry out this ritual for you.

You will need
Nothing.

Timing
When you bring your new baby home.

The spell
* As soon as you enter your home, carry the baby upstairs to the landing and say:
So shall you rise in life, in prosperity, success and happiness, and thereby do good to all creatures on the earth, in the sea and in the skies.
(If you do not have stairs, gently lift the baby upwards, still cradled in your arms.)

A spell to bond with a newborn infant

Mothers (and fathers) are supposed to fall instantly in love with their newborn child. There are all kinds of reasons why this may not occur – a prolonged labour, temporary separation after the birth, less than ideal conditions in hospital or at home immediately after the birth, tiredness and hormonal problems. Performing this spell is a good way of making a connection that will grow over the months and years. It can also be useful for a father who feels helpless or left out.

You will need
Nothing.

Timing
When the baby is quiet.

The spell
* Touch the centre of your brow and then your baby's. Say:
We are joined spirit to spirit.
* Touch your own closed lips and then the baby's. Say:
We are joined breath to breath.
* Touch your heart and then the baby's. Say:
We are joined heart and heart. So shall it be always even when we are apart.
* Repeat the ritual whenever you start to feel overwhelmed – as most parents do at times by a new baby.

40 SPELLS FOR RELIEVING PAIN

Pain is debilitating. If it is chronic, it may make it difficult for the sufferer to rest and can dominate waking life. While there is now much effective medical pain relief available, visualisation can also be a powerful tool in reducing pain or enabling the sufferer to cope with it. It works by causing the release of endorphins, the body's own feel-good, pain-inhibiting chemicals.

Many principles of magical pain relief occur independently across cultures. The most common are the removal of acute pain through light, the absorption of chronic pain into healing darkness, burying pain, washing pain away and appealing to a higher source (be it God, the Goddess, an indigenous deity or an angel) to take away the suffering.

While most spells for pain relief are carried out on our own behalf or on behalf of loved ones, I have also included a general ritual for taking away pain in the world, as a way of sending healing energies into the cosmos. These healing energies can get depleted as we ask – quite rightly – for help. For this reason, I would suggest that when you feel well enough you make some form of offering after all healing spells, be it in the form of spending time with or writing to someone who is sad or lonely, picking up litter, planting seeds, feeding birds or working in a small way to help a humanitarian cause.

A light path spell to dissipate pain

This is a good spell to help you settle in the evening and hopefully get a good night's sleep. Often, when we do relax after the day, chronic pain can kick in, especially if we have been overworking or overstretching ourselves physically and emotionally. The spell is good for all kinds of pain, chronic or sudden, and especially joint, back and bone pain, strong menstrual pains or powerful discomfort connected with the digestive system. The tactic of this spell is to externalise the pain so that it forms an outer shell of darkness around you, while you remain a separate whole within. You then shed the dark shell, using a pathway of light.

You will need

6 tea-lights in holders (8 if the pain is bad); a long table; an uncurtained window with no direct light shining in.

Timing

When it is really dark and you are in pain.

The spell

* Push the table so that one of its narrow ends is against the window. Create two parallel rows of tea-lights on the table, making a pathway whose reflection will shine in the dark window when the tea-lights are lit.

* Light the tea-lights, beginning with the ones nearest the window and working outwards.

* Sit so you can clearly see the pathway of light extending through the window into the darkness. Do not look back into the room.

* Picture the pain as a dark outer egg-like shell around your outline.

* Focus on the pathway between the lights, beginning with the lights nearest to you. Pause at each pair of lights and say:
I walk along the path of light and shed my shell of pain. Fade into the light, pain. You have travelled far enough with me along this road.

* Picture part of your shell of dark pain falling from you and being absorbed by each set of lights. Feel yourself becoming lighter and more at ease.

* When you have travelled along the light path, extinguish the tea-lights one by one, starting with those furthest from the window. As you extinguish each light, say:
Pain be gone. We travel no more together.

* Switch on the light and close the curtains, leaving the pain outside to be absorbed by the night.

A spell to control pain or discomfort

This spell is effective if you suffer regular predictable bouts of pain, perhaps a weekly migraine or a stress- or food-related skin rash. Like the previous spell, this one works on the basis of externalising the pain, this time by regarding it as an unwelcome visitor you choose not to admit to your home.

You will need

A relaxing herb- or oil-based bath product, for example chamomile, lavender or rose.

Timing

When you are relatively pain-free and relaxed.

The spell

* Have a bath using your chosen bath product, dry yourself and sit or lie in a warm comfortable place.
* Close your eyes and picture the pain as a dark tight knot in your body. Visualise it wherever it is principally located when it strikes. If you have skin problems, visualise a dark scratchy web.
* Still with your eyes closed, imagine that you are breathing in healing golden light. With each in-breath, its warmth melts the knot a little. Breathe out through your mouth with a soft sigh and imagine that darkness is coming out like a long black tendril of smoke. With each exhalation it builds up in to a shape in front of you. Continue to breathe in this way until you feel completely light inside.
* Open your eyes, blink and picture the dark form in front of you. The darkness that was your pain now has a definite, two-dimensional black outline.
* Give the shape a name and ask it to tell you about itself. Ask it what it is. It may be, for example a person who is a pain in the neck and causes your muscles to seize up; it may be undigested anger; it may be stress caused by constantly smiling and pleasing other people; it may be a financial problem you have avoided facing; it may be an accumulation of junk; it may be the exhaustion of juggling work and home life. Even a physically based pain may have psychological factors as a trigger. The black pain shape may not even belong to you but have been accepted by you as your responsibility. It may be, for example, someone else's bitterness that is tangling your guts or clogging up your gall bladder.
* Go to an external door, open it and say:
You are no longer welcome here, for you are not part of me, nor of my life. Call on me no more, for I shall not answer nor admit you into my home and life.
* Close the door firmly and return to where you were sitting or lying.
* Using your right thumb, gently press the spot where the pain is usually at its worst and say:
Whenever I feel pain here, I will close the door on my unwanted visitor.
* When you feel the onset or warning signs of an attack, touch the spot with your thumb and repeat in your head or aloud:
I close the door on my unwanted visitor.
* Picture yourself closing the door and the black figure retreating. If you have the chance, close an actual door.

A Slavic healing spell

The Zorya are the goddesses who bring dawn and dusk in Slavic culture. Each morning, Zorya Utrenyaya opens the gates of the palace belonging to her father Dazhdbog, the sun god, so that he may ride out. In the evening, her sister, Zorya Vechernyaya, closes the gates after her father's chariot has returned. A third Zorya, called Polunocnica, is goddess of midnight. Sometimes the three women are regarded as one goddess. At these transition times of the day and night, they will take away pain and illness. They are sometime pictured veiled in mist and will enfold the sick as well as valiant warriors.

There are numerous versions of this spell. This one was told to me by a Czechoslovakian woman who asked me to sign a translation of one of my books. I was talking about the gall stone pain that could suddenly debilitate me without warning and which seemed much worse in the evening and at night. The spell has also proved effective against earache and sore throats or tonsillitis. You can also use this spell to ease the pain of a baby or child if prescribed medical treatment or pain relief is slow to take effect. In this case, use a soft white woollen blanket and wrap the child in it as you speak the words of the spell.

You will need
A long white net curtain, very large transparent scarf or grey sarong.

Timing
Most effective as dawn is breaking or dusk falling or at midnight. Work at all three if you have a pain that returns or lingers. Alternatively, work at any time when you or a child needs relief.

The spell
- Hold the curtain, scarf or sarong around your back and bring the top up so that it covers your hair.
- Face the dawn, dusk or night sky and draw the curtain, scarf or sarong across like a veil, so that it covers your face and encloses as much of your body as possible. As you do so, say three times softly:

Zorya, sisters of dawn, twilight and darkest night, enfold me in your healing veil as you quietly fade away and disappear. May my pain with you also fade and disappear, Zorya of morning, eve and night.

An eighteenth-century charm to relieve the pain of toothache, neuralgia or a gum abscess

This strange little folk charm comes from England and was created long before antibiotics or effective pain relief. It comes from a time when most people still lived in the countryside, folk medicine was popular and few were literate. A family might have a copy of the charm or ask for it from a sympathetic priest and reproduce the letters, hence the variations that are found in words and spelling. The pain of an aching tooth or abscess is still one that troubles us as we wait for emergency dental treatment or when we cannot take sufficiently strong medication because we need to remain alert. It may take a week or more for a swelling to go down. Try this charm and picture all the people through the centuries who have put their faith in it and handed on their pain to a higher source of wisdom and healing. Cloves are a herbal remedy for toothache.

You will need

A small square of good-quality white paper; a fountain pen and black ink; 3 cloves; some thin white cord.

Timing

When tooth pain is acute.

The spell

❋ On the white paper write in small carefully formed letters the following words:

St Peter lay outside the gate and wept.
Jesus came by and said: 'Peter, why dost thou lie here waxing grief?'
Peter answered: 'Lord, my teeth do ache, That I can neither sleep nor wake.'
Jesus said back to him: 'Peter thy ache I take and that of all who bear these words for my sake.'
Peter smiled. The pain was gone.
Father, Son and Holy Ghost, and so the prayer is done.

❋ Fold the paper up as small as you can, enclosing in the centre the three cloves (to represent the Holy Trinity). Tie the cord around the paper, fastening it with three knots and saying:

Father, Son and Holy Ghost, and so the prayer is done.

❋ Carry the folded paper with you until the pain goes away or you receive effective treatment.

❋ Keep the charm in a drawer and copy the words from it next time you or a family member has toothache. Only then should you throw the old charm, cord and cloves away.

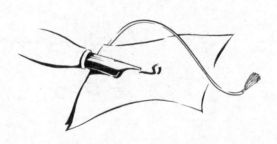

A Lithuanian spell to ease toothache

Many Lithuanian charms do not have the usual Christian references to the Virgin Mary, Christ and the saints. Some from pre-Christian times address the injury or pain directly, as though it were alive, and sometimes weave a story around it. This and the following two spells are adaptations of Lithuanian healing spells that have passed down through the oral folk tradition. There are some fascinating Lithuanian sites on the Internet where you can read more about the traditional healing charms.

You will need

A long, thin, jagged white stone.

Timing

When pain is acute.

The spell

- Hold the stone close to your mouth. Pull the stone downwards with a jerk and clasp it in your hands, as you do so saying three times:

  In the dark forest is a deep dark well. I draw you out, tooth, and cast you to the very bottom of the waters, where you will ache no more.

- If possible, cast the stone into running water, but otherwise into a bucket of very cold water.

A second Lithuanian spell to ease stomach ache

You will need

A small, perfectly round, smooth dark-coloured stone.

Timing

Whenever needed.

The spell

- Gently massage your stomach in circles with the stone, as you do so saying six times:

  The stomach ache has its own place. Roll yourself out. Smooth it away, Holy Mother, that the ache may return to its own land deep in the earth.

- Bury the stone (either in the earth or in a plant pot), as you do so saying three times:

  Like a stone to water go down. Get down stomach ache. Lie down and be still.

A Lithuanian spell to ease the pain of a broken bone, a dislocated joint or severe back pain

You will need

A bone-shaped stone; a small silver-coloured paper knife; a tea-light or red candle.

Timing

When pain relief wears off and you cannot take any more for a while or you are restless and cannot get comfortable at night.

The spell

* Light the tea-light or candle and set the bone-shaped stone close to it on a table or flat surface.

* Prodding the stone with the knife, push it away from the candle and say three times:
  Bone ache, in your wrong place. St George drive back the dragon that his fire may burn no more within me.

* Blow out the candle and say
  Bone ache, displaced bone, return to the place you were intended. Your fire is out.

* In an open place, throw the stone as far away as possible.

An ancient Egyptian ritual to take away a headache, an earache or pain behind the eyes when you cannot rest

The ancient Egyptians believed that the deities themselves suffered from illnesses and pain, such as headaches, and so linked their own healing work with that of the healing deities, who would cure their fellow gods. In Egypt you find dozens of spells, all different, that come from the same verse of one of the ancient papyri. They often take the form of a mini-drama, in which the healer and patient assume the roles of the gods.

You will need

A moonstone or cloudy crystal quartz; a small, clear glass bowl filled with still mineral water that has been left in starlight overnight.

Timing

When pain strikes.

The spell

* Recite the following:
  'My head,' said Ra, 'the light too bright. I must dim the sun and sleep awhile.'
  Mother Isis said: 'There is no time. Your boat must sail until Lady Nut enfolds you in her cloak of stars.'
  Ra said: 'The light too bright, the heat it sears me. I, Lord of Light, I seek the dark.'
  Mother Nut replied: 'Take then this star new risen that I have dipped for thee in the cool waters of the celestial Nile and press it to your temple.'

* Hold your crystal on the pressure points of your own temples and visualise the jagged pain flowing out into the gentle starlight.

* Continue reciting:
  Ra answered: 'The pain is eased. The sun will onward pass and fill the world with glory. The crops will glow with light and time shall not be broken. I thank thee mothers both for this thy remedy.'

* Plunge the crystal into the bowl of star water.

* Repeat all the above steps three times.

* Try to walk in the fresh air or at least spend two or three minutes sitting quietly with your hands over your eyes. Use the crystal water to splash on your temples and wrists.

A mirror and candle ritual to take away sharp or prolonged pain

Mirrors have a dual purpose in healing: to reflect light and to absorb illness or pain. Candle light is very gentle and will spread across the surface of the mirror, symbolically shedding warming light throughout the body, melting pain and enclosing jagged sensations. Repeat the ritual as often as you need.

You will need

3 or 4 small pastel-coloured candles; a small round or oval mirror; dried rose petals; a stick of pine or cedar incense; a few drops of spring water (shop-bought is fine); a soft dark cloth; a light-coloured cloth.

Timing

When you have sharp or prolonged pain.

The spell

* Arrange the candles in a semi-circle around the mirror and sit behind them facing the mirror. Light them from left to right.

* Look not at the candle flame directly but at the reflected light and picture the pain moving from you into the glowing surface of the mirror.

* Recite six time in a whisper:
  Fade with the light from here. Pain be contained, absorbed, diminished, a pale reflection, soon to cease.

* Blow out all the candles at once if you can – otherwise blow them out in rapid succession, as you do so saying:
  Pain fade from the body into the glass, and let me rest in darkness.

* Sprinkle the mirror with the rose petals, light the incense and waft it over, and drop a single drop of spring water on to the mirror.

* Rub the mirror with the soft dark cloth until it sparkles again.

* Wrap the mirror in the light-coloured cloth and place it on top of a high cupboard or in a drawer.

* Wash the dark cloth and hang it in the fresh air to dry.

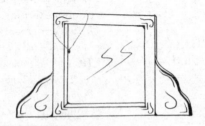

A spell for raising the threshold of pain

We all have different levels of resistance to pain. These depend in part on our physiological and psychological make-up. However, it is possible to raise the pain threshold through spiritual means – meditation is often used to increase resistance to pain. You can carry out this ritual before having an injection, surgery, dentistry or giving birth. The empowered pink or blue crystal can also be given to a child to hold while receiving an injection or dental treatment. The crystals can be re-empowered monthly.

You will need

A deep-blue candle; a stick of lavender or rose incense or lavender or rose essential oil and a burner; a blue lace agate, blue chalcedony or soft-blue angelite crystal, or pink rose quartz or manganocalcite; a soft purple amethyst or fluorite; a small blue drawstring bag.

Timing

In the early morning or at twilight, if possible when it is raining gently outside.

The spell

* Light the candle and set the incense or oil to burn.
* Hold the blue or pink crystal in your lightly closed power hand (the one you write with); hold the purple crystal in your closed receptive hand. Keep your hands relaxed and at waist height.
* Sit or stand in front of the candle, gazing into the flame, and raise your power hand to about shoulder height. Open it and say:
I fill with power to resist pain.
Return the hand to waist height.
* Raise your receptive hand to shoulder height. Open this hand and say:
I take away future pain.
Return the hand to waist height.
* Continue the hand actions and chants until the words have become a rhythmic flow in your mind. You may notice that the amethyst becomes noticeably heavier and darker, while the blue or pink crystal feels lighter and appears brighter or more translucent.
* Place the two crystals in the drawstring bag in front of the candle and incense or oil while the candle and fragrance burn through.
* Keep the bag in your medicine cabinet. Take the blue or pink crystal with you for any potentially uncomfortable treatment and hold it in your receptive hand. Afterwards light another candle and burn incense or oil as you repeat the ritual.

A lodestone healing spell to take away pain

As well as being used in love magic (see pages 28–9), lodestones have a role in healing and can absorb pain or illness. Keep a special lodestone (the rounded female ones are best) in a small red purse or drawstring bag. You can use this spell for yourself or for others, but lodestones are too heavy for children and babies or small or young animals.

You will need
A lodestone; a red purse or bag; a bowl of warm water.

Timing
At 10 pm (the healing hour).

The spell
* Gently touch the area of discomfort with the lodestone and, holding the rounded end in your receptive palm (of the hand you don't write with), move it in a gentle outward rhythm with small strokes. (You can pass the lodestone over the whole body if necessary.) As you work, repeat mesmerically:
  Draw out pain, draw out sorrow,
  And bring me/(name) peace until the
  morrow.
* When you can feel the power of the lodestone waning, place it in the bowl of warm water and leave it there for a minute or two.
* Remove the lodestone and allow it to dry naturally before returning it to the bag.
* Empty the water down an outside drain or gutter.

A ritual to heal the pain in the world

If life consists of moving energies, as science suggests it does, it would seem important to send into the atmosphere positive thoughts and healing in the hope that if enough people do it, we can actually make at least small positive changes. This spell is aimed at reducing pain and suffering in the world and was originally devised when so many children were being injured by buried landmines. This is a general version. You can change the words to fit any particular situation. If you can follow up the spell with a small positive gesture – be it in the form of money or time – to help ease human or animal suffering, the positive energies will increase in the practical arena as well.

You will need
A sphere made of clear crystal quartz, amethyst, rose quartz or jade (it need only be small); a pieces of black cloth; a piece of white cloth.

Timing
When you hear bad news on the radio or television or read it in the newspaper – perhaps of children injured by war or of hunger. If possible, work in sunlight.

The spell
* Rub the sphere with the dark cloth, as you do so saying:
  Take away the pain
  Of famine and of war.
  Bring relief from agony,
  So children laugh once more.
* When you feel ready, rub the sphere with the white cloth until it sparkles, as you do so saying:
  Bring help for the wounded,
  Relief from disease.
  Take away the misery
  Of poisoned lands and seas.
* Leave the sphere where light can fall on it and repeat the ritual regularly.

41 SPELLS FOR QUIET SLEEP AND PEACEFUL DREAMS

In the modern world, sleep disturbances are very common among adults and children alike. The frantic pace of life causes many to suffer from insomnia or nightmares. The need to finish chores or paperwork before bedtime, together with watching television, playing computer games or surfing the Net late at night can mean that the body is exhausted but the mind is still going at full throttle.

Gentle spells, incorporating or following a relaxing bath or shower, offer a gentle transition to sleep (once provided by nightly quiet times around the family hearth). There are many organic herbal or floral bath products on the market, costing little more than the chemically perfumed ones. These can help to still the mind as well as relax the body.

Candle light is another way of easing the transition between activity and rest. Traditionally, candle spells have always been used to keep away the fears of the night and slow the mind to a rhythm that will give beautiful and peaceful dreams.

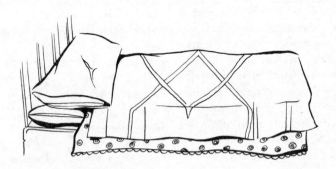

A Celtic sleep blessing

If we travel away from home a lot and spend nights in impersonal hotel rooms, or our family members are scattered in different places, bedtime can be when we feel most isolated and sad. But even if your family are living with you, this old blessing can be a wonderful way of connecting you all in love as you drift in to sleep. In a hotel room where I cannot light a candle, I focus on one bedside lamp and extinguish all other lighting in the room.

You will need

A pink or pale-green candle or a softly shaded lamp.

Timing

Before you go to bed (no matter if others are still up).

The spell

* Light the candle or switch on the single lamp and in its light picture the faces of all those you want to connect with.
* Say three times the following Celtic blessing, of which this is just one version, taught to me by a Scottish friend:

Sleep now peacefully,
Sleep now restfully,
Cradled lovingly
By kin and close company.
Weaver of dreams,
May nought disturb thee
Until morn rises
And gentle sunbeams call.

* Blow out the candle or switch off the lamp and send loving light to your family and to every corner of the room to protect you while you sleep.

A Celtic sleep circling prayer

The concept behind circling prayers is that you or the person you are blessing is encircled by the power of the blessing. This spell is very effective if you or a child cannot sleep. (I often wake in the middle of the night worrying or counting non-existent money to pay bills). An alternative method to the one given below is to draw a circle with your index finger deosil (clockwise) around yourself and/or a child. Recite the two circle blessings and picture an enfolding circle of light around yourself or the two of you. This is a version of a Celtic circle blessing still popular in Scotland.

You will need

A white candle; a pointed quartz crystal (very widely and cheaply available).

Timing

Before you go to bed or when you, a child or a loved one cannot sleep.

The spell

* Light the candle. Holding the crystal in your power hand (the one you write with) briefly touch the flame with the point and say:

Circle and enfold with blessing without ceasing.

* With the pointed crystal, draw around the candle – or, if you prefer, around yourself and/or the child/loved one – three deosil circles, as you do so reciting softly:

Circle me, Lord/Lady this night.
Keep peace within and dark without.
Drive away harm beyond my sight.
Circle me, Lord/Lady this night.
Keep peace within and danger without.
Circle me Lord/Lady this night
And banish fear until morning light.

Adapt the words to the plural if necessary.

* Blow out the candle and go to sleep, picturing the circle around you.

A candle protection spell for anxiety about being attacked or injured while you sleep

We all have periods when we feel vulnerable at night (see also page 399). There may have been a spate of burglaries or fires in the neighbourhood; you may be alone at night unusually or holidaying in a remote area. You have taken all precautions and logically you know there is no danger ... But still you may be awake tossing and turning, magnifying every noise or creak into an intruder or imagining disasters. This spell has a dual purpose: it will both protect you and settle you into a peaceful sleep until morning. You can use a lamp, torch or lantern if it would not be safe to light a candle. I devised this spell when I had a room in a very large hotel in Los Angeles with long empty corridors and some people were rattling my door late at night. In spite of reassurances about security, I could not settle, but I knew I had to work the next day and could not be tired. Fortunately, I had my small travel torch with me.

You will need

A white candle in a secure heatproof holder that may be carried safely or a light source you can hold freely in your hands (for example, a torch).

Timing

When fear is keeping you unnecessarily awake.

The spell

* Face north (approximately) and light your candle. Hold it in front of you and say:
  Candle bright,
  Shine your light
  Around me this night.
  Flame burn,
  Harm turn
  Away from me
  That I may be
  Safe until dawn
  To greet the morn
  Renewed by sleep's tranquillity.

* Face east, then south, then west, holding the candle and repeating the chant at each direction.

* Then spin around in each direction in turn, saying at each one:
  Bring quiet sleep this night until morning light.

* Return to the north again, blow out the candle or extinguish the light source and, as you get into bed, see the candle circle of light like a force field around the bed, the room and the whole building.

A spell to keep away nightmares

This is a very old spell, popular in many different cultures from ancient Greece to eastern Europe and China, where (according to a woman from Hong Kong who I met at a Chinese wedding in London) it was used to protect a bride from harmful influences while she slept on the nights before her wedding. It is a good spell to use if you are having a period of disturbed nights or frightening dreams. After two or three days you should find you are sleeping well and the dreams have ceased. In earlier times, this spell would have been carried out with well water.

You will need
A drinking glass half filled with tap water.

Timing
Just before you go to bed.

The spell
* Place the glass of water near your bedside in a place where you will not drink it if you wake from a half-sleep.
* Swirl the water five times widdershins (anti-clockwise), taking care not to spill any and saying:
  Nightmares, terrors and spectres of dread,
  Enter the glass and be held instead
  Of plaguing me.
  Sleep thus bring tranquillity.
* In the morning, as soon as you wake, whether or not you had a nightmare, empty the water down a sink, washbasin or drain, holding the glass in your receptive hand (the one you don't write with).
* Rinse out the glass three times and set it in the bedroom ready to be filled before you go to sleep the next night.

A five-angel or -fairy candle spell for a child or adult who does not like the dark

A number of children are frightened by the dark but find that a light in the bedroom keeps them awake. I also know adults who have found this spell useful, especially if they are sleeping alone in a house in a country area. You may need to repeat the spell regularly.

You will need
5 small scented tea-lights, each enclosed in a safe glass container with sand in the bottom — apple blossom, chamomile, jasmine, lavender, lilac, mimosa, rose, sandalwood, strawberry and ylang ylang are very relaxing.

Timing
Before bedtime.

The spell
* Light all five tea-lights so that the child can see them from the bed.
* Blow out the first tea-light and tell the child to sit with eyes open and picture the extinguished light as if it was still burning. Describe the extinguished light as a fragrance fairy or angel who will shine a magical protective light all night.
* One by one, extinguish the other tea-lights. As the room gets physically darker, help the child to 'see' the five light fairies or angels. Tell the child that he or she can call on them during the night if necessary.
* If the child becomes distressed at the idea of total darkness, re-light the first light and sit with them while it burns through, by which time the child should be asleep. If the child still wants a normal light on, go along with it, but explain that the candle angels cannot be so easily seen in electric light.

A dream catcher spell for children

Dream catchers, nets on a hoop, hung with beads and sometimes chimes, are widely available throughout the world. Hanging one over a child's bed can help them to overcome fears of the night and reduce nightmares. This spell is a traditional Native American one, based, like a number of indigenous spells, on telling a story as part of the spell. The concept in this case is that the repetition of the story each night increases the power of the dream catcher. After about a week, the child may be content just to hang the dream catcher in position nightly – or, if the child is old enough, may like to tell the story themselves before sleep. However, you might like to keep the story as part of the nightly settling process.

You will need

A dream catcher; a hook over or near the child's bed, or by the window.

Timing

Before bedtime.

The spell

* On the first night, show the child the dream catcher and allow them to touch it as you tell the following story in your own words. You can make the tale shorter or longer, and the child may add details:

Long ago, the Native North American peoples all lived in the same area of land. Day and night, Grandmother Spider Woman, who created humans and animals from clay, wove tiny nets of thread she called dream catchers. Mothers hung them over cradles so that babies would sleep peacefully. Bad dreams became entangled in the web and only the happy ones passed through. The sleeping babies laughed and clapped for joy. With the first rays of sunlight, the bad dreams broke free and returned to the place of shadows, but the good dreams sparkled like rainbows and stayed with the child all day. The day came when the Native American people were so many that the tribes travelled in different directions to find new hunting grounds. Grandmother Spider Woman could no longer visit all the cradles to keep her webs in order and so she taught her magical secret to the wise grandmothers, who taught their daughters to weave magical webs for their very own babies and for other babies and children around the world. And so this dream catcher was made and I bought it for you to keep you safe.

* Hang the dream catcher on the hook – or, if the child is old enough, help them to do it. Reassure them that the dream catcher will keep them safe until morning.
* In the morning, take the dream catcher down and shake it in the light to untangle any bad dreams caught there.
* Re-hang the dream catcher the next evening.

A herbal bath for quiet sleep

Although you can make your own bath herb sachets quite easily, if it is living a frantic life that made you stressed in the first place, you may not have time. There are many good-quality pure herb bath products on the market, some available via the Internet. Look for those containing a mixture of any of the following herbs and flowers, which are naturally sleep inducing: chamomile, carnation, elecampane, elderflower, eucalyptus, fennel, jasmine, hops, hyssop, lavender, lemon balm, lemon verbena, lilac, linden blossoms, marjoram (sweet), orange blossoms, passionflower, peppermint, rosemary, rose, skullcap, slippery elm bark, olive and valerian root. You can adapt this spell for a shower by using a herbal bath gel and lighting the bathroom so that the light shines on the shower cabinet. Wash gently widdershins (anti-clockwise) to remove tension and deosil (clockwise) to draw in the light.

You will need

A natural herbal bath product (not a bubble bath); small pink, purple or pale-blue tea-lights or candles, preferably scented.

Timing

After a hard day when your mind is still whirling.

The spell

* Light the tea-lights or candles in safe places in the bathroom, positioning them so that light will be reflected in the bath water.
* Fill the bath with warm, but not too hot, water and add the bath product.
* Relax in the water and inhale the fragrance.
* Create pools of light by swirling the water. Draw the light towards you, as you do so saying:
  Fragrance of garden, wood and field,
  Enter this light that I may yield
  To the softness of the eve
  And in this water day's thoughts leave.
* Push away any unlit areas of water and replace them with light pools, picturing all the tensions and stresses of the day past and the worries of tomorrow floating away and being replaced by the soft light.
* When you are ready, dry yourself and pull out the plug, as you do so saying:
  Flow from me, go from me, and be
  transformed by Mother Night into
  tomorrow's promises.
* Go to bed and lie with your eyes closed, picturing fields and woods filled with fragrant flowers.

A dream pillow spell

Sleeping on a dream pillow is a traditional way of inducing peaceful sleep, reducing insomnia and nightmares, and creating happy dreams. These pillows are still sold at country fairs and in rural gift stores and are available by mail order over the Internet. They can increasingly be found in microwaveable form in pharmacies and stores such as The Body Shop. Ordinary bed pillows also sometimes come fragranced – I have seen a number in both department and discount stores. You can, of course, make your own (see my *Fragrant Magic*, Quantum, 2003, for instructions), but it is quite easy to empower one you have bought. You can also empower one for a child, naming them in the empowerment. Most popular are pillows filled with chamomile, lavender or rose. Eucalyptus is good for snuffly adults and children. Traditionally, hops are used, but these alone can smell a bit like horses, so choose a pillow that is also fragranced.

You will need
A sleep pillow of any kind.

Timing
During the crescent moon.

The spell
* Rest your head on the pillow and whisper softly nine times:
May sleep come swiftly and gently. May Mother Night carry me into sweet dreams. May angels and all the gentle spirits of the night keep from me danger and dark dreams, that in the morning with joy and renewal I wake restored.
* Repeat the empowerment every night for a week, and thereafter weekly on a Monday.

A fragrance spell to create a beautiful sleep experience

From ancient Egypt, Greece and Rome come rituals that use fragrances to induce peaceful sleep and beautiful dreams. If you are not sleeping well or have disturbing dreams, perform this spell nightly for a week and thereafter when needed. It will harmonise sleep patterns if you are an insomniac and help you to rest if you have experienced a particularly pressurised few weeks. Even if all is well in your life, try to spend one night a week – or whenever you have time – creating a beautiful sleep experience from which you will wake relaxed and refreshed. This is one of my favourite fragrance sleep rites.

You will need
Rose or lavender essential oil, or rose or lavender cologne – or your favourite gentle fragrance; a small scented candle or tea-light in a deep holder filled with sand (in case you drift off).

Timing
Just before sleep.

The spell
* Set the phone to silent answer, switch off any fax machine and do not check your e-mails just before getting ready for bed. It is all too easy to slip back into social or work mode.
* Have a scented bath or shower, perhaps in candle light.
* Afterwards, when you are wrapped up warmly in your dressing-gown, sit in a soft light listening to gentle music, perhaps enjoying a herbal or milky drink.
* When you are totally relaxed, light the small scented candle or tea-light and place it somewhere safe in your bedroom. Sit on the bed facing it, well propped up on pillows.
* In the semi-darkness, smell the rose or lavender fragrance and imagine yourself in a beautiful rose garden, field of lavender or other flower-filled place. Say:
I walk through the fields of flowers to sleep, to gentle lands of beauty and of radiance, of magic and of joy, of loving friends and welcoming strangers; and so I walk through the fields of flowers to sleep.
* Sprinkle just a drop or two of the scent on your pillow to transfer the experience to the realms of sleep, as you do so repeating the chant.
* Blow out the candle, lie down and close your eyes, imagining yourself stepping through the flowers, field upon field, until at last you sink down among the fragrant blossoms into the waiting world of wonderful dreams.

A spell for obtaining healing through a dream

The ancient Egyptians, Greeks and Romans all had dream temples where people went to receive healing through a dream. While sleeping in the temple, one of the healing deities, such as the Greek god Aesculapius, came to them and either cured their illness or suggested a remedy. Dreamers may be tapping into a source of collective healing knowledge – a concept that becomes ever more credible as treatments and herbal remedies for illnesses that have been used in popular folk tradition are rediscovered by conventional medicine. If you are exhausted or unwell but there is no obvious cause and the illness does not warrant urgent medical intervention, or if you are not responding well to a prescribed treatment, you can seek healing through a dream. You may wish to ask God, the Goddess or one of the healing Archangels, Raphael or Cassiel, to send healing while you are asleep (see pages 681 and 682). Alternatively, picture this healing wisdom in the form of a Druid or Druidess, a sage, or a monk or nun, who were famed for healing. You can also use this method to ask for healing for someone you love.

You will need
A beeswax or white candle; a metal tray or broad-based metal candle-holder; a strip of white paper; a green pen.

Timing
On a Wednesday at 10 pm (the healing hour).

The spell
* At about 9.30 pm, have a bath, adding a few drops of a gentle healing essential oil such as chamomile, rose or lavender, or your favourite soothing bath product.
* Go to your bedroom, place the candle on the tray or in the holder and light it.
* Sit facing the candle and in its flame visualise the face of your chosen wise healer. Allow the form to build up quite spontaneously in the halo around the flame. Picture this person in your own way.
* Speaking to the healer you have envisaged, list each symptom and each area of pain, and tell them about your state of mind. Let flow quite naturally any related worries.
* Using the green pen, write on the strip of paper two or three key words to represent the symptoms or distress.
* Hold the edge of the paper to the flame until it catches light. Drop it on to the tray and let it burn away. Say: *I consign this illness/distress to the fire. Wise healer (name him or her if you wish), guide me in sleep to health or show me how I may be healed.*
* Blow out the candle and see the illness crumbling into tiny black dots, which are absorbed by the light as it flows into the cosmos.
* Close your eyes and float on fluffy white clouds into sleep. You may dream of your healer or of flowers and beautiful places, and wake feeling better. Or you may see in a dream clues to a cure. If, for example, you had a skin problem and dreamed of bathing in rose petals, a rose-based ointment or oil might help (check with a pharmacist or herbalist). If you dreamed of flowing streams, you might need to drink more water to cleanse your system of toxins.
* Repeat the ritual once a week until a solution or improvement comes or you unexpectedly meet someone in the everyday world who can guide you to the right treatment.

PART 8

SPELLS FOR ANIMALS

(*A.*)nimals and birds have been involved in our lives since early humans first domesticated wolves to act as hunting dogs. Indeed, the findings of three research teams, reported in *Science* magazine in November 2002, suggested that 95 per cent of all dogs evolve from three founding female wolves, tamed by humans living in or near China less than 15,000 years ago. Even dogs in the New World have their origins in eastern Asia. According to Carles Vila, of Uppsala University, Sweden (one of the team studying the New World dogs), American dogs travelled with the European colonists. From hunter to pampered urban pooch, the dog has maintained a relationship of mutual dependence with its human companions. Even today, it often plays a useful role in human society, acting as guard or guide to its owner.

The ancient Egyptians were devoted to cats rather than dogs, and the wealthy would accord their pet cats elaborate burials. The first authenticated accounts of cats as human companions in Egypt date from about 2000 BCE. It would seem that African wild cats or the smaller swamp cat kittens were adopted and, over generations, became domestic creatures. But cats, too, were originally domesticated for a purpose: to protect valuable grain stores and domestic larders from the rats and mice that breed rapidly in hot lands.

Animals have always been associated with magic because of their instinctive awareness, even foreknowledge, of danger and their ability to detect unearthly presences invisible to humans. In medieval times, cats were regarded as witches' familiar spirits or even as witches themselves. It was believed that witches assumed the guise of black cats for seven years at a time. In northern Europe and Scandinavia, the hare was the magical companion of the goddess of spring, Ostara or Oestre, from whose name we get the word 'Easter'. The hare is the source of the Easter rabbit.

The spells in this section can be cast to increase the intuitive connection and loving bond between us and our pets as well as to heal them and protect them from harm. There are also spells to get close psychically and physically to indigenous wildlife and to attract birds and tiny creatures into our garden (but persuade them to stay out of our houses). I have also suggested spells for better conditions for factory farm animals and exotic species kept in cramped zoos. (Some conservation programmes and parks, on the other hand, are excellent, and we can use magic when visiting them to draw the powers of the magnificent wild creatures that live and breed there into our own lives.)

The final chapter of this section of the book looks at animals as luck-bringers and natural protectors. The ancient Egyptians associated their deities with animal powers – for example, Thoth, the god of wisdom, was allied with the sacred black and white ibis, which once appeared in their thousands on the fertile banks of the Nile at the time of sowing. Even in the modern world, animal charms and amulets can be empowered by magic to endow us with those animal qualities that will bring power and success.

42 SPELLS FOR STRENGTHENING THE LINK WITH A PET

We are probably all aware of the strong bond of love that often evolves between owners and their pets. However, there may also be an intuitive link, whereby the pet will warn its owner of a dangerous person or situation by becoming unsettled or distressed. In fact, this kind of intuitive connection grows out of the love that operates on an everyday level. An animal knows when we are sick or sad and will sit quietly by us even if it is normally boisterous.

Spells can help from the very beginning of this special love affair, from guiding us to the right pet, to helping a new pet to settle, to developing a level of unspoken communication. This form of connection has all kinds of practical as well as spiritual benefits. It can enable us to call the animal back to us in a park or open space if it is out of ear shot and reassure it from a distance if we are going to be late home.

Animals, like children, are very receptive to magic because their minds and hearts are so open.

A spell to find the right pet

When we see an animal or bird for the first time, we usually know instantly whether or not it is for us. It may not be the one you planned to choose but the runt of the litter, a scruffy mongrel or a half-feathered bird. Sometimes we find the animal quite by chance – perhaps getting lost, seeing an animal sanctuary and deciding to go in, even if we were not consciously planning an addition to the family. Maybe the creature we intended to buy is ill or unavailable. At other times we are offered a pet out of the blue, just when we have decided we want one. As with any love spell, this one works by calling your special creature into your life at the right time. It can be cast whenever you feel that there is room in your life for a new furry or feathered family member.

You will need
A deep still pool or body of water; 3 small white stones.

Timing
When sunlight or moonlight is shining on the water.

The spell
* Drop one of the pebbles slowly into the still water so that it makes ripples, as you do so saying:
  Come swiftly to me, wherever you may be.
* Allow the ripples to disperse and then cast the next pebble, repeating the words.
* When the ripples have again dispersed, cast the third pebble, repeating the words. The animal will enter your sphere, usually in an unexpected way, within a few days. It may not be at all the kind of pet you thought you wanted, but you will fall instantly in love with it.

A smudging spell to find a special pet if you are uncertain about whether to buy one

It may be that a pet has died and you hesitate to find a replacement yet hate the emptiness left by the loss. Or perhaps there always seems to be a reason for putting off the decision, or the animals or birds on offer are not quite right. The sweetgrass braid (like a herbal plait) used in this spell is a very gentle form of smudge, said to represent the hair of the Spirit Mother.

You will need
A sweetgrass braid; a heatproof dish with a lip you can hold (wide and quite flat smudging dishes are available – or use an abalone shell that has natural holes so it does not get too hot); a feather (optional).

Timing
As the sun is setting.

The spell
* Light one end of the sweetgrass braid and blow on it gently so that the end glows red.
* Coil the sweetgrass on the dish and stand in the open air with the dish in your power hand (the one you write with), fanning it with the other hand or with the feather.
* Turn round deosil (clockwise) to face each of the main directions in turn, starting with West, the direction of the sunset. At each direction say softly three times:

North, East, South and West,
Send whom I will love the best.

- Face West again, lower the dish towards the ground, still gently fanning the smoke, and repeat the chant.
- Raise the dish high, fan the smoke and repeat the chant.
- Close your eyes, still facing West. You may see an image in your head or suddenly know the right place to find your pet. When you go to bed, you may dream of the creature or a place where you will find it. If none of these things happens, be patient and your pet will find you. If it is replacing a pet that has died, the new animal may coincidentally share its birthday with the former pet – or with yourself or a family member.

A spell to help a new pet settle in your home

When a new animal comes in to your home, the first days can be stressful for both of you. You may become anxious if the animal cries or whines, and this can increase the tension. This spell will help to familiarise you both with each other, and the animal with the unfamiliar territory, more speedily than would occur naturally.

You will need

An area of your home prepared in advance for the animal (somewhere where it can have privacy but not feel lonely); 4 small soft-brown or fawn earth-banded agate crystals; a blanket or garment belonging to you, such as an old coat or sweater.

Timing

Starting two days before the pet arrives.

The spell

- On the two nights before the pet arrives, place the agate crystals next to the bed legs or beneath the four corners of your own bed.
- Tuck the chosen garment or blanket at the foot of your own bed, so it will come into contact with your feet as you sleep.
- Touch the garment before you sleep and say softly six times:
  You are safe at home and warm, protected here from all harm.
- On the morning the animal is due to arrive, place its bed or cushion in the area set aside for it, and place the crystals at the four corners beneath.
- Tuck the garment or blanket on top of the pet bed, as you do so repeating the chant softly six times.
- When your pet arrives, show it the place you have prepared.
- If the animal has brought a blanket, place that on top of your own garment or blanket on the pet bed and repeat the chant six times. Even if the animal initially rejects the bed, before long it will have claimed the spot – and your home.

A spell to help a new pet find its place among other household animals or birds

Animals and birds can be quite as jealous of a new arrival as human children sometimes are of new siblings. Even a normally friendly creature may snarl or hiss and deny the newcomer access to the food bowl, or become annoyed if you fuss the new arrival. Time is a great healer of injured feelings, but a spell can speed the process, taking the edge off resentment and restoring your peace.

You will need
Nothing.

Timing
When all the animals or birds are in the same room, even if they are expressing hostility.

The spell
* Using the index finger of your power hand (the one you write with), draw an imaginary deosil (clockwise) circle of light to enclose yourself and your pets. Do this without moving.
* Within the circle of light, gently stroke each of your pets on the head and name him or her, beginning with the most senior animal (in age or rank) and moving slowly and softly down the hierarchy to end with the newcomer. Repeat this stroking and naming, following the same order, nine more times (so that you have done it ten times in all).
* Repeat whenever your pets are together.

A spell to introduce a new human – adult or baby – to a pet if the creature is jealous

An established pet, even a mild-natured one, can feel displaced if you introduce a new partner or a baby into the household, especially if they are used to monopolising your affections. Not just dogs but also cats and birds (especially parrots) can become very resentful. Together with reassurance and vigilance, magic can help to blend the newly increased family into a harmonious unit. In time, your pet may bond with the newcomer.

You will need
Nothing.

Timing
When you are alone in a room with the animal.

The spell
* Gently and rhythmically groom the pet, as you do so whispering:
  We must share our home in lovingness,
  Share our love and tenderness.
  Enough love to share and to spare.
  Love everywhere to spare and share.
* The next time the newcomer is present, stroke the animal and repeat the words.
* Repeat these steps daily until harmony is established.

A spell to call a pet telepathically from a distance

The telepathic link between human and animal is a natural one, and has been well researched and attested, but some creatures are slow to utilise the power (or too lazy). The ability is useful when you need to call an animal over a distance (see also page 546). A tuned in animal also becomes more able to alert you to dangerous situations. Horses as well as dogs and cats can develop this ability. As a result you will be able to start calling them before you arrive at the paddock, so they will be waiting for you at the gate.

You will need
A small pet treat.

Timing
When the house is quiet and you and the pet are alone.

The spell
* Wait until the pet is in another part of the house. Holding the pet treat in front of you, say the animal's name softly in your head, followed by however you usually call the animal to you, for example a whistle or a 'come on' – still silent.
* Turn the volume up gradually in your head, so that you are calling louder and louder. Picture a silver lead gently guiding the pet towards you.
* When the animal arrives, praise them and offer them the treat. If your pet is still not tuned in after a few attempts, start to call him or her aloud but softly, increasing the volume of your voice until the pet arrives. Persevere and you will eventually make the psychic link.
* Gradually increase the distance between you and your pet when you psychically call. In time, reward and praise will be sufficient, and you will not need the treat.

A spell to link emotionally with your pet if you must be apart for a while

One of my cats, Jenny, gets very upset when I go away even for a short time, although though there are still people in the house to care for her. I devised this spell to try to reassure her when I am working away. The spell also works if a pet must stay away overnight, for example at the vet's or in kennels while you are on holiday.

You will need
2 small matching amber, smoky quartz or rutilated quartz crystals.

Timing
When you must be apart from your pet.

The spell
* Place one of the crystals under your mattress and another under the pet's bed.
* When you must be apart overnight or longer, exchange the crystals. Take the pet's crystal away with you and put yours in their sleeping place.
* Each day when you have a moment, hold the crystal, picture your pet and talk reassuringly to them, promising you will soon be home.

A second spell to link emotionally with your pet if you must be apart for a while

You will need

2 halves of the same sea shell or an ornamental wooden or cardboard egg that splits into two halves (they are often on sale around Easter); a small dish of salt.

Timing

When you must be apart from your pet.

The spell

⁕ Keep the two halves of the shell or egg side by side in a room where you and the animal spend time.

⁕ An hour or so before either you or the animal go away, sprinkle a deosil (clockwise) circle of salt around the shells or eggs and say:

Within this circle we are together and will remain so until I/you return.

⁕ Repeat the chant before you go to sleep and when you wake each day until you are with the animal again.

A spell for taking a dog to obedience training or training a horse

Some animals find it harder than others to follow even simple instructions. While a training course can be helpful, the animal can sometimes become even more stressed and refuse to co-operate at all. This spell will increase both focus and concentration and help the animal to learn through linking emotionally with you. It is based on a finding that helper dogs who fail basic training courses can sometimes become first-class guides when they are deeply bonded to an owner.

You will need

A Bach Flower Remedy such as Cerato, Chestnut Bud or Impatiens (or your own choice of Remedy good for learning and for calm and focus).

Timing

Begin the night before the training starts.

The spell

⁕ The night before the training course starts or you are planning to start training your pet, add one or two drops (according to the animal's size) of Bach Flower Remedy to your pet's food or water, then place a drop under your own tongue. Say:

Together, we will learn together,
To walk as one together,
Through wind and weather,
Safe in street and field and park,
Safe in light and safe in dark,
Because we walk together.

⁕ Repeat the chant just before the training session.

A spell to help an animal or bird move house

Animals and birds are very aware of unfamiliar territories and for some a physical move is traumatic. The old remedy with cats is to smear their paws with a tiny amount of butter (keep them away from furniture and carpets). By the time they have licked it off they will be settled. This spell can be used with any household pet.

You will need

Plants from your garden that you have potted, or potted house plants; a small brown stone or crystal.

Timing

A week before the move.

The spell

* Place the potted plants in a semi-circle around the area where the animal sleeps. They will act as a shield.
* Each day up to and including the day of the move, place the crystal on the soil of one of the plants, if possible when the animal is resting in the area. As you do so, say:
Make your roots in me that you may flourish in new soil.
* On moving day, transport the plants together with the animal if possible, and rearrange the pet bed in a quiet corner as soon as you arrive.
* Put the crystal under the pet's bed in the new home.

A spell to move a horse, goat or sheep to a new stable or paddock

Larger animals can become very attached to their shelter, so you should prepare them gradually for any move. The amulet created in this spell is also good for travelling with your animal and during storms.

You will need

A beeswax candle; some hair or wool from the animal; a circle of wire, preferably copper, about the circumference of a tennis ball.

Timing

As soon as you have notice of a definite move, at 10 pm.

The spell

* Light the candle and pass the wire ring eight times over the flame, as you do so saying:
Be enclosed in light, insulated from change and all disturbances. Carry your security with you in this ring.
* Bind the wool or hair round and round the ring, as you do so saying:
Be enclosed in the warmth of your own protection, insulated from change and all disturbances. Carry your security with you in this ring.
* Place the ring in front of the candle and leave it there until the candle is burnt down.
* Hang the ring somewhere in the animal's stable or enclosure. Each time you visit the animal, touch the ring and repeat both empowerments.
* On the day of the move, ensure that the ring travels with the animal and put it in place as soon as the animal enters the new shelter.

A spell to bless small animals and birds

Small animals and birds can sometimes feel vulnerable in a household, especially if there is a lot of movement. If repeated weekly over a cage or enclosure, this blessing will create an aura of peace. You may notice that after a week or so even timid creatures become more sociable.

You will need

A soft-green jade and a pink rose quartz crystal, both smooth and of a size to fit easily in to your palm; a small dish.

Timing

In the morning, when the house is still quiet.

The spell

* Take up the jade in your power hand (the one you write with) and the rose quartz in the other hand. Hold the stones loosely, with your palms facing downwards, over the animal's cage and circle both hands slowly nine times widdershins (anticlockwise). As you circle, say:

Though you are small, you are blessed.
Though you are small, you are loved.
Though you are small, you are protected
And always will be while in my care.

* Keep the crystals in a dish beside the cage and repeat the spell weekly or whenever the creature is disturbed by loud noise or sudden movement.

A three-day spell for when you and your pet must part

There are many reasons why you may need to find a new home for a pet. You may need to move house and cannot take your pet with you; you may have a new partner or a new child in the home with whom the pet cannot settle; or someone in the family may develop an allergy to fur or feathers. When the parting becomes unavoidable, you need to unravel the bonds of love so that the creature can make a relationship with a new owner.

You will need

A light-brown candle; some strands of brown wool; a deep metal tray.

Timing

On the three nights before the departure.

The spell

* On the first evening, light the candle and burn three strands of wool one after the other in the flame, dropping each in the tray as it catches alight. For each thread say:

My love for you lives in my heart,
Yet we must part.
And so I loose the bonds,
That you may love again.

* When the candle has burnt one-third through, blow it out, sending the love to your pet's new home.

* Repeat the next night, this time burning only two threads in the candle and letting another third of the candle burn down before blowing it out.

* Repeat again on the third night, this time burning only one thread and leaving the candle to burn through.

A spell to stop your dog barking

Dogs may bark because they are intelligent and want to be the centre of attention or because they are so devoted that they hate being left, even for a short time — although that is no consolation to the owner. Placing a couple of drops of Beech, Cherry Plum or Chicory Bach Flower Remedy in the dog's water generally helps. If that is impractical for some reason, try this spell. Use a silent spray bottle if your dog hates the sound of water sprays. Ideally, work the spell when the dog is out of the house.

You will need
2 drops of any of the above Flower Remedies diluted in a plant spray bottle about one-third full of water; 2 moss or tree agate crystals, or Dalmatian jaspers; a plant pot filled with earth.

Timing
Early in the waxing moon phase, after dark.

The spell
* Starting near the dog's customary sleeping place, spray the inside of every threshold the dog has to go through to get to the front door (and any other exit it uses to go out for walks). As you spray, say continuously, starting softly and reducing the level of your voice so that you end up in a whisper:

Softer now and softer be;
Bark affection silently.
Loved you are and loved will be,
But loved much better silently.

* When you reach the front door, go outside and close it silently, then spray the front doorstep, as you do so repeating the chant. (Don't forget to take your key with you.)
* The next morning, again when the dog is not present, spray the crystals with the Flower Remedy mixture, repeating the words softly three times, once more ending in a whisper.
* Bury the crystals in the plant pot and keep it as near as possible to the dog's sleeping place.
* Spray the doors and repeat the chant monthly after dark, when you see the crescent moon in the sky.

A Bach Flower Remedies spell to stop a neighbour's dog barking

This and the following spell are not so much about strengthening the link with your own pet as about being able to live in harmony with one of your neighbour's. However much you like dogs, if a neighbour's dog barks repeatedly and for long periods, it is difficult not to become irritated, especially if it is early in the morning or at a time when you want a bit of peace and quiet.

You will need

2 drops of two of the following Bach Flower Remedies: Beech, Cherry Plum, Chicory (4 drops in all).

Timing

When the dog is barking.

The spell

* The minute the dog starts barking, sprinkle the Flower Remedy mixture along all adjoining walls and fences, working from back to front (starting with the back gate of the back garden, going in through the back door, moving along adjoining walls first upstairs and then down, and finally going out of the front door and along the front fence). To be on the safe side, spray along the thresholds and doorsteps of front and back doors as you cross them to come back indoors. As you spray, whisper or speak the following words in your head without stopping:

Softer now and softer be;
Bark affection silently.
Loved you are and loved will be,
But loved much better quietly.

* Repeat these steps every day for seven days and resume if the dog starts barking again.

A candle spell to stop a neighbour's dog barking

If the Flower Remedies spell above does not work, try this gentle candle binding. The problem should stop by the third binding if not before.

You will need

A beeswax candle of the kind made from a rolled strip of beeswax; some dried lavender or pot pourri; a tiny jade crystal; some cotton wool.

Timing

When the dog starts to bark.

The spell

* Unroll the beeswax candle and mould it into a rough image of a dog.

* Sprinkle the image with the dried lavender or pot pourri, push in the jade crystal for the mouth and wrap the image in the cotton wool.

* Place the wrapped image in a drawer in a shed or outhouse, as you do so saying:

(Name dog), please bark no more. I bind you with affection from making so much noise that I cannot think of you with affection.

* Take the image out every seven days and sprinkle more lavender or pot pourri on it, as you do so repeating the chant.

43 SPELLS FOR HEALING YOUR PETS AND RECEIVING HEALING FROM THEM

Animals, like young children, are remarkably receptive to healing powers. In this chapter I will suggest spells for healing pets, as well as ways of receiving healing energies from those creatures with which we are closely linked. Even if you have never healed before, the link of love will spontaneously open the channels of healing between you and your pet. While crystals are an effective tool, gentle loving touch is the most powerful healing medium.

The difference between healing magic and spiritual healing is really a matter of who is carrying out the healing and in whose name the healing is asked. Witches who heal might define their healing rituals as magic. Others, who work in the context of different philosophies, might talk of transmitting healing from higher sources. But, of course, many witches, myself included, also heal by asking the help of the Goddess, an angel or a higher source of spiritual energy. If you care about the person, animal or place you are healing and work with the purpose of relieving sorrow or suffering, that is spiritual, so this chapter, although part of a spell book, is about healing in its highest form.

If your animal is suffering from an acute condition or is not responding to treatment, I would, of course, recommend that you consult a veterinarian (some of whom these days also offer homeopathic treatments). But for a minor or chronic condition, or when an animal is stressed or cannot settle, a spell is an effective way of sending healing energies. A spell can also be a useful way of sending strength to an animal or bird that is being treated by a veterinarian, and may help the animal to respond faster to conventional medicine or surgery. Magic has the ability to kick-start a creature's own self-healing system. It can also help to maintain health in young, vulnerable, pregnant or old animals. If a pet is very old or sick, sometimes it is kinder to ease the passing rather than attempt futilely to make the animal better. This is a very positive form of healing.

The process is two-way. Animals can also heal us emotionally and physically. It has been shown that petting a cat lowers blood pressure in humans. Dolphins are truly magical in their healing powers, especially where children or conditions of the mind are concerned (see page 582). If you want to read more about animals as healers, see my *Psychic Power of Animals*, Piatkus Books, 2003.

If, despite healing, your pet dies, it does not mean that your work has failed. Healing can bring a gentle passing when recovery would have left a beloved pet with a poor quality of life.

A spell to raise the energy levels of a pet

Sometimes an animal may seem unwell, lacking appetite and energy, but the vet can find no physical problem. This spell is ideal for such cases. It is also useful if your pet is recuperating from an operation or treatment. Old animals may benefit from the regular performance of this spell. It will also calm a hyperactive or nervous animal.

You will need

4 jade or moss agate crystals (or a single crystal for a tiny pet or bird).

Timing

When your pet is listless and lethargic.

The spell

* Take up one of the crystals in your power hand (the one you write with), touching it first to the centre of your brow, then to the centre of your throat, then to your heart and finally to your solar plexus, saying for each: *May (name pet) be filled with life.* (Each of these places corresponds to one of the higher energy centres of the body.)
* Repeat with the other three crystals.
* Set the four crystals beneath the four corners of the animal's bed (or the single one in the bird's or small pet's cage). They will release energy slowly.
* Once every two weeks, wash the crystals under running water and repeat the spell. It will gradually enhance your pet's health.

A second spell to raise the energy levels of a pet

This spell is also good for calming very sensitive or noisy animals.

You will need

Your animal's water bowl; a green jade crystal.

Timing

When your pet is listless and lethargic.

The spell

* Fill the water bowl and place the crystal in it.
* Hold your hands, palms down, over the water, about 3 cm/1¹/₂ in above the bowl, and pass them deosil (clockwise) over the water bowl nine times, as you do so picturing soft green light entering the water.
* Leave the jade in the water for about an hour and then remove it.
* Give the water to your pet to drink. Wash the crystal under running water.
* Use jade water three times a week – more frequently if the pet has been unwell or is delicate.

A spell for empowering fish or pond life

You will need

An aquamarine crystal (for a fish tank) or a small green fluorite crystal (for a pond).

Timing

Ongoing.

The spell

* Place the crystal in the fish tank amongst the gravel or in the garden pond. Leave it in place. (It will be empowered by the water as well as empowering it.)

A spell for ensuring the continuing well-being of a healthy and active pet

Even the healthiest pet can benefit from having its energy levels topped up once a month. For city dwelling pets, a weekly psychic cleansing will help to remove pollutants, both physical and emotional. Try this spell also if a pet has been unwell, under stress or frightened for any reason.

You will need

A smoky quartz crystal, or a moss, tree or brown agate, together with a green jade, brown tiger's eye, green aventurine or yellow rutilated quartz crystal (both crystals should be smooth and of a similar size and shape).

Timing

When needed, preferably when the weather is calm.

The spell

* When the animal or bird is sitting or lying down, kneel or sit next to it, holding the jade, tiger's eye, aventurine or yellow rutilated quartz (for energising) in your power hand (the one you write with) and the smoky quartz or agate (for absorbing pollution and stress) in your other, receptive, hand.

* Very slowly and gently rotate your hands, moving the energising crystal deosil (clockwise) and the pollution-absorbing one widdershins (anti-clockwise) around the creature. Your hands should be about 9 cm/4 in away from the animal. As you move the crystals rhythmically, say as a soft chant:

Go away,
Flow away
Disharmony.
Flow in the air,
Flow to the sea.
Flow in its place
Vitality.

Continue rotating the crystals and chanting until the pollution-absorbing crystal feels heavy.

* Put the pollution-absorbing crystal down and work with only with the energising crystal, moving it gently around the pet in spirals, this time in silence, until you feel a sense of peace emanating from your pet.

* Wash the crystals under running water and put them together beneath the pet's bed overnight to finish the work.

* Keep the pair of crystals aside and use them for this spell.

A spell for soothing a sick or stressed pet

A specific incident – an attack by another animal or an accident – can cause a normally placid animal to become unusually timid or sometimes aggressive. It may take a number of repetitions of this spell to calm the animal, but each time will bring improvement.

You will need

Nothing.

Timing

Whenever necessary, but early evening is especially effective.

The spell

* Stroke your pet gently and rhythmically with your receptive hand (the one you don't write with), as you do so saying softly:

Light of healing enter here;
Comfort bring and consolation.
Light of healing, disperse fear.
Rest, grow strong and renewed be.

* As the animal relaxes, lighten the pressure and soften your voice until your hand is still and your voice fades into silence.
* Repeat the ritual when needed.

A spell for calming a nervous or timid pet

Your pet may be anxious in the presence of other animals, unfamiliar people, noise or sudden movement. This is often due to a very sensitive nature. Such animals are usually very psychic. To help your pet cope with everyday stresses, try a regular relaxation spell. Performing the spell at the same time each week will gradually help the creature to flow with the stream of life.

You will need

A rose quartz or amethyst pendulum; a pot of herbs.

Timing

Weekly, when the pet is sleepy.

The spell

* Hold the pendulum in your power hand (the one you write with) and stroke the pet on the back, from the head downwards, with your receptive hand. With the pendulum, follow your receptive hand (just above it), allowing the pendulum to spiral on its own path, absorbing any stress. Continue until you feel that the pendulum is heavy.
* Bury the pendulum in the pot of herbs for 24 hours and then wash it under running water and allow it to dry naturally.

A spell to heal a sick or injured animal

This method does not involve physical contact and so can be used to give extra strength when your pet is resting or is in pain and does not want to be touched. I have used spell this many times with my own animals. Try it also if you take in an animal from a rescue centre that may be traumatised.

You will need

A fibre optic lamp, shaded lamp or pool of natural light (sunlight or bright moonlight) – candles and animals tend not to be a good mix.

Timing

When your pet is asleep or totally relaxed.

The spell

* Place the lamp (if necessary) so that a pool of light surrounds it, and sit next to your pet.
* Say the pet's name several times very softly and then point both your index fingers towards the light. Then move the finger of your right hand in a circle to the right and the finger of your left hand in a circle to the left, as if you were making the circle of light bigger and more powerful.
* Point both your index fingers towards the light again, and then once more draw light circles, as you do so imagining the circles gradually enclosing you and the pet. As you work, recite a soft mantra or chant. My favourite is:
  Light of love intensify,
  Healing power from on high,
  From the Earth to the sky.
* When the circle of light is bright in your mind, hold your fingers in the light (if this seems strange, use the physical light pool) and with your fingertips draw in the light.
* Now hold your hands palms down and move your fingers fast, as though typing. Picture light drops falling from your fingers like gentle rain and entering your pet in those places where there is pain or discomfort. Continue until the visualised light fades, and leave the animal at rest in the physical light.

An absent healing spell for an animal

This spell is an adaptation of the previous one. Use it to heal a pet that is staying at an animal hospital for an operation or a pet belonging to a friend or relative. You can also use it to send healing to an endangered species, working with a picture of the relevant wild animal.

You will need

A lamp or golden-coloured candle; a photograph or symbol of the pet to be healed.

Timing

At the time of the treatment or when you are quiet at home.

The spell

* Turn on the lamp or light the candle. Set the photo or symbol of the animal in the light. Make the series of hand movements described in the previous spell, chanting the mantra and imagining the light.

A spell for bringing relief to an old or chronically sick pet

As pets get older, they may slow down and want to spend more time quietly. Some may not like being touched, especially if their joints are painful or stiff, or if they have an ongoing condition that makes them restless. This spell is a good way of bringing relief to the creature, together with a gradual improvement in strength and some healing. It may help an animal in pain to sleep through the night. The spell works best if the animal or bird is in the room with you when you perform it.

You will need

A brown candle; a ball of dough or modelling clay; some very small brown or sandy agates or brown glass nuggets.

Timing

Once a month on a Saturday evening at dusk, or when your pet is sick, in pain or unusually lethargic.

The spell

* Light the candle.

* Make a clay animal to represent your pet and set it where the light will shine on it.

* Press the crystals or glass nuggets into the clay at the points where the animal is in pain – or around the outline if there is a general energy problem. Also place a crystal on the paws or claws and another on the stomach of the clay representation. These are the main psychic healing centres in animals.

* Beginning with the problem spot, touch each of the crystals in turn, and say for each:
  Bless and protect, restore and heal.

* Blow out the candle and let the light travel into the model and into your animal.

* Leave the clay animal overnight near where your pet sleeps. When it is light, remove the crystals, wash them and roll the clay back into a ball, ready for the next time you use it.

A spell to identify a healing remedy

Sometimes when we buy a health supplement for a pet there are a number of very similar remedies, and the pet store owner or pharmacist can only offer general guidance. By linking in to the pet, it is possible to discover which will be the most effective.

You will need

A rose quartz, amethyst or clear quartz crystal pendulum; 3 hairs or a single small feather from your pet.

Timing

When needed.

The spell

* Attach the hairs or feather to the pendulum. Some pendulums have a tiny compartment to hold such things, but if not, fix them to the chain with a thread.

* Hold the pendulum up to the light, be it natural or artificial, and turn it nine times deosil (clockwise), then nine times widdershins (anti-clockwise), then nine times deosil again. As you turn the pendulum, say in your head:
  Make the connection,
  Give me direction.
  What best will heal/give health to (name of pet).

* Pass the pendulum slowly over each of the possible remedies. It will feel heavy and vibrate or actually pull down, as though pulled by gravity, over the correct remedy.

A spell to empower a healing remedy

Whether you have used the above spell to find the right remedy or have been prescribed medicine or health supplements for your pet, cast this spell to ensure that the healing powers are released to trigger the pet's own self-healing system.

You will need

Any green healthy plant in a pot.

Timing

Before giving the remedy.

The spell

* With your power hand (the one you write with) hold the bottle or tube of medicine just above the plant. With the other hand, draw imaginary green light upwards and direct it in slow waving movements in to the bottle.
* Still with your power hand, pass the bottle nine times deosil (clockwise) around the plant.
* Shake the bottle or tube to stir up the energies and then give it to your pet.

A spell to help an animal or bird recover from the death of another pet in the household

Even if pets were not emotionally close, the death of one can cause trauma in the surviving animal or animals. If the pet who has died was a close companion to another animal, the remaining pet may grieve and stop eating. This spell is effective for any grieving creature, be it a gerbil or a horse. It also works well when a human family member leaves the household to live somewhere else, leaving behind a grieving pet.

You will need

A black-and-white snowflake obsidian or any very dark crystal; a fabric item belonging to the deceased pet or human who has gone away (for example, an old blanket or scarf), or a small dish; some rose petals or any pink or white petals or blossoms; a small old box with a lid.

Timing

The evening after the animal has died or the family member gone away.

The spell

* Wrap the crystal inside the item belonging to the deceased pet or human, or place it in the dish.
* When you go to bed, transfer the obsidian, still wrapped in the fabric or in the dish, to a spot near the sleeping place of the surviving pet.
* In the morning, remove the obsidian, place it in the box and fill the rest of the box with petals. Put the lid on the box and bury it in the earth close to a spot the deceased pet or departed person used to like – or, if you have buried the pet in the garden, close to the grave.
* Leave the fabric item or dish close to the grieving animal's sleeping place for a further 24 hours.

An absent healing spell for pets or animals that are ill-treated or neglected

On page 482 I write about using a healing book to heal anyone who was sick and noted that you could include animals in it. Some people prefer to keep a special healing book for pets of friends and family members. You could include in this animals and birds at your local pet rescue centre and any farms or zoos where you know the creatures are kept in less than ideal conditions (see also pages 572 and 574). The more people who carry out a spell like this, the more powerful the vibes that are released into the cosmos to help the great number of sick and abused animals. It is a good supplement to more practical ways of offering help.

You will need

A small notebook; a small table or flat surface in your home; a pink cloth; a pen you keep only for your healing book; a pink candle; a pot of sage or thyme or any green plant.

Timing

Weekly at the same time if possible (10 pm is a good time for absent healing spells for animals as well as people).

The spell

* In your notebook, write the name of any animal who needs healing or any local animal organisation you know of that is caring for sick or neglected animals and birds.
* Place the cloth on the table. Light the candle and set it on the cloth. Set the plant where the light will shine on it.
* Open the notebook at the first page and read each name in turn, then say:
  May she / he / they be healed by the power of light and love.
* When you have read all the names in the book, add:
  May all those animals and birds I know and do not know who are sick or suffering be healed by the power of light and love.
* Blow out the candle and visualise the light travelling to all the creatures who need it, known and unknown.
* Leave the cloth, the plant, the candle and the book on the table. Have the book open at a different page each day. Take out any names of creatures that are healed. If an animal passes away, light the candle and speak a few words of blessing and thanks for their life, then blow out the candle. Remove their name from the book.

A spell to receive healing from an animal

If you have been suffering from pain and feel exhausted, or you are anxious or depressed, you can draw healing strength from your pets. Dogs, cats, horses and rabbits are most the most attuned to this purpose, but a bird that remains still for long periods can also give healing. Because pets have unconditional love for us, their healing strength often pours out almost effortlessly. Afterwards, give your pet extra attention. This will recharge his or her healing strength.

You will need

A quiet place where you can be alone or undisturbed.

Timing

In the early evening.

The spell

* Sit or stand facing the animal and create a circuit by placing both your hands on either of the animal's sides.
* Unless you are working with a cat, make eye contact (cats do not usually like being stared at).
* Keep perfectly still and for a minute or two focus on the animal's breath, until you are totally connected with the rhythm.
* Begin to breathe in time with the animal, even if it is panting or purring. On the in-breath visualise a soft pink light flowing from the animal into your body through the connection made with your power hand (the one you write with). On the out-breath allow imaginary darkness to flow out of your receptive hand in to the animal.
* When you are ready, slowly withdraw your hands and start to breathe normally.
* Gently groom the pet to remove any negativity that may have stuck to them. You may both feel tired, so settle down together, or if you are working with a horse in a stable or an outdoor rabbit, make sure they are comfortable and have extra food.

A second spell to receive healing from an animal

If you cannot sleep at night because of pain or worry, you will probably find that your pet is close by or will also be awake in their cage or sleeping place.

You will need

A bowl of warm water.

Timing

At night.

The spell

* Set the bowl of water at your side.
* Touch the animal with your power hand (the one you write with), as you do so saying:

Walk with me a little way and carry this burden/pain that it may be less heavy.

* Hold your other hand so that your fingertips just touch the bowl of water. Picture the strength passing from the animal through your power hand and flowing out of your body through your receptive hand in to the water. Continue for a minute or two.
* Pour the water away outdoors or under a flowing water source.
* Pat the animal and thank them.

A third spell to receive healing from an animal

This is a good spell to use if you need more energy or better health but there is no specific illness or pain.

You will need

An open-air place or an indoor one where your pet can move freely and there is plenty of greenery (indoors you can collect your pot plants together).

Timing

When the animal or bird is most lively during the day.

The spell

* Let the pet move freely while you follow its paths, if possible barefoot, so that you absorb energy through the energy centres in the soles of your feet. These are connected with your root energy centre, the power house of physical strength that rises through the body.
* When you are ready to go back indoors, take a small piece of greenery with you (or place one of the pot plants in a space that you frequently use). It will be filled with the vitality of the creature.

A spell for obtaining healing from fish

Fish in aquariums or pools are known to reduce human stress levels. Try this quick stress remedy.

You will need

An aquamarine, or a blue or pink coral; a net (if your fish are in a pond); a small bag or purse.

Timing

When you face a lot of stress.

The spell

* Place the aquamarine or coral in the fish tank or put it in the net and place it in the pond. Leave it there for an hour or two.
* Remove the aquamarine or coral from the water, wash it and allow it to dry naturally.
* Place the aquamarine or coral in the bag or purse and carry it with you whenever you face a stressful situation.

44 SPELLS FOR PROTECTING PETS FROM HARM

There are many hazards facing household pets, especially those that go out of doors. They may be attacked by larger animals, run over on the road, infected with viruses or parasites, or even harmed by a neighbour who hates animals. In the modern world, in which pets are protected and do not have to forage for food, some may lose their instinctive awareness of danger. Spells can be helpful to create barriers between a pet and potential harm and also to rekindle the creature's own sense of preservation.

Some of the spells in this chapter have been practised for hundreds of years, while others are modern, created to deal with the changing environment of our pets. Crystals appear in many of the spells because, of all natural remedies, they seem most to strengthen the pet's own innate self-protective abilities without affecting its physiological system. If you have crystals around your home or garden from other spells you have cast, they will already be having a positive effect on creatures of all kinds who come into their sphere.

A traditional protective turquoise spell for all pets, from horses to hamsters

If you choose only one protective crystal, make it turquoise. Down the ages and in different lands, turquoise has been tied to animals' collars to prevent them from straying or being stolen. It is also traditionally plaited into a horse's bridle or mane to guard it against stumbling. You can keep a small turquoise attached to a small animal or bird cage.

You will need

A small turquoise of any quality.

Timing

Ongoing.

The spell

* Empower the turquoise by leaving it outdoors for 24 hours at any time from the full moon to the end of the moon cycle to absorb protective sun-, moon- and starlight.
* Attach the turquoise to the animal's collar, cage or hutch.
* Wash and re-empower the turquoise crystal monthly.

A spell to prevent a pet getting lost, straying or being stolen

A pet that wants to move on will generally do so (especially if it is a cat). On the other hand, animals have been known to cross continents to find an owner who moved house while the pet was missing. The majority of domestic creatures who disappear get diverted while exploring or wander into places where they get shut in – or get very comfortable and forget the time, which may extend to days or weeks. A valuable animal may be stolen. Microchips and security collars are very effective in all these cases, but the old ways of our forebears are also useful. They relied on imprinting the creature's identity on the home, so deterring the animal from wandering far and drawing it back if it did, and putting off thieves and those with ill intent.

This and the following three spells are common to a number of lands. Many spells spread to America, Canada, Australia, New Zealand and South Africa from eastern and western Europe with colonists and migrants. This spell will work for any pet small enough to be lifted and also for birds if they are tame.

You will need

Nothing.

Timing

When you move to a new home or a new animal arrives in your house.

The spell

* Hold the animal up to the first mirror in place in the house (or the nearest to the front door), so that your pet sees itself in the new location not only on a physical but also on a psychic level.

A second spell to prevent a pet getting lost, straying or being stolen

This spell is not recommended for very tiny animals or birds, as it involves feeding them sugar. However, you may be able to find a sweetened food or vitamin supplement that agrees with them, in which case you can do the spell using that.

You will need
A grain of sugar.

Timing
At dawn (some versions of the spell say 9 am) on the first Friday after a new pet arrives in your home or you move house.

The spell
* Put a tiny grain of sugar into your pet's food or water bowl. It will henceforth know your house as home.

A third spell to prevent a pet getting lost, straying or being stolen

You will need
A dish of salt.

Timing
When a new pet arrives, or you move house, or you suspect that someone is being unkind to or taking an unusual interest in your pet.

The spell
* When the pet is settled or sleeping, scatter an unbroken widdershins (anti-clockwise) circle of salt round it. (If your pet is tiny, work around its cage or hutch.) Then make an unbroken deosil (clockwise) circle just outside the first, and finally another unbroken widdershins circle beyond that. As you work, whisper softly and continuously:
Keep safe within and safe without, peacefully, protectingly. So shall it be!
* If your pet moves out of the circles before you have finished the spell, repeat it at another time.

A fourth spell to prevent a pet getting lost, straying or being stolen

You will need
Three hairs or small feathers from your pet (7 hairs for a large animal) – shed or on the grooming brush; a clay or dough likeness of the creature; some fresh or dried rosemary or basil; some fresh or dried dill, mint or catnip (the latter very protective for cats); a small wooden, card or metal box with a lid; a long red cord.

Timing
During the waning moon.

The spell
* Push the hairs into the head of the clay likeness.
* Place the model in the box.
* If the herbs are fresh, add them to the box; if they are dry, sprinkle them on the clay.
* Tie the box with the red cord, knotting it nine times.
* Bury the box outside the door that the pet uses most. For a horse, you can bury the box in a paddock; for a small animal or bird kept indoors, bury it in the soil of a large pot plant near the animal's cage.

A traditional bell protective ritual

An effective form of protection is a shiny bell, used – like the horse brasses of old – to repel negative intentions towards your pet and return them to the sender. Horse brasses – circular brass discs adorned with emblems such as stars, the sun, stylised faces and wheels – were fastened to the bridle of a horse, especially carthorses and shire horses. The brasses would jingle as the creature moved, so driving off all harm. Horse brasses were highly prized and handed down through the generations. You may be able to buy a horse brass to hang in a stable, or a miniature one to hang over your pet's sleeping quarters. However, a bell is equally effective. Both can be empowered in the same way.

You will need

A small bell or horse brass; a small dish of soil; a small bowl of water; a green candle.

Timing

Late in the moon cycle, after dark.

The spell

* Light the candle.
* Dip the bell or horse brass three times in the dish of earth, saying for each time:
  Do not stray, keep away harm, from malice and from stranger, keep away danger.
* Plunge the bell or brass into the water six times, repeating the words for each plunge.
* Pass the bell or brass nine times above the candle flame, repeating the words for each pass.
* Suspend the bell or brass from the animal's collar or hang it in his or her sleeping quarters, somewhere where it will move in any air current.
* Re-empower the bell or brass once a month.

A spell to keep animals and birds safe from all harm

You will need

A small spray bottle (of the kind used for watering plants) filled with 250 ml/ ¹/₂ pt water; Cerato or Cherry Plum Bach Flower Remedy, or tea tree or pine essential oil.

Timing

Weekly, at any time.

The spell

* Add three or four drops of the Flower Remedy or five drops of the oil to the water in the bottle.
* Spray the water over all doorsteps and on the inside of any garden gates. If you have a cat, also spray along inside window ledges. As you spray, say repeatedly, as a chant:
  Remain within or swift return.

A spell for making an amulet to keep your pet from straying or being stolen and to guard against fears

This amulet, or protective charm, is especially good for protecting horses (see also page 562). You can make two amulets and keep one in the horse's travelling box if you take it to shows. If you repeat the chants three times to activate extra power, the amulet will also stop animals and birds being afraid in storms or when there are sudden loud noises, such as firecrackers.

You will need

Three hairs or feathers from the pet (7 for a large pet); a small loop of thin wire; some red thread; a dish of salt; a small bowl of water.

Timing

Any.

The spell

* Bind or tie the hairs around the wire to create a complete circle, securing them tightly with the thread. As you work, chant three times:

Protection safe
Wind in here,
From theft or loss

Or any fear.
Nought harm,
Peace calm.
Do not stray
Or unwillingly be led away.

* Add three pinches of salt to the water and stir them in with the index finger of your power hand (the one you write with), as you do so saying three times:

Salt and water, blessed be!
Create for (name pet) a sanctuary.

* Using your power hand and moving outwards, sprinkle three deosil (clockwise) circles of empowered water drops around the plaited ring, as you do so saying:

Three by three the power I raise,
Bringing lifelong peaceful days.
So shall it be.
Security forever see.

* Hang the ring close to the pet's sleeping area. If the creature becomes afraid, touch the amulet and repeat all three chants of the spell, one after the other, three times.

A spell for protecting a pet from the aggression of humans and animals

Your pet may come under threat from hostile humans or other larger or fiercer animals. Whether you are dealing with jealous rivals at a horse or dog show, or neighbours who hate animals, try this spell. It will cast around your animal an active circle of protection to repel anger and aggression. Do the spell while the bird or animal is not present, because the flashing light may disturb it.

You will need

An electric torch with a beam that can be set to flash on and off continuously; the animal's water bowl (filled with water); some dried mint or rosemary.

Timing

Late on a moonless night.

The spell

* Working by torch light in the open air, set the bowl of water on the ground, if possible soil or grass, so that the protective earth energies can rise into the water.
* Scatter a single widdershins (anti-clockwise) circle of mint or rosemary around the bowl, as you do so saying:

Spite and anger come not here.
Cruel humans cause not fear.
Fierce predators turn away
Your claws and jaws and do not stay.

* Set the torch to continuous flash and move around the herb circle in nine widdershins circles, waving the light also in widdershins circles as you move. Say as you work:

Sparks of light, beams of fire,
Drive from here all wrong desire.
Golden rays and radiant flame,
Repel all who come in evil's name.

* After the final circling, call out:

Be gone! Do not come again.

If you shake your fingertips, you may see the sparks emanating from them.

* Leave the bowl of water in the open air or near a window and give it to your pet first thing in the morning so that he or she can drink the protection. The effects are long-lasting.
* When the animal is especially vulnerable, visualise light sparks or beams and shake your fingers over your pet for protection.

A spell to desensitise dogs and horses to traffic noise and to keep cats away from roads

Both dogs and horses can be afraid of sudden loud noises, such as a road drill or a noisy motor bike. This can make road walking hazardous. This spell will calm the animal down. If you live in a city, you can also use it to help a cat develop road sense. It will protect urban pets against pollution, too.

You will need

An amber or malachite crystal; a stick of myrrh, patchouli or carnation incense, or a cedar smudge stick; a small purse or bag of the same colour as the crystal.

Timing

At 10 pm, during the waning moon.

The spell

* Set the crystal on a rock outdoors.
* Light the incense or smudge stick and, holding it above the crystal, make ever-widening widdershins (anticlockwise) smoke circles until you have enclosed the crystal in a smoke cocoon. As you work, say continuously and increasingly softly, so that your voice ends in silence:
  Be as a shield against disturbance and intrusion, against loud noise and pollution and all that frightens, confuses or endangers.
* Leave the incense or smudge to burn down safely next to the crystal.
* Carry the crystal with you in the purse or bag whenever you exercise the animal. If you have empowered the crystal for a cat, put it close to the cat flap or to the door that the cat uses to go out.

A spell to guide pets safely home, especially at night

If your cat enjoys frequent night time forays, you can empower a crystal to act as a homing beacon.

You will need

A green or orange cat's eye crystal or a moonstone of any colour.

Timing

On the night of the full moon.

The spell

* Set your crystal outside from moon rise (check the time in the weather section of a newspaper or *Old Moore's Almanack*) until sunrise (or when you wake).
* The next evening at dusk, place the crystal in a window facing the direction in which the cat leaves the house. Leave it there as a beacon.
* Wash and re-empower the crystal once a month.

A spell to guide safely home birds that fly free, such as pigeons, doves and birds of prey

You will need

A falcon's eye crystal (a blue form of tiger's eye).

Timing

On the day of the full moon.

The spell

* Set the crystal outside from dawn to sunset.
* The following dawn, place the crystal in the pigeon loft or aviary to guide your birds safely home.
* Wash and re-empower the crystal once a month.

A spell to reconnect domestic pets with their natural cycles

Animals and birds that live in apartments or in big cities may lose connection with nature. This can dull their instincts and sometimes make them over-dependent on human company. If possible, take larger pets to parks and woodland regularly and surround indoor pens or cages with green plants, especially tall herbs. For outdoor pets, have small bushes and greenery growing in aviaries and runs.

You will need

A big box of leaves, grass and greenery; a moss agate crystal.

Timing

Once a month.

The spell

* Take the box of greenery outside and give it to the animal to play in.
* As your pet is playing, take a handful of leaves and throw them in the air, so that some fall on the pet, as you do so saying three times:
  Power of nature rise and fall,
  Waken instinct with your call.
* Drape a little of the empowered greenery near to the animal's sleeping place and place a moss agate in it.
* Leave the moss agate out in the rain once a month and then replace it in the greenery.

A spell to protect your pet against parasites

With wall-to-wall carpeting and central heating, fleas are a year-round problem for many pet owners. Yet many owners are worried by the chemical toxicity of some commercial flea collars and sprays. This and the following spell work by empowering a natural remedy to trigger the pet's own resistance. They should decrease parasites to a level where you can successfully use a herbal flea collar to mop up any residual unwanted visitors. Empower the flea collar using the method described in the following spell for the dish of herbs.

You will need
An amethyst crystal.

Timing
When your animal has a problem with parasites.

The spell
* Place the amethyst in your pet's water. Pass your hands, palms down, slowly widdershins (anti-clockwise) a few centimetres above the water, as you do so, saying seven times slowly:
  Far from here your irritation,
  Far from here your infestation.
  From this place I banish you.
* After eight hours, take the amethyst out of the water and allow the pet to drink the water.
* Repeat weekly.

A second spell to protect your pet against parasites and infections

You will need
A dish of dried lavender, tansy and pennyroyal; 4 or 5 pots of eau de cologne mint or basil.

Timing
In the early morning, on the first day of the month.

The spell
* Place the dish of herbs outdoors in an open space, preferably on the earth or grass, and surround it with the pots of herbs.
* Walk very slowly around the herb pots (if possible barefoot) three times widdershins (anti-clockwise), then three times deosil (clockwise) and finally three times widdershins.
* To deter parasites, scatter the herbs under the pet's bed, around hutches or runs and outside each entrance door and downstairs window, as you do so saying:
  Come not here, you who fly or hop or creep; sleep outdoors.
* To keep flies away from pets' dishes, place the pots of herbs near the animals' feeding places.

A spell to light your pet's way home if lost

If a pet gets lost and conventional channels fail to produce a sighting, this spell may help to connect with the creature – which may have panicked and so have lost its bearings. If the animal was lost while exercising, especially if you travelled by car, it may be confused. However, as I said before, animals do find their way home, sometimes over hundreds of miles.

You will need
A shaded lamp; a picture of your pet.

Timing
When a pet has not returned, at dusk.

The spell
* As darkness falls, place the lamp in a window facing the street or the direction in which the pet usually leaves the house.
* Switch on the lamp and sit by it, softly calling your pet. Picture your animal guided by the soft beam of light and send calm, loving thoughts to add to the homing power.
* Say nine times:
  Come home now (name pet).
* Place the picture next to the lamp. Leave the lamp burning all night.
* Repeat each night.

45 SPELLS FOR ATTRACTING WILDLIFE AND DRAWING STRENGTH FROM EXOTIC CREATURES

Animals that live in the wild are becoming an integral part of the urban as well as the rural environment. Peregrine falcons, for instance, now nest in the ruins of the once famous Battersea Power Station, no more than a mile or two from the Houses of Parliament in central London. We can cast spells to attract such indigenous wildlife into our gardens and to help protect local wildlife habitats from destruction by building works or pollution. In return we can draw on the strengths and luck-bringing qualities of all kinds of creatures.

Conservation parks bring more exotic, and often endangered, species into our world. Again, we can utilise the powers and healing of these animals through magic, while at the same time sending our own positive energies to help others of the species that are being hunted to extinction or kept in cramped zoos or circuses.

The more we connect magically, as well as practically, with the natural world, the more we are able to tap into its treasure store of power, thus amplifying our own innate psychic and magical abilities. Each time we cast a spell (followed by practical action) to help an individual animal or bird, a group of creatures or a species, we are making this connection.

Just as indigenous people, such as the Native North Americans, the Australian Aboriginals and the New Zealand Maoris, have done for many hundreds of years, we can acquire wisdom from an archetypal or mythical animal or bird through contact with a real or visualised member of that species.

This chapter is a varied one. It opens up the concept of drawing magical energies from the world around us, a theme I develop more in Part 10 of this book.

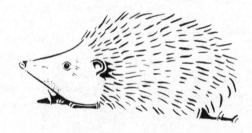

A spell for protecting animals and birds in the wild

Whether you have a bird table, enjoy watching videos about wildlife or like to visit conservation parks, you can enhance your connection with animals by performing your own magical spells to preserve wildlife and wildlife habitats for future generations. This spell should be performed in an open outdoor place. Choose somewhere where you won't be disturbed as you work.

You will need
Nothing.

Timing
In the afternoon.

The spell
* Kneel down and touch the grass, forest floor or earth with your hands, your knees and the soles of your feet. Say:
  I connect. Protect all creatures of the earth, those who roam across it, feed upon it or live beneath.
* Stand up and extend your arms upwards to make a V-shape above your head. Say:
  I connect. Protect all creatures of the air, from mightiest eagle to most fragile butterfly.
* Make a circle around you with your arms at waist height, so that you almost touch your back, and then bring your arms to the front again. Say:
  I connect. Protect all creatures of still waters, flowing rivers and the sea.
* Spend time in the open air and afterwards plan or do something practical to help animals, be it feeding the birds, joining a conservation society, writing to your local supermarket to protest at the sale of eggs from caged hens, or taking friends or family to a good conservation park where wildlife is cared for in natural surroundings.

A St Francis of Assisi ritual

St Francis, who lived during the early eleventh century, is patron saint of all animals and birds. However, he is most famed for his connection with wild creatures, which would come close to him and be silent as he spoke and prayed. He healed many of them. They were said to gather around him like a human congregation. The first environmentalist, he wrote a number of prayers that are still used at church services for animal healing and blessings. This is a version of a traditional St Francis Prayer that I heard only recently, when an area of land had been saved from developers in the West Country of England.

You will need
Nothing.

Timing
Any, but when feeding wild birds is good.

The spell
* Focus on an individual wild creatures or an endangered species to which you wish to send healing, or allow the healing to find its own path. Say:
  St Francis, who loved all creatures of the wild, we have lost the beautiful relationship to treat them with respect.
  We pray for all animals who are suffering as a result of our neglect or destructive ways.
  May right order be once again restored to the whole world and to the creatures who choose to live apart from the human world yet should enjoy its protection.

A second St Francis of Assisi ritual

This ritual is based on another St Francis prayer, spoken generally as a peace prayer (see page 628). However, it is also very appropriate for sending healing and protection to an endangered habitat, be it a piece of local wetland or an Amazonian rainforest.

You will need
A pink candle for a small area of destruction or a gold-coloured one for a large area.

Timing
On a Sunday evening, at dusk.

The spell
* Light the candle and, looking into the flame, name the area and creatures under threat.
* Still looking into the candle, recite softly three times:
  Lord, make me a channel of thy peace,
  ... that where there is hatred, I may bring love;
  That where there is discord, I may bring harmony;
  That where there is error, I may bring truth;
  ... that where there are shadows, I may bring light;
  That where there is sadness, I may bring joy.
* Name once more the threatened areas and the creature that will be harmed and blow out the candle, as you do so saying:
  Preserve them, St Francis.

Even if the cause seems hopeless, press on, saying the St Francis prayer once a week.

A third St Francis of Assisi ritual

This ritual is based on another general St Francis prayer that is effective for sending blessings to wild animals, birds and fish (especially those who are being hunted to extinction), as well as to factory-farmed or caged animals and birds. It takes the form of a walking or circling prayer (see also page 628) and, if practised on a regular basis, is a good way of releasing positive energies for wildlife preservation.

You will need
A natural outdoor circle, for example a circle of trees, a circular flower bed or a stone circle, or (for working indoors) a large white pillar candle.

Timing
In the early morning.

The spell
* If you are working indoors, light the candle and set it on a small table or in a holder on the floor.
* Walk in a continuous deosil (clockwise) circle around the candle or outdoor circle, as you do so naming an individual creature, group or species of animals or birds that needs protecting, and reciting:
  May the Lord bless you and keep you;
  May the Lord show his face to you and have compassion on you;
  May he turn his face to you and give you peace.
* Name another animal, bird or species that needs blessing, and repeat the circling and chanting.
* Continue naming, circling and chanting until you have named all the causes you wish to bless.
* Try to do some small practical thing to help one of the concerns you have named.
* Repeat monthly.

A St Blaise ritual to help animals and birds in badly run zoos and in circuses

St Blaise was a fourth-century saint associated with animals. Because he worked with fierce creatures, he is an ideal focus for protecting more exotic animals in captivity. Blaise was an Armenian bishop who became a hermit in a cave, where he was renowned for healing animals. Sick animals, gentle and fierce, would come to his cave, waiting patiently until he finished his prayers. Even the most ferocious became docile as they gathered around to hear him speak.

You will need
8 small pottery or plastic toy animals of ferocious species; a small, hand-held, battery-operated fan.

Timing
Early on a Friday morning.

The spell
* Arrange the animals on a table in two rows.
* Switch on the fan and spiral it over and around the animals, as you do so saying three times:
Good St Blaise from whom no creature ever was turned away,
Good St Blaise who calmed the fierce and helped the weakest in your care,
Good St Blaise, preserve, I ask and free from chains those who are captive now though innocent.
Good St Blaise, ease their plight that they may move once more in places likened to their own.
* Arrange animals randomly in your garden or among potted plants.

A spell to avert bad luck when encountering a magpie

The magpie is regarded in many lands as an omen of good or bad fortune. A single magpie is seen as unlucky, especially if encountered during the morning. I know a number of very cynical people who swear by this ritual.

You will need
Nothing.

Timing
When you see a single magpie.

The spell
* Bow three times and say:
Good morning, Mr Magpie, and how are you today?
Good luck will follow you all day.

A good luck magpie spell

There are a number of magpie divinatory rhymes that predict your fortune according to the number of magpies you see together. This spell strengthens the good luck in the predicted area. This is a very old rhyme and as such has gathered power down the years.

You will need
Nothing.

Timing
When you see a number of magpies together.

The spell

* Recite seven times very fast:
  One for sorrow,
  Two for mirth,
  Three for a letter,
  Four for a birth,
  Five for silver,
  Six for gold,
  And seven for a secret never to be told.

* Turn round deosil (clockwise) the same number of times as there are magpies and say:
  The wish is mine and it shall be,
  As the magpies told to me.

* Shout in to the air what you really want. If, for example, you saw three magpies, this might be a letter containing a job offer, a love letter, a letter bringing a long overdue cheque or a letter bearing good news from friends overseas.

A spell to empower a lucky elephant charm for your home

It is said that every home should have a model elephant for each external door. This ensures that bad luck remains outside and good fortune attaches itself to family members. Place an elephant also at the foot of the stairs and (a larger one) at the top. This will ensure that your fortunes continue to rise.

You will need
An elephant for each exterenal door in your home and one for the bottom and top of the stairs (small elephants are as lucky as large ones); a golden-coloured coin for each elephant.

Timing
When the crescent moon is visible in the sky, as soon as it is dark. (If it is too cloudy to see the moon, wait for a clear night.)

The spell

* Arrange your elephants left to right in ascending order of size on the doorstep and place a coin under each of them. Leave them until bedtime.

* Put the elephants in their places, at the doors and stairs.

* Re-empower the elephants (by taking them outside again and placing a coin beneath) whenever the sky is clear during the crescent moon.

A lucky frog spell to bring fertility and abundance into your life

The frog is a symbol of fertility and abundance in many cultures. Its seemingly miraculous cycle of transformation from egg through tadpole to frog gave it strong associations with rebirth and renewal. In ancient Egypt the appearance of vast numbers of frogs was associated with the Nile flood that brought fertility to the land. Heqt or Heket was the frog goddess, wife of the potter god, Khnum, who fashioned people from the Nile clay. She breathed life into them. Her amulet brought fertility to women and after death it promised resurrection. Perform this spell if you want to conceive a child, get a new venture moving or revive enthusiasm for a personal dream.

You will need

A green crystal such as jade, malachite, apple-green chrysoprase, aventurine or aquamarine; a soft green cloth; a permanent marker pen or black acrylic paint and a thin brush; a bowl of sparkling mineral water; a small green purse.

Timing

When it is raining outside.

The spell

* Take the crystal out in to the rain and say five times:

  Water flow fast, water renew
  Fertility, abundance. Bring life anew.

* Dry the crystal with the cloth, as you do so repeating the words five more times.

* Draw or paint a frog on the crystal.

* Using your power hand (the one you write with) make a single deosil (clockwise) circle of water drops very slowly around the frog. As you do so, repeat the chant five times more.

* When the paint is dry, place your frog crystal in the purse and carry it with you.

* Repeat the spell about once a month, when it is raining, touching up the drawing if necessary. If you have a pond in your garden, real frogs may arrive within a short time of casting the spell. They will increase the abundance flowing into your life.

A toad spell for prosperity

The three-legged Chinese toad is the power creature of Liu Hai the God of prosperity. Most Chinese lucky toads have a golden coin in their mouth. According to Chinese myth, a three-legged toad lives in the moon, its legs representing the three main lunar phases. During lunar eclipses, the toad swallows the moon.

You will need

A small ceramic, wooden or crystal toad (if you cannot get a Chinese toad with a coin in its mouth, set one of the gold coins from the circle beneath it after the spell); 12 gold-coloured coins; a stick of patchouli, peach, geranium or frankincense incense; an incense-holder.

Timing

Early in the afternoon on a Thursday, preferably in sunshine.

The spell

* Surround the toad with a deosil (clockwise) circle of gold coins.
* Light the incense and, holding it in your power hand (the one you write with) write in smoke over the toad and coin circle seven times: 'Prosperity be mine.'
* Set the incense, in the holder, in the centre of the coin circle, next to the toad, and leave it to burn through.
* Keep the toad in the south-east corner of the room you use for working out finances or under your work desk or table at home (with one of the coins beneath it if necessary). Place the 12 (or 11) coins in a circle around the toad.
* Re-empower the toad monthly *in situ* by lighting another incense stick and writing 'Prosperity be mine' seven times in smoke over the coins and toad and leaving the incense to burn through in the centre of the coin circle.

A lucky pig spell for good fortune in every way

Pigs are symbols of good fortune and prosperity in many cultures. In Chile and Peru, the three-legged lucky pig corresponds with the Chinese three-legged toad (see page 577). Piggie banks, with a slot for coins, are a symbol of accumulated wealth. Some have an opening in the bottom to retrieve the money when the pig is full; others are made of pottery and designed to be smashed once full. A new piggie bank should be started with a coin from the old one to ensure continuing prosperity.

You will need

A piggie bank; a gold-coloured candle; a gold-coloured coin that you have been given the day before the spell (for example as change in making a purchase).

Timing

On a Wednesday, as it gets light.

The spell

* Light the candle and place the piggie bank where the light will shine on it.
* Pass the coin around the candle flame seven times deosil (clockwise), saying for each pass:
  Increased be luck and prosperity.
* Put the coin in the piggie bank and silently make a wish for whatever good fortune you need in your life.
* Blow out the candle.
* Each day re-light the candle, pass another golden coin (from any source) seven times round the candle, as you do so chanting the words seven times. Put the coin in the piggie bank, repeating the wish silently or making a different one. Again blow out the candle.
* Continue these actions and the chant until the candle is burnt through or the pig is full. Then replace the candle or empty the piggie bank (keeping back one coin to start filling the pig again). Spend the rest of the money on a small treat you can share with your family or friends.

A lucky hare spell

The hare is a symbol of new beginnings and fertility. It is especially associated with spring and was the sacred animal of Ostara, Viking goddess of spring, and of Oestre, Anglo Saxon goddess of spring, whose name gives us 'Easter'. Lucky amulets were once made from a real rabbit's or hare's foot. You can still obtain these on silver key rings. Many people in the modern world, however, do not like carrying animal parts, even to bring good fortune. The following spell provides a less gruesome alternative. It was inspired by a chant, called 'The Hare's Song' used by a Sussex coven, part of which is included in this spell. I found it in the wonderful Witchcraft Museum in Boscastle, Cornwall, England. The original version talks about witches shapeshifting into hares. Use this adaptation to weave good fortune in to your charm, especially if you need a new beginning or new energy.

You will need

A rabbit charm, a silver rabbit's foot, or a ceramic or wooden rabbit or hare (or make your own from clay or wood).

Timing

The first day of the month – I March is the luckiest of all.

The spell

* Go into a wood or open space. Holding your rabbit or hare symbol in cupped hands, weave a path in and out of the trees or over the grass, as you do so reciting softly over and over again:
Then I shall go as a fleet-foot hare,
With rejoicing, laughter and little care,
And I shall go in our Lady's name,
Aye, until I come home again.
* Move and chant faster and faster.
* When you feel the power rising in you, stop, raise the symbol, still in cupped hands, high over your head and then bring it down fast in a straight line, as you do so calling:
Come joy, come laughter, come new beginnings.
* Set your hare in a green plant where it will catch the morning sunshine in your home.

An ancient Egyptian spell to assume the focus, courage and clear vision of a hawk of gold

To the ancient Egyptians, the powers of the deities were mirrored in mythical animals and birds. For this reason, sacred animals were kept at the temples of those gods and goddesses with whom they were associated. The old spells , such as this one and the one that follows, were originally intended to help the Ba spirit ascend to the Blessed Field of Reeds (situated along the Celestial Nile in the Milky Way) after death or to return to the world. The Ba, a hawk with a human head, represented the spirit that flew out of a mummified body and gave life to the spirit body that dwelled with the Blessed Dead. The hawk image linked it to Horus, the falcon-headed sky god. This spell comes from a very old translation, by E. A. Wallis Budge, of the *Papyrus of the Scribe Ani*. Ra is the Sun God. The Benu bird was a blue phoenix-like creature that appeared at the first sunrise of creation.

You will need
Nothing.

Timing
Close to sunrise or when you wake.

The spell
* Recite the following words five times very slowly and deliberately:
  I have risen up like the golden hawk which cometh from his egg. I fly; I alight like a hawk with the wings of mother-of-emerald of the south, with the head of the Benu, and Ra who hath entered into me.

An ancient Egyptian spell to travel where you wish

Like those of the spell above, the words of this one are given in the *Papyrus of the Scribe Ani*, so that his deceased spirit (or Ba) might recite them and assume the form of a swallow when it wished to travel back to his former home on Earth. However, you can use the words to bring travel opportunities into your life (see also page 435). Osiris was the god of rebirth.

You will need
A map or picture of where you wish to travel to.

Timing
In the early morning.

The spell
* Holding the map or picture in both hands, say slowly and deliberately six times:
  The Osiris Ani, whose word is truth, saith: 'I am a swallow, I am a swallow. Hail, O ye gods whose odour is sweet. I am like Horus. Let me pass on and deliver my message.'
* Turn six times very fast and say:
  Osiris, Ra, Horus, Osiris, Horus, Ra, I fly swift and I fly far.
* Keep the map or picture where the first light of day will shine on it.

A spell to absorb the strength of a wild creature

Each animal and bird has ideal strengths and qualities that mirror and amplify our own inner powers, some of which we may never have explored. So, for example, if one of your children were being bullied and school staff refused to listen to you, you might need the fierce protectiveness of mother wolf. If you wanted to rise high in your profession, you might seek the power of the eagle to soar. Conversely, you can use animal qualities to lower your profile at times when you need to remain unnoticed, for example if you find yourself in a dark, lonely place. At such a time, the mouse or the cat (who walks stealthily through the night) might be good animals to turn to.

You will need
Nothing.

Timing
Whenever you need a power animal's strength.

The spell
* Choose the animal whose strengths you would like to draw on. Imagine it, of human size, in front of you and listen to its breathing, be it slow and deep or tiny panting breaths.
* Match the creature's breathing, either aloud or in your head.
* On each in-breath, picture the animal's strengths flowing into your body, and on each out-breath, let go of any fears or weaknesses, seeing them flowing from you as rays of dark light or mist.
* Continue to inhale and exhale rhythmically, imagining the current scene through the eyes of your power creature. Feel its paws padding beneath you, its mighty strides or its scurrying feet.
* When you are ready, start to become aware of your separate human breath.
* Shake your fingers and feet and step out of your power creature's psychic energy field, thanking him or her for safe passage. Though you are now separate, you carry within you some of the residual strength of the creature with whom you temporarily merged in your mind.

A dolphin spell to reduce stress, insomnia and anxiety

Dolphins are perhaps the most magical of all wild creatures and appear to have the ability to heal humans – and especially children – of mental and neurological problems. Swimming with dolphins can often bring dramatic improvement in such conditions. It has also been found that listening to dolphin sounds and working with dolphin images has positive effects on stress-induced conditions and regularises sleeping patterns. If you cannot relax or sleep, try this spell.

You will need

3 or 4 small turquoise candles or tea-lights; some blue or green bath salts (not foam), if possible containing lavender or kelp; 5 or 6 tiny aquamarine or jade crystals; a CD of dolphin sounds (optional); a CD player that you can use in the bathroom or that can be heard from the bathroom (optional).

Timing

Once a week or after a very stressful day, before going to bed.

The spell

* Set the candles in the bathroom so that their light will shine into the water.
* Light the candles and put on the dolphin music if you are using it.
* Run a bath and add the bath salts, mixing them with your hands and saying as a slow rhythmic chant:
  Gentle dolphins of the sea,
  Healing, rest and peaceful dreams bring, I ask, to me.
* Once you are in the bath, drop the crystals, one by one, in to pools of light in the water, then swirl the light pools.
* Close your eyes and visualise dolphins swimming towards you. Reach out and touch them in your mind's eye. Ride on their backs through the white-capped waves. As the dolphins swim away, see them carrying with them any tension or pain you have been feeling.
* When you are ready, get out of the bath, dry yourself, remove the crystals and pull out the plug, watching the water swirling away and leaving you calm and restored.

PART 9

SPELLS FOR BANISHING AND BINDING

Banishing and binding spells have featured in magic since at least ancient Egyptian times. They can be used, for example, to end a destructive love affair or repel a physical or psychic attack against us or our family. Most binding and banishing magic is protective, though if an attack is vicious or prolonged, you may need to defend yourself actively by returning the negativity.

When casting banishing and binding spells you need to be extra careful not to encroach on the free will of others, however unpleasant they may seem to you to be. Some very respectable white witches believe it is acceptable to bind those who harm children (or anyone else who cannot defend themselves) or are cruel to animals. It is for you to decide how you feel about this issue. Where an adult is concerned, it is a different matter. If someone is leading your partner astray or abusing a friend, it is tempting sometimes to go in with bell and broomstick. Difficult though it is, however, you should offer only earthly support and masses of healing and protective magic until the person concerned is able to acknowledge that they need help to break away. We are only human, and it is easy to slip into the role of judge and jury, extending our bindings and banishings to people we do not like or who seem to us to be living in the wrong way.

One safeguard is to bind a person's actions rather than the person carrying them out. Likewise, you can banish the emotional hold that a person has over you or a family member. It is a fine line, and after more than 15 years I am still trying to get the balance right. The ultimate criterion is whether we are interfering with the general free will of the person whose actions we are seeking to banish or bind.

You can use binding and banishing spells very positively in your own life to lessen the hold of bad habits, fears or phobias and all that emotional luggage we drag around from the past (I still have suitcases full of bad memories and regrets in my psychic attic). These spells can thus be very empowering. Bear in mind, however, that when you banish anything from your life, you should replace it with something positive to prevent the old doubts and fears creeping back.

Carry out these spells when you are calm and quiet, and they will be very effective. If you are in a raging temper or a black despair after an unwarranted attack, it is best to dig the garden or scrub the kitchen floor instead, so transforming your energy into positive effort and leaving yourself calm.

46 SPELLS FOR BANISHING DESTRUCTIVE RELATIONSHIPS

Banishing spells are a very powerful way of removing the harmful effects of those who seek to undermine us or control us mentally or emotionally to feed their own ego. Be they a manipulative parent, a friend who seeks to diminish your self-confidence or an employer who repeatedly tries to make you feel small, those who seek to put us down in this way are often simply offloading their own inadequacies. Even highly successful people can sometimes feel like stupid children when they visit the parental home and find themselves being compared unfavourably with siblings or brothers- and sisters-in-law.

This chapter contains not just protective spells but also actively defensive ones. These spells will increase your confidence and activate your own self-defensive mechanisms each time you cast them. The more you cast them, the stronger your own defences will become, so that you are more assertive and less vulnerable to malice and attacks on your self-esteem — for the real effect of a curse or malicious remark is the negative change it causes in our perception of ourselves, leading us to doubt our own self-worth and ability to cope.

You will also find banishing spells in Chapter 7 (for ending a destructive marriage or love affair), Chapter 10 (for putting a stop to spite and unkindness directed at you and those you love) and Chapter 27 (for protection in the workplace).

A spell to reverse the effects of an attack on your self-esteem or confidence

Attacks may be quite low-key – snide remarks about your weight or dress sense, correcting things you say or pointing out a small omission in an otherwise perfect piece of work. However, the effects can build up so that you become unsure of yourself – and as a result even more open to undermining. This trend can be reversed. When the perpetrator realises that these tactics are no longer working, he or she will give up.

You will need

Half a cup of warm water; rosemary essential oil.

Timing

When you expect to be in contact with the person who undermines you.

The spell

* Add six drops of the rosemary oil to the cup of warm water.
* Set the cup between you and the person as they speak.
* When the person has gone, pour the water down a drain or under a running tap, as you do so saying:
  Your words I return unheeded;
  Your negative thoughts are not needed.
* Repeat the spell each time the person approaches you. Gradually you can reduce the number of rosemary drops until you are using plain water and then nothing at all. If you have to visit the person's home, carry the essential oil water in a small screw-top bottle in your bag and keep the bag between you and the person. Dispose of the water after the visit.

A spell to remove the effects of nastiness

Even now, in my mid-fifties, I still get very upset by sheer vindictiveness, whether from a stranger or from someone who knows my weak spots and does not hesitate to exploit them. This spell is a good way of building up your psychic defence system so that even someone who is thoroughly unpleasant has no lasting effect on your confidence. The spell is also good for protecting your family.

You will need

3 dark-coloured candles (black is traditional, though some people prefer dark-blue or indigo — you can sometimes buy very dark beeswax); some garlic salt; some dark wrapping paper.

Timing

As soon as possible after the encounter or in advance of an anticipated contact.

The spell

* Place the candles in a row and light them from left to right.
* As the wax begins to melt, drop a grain or two of garlic salt into each flame. Say for each:
Threefold your viciousness return,
Three times to you as candles burn.
Pick up the pain you cause to me / my family
That its effects in you may be.
I send only what is your own;
Carry it then you alone.
* Blow out each candle, as you do so saying:
I return this pain;
Send it not again.
* When the candles are cool, wrap them in the paper and keep them so that you can repeat the spell whenever you fear another attack.

A spell to reverse a negative or destructive influence

A great deal of negativity is offloaded in the name of 'for your own good' by those who say they love us or are concerned for our welfare. If this occurs on a regular basis, it is a form of mental abuse. As a result, we may feel that we are somehow at fault or we may come to rely unduly on the person who wields the power of approval. This spell also works well if a child or vulnerable family member is being bullied or manipulated. You can recite the chant whenever you know they will meet the abusive person.

You will need

The complete set of clothes you will wear the next day, including shoes and any coat and gloves.

Timing

The night before you see the person, just before bed.

The spell

* Turn each garment inside out and your shoes upside down, as you do so saying:
You do not do,
You do not do,
You do not do.
Your power is through.
Reversed on you.
* In the morning, leave a garment inside out (one that cannot be seen when you wear it) and repeat the chant as you dress.
* When you meet the person, stare once piercingly into their eyes, repeating the chant in your head. Then avoid all eye contact.
* Repeat as often as necessary. Eventually, you will feel the power balance changing.

A spell to repel a stalker or someone who will not stop intruding on your life

Stalking has become a real problem and can affect even those who are not famous. The police are generally very helpful, but a spell can also help to reduce this kind of intrusion. On a smaller scale of severity, there may be people in our lives who are constantly telephoning, e-mailing or visiting, bombarding us with their problems or with trivial requests, pestering us to spend time with them or demanding our attention at work. This spell, originally designed to put off an un-wanted suitor, is a very powerful way of cutting the connection and screening ourselves from invasion.

You will need

A length of dark-coloured cord; a dark-coloured candle; a metal fireproof tray; a handful of earth.

Timing

On a Saturday during the waning moon, when it is dark.

The spell

* Light the candle and place it on the tray.
* Tie a knot in the cord, name the stalker or intruder and say:
  You are bound from approaching me menacingly or needlessly.
* Hold the cord tightly at each end, with the centre in the candle flame. Say:
  Go from me, leave me, let me be free.
  Repeat the words faster and louder until the knot is burning, then drop it on to the tray to burn away.
* When the cord is at least partially burnt through, throw some earth over it, as you do so saying:
  I am free. No more trouble me.
* Throw some earth over the candle to extinguish it, as you do so repeating:
  I am free. No more trouble me.
* Dispose of the candle. Bury the cord under a tree, so that good can grow from it.

A spell to stop unpleasant or anonymous phone calls

Although telephone companies can put security into place to stop unwanted calls, you may want fast action if such calls are upsetting you and your family or come at night. This spell works whether you suspect you know the identity of the caller or the attacks are from an unknown source.

You will need

A lemon tea bag; a spoon; a small jar of sugared violets or tiny candies.

Timing

After a call or, if there are regular times, before you expect one.

The spell

* Use the tea bag to make a cup of lemon tea. With the tea bag still in the cup, stir the tea ten times widdershins (anti-clockwise), as you do so saying:
No more your threats or silent menace, nor more insinuation. Take back your words, swallow them, taste your own bitterness.
* Take out the tea bag and take three sips from the cup, repeating the words for each sip.
* Throw the rest of the tea away, as you do so saying:
Take back your words, swallow them, taste your own bitterness.
* Eat one of the violets or candies and place the rest next to the phone.
* If the anonymous caller rings, put down the phone at once (it is tempting to listen if you are trying to identify the caller or they are warning you about a family member, but do not collude with them in this way).
* Eat one of the violets or candies, make a fresh lemon infusion and repeat the spell.
* The calls will lessen and eventually should stop.

A spell to stop poison pen letters or vicious e-mails

Nasty letters and e-mails are best destroyed, although if the problem becomes bad, you should take them to the police. This spell will act as a deterrent by bouncing back the vicious words from whence they came.

You will need

Some dried nettles (available from health food stores and some grocers).

Timing

As soon as you can after you receive the communication.

The spell

* Leave the communication unread.
* Cast three widdershins (anticlockwise) circles of nettles (one of the most powerful defensive herbs) around the letter or the computer, as you do so saying:
Nasty words sting like nettles; vicious thoughts are viper venom. Your mail is returned unopened.
* Destroy the unopened communication (unless you are saving it as evidence).
* After three hours, clear up the nettles and throw them away.

A spell to stop attacks against your home and property

I suggested various ways of keeping your home safe in Chapter 24. This spell is effective if you live in an area with high rates of vandalism or burglary. It is based on an old magical principle called 'the sending'. In darker forms of magic, this would consist of leaving something nasty hidden outside your home to surprise any unwanted visitor. This spell is much more positive and will not in any way cause harm but will deter those who come to disturb or destroy. (Legitimate visitors and family members will be unaffected.) It works not by cursing but by turning the intruder's own negativity back on themselves.

You will need
A dark shiny tile (the kind used in bathrooms or kitchens; some dried nettles.

Timing
Early on a Saturday morning.

The spell
* Work in a place where light does not directly shine.
* Scatter dried nettles over the tile, as you do so saying:
  Those who come with dark intent see your own self and slink away, shamed into the shadows you have created.
* Hang or prop the tile outside your home, somewhere where it cannot be easily seen.
* Re-empower the tile monthly.

A spell to stop unusually large numbers of virus attacks on your computer

There are many viruses on the Internet, and even powerful security systems cannot always keep up with them. Some viruses leave beacons to attract others to your machine or to allow hackers to break into your personal files. Worms and Trojans can be particularly hard to get rid of. This spell may be helpful if carried out monthly as a supplement to more regular defences. Under the threefold law of magic, what is sent — good or bad — returns threefold to the sender.

You will need
Five very small mirrors.

Timing
Before you begin work using the computer.

The spell
* Hold up each mirror in turn, either to natural light or (if it is a dark day) to a lamp, so that light shimmers within it. Say for each mirror:
  Deny what should not enter here; send back to those who seek to wreak this harm. Three times three by magic laws, destruction sent shall confound sender.
* Place four of the mirrors, face up, at each corner of your computer. Place the fifth mirror, again face up, next to the computer connection to the phone line.
* E-mail the words of the spell to your own computer.
* Polish the mirrors every week, repeating the words for each one, and e-mail the words of the spell to your computer again.

A spell to sever a connection with negativity

The clutter in our mind tends to be a mixture of obligations we must meet urgently, tasks that could wait but which buzz around in the form of free-floating tension, and burdens imposed on us by others and which should not be our problem. This is a psychic cleaning spell for discarding what you need to discard if you are to deal with priorities and, most importantly, shedding the guilt and pressure the unnecessary clutter imposes on you.

You will need

Symbols of people who drain your energies (for example, critical faxes, troublesome e-mails, nasty work memos, shopping lists – belonging to others but which you end up doing – excessive requests from children's schools for funds, etc.); a box without a lid; some red wool; a sharp knife or scissors; a small box with a lid; potted plants that are already budding; potted seedlings; some dead leaves or petals.

Timing

Early on Saturday morning, before you start your weekend.

The spell

* Place all the symbols in the box without a lid, and bind the red wool around the box, fastening it with nine knots and saying:

Bind and wind nine times through
Obligations overdue,
Worries needlessly renewed.

* Using the knife or scissors, cut through the knots, as you do so saying:

Ties so binding,
Guilt unwinding,
Freedom finding.

* Without hesitation or anxiety, divide the contents of the box into three categories: responsibilities that you must deal with instantly, responsibilities that you must deal with at a future date but which will not be helped by worrying about them now, and insoluble matters – things that you can do nothing about or that have been draining or unfruitful.

* Surround the urgent responsibilities with the already budding plants.

* Place the less urgent responsibilities back in the box, and surround the box with the seedlings.

* Place the insoluble matters in the small box, cover them with the dead leaves or petals and put the lid on the box. Bury the box in the garden or place it on a high shelf.

* Spend half an hour relaxing.

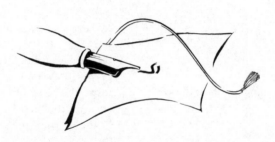

A spell to move out of the sphere of a destructive situation or person

Traditional spells such as this are sometimes carried out using graveyard dirt, but this is a practice that is not acceptable to a number of modern white witches, myself included. Earth from beside a river, stream or large tree is just as effective and much more positive. Collect some in advance and keep it in a jar with a pinch of salt.

You will need

A dish of stream, river or tree earth; some salt; a little water.

Timing

At dusk.

The spell

* Sprinkle salt on top of the earth and add three drops of water, as you do so saying:
  By salt, earth and water,
  Three by three,
  You can no longer reach to me.
  By salt, earth and water,
  Three by three,
  You no can longer preach to me,
  Teach to me.
  I will be free.
* Turn to face the sunset and scatter a straight horizontal line of the earth, salt and water mixture in front of you. Take a step backwards and make a second line. Step back again and make a third line.
* Stand behind the three horizontal lines, facing the fading sun, and say:
  By salt, earth and water,
  You cannot reach me.
  I start anew,
  Without you.
  Your power is through.
* Walk away from the sunset, scattering the remains of the mixture behind you. Do not look back.

A binding and banishing spell to break a negative influence, whether of an individual, a cult or an organisation

This spell first binds and then banishes, so it is very powerful. Use it if a vulnerable family member is being adversely influenced or you know that certain people are bad for your health, security or happiness.

You will need

A sharp knife; a piece of dead wood, preferably a fallen branch; a piece of rope.

Timing

During the waning moon, at dusk.

The spell

* Go outdoors and, using the knife, draw a deosil (clockwise) circle in the earth or on a paved area.
* Sitting within the circle, carve in the wood the name or a symbol of the person who is causing the problem. Say:
  May the influence be lessened, if it is right to be.
* Bind the wood tightly with the rope, as you do so repeating the words. Leave the piece of wood within the circle overnight.
* In the morning, either burn or bury the wood.

A banishing candle spell

This candle spell is the reverse of the attracting candle spell on page 27. It is a good spell to use if you are being intimidated by an organisation, whether a debt collecting firm or an official body, and will help you to banish fear and fight back effectively. You may need to carry it out a number of times, but each time the destructive hold over you (or a family member) will lessen.

You will need
A purple or dark-blue candle on a metal tray; a dark strip of paper and a white pencil or crayon.

Timing
At dusk on any night, though the spell will work faster if performed during the waning moon.

The spell
* Light the candle.
* Using the white pencil or crayon, softly write the name of the person or organisation threatening or manipulating you on the strip of paper, so that the point just touches the paper but the words you have written cannot be seen.
* Hold the paper in the flame and say:
  Be gone.
  Be done.
  I want no more of you.
  Your power to frighten me is through.
* Drop the flaming paper on to the tray to burn through or go out.
* Leave the candle to burn down.
* When the ashes of the paper are cool, bury them beneath a fragrant bush or plant.
* Phone or e-mail someone who makes you feel good about yourself or who can offer support, and then have a bath, ideally using a lavender or ylang ylang bath product.

A banishing candle and pin spell against abuse

This is an excellent spell for lessening the power of an abuser, whether past or present. It works for physical, sexual, racial or emotional abuse. Most of all, it gives courage to seek help or walk away. You are not sticking pins in to the abuser but merely attaching their power to the candle with the pin. When the pin falls out, their power lessens.

You will need
A dark-coloured candle on a metal tray; a long pin such as a hat pin; some small pieces of wool (optional).

Timing
During the waning moon, in the late evening.

The spell
* Holding the pin, name the person whose power over you you wish to lessen.
* Light the candle and, as the wax begins to melt, stick the pin carefully about a third of the way down the candle, so that it penetrates the wick within. Say:
  Sharp pangs cease.
  Power end.
  Into the candle flame
  Bend, pin, bend.
* Sit and let your sorrows burn away in the wax. If it helps, burn small pieces of wool in the flame, naming a sorrow for each one. When the pin falls from the candle, say:
  Fall, pin, fall.
  Let my heart be free from your thrall.
  Burn candle all.
* Blow out the candle. Dispose of the wax and the pin.
* You may need to repeat the spell.

A garlic spell for banishing hurt caused by someone in your life

You will need

Some garlic cloves; a knife; several plant pots; some potting compost.

Timing

Late summer to early autumn is best, but perform the spell when you have the need.

The spell

* Using the knife, engrave on one of the cloves of garlic a word to symbolise the hurt that has been inflicted on you. Do not name the person who caused the hurt.
* Bury the clove in one of the plant pots and water it regularly.
* Engrave a further clove and plant it every week. The person who threatens or manipulates you should move out of your life by the time the shoots of the first clove appear.
* When the plants are tall enough, transfer them to your garden.

A water spell to banish injustice or abuse

Water has traditionally been used to wash away sorrow, illness and injustice. Try this fast-flowing spell for removing harm or injustice and bringing on happier times.

You will need

A perfectly round black stone; a round white stone of the same size as the black one; a fast-flowing river or stream, or a waterfall.

Timing

On a Saturday morning.

The spell

* Hold the black stone tightly with both hands and endow it with your feelings of injustice or abuse. Focus on the effects on you rather than on the person causing the problem.
* Raise the stone to your forehead and press it against the centre of your brow. Say:
Bad thoughts and despair be gone.
* Cast the stone as far as you can into the water.
* Now hold the white stone, filling it with the determination to fight back, break free or win through.
* Raise it to your brow and say:
New thoughts, fresh hope, flow free in me. I will win through, survive and thrive.
* Cast the white stone into the water, as you do so calling out your own name five times.

47 SPELLS FOR LETTING GO OF GUILT, SORROW AND THE PAST

One of the most positive forms of banishing magic involves letting go of past regrets or current unwarranted guilt or fear. The inner world is very strong, and sometimes we defeat ourselves before we start a venture by listening to voices in our head reminding us of past failures or mistakes. Of course, it is important to learn from the past, especially if we have repeated an unhelpful pattern out of habit. But each new opportunity gives a chance to rewrite history and choose different avenues, so freeing ourselves of past burdens. Spells can help us to move on in this way. They can also cancel bad luck and reverse a downward trend, thereby opening new possibilities and bringing all kinds of potential benefits.

This chapter picks up on themes touched upon earlier in the book, but focuses specifically on clearing our private attic of emotional luggage so that we can live in the present and thus take charge of our destiny. In this way, we can make sure that our future is even better than our past.

A spell to wash away guilt, sorrow, anger and regrets

On page 171 I give a spell for washing away negativity and talk about the Roman baths at Bath, in Avon, Britain, which were sacred to the Celtic Romano goddess Sulis Minerva. This spell is more complex and takes much longer, but it is very effective for removing the kind of long-standing redundant emotions that make us hesitate to take opportunities in the present. It is especially powerful against experiences of childhood unkindness.

You will need

A miniature tablet of soap containing eucalyptus, rosemary or tea tree (natural purifiers); a paper knife or nail file.

Timing

Before taking a bath or shower.

The spell

* Think of a word or a symbol that you can engrave on the soap to express one aspect of your sorrow. (You can name a person who hurt you as long as you focus on banishing the effect they had or influence they still have rather than on the person themselves).

* Carve the word or image on the soap with the knife or nail file and then carve a square around it to mark the limits of the emotions and negative effects on your life.

* Carve a diagonal cross through the square and the symbol (of the kind found on hot cross buns). This is the old astrological sign for Mother Earth, who will absorb your pain. The act of crossing out the word or image also symbolises the removal of the pain.

* Use the soap in your bath or shower. When you have finished, let the soapy water flow away and say:

Flow and go;
It must be so,
For the past
It cannot last,
Nor sadness now.
Go anyhow.

Keep the soap just for yourself.

* If the image or word has faded, re-carve it, together with the square and the cross, before your next bath.

* As you repeat the ritual over time, the soap will eventually become too small to write on, and one day will be gone, like your sorrow.

A Russian spell to lay the past to rest

From Neolithic eastern and western Europe, the Baltic and Scandinavia comes the tradition of the old bone goddess of rebirth, called Baba Yaga in Russian myth. Long before she became a frightening fairy tale figure, she was a benign guardian who led people at the end of their lives through death and then restored them to new life. In time, she became associated with spiritual rebirth. In Germany she was called Mother Holle and in Scandinavia Hulda or Holda. On page 393 I give a spell to bury the hatchet. This is another variation on the same theme, from the Russian tradition. It is a gentle but potent method of marking the end, whether of sorrow, anger or self-destructive messages running on constantly in your head.

You will need
An animal or fish bone (from cooked meat or fish – or look for a fish bone on a beach), or a white stone or bleached twig in the shape of a bone; a sharp stone; some dark-blue or purple petals; a handful of caraway seeds.

Timing
At sunset on the last day of the month.

The spell
* Using the sharp stone, scratch on to the bone, white stone or twig a word or symbol of what stands in the way of your happiness, success or healing. As you write, allow the redundant emotions to pour into the bone or stone.
* When it is dark, find a place in your garden, or in a window box or pot plant, and bury the bone as deep as possible, as you do so saying:
  Baba Yaga, grandmother who carries all to rest, take these sorrows and transform them as you will.
* Cast the petals and caraway seeds over the place where you buried the bone, in tribute to Baba Yaga.
* The next morning, initiate a new project or make the changes you have planned but feared.
* If the old sorrows creep back, repeat the ritual. Go on repeating it for as long as you need, using a smaller bone, stone or twig each time.

A chimney spell for banishing sorrow

This spell will only work if you have an open hearth with a chimney (it doesn't matter if the chimney is blocked off).

You will need
5 white flowers.

Timing
At midnight.

The spell
* Sit by the hearth in complete darkness and whisper up the chimney what you wish to lose from your life.
* Leave the flowers in the hearth and go to bed.

A water banishing spell

This spell uses a stone and a crystal. The stone represents what you wish to lose from your life, and the crystal represents you as you will be without the burden.

You will need

A dark pointed stone, found anywhere; a crystal, carefully chosen and, if possible, bought new (it need only be small); a still pool or pond.

Timing

At dusk, any evening after the night of the full moon until the crescent moon is seen in the sky, about two weeks later.

The spell

* Go to the water. Hold the dark stone in your receptive hand (the one you do not write with) and the crystal in your power hand.
* Name what you wish to lose – regrets, sorrows, unfounded warnings or just a sense of flatness and greyness over your life.
* Cast the stone into the water and watch the ripples disappear.
* Dip the crystal three times into the water and say:
  Be reborn hope in me.
  Now I am free.
* Dry the crystal with a tissue or handkerchief and keep it with you. Touch it when you hear an old voice stopping you from moving forward.

A Celtic hearth spell for losing guilt or anger

If you do not have a hearth and open fire, you can carry out this spell either by using the ashes of a bonfire or by burning several incense sticks in holders on a tray, so that the ash accumulates.

You will need

Some ash.

Timing

Just before you go to bed, traditionally on St Brigit's Eve (January 31), but otherwise on the last day of any month.

The spell

* Use the cold ashes to write on the hearth (or, if you do not have a hearth, on any flat surface) a word or symbol of what you want to lose.
* In the morning, sweep up the ashes and throw them away.

A north wind guilt banishing spell

This is a slow-acting ritual for guilt that may have taken years to accumulate.

You will need

A branch with a number of dying leaves corresponding to each specific guilt, sorrow or regret (you can pull some off to get the right number).

Timing

When the wind blows from the North or north-east (hold up a long sock or scarf to work out the direction).

The spell

* Stand in the wind holding your branch.
* Name a guilt or sorrow for each leaf.
* Leave the branch in an exposed place and walk away without looking back. As the branch is stripped bare, you will be able to start anew. It does not matter if the wind changes during the ensuing days as long as you begin on the north wind.

A Lammas completion spell for overcoming feelings of injustice that cannot be put right

The old Celtic festival of Lughnassadh, at the end of July and beginning of August (or the first harvest of the corn) was associated with the completion of matters and was a time when judgements would be given and scores settled. In the Christian tradition, Lammas was celebrated at the beginning of August. A special loaf was baked from the first corn and placed on the altar. Fires, stemming from the pre-Christian festival, continued to burn in Ireland at Lammas until the middle of the twentieth century, and are being revived in some communities.

You will need

Some loose straw or dried grasses (you can use animal bedding straw, sold in small quantities for rabbits and guinea pigs); a small fire or a large dark-yellow beeswax or brown candle on a tray.

Timing

In late summer or early autumn, or whenever needed.

The spell

* Light the fire or candle.
* Using a few of the straws, knot a rough doll shape (called a corn dolly, and still made by crafts people).
* Burn a loose straw and say:
  The past is complete, all scores are settled. If justice cannot be done, so be it. I rest my case and my feelings.
* Hang the corn dolly as a symbol of hope over your door. When it crumbles, throw it away.

A crossroads spell to banish the effects of unfair treatment

Traditionally, crossroads were sacred to the ancient Greek Goddess Hecate. Here offerings were left to ask her blessings and to bring good fortune. She was protective especially to sailors, hunters and those falsely accused of wrongdoing. Like the bone goddesses, Hecate was once an underworld guardian and guide, and lady of rebirth. She thus became patroness of midwives.

You will need

A crossroads with soil (even a small flowerbed on a traffic island); a very small black crystal, such as jet, obsidian or onyx, or a small shiny black stone; a silver-coloured coin.

Timing

At dusk or when you know the crossroads will be deserted.

The spell

* Go to the crossroads. Press the crystal into the earth, as you do so saying:
  I was treated badly, accused unfairly, but now, Mother of the Crossroads, I can carry the burden no longer. I leave it in your care.
* Leave the silver coin at the crossroads, where it may be found and used.

A spell to lose the old voices in your head

Maybe it was a childhood teacher who told you that you would never succeed at anything (it was for me). Perhaps it was a parent or a grandparent who said you were the plain or stupid one and your sister was pretty and clever. Maybe an early partner or boss shattered your self-confidence, or an unwise fortune-teller predicted a future disaster. Although you are now successful and happy, the old voices may still haunt you in the still of the night, saying you don't deserve what you have and it may be taken away. This spell will enable you literally to lose the echoes.

You will need
A place with an echo.

Timing
When you know you will not be disturbed.

The spell
- Go to the echoing place and call out the put-downs that still trouble you. Call out as many as you wish, in rapid succession. Then call out:
  You are only echoes, and echoes you must stay. I walk away.
- Walk away from the place and take a roundabout route home, preferably crossing water so that the echoes of the past cannot follow.

A spell to shed sorrows from childhood or early adulthood

Sometimes I awake feeling once again a childhood hurt or the pain of a loss that occurred years before but never healed. We may avoid going to a place because it is filled with sad memories. This spell leads us back to the location of our sorrow and enables us to lay its ghosts once and for all.

You will need
Some sunflower seeds.

Timing
Any.

The spell
- Go back briefly to a place that holds sad memories for you. Don't tell anyone you are visiting. If you see someone you know, keep the encounter brief, light and pleasant.
- Walk around and if you encounter a sad memory, drop one of the tiniest sunflower seeds in to the nearest soil.
- Buy a postcard. Just before you leave (for example, on the railway station platform), write on the card 'Gone away' and throw it in a bin.

A ritual to finish business with someone who has gone away or died

The saddest words are those that come too late. If a family member has died with unkind words or an estrangement between themselves and you, they may return in a dream. Psychically or psychologically this usually heals the breach. If you do not have such a dream (and perhaps would not want one) or if the person is still alive and any contact with them would re-open bitterness, you can carry out a simple ritual to close the door gently.

You will need
Nothing.

Timing
Any.

The spell
* Go to a place where you and the other person were once happy together and say what you wish you had said to resolve the matter before the parting (speak in your head if there are people around).
* Find a local charity box and put some coins in it or go into the nearest church and light a candle for the person who has gone, in either case making a small donation.
* Leave the location, but stop on the way home and do something pleasurable so that the day contains happy memories.

A spell to stop nightmares about the past

When we are under stress, bad situations from the past can haunt our dreams and we experience again the sense of helplessness, shame or frustration in sleep that we once did in reality. Such feelings can spill over in to the day ahead. This is an easy way to banish the bad dreams.

You will need
A large paper butterfly or flower, as brightly coloured or iridescent as possible (often available from shops that sell greetings cards – or make your own).

Timing
Each night before sleep.

The spell
* Hold your butterfly or flower and say:
  When I experience (name bad situation) in my dream, I will see this butterfly / flower. Then I will know I am dreaming and can change the ending of the dream.
* Hang the paper image over your bed.
* Repeat the words as you lie down. Close your eyes and imagine the largest, most beautiful butterfly or flower in existence coming towards you. You should now see the butterfly or flower when the recurring nightmare begins. If not, keep repeating the spell; you will eventually see the butterfly or flower. Once this happens, you can change the ending of the dream while you are asleep. The nightmare should never return.

A spell to reverse bad luck

This and the following spell are two methods that work well to reverse bad luck and bring rapid results.

You will need

A pair of muddy shoes; a mop; a bucket of warm water to which has been added 4 drops of lemon or tea tree essential oil and 5 drops of patchouli or geranium essential oil (or a lemon and a floral washing-up liquid).

Timing

On a wet day.

The spell

* Put on the shoes and make a trail of muddy footprints across a tiled or laminated floor (for example in a kitchen) to represent bad luck.

* Take off the shoes when you reach the other side of the room and wash the floor with the water and oils (lemon or tea tree to remove bad luck and patchouli or geranium to bring good luck). As you work, say continuously:
  Bad luck wash away;
  Good luck stay.

* When the floor is clean, dip the soles of the shoes into the water and put them outside the door.

* Pour the water down an outside drain, as you do so repeating the chant.

A two-balloon spell to banish bad luck

This is a good spell for banishing family as well as personal misfortune.

You will need

2 identical silver helium balloons; a black shoe lace; a white ribbon.

Timing

A windy day.

The spell

* Tie the balloons in a safe place indoors.

* Attach the black lace loosely to one of the strings, as you do so saying:
  Bad luck, you are no longer welcome here:
  Disappear.

* Transfer the shoe lace to the second balloon, as you do so repeating the words.

* Attach the white ribbon to the first balloon, as you do so saying:
  Good luck stay;
  Fly not away.

* Release the second balloon, with the black lace attached, in to the sky, either in your garden or from an upstairs window.

* Keep the original balloon, with the white ribbon attached, somewhere safe for three days.

* On the fourth day, untie the ribbon and attach it to an object near the front door.

* Release the balloon in to the sky, for it has done its work.

48 SPELLS FOR OVERCOMING, ADDICTIONS, HABITS, FEARS AND PHOBIAS

Because addictions, irrational fears and phobias are usually rooted in trauma or a specific incident that has become locked into the psyche (and is usually triggered by stress), spells are a very effective way of banishing them, together with the original trigger. A spell will supplement any counselling or medical treatment you are receiving and, in less severe conditions, may activate the mind's own self-healing system. It would seem that a creative ritual somehow overrides the mind's irrational responses, thus resolving the problem.

A spell to overcome cravings for a cigarette

Smoking is one of the most common addictions I am asked to cast spells for. Not only is it bad for health but it is increasingly unwelcome in public places. This spell supplements nicotine patches and other medical remedies and may help you to stick to a course of treatment. The cigarettes used in this spell must on no account be smoked; if you have to smoke, use different cigarettes. Keep those for the spell in a locked drawer.

You will need

As many small white stones or glass nuggets as there are days in the month you start the spell; a box with a lid; a packet of 10 cigarettes.

Timing

The first day of a new month, in the morning.

The spell

* Set out the stones or nuggets in rows. Pick up each one in turn and say:
  I banish this addiction. I no longer crave cigarettes.
* Dispose of one stone or nugget and one cigarette in any eco-friendly way you like, first crushing the cigarette and repeating the words.
* Repeat these first two steps each morning, speaking the chant for each stone or nugget, then disposing of one stone or nugget and one cigarette. When all the cigarettes are gone, work just with the stones, keeping the empty packet in a locked drawer. If you lapse, add one stone for each day of lapse (but do not replace the cigarettes) and continue the ritual.
* On the last day of the month, when all the stones or nuggets are gone, destroy the empty cigarette packet. You are on the road to recovery.

An Earth spell for ending excess consumption of food, alcohol, cigarettes and so on

You can use this method to ease any compulsion or addiction, asking Mother Earth to absorb your inappropriate need. If you regularly over-eat, smoke or drink in more than one place, you may need to plant bulbs or herbs in the other places too. It can also help to use an essential oil or perfume with the same fragrance as the plant. Sniff it as a reminder if you have a sudden craving and cannot smell the actual plant.

You will need

A large pot or area of garden; some fragrant flowering bulbs or herbs, such as hyacinth, lavender, eau de cologne mint or lemon balm (fragrance is important).

Timing

On a Saturday morning.

The spell

* Plant the bulbs or herbs, as you do so saying:
  I sow with this plant/flower/herb the person I wish to become, free from compulsions. Every time I smell this fragrance, I strengthen my resolve and my own self-worth, which does not need stimulants or soothing substances to survive and thrive.
* Pat the earth with your fingers nine times.
* When you want to indulge in over-eating, smoking or drinking, take the food, cigarette or drink to somewhere private and shred it on a plate or pour it into an appropriate container, as

you do so repeating the chant in your head over and over again until the craving subsides.

- Throw most of the food, cigarette or drink away, but save a tiny quantity to take to your fragrant place when you have time.

- Bury it in the soil, as you do so saying in your head or out loud:
I bury this (name substance) that it may be taken by Mother Earth to be transformed through decay to new life.
- Inhale the fragrance.

A spell to lose weight healthily

Obesity is a major problem in the Western world and the diet industry is booming. Most diets fail because for many of us, myself included, food is an emotional issue. Once eating moves out of the hunger/pleasure zone into a way of swallowing anger or stilling negative thoughts about ourselves, we need to restore the emotional balance.

You will need
Rose or violet essential oil; a jar of rose-based pot pourri; a large glass bowl; some small dishes.

Timing
When you start a new diet.

The spell
- Set the bowl on the kitchen table or a surface near the fridge or larder.
- Whenever you are tempted to snack, add a few pieces of pot pourri to the bowl and smell the fragrance on your fingers, as you do so saying:

I do not need to compensate. I am complete and worthy of respect and admiration.
- Wait half an hour and see if you are still hungry, in which case eat something healthy with pleasure, as you do so repeating the words.
- Each time you get through a day following a sensible (rather than starvation) diet, add a single drop of rose or violet essential oil to the pot pourri, as you do so repeating the words. (Also add a drop or two of the oil to your night-time bath if you wish.) As the days go by, your bowl of pot pourri will smell ever more fragrant and will remind you of your increasing confidence and control.
- When the bowl is full, place the pot pourri in the little dishes and set them around the house. If you are tempted to lapse, smell each bowl in turn and repeat the words.
- When the fragrance is gone, you will be well on your way to success.

A spell for banishing panic attacks

Panic attacks are often our mind's way of alerting us to the fact that our life is spinning out of control; however, they may occur suddenly and without warning at a time when we need to maintain at least external control. Drugs can control panics attacks but they have side-effects and are only effective as long as you take them. In my experience, you need to use drugs or alternatively (and perhaps better) counselling or psychological techniques to overcome the root cause of the panic. Spells are a good supplement to such treatment, and you can repeat the words in your mind when a panic begins.

You will need
A tub of bubble mixture and a bubble blower.

Timing
On a sunny morning when you feel calm.

The spell
* Very slowly blow bubbles, breathing gently and regularly.
* Watch the bubbles, some rising high filled with rainbows, some breaking, some not forming at all, and let each one take its own course.
* Continue until the tub is empty and then say very softly:
  Each to its own destiny. So float from me all but harmony.
* If you start to panic, picture the bubbles rising and repeat the words in your head nine times. If the panic is still there, go back to alternately picturing bubbles and repeating the words. In due course, the time it takes to reduce the panic will become less.
* Repeat the spell weekly.

A self-blessing spell to reduce panic attacks or crippling fears

This is another good method of stopping panic or a sudden fear that freezes you into inaction. This spell activates your four higher chakras, or psychic energy centres, to allow harmony to flow through your system and de-activate the inappropriately activated flight mechanism that resides lower in your energy system.

You will need
A rose quartz crystal.

Timing
The first day of the month, at sunset.

The spell
* Using your power hand (the one you write with), hold the rose quartz crystal at the centre of your hairline and say:
  Blessed am I by this crystal and the light of evening.
* Hold the crystal at the centre of your brow and repeat the chant.
* Hold the crystal at the centre of your throat and repeat the chant.
* Hold the crystal at your heart and repeat the chant.
* Pass the crystal to your receptive hand and watch the light fade, taking with it your panic attacks.
* When you feel panic rising, press the crystal to any one of the above points (corresponding with the higher energy centres) and recite the words in your head. If you don't have the crystal, touch the points with the index finger of your power hand as you chant in your head.

A spell to overcome fear of elevators

A significant number of people, even those who are not normally claustrophobic, fear becoming trapped in a lift, especially if it is crowded or small. This fear is not entirely irrational, since lifts do get stuck – but quite rarely, and even then the problem is generally speedily resolved. If we are in a tall building or have heavy luggage, we do need to use an elevator. This spell will help even if your dislike of lifts is quite acute.

You will need

Your mobile phone; a stick of fern or frankincense incense.

Timing

On a windy day.

The spell

* Working outside if possible, light the fern or frankincense incense stick (both fragrances of travel) and write in smoke over the phone:
Fly free. Go upwards and go downwards, swift and safely again. So long as I speak, shall the power remain.
* When you next enter a lift, either phone a friend or relative you know will be home, or talk softly into the phone as if you were making a call. Continue until you reach your floor.
* Re-empower the phone every month or so, unless you have to use lifts daily, in which case do it weekly.

A spell to overcome a fear of heights or flying

On page 375 I give a spell to reduce the fear of flying. This spell works well also if you hate heights but have to climb a ladder to clear a blocked gutter, or your children want to go in a cable car or climb a church tower on a day out. It is also a good way of helping children overcome a fear of high places.

You will need

A box of children's coloured bricks.

Timing

A few hours before you have to fly or climb to a high place.

The spell

* Make a tall tower with children's bricks, saying continuously as you do so:
From high to low it shall be so, fear of heights do I not know.
* Take off the top bricks to reduce the size of the tower and repeat the chant.
* Rebuild the tower higher than before, as you do so saying continuously:
From low to high, towards the sky.
Birds have no fear, so why should I?
* Knock the tower down, as you do so saying:
High or low, it is the same.
Be gone fear, you have no name.
* Recite all three chants in your head just before you fly or climb.

A spell to overcome a phobia such as fear of spiders or of feathers

Even generally rational people may have a seemingly irrational phobia, perhaps with origins in a forgotten childhood incident. Such fears can cause problems in everyday life, especially if you cannot avoid the object of your phobia.

You will need

A picture of your fear (if necessary, keep the picture face down or just write the word); a pair of scissors.

Timing

During the lightest part of the day.

The spell

* Cut around the edges of the picture (working from the back if necessary), as you do so saying:

I cut you down to size.
You are diminished in my eyes.

* Cut the picture smaller and repeat the words. Go on doing so until you can cut no smaller.
* Throw all the pieces away in an outdoor dustbin or down a garbage chute, as you do so saying:

You are now very small.
Your power was not so great after all.

* Repeat the spell weekly using smaller and smaller pieces of paper and a smaller image. If you meet your fear, stop, take a deep breath and repeat the words of the spell in your head, picturing the bin or garbage chute disposing of your fear.

A computer spell to overcome a phobia

This is a computerised version of the above spell.

You will need

A computer with a drawing program or clip art.

Timing

On a sunny day or at noon on any day.

The spell

* Search the clip art or drawing program to find an image of your fear. If you cannot find an image, write your fear on the screen.
* Enclose the image or words in a box in the centre of the screen.
* Gradually reduce the size of the box containing the image or word.
* When you can shrink the box no more, press delete and call out:

Fear diminished, vanish from my life.

* Repeat weekly, starting with a smaller image or word and box each time.

A spell to overcome dependency on prescription drugs

What starts as a necessity to control chronic pain, a medical condition or depression can leave us with a dependency on prescription drugs (or those bought over the counter). Busy doctors may not realise there is a problem and may sign a repeat prescription for months after it has ceased to be medically necessary. Over-the-counter painkillers can also become a habit if you have a lot of headaches or joint pain. You should not come off any medication suddenly or without medical advice, but this spell is a good supplement to more conventional forms of treatment.

You will need

A small dish containing a few tablets; a dish of salt; a stick of myrrh, rose or violet incense; a purple candle; a dish of still mineral water.

Timing

On the last day of the month, after dark.

The spell

* Set the dish of tablets on a table. Around them place the salt (in the North), the incense stick (in the East), the candle (in the South) and the water (in the West). The directions can be approximate.
* Light the candle and then the incense from the candle.
* Make a widdershins (anti-clockwise) circle of salt around the dish of tablets, beginning in the North. As you do so, say:
I reduce your hold over me by the power of Earth.
* Return the salt to its place. Make a widdershins circle of incense smoke around the dish of tablets, beginning in the East. As you do so, say:
I reduce your hold over me by the power of Air.
* Return the incense to its place. Make a widdershins circle around the dish of tablets with the candle, beginning in the South. As you do so, say:
I reduce your hold over me by the power of Fire.
(If you prefer, you can leave the candle in place and circle the dish of tablets around the candle.)
* Return the candle to its place. Make a widdershins circle of water around the dish of tablets, beginning in the West. As you do so, say:
I reduce your hold over me by the power of Water.
* Return the dish of water to its place. Leave the dish of tablets inside the circles of salt and water until the candle and incense are burnt down.
* Repeat the spell weekly, with fewer and fewer tablets in the dish, until in the final spell you have only one.

A spell to reduce over-spending

This is a good way to help you get spending under control. Sometimes shopping for things we do not really need can give us a psychological boost when we feel unappreciated or helpless in a relationship or situation. If your problem is serious, use this spell to supplement counselling and debt advice. For ordinary over-indulgence in retail therapy, use the spell on its own.

You will need

A long piece of paper (the kind you use for a shopping list); 2 shorter pieces of paper; a pen; salt and pepper in shakers.

Timing

The night before a shopping trip.

The spell

* Using the long piece of paper, write a list of everything you would like to buy. Be honest with yourself and imagine you are walking round the stores. List your most frequent impulse buys.
* Cross through anything you do not need.
* Copy the remaining items on to one of the shorter pieces of paper.
* Sprinkle salt and pepper over the original list (with the crossings out) and say six times very fast:
Want is not need.
I banish your greed.
I am in charge,
And want is too large.
Be gone!
* Throw the first list away.
* Read through the second list and cross out anything that could be bought on another day. Cross out anything that you could avoid buying by mending what you already have. Cross out anything that you could buy more cheaply in an older version. (You may be able to cross nothing out.)
* Write the remaining items on the second short sheet of paper.
* Throw the second list away.
* Add to the third list an inexpensive item that you do not urgently need but that would give you pleasure.
* Scatter a deosil (clockwise) circle of salt, followed by a deosil circle of pepper, around the third list, as you do so saying:
Want is not need.
I need you indeed.
And with this small treasure (name your treat)
Shopping will be a pleasure.
* Take the list with you shopping, and stick to it – using the extra time to compare prices and different kinds or models, so you get what you really want. If you are tempted to impulse-buy, recite both chants in your head and re-read the list.

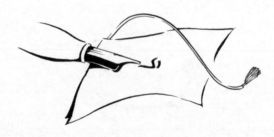

A spell to overcome dependency on alcohol

Whether you drink socially or enjoy a quiet drink at home to relax after a hard day, alcohol can become a habit. We may only realise this if we do not have alcohol at the usual time and find ourselves feeling restless and irritable. You can carry out this spell before going out if you know there will be alcohol served. Drink the whole glass of water before you go out. This spell should not be seen as a substitute for medical help or counselling if the problem is serious.

You will need

A large glass; a small bottle of your favourite alcohol that you have already opened.

Timing

When you are aware that you need (rather than would enjoy) a drink.

The spell

* Turn the cold tap in the kitchen sink full on. Drop three drops of alcohol, one after the other, into the flowing water, for each one saying:
  Join into the stream of life,
  Flowing downwards to the sea.
  Alcohol I do not need.
  I rule it, not it rules me.
* Fill the glass with tap water and turn off the tap. Repeat the chant and slowly sip some of the water.
* If the craving returns during the evening, repeat the chant again and sip some more water.
* Repeat the spell when necessary.

A spell to cut down on gambling

Whether your preferred form of gambling is buying scratch cards or visiting a casino, you may find you are spending more money on it than you would like. This spell is a good way of getting back to what is for you an acceptable level of spending.

You will need

A pot of loose change; a small fishing net.

Timing

On a Wednesday morning or before you foresee that you will be tempted to gamble.

The spell

* Place the money pot next to a sink and pick out a coin.
* Put the plug in the sink and turn on the cold tap. Drop the coin in and say:
  Money down the drain,
  Money spent in vain.
  Without any preamble,
  I no longer will gamble.
* Continue picking coins, dropping them and reciting until the sink is almost full of water.
* Turn off the tap. With the net (and if necessary your hands), fish out the coins, as you do so saying:
  Money caught back
  I will not lack.
  Saved from the drain,
  Not money in vain.
* When you have removed all the coins, take out the plug and repeat the first chant until the sink is empty.
* Let the money dry and then put it back in the pot to be used for the next spell.
* Repeat the spell weekly.

A spell for breaking bad habits of all kinds

Whatever the bad habit or addiction, it has probably built up over months and so will take time to overcome. This is a very gentle spell.

You will need

A large lavender bag or a small fabric animal, such as a bear, filled with lavender (available from gift and health food stores), or a purse filled with dried lavender; a purple ribbon.

Timing

On the first Friday in the month, and six subsequent Fridays.

The spell

* Hold the lavender-filled item and name your problem aloud, then say softly:

Bad habit slow made
Must slowly be broken,
But broken it will be,
For this I have spoken.

* Tie the ribbon securely around the bag or purse, as you do so saying:
You tie me to you, (name problem), but not for eternity. I loosen the bonds, and so it shall be.
* Loosen the ribbon slightly and repeat the first chant.
* Keep the lavender item in a drawer and each Friday loosen the ribbon a little, repeating both chants, and return the item to the drawer, so that by the seventh Friday (or maybe before), the ribbon has fallen off.

A general candle spell to reduce the power of an addiction or compulsion

Candle magic is a very gentle way of loosening the ties that bind us to destructive habits. It replaces the urgency with a soft healing light. This absorbs not only the compulsion but also the inner pain that is causing it.

You will need

A large red pillar candle; a deep metal or ceramic bowl of water.

Timing

During the waning moon, on a Monday at dawn (or as soon as you wake).

The spell

* Light the red candle (red represents the natural physical drives that have become excessive) and look into the flame, picturing all your anxieties, contradictions and inwardly directed destructive urges flowing into the candle flame.

* Say softly three times:
Leave me. Lose your power to drive me on a downward path, and let there be peace within me that I may rise anew.
* Extinguish the candle by plunging it, flame first, into the water, as you do so saying:
Be cooled, power to burn, to drive me against my will, and let there be peace within me that I may rise anew.
* Remove the candle from the water and throw it away.
* Pour the water down a drain, letting any remnants of the burning compulsion likewise go and feeling the promises of new life stirring.
* Go out into the fresh air and walk for a few minutes.
* Repeat the ritual every Monday morning when possible.

49 SPELLS FOR BINDING HARM AND ENCROACHMENT

Binding spells, like banishing spells, should be used with care, and only when you are in a positive frame of mind. They work best if you bind a specific action or behaviour that is harmful to you or to vulnerable friends or family members, rather than the perpetrator him- or herself. That way you avoid interfering with free will but restrict negativity directed at you – a perfectly permissible defensive action.

Should you bind those who harm children or animals or destroy places of beauty? Certainly you can bind individuals and organisations against polluting a specific area or exploiting a group of people you know to be especially vulnerable. It is asking rather a lot of any magical group, let alone an individual, to bind all polluters of all seas, but if enough people carry out localised defensive binding spells, then the protection can be extensive.

A gentle form of binding may be appropriate where friends or family are unthinkingly intruding on our personal space, asking one too many favours or expecting us to subsidise their lifestyle, even though we are ourselves struggling financially or are short of time to fulfil our own responsibilities. An 'enough, no further' spell can help you to detach from such demands, even if you are a very kind person who hates to say no to anyone.

Some of the areas of concern in this chapter you will have met in other places in this book, for example difficult neighbours. The spells here are all centred on the various binding techniques, which can be applied to many problems and areas.

A spell to bind troublesome neighbours

I have devoted the whole of Chapter 28 to this topic. It is included here because a gentle binding is an appropriate solution. This is an issue on which I get a great number of requests for help, especially in cases where neighbours are interfering with sleep patterns or being menacing. Try this quick spell. It makes use of an adaptation of a Scottish children's rhyme I learned when I taught in Fife, in Scotland.

You will need

A duster you have used that day.

Timing

When your neighbours start their noise or their children are kicking footballs at your windows.

The spell

* Open an upstairs widow, shake the duster out of it (not on your neighbours) and chant softly ten times:
  Neighbours, neighbours, stay away.
  Don't trouble me again today.
* Tie the duster (in a knot) to the handle inside the window from which you shook it, thus binding the neighbours from causing you further disruption.
* Repeat daily if necessary. A bonus is that you will have a well dusted house.

A spell for discouraging family members or friends from relying on you too much

If you have a gentle nature, you can end up as on-tap babysitter, DIY expert, chauffeur and social secretary to your friends and relatives. Although I have a frantic schedule, I work from home and so on a bad day can clock up nearly 100 miles of taxiing family members – surprising since I live on an island that measures only 37 by 25 kilometres (23 by 16 miles)! This spell will not stop you being ready to help, but it will make you give off fewer 'available any time' vibes and help you to say no when the snow is knee-deep, you have a temperature hotter than the Amazonian jungle and your favourite programme is on television. In this spell you will be binding yourself.

You will need

A photograph of yourself in a frame; a thin, pink, silk ribbon.

Timing

At the start of a new week.

The spell

* Tie the ribbon around the photograph and secure it with a double bow. Say:
  I bind myself from saying yes when really I mean no.
  I bind myself from smiling on when crossness I would show.
  I bind myself from being weak
  When stronger words I would speak.
* Keep the bound picture somewhere where you can see it and touch the ribbon whenever you are tempted to weaken under pressure.

Two binding spells against sexual harassment

Even today, with a high level of legislation in the workplace, sexual harassment can be a problem, especially if you are young. There may be entrenched workplace predators, both elderly Lotharios and young bloods eager to demonstrate their sexual allure, who regard a new arrival as prey to be stalked. Some men, especially in a mainly male environment, assume that all women are there to be groped. They may make the kind of offensive remarks best left in the locker room as part of ordinary conversation and assume that a business trip with a female colleague means a double room booked in the name of Smith. Men, too, can suffer under bosses who assume that PA duties extend beyond the office. Official complaints may be counter-productive or not taken seriously. But even if you are successfully pursuing legal or official channels, these very simple spells are a an effective way of getting those who behave inappropriately to back off fast. The first is intended for use with a man, the second with a woman

Spell I: When a predatory man extends octopus hands or makes an offensive remark, twist a phallic shaped crystal or stone sharply widdershins (anti-clockwise) three times between your hands, saying in your head:

So are you bound. Feel the discomfort of your lechery.

Spell 2: If the predator is female, use an ammonite or spiral-shaped shell, cupping your hands firmly round it whenever you feel intimidated and saying in your head:

You come too close; your intimacy is neither welcomed nor reciprocated.

Hold the shell in your power hand (the one you write) with and draw a large circle in the air, an arm's width from you, all round your body to mark out the exclusion zone, as you do so repeating five times:

I bind you from this sphere.

A spell to bind someone who is threatening you or a vulnerable family member

Threats can take many forms, from the intimidation of one of your children to bullying by an organisation. Though it may be hard to prove that the perpetrator is being menacing (as many bullies are quite clever), you can use a binding spell not only to block the threats but also to galvanise the victim's fight-back mechanism, which often causes a shift in the power dynamic.

You will need
A small box with a lid; a chain, padlock and key.

Timing
On a Tuesday, at midnight.

The spell
* Open the box and blow into it three times. Say:

Your threats are empty, your power that of the weak who prey on vulnerability. Seek to reclaim it if you will. I bind you from harming me/(name) under threat and lock away the key.

* Put the key in the box, wrap the chain around the box and close the padlock.
* Take the box to the local rubbish tip and throw it in to a deep pile of rubbish, as you do so repeating the words in your head and then blowing three more times.

A spell to bind racial prejudice towards you or someone you care about

Racial prejudice exists both subtly and more openly, usually against people who cannot defend themselves or take full advantage of protective legislation. People of all cultures may experience prejudice, especially if they are in a minority in an area.

You will need

6 small candles, one in each of the following shades: dark- and light-brown, pink, white, pale-yellow, black; a large flat metal tray; a very thin cord.

Timing

On a Sunday morning.

The spell

* Set the candles, equidistant from each other, in a circle. They should be as close together as possible.
* Beginning anywhere in the circle, light the candles in a deosil (clockwise) direction, one from the other. As you do so, say:

So are there no divisions between us all, but love and light.

* As the wax from all the candles runs together into a collective pool, press the cord down into the central area of wax, as you do so saying:

Be bound those (or name a person) who seek divisions. Candle power exert thy might.

* When the candles are burnt through, embed the cord even further into the wax, as you do so saying:

Bound are those (or name person) who cause division,
Free no more by day or night,
Free no more to spread their spite.
Thus is wrong restored to right.

* Carefully cut around the wax as it hardens, so that the cord is contained in a circle of wax.
* When the wax is cold, dispose of the cord, still within the wax.

A lunar justice spell for restraining those who accuse you unfairly

Unfair accusations can come from many sources – a family member or friend who accuses us of causing trouble not of our making, a colleague who blames us for someone else's mistakes or wrongly accuses us of copying another person's ideas, a police officer who serves us with a shoplifting or motoring charge, or an ex-partner who alleges in a custody dispute that we have not cared properly for our children. Though we may be certain we can prove our innocence, the stress may be so great that we feel helpless. Gossip may also spread, so fuelling the original accusation. A spell can bind the gossips as well as any individual, known or unknown, who is pursuing an unremitting vendetta against you (see also the next spell). Hazel is the traditional tree of wisdom and justice. The Vikings surrounded their judicial gatherings with hazel staves to mark their limits.

You will need

A bag of unshelled hazel nuts or 12 small twigs from a hazel tree, or any unshelled nuts or oak twigs; a black cord.

Timing

On the night of the full moon and the two nights following.

The spell

* When the moon has risen, surround yourself with a widdershins (anti-clockwise) circle of hazel nuts or twigs.
* Loosely bind your hands with the cord.
* Turn around in the centre of the circle nine times widdershins, as you do so untying the cord and saying:
  Let the matter proceed with all swiftness to a positive conclusion that I may be free of its bonds.
* Holding one end of the cord in your power hand (the one you write with), turn around nine times deosil (clockwise), as you do so saying:
  May (name accuser, which could be an official body, or if unknown say 'the accuser') be bound from causing me stress or speaking with malice against me until the matter is resolved with all swiftness to a positive conclusion and I am free of its bonds.
* Take the hazel nuts or twigs and cord home and repeat the spell on the following two nights, when the moon has risen.
* On the third night, leave the hazel circle in place after the spell and keep the cord in a dark indoor place until the matter is resolved. You can then throw it away.

A spell to bind an anonymous accuser

There is nothing more upsetting than an accusation from an unknown source, as you can end up suspecting everyone you know. Official bodies are not always very helpful in revealing who made the complaint, and may feel bound to investigate it. This is an occupational hazard for anyone in the public eye, but, as I know, it can be totally devastating when such an unknown source of hatred pours towards you. This is a version of an old Egyptian spell.

You will need

Some vinegar in a bottle with a shaker.

Timing

When it is really dark and the stars and moon are not visible.

The spell

* Stand outdoors, facing away from your home. Pointing the index finger of your power hand (the one you write with) towards an invisible and unknown person and say:

You, you shall be restrained, you without face or voice, who whisper your poison only under cover of darkness. I send back your viciousness to pick up as you will or move on. You, you are restrained and shall not follow me.

* Turn and drop a trail of vinegar behind you as you walk back to the house. Do not look back.

A spell to bind unjust entry of your home by bailiffs, debt collectors or officials

Most people who fall foul of bailiffs or debt collectors are unfortunate rather than deliberately obstructive – as a young single mother of two small children I myself once fell foul of unscrupulous money lenders. Although the regulation of debt collection has improved vastly over the years, I still hear alarming stories of unnecessary pressures placed on people who are stressed enough already. Debt collectors may phone during evenings or call after dark in contravention of guidelines and make veiled threats, which – especially if you live alone – can be very frightening. There are, however, official bodies to which you can complain about harassment. Do get help from your local Citizens Advice Bureau. This and the following spell – the first from the American folk tradition and the second a custom from the English Midlands – may help.

You will need

4 copper-coloured coins.

Timing

When necessary.

The spell

* Place the coins, heads upwards, to form a diagonal cross at the bottom of your doorstep, as you set them down saying:

You shall not enter here
Bringing fear.
Only with courtesy
May you visit me.
You shall not enter here
Bringing fear,
So turn away.

* Leave the coins in place indefinitely.

A second spell to bind unjust entry of your home by bailiffs, debt collectors or officials

You will need

A pot of marigolds.

Timing

When you are expecting an unpleasant caller, especially if you are being threatened with legal action.

The spell

* Set the pot of marigolds on a flat surface just inside the front door.

* Just before the caller is due, sprinkle a little of the soil from the pot on the doorstep.

* When the caller has gone, scoop up every tiniest grain of soil and put it back in the marigold pot, as you do so saying:

Now you are bound from returning, you and your kind. Be gone from my mind and my life until the matter is resolved with justice to my satisfaction.

A spell to bind rumours or lies being spread about you

Whether you have fallen foul of the local gossip or your partner's jealous ex is spreading nasty rumours about you, it can be hard to tackle the problem directly without causing denials and an escalation of the trouble as your words are twisted further. This spell is a good defence against such malice.

You will need

A long piece of white lined paper; a black pencil; a red pen; a white cord.

Timing

On a Wednesday, before sunset.

The spell

* Starting at the top of the piece of paper, write the name of the person spreading the lies on each line faintly in pencil.

* When you have filled every line, write your own name heavily in red pen over the accuser's name, starting at the bottom and filling every line.

* Roll the paper in to a scroll and tie it tightly with the cord, knotting it nine times and saying for each:

I bind your tongue from blackening my name. You stand corrected.

* Keep the scroll in a drawer, flattened under a heavy weight.

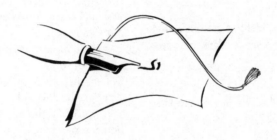

A spell for preventing an angry or violent person from entering your home or attacking you or a loved one

If there is someone you fear, be it an ex-partner, a relative who visits only to cause trouble, a neighbour whose complaints become menacing or someone who lives with you whose rages are unbearable, you can supplement very necessary official support with a spell. No one should live in fear of another, but bullies, physical and mental, often succeed by making the victim feel to blame. As well as restraining the bully, this spell may provide you with the sense of power to seek help.

You will need

Some red dough (children's play dough or ordinary dough with food colouring added); a freezer bag with a tag that ties.

Timing

An hour or so before you know or fear the anger will erupt.

The spell

* Make a very small dough figure.
* Place the figure in the freezer bag and tie the bag tight, as you do so saying:
So are you bound from rage and anger, from causing danger and harming me/(name victim). I freeze your violence in immobility. So must it be until I am free of you.
* Put the bag in the coldest part of the freezer or freezer compartment of a fridge, as you do so repeating the words.
* Throw away the rest of the dough.
* When the angry person appears again in your life, repeat the spell, throwing away the frozen figure from the previous spell in a bin outside your home or down a garbage chute.

A spell to bind a person who is causing harm to children or vulnerable people

It is very hard not to act as judge and jury if you know a person is a danger to those who cannot defend themselves. This spell avoids negativity on your part but is quite powerful, so carry it out without expressing any anger or outrage.

You will need

Some clay or modelling dough; a stick of myrrh incense; a dark-coloured drawstring bag.

Timing

At 10 pm (the healing hour) – to keep the spell positive.

The spell

* Make a small featureless doll to represent the potentially dangerous person.
* Light the incense stick and weave a smoke curtain around the figure, as you do so saying:
Turn away your eyes from (name potential/actual victims). Do not approach with harm in your heart. Depart in peace. Turn away your eyes.
* Leave the incense stick to burn away next to the doll.
* When the ashes are cool, sprinkle them on the doll and place the doll in the bag. Hide the bag away in your home, somewhere where it will not be disturbed. As the figure crumbles, so the danger will diminish.

A spell for gently restraining a person who is constantly bothering you

There are many forms of lame duck that come quacking into our lives and never go away. Your personal one may be a colleague who checks every minute detail with you before acting and plays helpless when there is anything even remotely new to sort out, a needy client who has obtained your home phone number and calls at all hours, a friend who wants to re-run every detail of her tangled emotional life as a nightly soap opera while you are trying to cook dinner, or a neighbour who watches for your light to go on before popping round and staying until you make the bedtime cocoa. Whatever the nature of your duck, you may need a spell to restrain them gently from monopolising your time.

You will need
A small ball of pink knitting wool; a small fabric doll.

Timing
On a Friday, at sunset.

The spell
* Place the doll on a flat surface and speak to it softly, naming it as though you were speaking to your lame duck. Say:
I cannot be what you ask of me,
And so, you see,
Bound you must be,
Not maliciously
But to discover your own ability
And not rely on me.
* Wind the doll up in the ball of wool, as you do so repeating the words. Tie the wool in a loose bow.
* Keep the doll bound in wool in a drawer for seven days, together with soft scented things.
* Unwrap the doll, as you do so saying:
Now be free yourself to see.
And not just me.
* As soon as possible after the unwrapping, take the doll and hide it in the person's home, maybe down the back of a sofa or near their workspace. If you cannot do this, put the doll in a large envelope with their name on it, leaving the envelope unsealed. Put the envelope in a high place in your own home.

A spell for keeping a lock on your finances if others are always demanding you subsidise them

As I said on page 428, parents tend to help adult children out financially far more today than they did in the past, and this can be emotionally rewarding. But if you are always subsiding what seems to be a very comfortable lifestyle for other family members or friends while you are struggling, it may be time to put a temporary lock on your finances. This spell does not stop you helping family and friends when they have a crisis but does prevent you from becoming the limitless overdraft or the cashpoint that never runs out of money.

You will need

A small jar with a screw-top lid; coins of different denominations; as many bay leaves as there are people who regularly borrow from you (the culinary kind is fine).

Timing

On a Wednesday evening.

The spell

* Rest the lid on top of the empty jar and, working widdershins (anti-clockwise), surround it with a circle of coins. The coins need not be touching. As you make the circle, say:
  Money is not endless.
  This money is my own.
  Though I dearly love you,
  I am not an endless loan.

* Drop the coins, in the order that you set them, one by one in to the jar, repeating the words for each.

* Add the bay leaves to the jar, for each one naming a person who regularly borrows from you and saying:
  The account is now closed, except in emergency.

* Screw the lid firmly on the jar, as you do so repeating the words of the previous step.

* Bury or hide the jar where no one will find it.

PART 10

SPELLS FOR
THE PLANET

While many of the spells in this book are directed towards personal or family needs, there is a place in both private and group spell-casting for working with planetary concerns. As I said on page 613, it is impossible to bind all people against, for example, polluting the earth. But it is possible to work with local ecological and humanitarian issues and to send more general healing into the cosmos, where it will add to the collective pool of positive energy.

We know that the fluttering of the wings of something as small as a butterfly causes a minute shift in global energy. When we cast positive spells for the planet, we are in effect topping up the store of power for good. If we all did a little of this work, we could provide a lot of power to counter the evil and destruction wreaked by humans, as well as the adverse effects of natural disasters.

The Age of Reason and industrialisation encouraged urban humankind to regard the Earth as a larder and fuel store that could be raided as necessary and need never be replenished or kept clean. In the last 30 years, however, this misconception has begun to be overturned, and we have seen the birth of Green spirituality. This movement takes many forms, but the unifying principle may perhaps best be encapsulated in a Malaysian proverb: 'We have not inherited the Earth from our forebears but borrowed it from our descendants.'

One of the founding articles of the environmental movement is the Gaia Hypothesis, which takes its name from the ancient Greek earth mother, Gaia. The Hypothesis was first proposed in the early 1970s by James Lovelock, a British biologist working for the Jet Propulsion Laboratory of the National Aeronautics and Space Administration in Pasadena, California. Lovelock argued that the Earth was a biologically self-regulating mechanism, and in the following three decades his theory has gained credence. It would seem that all those who depend upon the Earth are actually microcosmic reproductions of the Earth herself. She provides resources for all of these dependants, including healing medicines for every ill of the mind, body and psyche, in the form of plants and minerals. Thus when we harm the Earth (spiritually as well as physically) we are damaging our own life support system and that of our descendants. This idea, so recently rediscovered in the dominant Western culture, in fact dates back to the beginning of human consciousness, and has never disappeared from the philosophies of many indigenous peoples, such as the Native North Americans and Australian Aborigines.

On 22 April 1970, 20 million Americans of all ages and from all walks of life demonstrated for a healthier environment. As a result, an annual Earth Day was instigated by Senator Gaylord Nelson of Wisconsin. Since then, the event has spread throughout the world. On its 30th anniversary, in 2000, millions of people from across the world gathered to address ecological issues. Earth Day, and the weekends before and after it, are a good focus for environmental spell-casting, as is the vernal equinox (21 March in the Northern Hemisphere) and World Environment Day (6 June).

As I have said many times in this book, we must put back into the spiritual pot what we take out of it. Altruistic spells form a kind of repayment for those (perfectly acceptable) rituals that we perform for our own needs and for the needs of loved ones. However, there is a bonus that comes as a result of casting spells for the Earth and for people we do not know personally. Under the threefold magical law (see page 11), if you ask for world peace, peace will also appear in your own life. If you ask for abundance in lands where there is starvation, money will also flow into your own pocket.

Mother Earth spells are a very uplifting form of magic. Especially when followed by a small gift of time and practical effort, they make a real difference to a world that we may sometimes feel as individuals we have little influence over.

50 SPELLS FOR PEACE BETWEEN AND WITHIN NATIONS

One of the greatest gifts we can pass on to future generations is a peaceful world. By far the majority of people in the world are united in the desire to live in a safe and conflict-free society. As well as practical action, which may not be possible in authoritarian regimes, private rituals for peace are a potent way of increasing the underlying energies that may ultimately turn the tide towards a more harmonious world.

Spells and prayers for peace are closely entwined. Some of the best peace spells incorporate prayers from different faiths as a focus for calling upon greater powers than our own in cases of war between nations or persecution of the weak by the strong. I do not believe that it matters what name we use for higher powers – or whether we give them a name at all (some consider this source of the energy as the evolved spiritual essence within individuals). I know others would disagree, and that is their prerogative.

Many people, both old and young, observe Remembrance Day as a memorial to those who have lost their life in war, pausing to pay their respects at the 11th hour of the 11th day of the 11th month. This time and date is a good focus point for casting spells for peace. With terrorism as great a threat as war for many of us today, September 11th is another date that can be focused on. Other good occasions for peace workings are any of the World Peace Days (of which a number have been created) and the midsummer and midwinter solstices.

There is a wide variety of spells that can be woven for peace, some of which can join us with other spell-casters united in a common aim. This chapter gives a representative selection.

A candle spell for peace between religious or ethnic factions or within nations with which you have a personal connection

You may have a friend from a persecuted minority, a family member serving in the forces in a conflict area or a relative who is an aid worker in a war-torn region. If so, try this spell.

You will need
3 white lilies (or white roses) in a vase; a pink or beeswax candle on a metal tray.

Timing
At 10 pm.

The spell
* Light the candle. Place the vase of lilies (symbols of peace) or roses near the candle, so that the light shines on them.
* Pick a single petal from one flower and singe it in the flame, then drop it on to the tray to burn or not. Say:
For those who suffer/have suffered persecution during the conflict in (name place).
* Pluck a petal from another flower, singe it and let it fall onto the tray. Say:
For those who bring/brought relief during the conflict in (name place).
* Pluck a petal from the third flower, singe it and let it fall on to the tray. Say:
That persecution and conflict may end in/not return to (name place) and peace be lasting.
* Leave the candle to burn down.
* Bury the singed petals. When the flowers die, bury them in the same place as the petals.

A Hebrew circling ritual for peace

I was taught this chant by a Church of England clergyman in London when I worked there as a teacher. I have used it in many times of conflict – personal, national and international. More recently I have worked with it as a circling prayer. Perform this spell either alone or with a group of friends or fellow peace workers. *Shalom* means 'peace'.

You will need
A white candle for each person present.

Timing
On a Friday, at dusk.

The spell
* If alone, light your candle. If in a group, light the first candle. The second person should then light their candle from the first person's, the third from the second's, and so on.
* Begin to walk in a deosil (clockwise) circle or spiral, as you do so chanting softly and rhythmically over and over again:
Shalom, my friend, shalom, my friend, shalom, shalom, shalom, my friend, shalom, my friend, shalom, shalom.
If you are in a group, the second person can begin chanting when the first person is beginning the second phrase, and so on.
* Gradually slow your steps and let the words fade into silence, until – if you are in a group – the last person to start chanting makes the final 'shalom, shalom'.
* To close the ritual, say (together as one if you are in a group):
May there be peace throughout the whole world.

A five-flower spell for ending racial or religious hatred in an area

This is a good spell to perform if you, your family or your friends have experienced problems as a result of racial or religious tensions. It can also be used to send healing to areas where there have been divisions over many years, or even centuries, for example the Middle East and Northern Ireland.

You will need
5 white flower heads; a clear glass bowl of still mineral water; some seeds.

Timing
At dusk.

The spell
* Go out in to the open air. It does not matter if it is raining. Set your bowl in a sheltered place, on some earth, and float the five flower heads on the surface of the water, as you do so saying:
Fill with peace this water, that unity may flow and grow where there is now division.

* Leave the flowers on the water until noon the next day.
* Remove the flowers. Write the name of the country experiencing division with a stick in the soil and pour the flower essence water onto the soil, as you do so saying:
So spreads harmony, so increases unity, from the roots upwards rising.

* Plant some seeds in the newly watered soil as a symbol of the unity that may slowly grow. Follow the outline of the letters with the seeds if you wish.
* Keep the flowers in a dish of water until they die, and then add that water to the soil where you planted the seeds.
* Do something to bring unity into your own life, perhaps by mending a petty quarrel or bringing together in a joint venture two people who have differences of opinion.

A continuous candle peace ritual

I received this ritual by e-mail from a friend of a friend in America. The original source was not credited. I am sure whoever created it will not mind me passing it on, even if the form has been somewhat changed in transmission. I sent the e-mail on to several people, and I know that they, too, passed it on. The original candle was lit on 11 September 2001.

You will need
A candle (preferably a long-burning church one).

Timing
Any.

The spell
* Light the candle, as you do so saying:
There is not enough darkness in the world to put out the light of one candle.
You may like to dedicate the candle to peace everywhere, in memory of those who lost their lives on 11 September in New York and all who have suffered as a result of terrorist attacks before and since.

* E-mail, phone or write to someone you know will carry on the ritual, giving them instructions and asking them to pass the message on in turn. The idea is that someone else should light a candle before yours has burnt down.

A St Francis peace circling ritual

On page 573 I use part of the St Francis peace prayer in a ritual for healing and conserving animals in the wild. Here I use a slightly different version of the whole prayer (variations are due to differences in translation). This ritual focuses particularly on those who have been injured or whose homes and livelihoods have been destroyed by war or fighting. You can work the ritual alone or with others (each of whom should have their own bowl of petals or leaves). If you work as a group, speak the words of the prayer slowly in unison. Work in an open space.

You will need

Some petals from dead or dying flowers mixed with petals from one living flower – or a mixture of dead and newly plucked leaves; a bowl or basket.

Timing

In the late afternoon, when there is a breeze.

The spell

* Place the petals or leaves in the basket or bowl.
* Walk three times in a deosil (clockwise) circle and then once in a widdershins (anti-clockwise) circle. Keep walking in this pattern of reverse circles until you have recited the following chant 12 times, as you go scattering the petals or leaves:

Lord, make me an instrument of your peace.
Where there is hatred, let me sow love;
Where there is injury, pardon;
Where there is doubt, faith;
Where there is despair, hope;
Where there is darkness, light;
And where there is sadness, joy.
Grant that I may not so much seek
To be consoled as to console;
To be understood as to understand,
To be loved as to love;
For it is in giving that we receive,
It is in pardoning that we are pardoned,
And it is in dying that we are born to eternal life.

* Stand facing the direction of the sun or the brightest area of the sky and name the places for which you seek peace. (If you are working in a group, you can take it in turns to speak a place name until there are no more you wish to name.)
* End by saying:
May they be blessed.
* Scatter any remaining petals.

A spell to create a candle web for world peace

This is a very simple but potent method of joining with the energies of others in different places and different time zones for peace. I have discovered that if you work at a set time each week, time zone differences do not seem to matter. I have revised this spell over the years; this is the most effective form so far.

You will need

A pure-white candle.

Timing

At 10 pm (the healing hour), on a Sunday.

The spell

* Light the candle near a window or in a sheltered part of your garden.
* Look through the candle flame in to the darkness and picture the light beams travelling in all directions and crossing other light beams from other candles in other places.

* Say softly three times into the candle flame the World Peace Organization's prayer:
  May peace prevail on Earth.

* Blow out the candle and send the light to wherever there is most need for peace (trust the cosmos to find the right place).
* Repeat weekly.

A Native North American peace ceremony

The Native American prayer used in this ritual is often recited at world peace ceremonies. It can also can form the focus for a private or group ceremony when news is received of a massacre, tragedy, war or act of terrorism.

You will need

A sage or cedar smudge stick or firm incense stick for each person taking part; a candle or other source of flame.

Timing

In the early morning.

The spell

* Holding the smudge or incense stick in your power hand (the one you write with), light it from the candle or other source of flame.
* When the tip is glowing, fan the smoke with your other hand and turn to face each of the four directions in turn (you can use approximations), beginning with the direction in which you can see the sun or the brightest patch of sky.
* Return to the direction of the sun or brightness. Lower the smudge or incense to the Earth and then raise it to the sky.
* Turn slowly, holding the smudge or incense just above waist height and fanning the smoke with the opposite hand so that it spirals as you turn. As you turn, recite six times:
  Great Spirit of our ancestors, I raise my pipe to you; to your messengers, the four winds; and to Mother Earth, who provides for your children. Give us the wisdom to teach our children to love, to respect and to be kind to each other so that they may grow with peace of mind.
* Allow the smudge or incense and the candle or other source of flame to burn through in a safe place.

A war memorial ritual

Perform this spell if you see your family surname on a war memorial or in a book of remembrance.

You will need

Nothing.

Timing

When you see the family name.

The spell

* Touch the name with your power hand (the one you write with). If this is not possible, say it three times.
* Touch your heart, silently giving thanks.
* If possible, leave a small donation to help with the upkeep of the memorial or church.

A candle vigil for a national or international tragedy

This spell can be worked following a tragedy caused by war or terrorism, or the anniversary of the assassination of a loved figure for peace. Carry it out alone or in a group. Although vigils customarily last all night, you can carry this one out for just for an hour or two – perhaps from 10 pm (the healing hour) until midnight, or for the hour before dawn or dusk. You can ask a family member or friend to carry out the vigil at the same time if they cannot be with you. If you are working as a group, pre-arrange who will light and be responsible for the tea-lights, replacing them before they go out.

You will need

A large long-burning white candle (plus a spare in case it goes out and will not re-light); sufficient white tea-lights or small white candles to have eight burning constantly throughout the vigil, plus one for every person present.

Timing

Any (see above).

The spell

* Light the large candle and around it make a circle of eight tea-lights or smaller candles (do not light them yet).
* Speak a few words to define the purpose of the ritual.
* Light the first tea-light from the central candle, as you do so saying:
  So I light the flame of peace that it may spread throughout the whole world.
* Moving deosil (clockwise) light each of the tea-lights from the previous one, for each tea-light repeating the words above.
* The vigil is thereafter silent. Replace any tea-lights before they die, lighting the replacement light from the dying one and repeating the words above in your head.
* At the appointed end of the vigil, you (and any present) can ask for a personal blessing concerning peace and say:
  May the light kindled this day burn on in my life / our lives and in the world. Blessings be!

A Hindu ritual for peace

You will need

A small bonfire or a large red candle embedded in a bucket of sand or earth; some dried thyme or coriander seeds.

Timing

Any.

The spell

* Light the bonfire or candle.
* Walk seven times deosil (clockwise) around the fire or candle, scattering the dried thyme or coriander seeds in to or towards the flames as you go and reciting for each round the following words (from a well-known Hindu prayer):
  May there be peace on Earth.
  May the waters be appeasing.
  May herbs be wholesome,
  And may trees and plants bring peace to all.
  May all beneficent beings bring peace to us.
  And may thy peace itself bestow peace on all,
  And may that peace come to me also.

A remembrance for those who have died in war or acts of terrorism

There are a number of official occasions in different lands for remembering war or an atrocity. As well as attending more public ceremonies, you can use a quiet moment for a remembrance of your own. This need not be on a publicly recognised anniversary but could be on the anniversary of the death of a family member in war, or of a day when the tragedy of war touched your life or that of someone you know.

You will need

Some poppies, or any white and red flowers; a bridge over flowing water.

Timing

Just before dusk, or at a significant time in the event you are marking.

The spell

* Standing facing upstream, cast your flowers one by one in to the water, so that they are carried under the bridge.

* Name the person or people on whom you are focusing and recite softly the words of the British poet Laurence Binyon, who lived through both World Wars. They come from the poem 'For the Fallen', written in 1914:

They shall grow not old, as we that are left grow old.
Age shall not weary them, nor the years condemn.
At the going down of the sun and in the morning
We will remember them.

* Cast a final flower into the water, as you do so saying:

May she/he/they and those they left behind know peace.

* Leave the bridge from the direction in which you came.

A Druidic peace ritual

This ritual is based on a simple Druid chant ceremony. You can work it alone or with as many people as you like (standing in a circle but not touching one another). If you are working in a group, you can speak in unison or decide in advance who will say each chant. Work outdoors.

You will need

A compass; a lantern (if you are working after dark).

Timing

At one of the solar transitions of the day – dawn (East), noon (South), dusk (West) or midnight (North).

The spell

* Light the lantern if necessary. Set it in the middle of the area you are working in. Using the compass, find the four main directions.

* Face the direction that corresponds to the time of day you are working at – for example, East if you are carrying out the rite at dawn. Say:

May there be peace in the East/South/West/North.

* Moving deosil (clockwise), face each of the directions in turn and repeat the chant.

* Face the direction you began with or the centre of the circle if you are working in a group, raise your arms upwards and outwards, and say:

May there be peace throughout the whole world.

A Celtic peace ritual to ensure safe return from war, or from aid or peace-keeping duties

This is a Celtic Christian peace ritual that may derive from even earlier times. I first learnt it from some Americans I met in Los Angeles whose ancestors originated in Ireland. They used it when their brother was serving in Vietnam, but it applies as well to any nation's soldiers, aid workers or peacekeepers. You can also use the ritual to minimise the loss of civilian life in war-torn places or for anyone you know serving in the forces in peacetime. I have seen longer versions of the prayer. If possible, work in the absent person's home – otherwise name them and use your own home.

You will need

A glass bowl of sparkling mineral water; some salt; a silver-coloured knife.

Timing

Every first Sunday of the month during the absence, in the morning

The spell

* Make sacred water by placing three pinches of salt in the bowl of mineral water and stirring it three times deosil (clockwise). If you wish, you can use the knife to make a cross, either the Christian equal-armed cross or the diagonal cross of the Earth Mother, on the surface of the water.
* Going from the top to the bottom of the house, walk from room to room, sprinkling water drops around doors, windows and beds, as you do so reciting softly:

The peace of God, the peace of men
Be on each window, on each door,
Upon each hole that lets in light,
Upon the four corners of the house,
Upon the four corners of the bed,
Upon each thing my eye takes in.
And safe (name) once more return.

A new year's earth spell for all touched by conflict

You will need

A plant pot; a plastic bag; some seeds.

Timing

On new year's morning.

The spell

* Go outdoors, pick up a handful of soil and allow it to trickle through your fingers, as you do so saying:

Mother Earth, protect all who walk upon you and let them live in peace this year.

* Place a little of the soil in the plastic bag and take it away with you. Use it to plant the seeds in the pot, as you do so repeating the chant.
* Next new year's day morning, return the soil, and hopefully the grown plants, to the place you took the soil from and repeat the spell.

51 SPELLS FOR DEALING WITH DISASTERS

In the modern world, we understand much more about the causes of natural disasters, such as floods and drought. We have also seen how humans can contribute to famine by corrupt or inefficient government and management of resources. But in spite of modern advance warning systems, earthquakes, tidal waves, floods and hurricanes still cause great devastation, especially in places where housing is relatively basic and where relief cannot easily reach.

Mother Earth is not always gentle, and destruction is as much a part of her cycle as birth and growth. An earthquake or tornado is no respecter of the most luxuriously constructed human edifice. I was caught in the 1994 Los Angeles earthquake and can still recall the disbelief of hotel guests that room service simply was not going to happen as – eight kilometres (five miles) from the epicentre – the ground and walls shook. While the effects of a natural disaster on more affluent nations are, obviously, more easily coped with (in the Third World such an event can be catastrophic), there are nevertheless still people in the richer countries who struggle to provide for themselves and their families. For them the consequences of an earthquake or hurricane may be very serious. Moreover, a fatality caused by a natural disaster will be a cause of grief wherever it happens.

Once sacrifices were offered to the deities in order to ward off natural disasters. In the modern world, charms and amulets are still a popular form of personal defence against their effects. Angels are also often invoked for protection. I have included both these forms of magic in this chapter.

Where possible, try to follow your spell with some form of practical aid or support, however small. It need not be financial.

An angels of the rains spell to end drought or to bring clean water to an area

You can cast this spell to bring clean water to the local population of any area in the world, as well as to relieve the effects of drought. You can also use the spell if there are temporary water shortages in your own area. Matariel, Ridya and Zalbesael are the angels of rain (see page 639).

You will need

A photograph of the drought-affected area or of the people who need clean water; a glass bowl of tap water or filtered water; an area of dry earth or sand (or put some in a box or on a tray).

Timing

During the coolest part of the day, while it is still light.

The spell

* Name the place that needs clean water or relief from drought.
* Scatter ever larger deosil (clockwise) circles of water drops over the dry soil or sand, as you do so chanting continuously:
  Matariel, Ridya, Zalbesael, Matariel, Ridya, Zalbesael.
* Pour the rest of the water into the soil, then shake the wet soil on to an area of open earth.

A Suiel angelic charm against earthquakes

Suiel, angel of earthquakes, is the special guardian of earthquake zones. Earthquakes and strong tremors have also been known to occur in seemingly unlikely places such as Birmingham, in the centre of England. If you have experienced a quake or know your home is on a geological fault line, perform this spell every three months. This is also a good spell to cast if you are going to holiday in a place that is within a recognised earthquake activity area, especially if there have been earthquake warnings around the time you will be travelling. Although you can't expect to stop an earthquake, you can minimise its effects on yourself and loved ones, as well as on your property and possessions. Suiel is often depicted wearing dark-red, with sharp golden rays shooting from his halo.

You will need

A purse filled with sage, coriander seeds and basil; a dark-red or indigo candle.

Timing

Every three months in an earthquake zone, or when there are warnings of an earthquake in an area you will be visiting.

The spell

* Light the candle and set the purse of herbs in front of it.
* Look into the flame and say:
  Wise Suiel, Master of Earthquakes, spare me/those I love from the effects of earthquake, shake and tremor. Guard home and property and pass gently that the Earth may remain firm beneath my feet.
* Pick up the purse and shake it above the candle flame slowly ten times (holding it high enough so that it will not catch fire), repeating the words for each shake.
* Return the purse to the front of the candle and leave the candle to burn down.
* When the candle has burnt down, place the purse above a door or

window lintel at home or pack it in your suitcase.

* If you live in an area of earthquake activity, replace the herbs in the purse every three months, scattering the old herbs on to earth.

A fire spell to relieve harsh winter conditions

In January 2003, western Europe and parts of America, as well as more usually cold places, were gripped by icy weather. Extremes of temperature are an effect of global warming, and incidences may increase unless we can reverse the process. Old people, babies and the sick suffer especially in cold weather, particularly in lands where temperatures plummet below zero. Oertha is the angel of the North. He has a flaming torch that he holds to stop his own great power freezing the world. Picture him shimmering with ice, with icicles for a halo. He exudes not coldness but what is sometimes called 'fire ice', blazing with inner light.

You will need

A small block of ice or some ice cubes; a jar of a hot spice such as ginger or chilli; a wooden spoon; an old saucepan.

Timing

At the beginning of a cold snap or when you hear news of areas hit by very cold temperatures.

The spell

* Working in a warm room, sprinkle a little of the spice on top of the ice and say:

    Oertha, warm the winter cold and relieve all who are suffering the effects of ice and snow and biting Arctic winds.

* Transfer the saucepan to the stove and, as the ice begins to melt, stir in to it deosil (clockwise) the spice you added, so that it colours the water. Go on stirring until the ice has gone and the mixture has become warm, as you do so chanting continuously.

* When steam appears, turn off the heat and, if possible, pour the hot liquid on to an icy area outdoors, otherwise pour it down the sink, turning on the cold tap so that the mixture hisses as it disappears.

An Australian Aboriginal spell to bring rain or reduce unbearable heat

Traditional Australian Aboriginal annual rain rituals are the most effective method I have discovered of reducing the adverse effects of excessive heat on the vulnerable, both your own friends and family members and more generally in lands where the temperature has become unbearable as a result of global warming. Aboriginal rock art was originally created between 10,000 and 40,000 years ago. Many of the images, especially those depicting deities or ancestors, were considered to contain the essence and magical power of the form represented. Some still maintain their original magical significance. For example, in Kimberley, in western Australia, may be found paintings of the Wandjinas, the spirits of rain, sometimes called the Lightning Brothers. The Wandjinas are depicted with spots around their heads, to invite thunder and lightning to bring rain, but without mouths, so that the seasonal waters will not flood the Earth. They are repainted at the appropriate times before the rainy season so that they will retain their power. This is also a good anti-drought spell.

You will need

A piece of rock or slate; red, yellow and blue chalk or permanent coloured pens; a jug of tap water.

Timing

When an extreme heat wave is forecast or you hear of countries where people are being affected by unusual heat.

The spell

* Copy the image above onto the rock or slate, adding spots around the heads to indicate rain. Lay the slate flat, picture uppermost, outdoors on dry earth or concrete.
* Pour the water deosil (clockwise) in a steady stream around the outside of the rock or slate (making sure it does not splash the drawing), as you do so saying continuously:
  Awake and cool the Earth.
* When you have used all the water, take the picture inside and prop it up so that the figures face a door that opens on to the outdoors.
* Retouch the image when necessary, repeating the ritual.

A spell against famine

One of the cruellest facts is that while a considerable proportion of people in the Westernised world are affected by obesity, eating disorders and the effects of crash dieting, many in the Third World do not have enough to eat. This spell works on the principle of fairer distribution of resources through magical means.

You will need

2 small deep dishes containing fruits, nuts and seeds (you can use a fruit and nut muesli), the first dish filled to the brim, the second almost empty; a pair of kitchen scales with a large pan on either side; a scoop or spoon.

Timing

At the beginning of the month, in the morning.

The spell

* Set the two dishes on a table, one on either side of the scales. Holding the almost empty dish, say:

  Too little or too much,
  Neither can be right.
  Divide resources equally
  And put injustice right.

* Tip the contents of each dish into one of the pans of the scales. If some of the contents of the fuller dish does not fit, leave it in the dish.

* Take some of the contents of the full side of the scales and add it to the almost empty side, as you do so repeating the words.

* Keep taking from the full side of the scales and adding to the emptier side, repeating the words for every spoon- or scoopful you move.

* Top up the original full side with anything left in full dish and redistribute this also, chanting as before.

* When the scales balance, refill the dishes, each with the contents of its respective scales pan. Say:

  Too little or too much,
  Neither can be right.
  Resources divided equally
  Do put injustice right.

* Use the contents of both dishes to make a cake or pudding to share with family or friends.

* Each day during the following week, avoid buying a small snack or luxury item, donating the money instead to a charity that feeds people in famine-hit areas and, most importantly, buys them seeds and farming equipment.

A spell against whirlwinds, hurricanes and tornadoes

As I mentioned on page 507, it was once believed that women newly delivered of a child had the power to quell storms and tempests. Witches were also credited with this ability. The effects of hurricanes reach people living far from the epicentre, but even if you are too distant to experience any of them, you may wish to carry out this spell as a way of sending spiritual support to those whose lives and homes are threatened. Obviously, you will not be able to turn back a hurricane single-handedly (or even as a group effort), but if enough people focus on minimising damage, the spell will not be in vain.

You will need

A long scarf that knots easily; a large plastic bag (a supermarket one will do); an electric fan (if you are casting the spell far from the hurricane).

Timing

When the wind begins to rise or when you hear that a hurricane is forecast in another part of the world.

The spell

* Hold the scarf up to the wind or the fan so that it fills with air. Tie the ends of the scarf quickly in three knots, saying for each one:

  You are bound from wreaking devastation.

* Place the scarf in the bag and knot the bag tightly three times, repeating the words for each knot. Keep the bag (well away from children) in a safe place indoors for the duration of the adverse winds.

* When the danger is passed, untie the bag and unknot the scarf in the open air, as you do so saying:

  You are free to go on your way in peace. I thank you.

A spell to redress poverty in under-resourced countries

Many people in the Third World are paid so little for their work that poverty is a real problem. Even small children often have to work long hours in order for families to survive. This spell, like the previous one, focuses on the magical redistribution of material resources. Performing it may seem like an insignificant action in the face of a huge problem, but every little contributes to an increase in positive energy. If you follow up the spell by buying, where possible, only Fairtrade goods and patronising stores that do not take goods from sweat shops, you will also be helping to swing the tide in a practical sense.

You will need

A large tub of mixed gold- and silver-coloured or clear glass nuggets; a long piece of white cord; a dark-coloured candle on a flat metal tray; a dish.

Timing

At the beginning of the month, in the morning – if possible as sunshine reflects on the table on which you are working.

The spell

* Place the white cord across the middle of the table and tip most of the glass nuggets on one side of it. Say:

The gulf between rich and poor, between have and have not, between wealth and dearth, between greed and need, is too great. May the treasures of the Earth be more fairly distributed.

* Light the candle and place it on the almost empty side of the table.
* Lift the cord and, holding it taut (you may have to hold it part way along and let some hang down on either side), place the centre of the cord in the candle flame until the cord breaks. Repeat the chant.
* Using both hands, scoop all the nuggets together in the middle of the table.
* Carefully lift the candle from the holder and pass it in a circle around the heaped nuggets, as you do so repeating the words.
* When the candle is burnt down, put the nuggets in a dish where the morning sun will light on them.
* Spend a little time researching which large stores local to you stock goods that are produced using only fair labour. Find out the location of your nearest Fairtrade store (for example Traidcraft).

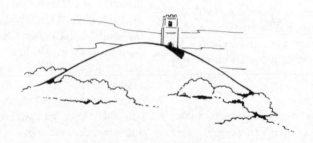

A spell against urban decay and inner-city or rural poverty

You may know of a community that is struggling, have friends who are living on the breadline, or perhaps suffer financial hardship yourself — living in substandard housing and sending your children to a school where there are problems linked with deprivation. Any of these situations could be the focus of this spell, or you could centre it on a larger area where economic conditions are difficult, perhaps because mining or manufacture no longer exist, or there is high unemployment and a lack of public transport.

You will need

Pictures of urban wastelands or villages where the local people can no longer afford to live; some greenery in a vase; 11 black stones; 12 white stones.

Timing

At any transition point — for example, the beginning of a week, month or year.

The spell

* Set the pictures in a circle and place the greenery in a circle around the pictures. Beyond the greenery make a circle of the 11 black stones plus one of the white stones.
* Touch the white stone and say:
  May light and life return.
* Each day, when you have time, replace a black stone with a white one and bury the black stone. After the burial, touch the new white stone in the circle and repeat the words. Replace any dying greenery.
* When you have all 12 white stones in place, the spell is done. During the intervening days, write a letter to a newspaper or politician about an issue of local concern, or find out about local groups or charities that support the regeneration of communities.

An anti-flood angel spell

Matariel, Ridya and Zalbesael are traditionally angels of rain. They are invoked to protect against floods and drought and to bring clean water to an area (see also the spell on page 634). Visualise these angels constantly moving in robes of grey and blue, their dark-grey wings shedding raindrops. With global warming and the modern practice of building homes on flood plains, floods have become a more widespread problem. You can also cast this spell to send positive energies towards relief efforts when there are bad floods.

You will need

A glass bowl of sparkling mineral water; some salt; a silver-coloured knife (for example a paper knife); a map of the area where you live or of the affected area (or draw an approximation).

Timing

During heavy rain, or when there is a flood warning or news of a flood disaster far away.

The spell

* Add three pinches of the salt to the water and stir it three times widdershins (anticlockwise) with the knife.
* Sprinkle water drops widdershins around the four sides of the map, as you do so repeating as a continuous chant:
  Zalbesael, Ridya, Matariel, Zalbesael, Ridya, Matariel, take away the water, take away rains, take away the flood.
* Pour away the rest of the water outside your home and keep the map folded in a dry, warm place until the danger is past.

A spell bag against tidal waves and high seas

This spell is especially relevant to all those who live in coastal areas or near tidal rivers, as well as for all who suffer the effects of land erosion. Climatic changes and dramatic weather patterns, even thousands of miles away, can cause a sudden rise in sea levels that results in major flooding and, in the long term, erosion of coastal areas. Where I live, on the Isle of Wight, in southern England, the soil is soft clay, and every year more and more of it falls into the sea. When I moved to the island 14 years ago, it was a long steep climb to a local beach. Now the beach is almost level with the road.

You will need

A pinch of sea salt; a pinch of dried powdered kelp (available from health food stores) or a piece of dried seaweed; a small sea shell or sea pebble; some coral or a tiny aquamarine; a turquoise purse; a small paper or fabric fish, or a fish charm; a bowl filled with small stones of any colour, collected from the land.

Timing

When high tides are forecast.

The spell

* Working in as bright a natural light as possible, fill the purse with the sea salt, kelp or seaweed, sea shell or pebble, coral or aquamarine, and fish. Close the purse and say:

The sea shall safely be contained.

* Surround the purse with three concentric circles of land stones extending outwards, repeating the words as you complete each circle.
* Leave the purse within the stone circles for 24 hours and then transfer it to a high, open, indoor place, such as an upstairs shelf, that faces the direction of the sea or nearest tidal water (however distant). Surround the purse with a single circle of stones, as you do so repeating the chant.
* Return the remaining stones to the land. The spell will last for approximately six months.

A charm against volcanic eruption

Volcanic eruption not only causes devastation to those living around the volcano but also affects tides and climate over a wide area. Pele, the Hawaiian goddess of volcanoes, is the focus for most anti-volcano spells. She is still revered in Hawaii, and altars to her are set up near lava streams. She is often described as a hag sitting by the fires in her volcanic cavern, lit only by a single blue flame. This spell will also protect your home from misfortune.

You will need

Two small pieces of lava or pumice stone (the latter available cheaply in health food and beauty stores), one lighter in colour than the other; a metallic-grey candle.

Timing

Ongoing.

The spell

* Light the candle.

* Take up the lighter-coloured lava or pumice stone in your power hand (the one you write with) and the darker one in your receptive hand. Pass the stones in spiralling circles high over the candle flame, being careful not to burn yourself. As you do so, say:
Grandmother Pele, may the fires remain within the Earth.

* Set the lighter stone near the centre of your home and the darker one near the front door.

* When you learn of volcanic activity anywhere in the world, repeat the words nine times over the dark stone each morning when you rise.

* When the danger is over, float the dark stone away on water (for example a pond). As it floats away, say:
Grandmother Pele, receive your own as tribute.

* Replace the dark stone as soon as possible.

A spell bag against forest fires and fires caused by lightning

In recent years, forest fires have devastated vast areas of Africa, Australia and western America. With its unusually high summer temperatures, 2003 saw serious forest fires in Spain, Portugal and the south of France. Our ancestors kept pieces of lightning-blasted oak and ash near the fire as a charm against lightning bolts and conflagration – a necessary precaution in a time when the land was far more densely forested than nowadays and homes were made of wood.

You will need

A stick of ginger, cinnamon or dragon's blood incense; an incense-holder; a small piece of meteorite, tektite, olivine or moldavite, or a silver-grey haematite; a small charred piece of wood; some dried ginger or cinnamon; 3 bent iron nails; a red purse; a bowl of tap water.

Timing

During a very hot dry period or when electrical storms are forecast, at noon if possible.

The spell

※ Light the incense stick and set it in the holder near the purse. Place the meteorite (or other stone), charred wood, ginger or cinnamon and bent nails in the purse and close it.

※ Write in incense smoke over the purse three times:
May the fires not rage unchecked, but be cooled and die.

※ Plunge the incense stick in to the water so that it hisses. Throw away the incense stick and the water.

※ Keep the purse near the hearth or in the warmest room in the house, somewhere where it will not be found.

※ Renew every six weeks in the hot dry season if you live near forests, otherwise every six months.

52 SPELLS FOR COMBATING ENVIRONMENTAL DESTRUCTION

As caretakers of the Earth, it is our duty to work against pollution and the squandering of the Earth's resources. As individuals, of course, our influence is limited and our own resources finite, but we do have an influence. If we refuse to buy fast food from companies that destroy rainforests, choose goods with eco-friendly packaging, monitor local woodlands and wetlands and support a conservation movement, our input over the months and years can be significant. We can also work to prevent others from destroying the environment, protesting when governments exploit habitats to gain access to cheap fuel, corporations waste resources by over-packaging goods, and farmers fill animals with chemicals whose safety has not been proven in the name of low-cost food.

Significant steps forward have already been made as a result of individual and collective intervention. Some endangered species are being successfully returned to the wild. Otters, for example, after being threatened with extinction during the 1980s as a result of industrial pollution and destruction of their habitats, have returned to rivers and canals in the UK during the last five years. What is more, they are also being seen in the urban environments from which they disappeared hundreds of years ago, for example along canal and river banks in the centre of Leeds, Bristol, Norwich, Doncaster, Newcastle and Glasgow. Similar wildlife initiatives are succeeding worldwide.

This chapter is about using magic to supplement practical efforts to counter the devastation of the Earth. Whether you carry out the spells alone or with like-minded friends and family, they will generate positive results over time, joining with the energies of spells and planetary healings carried out by people all over the world.

A spell for reversing global warming and pollution

Each individual spell you work releases positive energy against the ongoing destruction of the Earth's resources, so never feel that your ecological magic is disappearing down a black hole. It has taken two centuries (from the beginning of the Industrial Revolution) to build up to the present ecological crisis. It will take equally long to halt and then reverse it. But each spell, and each individual practical step, counts.

You will need

A globe (available from toy stores); a bowl of pure sparkling mineral water.

Timing

At the beginning of the month or year, in the morning, preferably when the light is bright.

The spell

* Stand the globe on a flat surface where it can turn freely, either near a window or, if it is fine, in the open air.
* Spin the globe deosil (clockwise) and let it come to a halt in its own time. Say:

The world turns. It supports life, the birds in the air, the fish in the sea and all who walk or run or crawl over the land. Why then should we damage our mother?

* Dip the index finger of your power hand (the one you write with) into the water. Using that finger, turn the globe once widdershins (anti-clockwise), as you do so saying:

So may destruction be halted and all harm reversed. Mother Earth, hear and be healed.

* Dip your finger and turn the globe five more times widdershins, as you do so, repeating the second chant.
* Finally, let the globe spin freely deosil and say as it turns:

Harm no more, despoil no longer, pollute, corrupt, slash, burn or litter Mother Earth. The world turns.

* Repeat the spell on the first of every month or whenever you hear of an ecological disaster.

A spell to help deal with an oil or chemical spillage at sea

An oil slick at sea can pollute many hundreds of miles of coastline, killing seabirds and marine life and ruining beaches for months or even years. Modern clean-up techniques are efficient, but small amounts of oil can still come ashore, continuing the pollution long after the original damage. Some marine life may never recover. In addition, toxins may have entered the food chain through affected fish and plants.

You will need

An oil burner; lemon, pine or mint essential oil.

Timing

When there is a disaster or potential spillage.

The spell

* Add five or six drops of essential oil to warm water in the burner.
* Light the burner and, as the oil heats and the perfume is released, say:

Be transformed to fragrance. Do not pollute, damage or injure bird, fish, sea creature nor shore. Be no more a danger. Leave all as before, living and clear.

* When the bowl of the oil burner is almost dry, add more warm water. Continue to do so until the fragrance fades.
* Blow out the flame, and when the oil burner is cool, clean it.

A second spell to help deal with an oil or chemical spillage at sea

You will need

Bath salts that do not contain chemicals (read labels carefully); lavender or rose essential oil; a rose- or lavender-fragranced candle.

Timing

When there is a disaster or potential spillage.

The spell

* Light the candle in the bathroom and place it where its light will be reflected into the water of the bath.
* Run a warm bath (but do not add the bath salts).
* Turn off the taps and add five or six drops of the essential oil, so that they float on the surface of the water.

* Get in the bath and swirl the oil, as you do so saying:
  Be dispersed, darkened waters.
  Far away may you be
  Absorbed by the sea.
* Add the bath salts to the bath and mix them with the oil, as you do so saying:
  Be dissolved; do no harm.
  Keep life safe in sea.
  May healing be granted
  That cleansed all may be.
* When you are ready, take the bath plug out. Let the foam and water flow away and leave the cold tap running until the bath is completely clear of oil and residue from the bath salts.

A weekly incense spell against pollution or destruction

Carry out this spell whenever you have half an hour in the evening. It will release positive energies into the cosmos to counter negative intentions or actions against the environment.

You will need

A stick of your favourite incense; a picture or poster of the place or species under threat; a CD of sounds connected with the endangered environment (for example rainforest sounds, dolphin song or birdsong).

Timing

In the evening.

The spell

* Place the picture or poster on the wall. Light the incense beneath it.
* While the incense burns, play the CD. Sit listening to it quietly, seeing images of the restored or untouched area.
* The following morning, carry out a small practical action to help an environmental concern in your own neighbourhood.

A spell to heal polluted oceans, rivers, lakes and streams

Ongoing water pollution from untreated sewage, wastes and chemicals continues in spite of legislation. In too many places, the sea, streams and rivers are not safe for our children to swim or paddle in. In some countries, drinking water is treated with so many chemicals that it rarely tastes good, while in others it still cannot safely be drunk from the tap, even in urban developments (see also the spell for clean water on page 634). This is a lovely new year's eve spell – and you can take the purified water to a water source on new year's day, making a wish for the planet for the coming year on dropping a few drops in.

You will need

A small bottle of pure still mineral or filtered water; a bottle of your favourite Bach Flower Remedy (optional); a clear quartz crystal small enough to fit in the bottle; a white candle.

Timing

After dusk.

The spell

* Wash the crystal well and leave it to dry naturally. Light the candle and open the bottle of water.
* Place the crystal in the bottle of water and add a drop of the Bach Flower Remedy if you are using it. Say:
  Be cleansed and clean; flow pure and wholesome; be filled with healing and blessing. You, the source of life, live once more.
* Put the lid on the bottle and leave the bottle next to the candle while it burns down.
* Place the water outdoors, leaving it there until the following noon.
* As soon as possible after noon, pour the water into a stream, a river or the sea, keeping the crystal in the bottle. Repeat the words as you pour.
* When the bottle is empty, bury the crystal on the shore.

An Earth spell for reforestation

This spell involves planting a tree. You might do this as part of a local tree planting day or in memory of a loved one (some charities have woodlands where you can do this). A tree can also mark a significant occasion such as a birth, a wedding or a house move. A fully grown birch tree provides enough oxygen for a family of four. The loss of rainforests has had a dramatic effect not just on the lives of those who lived in them (humans, wildlife and plants) but also on the health of the whole planet. The rainforests have been called the lungs of the Earth. Every tree planted, however small, has a symbolic as well as an actual significance.

You will need

A sapling and everything necessary to plant it.

Timing

Any.

The spell

* Plant your tree and then circle it slowly five times, as you do so saying in your head:
  For one tree planted, grow five, for five, ten and then a hundred. Thus shall the Earth be green again and breathe anew.

A Gaia or Mother Earth healing spell against all pollution

As I said on pages 623–4, Gaia, the ancient Greek Earth mother, has come to represent the Earth as a sentient being. Although we may prefer to cast our spells on wild seashores and in glorious forests, working in a local 'beauty' spot that has been defaced by litter or graffiti is a good use of our energies.

You will need

Enough stones, shells or branches to make a circle large enough to stand and turn in; a bag (a carrier bag from a supermarket will do); some gloves or a stick.

Timing

The evening before a partial or total lunar eclipse (consult a diary, the weather section of a newspaper or *Old Moore's Almanack*).

The spell

* Make a circle of the stones, shells or branches and stand in the centre.
* Raise your arms upwards vertically, with your palms flat and outstretched, until your arms are at a right-angle to your body. Say:

Gaia, Mother, I am sorry that this beautiful place has been polluted by your children. I call from the skies for healing and restoration to fall like rain and make all beautiful again.

* Turn nine times widdershins (anti-clockwise), still with your arms raised and your palms, flat, as you do so saying:

Undo what has been done in thoughtlessness, carelessness and indifference, that loveliness may return to this place once more.

* Leave the circle and, using the stick or gloves and the bag, pick up a few pieces of litter, as you do so repeating both chants in your head.
* When you get home, contact whoever owns the place to see how things might be improved, perhaps by the introduction of regularly cleared refuse bins or a group cleaning day.
* Return to the spot periodically, repeat the spell and pick up a little more litter each time. You may notice a gradual improvement within a relatively short period.

A spell to heal the ozone layer

The effects of global warming are as yet only partially understood, and there are many disagreements about the causes of the hole in the ozone layer. However, chloro fluoro carbons (or CFC gases) are implicated. In spite of legislation, the problem is increasing. This spell may seem fairly useless against such a huge problem. However, if enough people are working towards saving the planet magically as well as practically, in time these positive energies may cause the tide to turn, forcing cynical corporations and governments to tackle the issues before it is too late.

You will need

A high place away from buildings or trees; some sunflower seeds in a pouch or purse you can wear around your waist or neck.

Timing

Between noon and 3 pm.

The spell

* Stand as near to the top of the high place as possible and raise your arms over your head so they join in an arch. Say:
May the skies be healed.
* Return your hands to your sides and then repeat the arm-raising action and the chant six more times.
* Open your purse and turn slowly widdershins (anticlockwise), scattering seeds and saying:
May cynical minds be opened and pollution cease, Sunday, Monday, Tuesday, Wednesday, Thursday, Friday, Saturday, every day.
* Turn seven times deosil (clockwise), scattering more seeds and saying:
May those who care their power increase, Sunday, Monday, Tuesday, Wednesday, Thursday, Friday, Saturday, every day.
* Scatter the remaining seeds on your way down the hill. Most will be eaten by birds and animals, but some may take root and grow.

A spell to send protection to an endangered piece of land or species of plant, bird or animal

Chapter 36 of this book is devoted to absent healing, in which you focus on a person, creature or place and send healing light. This technique is effective as a defence when official or unofficial protests have failed to stop the destruction of land, perhaps for a road or for housing. You can carry out the spell alone or with others, each in your own home, at an agreed time on the day the destruction begins.

You will need

A picture, illustrated newspaper article or protest material showing the area and the creatures and flora under threat; a stick of rose or chamomile incense; an incense-holder; a white or beeswax candle; candles or a fibre optic lamp to shed light (optional); a glass bowl of water; a dish of fresh or dried petals; a piece of white fabric.

Timing

At noon, if possible in sunlight.

The spell

* Work in a pool of light. If there is no sunlight, create a circle of light using the candles or fibre optic lamp.
* Set the picture, article or protest material in the pool of light. Light the incense (to represent Air) and place it in its holder in front of the picture, article or protest material.
* Place the bowl of water (to represent Water) behind the picture, article or protest material, so that the light reflected in it shines on the picture.
* Light the white or beeswax candle (to

represent Fire) and set it to the left of the picture, article or protest material as you face it, so that it, too, reflects light on the picture.
* Place the dish of petals (to represent Earth) to the right of the picture, article or protest material.
* Sprinkle some of the petals over the picture, article or protest material, as you do so saying:
Within this circle four powers meet,
Fire, Earth, Water, Air.
Destruction follows without care.
But save, I ask, the creatures
And the plants growing there.
* Pass the smoke from the incense nine times around the pool of light, as you do so repeating the chant nine times.
* After the last chant, hold the incense above the circle, make a spiral of smoke and say:
Protect the innocent from the destruction
wreaked by humans in the name of progress.
* Plunge the incense stick, lighted end first, into the water, as you do so repeating the second chant.
* Leave the candle or candles to burn down, then pour the water away in to earth or down a flowing water source. Place the picture, article or protest material together with any loose petals on the white fabric and leave it where it can catch the light every day. Leave the dish of petals next to the picture. Scatter a few petals on the picture each day, as you do so repeating the second chant. When all the petals are gone, the spell is finished.

A spell for temporarily moving or turning an earth dragon around

'Dragon lines' is the name the Chinese give to positive lines of energy that flow through the earth, bringing peace and prosperity to the land. They can be seen over large areas of landscape as dragon outlines etched on to the various contours, complete with back, scales, head, tail and limbs. If an area of land is being carved up, for instance to construct a motorway, the Earth dragon must be persuaded to turn round (so that his tail, which will re-grow, is damaged rather than his head) or to move out of the way rather than trying to defend the territory. While local Earth groups will probably be carrying out rituals, individual power is also important. If enough people carry out rituals, the earth dragon will turn or move and life will one day come back to the area.

You will need
Some dried tarragon; a stick of dragon's blood incense; a clay model or drawing of a dragon.

Timing
In the weeks before the destruction is due and on the day the destruction begins.

The spell
* Go to the land under threat and encourage others to do so.
* Scatter a little dried tarragon, the dragon's herb, on to the grass in the area where you identify the dragon's head on the landscape.
* Ask the dragon softly to turn around or to move when the destruction begins, so that his power will be conserved for the hard task of bringing life back to the area afterwards.
* At dawn on the day work begins, light the stick of dragon's blood incense.
* Sprinkle a little tarragon over the clay model or drawing of the dragon, as you do so repeating your entreaty.

A spell to restore life to polluted or abandoned urban wasteland

If you live or work in a city, especially one where industry has declined, you may see areas of waste ground on which plants or flowers are trying to grow. Carry out the following spell at home, focusing on one particular piece of ground that you pass regularly.

You will need

A pot of your favourite culinary herb (for example sage or thyme); a stick of rose, chamomile or lavender incense; an incense-holder.

Timing

If possible, on a morning when it is or has been raining.

The spell

* Light the incense stick and, holding it in your power hand (the one you write with), circle the pot of herbs nine times, as you do so saying:

May the unlovely become filled with beauty, the abandoned be cared for and the wastelands grow.

* Write with incense smoke in the air over the pot of herbs a word or phrase that sums up your hopes for the unlovely place.
* Leave the incense in a holder to burn through.
* When you have time, plant the pot of herbs in or near the unloved place. You might choose an area behind a bus shelter, an abandoned concrete tub in front of your office or a children's playground that is mainly concrete and cigarette butts.
* Repeat the ritual in a week or so. Do not despair if the plant has been ripped up or died. Replace it. If you persist, seeds will take root in the earth and nature regenerate the land a little at a time.

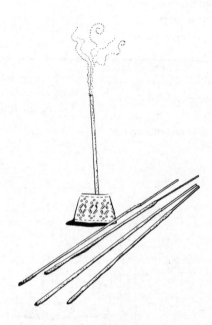

A five-candle spell to stop the Earth's resources being squandered

Waste is one of the most serious ways in which the Earth's resources are dissipated, be it over-packaging, dumping what could be recycled or fly-tipping in the countryside. This spell can be cast while you are relaxing after a long day and playing gentle music with an environmental theme. You can invite friends or family to join you. They can each light a candle and express their own environmental concerns.

You will need

5 fast-burning candles: a pure-white one, a green or brown one, a yellow one, a red or orange one, and a blue one; a small table or flat surface midway down each wall; a small table in the centre of the room; a taper.

Timing

In the evening.

The spell

❋ Light the white candle, place it in the centre of the room and say:
May the Earth's resources be conserved and squandered no more.

❋ Place the green or brown candle in the North (approximate directions are fine) and use the taper to light it from the central candle, as you do so repeating the chant. Name one area of waste that concerns you.

❋ Place the yellow candle in the East and use the taper to light it from the central candle, as you do so repeating the chant. Name another area of waste that concerns you.

❋ Place the red or orange candle in the South and use the taper to light it from the central candle, as you do so repeating the chant. Name another area of waste that concerns you.

❋ Place the blue candle in the West and use the taper to light it from the central candle, as you do so repeating the chant. Name another area of waste that concerns you.

❋ When all the candles are lit, repeat the chant and list in order all four concerns.

❋ Leave the candles to burn through while you relax and enjoy a light supper (choose unprocessed and raw or lightly cooked ingredients) and listen to music or, if with others, talk quietly.

❋ Consider one measure you can take but have not yet adopted to reduce waste or a local issue that you could become involved with.

❋ As each candle dies, repeat the chant, allowing the room to become darker.

53 SPELLS FOR THE HEALING AND REGENERATION OF RESOURCES

This final chapter of spells draws together many strands from earlier in the book. Healing and regeneration are two of the most important purposes of spells. What is more, as we focus on global and environmental issues, blessings fall unsought into our lives on a personal level.

One of the most important human resources is ancient wisdom. Much indigenous wisdom has continued in an unbroken tradition for hundreds, and in some cases thousands, of years. Though many indigenous cultures have been damaged, a number of them, notably the Native North American ones, are enjoying a revival. They have much to teach humanity about integration and responsibility for the Earth, and their revived ceremonies can enrich the spells and rituals of other lands.

Some of the spells in this chapter make use of natural spell-casting materials, such as sand and clay (symbols of rebuilding from the roots upwards). Others call upon angelic assistance in matters where humans seem to have reached an impasse.

Mother Earth is remarkably resilient, as are people and wildlife, so the spells end hopefully, as they began, with optimism and trust.

A soil fertility spell from the Andes

Among the Inca people of the Andes one of the most important festivals was held in August and was called the Rite of the Planting. The King would ritually break the soil to awaken the fertility of the Earth and to mark the symbolic union of King, as representative of the people, and Mother Earth, who was called Pachamama. This sealed the bargain by which the Earth would bring fertility to crops, people and animals, and in return would be offered tributes of the finest of the crops at the harvest. Among some tribes, gifts of gold were buried in the Earth at the time of planting. Christianised folk versions of these rites are still practised in Peru at the time of planting, while similar rituals appear in other cultures. Breaking the earth is a good way of ritually marking the beginning of a period of regeneration and planetary healing. It symbolically represents the breaking of the barrier between desire and the launching of the dream in reality.

You will need

A patch of relatively hard earth (or a large plant pot filled with soil – use a trowel to break it); a garden fork or spade; some water; some seeds or seedlings; an Earth crystal such as moss agate or jade, or a gold or silver earring, or a very thin metal ring.

Timing

At sunrise.

The spell

* Begin to dig, as you do so reciting:
  The Earth is our Mother. We wake her from her sleep. We call her fertility into our lives at this time of planting. Wake, Mother Earth, I have need of your gifts.
* When you have dug a hole, plant a few seeds or seedlings, saying in your head what you are planting in your life (both in terms of hopes for the planet and personally) and how you wish it to grow over the coming months. Talk as though to a kind wise mother.
* Pour a little water in to the hole and repeat the chant.
* Drop the crystal, earring or ring in to the hole, as you do so saying:
  I bring you gifts, Mother Earth, not only this crystal/gold/silver, but a promise to tend and care for you and all your creatures as fair exchange. Bless me likewise with growth and with fertility.
* Fill the hole and mark the spot where you planted the seeds or seedlings.
* Tend the seeds or seedlings regularly, and in addition – even if you live in a city – try to do something once a week, however small, to improve the environment.
* If the seeds or seedlings fail to grow, repeat the ritual, turning the soil gently and adding more of them. Even with magic, we sometimes have to accept that everything has its right time; if you persevere you will get there, even if the end results are not exactly as originally envisaged.

A sand spell for the regeneration of the Earth and her resources

One of the most simple forms of magic is to stand on sand by an ocean, lake or river and write with a stick you find there an image or words to represent what you wish to bring into being.

You will need

A sandy shore near the sea or a tidal river, or a sand box and a jug of water; a stick; shells, pebbles or seaweed.

Timing

Just before high tide if you are near tidal water, or just before dusk.

The spell

* With the stick, write a word or words to represent what you wish to regenerate, whether an area, an endangered species or something more general, such as the air quality.

* Enclose the words in a deosil (clockwise) circle of stones, shells or seaweed.

* If you are on the shore, watch the sea cover your message – if you wish, standing in the circle and feeling the sea tug it away. If you are working with a sand box, pour water over the words until they are gone. Say:

Water carry this from me,
From the rivers to the sea
That restoration there may be.

A second sand spell for the regeneration of the Earth and her resources

As well as by the sea or a river, you can also carry out this spell in a dry sandy place (or a children's sand pit large enough to walk round).

You will need

A sandy shore near the sea or a tidal river, or a sand box and a jug of water; a stick; shells, pebbles or seaweed.

Timing

Just before high tide if you are near tidal water, or just before dusk.

The spell

* With the stick, write a word or words to represent what you wish to regenerate, whether an area, an endangered species or something more general, such as the air quality.

* Enclose the words in a deosil (clockwise) circle of stones, shells or seaweed.

* Remove the circle by walking round and round it widdershins (anti-clockwise) and then inside it, erasing the word or words with your bare feet. As you do so, chant continuously:

Sand, I thus consign to thee
What it is I wish to be.
Though now invisible, gone to grains,
Within the sand the power remains.

A spell to create new life and growth after decay and destruction

In Africa, women make the vast majority of pots for everyday use. These pots have great magical significance as representations and containers of the life-giving powers of the potter and through her the Great Mother. In west Africa, the senior potter in a village is generally also the midwife. Focus this spell on a special environmental project, either local or global.

You will need

Some colourless modelling clay; some yellow candles (optional); some symbols of fertility, for example a few grains, nuts, olives or seeds.

Timing

In the morning, if possible in sunlight.

The spell:

* Work outside if possible. If there is no sunlight, light some yellow candles. Take a large ball of the clay and fashion a coil pot as a symbol of regeneration and new life. As you work, picture the golden light entering the clay and repeat:

Earth give birth,
Make of worth
This vessel of fertility.

* Name the special ecological project that is dear to your heart.
* Leave your pot to dry in the sun.
* When the pot is dry, place in it the symbols of fertility, repeating the chant and naming your project again.
* Each day add fresh fertility symbols to your pot, repeating the words and again naming the project.
* On the seventh day, bury the contents of the pot in the earth and keep the pot until it crumbles, when you should bury it too, to return the clay to the soil.

A Slavic Matka, or moist mother Earth, spell

Mata Syra Zjemlja, or Matka, is the Slavic Earth mother, whose name means 'moist mother Earth'. In Christian times she has become closely associated with the Virgin Mary. Indeed, one of her most important days, on which none may dig or plough, coincides with the Assumption of the Virgin Mary, on 15 August. She was not worshipped as a goddess but as the Earth itself.

You will need

A spade; a few seeds.

Timing

In spring.

The spell

* When you feel spring in the air, dig a very small furrow in a flower bed.
* Drop in a few seeds and cover the furrow over, as you do so asking for protection from illness and misfortune for yourself and your family, and adding a blessing for the Earth, that she may likewise be protected from harm.

A solitary or group ritual for Earth Day or any other environmentally significant occasion

On page 624 I write about Earth Day, but this ritual can be carried out on any environmentally significant day, for example the spring equinox. You can also use it to send concentrated power when there is a specific threat of environmental disaster. It is one of my favourite rituals and is wonderful if you can find an open-air labyrinth to perform it in.

You will need

Seeds or petals (optional).

Timing

In the morning.

The spell:

* Go to an open area and walk around it, allowing your feet to guide you. If you are working as a group, you can pre-arrange to walk in ever larger spirals or a deosil (clockwise) circle. as you begin to walk, chant three times:

I am the rain, and the rain falls and sanctifies me.

* If you are working in a group, the next person now repeats the rain chant three times and then chants the following chant three times. If you are working alone, chant both yourself:

I am the wind, and the wind blows and sanctifies me.

* If you are working in a group, the third person now repeats the rain and wind chant three times and then chants the following chant three times. If you are working alone, chant all yourself:

I am the sun, and the sun warms and sanctifies me.

* Keep walking and chanting according to this pattern, adding natural forces until no more come.

* Alone, in turn or in unison, name the powers in the order they were invoked and say:

Heal and bless the Earth, mother of us all.

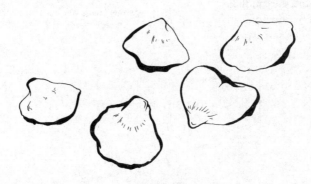

An Archangel Gabriel spell for regenerating the planet and the Earth's resources

On pages 680–2 I suggest ways you can use Archangel powers in rituals. All the Archangels can be invoked to lend their energy to planetary spells, but I have found Gabriel and Cassiel especially good. Although Gabriel's special concern is protecting water creatures and cleansing polluted waters, invoking him is effective whenever there has been destruction caused by war, greed, vandalism or exploitation. Sometimes called the Archangel of the Moon, the Messenger Archangel and the Heavenly Awakener, Gabriel is often pictured holding a sceptre or lily, clothed in silver or the blue of the night sky, with a mantle of stars and a crescent moon for his halo.

You will need

A silver-coloured candle; a moonstone; a stick of jasmine or mimosa incense.

Timing

On the new moon (especially the day before the crescent is visible in the sky), at dusk.

The spell

* Face the direction of the setting sun and light the candle and then the incense from the candle.
* Hold the moonstone in your open cupped hands and say:

Wise Gabriel, as the sun goes down, protect all Earth's creatures and places spoiled by war, greed or exploitation. May night heal and day reveal rebirth.

* Pass the moonstone carefully through the candle flame, as you do so repeating the words.
* Write in incense smoke over the stone:
Be healed and reborn.
* Set the moonstone between the candle and the incense while they burn through, so that the light and fragrance will enter the moonstone.
* In the morning, leave the moonstone near a window to absorb the light of day.
* Just after dark, hold the moonstone towards the moon (if it is now visible), turn it over three times and repeat the chant. Leave the moonstone near a window to absorb any moonlight.
* The following day, bury the moonstone in a local place where there is ugliness or vandalism.
* Repeat monthly, with a new moonstone each time, burying the new stone in another unlovely place, so that the Gabriel power spreads and grows from beneath the earth.

An Archangel Cassiel spell for the preservation and revival of ancient wisdom, especially from indigenous sources

Cassiel (see page 682) is the Archangel of stillness, compassion, contemplation, patience and balance. He is associated with the planet Saturn and so is a moderator of human excess. His effects are felt slowly but tend to be long-lasting. Cassiel is pictured in traditional magic with a beard and riding a dragon. However, you may find it easier to visualise him swathed in dark robes, with indigo flames in his halo and autumnal brown wings.

You will need

An indigo candle; a stick of patchouli, thyme or vetivert incense; an onyx, jet or obsidian crystal, or a round black stone or dark-coloured paperweight; some pure-white unlined writing paper; an envelope; a green or dark-red pen.

Timing

On Saturday evening, after dark.

The spell

* Light the candle and incense.
* Using the red or green pen and white paper, write your request to Cassiel for the regeneration of ancient wisdom (especially in any indigenous culture that has been partially destroyed), the conservation of old buildings and sacred sites, and the revival of interest in folklore. The letter can be as long as you wish.
* Sign your name and put the letter in the envelope. Leave the envelope blank.
* Pass incense smoke over the sealed letter in spirals and say:
  Cassiel, Archangel of Compassion, may this matter be completed in your time, not mine.
* Turn the letter over and drip just one drop of hot candle wax on the seal, as you do so saying:
  The matter is sealed, Lord Cassiel, and I wait with patience, knowing all is safe in your hands.
* When the wax is cool, turn the letter over once more and put the dark crystal, stone or paperweight on top of it.
* Leave the letter in candle light until the candle and incense are burnt through.
* Keep the letter in the bottom of your business or desk drawer and after a month put it with papers you are storing long-term.
* Read some old wisdom or folklore so you can share the knowledge with friends or family.

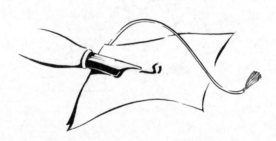

A spell for mutual exchange with the devas of the land

The term *deva* means 'shining one' in Sanskrit. Devas, or adhibautas, represent the higher forms of nature essences. Akin to angels, they are the opalescent beings who watch and direct the natural world. They communicate with people either through channelling or psychic communication, or directly through the healing and restorative properties of herbs, flowers and trees. Even if the idea seems strange, you can use the concept to work with the underlying creative patterns of nature.

You will need

A botanical garden, park or garden where flowers are growing; some seeds or seedlings.

Timing

When the weather is fine.

The spell

* Sit facing the flowers, either on the grass or on a blanket. Touch the earth or grass with your hands, pressing your palms down. Say six times:
Wise devas of the Earth mother, I offer my energies, as I take yours every day of my life.
* Lift your hands and then press them down again, palms down. Say six times:
Wise devas of the Earth mother, I offer my healing, as I take yours every day of my life.
* Lift your hands and then press them down again, palms down. Say six times:
Wise devas of the Earth mother, I offer you my protection, as I daily call on yours.
* Lift your hands and then press them down again, palms down. Say just once:
Wise devas of the Earth mother, I offer you my service and my blessings.
* Spend time among the flowers. When you go home, plant the seeds or seedlings. If possible, plant one of the flowers with which you worked in the devic energy exchange.

A spell to cleanse the planet of toxins

Toxic waste is one of the chief causes of pollution of the planet. How can a single spell help? If the fluttering of a butterfly's wing can subtly alter the energy of the universe, then carrying out a positive spell, can help to turn the tide.

You will need

A bowl of water; vegetable food dye in any dark colour.

Timing

On a Friday or Sunday, at the brightest time of the day.

The spell

⁕ Drop the food dye slowly onto the surface of the water, saying:

May pollution cease and toxins wash away.
Let the planet be pure once more.

⁕ Swirl the water until it turns dark and say:
Pollution will stop and toxins be washed away. They will not stay.

⁕ Pour the dark water away under running water, such as a cold tap in the sink, as you do so repeating:
May pollution stop and toxins wash away.
Let the planet be pure once more.
Continue until the bowl is quite clean and the tap water flows pure again.

⁕ When the water is clear, find out how you can help with the problem in a small way, perhaps by recycling your own waste.

A dough spell for the regeneration of the Earth's resources

One of the earliest principles of magic was absorbing energies through food. Hence the pre-Christian hot cross buns or cakes, marked with the astrological sign for the Earth, were sacred to the Earth mother, whose power you absorbed when you ate the bun or cake (see page 188). For this spell you can focus on a specific environmental concern or work for general regeneration and let the cosmos direct the energy to where it is most needed.

You will need

The ingredients to make a dough, or a packet mix.

Timing

On a Friday morning.

The spell

⁕ Working in a warm room, mix the ingredients thoroughly with your hands (even if you are using a packet mix), as you do so picturing the dough filled with light and saying softly and continuously:
Creating Mother, bring rebirth
To what is spoilt here on the Earth.

⁕ When you are ready, create out of the dough two featureless round, pregnant-looking Earth mothers with rounded breasts and belly.

⁕ Cook your Earth mothers. Eat one of them while it is still warm, to absorb the energies, and return the other to the earth.

⁕ Take an action, however small, to assist regeneration.

A Native North American Earth healing ritual

The revival of Native North American spirituality has greatly enriched other parts of the world. Although we cannot and should not try to recreate precise ceremonies, wisdom from this source can form a vital core for our own healing work. I think this is an appropriate final ritual for this book.

You will need
Sufficient stones or flowers to create a circle you can sit in.

Timing
Any.

The spell
* Using the stones or flowers, create a circle.

* Sit in the centre of the circle, reciting softly as a mantra the wise prayer of the late great medicine man, Black Elk, holy man of the Oglala Sioux, who was at the Massacre of Wounded Knee as a child:

Grandfather, Great Spirit, once more behold me on Earth and lean to hear my feeble voice. You lived first, and you are older than all need, older than all prayer. All things belong to you — the two-legged, the four-legged, the wings of the air, and all green things that live. You have set the powers of the four quarters of the Earth to cross each other. You have made me cross the good road and road of difficulties, and where they cross, the place is holy. Day in, day out, forever more, you are the life of things.

PART II

Spell-Casting – Creating Your Own Spells

Now that you have read, and perhaps tried casting, some of the spells in this book, you will probably want to create your own spells. This part of the book will give you detailed information about how to construct a spell. In Chapter 57 I have also suggested ways of casting one very special spell for yourself, to fulfil your dreams.

This part of the book includes information about the best times for different kinds of magic (such as the phases of the moon) and the meanings of different colours, herbs and so on, so that you can customise your spells to make use of exactly the right energies at the right time. Spell-casting is just like making a cake. You use a basic recipe, but then you add that special extra ingredient that makes that recipe from a bestselling cookery book uniquely your own. At first you learn the procedures and timings for success, but after a while you start to know instinctively whether to turn the oven up slightly or leave the cake for five minutes longer than the recipe suggests. It's the same with spell workings. The more you cast spells of your own, the more you will adapt pre-written ones (such as those in this book). You will know instinctively when to add an extra scoop of herbs or leave a candle burning instead of extinguishing it. You will suddenly feel that a particular moment is right – just as the moon appears from behind a cloud, the wind billows the trees in the garden or a rainbow arches over your office. You may find yourself dropping everything to take advantage of a moment that may not come again.

You can – and may frequently – carry out homemade spells with what is to hand: a white kitchen candle, some salt and a pot plant. When you have ten minutes of unexpected peace and quiet and a pressing need for some magical input into your world, spontaneous spell-casting is absolutely unbeatable. However, spell-casting is also a good way of marking out your own time and space.

Try to carry a notebook and pen around with you, as ideas for spells can materialise anywhere – when you are walking the dog, doing the shopping or travelling to work. (My daughter, Miranda, created a spell when her train was stuck for an hour between Basingstoke and London Waterloo to stop people bellowing into their mobile phones.) In formal magic, this kind of book is known as a Book of Shadows. You can also use it to make a note of any new crystals or flowers you have worked with, as well as recording your own spells and your adaptations of mine. In time your spell journal will swell the living tradition of magic and some day be a wonderful gift for a son, daughter or younger relative who expresses an interest in magic.

As you weave your own spells, perhaps using some of mine to give you ideas, you will become more powerful and confident in your daily life, more intuitive and spiritually aware.

54 THE BASICS

reating your own spells is remarkably easy, and the steps I suggest in this chapter are just guidelines. You may decide to plan a spell in detail, working out in advance where and when you will carry it out and what you and anyone else joining you will say or do. But spontaneous spells should also have a place in your magical repertoire. If you are suddenly moved by a beautiful sunset on a seashore or a rainbow in an urban park, you will find you instinctively use the right words and actions to create a spell with sticks and stones or just your imagination.

As you continue to work with magic, you will become increasingly aware that what you once regarded as junk – at car boot or garage sales, markets and tourist shops at holiday resorts – is essential magical equipment. Glass fruit bowls, Gothic-style candle-holders, small charms, toy cars, statues – all of these are useful materials for your magical store.

Most towns have at least one good New Age store. If what you need is not in stock, the staff will often be prepared to order it for you if you are carrying out an important ritual. If you live in a remote area, there are a number of good companies online who will supply you by mail order. Those that specialise in only one or two kinds of product generally offer the highest quality and the best value.

Trade and craft markets are ideal for buying beeswax candles and candles with the colour all the way through (as opposed to those that are dipped). You will also find lavender bags, dried rose petals, ribbons and items such as tiny dolls and hand-crafted cords for knot spells.

An old fashioned grocery or delicatessen may sell a wealth of loose herbs and dried flowers. A herbal pharmacy is another good source of unusual dried herbs and spices, while at arboretums, botanical gardens and independent garden centres you will find experts who love talking about different plants and can guide you to seasonal varieties. Whether or not you have a garden, you can grow pots of herbs for spells and to release ongoing positive magical energies into your home and workplace. And don't forget the local supermarket. This may be a treasure house of culinary dried herbs and spices, scented candles, pot pourri, natural bath products and, increasingly, incenses and essential oils.

How to write and cast a spell

The following questions should be considered when you are planning a spell. If you are new to spell-casting, you may find it useful to make a note of the ones that are relevant to your particular spell. (Even an experienced practitioner may find it helpful to consider the structure of spells that have become second nature.)

Making preparations

1. What is the spell for?

Spend time identifying precisely what you are asking for and the way in which you hope or expect the wish will manifest.

2. What is your time scale?

Do you anticipate results 'by the time this moon is through', 'when the leaves are on the trees' or in an unspecified period? Does the spell need to be repeated daily for a week, monthly, when the need arises or when the fragrance of a spell bag fades?

3. What is the focus of the spell?

Most spells focus on a central symbol. Such a symbol might be, for example, a crystal that is empowered and carried as a talisman after the spell, a purse of herbs, a plant that is sent after the spell to someone who is ill, a lucky charm, a tree, a written message or a tarot card. Consider what is most suitable for your own spell. Do you already have a relevant symbol in your personal magical collection or do you need to order, buy or find one? If this proves difficult or you need to do the spell in a hurry, is there a suitable substitute – or do you want to wait and go for the more special option? If you want to use melted wax as a symbol, work with a wax rather than a church candle.

4. What other materials do you need for the spell?

Are you using the elemental substances – salt (Earth), incense (Air), a candle (Fire) and water (Water). What fragrance should the incense be? What colour should the candle be? Should it be slow-burning? Should the water be sparkling, still, from a tap, rainwater or water or made sacred with salt? Should it be left out in sun- and moonlight for a period before the spell? If you are using coins for a money spell, what metal should they be? How many do you need? You might like to write a checklist before you perform the spell.

5. Can you add significance by use of colour or fragrance?

If you refer to pages 690–7, you will see that each plant and incense has a magical meaning. By using specific fragrances – for example rose or lavender for gentle love, or ginger or rosemary for passion – you can make a spell more focused. You can also mix and match, for example, using one lavender and one ginger incense stick if you want a considerate but exciting lover. Similarly, the colours that you choose are significant, a pink candle being more appropriate for tender love and a red one for unbridled passion.

6. What accessories do you need?

Think through the spell. Will you need bowls for salt or water, or holders for incense and candles? If so, how many and how large? Do you need spoons? If you are burning something in a candle, is the holder fireproof and sufficiently large to hold the burnt material. If you need a pool of wax, will the melted candle be able to flow freely enough to form one? If you are using a smudge stick, do you need a holder for when you are not holding it? Do you need matches or a taper? Do you need pens, paper, knives or scissors? Do you have spares?

7. Where will you carry out the spell?

Can you carry out the spell on a table indoors? Will the table need a cloth, or a fireproof tray? Will you need extra lighting, such as lamps and candles? Where will they be positioned? Do you want to create a special place for casting spells that you can leave partly ready and that will be undisturbed? If you are working outdoors, is there a flat rock or surface you can work on? Is there a sheltered place so that outdoor incense, garden torch candles or smudge sticks will stay alight? Do you have spares in case candles go out? Do you need to go to a special place such as the sea and use the natural materials found there? If so, do you need to take a small rucksack with any crystals, coins, flowers, matches, candles and so on?

8. What about safety?

Whether you are working indoors or out, is there somewhere you can leave candles to burn down safely? Where can you safely make a fire – a hearth indoors, a barbecue or bonfire pit, a metal bucket filled with sand? Are you happy that candles, smudge sticks and incense sticks won't set fire to soft furnishings or to your sleeves? Do you know what to do if this does happen? (Cut off the air supply to a candle or oil. Don't pour water over oil or wax, but you can pour it over incense.) How can you carry out a spell in a beauty spot without causing damage or danger, for example if you are using fire near trees or dry undergrowth? Do you need to modify the spell accordingly?

Structuring the spell

9. How many people will be casting the spell?

Will you be casting the spell alone or together with family friends or a group? Will you be working with a person you are healing? Will the spell need planning and leading or will it happen spontaneously? (A rough plan of who does/says what may be useful to avoid awkward gaps and interruptions.)

10. When will the spell be cast?

Does the spell require a particular day, season, phase of the moon or phase of the sun (see pages 671–80)? Is there a special day whose angelic or planetary influence would be helpful (see pages 680–2)? If it is a two- or three-day or a weekly spell, what beginning and ending days are best for the energies? Is the schedule feasible? Will getting up at seven dawns really suit your lifestyle or would it be better to start the spell at the weekend, beginning at dawn on the first day and moving the start time to whenever you usually wake for the remaining days?

11. How will the spell evolve?

Go through the five stages discussed on pages 11–12 and consider how these can be naturally encompassed in your spell. How will you begin? How will you raise and release the power? Should you plan a chant and movements in advance or let everything unfold of its own accord? Will your spell have distinct different stages at all or will they merge? Occasionally, you may want your spell to fade into stillness and silence, in which case you will slow down rather than build up to a climax.

12. Do you need any psychic protection?

If you are working a quick simple spell, will you be relying simply on your own innate protective radar or your guardian angel to keep you safe? (This would be quite adequate.) If you are carrying out a more complex ritual, or one in which you are banishing anger or sadness, do you want to cast a circle or light protective candles round the room (see pages 13 and 683–4). If you are carrying out a formal ritual or one in which you are releasing negativity, do you want to cleanse the working area before you begin, for example by sprinkling dried lavender on the floor and then sweeping or vacuuming it up in widdershins (anticlockwise) circles? If you are working outdoors or in an uncarpeted area, would you prefer to dip a long twig in water and sprinkle the drops over the area you will be working in (called 'asperging')? If you are working on a carpet, do you want to sprinkle a few drops of perfume on the carpet before the spell?

Getting ready

13. Can you begin the spell at the appointed time and carry it through smoothly?

Is everything you need set out in the working area, so that you don't have to stop to look for matches or find that you can't get the lid off the herbs in the middle of a chant? Check from the list you drew up earlier where everything should be.

14. What about personal preparations?

Are you happy performing the spell in your oldest jeans or your smartest city suit (perfectly acceptable if circumstances dictate) or would you prefer to change into something loose and comfortable that you keep for spell-casting (as opposed to walking the dog)? Do your clothes have drapy sleeves or hems that could catch in candle flames? Would you feel more relaxed and less everyday if, before casting the spell, you had a bath in lavender- or rose-scented water? Would it help to spend five minutes before the spell gazing into a candle flame and breathing gently and rhythmically? Have you turned off mobile phones and so on and arranged things so that you won't be disturbed except in an emergency? (If you are working with others, this quiet pre-spell time may be spent sitting in a circle, perhaps focusing on a central candle or crystal in the centre. This will help you all to merge your energies and move away from the everyday world.) However, don't let the need for preparations constrain you. You may hit a spell head-on when you have only five minutes before collecting a child from school. I have cast some of my best spells on the wing.

The spell

15. Are you in position to begin the spell?

Do you know where the relevant directions are in relation to the table on which you are working? (Use a compass beforehand or guess at approximate positions from known geographical locations – when I am at home on the Isle of Wight, East is always Ryde High Street.) Are the elemental substances in the right place (Earth in the North, Air in the East, Fire in the South and Water in the West)? Can you walk round the table you are using for the spell and can you easily reach everything you need? Do you know where anyone else involved will be standing and, if you are having a circle, where you intend to start casting it from? Which way will you face? North is the most popular direction for magic, but you may alternatively start facing East if you are working with the rising sun or the spell is for new beginnings; South if you need full power; or West if you are working with the setting sun or performing letting go magic.

16. How will you begin the spell?

Will you simply light the candles and incense? If you are carrying out a formal ritual, will you ring a bell three times at each of the four main directions (beginning in the North and going deosil – clockwise)? Will you greet the four directions, facing outwards to speak to the guardians of the North, East, South and West in turn (sometimes known as the Guardians of the Watchtowers), asking for their blessing and welcoming them? If you are working with other people, should one person stand at each direction, turning outwards and greeting the individual guardian? If your spell is less formal, will you stand and hold the focus over the centre of the table, stating the purpose of the spell and asking for help and protection in your work from an Archangel or your favourite deity? At this point, don't forget to state the obvious, saying aloud that your spell is being carried out with the purest purpose and for the highest good.

17. How will you carry the spell through?

Once you have begun the action you planned (for example, chanting, moving or adding water to a substance), relax and let it all happen. A spell is not a test of memory or your ability to follow rules. It comes from the heart, and if it changes completely during casting from what you planned, then you know your unconscious wisdom is taking control and the spell will be very powerful.

18. How will you close the spell?

If you greeted the guardians at the beginning of the spell, you should thank and bid each of them goodbye in turn, starting in the West and ending in the North. If you rang a bell three times at the four directions, you should repeat the ringing, this time starting in the West and finishing in the North. If you cast a circle, you should slowly uncast it (see page 684). If your spell was less formal, how will you thank whoever protected you? Will you do this spontaneously or will you pre-arrange some words? Finally, you should say, 'The spell is ended. Blessed be!'.

After the Spell

19. How will you clear up and dispose of what is no longer needed?

Clearing up together is a good way of bonding with those you have worked with. If you worked alone, it will help you settle yourself back into everyday life after the spell. Will you need to bury any items? Will you need to throw things away in a special place? Dispose of what must be disposed of quietly and respectfully, even if you are putting candle wax in the garbage.

20. How will you ground yourself and return to the world?

Will you eat a light meal, sharing it with those you worked with if your spell was performed in a group? Will you go for a walk in nature? Will you do some kind of physical work or exercise to bring your awareness back into your body? Will you walk barefoot on the grass? Will you do some gardening or listen to gentle music? If it is still early, take a small practical step towards bringing your wish into reality by earthly means (if it is late, do this in the morning).

21. How will you learn from the spell?

Either during the evening or the next morning (while the spell is still fresh in your mind), write down any chants you created or actions you carried out that were especially effective, together with the names of any herbs or incenses that were very evocative. You can also note ways in which you might modify or develop the spell in future. Write down the date and time of working so that you can monitor results and will have a record of when (if at all) you need to follow up the spell.

55 MAGICAL TIMES, PLACES AND POWERS

The following information is not intended as a full magical course but to offer guidance as to the best times and places to cast your own spells. If you want more detailed and in-depth information, my *A Practical Guide to Witchcraft and Magick Spells*, Quantum, 2001, includes much magical background knowledge and a variety of techniques. You will also find useful material on my website, www.cassandraeason.co.uk. In addition, I run workshops and private classes on magic and ritual, mainly in the UK and Sweden. Details of these, too, can be found on my website, as well as on the Swedish www.planet.se.

The moon

This is perhaps the single most important influence on magical timings. The three phases of the moon represent different kinds of energy, and you should choose a phase appropriate to your spell. For projects that will take months or even a year or more to bring to fruition, you can repeat a wish or empowerment nightly during each waxing moon period.

The waxing (or increasing) moon

From when the crescent first appears in the sky to the day the full moon rises. The light increases from right to left during this period. The closer to the full moon, the more intense the energies.

Use the waxing moon for ...
* Making a new beginning
* Working towards a longer-term goal
* Improving health
* Gradually increasing prosperity
* Attracting good luck
* Enhancing fertility
* Finding friendship, new love and romance
* Hunting for a job
* Making plans for the future
* Increasing psychic awareness

The full moon

Strictly speaking, the moon is only full at the second it rises; thereafter it wanes. In practice, however, the moon is considered to be full from moon rise to moon set on the night of the full moon. The hours immediately around that period and also, to a lesser extent, the following day can also be counted as part of the full moon period. The day of the full moon is the day of full power, but also of instability, as – astrologically – the Moon is in opposition (or in the opposite side of the sky) to the sun.

Use the full moon for ...

* Fulfilling an immediate need
* Boosting power or courage immediately
* Changing career or location
* Travelling
* Protecting psychically
* Healing acute medical conditions
* Raising a large sum of money needed urgently
* Consummating love
* Making a permanent love commitment
* Ensuring fidelity, especially in a relationship that is looking shaky
* Bringing about justice
* Fulfilling ambition
* Gaining promotion

The waning (or decreasing) moon

The moon decreases from right to left until, finally, the crescent disappears from the left. About two and a half days later the crescent reappears on the right. The two and a half days when the moon is not visible in the sky (sometimes known as 'the dark of the moon') mark the beginning of the new moon. Magic is rarely performed when the moon is dark. Waning moon magic should not be thought of as dark or negative but rather a process of bidding farewell to what is no longer wanted or helpful.

Use the waning moon for ...

* Removing pain and sickness
* Removing obstacles to success and happiness
* Lessening negative influences
* Reducing the hold of addictions and compulsions
* Banishing negative thoughts, grief, guilt, anxiety and destructive anger
* Banishing the envy and malice of others
* Ending relationships gently

The sun

There are four main sun times that are used magically: dawn, noon, dusk and midnight. Sun magic is faster and more intense than moon magic and is good for moving matters rapidly.

Dawn

The time of dawn varies each day (the precise time can be found in *Old Moore's Almanack*, a diary or the weather section of a newspaper). Dawn is associated with the East and with spring, and is represented in ritual by facing East. However, since the sun in fact rises in the true East (and sets in the West) only on the equinoxes (because of the tilt of the Earth), you may wish to work with its actual position in the sky at daybreak.

Use dawn magic for ...
* Creating new beginnings
* Initiating a project
* Creating hope
* Stirring up positive energies at a time when life is going badly
* Improving health
* Improving career prospects
* Bringing good fortune
* Improving financial matters
* Bringing new love and trust

Noon

'Be not sad; be as the sun at midday' says a passage in the I Ching. Noon represents the South and summer. These energies are similar to those of the full moon, but more concentrated. The full moon will give you more enduring power.

Use noon magic for ...
* Creating a sudden burst of power, confidence, strength or passion
* Bringing a fast infusion of money
* Sending absent healing for serious or acute conditions

Dusk

The time of dusk also varies from day to day. Dusk corresponds with the West and with autumn.

Use dusk magic for ...
* Letting go of the regrets of the day or of your life
* Completing unfinished tasks or issues
* Reducing pain and illness
* Reducing debt
* Bringing love in maturity
* Bringing justice and just reward

Midnight

This is an important sun time, as it corresponds with the beginning of the new day. Midnight is associated with the North and with winter.

Use midnight magic for ...

* Overcoming grief and sorrow
* Contacting wise ancestors
* Bindings and banishings of all kinds

The seasons

Seasonal rituals are slower-acting than both sun and moon spells, but they have long-lasting results. Each season represents a quadrant, or quarter, of the Wheel of the Year. The seasonal timings given in this book refer to the Northern Hemisphere. If you live in the Southern Hemisphere, you will need to add six months to the timing stated.

Spring

* From the spring equinox (on or around 21 March) to the summer solstice (on or around 21 June)
* Direction: East
* Colour: yellow
* Quadrant: Air, which promises the impetus for change and growth
* Plants: celandine, cinquefoil, crocus, daffodil, honeysuckle, primrose, sage, tansy, thyme, violet
* Ingredients: eggs, spring flowers, leaves in bud, sprouting pots of seeds, pottery or china rabbits, birds, feathers

The spring, or vernal equinox, marks the transition point between the dark and light halves of the year. At the spring equinox, the sun rises due East and sets due West, giving exactly 12 hours of daylight and 12 hours of darkness. At this time, the first eggs of spring were painted and offered on the shrine of the Anglo Saxon Goddess Eostre and the Norse Ostara, to whom the hare was sacred. Bonfires were lit and the corn dolly of the previous harvest (or in Christian times a Judas figure) was burned on the Easter fires. The ashes were scattered on the fields for fertility.

Use spring magic for ...

* Bringing new hope
* Creating new beginnings
* Starting new relationships
* Enhancing fertility (in all its aspects)
* Working with pregnancy, babies and children
* Working for new-flowering love

Summer

* From the summer solstice (on or around 21 June) to the autumn equinox (on or around 21 September)
* Direction: South
* Colour: red
* Quadrant: Fire, which promises dynamic results, inspiration and success for any venture
* Plants: chamomile, elder, fennel, lavender, St John's wort, verbena
* Ingredients: brightly coloured flowers; oak boughs; golden fern pollen (said to reveal buried treasure wherever it falls); gold-coloured coins; orange or red candles; scarlet, orange or yellow ribbons

The summer solstice marks the high point of the year. It is the longest day and is the zenith of summer magic. Modern Druids still celebrate this festival of light with ceremonies at midnight, dawn and noon, beginning on the eve of the solstice. Traditionally, great fire wheels are rolled down the hillsides in honour of the triumph of the sun god.

Use summer magic for ...

* Achieving success, in career and otherwise
* Working for happiness
* Maximising strength
* Resolving issues of identity
* Creating wealth
* Enhancing fertility
* Working for travel
* Working for adolescents and young adults

Autumn

* From the autumn equinox (on or around 21 September) to the winter solstice (on or around 21 December)
* Direction: West
* Colour: blue
* Quadrant: Water, which augurs well for rituals of reconciliation and harmony, both within oneself and with others
* Plants: fern, geranium, myrrh, pine, Solomon's seal
* Ingredients: coppery, yellow or orange leaves; willow boughs; harvest fruits such as apples; pottery or china geese; woven knots of corn, wheat or barley; dried grasses; copper or bronze coins

The autumn equinox was traditionally celebrated as the 'second green', or harvest of vegetables, fruit and any remaining crops, and was also known as 'harvest home'. (The first corn harvest was at the beginning of August.) The autumnal harvest supper pre-dates Christianity. On the day when equal hours of darkness and light heralded winter, this feast constituted a sympathetic magical gesture. By displaying and consuming the finest of the harvest, the celebrants sought to ensure that there would be enough food during the winter.

Use autumn magic for …

* Bringing to fruition long-term goals
* Reaping the benefits of earlier input
* Enhancing relationships, especially concerning the family, adult children, brothers and sisters, and friendships
* Ensuring material security

Winter

* From the winter solstice (on or around 21 December) to the spring equinox (on or around 21 March)
* Direction: North
* Colour: green
* Quadrant: Earth, which promises rest, regeneration, wisdom and psychic awareness
* Plants: bay, cedar, feverfew, holly, juniper, pine, rosemary
* Ingredients: evergreen boughs (especially pine or fir), red and green candles, small logs (especially oak and ash) found naturally

Celebration of the winter solstice pre-dates organised religion. When early humankind saw the sun at its lowest point and the vegetation dead or dying, they feared that light and life would never return, so they lit great bonfires from logs, hung torches from trees and decorated their homes with evergreens to persuade the other greenery to grow again. This mid-winter magic forms the origins of Christmas festivals around the globe.

Use winter magic for …

* Removing unwanted influences
* Ending redundant phases
* Making long-term money plans
* Working for the home
* Working for older members of the family

The tides

The tides can be used to work magically for the sea or any other body of water.

The in-coming tide

This tide heralds new beginnings. Use a sharp stone to engrave on a second stone what you want to begin – a relationship, a new job or even a new approach to a problem. Throw both stones as hard as you can into the in-coming tide and see yourself taking that first step towards happiness or success.

The turning tide

This tide harnesses the full power of the sea and can be used when you need to make a tremendous leap in your life or when you have taken the first steps in a new venture or relationship but don't seem to be getting anywhere. As the tide turns, throw a symbol of what you desire on to the waves – for example, fruit for fertility, a coin for wealth, flowers for love, a toy boat for travel, a key for a new home, an old car key for a new car or the name of a desired lover carved on a stone.

The out-going tide

This tide is good for kicking bad habits or redundant relationships. Using a sharp stone, engrave on a second stone what you want to off-load – a habit, a relationship, a responsibility. Cast the second stone in to the out-going tide and watch what you no longer want receding with it. Bury the first stone.

The planets and the days of the week

Each of the planets rules a day of the week. You can use its associated metals, incense and so on to strengthen a spell worked on that day.

The sun/Sunday ☉

* Element: Fire
* Colour: gold
* Crystals: amber, carnelian, diamond, clear crystal quartz, tiger's eye, topaz
* Incense: cloves, cinnamon, frankincense
* Trees: bay, birch, laurel
* Herbs and oils: juniper, rosemary, saffron, St John's wort
* Metal: gold
* Astrological rulership: Leo

Sunday, the day of the sun, is good for spells for personal fulfilment, ambition, power and success. It will help to increase the flow of the life force, enabling you to assert or strengthen your identity and individuality. Use the sun for innovation of all kinds and new beginnings. It is potent also for energy, joy, health, prosperity, spiritual awareness and self-confidence. It will bring wealth and prosperity where there is poverty and failure and will help to break a run of bad luck. The sun is for all matters concerning fathers.

The moon/Monday ☽

* Element: Water
* Colour: silver or white
* Crystals: moonstone, mother of pearl, pearl, selenite, opal
* Incense: jasmine, myrrh, mimosa
* Trees: willow, alder
* Herbs and oils: chamomile, lotus, poppy, wintergreen
* Metal: silver
* Astrological rulership: Cancer

Monday, the day of the moon, is good for spells concerning the home and family matters, especially the mother, children and animals. Its prime focus is fertility, and it rules over all the ebbs and flows of the human body, mind and psyche. The moon will provide protection, especially while travelling, and will aid psychic development, clairvoyance and meaningful dreams. It is potent for all sea and gardening rituals and for herb magic and healing – as well as for keeping secrets.

Mars/Tuesday ♂

* Element: Fire
* Colour: red
* Crystals: garnet, bloodstone, ruby, jasper
* Incense: dragon's blood, ginger, mint, thyme
* Trees: cypress, holly, pine
* Herbs and oils: basil, coriander, garlic, pepper, tarragon
* Metal: iron, steel
* Astrological rulership: Aries (co-ruler of Scorpio)

Tuesday, the day of Mars, is good for spells for courage, change, self-assertion, taking the initiative, independence and separateness from others. Mars is the Roman warrior god, and also represents aggression, competitiveness and anger, all qualities that can be used positively for altruistic purposes such as standing out against injustice and protecting loved ones or the vulnerable when they are under threat. Mars can be used to overcome seemingly impossible odds, to defeat opposition and to enhance health and vitality. This planet also rules over passion and the consummation of love.

Mercury/Wednesday ☿

* Element: Air
* Colour: yellow
* Crystals: agate, citrine, falcon's eye, jasper, malachite, onyx
* Incense: lavender, lemongrass, mace
* Trees: hazel, ash
* Herbs and oils: dill, fennel, parsley, valerian
* Metal: aluminium, mercury
* Astrological rulership: Gemini, Virgo

Wednesday, the day of Mercury, is good for spells for money-making ventures, clear communication, persuasion, adaptability and versatility, improving memory and sharpening logic, learning, examinations and tests, mastering new technology, short-distance travel and short breaks, and conventional methods of healing, especially surgery. It is also potent for business negotiations, overcoming debt, and repelling envy, malice, spite and deceit. Mercury is a fleet-footed messenger god who carries the healing caduceus, a staff with entwined serpents.

Jupiter/Thursday ♃

* Element: Air
* Colour: blue, purple
* Crystals: azurite, lapis lazuli, sodalite, turquoise
* Incense: agrimony, cedar, sandalwood, sage
* Trees: beech, oak
* Herbs: borage, cinquefoil, coltsfoot, hyssop, mistletoe
* Metal: tin
* Astrological rulership: Sagittarius (co-ruler of Pisces)

Thursday, the day of Jupiter, is good for all forms of increase and expansion, be it in the realm of money, career, power or joy. Jupiter rules over fulfilment of objectives, most usually those that are socially orientated. He is also potent for leadership, conscious wisdom, creativity, extending one's influence in the wider world, idealism, justice and the law, authority and altruism. Jupiter's influence extends over marriage, permanent relationships (business and personal), fidelity, loyalty and male potency (in both the human and the animal kingdom). Jupiter can lead to excesses, such as greed and gluttony, but can also, paradoxically, be used for banishing these.

Venus/Friday ♀

* Element: Earth
* Colour: green, pink
* Crystals: amethyst, emerald, jade, moss agate, rose quartz
* Incense: geranium, rose, strawberry, vervain
* Trees: almond, apple, birch
* Herbs: and oils: feverfew, mugwort, pennyroyal, verbena, yarrow
* Metal: copper
* Astrological rulership: Taurus, Libra

Friday, the day of Venus, is associated with love and all forms of love magic (especially to attract love). Venus is also invoked for beauty, the arts, crafts, relationships, friendships, blossoming sexuality, the acquisition of beautiful possessions, and the slow but sure growth of prosperity (Venus rules all matters of growth). Like the moon, she can be invoked for horticulture, the environment, fertility and women's health matters. Since she can be associated with excessive and unwise love affairs, her spells can, paradoxically, be used to reduce the influence of destructive lovers and possessiveness.

Saturn/Saturday ♄

* Element: Earth
* Colour: black, grey
* Crystals: haematite, jet, lodestone, obsidian, smoky quartz
* Incense: aconite, cypress, patchouli
* Tree: blackthorn, yew
* Herbs: aspen, bistort, comfrey, horsetail, Solomon's seal
* Metal: lead, pewter
* Astrological rulership: Capricorn (co-ruler of Aquarius)

Saturday, the day of Saturn, is potent for spells concerned with unfinished business, with endings that lead to beginnings. It is a good day for all slow-moving matters and for accepting limitations, as well as for overcoming obstacles that are long-standing or need careful handling. It can also be used for lifting depression or doubts, meditation, long-term psychic protection, locating lost objects (as well as animals and people) and regaining self-control over bad habits or emotions. Saturn can be used to slow down the outward flow of money and to encourage those who owe you favours or money to repay. He will help banish pain and illness and bring acceptance of what cannot be changed. Saturn is in a sense the shadow side of Jupiter – in other words, the reality factor. He represents the constraints of fate, time and space, but can also turn challenge into opportunity, if you are prepared to work hard and persevere.

Archangels

The seven Archangels figure in various magical and religious traditions, and their attributes vary accordingly. The following are the most commonly accepted correspondences, and are the ones that have been most generally adopted in magic. You can use the Archangels as a focus for any spell, even if it is not their own day, by using their associated candle colour, crystals and incenses.

Michael

* Archangel of: the sun and Sunday
* Candle colour: gold
* Crystals: citrine, pure crystal quartz
* Incense: frankincense, orange

Michael, the initiator, brings illumination and inspiration in many spheres of life, through the efforts of our individual creative spirit. He is the guardian of all who stand alone with their unique vision for bettering the world and are not prepared to compromise their ideals for the sake of money or fame. He can be invoked in ritual for creative ventures; original ideas and individuality; contact with deities, the higher self or spirit guides; the revival of barren land despoiled by industrialisation; and the cleansing of air pollution. In a magic circle, Michael may be invoked as guardian of the South.

Gabriel

* Archangel of: the moon and Monday
* Candle colour: silver
* Crystals: moonstone, opal
* Incense: myrrh, jasmine

Gabriel, the integrator, brings increased spiritual awareness, mystical experiences, astral travel and significant dreams. He offers spirituality within the family and work environment. He can be invoked for protection against inclement weather, travel across water, removal of sorrow and diminution of self-destructive tendencies – replacing them with the gentle growth of new hope. Gabriel also rules rituals to protect water creatures and to cleanse polluted seas, lakes and rivers. In a magic circle, Gabriel may be invoked as guardian of the West.

Samael

* Archangel of: Mars and Tuesday
* Candle colour: red
* Crystals: garnet, bloodstone
* Incenses: allspice, dragon's blood

Samael, the avenger, is the angel of cleansing and of righteous anger. He offers protection to the weak and vulnerable, and cleanses doubts and weaknesses, replacing them with the spiritual courage to stand against what is corrupt, especially abuse of power. Samael can be invoked in rituals to relieve those in war-torn lands and to protect minorities who are being oppressed. He can also be called upon for the protection of endangered species. Samael is closely associated with the Archangel Uriel (who brought alchemy to humankind). Indeed, the associations above apply equally to either Archangel. In a magic circle, Samael (or more often his counterpart Uriel) may be invoked as guardian of the North.

Raphael

* Archangel of: Mercury and Wednesday
* Candle colour: yellow
* Crystals: citrine, yellow jasper
* Incense: lavender, clover

Raphael, the harmoniser, offers healing of all kinds, as well as protection to children. He guides and sustains all travellers (emotional and spiritual as well as physical), particularly those who are lost. He can be invoked in all health matters and will heal technological and chemical pollution, together with the adverse effects of modern living. He provides spiritual knowledge and insight and alleviates the worries of daily life that keep us bound to the Earth. Most importantly, he shows us how to teach others our own spiritual insights. In a magic circle, Raphael may be invoked as guardian of the East.

Sachiel

* Archangel of: Jupiter and Thursday
* Candle colour: blue
* Crystals: lapis lazuli, turquoise
* Incense: sandalwood, sage

Sachiel, the divine benefactor, is the angel of charity. He works constantly to help others and to improve the lives of humankind. He can therefore be invoked in all rituals to bring better harvests (both physical and emotional) and to increase abundance and prosperity – not just for a minority but for the good of all. He restores run-down areas where unemployment is great, blending new skills with traditional knowledge.

Anael

* Archangel of: Venus, Friday
* Candle colour: green
* Crystals: jade, rose quartz
* Incense: valerian, rose

Anael, the regenerator, is the angel of pure altruistic love, both of one's fellow beings and of all creatures in the universe. He can be invoked for all matters of forgiveness, be it of ourselves – for what is past – or of others, that we may be free from their thrall. Anael brings harmony to places and people, together with the restoration of natural balance, healing rainforests, bringing wildlife habitats to the city and spreading greenery everywhere. His fertility is that of the whole Earth, rich in fruit, flowers, people and creatures of all kinds, whether wild or domestic.

Cassiel

* Archangel of: Saturn and Saturday
* Candle colour: purple
* Crystals: obsidian, jet
* Incense: cypress, thyme

Cassiel, the conservator, is called the angel of solitude and of temperance. He is, traditionally, invoked for investment and speculation, and he is associated with patience and compassion. Cassiel can form a focus for rituals to reverse bad fortune. He also helps to conserve, be it ecological resources and places in their natural state or history and tradition, as a legacy for future generations.

56 MAGICAL TECHNIQUES, ENERGIES AND MATERIALS

This chapter will provide you with all the remaining information you need to create your own unique spells.

Circle-casting

Circle-casting is in fact part of a more formal magical tradition. However, for special rituals or when you feel the need for protection, you can use this technique to create a space around you that is both safe and powerful. You can make your circle in a number of ways:

* Make a physical circle with stones, shells or crystals, setting them out deosil (clockwise) around yourself. After the ritual, remove the circle widdershins (anticlockwise).
* Make a physical circle with tea-lights and light them deosil from inside the circle. You could put a larger green candle in the North (for Earth), a larger yellow candle in the East (for Air), a larger red candle in the South (for Fire), and a larger blue candle in the West (for Water). Uncast the circle by blowing out the candles in reverse order of lighting.
* Use a symbolic miniature circle, such as a circular metal tray or a garden stepping stone. Sit or kneel facing it, looking northwards. If you like, you can draw around the outline deosil with a crystal point to empower the circle and widdershins to uncast it after the spell.
* Use a natural existing outdoor circle, such as a grove of trees or a ring of flowers or toadstools. Always ask permission of the natural essences of the place first. You do not need to cast or uncast this kind of circle, as the natural energies will hold the power and protection.
* Draw a deosil circle in earth, snow or sand, using a stick, a magic wand or a sword. Rub it out widdershins after the spell or leave it for the elements to take away. Chalk on paving stones also works well.
* Make a circle with incense smoke or water drops in which salt has been mixed. This kind of circle will disperse itself naturally.

If you wish, you can cleanse your circle area as described on pages 667–8 before casting. Put your ritual table or altar in the centre of the area, all set up for the spell, before you cast the circle. Use a compass to find North (or estimate a symbolic North) and start casting from there. Some practitioners light any necessary candles or incense before casting the circle, but you may prefer to light them afterwards.

Symbolic circle-casting

This is the most common method of casting a magic circle. The circle is cast in the air, about waist-high, with a pointed crystal held in your power hand (the one you write with). Alternatively, you can use the index finger of your power hand, a magic wand or an athame (a black-handled ritual knife).

You can walk round the perimeter of your visualised circle, starting in the North and going deosil (clockwise), to make it. Alternatively, you can stand in the North, facing outwards, and make a sweeping deosil movement of your hand, as you do so visualising a circle of gold, white, silver or blue light. The circle should be large enough to enclose yourself and the table/altar, allowing enough room for you to move round.

You can also visualise the circle appearing around you. Stand in the centre of your working area, facing North. Holding your pointed quartz crystal, wand or extended index finger waist high, turn slowly in a circle, but remain on the same spot. Picture light flowing outwards and then into a circle around you and where you are working.

If working in a group, some practitioners like to cast the circle first and then welcome other members in to it, sealing the circle after everyone has entered by making a diagonal slashing movement of the power hand, wand or athame, first up and then down. However, I personally think it is more powerful to cast the circle around the group. Ask the group members to stand in a circle and walk deosil around them, as you do so making the circle, be it visualised or marked out with incense or salt water. You then enter the circle, at the place where you began casting it, through a visualised doorway, sealing it afterwards.

Uncasting the circle

However you have cast your circle, to uncast it, you simply reverse the process. So you might walk widdershins (anticlockwise) around the periphery of the circle, starting from where you completed it, mentally drawing the light back into your crystal, wand or finger. Alternatively, stand in the centre of the light circle and turn slowly widdershins, remaining in the same spot and envisaging the light of the circle receding inwards and finally disappearing.

You will find words for casting and uncasting a circle on page 13, but you can create your own.

The four elements

Throughout this book I have used the four elements, Earth, Air, Fire and Water, in spell-casting, just as witches and magicians have done for hundreds of years. In ancient Greek times, it was believed that all life contained the four elements. By combining them magically, it was thought that you could create a magical space and power – the fifth element, called Ether or Akasha – where thoughts could be magically transformed into actuality.

Each element has a number of magical associations. You can create your own spells simply by using some of the materials as a focus and weaving chants around the images I have suggested.

Earth

* Direction: North
* Time: midnight
* Season: winter
* Colours: green, brown
* Magical qualities: stability, common sense, practical abilities, caretaking of the Earth, protectiveness, upholding of tradition, love of beauty, patience, perseverance, generosity, acceptance of others, nurturance
* Rules over: abundance and prosperity, fertility, finance, law and order, institutions, authority, motherhood, the physical body, food, home and family, animals, the land, agriculture, horticulture, environmentalism
* Deities: Earth and creating goddesses from any tradition (for example Nerthus, the Viking Earth mother, and her successor, Frigg, wife of Odin and patroness of women and childbirth; the Virgin Mary; Gaia, the ancient Greek Earth mother)
* Places: megaliths, stone circles, groves, forests, homes, temples, the crypts of churches and cathedrals, ley or psychic power lines in the earth, caves
* Power animals: bear, bull, serpent, snake
* Zodiacal signs: Taurus, Virgo, Capricorn
* Sacred substance: salt

Air

* Direction: East
* Time: dawn
* Season: spring
* Colours: yellow, grey
* Magical qualities: logic, clear focus, an enquiring and analytical mind, the ability to communicate clearly, concentration, versatility, adaptability, the quest for truth, commercial and technological acumen, healing powers
* Rules over: new beginnings, change, health and healing, teaching, travel, house or career moves, knowledge, examinations, the media, science, ideas, ideals, money-spinning
* Deities: sky gods such as Odin (the Viking father god) and Tiwaz (the Viking god of the Pole Star and warrior god), also messenger and healing deities, such as the Roman Mercury
* Places: mountain tops, hills, towers, steeples and spires, the sky, pyramids, open plains, tall buildings, balconies, roof gardens

* Power animals: eagle, hawk, birds of prey, the white dove
* Zodiacal signs: Aquarius, Gemini, Libra
* Sacred substances: incense, fragrance oils

Fire

* Direction: South
* Time: noon
* Season: summer
* Colours: red, orange, gold
* Magical qualities: fertility in all aspects of life, creativity, light-bringing, power, passion, joy, initiation, transformation, courage, mysticism, clairvoyance, prophecy, spirituality
* Rules over: ambition, achievement, illumination, inspiration, all creative and artistic ventures, poetry, art, sculpture, writing, music, dance, religion and spirituality, psychic powers — especially higher ones such as channelling, innovation, sexuality, the destruction of what is no longer needed, binding and banishing, protection
* Deities: all Fire gods and goddesses and deities of light (for example Thor, the Viking thunder god; Freyja, the Viking goddess of beauty and fertility; and Vesta, the Roman goddess of the sacred hearth)
* Places: hearths, bonfires, deserts, volcanoes, sacred festival fires, hill-top beacons, conflagrations, solar eclipses
* Power animals: stag, lion, dragons and the legendary golden phoenix (symbol of transformation and rebirth, which burns itself on a funeral pyre every 500 years, only to rise again golden from the ashes)
* Zodiacal signs: Aries, Leo, Sagittarius
* Sacred substances: candles, a small fire

Water

* Direction: West
* Time: dusk
* Season: autumn
* Colours: blue, silver
* Magical qualities: intuition, empathy, sympathy, healing with crystals and herbs, inner harmony, peace-making, unconscious wisdom, divinatory powers (especially those connected with water), ability to merge and interconnect with nature, the cycles of the seasons, the life cycle
* Rules over: love; relationships; friendship; dreams; the cycle of birth, death and rebirth; purification rites; healing; the use of the powers of nature; water and sea magic; moon magic; travel by sea
* Deities: all sea and moon deities (for example Ran, the Viking sea goddess, and Diana, Graeco Roman goddess of the moon and of witches)
* Places: the ocean, rivers, lakes, pools, sacred wells and streams, marshland, flood plains
* Power animals: frog, dolphin, all fish — especially the salmon
* Zodiacal signs: Cancer, Scorpio, Pisces
* Sacred substance: water

Colours

Using colours is one of the easiest ways to direct a spell towards a particular goal. Colours can be introduced in the form of candles, flowers, crystals, coloured purses to contain herbs, charms for healing and so on.

White

* Limitless potential
* Boundless energy
* Innovations
* Originality (also orange)
* Ambitions and success
* New beginnings
* Free-flowing life
* Purity
* Healing
* The quest for what is of worth
* Attracting rituals

Crystals: diamond, moonstone, fluorite, clear crystal quartz, pearl, opal, Herkimer diamond, zircon

Red

* Action
* Survival
* Change
* Courage
* Overcoming obstacles
* Determination
* Will power
* Physical strength
* Stamina and endurance
* Binding rituals
* Passion
* Campaigns and crusades

Crystals: red jasper, red tiger's eye, banded red/brown agates, blood agate, garnet, ruby

Orange

* Confidence
* Joy
* Self-esteem
* Creativity
* Independence
* Strong identity
* The media
* Originality
* Abundance
* Fertility

* Good health
* Balance
* The workplace

Crystals: amber, aragonite, carnelian, celestine, coral, mookaite, topaz, chrysoberyl, banded orange agate, zincite

Yellow

* Logic and the mind
* Knowledge of all kinds
* Business acumen
* Communication
* Technology and science
* Short-term local travel
* House moves
* Speculation, loans and credit matters
* Honesty

Crystals: ametrine, citrine, golden amber, yellow jasper, topaz, lemon chrysoprase, rutilated quartz, yellow calcite

Green

* Love
* Harmony
* Good luck
* Growth and gradual increase
* Concern for the environment
* Beauty
* Altruism
* Protection, especially for forests and endangered species and against pollution
* Gradual healing and recovery after illness

Crystals: amazonite, aventurine, chrysoprase, emerald, jade, green and ocean jasper, malachite, moss agate, moldavite, olivine/peridot, tourmaline

Blue

* Ideals
* Ideas
* Expansion of both perspective and physical horizons
* Leadership and authority
* Justice
* Integrity
* Career
* Long-term or long-distance travel
* Long-distance house moves
* Success
* Clean air
* Sea rituals

Crystals: aqua aura, aquamarine, blue chalcedony, blue lace agate, blue quartz calcite, kyanite, lapis lazuli, sapphire, turquoise

Purple

* Inner vision
* Psychic development
* Spirituality
* Peaceful dreams
* Inner peace
* Unconscious wisdom
* Healing, especially of the mind and emotions
* Ancient wisdom

Crystals: amethyst, bornite (peacock's eye), fluorite, lepidolite, sodalite, sugilite, super seven

Pink

* Unconditional love
* Reconciliation
* Gentleness
* The mending of quarrels
* Patience
* Children and the vulnerable
* The healing of abuse of any kind
* The home and family

Crystals: morganite, coral, kunzite, pink chalcedony, rhodochrosite, rose quartz, manganocalcite, tourmaline

Brown

* Nurturing powers
* Acceptance of frailty in self and others
* Earthing power
* Property and DIY
* Official organisations
* Banks and finance
* Animals
* Older people
* Protection of all kinds
* Earth rituals

Crystals: desert rose, Dalmatian jasper, leopardskin or snakeskin jasper, all sandy jaspers, brown zircon, petrified wood, chiastolite, fossils, rutilated quartz, tiger's eye

Black

* Endings
* Transitions
* Regeneration
* Acceptance of life as it is
* The confrontation of mortality
* Banishing
* Combating pollution
* Countering depression

Crystals: Apache tear, jet, obsidian, snowflake obsidian, black onyx, staurolite, black pearl, black opal, tektite

Grey

* Compromise
* Adaptability
* The ability to merge into the background or maintain a low profile
* The keeping of secrets
* Psychic protection
* The reduction of anger, grief or guilt

Crystals: smoky quartz, lavas, grey banded agate, laboradite, meteorites

Silver

* Intuition and sudden insights, especially in dreams
* Hidden potential
* Fertility
* The cycle of the year and the seasons
* Sea and moon and star magic
* Prosperity

Crystals: haematite, moonstones, iron pyrites

Gold

* Wealth
* Aiming high
* Great good fortune
* Perfection
* Wishes coming true
* Sun magic

Crystals: amber, cuprite, polished pyrites, tiger's eye, topaz, citrine

Herbs

These herbs are intended only for magical use, in sachets or as infusions to protect the home, workplace, property and so on. They should not be taken internally without medical advice. Some are not suitable for pregnant women or those with certain medical conditions and all need careful dosage.

Angelica (*Angelica archangelica*)

Energy, health and long life; protection, especially for children and against attacks on the home, pets or possessions.

Anise/aniseed (*Pimpinellla anisum*)

Protection against all negative influences and against nightmares; calming of fears and phobias.

Basil (*Ocimum basilicum*)

Faithful love and trust in love; abundance of all kinds; prosperity; protection; passion; eases stress and anxiety; helps indecision and insomnia; conquers fear of flying.

Bistort/snakeweed/dragon's wort (*Polygonum bistorta*)

Fertility; courage; deters malice in others; good for dragon energies.

Blue cohosh (*Caulophyllum thalictroides*)

Protective, especially for women; good for overcoming fears and abuse of all kinds; effective for birth rituals and female rites of passage, such as the onset of menstruation and the menopause.

Chamomile, Roman (*Chamaemelum nobile*) and chamomile, German (*Matricaria recutitao*)

The most gentle and soothing of herbs, sometimes called the children's herb; can be used in all healing rituals, especially those for babies' and children's ills; heals sorrow in love; restores confidence after a period of bad luck; protection; good for money and family matters.

Dandelion (*Taraxacum officinale*)

Love; long life; gets things moving after stagnation; protection, especially psychic attack; counters addictions and pollution of all kinds.

Echinacea/purple cornflower (*Echinacea angustifolia*)

Personal power; trust in self; stimulates the immune system and so is good in all healing rituals; intuition.

Elecampane (*Inula helenium*)

Attracts love; deters hostility and spite; speeds healing.

Fennel (*Foeniculum vulgare*)

A herb of courage; banishes and keeps harm away from people, places and animals; good for travel rituals and house moves.

Fenugreek (*Trigonella foenumgraecum*)

Increased prosperity over a period of time; protective of home, possessions and workplace.

Feverfew (*Tanacetum parthenium*)

A cleansing herb; protects travellers and all who must go in to unfamiliar or hostile environments; reduces stress and anxiety.

Juniper (*Juniperus communis*)

Purifies homes; protects against accidents, thieves and all forms of illness; increases male potency.

Kelp/bladderwrack (*Fucus visiculosus*)

Protective for all sea travel; prosperity in the home; general improvements to health and energy levels.

Marjoram (*Majorana hortensis*) and sweet marjorum (*Origanum marjorana*)

Protection; love; happiness; health; relieves stress, depression; encourages intuition and the ability to discover the truth about people.

Milk thistle (*Silybum marianum*)

Protects mothers, babies and the young, both human and animal; repels cruelty; a good healing and calming herb for all purposes.

Mint (*Mentha aquatica*) and peppermint (*Mentha piperita*)

Purifies; drives away negativity from objects and places; a natural protector of travellers; money; health; love; passion; success.

Mugwort (*Artemisia vulgaris*)

Drives away danger and negative paranormal influences; fertility; physical, mental and psychic powers; gives prophetic dreams.

Nettle (*Urtica dioica*)

Defensive and cleansing; repels strong attack or danger against self, family and home.

Parsley (*Petroselinum sativum* and *Petroselinum crispum*)

Purification herb; keeps away all harm; alleviates grief and sorrow; banishes misfortune; money; passion.

Rosemary (*Rosmarinus officinalis*)

Drives away illness, malevolence of all kinds and nightmares; improves memory and concentration; love; fidelity; prosperity.

Sage (*Salvia officinalis*)

Longevity; good health; contentment; increases the ability to concentrate; protection of the home and family, also creatures, places and nations; prosperity; wisdom.

Saw palmetto (*Serenoa serrulata*)

Male potency; empowers any who are afraid or bullied.

St John's wort (*Hypericum perforatum*)

Invincibility; courage; power; fertility; brings relief from depression; attracts wealth.

Tarragon (*Artemesia dracunculus*)
Associated with dragons and serpent goddesses; shedding of old burdens, guilt, fears and destructive relationships.

Thistle, blessed, and thistle, holy (*Carduus benedictus*)
Drives away negativity when placed in a room; protects when placed in a spell bag; good for contacting angels; protection when travelling.

Thyme (*Thymus vulgaris*)
Psychically cleanses the home and land; divinatory; brings health; improves memory; drives away nightmares and phantoms of the night; growing wild is said to indicate a place of concentrated earth energies.

Valerian (*Valeriana officinalis*)
Reconciliation; reunites those parted by circumstance or distance; reduces despair, tension, anxiety, insomnia and pain associated with stress-related conditions; protects against hostility.

Vervain (*Verbena officinalis*)
Protects the home; attracts the blessings of nature spirits and guardians of the land, on which even urban homes are built.

Vitex/chaste tree (*Vitex agnus castus*)
Fertility; new ideas and new stages of life; the conception and safe and easy birth of a child.

Magical flowers

You can use these flowers in spells, fresh or dried in pot pourri or as essential oils or flower essences.

Geranium (*Pelargonium graveolens*)
Heals domestic conflict and trouble in the workplace (take a pot into a troubled office); gentle love and trust; money.

Hyacinth (*Hyacinth orientalis*)
Self-esteem; rebuilding of trust after betrayal; domestic happiness; increasing beauty and attracting beautiful things into your life.

Jasmine (*Jasminum grandiflorum*)
Love; increases sexual desire; optimism; moon and night magic.

Lavender (*Lavandula*)
Love, especially self-love and gentleness; happiness; health; guards against cruelty and spite; helps grief, sorrow and guilt; reduces stress and the power of addictions; new beginnings; healing.

Lily of the valley (*Convallaria majalis*)
Restores happiness after sorrow or loss; fairy and deva magic; mothering issues.

Marigold (*Calendula officinalis*)
Increases positive energies in a room or building; protective, especially at night and in domestic matters; resolution of legal problems and obtaining justice; increase of love and fidelity.

Narcissus (*Narcissus poeticus*)
Self-esteem and self-confidence; inner beauty and radiance; protects against emotional abuse and those who steal ideas or credit for your work.

Nasturtium (*Tropaeolum majus*)
Optimism; abundance, especially in the form of new sources of income; business success.

Passion flower (*Passiflora incarnata*)
Helps with acknowledging and expressing strong feelings positively and being open to love and life; passion; prosperity; soothes anxiety, panic attacks and phobias.

Rose/rose otto (*Rosa damascena*), rose absolute (*Rosa centifolia*)
The ultimate gentle healing flower of love and reconciliation; self-esteem; healing the young, the very old, anyone who has suffered abuse and the vulnerable; probably the best flower for any love or fertility magic; reduces stress and prevents insomnia; relieves psychosomatic conditions, eating disorders and other addictions.

Snapdragon (*Antirrhinum majus*)
Reduces anger, especially if directed inwards; prevents spite and malice in the workplace or from neighbours; courage.

Violet (*Viola odoratoa*)

Healing; gentle love; self-confidence; domestic happiness; getting one's talents recognised; keeping secrets.

Trees

You can work magically with trees that are growing in a woodland, a park or your garden, with miniature pot trees, with leaves, with berries, with nuts, with blossoms, with the tree oil or incense or with the wood or bark.

Apple (*Pyrus malus*)

Brings fertility in every way; increases self-love; gradually restores health and optimism; a symbol of long life and lasting good health.

Ash (*Fraxinus excelsior / Fraxinus Americana*)

A father tree; attracts travel opportunities, especially across seas; career advancement; courage; confidence; good for weight- and food-related disorders; power; prosperity; healing.

Beech (*Fagus ferruginea*)

Unconscious wisdom; healing; a sense of connection with the Earth and with others; good for domestic matters; protection; formal learning and traditional knowledge; accelerates welcome change.

Birch (*Betula pendula alba* or *lenta*)

A mother goddess tree; new beginnings and opportunities; protects mothers and their young; a symbol of cleansing, health, wisdom and moon magic.

Elder (*Samambucus canadensis* or *nigra*)

The fairy tree that makes anything seem possible; tree of the white (moon) goddess of the Celts; protects the home; gives ability to see other dimensions; increases clairvoyance; absorbs negativity.

Eucalyptus (*Eucalyptus regnans*), **blue gum tree** (*Eucalyptus globules*)

Cleansing; healing; frees stagnant or blocked energies and helps a person to move forward; clears physical and mental blockages.

Fig (*Ficus carica*)

Fertility and the blossoming of creativity; wisdom; harmony and balance; good for travel to faraway places.

Laurel, bay (*Laurus nobilis, Pimenta racemosa*)

Protects against illness and malice; restores trust after infidelity; reduces stress and anxiety; the best tree for fidelity, happy marriages and families and to attract abundance to the home; female fertility.

Magnolia (*Magnolia glauca*)

Love and loyalty; reduces the power of addictions and obsessions, especially smoking; restores strength after a long illness or major setback; domestic joy.

Maple (*Acer rubrum*)

Long life; health of children; fertility; riches of all kinds; pleasure; restores confidence; brings luck.

Mimosa (*Acacia dealbata*)

Removes a sense of isolation, especially for older people; calms anxiety; relieves depression and nightmares; new love and passion; money.

Oak (*Quercus alba*)

The father tree; tree of the Druids; wisdom, knowledge and power; drives away fear and impotence, physical and emotional; independence; confidence; long-term prosperity.

Orange (*Citrus sinensis*)

Marriage and faithful love; self-esteem and confidence; brings a sense of well-being and fertility in every way; soothes anxiety, insomnia and bad dreams; abundance; health; and inner radiance.

Peach (*Amygdalus persica*)

Marriage and birth; abundance; happiness; fertility; long life; a sunshine tree of sensuality and physical pleasures.

Pine (*Pinus*), spruce (*Picea excelsa*)

Drives away all harm to home and family, especially to newborn infants; a Fire tree, used for cleansing negativity and malice; strengthens friendship in adversity; inspiration; good for travel and for guarding property and premises.

Poplar/aspen (*Populus tremuloides*)

Called 'the shiver tree' because it was believe to cure fevers and chills (as its own leaves trembled even when there was no wind); gentle healing of the body, mind and spirit; relieves stress; attracts money.

Walnut (*Juglans regia*), butternut (*Juglans cinerea*)

Fertility and abundance; traditionally a tree where witches meet; health; increase of mental powers; happy marriage; granting of wishes.

White willow (*Salix alba*)

A mother and moon goddess tree; protection; harmony with the cycle of the seasons and the moon; makes wishes come true; increases psychic energies and brings an understanding of the emotions of others.

Wild cherry (*Prunus serotina*)

Reconciliation; inner tranquillity; fertility; new love.

Incenses

These may be found both in the form of incense sticks (the easiest to use) and as powdered incense that you burn on heated charcoal blocks.

Allspice
Money; strength; action.

Benzoin
Money; increased mental powers and concentration.

Cedar/cedarwood
Healing; cleansing redundant influences and negative thoughts.

Cinnamon
Passion; money; psychic awareness.

Cloves
Love; money; repelling hostility; improved memory.

Copal
Protection; purification – especially good for cleansing crystals.

Cypress
Transition to a new phase of life; letting go of sorrow.

Dragon's blood
Love; protection; passion; male potency.

Fern
An initiator of change; travel; fertility.

Frankincense
Courage; joy; strength; success; travel; career; use in formal rituals.

Gum Arabic (acacia)
Dreams; meditation; psychic protection and development.

Hyssop
Known as 'the holy herb'; for making a love commitment; healing; all forms of protection, especially from psychic attack; cleanses artefacts that are associated with sorrow.

Lemongrass/lemon
Repels spite; protects against malice and gossip; passion; psychic awareness; travel.

Lemon verbena
Breaking a run of bad luck; love; protection against negativity.

Lilac
Joy in all domestic matters; acceptance of the frailty of self and others.

Moss
Good fortune; prosperity; money; permanence, whether in job or relationship; water magic and environmental rituals.

Mistletoe
Known to the Druids as 'the all-healer'; healing sorrows; male potency; overcoming injustice; finding what is lost.

Myrtle
Fidelity in love; marriage; mature love; domestic happiness; matters of property and security.

Myrrh
Healing; peace; purification; overcoming grief; protection; inner harmony; use in formal rituals.

Nutmeg
Fertility; healing, especially of environment; gradual increase of wealth.

Orange blossom
Marriage and permanent relationships; restoring trust; increasing confidence and hope.

Poppy/opium
Divination; fertility; making oneself less visible in difficult situations; good luck; peace and peaceful sleep.

Sandalwood
Spiritual and psychic awareness and healing; money; sexuality; use in formal rituals.

Strawberry
Innocent love; friendship; happiness.

Vanilla
Love; passion; increases mental powers; harmony in the home; attracts abundance.

Vetivert
Love; breaks a run of bad luck; money; protects against theft and all negativity.

57 THE FINAL SPELL

"And finally, the best spell of all ... one created by you to fulfil your secret dream. It is the good fairy spell, the one you will carry out alone in a beautiful place that you love – or in your own backyard with no special tools, choreographed actions or pre-ordained words.

We all have a dream that may seem improbable but is attainable, given patience, perseverance, supreme effort and a lot of luck. I grew up in the back streets of an industrial city, and I still struggle with insecurity, but I did get to write books that are published. This was my burning ambition from childhood, but I did not begin writing professionally until I was 40 years old. Yours may be a dream you have never spoken of or, like mine, one you stopped talking about because others dismissed it as fantasy.

This spell will be powerful because it is endowed with all the hopes and desires that get us up in the morning and keep us smiling, because we believe that one day life will get gloriously better. Your dream might be to fulfil a life-long ambition to be a writer or musician, it might be to have good health, to conceive a longed-for baby, to earn enough money never to have to worry again how you will pay the bills, or to meet someone who will see you as you are and love you without trying to change you to fit their dream. Whatever it is, this spell will make it come true.

The following suggestions are ones that people I know have used successfully, but feel free to create your own scenario.

The best spell of all

* Like a child, gaze at the stars, pick one, clench your hands tight and say over and over:

  I wish, I wish, I wish ...

  Then whisper or shout your dream. Keep tracking your special star as a reminder.
* Stand on a deserted beach and whisper your wish into a shell, then cast the shell as far as you can on to the seventh wave.
* Build a sandcastle and adorn the highest turret with a word expressing your wish. Watch the in-coming tide crash into the castle, releasing the energy.
* Write your wish with a stick in the snow, then let the falling flakes erase it.
* Write your wish in icing sugar or cream on the top of a cake, then eat it, enjoying every mouthful – and for once not counting the calories.
* Tie the wish to the string of a kite or a balloon. Let go of the string on a windy plain or from an upstairs window and watch your wish float out into the world.
* When you next see a rainbow, walk or drive towards the rainbow's end. Stop before the rainbow fades, even if you haven't reached the crock of gold (people only find it in fairy tales), and wish on the rainbow as it arches overhead or across the horizon. Double rainbows are especially powerful.
* Jump in sunlit puddles while it is still raining and sing your wish aloud.
* Tell your wish to the wind or your cat or your newborn baby.

One day your wish will come true, not because I say so but because we all carry within us nuggets of pure gold, and one day we can spend that magic treasure on happiness.

You do not have to keep the special spell to be performed just once in your lifetime. Indeed, you may need to repeat it weekly, monthly or yearly. If necessary, compromise over the setting. Cast your wish spell in a sooty park or on a cold railway station platform. If you are having a miserable day out with the family or a lover, go off for a few minutes and cast it. If your boss is giving you a hard time, escape to the concrete square opposite work and cast it. If the bank's call centre on the other side of the world has just told you that your mortgage payment bounced, go out in the garden and cast your wish spell.

Repeat the wish over and over again, believe in your own magic and don't let anyone take the dream away.

GLOSSARY

This is a glossary of terms associated with witchcraft and spell-casting. They have not all been used in the book, but you may find these explanations useful if you come across the terminology in your further reading.

Akasha: The fifth and greatest element, formed by the combination of the elements of Earth, Air, Fire and Water that were considered in classical times and by alchemists to be the components of all life and matter. Also sometimes called Spirit or Ether.

Akashic records: The collective memory bank on the spirit plane said to hold the experiences of all people, past, present and future.

Alban Arthuran: The festival of the mid-winter solstice, named after King Arthur, the legendary Sun King, which takes place on or about 21 December in the Northern Hemisphere.

Alpha waves: Brain waves, cultivated in psychic work, that are associated with a very relaxed state of mind in which it is possible for intuitive faculties to find expression.

Amulet: A charm carried on a person or placed in a house to offer protection against danger and illness. When charged with healing energies, it becomes a talisman and can attract health and good fortune.

Anima: The term coined by Carl Gustav Jung to represent the female power within men as well as women.

Animus: Jung's term for the male power within women and men.

Ankh: An Egyptian symbol of eternal life.

Archangels: Higher orders of angels, celestial beings featuring in the cosmologies of the three major religions of the Western world, Christianity, Judaism, and Islam, as well as in many other world religions.

Athame: A double-edged knife used in formal ritual magic.

Auric field/aura: The personal energy field around all animate life, visible to clairvoyants.

Beltane: The Celtic festival of summer, beginning on 30 April and lasting for three days.

Bicarmel mind: A way of thinking that uses both hemispheres of the mind, the logical and the intuitive, rather than the left (logical) hemisphere predominating as is normal in adults.

Book of shadows: A personal book of reference containing magical spells, herbs, flowers, incenses, moon phases, and so on.

Caduceus: The staff of the classical messenger of the gods (Hermes to the

Greeks and Mercury to the Romans), shaped like two snakes, entwined in a double circle.

Cardinal: Principal, as in the four cardinal directions set round a circle – North, South, East, and West. Also a term applied to the astrological signs of Aries, Cancer, Libra and Capricorn, because when the Sun moves into these signs it marked the start of a new season. Those born under a cardinal sign manifest this quality as a desire to initiate and to take command of people and situations. *See also* Fixed, Mutable.

Cauldron of Undry: A magical cauldron, one of the original four Celtic treasures, that could provide an endless supply of nourishment and had great healing and restorative powers. Believed by some scholars to be the inspiration for the Holy Grail.

Censer: A container for granular incense that is burnt on charcoal. Also called a thurible.

Chalice: A cup or goblet made of glass, crystal, pottery or metal, traditionally silver, used in ceremonies to represent the Water element and to hold wine, juice or water.

Charge: A declaration of the power and benevolence of the Goddess (or god) in Wicca, similar to the Creed in other religions. It is spoken usually in the first person and is sometimes believed to be the words of the Goddess channelled through the speaker.

Ch'i: The invisible life force, the flow of positive energy through everything, promoting growth, health and vitality.

Clairaudience: A natural psychic ability to hear sounds beyond the range of the physical sounds and the physical ear, sometimes from other dimensions. Mediums often communicate with spirits by hearing their voices and so can convey messages to relatives or friends in whom the ability is not so developed.

Coven: A meeting of any group, numbering from two to 13 practitioners, who meet together to perform magick.

Deosil: Clockwise, or, literally, 'in the direction of the sun'. The direction used in creating a circle, in all forms of attracting magic and for giving healing energies. *See also* Widdershins.

Devas: The angelic beings who watch and direct the natural world. In formal magick, one deva rules over each segment of a magical circle and one of the four elements of Fire, Water, Air and Earth. Also known as the Devic Lords of the Watchtower.

Dhoop: An incense stick like a slender rope, from India.

The divinity: Generic term for the ultimate source of goodness, light and creation.

Djinn: An invisible, shapeshifting creature of fire and air, originating in the Middle East. In Islamic tradition, djinns live in a parallel universe and so are invisible, created, it is said, before mortals from smokeless fire.

Druids: Celtic high priests and wise men (and women) who preserved a common culture, religion, history, laws, scholarship, healing, magic and science amongst the disparate Celtic tribes. There is historical evidence of Druids in Ireland, England, Wales and Gaul, and it would seem that they also held sway in the Celtic settlements of Spain, Italy, Galatia and the Danube valley, although under a different name.

Eightfold Wheel of the Year: An ancient magical and spiritual division of the year, formalised by the Celts, though possibly dating back to the first agricultural societies.

Elementals: The forces or energies that in nature and magic give shape to living things and bring thoughts and desires into actuality.

Equinox: The two times of the year when day and night are equal – namely, the spring equinox around 21 March (21 September in the Southern Hemisphere) and the autumn equinox around 21 September (21 March in the Southern Hemisphere). In Celtic myth these were the times when the twin gods of light and darkness fought each other for control.

Esbat: A monthly coven meeting traditionally held 13 times a year, during each full moon.

Evil eye: A way of transmitting negativity to another person, not as a deliberate curse but through feelings of envy, jealousy or resentment.

Evocation: The summoning-up of angels (and sometimes demons) in order to bind them to perform tasks.

Fixed: In astrology, a term applied to the signs of Leo, Taurus, Aquarius and Scorpio because the Sun enters them in the middle of a season. Those born under these signs exhibit stability and a tendency to continue in a predetermined path. *See also* Cardinal, Mutable.

The Goddess: The archetype or source energy of the feminine ultimate power or principle. All the named goddesses are aspects or particular qualities of the Goddess in different cultures.

Grail: The chalice that Christ used at the Last Supper, in which His blood was collected after the crucifixion.

Grail guardians: Nine maidens, sometimes associated with the guardians of sacred wells or with the nine priestesses of the Isle of Avalon, who included Morgan le Fay, Arthur's half-sister, and Vivien, the Lady of the Lake in Arthurian tradition who accompanied Arthur on his funeral barge. In some Grail legends, the Knights Templar were the traditional guardians of various holy relics, including the Grail Cup, that were brought back from the Crusades.

Grail treasures: The main elemental ritual items in magic, associated with the treasures of the Celts, and having parallels in Christianity.

Handfasting: A popular marriage rite among Wiccans, named after the focal point of the rite in which a couple's right hands are loosely joined by a cord to symbolise the uniting of the two people, body, mind and soul.

Hedge witch: A lone witch; the name comes from the practice of village wise women surrounding their homes with a hedge of hawthorn, a magical tree that afforded privacy from the curious.

The Horned God: The male principle in Wicca, Lord of the Hunt, the Herds, Winter and the Underworld. Known to the Celts as Cernunnos, the generic name for 'horned one'.

Imbolc: The Celtic festival of early spring. A fire festival, christianised as Candlemas on 1 February. Also known as Oimelc.

Immanent: Usually refers to a god or the Goddess; indicating that they are manifest within the object of their creation, as the divine spark within people. *See also* Transcendent.

Inner-plane teaching: Contacting through meditation or rituals the cosmic memory bank or Akashic records in order to tap into the great existing magical systems and wisdom without external formal teaching.

Invocation: The process by which the wisdom and benign powers of the natural world and of higher planes of consciousness, associated with the evolved self and divine power, are drawn into oneself. Medieval magicians would invoke spirits to take over their bodies — dangerous and mind-blowing.

Karma: The concept that the good and bad deeds and thoughts accumulated in an individual lifetime may either progress us forwards to spiritual perfection or mean we need to learn lessons in subsequent lives in order to right our mistakes.

Litha: The Celtic festival of light, held around the midsummer solstice, on 21 June in the Northern Hemisphere.

Lughnassadh: The Celtic festival of the first corn harvest, held from 31 July to 2 August in the Northern Hemisphere. Christianised as Lammas ('loaf mass'), the day on which loaves of bread were baked from the first grain harvest and placed on the altar to symbolise the first fruits.

Mabon: The second Celtic harvest festival of the autumn equinox, around 22 September in the Northern Hemisphere.

Medicine Wheel: A concept central to all Native American magic. The wheels link the celestial, human and natural cycles. Also known as the Circle of Power.

Mojo: A small bag containing between one and 13 symbolic objects — but always an odd number. It protects or provides energies and is always kept hidden. Mojos come from the US Hoodoo tradition, which draws upon African religions and also incorporates Native American and European magic.

Morphic resonance: The spreading of good will and positivity, through magic and good deeds, to increase the benign energies of the Earth and cosmos.

Mother goddess: The giver of all life and fertility and mother of the animals, worshipped by hunter-gatherer societies since paleolithic times. In the shamanic religions in Siberia and Lapland, the Mother of the Herds is still a central icon of power. During the neolithic period, the Mother goddess was the bringer of fertility to the land as well as to animals and humans. Gradually, she came to be seen as the wife of the great sky gods. She survives in the form of Mary in the Christian religion.

Mutable: The mutable signs of the zodiac are Sagittarius, Gemini, Virgo and Pisces, as when the Sun enters them the seasons are about to change. Those born under them are correspondingly versatile and ready to compromise. *See also* Cardinal, Fixed.

Oimelc: *See* Imbolc.

Ostara: The Celtic festival of the spring equinox.

Pentacle: A ritual item, symbol of the Earth, consisting of a flat, round disc, engraved with a pentagram.

Pentagram: A five-pointed diagram, one of the most sacred geometric forms in magick. Each of the five points represents one of the five elemental powers. The uppermost, single point is symbolic of Spirit, or Akasha.

Poppet: A featureless doll made of cloth that is filled with herbs and used in healing or as a talisman to attract love or fertility. It may also be made of clay and used as a focus for positive magick to bring health or happiness to the person represented by it.

Power hand: The hand you write with, used to transmit assertive and creative energies. *See also* Receptive hand.

Quarters: The four segments of a magical circle. Each is associated with specific archangels, colours, crystals, herbs, incenses, ritual tools, etc.

Receptive hand: The hand you do not write with. Used for receiving energies. *See also* Power hand.

Rede: A rule or moral code. The Wiccan Rede states: 'An it harm none, do what you will', and so ensures that all magic has a positive intent.

Sabbat: One of eight special days of the year on which Wiccan celebrations are held – the solstices, the equinoxes and the Celtic fire festivals.

Samhain: The Celtic fire festival of the new year, celebrated at the end of summer, from 31 October to 2 November.

Scrying: Seeing magical images in a reflective medium, such as a crystal ball, mirror or a natural moving source of inspiration, such as fire, water or clouds. The word 'scry' comes from the Anglo-Saxon word descry, which means 'to perceive dimly'.

Shamanism: Possibly the oldest spiritual practice in the world, continued today in communities as far apart as India, Australia, Japan, China, Siberia, Mongolia, Africa, among the Bedouins in the Middle East and in North, Central and South America.

Sky-clad: Naked.

Sky gods: The powerful patriarchal gods of the classical and Viking world, for example Zeus of the Greeks, Jupiter of the Romans, Odin of the Vikings and Thunor of the Anglo Saxons. They gained supremacy over the Earth mother who appears as their wife-consort, full of human foibles.

Solstice: One of the main astronomical points of the year. The summer solstice (21 June, or 21 December in the Southern Hemisphere) marks the sun at its height and greatest power. The winter solstice (21 December or 21 June in the Southern Hemisphere) is the shortest day, when the sun is at its weakest and it was feared by early humans that the sun would die.

Spirit guides: Guardians from another dimension who advise and protect humans. They may be deceased relatives, wise teachers, for example Native Americans, angels or evolved essences who never assumed mortal form.

Talisman: A charm or amulet that has been charged with specific healing or magical energies to make it powerful and to attract health, wealth or luck. It tends to become more powerful the more it is used.

Tarot: A pack of 78 illustrated cards often used in rituals to represent people or qualities that are being sought in a spell.

Threefold Law: A law in Wicca that states that whatever you do or send to others, good or bad, will be returned to you threefold – a great incentive to positive thought and action.

Thurible: *See* Censer.

Transcendent: Term used of god forms to express the belief that their existence extends beyond and is separate from creation. *See also* Immanent.

Triple goddess: A concept of a deity found in many cultures. May represent the three main phases of the Moon – maiden, mother and crone – or, as in Celtic tradition especially, three sisters.

Tulpa: A thought form created by medieval occultists seeking mastery over the elemental beings that they fashioned by their incantations. In extreme cases a tulpa might destroy its creator – hence the warnings of the Threefold Law.

Wheel of the Year: *See* Eightfold Wheel of the Year.

Wicca: A contemporary, neo-pagan religion that regards the divine life source as a part of nature, not a force beyond creation. This divine source of life is manifest as the god and goddess within everything living, male and female, animal, bird, tree and flower. Sometimes regarded as the oldest religion in the world.

Wiccan Rede: *See* Rede.

Widdershins: Anti-clockwise, moonwise, or against the sun. The direction used in closing a circle, banishing or removing pain and in banishing magick generally. *See also* Deosil.

Yin and yang: The complementary components of everything in life, according to ancient Chinese philosophy. Yang is the original sun concept of light, power, masculinity, assertiveness, logic and action. It controls heaven and all things positive. It is balanced by Yin, the original moon concept of darkness, receptivity, femininity, intuition, acceptance and inaction. Yin controls the Earth and all things negative.

FURTHER READING

alchemy

Holyard, E. J., *Alchemy*, 1990, Dover Publications

Jung, Carl Gustav, *Alchemical Studies*, 1983, Princetown University Press

amulets and talismans

Gonzalez-Wipler, Migene, *Complete Guide to Amulets and Talismans*, 1991, Llewellyn

Thomas, Willam, and Pavitt, Kate, *The Book of Talismans, Amulets and Zodiacal Gems*, 1998, Kessinger

annual almanacs

Llewellyn's Almanac, Llewellyn

Llewellyn's Pocket Planner and Ephemeris, Llewellyn

Old Moore's Almanack, Foulsham

Tybol Astrological Almanac, 27 Heversham Avenue, Fulwood, Preston PR2 9TD

Witch's Almanack, Foulsham/Quantum

angels, faeries and nature spirits

Bloom, William, *Working with Angels, Faeries and Nature Spirits*, 1998, Piatkus

Burnham, Sophie, *A Book of Angels*, 1990, Ballantine

candle magic and candlemaking

Bruce, Marie, *Candleburning Rituals*, 2001, Foulsham

Buckland, Ray, *Advanced Candle Magic*, 1996, Llewellyn, St Paul, Minnesota

Eason, Cassandra, *Candle Power*, 1999, Blandford

Guy, Gary V., *Easy-to-make Candles*, 1980, Dover Publications

Heath, Maya, *Ceridwen's Handbook of Incense, Oils and Candles: Being a Guide to the Magical and Spiritual Uses of Oils, Incense, Candles and the Like*, 1996, Words of Wisdom International Inc.

Innes, Miranda, *The Book of Candles*, 1991, Dorling Kindersley

Larkin, Chris, *The Book of Candlemaking: Creating Scent, Beauty and Light*, 1998, Sterling Publications, New York

Pajeon, Kala and Pajeon, Ketz, *The Candle Magic Workbook*, 1991, Citadel Carol, New York

CELTIC SPIRITUALITY

Anderson, Rosemarie, *Celtic Oracles*, 1999, Piatkus
Ellis-Berresford, Peter, *The Druids*, 1994, Constable Robinson
Green, Miranda, *Dictionary of Celtic Myth and Legend*, 1992, Thames & Hudson
Matthews, Caitlín and John, *The Encyclopaedia of Celtic Wisdom*, 1994, Element
Nichols, Ross, *The Book of Druidry*, 1990, Aquarian/Thorsons

CHAKRAS

Dale, Cyndi, New Chakra Healing, *The Revolutionary 32-Center Energy System*, 1996,
   Llewellyn
Karagulla, Shafica and Van Gelder Kunz, Dora, *Chakras and the Human Energy Field*,
   1994, Theosophical University Press

COLOUR HEALING AND MAGIC

Buckland, Ray, *Practical Color Magic*, 1996, Llewellyn, St Paul, Minnesota
Klotsche, Charles, *Color Medicine: The Secrets of Color/Vibrational Healing*, 1993, Light
   Technology Publications
Sun, Howard and Dorothy, *Colour Your Life*, Piatkus, 1999

CRYSTALS

Bourgault, Luc, *The American Indian Secrets of Crystal Healing*, 1997, Foulsham/
   Quantum
Cunningham, Scott, *Encyclopaedia of Crystal, Gem and Metal Magic*, 1991, Llewellyn, St
   Paul, Minnesota
Eason, Cassandra, *Crystal Healing*, 2002, Foulsham
Eason, Cassandra, *Crystals Talk to the Woman Within*, 2000, Foulsham/Quantum

DOWSING

Bailey, Arthur, *Anyone Can Dowse for Better Health*, 1999, Foulsham/Quantum
Lonegren, Sig, *Spiritual Dowsing*, Gothic Images, 1986, Druids

FLOWERS, TREES AND PLANTS

Graves, Robert, *The White Goddess*, 1988, Faber and Faber (in my opinion the best
   book on the tree alphabet and tree lore)
Tompkins and Bird, *The Secret Life of Plants*, 1974, Avon Books, New York

FLOWER REMEDIES

Barnard, Julian, *A Guide to the Bach Flower Remedies*, 1992, C W Daniel & Co.
Harvey, Clare G., and Cochrane, Amanda, *The Encyclopaedia of Flower Remedies*, 1995,
   Thorsons/HarperCollins
Korte, Andreas, *Orchids, Gemstones and the Healing Energies*, 1993, Bauer Verlag

GODDESSES

Budapest, Z, *The Holy Book of Women's Mysteries*, 1990, Harper Row, New York
Farrar, Janet and Stewart, *The Witches' Goddess, The Feminine Principle of Divinity*, 1987,
   Phoenix Publishing Inc., New York
Gadon, Elinor, *The Once and Future Goddess*, 1990, Aquarian/Thorsons
Starhawk, *The Spiral Dance*, 1999, Harper Row, San Francisco

healing

Brennan, Barbara Ann, *Hands of Light: A Guide to Healing Through the Human Energy Field*, 1987, Bantam Publishers

Eden, Donna, *Energy Medicine*, 1999, Piatkus

herbalism

Cunningham, Scott, *The Encyclopaedia of Herbs*, 1997, Llewellyn, St Paul, Minnesota

Lipp, Frank J., *Herbalism*, 1996, Macmillan

Rodway, Marie, *A Wiccan Herbal*, 1997, Foulsham/Quantum

incenses and oils

Cunningham, Scott, *The Complete Book of Oils, Incenses and Brews*, 1991, Llewellyn, St Paul, Minnesota

Dunwich, Gerena, *The Wicca Garden, A Witch's Guide to Magical and Enchanted Herbs and Plants*, 1996, Citadel, Carol, New York

native americans

Meadows, Kenneth, *Earth Medicine*, 1996, Element

Page, James Lynn, *Native American Magic*, 2002, Foulsham/Quantum

Wallace, Black Elk, and Lyon, William, *Black Elk: The Sacred Ways of a Lakota*, 1990, Harper and Row, New York

psychic phenomena

Sheldrake, Rupert, *Dogs that Know When Their Owners Are Coming Home and Other Unexplained Powers of Animals: An Investigation*, 1999, Crown Publishing

psychic protection

Eason, Cassandra, *Psychic Protection Lifts the Spirit*, 2000, Foulsham/Quantum

Fortune, Dion, *Psychic Self-Defence*, 1988, Aquarian

seasonal magic, old festivals and mythology

Cooper, J. C., *Aquarian Dictionary of Festivals*, 1990, Aquarian/Thorsons

Green, Marian, *A Calendar of Festivals*, 1991, Element

Stewart, Bob, *Where Is St George? Pagan Imagery in English Folksong*, 1988, Blandford

Walker, Barbara, *The Woman's Encyclopaedia of Myths and Secrets*, 1983, Pandora

Willis, Roy, *World Mythology*, 1993, Piatkus

shamanism

Castenada, Carlos, *Journey to Ixtlan*, 1972, Penguin

Devereux, Paul, *Shamanism and the Mystery Lines*, 2000, Foulsham/Quantum

Wahoo, Dhyani, *Voices of Our Ancestors*, 1987, Shambhala

WESTERN MAGICAL TRADITION AND THE GOLDEN DAWN

Gilbert, R. S. *Revelations of the Golden Dawn*, 1997, Foulsham/Quantum

Matthews, Caitlin and John, *The Western Way: A Practical Guide to the Western Mystical Tradition*, 1986, Arkana

Regardie, Israel, *The Golden Dawn: A Complete Course in Practical Ceremonial Magic*, 1989, Llewellyn, St Paul, Minnesota

WITCHCRAFT AND MAGIC

Bruce, Marie, *Everyday Spells for a Teenage Witch*, 2004, Foulsham/Quantum

Bruce, Marie, *How to Create a Magical Home*, 2004, Foulsham/Quantum

Bruce, Marie, *Magical Beasts*, 2003, Foulsham/Quantum

Buckland, Raymond, *Buckland's Complete Guide to Witchcraft*, 1997, Llewellyn

Cunningham, Scott, *Living Wicca, A Guide for the Solitary Practitioner*, 1994, Llewellyn

Eason, Cassandra, *The Complete Guide to Magic and Ritual*, 1999, Piatkus

Eason, Cassandra, *Every Woman a Witch*, 1996, Foulsham/Quantum

Eason, Cassandra, *Fragrant Magic*, 2003, Foulsham/Quantum

Eason, Cassandra, *Magic Spells for a Happy Life*, 2003, Foulsham/Quantum

Eason, Cassandra, *The Practical Guide to Witchcraft and Magick Spells*, 2001, Foulsham/Quantum

Fortune, Dion, *Applied Magick*, 2000, Samuel Weiser, New York

Fortune, Dion, *Moon Magick* (fiction), 1985, Aquarian

Fortune, Dion, *The Sea Priestess* (fiction), 2000, Samuel Weiser, New York

Steele, Tony, *Water Witches*, 1998, Capall Bann Publishing

Valiente, Doreen, *Natural Magic*, 1985, Phoenix Publishing Inc., New York

WITCHCRAFT HISTORY

Adler, Margot, *Drawing Down the Moon*, 1997, Penguin, USA

Briggs, Robin, *Witches and Neighbours, The Social and Cultural Context of European Witchcraft*, 1996, HarperCollins

Crowley, Vivienne, *Wicca, The Old Religion on the New Age*, 1989, Aquarian/Thorsons

Guiley, Rosemary Ellen, *The Encyclopaedia of Witches and Witchcraft*, 1989, Facts on File, New York

Murray, Margaret, *The God of the Witches*, 1992, Oxford University Press

USEFUL CONTACTS

Cassandra Eason's website can be found at: www.cassandraeason.co.uk.

CANDLE SUPPLIERS AND CANDLEMAKING EQUIPMENT

Australia
Price's Candles Ltd
80–82 Bryant Street, Padstow, NSW 2211
Web: www.prices-candles.co.uk

Lyndon House International Inc.
12605A–127 Avenue, Edmonton, Alberta, T5L 3ES

UK
Price's Candles Ltd
16 Hudson Road, Bedford MK41 0LZ
Web: www.prices-candles.co.uk

USA
Wax Wonder
221 North Main Street, Versailles, Kentucky 40383

COLLECTIBLES

Australia
G &M Treasures
PO Box 133, Kippas, ACT 2615
(Fantasy figures, pewter figurines)
Web: www.treasures.com.au

UK
The Faerie Shoppe
105 High Street, Marlborough, Wiltshire; 3 Montpelier Walk, Cheltenham, Gloucestershire; 6 Lower Borough Walk, Bath, Avon (All things faerie)
Web: www.fairyshop.co.uk

Snapdragon
12 South Park, Sevenoaks, Kent, TN13 1AW (All kinds of faerie collectibles, dragons, etc.)
Web: www.giltedgedgoblins.com

USA
Light as a Feather
Eric Torgeson, 216 Palisade Drive, Eureka Springs, Arizona 72631
(Hand-sculptured glass faeries)

Joyce Wiseman
PO Box 333, Comptche, CA 95427
(Mermaids, faerie dolls, mermaid and faerie cards)

CRYSTALS, AMULETS, MAGICAL SUPPLIES, ETC.

Australia
The Mystic Trader
125 Flinders Lane, Melbourne 3000
(Mail order as well as personal service)

Mysterys
Level I, 314–322 Darling Street,
Balmain, New South Wales 2041
(Wiccan supplies by mail order)
Web: www.mysterys.com.au

South Africa
The Wellstead
I Wellington Avenue, Wynberg, Cape
7300 (Mail order)

UK
Futhark
18 Halifax Road, Todmorden,
Lancashire OLI4 5AD (Occult,
magical and alchemical supplies of all
kinds by mail order)

Mandragora
Essex House, Thame, Oxfordshire
OX9 3LS (Mail order)

Mysteries
9–II Monmouth Street, London
WC2H 9DA (Shop and mail order for
absolutely everything for the New Age,
plus good advice)
Web: www.mysteries.co.uk

Pentagram
II Cheapside, Wakefield, West
Yorkshire WFI 2SD (International
mail order and personal service for
everything for the New Age, Wicca and
the occult)

USA
The Crystal Cave
415 West Foothill Blvd, Claremont,
CA 91711 (Mail order suppliers
stocking a huge variety of crystals and
stones, including unusual ones)

Eye of the Cat
3314 East Broadway, Long Beach, CA
90803 (Mail order crystals and other
New Age commodities)

Open Door Metaphysical Shoppe
428 North Buchanan Circle, Suite 16,
Pacheco, CA 94553 (Mail order New
Age supplies)

Spirit Search Emporium
Sun Angel Innovations, 1075 North
Miller Road, 230, Scottsdale, A2
85257, Arizona
Web: www.sun-angel.com

DRUIDS
UK
The Order of Bards, Ovates and
Druids
PO Box 1333, Lewes, East Sussex
BN7 IDX (Worldwide contacts and
training programme)
Web: www.druidry.org

EARTH ENERGIES
Australia
Dowsers Society of New South Wales
c/o Mrs E Miksevicius, 126 Fiddens
Wharf Road, Killara, NSW 2031
Web: www.divstrat.com.au/dowsing/

Southern Tasmania Dowsing
Association
PO Box 101, Moonah, Tasmania,
Australia 7009

UK
British Society of Dowsers
Sycamore Barn, Hastingleigh, Ashford,
Kent TN25 5HW
Web: www.britishdowsers.org

Findhorn Foundation
The Park, Forres, Scotland IV36 OTS
(Workshops and courses that teach
about meditation, consciousness and
nature spirits)
Web: www.findhorn.org

USA
The American Society of Dowsers
Dowsers Hall, Danville, Vermont,
05828-0024
Web: www.dowsers.org

FLOWER AND TREE ESSENCES
Australia
The Australian Flower Remedy Society
PO Box 531 Spit Junction, New South
Wales 2007

The Australian Bush Flower Essence
Society
45 Booralve Road, Terrey Hills, New
South Wales 2084
Web: www.ausflowers.com.au

Pacific Essences
PO Box 8317, Victoria, V8W 3R9
Web: www.pacificessences.com

Sabian
PO Box 527, Kew, Victoria, Australia
3101 or The Sabian Centre, 11
Selbourne Road, Kew, Victoria 31031
Web: www.sabian.org

UK
Bach Flower Remedies
Healing Herbs Ltd, PO Box 65,
Hereford HR2 0UW
Web: www.healingherbs.co.uk

USA
Alaskan Flower Essence Project
PO Box 1329, Homer, AL 99603
Web: www.alaskanessences.com

Desert Alchemy
PO Box 44189, Tucson, Arizona, AZ
85733
Web: www.desert-alchemy.com

HERBS AND OILS – PROFESSIONAL ORGANISATIONS
Australia
The National Association of
Herbalists
PO Box 65, Kingsgrove, NSW 2208

UK
The National Institute of Medical
Herbalists
56 Longbrook Street, Exeter, Devon
EX4 6AH
Web: www.nimh.org.uk

The International Federation of
Professional Aromatherapists
82 Ashby Road, Hinckley,
Leicestershire LE10 1SN
Web: www.ifparoma.org

The Herb Society
Sulgrave Manor, Sulgrave, Banbury
OX17 2SD
Web: www.herbsociety.org.uk

HERBS AND OILS – SUPPLIERS
UK
G Baldwin and Co.
171–173 Walworth Road, London
SE17 1RW (Largest range of herbs
and herbal products in the UK with
extensive mail order)
Web: www.baldwins.co.uk

Gerard House
736 Christchurch Road, Bournemouth
BH7 6BZ (Dried herbs by mail order)

Neals Yard Remedies
8–10 Ingate Place, Battersea, London
SW8 3NS (Oils by mail order)
Web: www.nealsyardremedies.com

USA

The American Herbalists Guild
1931 Gaddis Road, Canton, GA
30115
Web:
www.americanherbalistsguild.com

Joan Teresa Power Products
PO Box 442, Mars Hill, NC 28754
(Unusual herbs, plants, oils, incenses,
etc. by mail order)

The Sage Garden
PO Box 144, Payette, ID 83661
(Herbs, oils, amulets and incenses by
mail order)

Meditation and Visualisation Music
UK

New World Cassettes
Building 35, Shepperton Film Studios,
Studios Road, Shepperton, Middlesex
TW17 0QD (Music by mail order;
free catalogue)
Web: www.beechwoodmusic.net

New World Music
The Barn, Becks Green, St Andrews,
Beccles, Suffolk NR34 8NB (Music
by mail order)
Web: www.newworldmusic.com

Stress Busters
Beechwood Music, Littleton House,
Littleton Road, Ashford, Middlesex
TW15 1UU (Music of pan pipes,
rainforest, surf and whales)

USA

Raven Recordings
744 Broad Street, Room 1815,
Newark, New Jersey 07102
(Meditation music, videos and tapes by
Gabrielle Roth, founder of the
5Rhythms™ dance practice)

Paganism
Australia

Novocastrian Pagan Information Centre
Laren, PO Box 129, Stockton, New
South Wales 2295

The Pagan Alliance
PO Box 823, Bathurst, New South
Wales 2795 (An umbrella movement
for pagan organisations)

UK

The Pagan Federation
PO Box 7097, London WC1N 3XX
Web: www.pflondon.myby.co.uk

Shamanism
UK

Eagle's Wing Centre for Contemporary
Shamanism
PO Box 7475, London WC1N 3XX
Web: www.shamanism.co.uk

Faculty of Shamanics
Kenneth and Beryl Meadows, PO Box
300, Potters Bar, Hertfordshire
EN6 4LE
Web: http://shamanics.org

USA

Dance of the Deer Foundation
Center for Shamanic Studies, PO Box
699, Soquel, CA 95073
Web: www.shamanism.com

Spiritual Healing
Australia

Australian Spiritualist Association
PO Box 248, Canterbury, New South
Wales 2193

Canada

National Federation of Spiritual
Healers (Canada), Toronto, Ontario
Spiritualist Church of Canada
1835 Laurence Ave East, Scarborough,
Ontario, M1TR 2Y3

UK
British Alliance of Healing
Associations
Mrs Jo Wallace, 3 Sandy Lane,
Gisleham, Lowestoft, Suffolk
NR33 8EQ.

National Federation of Spiritual
Healers
Old Manor Farm Studio, Church
Street, Sunbury on Thames, Middlesex
TW16 6RG
Web: www.nfsh.org.uk

USA
World of Light
PO Box 425, Wappingers Falls, NY
12590 (List of healers)

wicca and goddess
UK
Fellowship of Isis
Lady Olivia Robertson, Clonegal
Castle, Enniscorthy, Co. Wexford, Eire
(Worldwide network of Goddess
worshippers)
Web: www.fellowshipofisis.com

The Museum of Witchcraft
The Harbour, Boscastle, Cornwall
PL35 0HD
Web: www.museumofwitchcraft.com

USA
Circle Sanctuary
PO Box 219, Mount Horeb, WI
53572 (Contacts with 700 pagan
groups, networks, etc.)
Web: www.circlesanctuary.org

Covenant of the Goddess
PO Box 1226, Berkeley, California
94704
Web: www.cog.org

The Witches' Voice Inc.
PO Box 4924, Clearwater, Florida (A
resource organisation with worldwide
links)
Web: www.witchvox.com

INDEX OF SPELLS

Courage

Horseshoe spell for overcoming seemingly impossible odds 138

Iron nail spell for the courage to keep a difficult resolution 138

Signet ring ritual to establish your identity and enable you to make your mark on the world 141

Spell to give you the courage of your own convictions 139–140

Spell to make you courageous and confident whatever the obstacles 146

Stone spell for helping you to endure and improve an intolerable situation 140

Storm spell for courage 139

Death

Memory box ritual for when a relation has departed 419

Ritual to ease the passing of a friend or family member 485–486

Debt problems

Candle spell for balancing the books 301

Cobweb spell for clearing financial chaos 306

Credit card spell to reduce plastic borrowings 307

Dark and light candle spell to reverse a run of bad financial luck 304–305

Longer-acting shopaholic spell 309

Misty bathroom spell 309

Misty day spell 308

Radio spell to reverse a run of bad financial luck 300

Rainy day spell to wipe the slate clean 305

Sand and sea spell to reduce debt 302

Sea spell to turn the tide on debt 304

Seven-day spell for turning loss into profit 301

Spell for balancing the books 300

Spell for spending wisely 308

Spell to call in what you are owed or to get more money from an employer 306

Spell to deal with unpleasant demands 310

Spell to help you or a family member with debt problems 303

Spell to recover debts owed to you 173

Spell to stop money flowing out too quickly 302

Disasters

Angels of the rains spell to end drought or to bring clean water to an area 634

Anti-flood angel spell 639

Australian Aboriginal spell to bring rain or reduce unbearable heat 636

Charm against volcanic eruption 641

Fire spell to relieve harsh winter conditions 635

Spell against famine 636–637

Spell against urban decay and inner-city or rural poverty 639

Spell against whirlwinds, hurricanes and tornadoes 637

Spell bag against forest fires and fires caused by lightning 642

Spell bag against tidal waves and high seas 640

Spell to redress poverty in under-resourced countries 638

Suiel angelic charm against earthquakes 634–635

Dreams, realising

Meteor spell for a life-changing wish or seemingly impossible dream 183

Pole Star spell for achieving a dream that seems ambitious or far off in time 182

Environment

Archangel Cassiel spell for the preservation and revival of ancient wisdom, especially from indigenous sources 659

Archangel Gabriel spell for regenerating the planet and the Earth's resources 658

Dough spell for the regeneration of the Earth's resources 661

Earth spell for reforestation 646

Five-candle spell to stop the Earth's resources being squandered 652

Gaia or Mother Earth healing spell against all pollution 647

Native North American Earth healing ritual 662

Sand spell for the regeneration of the Earth and her resources 655

Second sand spell for the regeneration of the Earth and her resources 655

Second spell to help deal with an oil or chemical spillage at sea 645

Slavic Matka, or moist mother Earth spell 656

Soil fertility spell from the Andes 654

Solitary or group ritual for Earth Healing Day or any other environmentally significant occasion 657

Spell for mutual exchange with the devas of the land 660

Spell for reversing global warming and pollution 644

Spell for temporarily moving or turning an earth dragon around 650

Spell to cleanse the planet of toxins 661

Spell to create new life and growth after decay and destruction 656

Spell to heal polluted oceans, rivers, lakes and streams 646

Spell to heal the ozone layer 648

Spell to help deal with an oil or chemical spillage at sea 644

Spell to restore life to polluted or abandoned urban wasteland 651

Spell to send protection to an endangered piece of land or species of plant, bird or animal 649

Weekly incense spell against pollution or destruction 645

Families

Blessing for a special meal 150

Blue lace agate spell for gentleness if a critical or trouble-making family member or friend is present 493

Cake spell for emotional security and stability 72

Candle ceremony for the birth of a baby 420

Christening or naming ritual for a new baby 420

Dedication spell on marriage or moving in together 75

Spell to empower a lucky elephant charm for your home 575
Spell to make a game of chance charm 294
Spell to make a speculation mojo 294
Spell to win competitions 296

Guilt
Celtic hearth spell for losing guilt or anger 598
North wind guilt banishing spell 598
Russian spell to lay the past to rest 597
Spell to wash away guilt, sorrow, anger and regrets 596

Happiness
Blessing for a special meal 150
Candle spell to recover optimism after a series of setbacks 174
Hospitality spell to welcome visitors and new friends into your life 151
Mystic nut spell for inner stillness 156
Spell bag to bring fun and excitement into your life 35
Spell for a happy family 152
Spell for finding true happiness 158
Spell to attract fun into your life 157
St Teresa of Avila walking chant 156
Triple spiral spell for personal harmony 155
White candle blessing before a gathering 152–153

Healing – people
Ancient charm for reducing the pain of a burn, scald, inflammation or rash 469
Ancient Egyptian water spell to heal yourself or others of skin irritations and allergies, cuts, burns wounds and internal lesions or inflammation 464
Anglo Saxon rusty nail spell to bury migraines, sore throats or any sharp pain 473
Basic absent healing spell 476
Clear crystal pyramid spell for healing a specific illness or pain in another person 462
Crystal ball moon healing spell 477
Crystal pyramid spell for reducing personal stress levels or alleviating anxiety that is making a medical condition worse 463
Dark and light absent healing spell for debilitating conditions and viruses 481
Druid mistletoe healing rite on the sixth day of the moon 483
Egg spell to bury a menstrual or reproductive problem 472
Eight-candle spell for someone undergoing an operation or beginning a difficult course of treatment 478–479
Garlic spell to bury an illness 471
Gentle pyramid healing spell 480
Healing herb ritual using a cloth doll or poppet 484
Holed stone spell for absent healing 478
Incense absent healing spell for a person who is far away or refuses help 485
Monthly absent healing ceremony using a healing book 482
Onion spell to bury an illness 472
Opaque crystal pyramid spell to absorb a pain or relieve backache, rheumatism or arthritis 460–461

Pendulum spell to heal yourself using the forces of nature 466–467
Ritual to ease the passing of a friend or family member 485–486
Salt, water and candle spell for helping the body to fight an illness or to prepare for an operation or medical intervention 470
Self-healing spell using stone water 468
Spell for burning away an illness, fever or addiction that is weakening a loved one 471
Spell for healing a child 465
Spell for obtaining healing through a dream 538
Spell to direct crystalline pyramid energy towards someone suffering from an acute illness or an illness that is not responding to treatment 480
Spell to help you keep a positive attitude to an illness and thereby encourage healing 461
Spell to send love and light through a pendulum 477
Spell to slow blood flow, to relieve anaemia and blood disorders, and to lower high blood pressure 473
Stone spell to bury a headache or pain 472
Three Marys rain chant spell 474
Water spell to remove warts, verruccas, viruses of any kind, fungal infections and gall or kidney stones 467

Health
American apple spell for health
Apple spell for health and vitality 129
Beauty pathway spell for health and vitality 133
Candle spell to recover optimism after a series of setbacks 174
Celtic nine-quartz crystal spell for health 128
Copper spell for maintaining health 135
De-stressing spell 134–135
Dolphin spell to reduce stress, insomnia and anxiety 582
Fruit spell for good health 129
Italian tomato spell for good health and prosperity 130
Rainbow spell to absorb the life force 131
Salt spell for health 132
Self blessing spell to reduce panic attacks or crippling fears 606
Solar empowerment spell for health 132–133
Spell for banishing panic attacks 606
Spell for boosting energy levels 134
Spell to help you keep a positive attitude to life and maintain well-being 136
Spell to lift your mood if you can't break out of a cycle of depression 172–173
Three-horseshoe protection rite to keep sickness and poverty from the home 344

Holidays
23rd Psalm ritual for when you are taking children on holiday 433–434
Computer drawing spell to fulfil a travel dream 436
Dandelion clock travel spell 436
Incense air ritual to make a dream of long-distance or long-term travel possible 435

Spell to make a lucky knot cord 239
Spell to recover debts owed to you 173

Self-esteem
Daily spell for confidence and self-esteem 147
Rainy day spell for confidence and self- esteem 143
Spell for increasing self-love and self-esteem 146
Spell to bolster your self-esteem when it has taken a knock 148
Spell to reverse the effects of an attack on your self esteem or confidence 586
Visualisation spell for protecting or recovering self-esteem 382–383

Sex
Earth, air, fire and water spell to maintain or restore passion in an established relationship 84–85
Ritual for combining passion with tenderness 86
Ritual to encourage expression of love in a long-standing relationship 88
Slavic spell for love and passion eternal 85
Spell to call an overworked or overstressed partner to your bed 87
Spell to relieve male sexual dysfunction 100

Sex – harassment
Banishing candle and pin spell against abuse 593
Hathor mirror spell for businesswomen under threat 381
Spell to repel a stalker or someone who will not stop intruding on your life 588
Two binding spells against sexual harassment 615

Skills
Bardic spell to improve your memory and concentration 160
Bouncing ball spell to generate enthusiasm 163
General study spell 164
Spell to improve your skill in a sport or art 166
Spell to increase possibilities 164–165
Spell to learn another language 165
Spell to master new technology 166

Sleep
Candle protection spell for anxiety about being attacked or injured while you sleep 533
Celtic sleep blessing 532
Celtic sleep circling prayer 532
Dolphin spell to reduce stress, insomnia and anxiety 582
Dream catcher spell for children 535
Dream pillow spell 536–537
Five-angel or fairy candle spell for a child or adult who does not like the dark 534
Fragrance spell to create a beautiful sleep experience 537
Herbal bath for quiet sleep 536
Spell for obtaining healing through a dream 538
Spell to keep away nightmares 534

Sorrow
Chimney spell for banishing sorrow 597
Ritual to finish business with someone who has gone away or died 601

Russian spell to lay the past to rest 597
Spell to shed sorrows from childhood or early adulthood 600
Spell to wash away guilt, sorrow, anger and regrets 596

Step families
Spell for getting on well with in laws and step relations 423
Spell for welcoming new younger members into the family 425

Stolen items
Garlic spell for restoring what has been lost or stolen, physically, financially or emotionally 172
Soap and water tablet spell to recover what has been stolen 171
Spell to avoid losing possessions or becoming a victim of theft while on holiday or in transit 373
Spell to deter a neighbour who keeps borrowing and never returns your property 394

Technology
Spell to stop unusually large numbers of virus attacks on your computer 590

Tests – passing
Another spell to pass examinations or written tests 161–162
General study spell 164
Spell for passing a driving test 163–164
Spell to pass an oral test or practical examination 162
Spell to pass examinations or written tests 161

Travel
23rd Psalm ritual for when you are taking children on holiday 433–434
Ancient Egyptian spell to travel where you wish 580
Celtic blessing for travel across seas 364
Celtic blessing spell for a child upon a journey 353
Celtic blessing spell for when a child is abroad and has not contacted you 362
Chinese happy travel charm 432
Computer drawing spell to fulfil a travel dream 436
Dandelion clock travel spell 436
Druid spell to enclose you in safety if travelling becomes hazardous 366–367
Incense air ritual to make a dream of long-distance or long-term travel possible 435
Lady of Guadelupe travel charm 430
Making a magical protection amulet for long-term or long-distance travel 368
Mojo bag for a regular traveller 431
Ritual for creating a safe path when walking alone 376
St Christopher spell for a safe journey or holiday 365
St Julian the Hospitaller prayer for a friend or family member who is backpacking 430
St Patrick spell for protecting travellers in remote or hazardous places 364
Scottish spell for protection when travelling 366
Second dandelion clock travel spell 437
Sewing spell for protection of children when they are outside the home 354

INDEX

shields, psychic 311, 395
shoes
    family spells 427
    prints 33
    and protection 342
    and starting a new job 450
shopping wisely 307–308, 309
Sidney, Sir Philip 83
signet rings 141
silver 690
    and abundance 262, 263
    candles 64, 93
    heart symbol 21
    moon metal 93
    turning three times 21, 266
    see also coins; money
Simon and Garfunkel 111
six (number) 20
skills, new 125, 159
    spells for 160, 164–166
    see also talents
skin complaints 464, 469
sky clad 705
sky gods 705
Slavic spells
    fertility 99
    healing 524
love 56, 85
sleep 531–538, 582
smoke *see* incense; smudging
smoking 604–605
smudge sticks 236, 260, 321
smudging spells
business success 236
finding a pet 542–543
money 260
    moving house 448
    new beginnings 411
    peace 629
    protection 321–322, 331, 374–375, 378
    travel 432
snakes
    new beginnings 409
snapdragon 694
snow
    reconciliation spells 490
soap
    banishing spells 596
socialising
    at work 201
Solomon, King 71
solstice 705
Song of Solomon 44, 71
sorrow
    banishing spells 595–598, 600
soul mates 37
spectacles
    protective spells 382
speculation
    financial 255–256, 287
spells 292–295
spell bags
    career spells 220

fire disasters 642
harmony in the workplace 197
love spells 34–35
protective spells 347, 348
see also mojos
spells 7–8
    action 11–12
    beginning 669
    casting 663–670
    defining the focus of 11
    definition 7
    ending 669
    ethics of 11, 15, 17, 40, 583–584, 613
    five stages of 11–12
    focus of 666
    formal 7, 8, 11
    and free will 11, 583
    grounding the power 12
    informal 7, 8, 11
    learning from 670
    location 667
    materials needed 666
    positioning equipment and participants 669
    preparing yourself 668
    raising the power 12
    releasing the power 12
    structuring 667–668
    timing of 663, 668
    writing 666–670
spices
    abundance spells 276–277
    and financial speculation 292, 293
    sachets 293
spiders
    fear of 608
    money spells 306
spirals
    happiness spells 155
spirit guides 13, 705
spiritual healing 457
absent 475–486
contact 459, 460–474
    see also healing
spite
    at work 384–385
sport, improving at 166
spring 674
    fertility spells 90
Sri 94
stalkers 588
stars
    wish spells 181–182
statues
    protective 335
steam 36
stelae 464
Stella Maris 110, 353
stepchildren
    incorporating into new family 66–67, 72, 75, 423, 425
stepping stones 221
stolen
    ideas 384